Precarious Li\

Precarious Lives

Job Insecurity and Well-Being in Rich Democracies

Arne L. Kalleberg

polity

First published in 2018 by Polity Press

Polity Press
65 Bridge Street
Cambridge CB2 1UR, UK

Polity Press
101 Station Landing
Suite 300
Medford, MA 02155, USA

ISBN-13: 978-1-5095-0649-1
ISBN-13: 978-1-5095-0650-7(pb)

A catalogue record for this book is available from the British Library.

Library of Congress Cataloging-in-Publication Data

Names: Kalleberg, Arne L., author.
Title: Precarious lives : job insecurity and well-being in rich democracies / Arne L. Kalleberg.
Description: Cambridge, UK ; Medford, MA : Polity Press, 2018. | Includes
   bibliographical references and index.
Identifiers: LCCN 2017050804 (print) | LCCN 2017054523 (ebook) | ISBN
   9781509506538 (Epub) | ISBN 9781509506491 (hardback) | ISBN 9781509506507
   (pbk.)
Subjects: LCSH: Precarious employment--Social aspects--Developed countries. |
   Job security--Social aspects--Developed countries. | Manpower policy--Developed
   countries. | Public welfare--Developed countries.
Classification: LCC HD5858.D43 (ebook) | LCC HD5858.D43 K35 2018 (print) |
   DDC 331.25/96--dc23
LC record available at https://lccn.loc.gov/2017050804

Typeset in 10.5 on 12 pt Plantin by Servis Filmsetting Ltd, Stockport, Cheshire
Printed and bound in the UK by CPI Group (UK) Ltd, Croydon, CR0 4YY

For further information on Polity, visit our website:
politybooks.com

Contents

Contents

Figures

Acknowledgments

How institutions and cultures shape labor markets has been a recurring theme in my research for many years. So too have been the topics of how political, economic, and social forces influence employment relations and individuals' well-being. The concept of precarious work brings together all these themes and provides a narrative of how institutional and cultural forces have transformed employment relations and impacted individuals and families. These topics are both timely and important for debates in economic sociology; the sociology of work, occupations, and organizations; and the study of social stratification and inequality; to name only a few of the many areas of research for the questions raised by the new age of precarious work. The consequences of precarious work also underscore political and policy issues that need urgent action by governments, business, and workers.

In writing this book, I have benefitted from the advice and feedback of many colleagues and friends, who have been generous in sharing their knowledge. I owe a special debt to the Russell Sage Foundation for providing me with a year's residency as a Visiting Scholar in 2016–17. There, I had the opportunity to work intensively on the book and receive very helpful feedback and advice from the other scholars and staff (and great lunches!).

My arguments were honed from the feedback I received from numerous presentations at seminars and conferences. In the United States, at: Columbia University; Duke University; Emory University; University of Hawaii; University of Michigan; New York University; University of North Carolina at Chapel Hill; University of Oklahoma; Princeton University; and Vanderbilt University; as well as at the Russell Sage Foundation and meetings of the American Sociological

Association. At international venues: Academia Sinica, Taipei, Taiwan; Alliance Manchester Business School, United Kingdom; Carlos II University of Madrid, Spain; Chung-Ang University, Republic of Korea; National Research University Higher School of Economics, Moscow and Saint-Petersburg, Russia; Norwegian School of Economics (NHH) in Bergen, Norway; Said Business School, Oxford, United Kingdom; Seoul National University, Republic of Korea; University of the South Pacific, Suva, Fiji; and the Wissenschaftszentrum Berlin für Sozialforschung (WZB), Germany; as well as at annual conferences of the International Working Party on Labour Market Segmentation (in Athens, Greece and in Manchester, United Kingdom); and of the 8th Nordic Working Life Conference, in Tampere, Finland.

I was also fortunate to have been able to persuade colleagues to give me critical and constructive reviews on parts of the book. I am especially grateful to the extensive comments and incisive critiques by Heidi Gottfried, John Stephens, and Steve Vallas.

I am also indebted to many others who gave me helpful feedback and suggestions on various portions of the book, including: Kenneth (Andy) Andrews, David Brady, Gøsta Esping-Andersen, Duncan Gallie, Kevin Hewison, Hande Inanc, Larry Liam Ching Liu, Sophie Moullin, John Myles, Jill Rubery, Michael Schultz, Guy Standing, and Leah Vosko. I also thank the reviewers for Polity (Harriet Bradley, Mary Brinton, Rachel Dwyer) for their perceptive and helpful comments. I owe special thanks to Galo Falchettore and Michael Schultz for their great help with the figures presented in the book. I also thank Jonathan Skerrett, my editor at Polity, whose combination of vision, persistence, and constructive feedback encouraged me to write this book and kept its completion on track.

Finally, I am grateful to my wife Judith. Her good sense and humor have been constant sources of support for more than a half-century. Together, we have experienced many of the changes that I've written about in this book. The era of precarious work presents new challenges for the young, and so we must look to them. In that spirit, I dedicate the book to my grandchildren: Elise, Margit, Jack, and Morgan.

Arne L. Kalleberg
University of North Carolina at Chapel Hill

Abbreviations

AfD	Alternative for Germany
CME	coordinated market economy
DPJ	Democratic Party of Japan
DPP	Danish People's Party
EPL	employment protection legislation
ESS	European Social Survey
GDP	gross domestic product
IEWB	Index of Economic Well-Being
ISSP	International Social Survey Programme
LDP	Liberal Democratic Party of Japan
LME	liberal market economy
NEET	not in education, employment, or training
NGO	non-governmental organization
OECD	Organisation for Economic Co-operation and Development
PRT	power resources theory
SER	standard employment relationship
SMEs	small and medium-sized enterprises
TANF	Temporary Assistance for Needy Families
UBI	universal (or unconditional) basic income
UI	unemployment insurance
VoC	varieties of capitalism
WVS	World Values Survey

Introduction

Recent news reports and observations by social scientists have revealed some alarming facts about work and workers in various rich democracies. Here is a sampling:

- More than 40 percent of young people in Europe are caught in a cycle of low-paid, temporary jobs, leaving them with feelings of being excluded from society as well as suffering from severe stress, depression, and persistent self-doubts about their abilities and possibilities for the future, along with increasing the ranks of the working poor in Europe. Since 2012, just 20 percent of temporary workers have been able to find full-time jobs (Alderman 2017).
- A Gallup survey of employed US adults, aged 18 or older, found that about a third of them in 2013 were worried about being laid off, more than twice the number in 2008 (Saad 2013). This has raised alarms since enduring job insecurity and the associated stress have stronger negative effects on poor health than smoking or hypertension and can lead to coronary heart disease and cancer (Parramore 2012).
- Forty-five percent of United States residents do not have enough income to cover basic expenses, plan for college and other important life events, or save for unexpected health bills and other emergencies, according to a recent report. In addition, over half of children in the US live in families that do not earn enough to obtain economic security (Rich 2011).
- At least one million Japanese today – most commonly young adults and more often men than women – are socially withdrawn and live a tenuous existence. Called *hikikomori*, these individuals often remain in a single room disconnected from contact with others. A

dramatic action by one who was detached from family and friends was committed by a 25-year-old temporary worker who was afraid he had lost his job and distressed by his job insecurity and precarious existence: he killed seven random people in the summer of 2008 in the Akihabara electronics district of Tokyo (Allison 2013: 3).

- In Tokyo's Hibiya Park, 500 temp workers set up a tent village to protest the worsening of their precarious existence after the collapse of Lehman Brothers in 2008, thereby raising public awareness of the dire living conditions experienced by the growing numbers of precarious workers in Japan (Gottfried 2015: 112).

- In Japan, men who have non-regular, insecure jobs are only half as likely as regular workers to get married, since women disdain marrying these *furita* men (i.e., those with non-regular jobs) because they regard them as being unable to fulfill their obligations to provide economic security for the household (Allison 2013: 33).

- In South Korea, non-regular workers called public attention to the insecurity and oppressive nature of their jobs by demonstrating on top of factory chimneys, atop a 50-metre-high power transmission tower, on a bridge over the Han River, and on the roof of the National Assembly. Non-regular workers also staged a strike lasting more than five years as well as engaged in hunger strikes, hair shaving, and even suicide (Shin 2013: 350).

- More than 60 percent of Italians aged 18 to 34 are still living with their parents and a third of these are in their early thirties, which is three times the number in 1983 (*Daily Mail* 2010), giving rise to their being labeled *bamboccioni* or "big babies." Moreover, 37 percent of men aged 30 in Italy today have never lived away from home. In Spain, 80 percent of youth under 30 still lived with their parents in 2015 (*The Local.es* 2016). In the United States, almost a third of young adults aged 18 to 34 lived with their parents in 2014, the highest rate since the Great Depression (Haynie 2016).

- The relative frequency of news coverage related to economic uncertainty was higher in January 2017 than at any previous time in the two decades during which the index has been computed, and was more than three times the average level of uncertainty during these two decades, according to the Global Economic Policy Uncertainty Index. This index is based on the archives from major newspapers in eighteen countries representing more than two-thirds of the global economy (Rampell 2017).

- EuroMayDay has become an annual event to protest the growing insecurities resulting from transformations in work. First held in Milan, Italy, on May 1, 2001, this yearly happening has since spread to dozens of European cities and to Asian countries such as Japan, and has attracted hundreds of thousands of people to the streets to call attention to the plight of millions of vulnerable workers and migrants who are subject to exploitation and discrimination in these countries.

These examples illustrate some of the consequences of the rise of *precarious work* in modern societies. By "precarious work" I mean work that is *uncertain, unstable,* and *insecure* and in which *employees bear the risks* of work (as opposed to businesses or the government) and *receive limited social benefits and statutory entitlements* (Vosko 2010; Kalleberg and Hewison 2013; Breman and van der Linden 2014). Precarious work has emerged as a serious challenge and a major concern in the contemporary world. It has widespread consequences not only for the quantity and quality of jobs, but also for many other outcomes, whether non-work individual (e.g., mental stress, poor physical health, uncertainty about educational choices), family (e.g., delayed entry into marriage and having children), or broader social (e.g., community disintegration and disinvestment). Moreover, precarious workers' insecurities and fears have spilled over into forms of protest that call for political responses to address these concerns.

While work has always been to some extent precarious, especially for more vulnerable groups in the population such as women and minority men, there has been a recent rise in precarious work especially for majority men in rich, democratic, post-industrial societies. The growth of precarious work has also accelerated the exclusion of certain groups from economic, social, and political institutions, such as when people are unemployed for long periods of time, left outside systems of social protections, and disenfranchised from voting and participation in the political process.

The upsurge in precarious work in some rich democracies (such as the United States) began in the mid-to-late 1970s and 1980s, while it occurred a bit later in others. In all cases, the consequences of precarious work were exacerbated by the global economic crisis of 2008–9. Pressures on governments to implement policies of fiscal austerity and welfare state reorganization accompanied – and are partly responsible for – the rise in precarious work, as countries have struggled to respond to weakening financial situations and an increasingly fragile global economy. These developments have created challenges for state policies and for businesses and labor as they strive to adapt to the changing political, economic, and social environment. This also raises important questions for social scientists seeking to understand the sources of these changes in employment relations and their likely consequences for workers, their families, and societies.

The recent rise of precarious work is associated with major economic shifts in the global economy and, as is common in major transitions, has created a great deal of uncertainty and insecurity. Governments and businesses have sought to make labor markets more flexible to compete in an increasingly competitive world economy. This has also led to the retrenchment of welfare and social protection systems in many countries and to a reconfiguring of the relationships between national and local levels of government and between public and private providers of social welfare protections. This has shifted the risks and responsibility for many social insurance programs to individuals and families.

Why has there been a rise in precarious work in rich democracies, with their high standards of living and privileged positions in the world economy? How and why do people experience precarious work differently in countries with dissimilar institutions and cultures? This book addresses these puzzles as it describes and explains how institutions and politics have shaped precarious work and its impacts on individuals and their families in rich democracies.

I argue that while the growth of precarious work is common to these rich democracies, its incidence and consequences differ depending on the countries' social welfare protections and labor market institutions. Relations between the state and markets are central to explanations of differences among employment relations, and hence to variations in the experience of precarious work. Social welfare protections and labor market institutions, in turn, result from a country's political dynamics (Sabel 1982) and the power resources and relations among the state, capital, labor, and other civil society actors and advocacy groups (such as non-governmental organizations [NGOs]) that shape the degree to which workers can protect themselves and their families from the risks associated with work and flexible labor markets. Moreover, cultural variations in social norms and values – such as those underlying the gender division of labor, whether families are characterized by dual earners or a male breadwinner–female homemaker model, and the importance placed on equality and the desirability of collective as opposed to individual solutions to social and economic problems – help to generate and legitimate a country's institutions and practices. Work and employment relations are also shaped by the demography of a country's labor force, such as its age distribution and patterns of immigration.

I develop and demonstrate my thesis about the impacts of social welfare protections and labor market institutions on precarious work and its consequences by comparing six rich democracies: Denmark, Germany, Japan, Spain, the United Kingdom, and the United States. These six countries represent diverse models of capitalism: social democratic nations (Denmark); coordinated market economies (CMEs; Germany, Japan); Southern Mediterranean economies (Spain); and liberal market economies (LMEs; the United Kingdom and United States). These countries differ in their employment and social welfare regimes and exemplify the range of ways in which institutional, political, and cultural factors affect precarious work and its outcomes. They also typify dissimilar responses of governments, employers, and workers to the macrostructural economic, political, and social factors driving the growth in precarious work and creating pressures for greater austerity and reorganizations among welfare and labor market institutions.

Studying precarious work and its consequences for individuals and their families is both timely and urgent. Rising insecurity and austerity have led to a variety of protests, ranging from mass mobilizations (such as Occupy), to confrontations with governments and businesses sponsored by traditional unions, to more stable social movements based on identity groups such as immigrants, race/ethnic groups, and gender. The consequences of precarious work have also inspired populist political movements in all these countries, with accompanying threats to democracy. Coming as it does after years of relative stability and prosperity, the recent rise of precarious work and the rollback of workers' hard-won gains during the post-World War II period also raises the menace of desperate actions by anxious people, such as by young adults who see little hope for the future. For these reasons, the recent rise of precarious work – along with its impacts on well-being – raises pressing political and policy issues that constitute a call to action on the part of governments, business, and workers.

Fortunately, the negative consequences of precarious work are not inevitable, as technology, globalization, or other inexorable forces do not determine them. Labor market and social welfare protection institutions are subject to the control of political actors, and, as I show in this book, some countries have been able to address the consequences of precarious work more successfully than others by reestablishing and expanding social safety nets, managing labor market transitions more effectively, and implementing social and economic reforms that are targeted at the needs and choices of increasingly diverse labor forces.

Research that examines how political, economic, and social institutions affect labor market outcomes and inequality typically makes trade-offs between specificity and generality. Some studies of precarious work and its consequences have tended to focus on specific countries, regions, or occupations and thus have been unable to assess how differences in a variety of macro-level structures and institutions affect these processes. Other studies compare relatively large numbers of countries, using typologies to distinguish distinct types that often gloss over important differences between countries within a given kind of employment or welfare regime.

My approach in this book, by contrast, is to consider a small number of countries that represent diverse models of capitalism. This strategy complements the more detailed and broadly comparative investigations of these countries, as it enables me to drill down on the features that may be distinctive to countries. By combining in-depth discussions of the labor market and social welfare contexts of these countries with quantitative empirical information on the extent of precarious work and indicators of well-being, I can observe the variability in precarious work and its consequences in these rich democracies.

The book provides evidence about precarious work, its relationship to social, economic, and political institutions, and its consequences for economic and non-economic forms of inequality. The book is not intended as a research monograph that furnishes detailed empirical analyses of these issues. Rather, I aim to offer an overview of the diversity associated with precarious work and its consequences and, by so doing, to identify key policy interventions needed to address precarious work and the actions on the part of social and political actors that could implement them. I also seek to contribute to the expanding body of empirical research by social scientists about how political, economic, and social institutions affect labor market outcomes and inequality.

Overview of the Book

I develop my argument about the rise of precarious work and its consequences for various aspects of well-being in rich democracies in four parts.

The first part provides the theoretical foundations for explaining precarious work and outlines the major differences among the six countries in their social welfare and labor market institutions and policies. Chapter 1 discusses the theoretical underpinnings of the notion of precarious work and summarizes the reasons for its recent rise in rich democracies. The chapter also sketches the conceptual model that I use in subsequent chapters to examine how countries differ in precarious work and its consequences. This model is a *multi-level* one, linking macrostructural institutions and policies to mesostructural features of employment relations and microstructural outcomes for individuals and their families.

Chapter 2 summarizes how countries differ in their social welfare protection and labor market policies. People in countries with more *generous social welfare benefits* are likely to be more secure both in their jobs and in their economic situations. Two significant labor market policies are *active labor market policies* that are designed to help working-age people obtain jobs and transition from unemployment to employment; and *employment protection* laws and regulations that denote the extent to which employment of regular workers is protected and the use of temporary workers is restricted by labor and other laws. Country differences in these social welfare and labor market policies result from the political dynamics underlying employment relations, especially the degrees to which workers can obtain *collective power resources* and align with political parties to advance their interests (e.g., Huber and Stephens 2001).

The second part of the book looks at country differences in the manifestations of precarious work. Chapter 3 provides an overview of common indicators of precarious work: nonstandard work arrangements such as temporary and involuntary part-time work. I show that the incidence of temporary work is relatively low in the LMEs of the United Kingdom and United States, which have few employment protections and whose labor markets have historically been flexible. By contrast, precarious work (especially temporary work among young people) is relatively high in Spain, with its high levels of employment protections and fewer restrictions on the use of temporary work.

Chapter 4 discusses various objective and subjective indicators of job insecurity, which is the most direct individual-level expression of precarious work. I show that active labor market policies as well as high degrees of worker power (reflected in high union density and collective bargaining coverage) all tend to reduce objective and perceived job insecurity.

The third part examines country dissimilarities in three dimensions of well-being: economic insecurity; the transition to adulthood and family formation; and subjective well-being. Chapter 5 looks at country differences in economic insecurity, including earnings inequality, low wages and poverty, social wages, economic instability, and perceived economic insecurity. Variations in social welfare protection institutions and policies play a major role in explaining why countries differ in these components of economic insecurity.

Chapter 6 discusses how the difficulties faced by young people in finding stable, regular jobs impede their ability to gain a foothold in the labor force and to establish career narratives that enable them to form their own families. Youth unemployment is particularly high in Spain, with its high levels of employment protection that relegates young workers to temporary jobs. Difficulties establishing families are especially pronounced in Japan, with its male breadwinner–female homemaker family model and rigid markers of the transition to adulthood.

Chapter 7 considers country differences in subjective well-being, an overall indicator of the quality of life. The generosity of social welfare protections, along with high levels of active labor market policies, enhances subjective well-being in a country.

The final part of the book summarizes some of the responses to the rise of precarious work. Chapter 8 discusses the protests generated both "from below" by workers and social movements and by government policies enacted "from above" to try to address the negative consequences of precarious work. I also outline the elements of a new political and social contract between workers and their employers and government that has the potential to collectivize the risks raised by precarious work and the kinds of actions that are needed to implement such a contract.

The conclusion summarizes the main findings of the book and speculates on possible future scenarios for employment relations.

Part I

Theoretical Foundations

1

The New Age of Precarious Work

[I]t is the insecurity of the present and uncertainty about the future that hatch and breed the most awesome and least bearable of our fears. (Zygmunt Bauman 2007: 26)

[T]he more work relations are "deregulated" and "flexibilized," the faster work society changes into a risk society incalculable both in terms of individual lives and at the level of the state and politics, . . . one future trend is clear. For a majority of people, even in the apparently prosperous middle layers, their basic existence and lifeworld will be marked by endemic insecurity. (Ulrich Beck 2000: 3)

Though it may start in one place, precarity soon slips into other dimensions of life. Insecurity at work, for example, spreads to insecurity when paying bills, trying to keep food on the table, maintaining honor and pride (in one's community or head of household), finding the energy to keep going. It is not only a condition of precarious labor but a more general existential state – a state where one's human condition has become precarious as well. (Anne Allison 2013: 9)

These quotations speak to a widespread concern about the lack of predictability, uncertainty, and insecurity in work, the family, and society that characterize rich democracies. Much of this insecurity and uncertainty is rooted in precarious *work*, which has far-reaching consequences for people's lives.

In this chapter, I provide an overview of precarious work and reasons for its recent rise in post-industrial capitalist democracies. I argue that precarious work is an increasingly important aspect of employment relations that has pervasive effects on job and economic insecurity, the transition to adulthood, family formation, and overall well-being. My conceptual model identifies ways to study empirically the manifestations and consequences of precarious work. I also provide an overview of how and why countries are likely to differ in the incidence and consequences of precarious work.

Precarious Work: Theoretical Foundations

Two general theoretical perspectives underlie social science studies of precarious work (see Kalleberg and Vallas 2018). The first, largely contributed by economic and organizational sociologists, uses the term "precarious work" to denote the many and various forms of work that may not be "new" but are redefined by employers and used by them in new contexts of production and in ways that cheapen the cost of labor, increase employers' flexibility, reduce the permanent workforce, shift employment risks to workers, and, perhaps not coincidentally, reduce labor's capacity for organization. As a general way of referring to the risks and insecurities connected to the complexities of contemporary work arrangements, the notion of precarious work offers advantages over commonly used but more specific designations, such as the dichotomies between formal and informal or standard and nonstandard work.

Precarious work arrangements include a variety of ways in which individuals are connected to work and employment, all of which are generally uncertain and often lack social protections. Major types of precarious work arrangements include: temporary work; contract work (comprising both independent contractors and employees of contract companies); involuntary part-time work; irregular and casual employment; and own-account self-employed persons (those who are classified as self-employed and do not have any employees themselves). The varied terms used to describe these types of precarious work include: contingent work; non-regular work; atypical work; market-mediated work arrangements; alternative work arrangements; nontraditional employment relations; flexible staffing arrangements or work practices; vulnerable work; disposable work; and new forms of employment.

The idea of precarious work is of course not new. It was intimately related to Marx and Engels's notion of a reserve army of labor, which was integral to Marx's critique of capitalism in Volume I of *Capital*. Indeed, Marx referred to the proletariat as a class that was typified by precariousness. The recent emergence of the emphasis on precarious work dates to the European responses in the 1950s and 1960s to poverty and low-wage work, though it became linked to politics through the radical Italian *Autonomia* movement, which emphasized the idea of precarious work as part of its analysis of the changes in production that led to new working-class politics based on the idea of immaterial labor (i.e., services that are not material goods) (Hewison 2016). It grew in prominence in the early 2000s as a rallying and organizing cry for social movement struggles, especially in Western Europe (Neilson and Rossiter 2005; Casas-Cortés 2009), where workers felt increasingly vulnerable to the consequences of neoliberal economic reforms that demanded the implementation of more flexible labor markets. Feeling deserted by unions and devalued by businesses, and struggling with a shrinking welfare system, Europeans began to organize around the concept of precarious work, which denoted a situation of living and working without stability or safety net. The concept of precarious work then spread to the United States, the industrial countries of East Asia (e.g., Japan, Korea, Taiwan), Australia, and elsewhere, as all these countries have undergone similar pressures for greater labor market flexibility and the resulting transformation of work and employment relations.

Precarious work, especially as conceptualized by European social scientists, has a normative bias that suggests a negative set of affairs (Mitropoulos 2005). It is often seen as a loss of social protections or other benefits associated with the so-called standard employment relationship (SER) that were once provided by employers or governments (e.g., Stone 2012; Adams and Deakin 2014). This defines precarious work against a normative state of affairs that departs from the post-World War II norm of secure employment with an employer, in which work is done full-time, full-year, on the employer's premises under his or her supervision, enjoying extensive statutory benefits and entitlements, and having the expectation of being employed indefinitely (see chapter 3 for a fuller discussion of the SER). Precarious work thus falls below socially accepted normative standards by which workers have certain rights and employment protections associated with economic life. Precarious workers lack a secure work-based identity and their jobs provide few benefits and low pay, and offer little hope for advancement to better jobs. Precarious work is also often equated with poor-quality, "bad" jobs and thus has been used as a synonym for poor job quality, high-stress jobs and working conditions, and so on. However, job quality is a much broader concept and while bad jobs are usually precarious, equating these concepts detracts from the uncertainty, riskiness, and other features that are distinctive about precarious work.

Viewing precarious work as the shifting of risks to workers regards it as a *process* – namely a swing in power relations from labor to capital, generally mediated by the state – rather than as a specific condition. For this reason, precarious work is sometimes seen as a useful concept in Europe, the United States, and the more developed countries of Asia, where there have previously been social protections and where the notion of standard work retains some of its normative value. In other countries in Asia (as well as Africa, parts of South America, and other less developed areas of the world), however, where precarious employment has always been the norm, this terminology may be less relevant. Even in many developing economies, though, being locked into precarious work with little opportunity to obtain better and more secure work can also viewed as a loss, in this case, for the chance to obtain the benefits of modernization and development. In these ways, precarious work reflects both *changing* employment conditions and the *loss* of conditions held or aspired for.

While linking precarious work to departures from a SER might be reasonable when considering the kinds of rich democracies examined here, it is important to recognize that this view is limited historically and cross-nationally. The SER was never the modal type of work arrangement in any society at any time; it was only slightly realized in advanced industrial countries and was uncommon in other areas of the world. Thus, most of the work relations under Fordism were outside the SER and excluded large groups of the population in these countries, such as women and immigrants, being predicated on the assumption of a male breadwinner–female homemaker model of the family (Neilson and Rossiter 2005). Moreover, wage relations have historically taken many forms besides the SER, such as the cottage industries in pre-industrial economies and in the Third World generally.

Furthermore, the concept of precarious work is not tied to a specific form of employment but encompasses the range of factors that contribute to whether a type of work exposes the worker to employment instability, a lack of legal and union protections, and social and economic vulnerability. Rodgers (1989) was one of the first in the academic mainstream to examine the nature of precarious work, as he identified four major dimensions of precarious work related to the employment relationship: (1) temporal (related to the continuity of employment); (2) organizational (control over work and its scheduling, working conditions); (3) economic (pay); and (4) social (welfare and legal protections). Vosko, MacDonald, and Campbell (2009), among others, extend this definition, incorporating self-employed workers and different forms of work-related insecurity. Building on these and other foundations, I emphasize three key aspects of precarious work.

1 Work that is *insecure* and *uncertain*, two aspects of the temporal dimension. Job insecurity implies a high risk of job loss and a future orientation characterized by expectations of not being able to find other, comparable jobs. Uncertainty denotes unpredictability on the job, such as having irregular and volatile work schedules, that is rooted in workers' lack of control over the conditions and terms of work.

2 Work that provides *limited economic and social benefits*, such as a living wage as well as health insurance or retirement benefits. This also has a temporal component, as precarious workers have little potential for advancement to better jobs and thus the prospects are bleak for improved economic and social rewards.

3 Work that has limited *statutory entitlements* provided by labor laws, regulatory protection, and labor rights.[1]

The extent to which work is precarious depends largely on the power of workers, as I will argue in the next chapter, and so I expect these three dimensions of precarious work to be generally positively interrelated. In cases where workers have high levels of collective market power, for example, they are likely to be able to pressure employers and governments to provide work that is relatively secure, well-paying, and protected by regulations and rights. This is especially likely during periods of high economic growth that are accompanied by high demand for labor, a situation that tends to enhance the power of workers. By contrast, in cases where workers have little power or control, jobs are apt to be characterized by high levels of precarious work on all three of these dimensions.

A second, broader, theoretical perspective on precarious work is that adopted by many foremost contemporary social science thinkers, who have used a more general ontological concept of *precarity* to describe a new phase of capitalism characterized by a lack of predictability or security. In their view, precarity results from forces such as globalization, rapid technological advances especially in information and communication, and political and economic policies related to the neoliberal revolution characterized by privatization, deregulation (and re-regulation) of markets, and a continued decline in the power of labor relative to capital.

This broad view of precarity was coined by Pierre Bourdieu (1998: 85), who saw *précarité* as a new form of domination in contemporary capitalism that is a permanent state designed to force workers to submit to their exploitation. He saw precarity as transforming society and as the root of problematic social issues in the twenty-first century that required the strengthening of the nation-state to combat.

In a similar vein, Giddens (1991) saw "reflexive modernization" as creating an "ontological insecurity" in social life, or an increased awareness of risk and insecurity that is largely produced by modern science and technological advances. Beck (1992, 2000) too maintained that rapid technological change and features of modern society such as global terrorism and the rise of radical Islam, economic crises and political decisions to promote austerity, climate change, and turbulence in financial markets have created a second age of modernity and a new political economy of insecurity, or a "world risk society" that is characterized by precarity, in which, among other things, work in developed countries of the West will increasingly take on the features usually associated with the informal economies of developing countries, which he termed the "Brazilianization of the West" (Beck 2000). He argued that this second modernity – typified by growing social inequalities, ecological crises, and an increasing individualization of work – represented a shift from the first modernity which took institutional shape in Europe in the post-World War II period and which was centered on paid employment and typified by the standardization of work, full employment, the welfare state, and exploitation of nature.

Moreover, Bauman (2000, 2007) identified a new era of "liquid modernity" whereby globalization, rapid technological change, and growing marketization have undermined the solid, stable institutional structures of work, society, power, and politics. This has led to the destruction of social bonds and unmooring individuals from social institutions, and so modern life is characterized by temporariness, vulnerability, and constant change, making "uncertainty the only certainty."

Further, Butler (2004) pointed to precariousness as a fundamental condition of life in the post-9/11 era that denotes the shared vulnerabilities that underscore the fragility of human existence. More recently, she argues (2015) that precarious economic conditions are not temporary but a new form of domination over ever-larger portions of the population (cf. Bourdieu 1998). This suggests that we are now observing a new stage in the political economy of modernity, replacing "organized capitalism" (Lash and Urry 1987).

The plight of the persons most affected by globalization and the other macrostructural changes was recently popularized by Standing's (2011) notion of the "precariat," a portmanteau word combining "precarious" and "proletariat" that refers to the broad group of people who lack key citizenship rights along with the various forms of security that formed the basis of the World War II citizenship agenda: job, employment, labor market, representation, income, and skill reproduction security. Those most likely to belong to the precariat are the young, women, the old, and immigrants (who are both a major reason for the growth of the precariat and its main victims). The precariat has minimal trust relationships with capital or the state and experiences anger, anomie, anxiety, and alienation. Precarity breeds a pessimistic view of life and the future, a loss of individual well-being, and disruptions in the transition to adulthood and family formation as people lack an ordered life plan. As Standing (2011: 24) describes this group:

> It [the precariat] is being in a status that offers no sense of career, no sense of secure occupational identity and few, if any, entitlements to the state and enterprise benefits that several generations of those who saw themselves as belonging to the industrial proletariat or the salariat had come to expect as their due.

The broader conception of precarity embraced by the second set of theorists identifies many of the social, economic, political, and cultural forces that have led to a pervasive sense of vulnerability and insecurity in contemporary capitalist nations. Manifestations of precarity are the general anxiety experienced by people resulting from events such as the terrorist attack in the United States on 9/11 and more recent acts of violence in France and other European countries, the specter of climate change, and the disruption produced by rapid technological changes, among many others. The resulting politics of fear that are rooted in these forms of precarity are reflected in the rise of right-wing, anti-immigrant parties and sentiments in countries such as the United Kingdom, France, Germany, the Nordic countries, and the United States, to name a few.

My arguments about precarious work draw on both of these general theoretical perspectives, which complement each other in important ways. The first, grounded in the dynamics associated with the transformation of employment relations in post-Fordism, provides the conceptual basis for understanding how economic and political factors – such as the spread of neoliberalism – have led to the emergence of precarious work. This perspective also lends itself more to empirical analysis and, as I will show in subsequent chapters, there has been a decline in long-term employment relations and a rise in nonstandard work arrangements of various kinds in the rich democracies, among other indicators of precarious work. By contrast, the writers I have cited who adhere to the second, broader and more abstract, perspective have produced little empirical support for their claims. Nevertheless, this second view is useful as it alerts us to the widespread effects of precarious work on individuals' well-being and its profound impacts on far-reaching social, economic, and political events. Both theoretical approaches underscore the necessity of comparative research in order to appreciate how macro institutions and structures shape precarious work and its consequences.

Explaining the Recent Rise of Precarious Work

[U]nemployment and underemployment – or, to use the nicer-sounding modern terms, . . . precarious forms of work and income – were historically the rule. (Ulrich Beck 2000: 13)

Why has precarious work become such a focus now, when capitalism has had continual crises and work and life have always been to some extent uncertain and insecure? As I noted in the previous section, precarious work was integral to Marx's critique of capitalism and work has always been insecure for both capital and most of the population in any society, as noted in the quotation here from Beck. Precarious work existed long before World War II and, while work is more precarious now for some people than it was in the early postwar period (especially for majority-group men in a society), it is undoubtedly less precarious for minority-group men and women than it was before World War II. We should therefore not romanticize about the security and advantages associated with work in the Post-World War II Golden Age of Capitalism, especially for those women and minorities, who have always been more subject to uncertain, insecure, and risky work relations.

The rich democracies that I focus on in this book represent a relatively privileged set of countries. The concept of precarious work means different things in developing and less industrial countries. While I argue that work has become more precarious in rich democracies in recent years, work in these countries is not nearly as precarious as in countries in the developing world and the Global South as well as in pre-industrial times.[2]

Precarious work is thus an old phenomenon that has re-emerged as a concern in the rich democracies over the past three decades. The latest rise in precarious work is a return to a more "normal" situation that characterized work for much of human history. The shift from the postwar "age of security" to the "age of flexibility" that began in the mid-1970s in the United States (and later in some of the other countries discussed here) can usefully be described by Karl Polanyi's notion of a "double movement." In *The Great Transformation* (1957 [1944]), Polanyi explained the organizing principles of industrial society in the nineteenth and twentieth centuries in terms of a struggle between unfettered markets and social protections. One side of this double movement was guided by the principles of economic liberalism and laissez-faire that supported the establishment and maintenance of free and flexible markets (i.e., the first Great Transformation in the nineteenth century). The other side of the double movement was dominated by pressures toward establishing social protections to help people cope with the psychological, social, and ecological disruptions that unregulated markets imposed on people's lives. Precarious work thus ebbs and flows and this has a lot to do with the kinds of social protections and state supports that are available at various time periods.[3]

The latest upsurge of precarious work in rich democracies was fueled by a variety of macro-economic, political, and sociological forces that challenged the postwar Keynesian institutional structure that emerged in industrial capitalist countries after World War II. This "Second Great Transformation" (e.g., Webster, Lambert, and Bezuidenhout 2008) fundamentally altered the postwar institutional structure of the labor market and transformed the traditional employment relations of the postwar period (see Kalleberg 2009, 2011; Levinson 2016).

Changes in the global economy played a big role in creating the conditions that generated precarious work. Increased international competition put pressure on businesses, especially in the core sectors of the economy, to become more efficient in their production of goods and services and more flexible in their relations with their employees and to cut costs. Employers in these core sector businesses (which were usually in manufacturing) experienced considerable uncertainty, risk, and instability compared to the more stable and high-growth period that preceded it. (Periphery sector firms had always existed in highly competitive, risky economic situations.) Indeed, it is the growing precarity of capital resulting from globalization and increased price competition that fueled employers' perceived need for greater flexibility in the employment relationship. While the high growth rates of the post-World War II period provided employers with considerable flexibility, the lack of growth in recent years made flexible employment relations both more necessary and more elusive.

These competitive pressures for greater flexibility were accompanied by political forces that led to a decline or removal of statutory and regulatory protections for workers through labor market institutions such as unions, minimum wage laws, and social protection legislation. These rollbacks were facilitated by (and in turn accelerated) declines in union strength, collective bargaining coverage, and other indicators of workers' power.

The reduction of government regulations in the labor market was accompanied by a shift in the balance of power to employers, who restructured employment systems (depending on the strength of the state and labor and the society's institutions) so as to evade institutional constraints and achieve greater flexibility, in order to reduce costs and to enable them to adjust the sizes of the workforces to market conditions. Forms of corporate restructuring included: offshoring and subcontracting production to lower-wage and less regulated areas of the world; shifting business risks by exploiting national and local differences in taxes and labor laws (such as those involving the use of temporary and contract workers) as well as opportunities for segmenting labor markets over space and national/ethnic divides; and expanding multinational corporations to make use of tax advantages and other ways of reducing costs and increasing profits.

These forms of corporate restructuring were powered by the growing financialization of corporations in the United States and many other countries. Financialization refers to "a pattern of accumulation in which profit-making occurs increasingly through financial channels rather than through trade and commodity production" (Krippner 2005: 181). It reflects a changing conception of the firm from an organization committed to specific product markets and to producing goods and services (managerial capitalism) to one that regards it as a tradable bundle of assets (finance capitalism). Accompanying this change was the replacement of the stakeholder model of corporate governance (which emphasized the welfare of managers, employees, suppliers, customers, creditors, and the broader community) by the shareholder model of corporate governance in the mid-1980s that gave primacy to the interests of investors and shareholders. Financial capitalism put pressure on corporate managers to increase profit margins and judged them by their ability to produce financial returns for shareholders. Financialization exposed many workers to outsourcing and downsizing, even by highly profitable firms seeking to make even more profits.

The political, economic, and ideological motivations behind many of these responses to global competition can be summarized by the notion of the neoliberal revolution, a political-economic perspective that emphasized the centrality of markets and market-driven solutions, privatization of government resources, and removal of government protections. Harvey (e.g., 2005) describes neoliberalism as a political project that was enacted by capitalists to limit the power of labor in response to what they perceived as labor's economic and political threats in the late 1960s and 1970s. Capitalists carried out this collective struggle on a number of fronts, including: promoting an ideology that emphasized market solutions and individual responsibility for economic issues; supporting political efforts to deregulate markets and weaken unions; adopting economic policies to promote offshoring and cost reductions; and implementing technological changes to automate work and reduce the need for labor.

The neoliberal revolution spread throughout the world and underscored the desirability of creating and maintaining greater flexibility in labor markets. Richard Freeman (1995: 63) succinctly described this view by referring to the 1994 *OECD Jobs Study* (OECD 1994):

> Throughout the 1980s, the superior performance of the U.S. in job creation compared to OECD-Europe [Organisation for Economic Co-operation and Development – Europe] suggested that labour-market flexibility, U.S.-style, was the panacea for European unemployment problems. Remove labour-market regulations, eliminate job-protection laws, reduce unemployment benefits, weaken unions, decentralize wage-setting, and presto! European unemployment would vanish. That, at least, is the crude version of the conventional wisdom of the decade. In more sophisticated form, this is the message of the *OECD Jobs Study*.

The primacy of flexible labor markets was reinforced during the economic crises in the early part of the twenty-first century in Europe, the United States, and Asia, which contributed to political demands on the part of governments for greater austerity and retrenchment in welfare protections and a greater reliance on "personal responsibility" rather than collective solutions, thereby eroding the solidarity character of many labor market and welfare institutions. These ideological changes associated with the adoption of neoliberalism represent deviations from the cultural logics previously underlying employment and social protection systems in the post-World War II period that emphasized the importance of secure work and economic security.[4]

Precarious work results from many of the features of neoliberal globalization: greater capital mobility in search of lower costs; financialization; privatization; the adoption of austerity policies to address budget deficits and cutbacks in social welfare protections in Europe after the economic crisis of the 2008–9 period; and the expansion of inequality in industrial countries. As Schram (2013: 13) observes: "neoliberalism begets precarity."

Several other key macrostructural forces that were relatively independent of politics fueled the expansion of precarious work in the contemporary period. Technological changes were an important source of precarious work. Advances in technology shortened product cycles and put greater premiums on obtaining flexibility in manufacturing processes. Production processes emphasizing flexible specialization began to replace mass production as the main way of manufacturing products, a development that Piore and Sabel (1984) referred to as the "Second Industrial Divide." Flexible specialization was facilitated by technological changes such as the rise of computerization and advances in information and communication technologies, which made possible greater connectivity among people, organizations, and countries, which made it relatively easy to move goods, capital, and workers within and across borders at an ever-accelerating pace. Such spatialization freed employers from conventional temporal and spatial constraints and allowed organizations to become more spatially decentralized and to export work activities to all parts of the world. Employers could locate their business operations optimally and access cheap sources of labor as well as exert greater control over decentralized and spatially dispersed labor processes (Wallace and Brady 2001).

These technological changes further drove the trend toward global markets as well as made it less advantageous for companies to make fixed investments in their workers. New information technologies also facilitated the downsizing of the organization's formerly "permanent" workforce as they eliminated the need for some layers of middle management and provided the infrastructure that enabled outsourcing and offshoring. Technological advances permitted the automating of some routine jobs in manufacturing and in clerical operations and created conditions for redefining work in other occupations. Managers, for example, now more often did what their secretaries used to do for them, scanners replaced clerks in stores, and self-serve check-in kiosks substituted for ticket agents at airports. Employers were motivated to get rid of their least skilled workers so they could hire workers who were better trained and more adept working with new technology. Technological advancements in automation and robotics have enhanced efficiency for employers but increased precarity for workers who are more at risk of being replaced by machines. Fears about a jobless future are likely overblown, but reflect the real concerns that many formerly middle-class workers have about their skills becoming obsolete and their being displaced from formerly well-paying and secure jobs.

The continued expansion of the service sector also led to the increased need for 24/7 staffing. While businesses and governments have a choice in how they organize such service jobs, the pressures already described – such as those related to cutting costs – created a demand for part-time and temporary workers.[5] The enlargement of the service sector was itself partly due to some of the macrostructural changes discussed so far, such as technological changes that enhanced the efficiency with which goods are manufactured, thereby reducing the number of jobs needed to make these goods, as well as the internationalization of production, which shifted manufacturing jobs from advanced industrial countries to less developed, lower-wage areas of the world. The growth of the service sector also reflects demographic changes, such as population aging (which increases the demand for health and care occupations, among others), and growing labor force diversity in gender, race, ethnicity, and immigration status.

In addition to these demand-side factors, changes in the labor forces of advanced industrial countries also contributed to the expansion of precarious work. The continued increase in the female workforce created a pool of workers who often preferred to work part-time.[6] The rise in low-skilled immigration from Latin America in the United States and the growth of migration within (and into) the European Union produced greater numbers of vulnerable workers with relatively little labor market power, who were often forced to take insecure and uncertain jobs due to a lack of alternatives. And the expansion of educational attainment in many industrial countries led to widening divides between high- and low-skilled workers and provided opportunities for employers to exploit less educated workers who had relatively little labor market power. Moreover, the entry into the global economy of China, India, and the former Soviet bloc countries in the 1990s doubled the size of the global labor pool, further shifting the balance of power from labor to employers (Freeman 2007).

Precarious work is historically and culturally specific, as I have discussed, which points to the need to examine its consequences within specific historical contexts and time periods. My focus in this book will be on the period beginning in the late 1970s and 1980s, which was the start of the recent era of precarious work in these rich democracies. This current era of precarious work is distinct from the character and consequences of past manifestations of precarious work in several ways.

First, while precarious work has always existed, it has now moved from a peripheral position under Fordism to a more central, core position under post-Fordism, especially given the prominence of immaterial labor that does not involve the production of goods (Hardt and Negri 2000). In addition, while women and racial/ethnic minorities have always been exposed to precarious work, as I have noted, job insecurity and risks of work have now spread to formerly advantaged men. In a sense, there has been a redistribution of precarious work, such that native men now work in insecure and risky jobs along with everyone else, creating a sense of relative deprivation among them that has helped generate social and political protests in various ways (see chapter 8). Highly skilled as well as low-skilled workers are now more insecure; temporary work characterizes all types of occupations, for example, not just low-status jobs. In a sense, everyone is now a temporary worker, though of course some people are more temporary than others.

Second, global competition has made it more possible for businesses to shift jobs around the world, as my discussion of spatialization indicates; this has been facilitated by innovations in communication and information technologies such as digitization.

Third, the consequences of unemployment have become more severe, due to lower financial supports for the unemployed in many countries and the tendency for long-term unemployment to increase as a proportion of total unemployment, especially since the 2008–9 recession. These direr consequences of unemployment have amplified people's sense of insecurity as they enhance the costs of joblessness.

Finally, precarious work now is different from the past in that many of the structures that facilitated human interaction and welfare in prior risky periods (such as the family or community-based organizations) have been weakened, due to the new institutional arrangements that accompanied the growth and prosperity of the post-World War II period. Hence, there is a decline in the capacity for collective action, on the part of both the corporate elite (Mizruchi 2013) and individuals (Fraser 2015).

Some writers have challenged the assumption that precarious work is really increasing in rich democracies. These objections generally equate precarious work with specific measures such as temporary work or other nonstandard employment relationships, and have questioned how much of a quantitative shift away from standard employment relations there has really been. Many of these criticisms have questioned how much growth of temporary work there has been in LMEs such as the United Kingdom (e.g., McGovern, Smeaton, and Hill 2004; Fevre 2007; Doogan 2009) and the United States. In these countries, data on trends in temporary work often seem to suggest that there has not been much of an increase in this form of precarious work. However, as we will see in chapter 3, the relatively low levels of, and small increases in, temporary work in these countries are due largely to the nature of their labor market institutions such as low employment protections for regular workers; there has been much greater growth in temporary work in other countries. Moreover, the growth of precarious work is not only reflected in increases in certain types of work arrangements such as temporary work, but also by reductions in social and statutory protections in what otherwise might be considered standard employment relations.

Other disputes over the assumption of rising precarious work come from analyses that use specific indicators of one of the dimensions of precarious work, usually job instability. Thus, studies of trends in indicators such as tenure with an employer for a long time revealed the existence of considerable stability, leading some to conclude that there has been relatively little change in employment relations (e.g., Auer and Cazes 2000). These challenges are also hotly debated, though a consensus has emerged that job instability has generally increased, especially for prime-age men, and I will show in chapter 4 that there has been a decline in the length of time prime-age men generally work for an employer.

These controversies about the extent to which there has been a rise in precarious work underscore the unsettled nature of this question and the need for systematic conceptualization and empirical study that is grounded in the experiences of diverse countries. These constitute central tasks of this book.

Causes and Consequences of Precarious Work:
A Conceptual Model

Figure 1.1 describes my conceptual framework for studying the causes, manifestations, and consequences of precarious work.

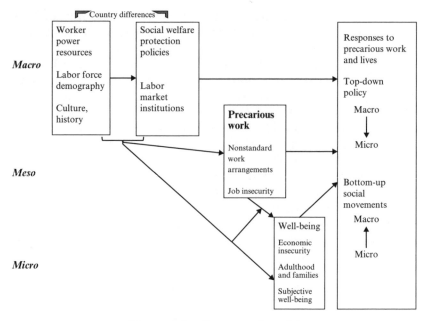

Figure 1.1   Conceptual model

The model identifies the interrelations among phenomena operating at *multiple levels of analysis:* at the macro, meso (middle), and micro levels. Country differences represent macro-level social, political, economic, and cultural forces. Precarious work refers to the meso-level employment relations between employers and their workers. Macro- and meso-level structures are the fundamental institutions of capitalist systems that have important implications for micro-level outcomes such as workers' well-being. Finally, precarious work and negative outcomes such as high economic insecurity, difficulties in making the transition to adulthood and forming families, and low subjective well-being may produce social and political movements to protest these conditions. The latter are examples of how micro forces can lead to macro-level changes. In addition, macro-level government policies might have meso- and micro-level consequences.

The model also summarizes my assumptions about the causal relations among the key components. A direct arrow from one box to another (e.g., from the first two boxes representing "country differences" to "precarious work") denotes my assumption that the former are causes of the latter. The arrow from "social welfare protection policies and labor market institutions" to the arrow between "precarious work" and "well-being" signifies my assumption that labor market and welfare institutions affect how precarious work translates into well-being (e.g., precarious work is less consequential in countries with generous welfare systems).

The remainder of this chapter provides an overview of these components.

Country Differences

Social scientists disagree in their views about how and why countries differ in their economic and employment institutions and whether these differences are likely to converge or diverge over time. *Universalistic* theories generally assume that forces such as globalization, market forces, and changes in technology are so strong that nations at similar stages of development must adapt to similar organizational logics. This weakens the impact of institutional contexts such that country differences should be minimal and decline over time, leading to an evolutionary development and convergence among advanced capitalist nations. Examples of universalistic schemes are the industrialism (e.g., Kerr et al. 1960) and post-industrial (Bell 1973) theories, which argued that technology and knowledge, respectively, would lead to skill upgrading in all capitalist countries. On the other hand, Marxist perspectives (e.g., Braverman 1974) predicted there would be an increasing degradation of skills in capitalist countries.

By contrast, *neo-institutional* theories argue that the different social, economic, and political structures typical of capitalist societies produce divergences among them in their employment systems and institutions. I adopt this perspective in this book and draw on two influential neo-institutional theories of national diversity among capitalist countries to identify the employment, labor market, and social welfare protection systems that shape the nature and consequences of precarious work for individuals and their families: the "varieties of capitalism" (VoC) or "production regime" theory approach (Hall and Soskice 2001); and the power resources theory (PRT) (e.g., Stephens 1979; Korpi 1983, 1985; Esping-Andersen 1990).

While both VoC and PRT emphasize a wide range of structures and policies that are important for understanding country differences in precarious work and its consequences, they tend to highlight somewhat different institutions. The VoC theory is especially relevant in accounting for differences in *labor market institutions* such as active labor market policies and collective bargaining. These institutions are linked to the *employment systems* within a country – especially educational and skill formation systems – and associated patterns of labor market mobility.[7] On the other hand, the PRT emphasizes how the differential *power resources of workers* through political parties and unions help to produce variations in the inclusiveness of welfare provisions and the degree of unemployment insurance (UI) protection and social spending generally. The PRT can also be considered a refined version of the argument made by Polanyi (1957 [1944]), whereby worker power helps to create welfare states that reduce workers' dependence on the market and employment (Pierson 2000).

I examine differences among these countries, then, in two key *social welfare protection policies*: (1) the generosity of *welfare spending*, or those monies (both public and required from private sources) that are designed to provide protections against illness, old age, disability, poverty, and other kinds of difficulties faced by persons over the course of their lives; and (2) the degree to which unemployed persons receive financial support (usually in the form of *UI* payments). These financial supports provide a cushion or economic safety net to support people during times of unemployment. These social welfare protection policies are especially important for reducing the degree of economic insecurity.

I also assess country differences in two key *labor market institutions*: (1) the nature and extent of a country's *active labor market policies*, which are designed to help workers transition between jobs and from unemployment to jobs; and (2) the degree of *employment protections* for "permanent, regular" workers and the rules governing the use of temporary and other nonstandard workers. These labor market institutions and policies are especially important for impacting objective and subjective levels of job insecurity.

These social welfare protection and labor market institutions are shaped in important ways by *labor force demographic* differences among countries. Age, gender, race and ethnicity, immigration status, and education are key factors that affect the degree to which a person experiences precarious work. The impacts of welfare and labor market institutions differ among demographic groups and life stages: e.g., active labor market policies are more relevant to younger and middle-aged workers in the prime of their careers than to older workers who may soon retire; while the degree of employment protections – by providing greater job security to older workers – may make it more difficult for young people to become established in the labor market, and help to foster a duality in the labor market between relatively protected insiders and vulnerable outsiders (which include young workers, women, and immigrants, depending on the country).

In addition, pension benefits (a form of welfare spending) are more salient for older workers approaching retirement than younger workers who have their working lives ahead of them.

Gender illustrates the important role of demographic characteristics as a source of welfare systems in these countries. A nation's need for women in the labor force (as in Scandinavian countries by the 1960s or Germany and Japan more recently) creates pressure on governments to expand childcare and other benefits related to balancing work and family. Moreover, greater female labor force participation also creates a stronger interest group able to push for its political demands for welfare services (see Huber and Stephens 2001).

Cultural differences may also influence how precarious work is interpreted and experienced. Gender role expectations – such as the desirability for a woman of marriage to a male breadwinner – affect the implications for family formation of men not being able to obtain secure and stable employment. Strong extended family networks and support systems may enhance levels of subjective well-being despite the presence of job and economic insecurity. And cultural logics and norms related to work (and non-work), and the importance of social rights to secure work and economic security, affect subjective perceptions of insecurity and well-being (and reactions to them).

Finally, countries' *historical* experiences have shaped all the differences among institutions and cultures that I have discussed. To some degree, "history" represents a residual, catch-all category for differences in precarious work and well-being among the six countries I study that are not captured by those welfare state and labor market institutions (and other forces) that I consider explicitly. Countries' historical experiences have also created a path dependency that helps shape the directions countries might take in the future to address precarious work and its consequences.

Conceptualizing Precarious Work

There are two main approaches to conceptualizing (and hence measuring) precarious work, which I defined earlier in this chapter as consisting of three main components: (1) insecurity and uncertainty associated with jobs; (2) limited economic and social benefits; and (3) lack of legal protections. One approach focuses on the form of the *employment relationship*, differentiating between the SER and various forms of nonstandard work arrangements. This view assumes that dissimilar types of employment relations will differ in the three dimensions of precarious work. Many of the social welfare protections and labor laws developed in welfare regimes were predicated on the idea of a SER and were available only to those in such work arrangements, for example, and so social and legal protections and the continuity and predictability of employment were closely linked to wage levels and work-related benefits and wage growth over time. I examine country differences in nonstandard employment relations in chapter 3.

A second approach emphasizes the insecurity associated with jobs, which can be assessed both objectively (e.g., the probability that a person will lose a job and/or obtain a comparable new one) and in terms of workers' subjective perceptions of these objective realities (and the degree to which one is concerned about these realities). I consider differences in objective and subjective job insecurity in chapter 4.

Each of the three dimensions of precarious work is potentially problematic for workers, though their relative incidence and difficulty may differ across time and country. For some persons, the main concern is the uncertainty and insecurity associated with precarious jobs, particularly in situations where there are few opportunities to acquire new skills and find new jobs. For others, it may be the economic insecurity resulting from periods of joblessness, especially in countries where social benefits are closely tied to employment. Moreover, policies that impose austerity by removing or decreasing economic and social benefits, or reduce statutory entitlements for some (such as immigrants), will also lead to precarious work, whether the employment contract is temporary or not. Workers in otherwise standard employment relations, for example, may no longer have the social protections associated with their jobs and so many are precarious regardless of their levels of job security. And in countries where social welfare and legal protections are not tied closely to the nature of the employment relationship, as with part-time jobs in the Netherlands, jobs may be relatively insecure but labor laws and rights may still protect all workers, making nonstandard jobs less precarious overall.

This discussion of precarious work points to the importance of labor market and social welfare protection institutions and policies for influencing workers' risks in the labor market, and thus their job and economic insecurity. While national institutions do matter for producing country differences, there is a great deal of variation within countries by local areas, industries, firms, and so on.[8] While all jobs are generally more risky and precarious now than during the decades after World War II, some jobs are clearly more precarious than others

(Neilson and Rossiter 2005). Firms within an industry or in different industries may also organize work in different ways: firms have considerable discretion as to which kinds of employment and wage policies to adopt in responding to similar market pressures, within parameters established by the employment and welfare regimes of countries.

Well-Being

I summarize the consequences for individuals resulting from precarious work in terms of three major aspects of well-being: economic insecurity; the transition to adulthood and family formation; and subjective well-being or happiness. Widening the lens to examine diverse consequences of precarious work highlights its wide-ranging effects on people's lives.

Economic insecurity denotes concerns about having sufficient economic resources to provide for oneself and one's family. This depends on one's (and the family's) human and social capital resources as well as on characteristics of the welfare state. Chapter 5 focuses on country differences in objective and subjective economic insecurity.

Transition to adulthood and *family formation* refers to the ability of young workers to find full-time work in stable jobs and so to make a successful and timely transition to adulthood by moving out of the parental home and establishing their own families. These topics are the subject of chapter 6.

Subjective well-being represents a person's overall affective evaluation of the quality of one's life and is generally measured by concepts such as life satisfaction or overall happiness. The concept of subjective well-being has attracted a great deal of attention from social scientists – notably economists, sociologists, and political scientists in addition to the traditional disciplines of psychology and philosophy – who see this as a means of evaluating the impacts of non-economic as well as economic utilities on one's overall quality of life. I examine country differences in subjective well-being in chapter 7.

Workers are not a homogenous group, of course, and people differ in the degree to which they have precarious work and the extent to which this is a problem for them. Individuals differ in their motives for working in their jobs, whether they voluntarily choose jobs that might be considered objectively to be precarious (as when a temporary or part-time worker chooses these work arrangements to accommodate their family or other needs) or if they work in such jobs involuntarily. Assessing individuals' motives and preferences is thus important when assessing the degree to which a type of work presents a problem or an opportunity for the worker.

Consequences of precarious work differ among individuals, depending on their vulnerability in terms of their labor market power. In some countries, such as Germany, Japan, and Spain, there are relatively high levels of dualism in labor markets and social welfare systems in which a core of regular workers is well protected while those who are more peripheral are not. This tends to be true of immigrants in most countries, especially those who have not acquired legal residence. Vulnerability to precarious work also differs by age, with the youngest and oldest workers most at risk, as are minority workers and women and those with relatively little education.

Hence, precarious work is double-edged. On the one hand, it means insecurity and instability for many people, especially those who are more vulnerable because they lack labor market power (such as undocumented workers, who are probably the most precarious workers of all in these rich democracies). On the other hand, the flexible employment relations associated with precarious work may provide those who possess skills that are in high demand (such as highly skilled computer programmers or knowledgeable consultants) the opportunity to benefit from being able to move more freely from one employer to the next. For them, insecure and unstable work may provide greater flexibility, rewarding some types of creativity, promoting individualism, and enabling some forms of social and geographic mobility (Horning 2012).

Responses to Precarious Work and Lives

The proliferation of precarious work undermines the socio-political stability that Fordism (with its associated Keynesian policies and expanded welfare state) had provided in the early post-World War II period in the rich democracies. The consequences of precarious work and precarious lives have triggered responses in the form of social and political movements that have sought to mitigate the most serious costs for workers and their families and have deeply affected the politics of post-industrial countries. Two main types of responses can be categorized as those emanating from the "bottom up" as workers seek to create macro-level structural changes through social movements of various kinds; and from the "top down," whereby governments (perhaps prodded by protest movements) enact policies (such as more generous welfare policies) to protect workers from the consequences of precarious work. These responses to precarious work and lives are discussed in chapter 8. There I also suggest policy ideas about how precarious work can be addressed, including the components of a new political and social contract among workers, employers, and the government that would alleviate its more negative consequences.

Summary and Conclusions

Precarious work denotes the extent to which work arrangements are: (1) insecure, unstable and uncertain; (2) associated with limited economic rewards such as wages and associated benefits, and provide few opportunities to obtain greater economic rewards over time; and (3) not accompanied by legal and social protections and rights. Precarious workers largely bear the risks of work, as opposed to employers and governments.

The idea of precarious work has gained wide currency among social theorists as a way of describing the condition of growing insecurity and uncertainty in contemporary capitalism that results from processes of globalization, technological change, the weakening of workers' power, and the political and cultural dynamics associated with the spread of neoliberalism. The past three decades have witnessed a rise of precarious work, which contrasts sharply with the period of relative growth, equality, and stability in Europe, the United States, and East Asia in the first three decades after World War II. This growth of precarious work represents a partial return to the market-mediated employment systems and relative lack of social protections that preceded the development of Keynesian welfare states, and has created considerable uncertainty and insecurity about the future of jobs and careers as well as economic situations and family formation, among others.

While precarious work is a worldwide phenomenon, it affects individuals and their families differently, depending on a country's social welfare protection and labor market institutions as well as its cultural norms regarding the gender division of labor, the importance of work and stable careers for a person's identity and ability to get married and start a family, and cultural values and norms related to rights to secure work and economic security.

My conceptual model summarizes my assumptions about the interrelations among the causes, manifestations, and consequences of precarious work. It is a multi-level model that links macro structures (such as country differences in institutions) to meso-level structures

(employment relations and precarious work) and to micro-level outcomes for individuals. The various chapters in this book will unpack
the components of this conceptual model.

The next chapter discusses the country differences suggested by
this conceptual framework in more detail, and outlines how variations among the advanced capitalist democracies in worker power,
and in social welfare protection and labor market institutions and
policies affect precarious work and its consequences.

2
Social Welfare Protection and Labor Market Institutions

Variations in public social provision have big effects on social life . . . social programs and regulations significantly modify employer and union behavior. (Paul Pierson 2000: 791, 793)

Labor market institutions have an important impact on firms' choices on how to respond to competitive pressures. (Eileen Appelbaum et al. 2010: 1)

Precarious work is a global phenomenon, affecting individuals, families, organizations, and governments in all post-industrial nations.[1] All of these countries face pressures due to the social and economic forces associated with more intense globalization, technological advances especially in information and communication technologies, greater mobility of capital and labor, new forms of organizational interdependence, and shifts in the balance of power between employers and workers that have weakened unions (see the case studies in Gautié and Schmitt 2010). At the same time, differences among countries in their institutions, cultures, and historical trajectories produce national diversities in the incidence as well as the consequences of precarious work, as the quotations here suggest. Identifying such country differences is the major goal of this chapter.

I draw on the two prominent theories of national diversity among capitalist countries described in the previous chapter – the varieties of capitalism (VoC) theory and the power resources theory (PRT) – to pinpoint the key dimensions of labor markets and welfare systems that shape the characteristics and consequences of precarious work for individuals and their families. I argue that the main sources of cleavages among countries suggested by the VoC and PRT approaches can be fruitfully studied by looking at the six countries that I examine in this book: Denmark, Germany, Japan, Spain, the United Kingdom, and the United States. I then show empirically how the key social welfare protection and labor market institutions and policies differ among these six countries.

Classifying Institutional Differences Among Countries

The VoC theory derives from economic perspectives on institutions and economic efficiency and emphasizes how economic activity is coordinated between employers and firms.[2] Different systems result from the various ways that countries solve problems related to the organization of production. VoC distinguishes between LMEs and CMEs that differ in five main ways in which production is organized and companies coordinate production: the industrial relations system; the vocational training and education system; corporate governance; inter-firm relations; and relations with their own employees (Soskice 1999; Hall and Soskice 2001). The interrelations among these institutions are assumed to produce high degrees of stability within each type of capitalism. VoC then clusters nations into distinct groups depending on how these spheres interrelate. In LMEs, market mechanisms dominate, collective bargaining is decentralized and uncoordinated, labor is relatively weak, relations between employers and unions are adversarial, there is limited non-market coordination between companies, and the state plays a relatively small role in the economy. By contrast, CMEs organize production more through non-market mechanisms such as coordinated bargaining and social partnerships between strong unions and robust, centralized, synchronized employer associations (Soskice 1999). Examples of ideal-type LMEs are the United States, the United Kingdom, and Canada; examples of CMEs are Germany, Japan, and the Nordic countries.

The VoC theory's emphasis on the significance of employers and firms contrasts with an older neo-institutional theory of country differences, the PRT. The PRT stems from political and sociological perspectives and focuses on how the balance of class power – reflected in the strength of unions and political parties within countries – provides social protections for individuals that help them to mitigate social and economic risks. The PRT emphasizes the relative power resources of employers and workers, their ability to achieve their distinct interests, and the role of the state in mediating the relations between them. The theory thus overcomes a criticism of VoC that it underplays the importance of political dimensions of economic activity (e.g., Wood 2001).

Esping-Andersen's (1990) influential application of the PRT to explaining differences among welfare states distinguished among three diverse ideal-type welfare regimes: liberal welfare states (US, UK, Canada) where work is idealized over welfare and entitlement rules are strict and dominated by modest social insurance plans and transfers, and means-tested assistance; conservative welfare states (Germany, France, Italy) that are characterized by efforts to link social rights and benefits to class and status, as well as preserving traditional families and motherhood by creating disincentives for mothers to work; and social democratic countries (e.g., in Scandinavia) in which social rights that enable people to maintain a socially acceptable standard of living without reliance on the labor market (i.e., principles of decommodification) were extended to the entire population.[3]

There is substantial theoretical and empirical overlap between country differences in the coordination of production (as in the VoC approach) and the degree of egalitarianism and social protections (as in the PRT). Hence, industrial relations and employment systems and labor market institutions emphasized by the VoC approach have strong parallels in social protections and degree of inequality (Thelen 2014). Welfare states are embedded in production regimes, as patterns of relations among firms, financial institutions, and the state facilitate conditions (such as skill formation systems and wage restraint) that enable the creation of welfare states that differ in their level of generosity (Huber and Stephens 2001). It is thus not surprising that the VoC and PRT categorize groups of countries in similar ways, despite emphasizing different institutional structures.

Bruno Amable (2003) provides a more systematic classification of models of capitalism that moves beyond the dualistic conceptions of national diversity inspired by the VoC and PRT. He first identifies five fundamental institutional areas that characterize capitalist societies: (1) product market competition; (2) labor market institutions and the wage-labor nexus; (3) financial intermediation sector and corporate governance; (4) social protection and the welfare state; and (5) education. He then develops quantitative indicators for all of these dimensions and derives an empirically based typology that yields five types of capitalist systems: (1) a market-based system; (2) a social democratic system; (3) Continental European capitalism (a "state capitalist" or state-coordinated form of capitalism); (4) South European ("Mediterranean") capitalism (where the family plays a strong role in welfare provision); and (5) Asian capitalism (a meso-corporatist, "productivist" type in which more coordination and welfare are provided at the company level). This empirical typology, derived from his theoretical analysis, thus further subdivides conservative welfare states into three types, in addition to the social democratic and liberal market models identified by other theories (see also the discussion by Schröder 2009). Amable's typology identifies key country differences that are relevant to studying precarious work and its consequences, especially collective wage bargaining, skills, training, and education. I will use it here as the basis for choosing strategically a small set of countries to represent the social welfare protection and labor institutions associated with the different models of capitalism.

Six Countries

While typologies are useful for summarizing broad differences among groups, the boundaries of clusters are often ambiguous, and there may be considerable heterogeneity across (and within) countries within regime types. Comparing a relatively few countries characterizing different models of capitalism permits an assessment of the impacts of institutions with greater precision and avoids the tendency to reach a set of nation-specific conclusions, thereby facilitating generalizations about more basic processes.

The six countries studied here represent the key distinctions emphasized by the neo-institutional typologies already outlined. When discussing these countries, I will typically do it alphabetically, which also corresponds in this case to social democratic, CME, and LME, respectively. In some instances, though, I will tailor my discussion to the topic, such as countries that are especially high and low on a policy area.

Denmark is a small (population of about 5.7 million in 2017)[4] European country that illustrates the social democratic model and is the clearest example among the six countries of an inclusive regime characterized by high levels of social protections for all citizens, and high involvement of the government in public policy. It has the largest public sector of all the countries, with about 35 percent of total employment in the public sector in 2013 (OECD 2015b). The "Danish model" is characterized by industrial self-governance, regulated by rules set up primarily through centralized negotiations between representatives of employers and employees. The policy of "flexicurity" is another key feature of the Danish model, whereby employers have great flexibility in hiring and firing workers but this is accompanied by giving workers considerable assistance in transitioning to new jobs once unemployed.

Germany has a population of about 82 million in 2017 and is Europe's largest and strongest economy ($3.23 trillion in gross domestic product [GDP]) (Thesing, Randow, and Kirchfield 2010); its GDP per capita has increased more than any other G7 country over the past decade (*The Economist* 2012) after a period of relatively poor performance. Germany is the classic Christian Democratic, Continental European CME in which the organization among economic actors occurs primarily at the industry sector level. The government has traditionally been highly involved in the economy (especially in the manufacturing sector, though not as much in the industrial relations system as Denmark) and its social protection system is employment-based, with social insurance being financed by contributions. Germany relies on a manufacturing-based export economy: almost all the economic growth in Germany from 2001 to 2007 was due to exports, and more than half of its exports were in vehicles, machines, electronic devices, and chemicals (*The Economist* 2012), though manufacturing now employs less than 20 percent of workers. Germany's public sector is relatively small compared to Denmark's, comprising about 15 percent of total employment in 2009 (OECD 2015b).

Japan is an East Asian country with a population of about 127.5 million in 2017. It illustrates the Asian social insurance welfare state in which social policies (including social protections) are subordinated to – and designed to facilitate – economic development and growth (Holliday 2000). Japan is characterized by company-level coordination: the government is also highly involved in production markets, but in contrast to Germany, Japan is group- rather than industry-coordinated, such as via the *kereitsu* (a conglomeration of businesses producing a variety of products and linked together by cross-shareholdings). Firms are central to the coordination of the Japanese economy as well as to employment relations, and the division between large and small firms helps maintain a dualistic labor market. Japan also has the smallest public sector of all the six countries, consisting of only about 8 percent of total employment in 2013 (OECD 2015b).

Spain has a population of about 46.4 million in 2017 and is an example of the Southern Mediterranean model of a coordinated economy. The Spanish model has features in common with both the German and Japanese CMEs (with their relatively concentrated ownership of firms and strong state intervention in markets) and LMEs, especially with Spain's reforms designed to enhance labor market flexibility in the wake of the disastrous 2008 economic crisis. A moderate level of social protection characterizes Spain's welfare system, with expenditures focused on pensions and poverty reduction and a reliance on the family as a key source of welfare provision. Spain's public sector makes up about 17 percent of total employment in 2013 (OECD 2015b).

The *United Kingdom* is a LME and welfare state with a population of 66 million in 2017. There is relatively low involvement of the government in the economy and relatively weak social protections that emphasize poverty reduction (though it is distinctive among LMEs in its universal National Health Service, set up under a Labour government in 1948). At the same time, it has a relatively large public sector, comprising about 24 percent of total employment in 2013 (OECD 2015b). The labor market in the UK changed from a system that bore some resemblance to that of other Continental European countries to one more like the US in a relatively short time due to the institutional changes initiated by the Thatcher government in the 1980s, which loosened employment regulations and made social welfare protections (such as UI) more targeted and less generous.

The *United States* is also a LME and welfare state, with a population of about 324.5 million in 2017. Like the UK, the US is typified by relatively low government involvement in the economy, which is reinforced by strong ideological commitments to free product and labor markets and individualism. Labor regulations and other government interventions in the labor market are fragmented among jurisdictions at the federal, state, and local levels. Public sector employment in the US is about the same as in Germany, about 15 percent in 2008 (OECD 2011). Union membership is low and employees have little collective bargaining power and few institutionalized employment guarantees. Social protections are generally weak and benefits are means tested.

The categorization of country differences derived from the VoC and PRT models reflects the historical periods when these typologies were developed, when countries were reacting in different ways to similar global historical forces (i.e., the early 1980s in the case of the "three worlds" of welfare capitalism; and the 1990s for the VoC approach). As such, these typologies were static and mainly oriented to explaining diversity in manufacturing economies; the shift to services has changed the political dynamics as service employers and workers have interests that are often different from those in manufacturing, such as a greater need for general skills and for more continuous ("24/7") staffing patterns. While the six countries still represent key institutional differences, then, we need to consider the changes that have taken place in recent decades. All six of these countries have liberalized their social welfare protection and labor market institutions in response to economic, social, and political pressures for greater flexibility, the same forces that are behind the recent rise of precarious work that I discussed in the previous chapter.

Varieties of Liberalization of Social Welfare Protection and Labor Market Systems

Kathleen Thelen (2014) identifies three divergent ways in which industrial countries have liberalized their political economies in response to the kinds of changes identified in the previous chapter. The approach adopted was dependent on the constellation and dynamics of political, economic, and social forces that characterize the country. The six countries illustrate all three of these forms of liberalization: embedded flexibilization; dualization; and deregulatory liberalization.

Embedded flexibilization (Denmark) involves the adoption of greater labor market and social welfare flexibility within an inclusive framework defined by a broad set of collective bargaining structures and strong union presence. Along with state policies to minimize wage inequalities, this has resulted in a collectivization of the risks produced by liberalization policies.

Dualization (Germany, Japan, Spain) entails the protection of "core" workers from market risks at the expense of "peripheral" workers who are relatively unprotected from these risks. A protected group of insiders or core workers enjoy long-term contractual relations and relatively high levels of security while those in the periphery, or outsiders, are often employed in non-regular jobs with relatively few protections.

Japan's economy has traditionally been dualistic, while dualism in Germany is more recent as it emerged within the past thirty years or so and was precipitated by deindustrialization and the failure of unions to organize workers in the private service sector. Spain has long been characterized by strong employment protections for regular workers and a strong divide between insiders and outsiders.

Germany went through several processes of liberalization, first in response to economic crises[5] after the reunification between East and

West Germany in 1990, and then in the early 2000s as the German government sought to further deregulate its labor market to combat slow growth and high unemployment, and to increase employment levels through the Hartz reforms (see chapter 3). Germany's liberalization response to the pressures for greater flexibility and austerity was a dualistic one. Employer coordination and relatively strong employer–union relations remained in the core manufacturing sectors, though there was a decline in the number of regular workers, in apprenticeship opportunities, and in collective bargaining coverage. Liberalization instead took place primarily among the unprotected, peripheral manufacturing sectors as well as in the growing service sector.

The Japanese liberalization response to economic crises in the 1990s and 2000s has also been a dualist one, which is consistent with the long history of dual labor markets in Japan. Workers in the core, protected economy have been better able to defend their positions at the expense of a growing number of workers in non-regular, less protected, employment relationships (see Peng 2012).

In Spain, pressures since the 1980s to make labor markets more flexible have also led to increased labor market dualism between a primary sector consisting of workers in larger firms, multinational companies, and state-owned organizations who have open-ended contracts with increasing wages that are tied to prices and social benefits, and a secondary sector composed of workers (mostly young persons and women) who have temporary contracts and precarious working conditions.

Finally, *deregulatory liberalization* (in the United Kingdom and United States) involves the replacement of collective mechanisms of labor regulations by the imposition of market processes, resulting in the shifting of the risks of work to individuals. In these countries, "institutions and mechanisms for collective regulation are explicitly set aside in favor of arrangements that re-impose the discipline of the market" (Thelen 2014: 13). The political decisions made by Conservative governments in the UK resulted in a liberalization of regulations on employment relations. This weakened labor market institutions in the UK and made them more like those in the US. In both countries, the spread of neoliberalism led to a rollback of institutional protections and an individualization of risk.

While dualism of the sort found in Germany, Japan, and Spain is relatively low in the LMEs, there is still a divide between "good" and "bad" jobs in these countries. In the US, there have always been gaps in the labor market produced by race and gender; more recently, education has grown in importance in providing workers with individual market power and creating divisions in the labor market (see Kalleberg 2011). In the UK, a key source of labor market dualism is between those in regular and those in nonstandard jobs (McGovern, Smeaton, and Hill 2004).

We should also recognize that insider/outsider dualism is not necessarily worse than deregulatory liberalization in terms of precarious work and the quality of jobs. Divisions between those in relatively good and bad jobs might be preferable, for example, to making everyone equally precarious.

These strategies of liberalization have altered the social welfare protection and labor market institutions of these six countries. Differences among them are rooted in variations in the degree to which workers can acquire power vis-à-vis their employers through unions and political parties. I elaborate this argument in the next section.

Worker Power Resources

Worker power, an important manifestation of the PRT, is a relative concept; workers may obtain power in relation to other workers as well as to their employers (cf. Lukes 1977). Workers can also exercise power resources individually or collectively, though the latter is more salient for achieving broad social change, and the PRT literature emphasizes differences among countries and over time in the extent to which workers are able to organize for collective action through unions or political parties that represent their interests.

I focus here on the collective power of workers in relation to employers and the state that is exercised through unions. The degree to which workers can organize in pursuit of their interests through unions and collective bargaining is crucial for reducing both the incidence and impacts of precarious work. Unions enable workers to realize their economic interests by exerting collective power in the form of bargaining and establishing other institutionalized arrangements in relation to employers. Some unions also provide workers with associational power (e.g., Wright 2000) that helps them to restrict labor supply and stimulate demand.

The emphasis on worker power as a key determinant of work relations has a long tradition in neo-Marxian theories of class (e.g., Edwards 1979). The PRT argues distinctively that conflicts of interest among classes could also alter capitalist systems non-violently through democratic institutions (such as political parties) by engaging in a "democratic class struggle" (Korpi 1983, 1985; Stephens 1979).

The state provides the legal framework for collective organization and the operation of markets. Hence, the history of political class coalitions is the key cause of differences in welfare states across countries (Esping-Andersen 1990). As Huber and Stephens (2001: 17) put it:

> The struggle over welfare states [*and many other aspects of stratification*] is a struggle over distribution, and thus the organizational power of those standing to benefit from redistribution, the working and lower middle classes, is crucial. It matters, of course, how this organizational power is politically articulated, and political parties perform the crucial mediating role.

The relative dominance in government of three political blocks was the key factor shaping the development of welfare state policies in advanced industrial democracies during their period of expansion (about 1945–73). The supremacy of political parties, in turn, was closely related to the strength of unions along with religious cleavages. Differences among these countries in their partisan politics were represented by: Social Democracy and its leftist allies; Christian Democracy; and right and center political parties (see Huber and Stephens 2001).

The Danish Social Democrats, often in coalition with one or two centrist parties, dominated Denmark's government during the period of welfare state expansion. A strong alliance between unions and Social Democrats was the main impetus behind the formation and expansion of a universalistic, citizenship-based, generous welfare state that was financed by the Danish state via taxation. The state plays a big part in facilitating coalitions, such as those between manufacturing interests (which are less dominant than in countries such as Germany) and employers in the service sector.

By contrast, the political dominance of the Christian Democratic party in Germany and its alliance with strong unions located mainly in manufacturing industries encouraged the expansion of a welfare system in which entitlements were based on employment and the principle of insurance as opposed to being citizenship-based (see Huber and Stephens 2001).

Japan's government has been dominated (with only a few exceptions) since the mid-1950s by the Liberal Democratic Party (LDP), a conservative political party (despite its name). The LDP's power was based on a coalition of big and small business interests and farmers that, along with the relative weakness of unions, enabled it to enact welfare and labor market policies that promoted economic development.

In Spain, the advent of democracy after the drafting of the Constitution in 1978 led to the political dominance of Social and Christian Democrats. In alliance with unions, this led to key changes in the Spanish economy such as the privatization of state-owned companies and the decline of the paternalistic orientation of management and the state toward employees that was characteristic of Francoist industrial relations.

Primarily right and center secular parties have controlled the government of the United Kingdom with some representation by social democrats and their leftist allies. The policies of the Conservative governments led by Margaret Thatcher and John Major (1979–97) led to a reduction in worker power and the liberalization of welfare and labor market institutions.

Right and center secular parties have also dominated the United States, but unlike in the UK, social democratic and leftist parties have had relatively little influence in the government. The presidency of Ronald Reagan (1980–8) paralleled that of Thatcher in many ways, and contributed to the continued decline of unions and the liberalization of social protections and labor market institutions. The paucity of worker power enabled US employers to reduce institutional protections for workers, such as government regulations and standards in labor markets. Employers could do this essentially without taking into consideration the views of workers, who were unable to act as a countervailing force (Galbraith 1952) due to their relatively weak position.

Political institutions shape state policies and the resources available to workers. The power of workers as exercised through unions depends to a considerable extent on their links to political parties; state regulations can strengthen unions' bargaining strength and guarantee coverage of collective agreements (e.g., Marks 1989). Hence, the political strength of unions reflects their size of membership, relations to political parties, and the electoral success of these parties.

Unions

Most researchers measure union power by union density, or the proportion of employees who belong to a union. A second, related,

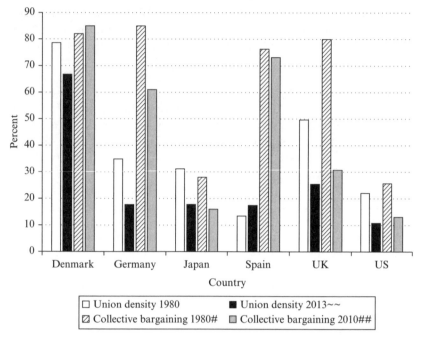

Figure 2.1   Union density and collective bargaining coverage, 1980, 2010, and 2013

~ Japan 2012; # UK 1979; ## Denmark 2007; Japan and Spain 2008

Source: OECD data

indicator is the degree of collective bargaining coverage, which reflects the extent to which employment and working conditions are affected by collective negotiations. The proportion of wage-and-salary employees covered by collective agreements generally measures collective bargaining scope. These two indicators are usually highly related, though in Continental Europe union density is considerably lower than the degree of collective bargaining coverage, as patterns of coordinated bargaining provide non-union members in certain industries with the benefits of unions' collective power.

   Figure 2.1 presents trend information on union density and collective bargaining coverage in the six countries. Denmark ranks the highest among the six countries in union density, with about two-thirds of the labor force belonging to a union, though this has declined from nearly 80 percent in 1980 to about two-thirds in 2013. Collective bargaining coverage is even higher than union density (about 85 percent in 2007), despite the reduction in union membership.

Germany's union density has decreased markedly in the past quarter century, declining from about 35 percent of the labor force in 1980 to about 18 percent in 2013; sector-wide collective bargaining arrangements have also weakened and coverage has declined greatly, from 85 percent in 1980 to 61 in 2010 percent (see also Bosch, Mayhew, and Gautié 2010: 101–2). There are still relatively strong unions in the manufacturing export sector, however, as well as in publicly owned companies in the service sector. The placement of worker representatives on company supervisory boards (co-determination) enhances worker power and facilitates long-term innovation goals.[6]

Union density in Japan (about 18 percent in 2012, down from 31 percent in 1980) is at about the same level as in Germany and Spain, though the extent of collective bargaining coverage is much lower (16 percent in 2008, down from 28 percent in 1980), exceeding only the low level found in the United States. Whether the behaviors of Japanese enterprise unions are independent of firms has been the subject of much debate, but there appears to be wide agreement that Japanese unions bargain hard for the interests of their members on the bread-and-butter issues of wages and job security. Although the volume of strike activity in Japan is considerably lower than in the United States and Britain, it is higher than in Germany, and there is strong reason to think that the militancy of combined Japanese unions in the annual "spring offensives" has been an important force in narrowing the wage gap between Japan and other industrial countries (Shirai 1983; Imai 2011).

Union density in Spain has increased slightly (from 13.5 percent in 1980 to about 17.5 percent in 2013) and is now comparable to that in Germany and Japan. The low level of union density is a legacy of the Franco era, in which democratic unions were illegal and employers and employees were combined in a single syndicalist organization that was controlled by the state (Aguilera 2005). Collective bargaining coverage is not closely dependent on union density and is relatively high, being nearly three-quarters of the labor force, second only to Denmark among the six countries. All workers benefit from collective bargaining agreements (either firm, industrial sector, or national) regardless of whether they are union members. Moreover, the influence of unions is leveraged due to their involvement in works councils, which are present in about 80 percent of firms (Aguilera 2005).

Union density in the United Kingdom has declined considerably in recent years, from about half of wage-and-salary workers in 1980 to about a quarter in 2013 (though this percentage is second only to Denmark among the six countries). As in the US, collective bargaining coverage depends mainly on union density, and the percent that is covered by a collective agreement has fallen from 80 percent in 1979 to less than a third in 2010. As already noted, the decline in collective worker power in the UK can be traced to the policies of the Conservative governments in the 1980s and 1990s, who implemented a series of liberalizing reforms that attacked and weakened labor unions by reducing their bargaining power and organizing capability. These reforms also reduced the size of the public sector through privatization and increased local as opposed to industrial sector bargaining, which helped decrease the proportion covered by collective bargaining agreements. These reforms, along with the decline of unions, brought the UK closer to the free-market situation characteristic of the US and away from the Continental European social and economic models.

Union density in the United States is the lowest among the six countries, with less than 11 percent of wage-and-salary workers belonging to a union in 2013, which is a decrease from 22 percent in 1980. By contrast, union density in the public sector remains higher and stable, at 35.9 percent in 2012. The relatively low union density is matched by low collective bargaining coverage (about 13 percent in 2010), which is again the lowest among the six countries.

Labor Force Demography

The sphere of reproduction (the household) is intimately related to the domain of production (the employment relationship and work arrangements) and so the insecurities and stresses associated with work are transmitted into the household, creating difficulties associated with the social and economic care and perpetuation of human beings from one generation to the next. Hence, who works in the labor force and who doesn't are central for understanding differences in social welfare protection and labor market institutions. A country's labor force demography is closely related to sources of worker power and the political dynamics and policies that affect both these institutions and the experiences associated with precarious jobs.

I focus here on three key dimensions of labor force demography: gender, age, and immigration.

Gender

Women's labor force participation is central to explanations of country differences in welfare regimes. As more women enter the labor force, there will be increased demand for public social services that allow women to spend time at work, such as childcare. The expansion of such services in turn creates more jobs for women, as women generally do these. The greater representation of women in the labor force also constitutes a source of political mobilization prompting social movements and political organizations to push for further growth of public social services (Huber and Stephens 2001).

Women's labor force participation varies among the six countries. Denmark has the highest labor force participation among women aged 15–64, according to OECD statistics, with over three-quarters of women in the labor force (76 percent in 2000, 77 percent in 2016). By contrast, the OECD average increased from 59 percent in 2000 to 64 percent in 2016. It is thus not surprising that Denmark has long been a leader in female-friendly policies that emphasize the public sector's provision of services and goods. The high proportion of public sector employment in Denmark supports the security and quality of care work as well as high female employment.

Germany's level of female labor force participation has increased substantially since 2000 (from 63 percent in 2000 to 74 percent in 2016). Germany was slower to modernize its social insurance welfare system with the growth of women workers (Esping-Andersen 1990). This was due in large part to the persistence of the male breadwinner–female homemaker ideal in Christian Democratic Germany, which tended to slow labor force integration of women and preserve gender stratification. Barriers to women working included tax and benefit schemes that did not incentivize women to enter the labor force and relatively poor and insufficient childcare.[7]

On the other hand, women's labor force participation is relatively low in Japan (68 percent in 2016), though this represents an increase from 2000 (60 percent). Spain, though, is the country that saw the largest increase during this period, rising to 70 percent in 2016 from only 53 percent in 2000. In the United Kingdom, female labor force participation increased from 69 percent in 2000 to 73 percent in 2016. By contrast, there was a comparable percentage decrease in the United States, from 71 percent in 2000 to 67 percent in 2016; nearly a third of the decrease in women's labor force participation in the US relative to other OECD countries was due to the greater expansion of family-friendly policies including parental leave and part-time work entitlements in the other OECD countries (Blau and Kahn 2013).

Part-time work is a major feature of women's labor force participation. Much of this is voluntary, as working less than full-time enables women to balance their work in the labor force with their familial responsibilities for child rearing and household activities. But some of this is involuntary as women are forced to work part-time due to the lack of acceptable full-time jobs and paucity of social services (such as adequate childcare) that enable them to work full-time.

The increases in female labor force participation in Germany and Japan were powered mainly by the growth of women's part-time work, as the percentages of women working part-time (relative to their total employment) in Germany grew from 38 percent in 2000 to 47 percent in 2016 and from 29 percent to 37 percent in Japan, producing a transition from a male breadwinner family to a 1.5 earner family. In Spain, part-time employment, which grew from 17 percent in 2000 to 24 percent in 2016, played a more limited role in the substantial expansion in female labor force participation (MacInnes 2009). The proportion of women working part-time declined slightly in the United Kingdom, from 44 percent to 42 percent in 2016, while it remained constant in the United States over this period at 25 percent. The OECD average also increased slightly, from 29 percent in 2000 to 31 percent in 2016.

Age

The age structure of the labor force and population is inextricably tied to the demands for social welfare protections and the ability of countries to meet these needs (e.g., Esping-Andersen 1990). It also affects labor market institutions such as the requirements for education and skill formation and active labor market policies. An aging population puts greater pressure on social welfare systems to provide retirement and other social benefits, while at the same time, a higher ratio of older to younger persons makes it difficult for countries to generate the revenues (through taxes, for example) to meet these needs.

All six countries experienced a rise in the proportion of the elderly population (i.e., those over 65) since 2000, according to OECD statistics. Japan experienced the biggest increase, from 17 percent in 2000 to 25 percent in 2013. Germany has the second highest proportion of elderly persons, rising from 17 percent in 2000 to 21 percent in 2014, while the proportion over 65 increased in Denmark from 15 percent in 2000 to 18 percent in 2013. The increase in Spain was modest (from 17 percent in 2000 to 18 percent in 2014) as it was in the UK (16 percent in 2000 to 17 percent in 2014). In the US, the proportion of elderly persons increased from 12 percent in 2000 to 15 percent in 2014.

The aging of the population in these countries was accompanied by relatively low birthrates, resulting in a decline in the percentage of the working age population (defined in these OECD statistics as the percent who are 15–64) in some of these countries. The drop was especially severe in Japan, falling to 62 percent in 2013 from 68 percent in 2000. The percentage of the population of working age fell from 67 percent in 2000 to 65 percent in 2013 in Denmark, and from 67 percent and 69 percent in 2000 to 65 percent and 67 percent in 2014 in Germany and Spain, respectively. By contrast, the percentage of working age persons remained constant over the period from 2000 to 2014 in the UK (at 65 percent) and the US (66 percent), which was also the OECD average.

Immigration

Immigration is a major way for societies to counteract the effects of aging and to bolster the proportion of persons of working age. The emphasis on immigration helps to explain why the percentage of working age persons remained relatively constant in countries such as the UK and US, while it declined in Japan, a country that has been especially resistant to incorporating immigrants (though it does allow a trickling of migrants from other parts of Asia and South America), making their situation of low fertility coupled with a rapidly expanding elderly population even more perilous.

The expansion of globalization and internationalization of production described in the previous chapter has accelerated labor mobility as well as cross-border flows of labor in addition to products, services, and capital. A key aspect of international labor mobility is immigration. Globalization and international competition have also promoted a certain type of precarity involving migrant groups. As already noted, for example, German companies shifted production across the border to Eastern Europe, while precarious labor crosses the border from Eastern Europe to Germany and other countries. Immigration among the countries belonging to the European Union has also accelerated due to the EU's rules allowing relatively free movement of workers among member states.

While immigration provides a source of labor supply, it also creates challenges for social welfare protection and labor market institutions, as societies need to either integrate immigrants into these systems or else deal with the consequences of not doing so. Efforts to integrate immigrants are often met with political resistance, as witnessed by the emergence of the right-wing anti-immigrant parties, as I will discuss in chapter 8.

Certain important kinds of immigration also produced a greater surplus of low-skilled labor and encouraged employers to create low-wage jobs. In the United States, for example, the increase in relatively low-educated Mexican immigrant labor has provided a large supply of workers who have comparatively few alternatives in the labor market and so are more willing to work for low wages and less disposed to challenge their employers. Immigrant workers with relatively few labor market options tend to be more subservient and compliant and thus more likely than native-born workers to take on low-wage jobs that have no benefits and are more difficult and dangerous (Waldinger and Lichter 2003). The increase of low-skilled immigrants is associated with the growth and persistence of low-skilled, low-wage jobs in industries such as farming, restaurants, hotels, day-care centers, meatpacking, and construction. Immigrants have much higher employment rates in the United States – and much lower wage rates – than in countries such as Denmark, where unions have been able to maintain higher wage levels at the lower end of the labor market.

These three aspects of labor force demography – gender, age, and immigration – along with the worker power resources discussed earlier in the chapter are central to explanations of country differences in social welfare protection and labor market institutions, along with the persistent but often more ambiguous cultural and historical factors. I represented this assumption by the causal link between the first two boxes in figure 1.1. I now turn to the institutions and policies themselves, showing how the forces discussed in this chapter are reflected in differences among the six countries.

Social Welfare Protection Policies

Modern welfare states began in the early part of the twentieth century in Europe and migrated across the Atlantic to form the framework of the New Deal in the US in the 1930s and 1940s. In the thirty years after World War II, most industrial countries developed welfare states and labor market institutions that were designed to provide protections for workers (Huber and Stephens 2001). Generally, the real maturation of welfare states occurred from the 1960s and 1970s onwards and provided relative security for workers in many countries that experienced growth, though workers in some countries (and some within a country) were better off than others.

The types and inclusiveness of labor market and social welfare institutions were produced by specific patterns of historical development resulting from the relative power of workers, the presence of political parties to support workers' interests, patterns of family support and relationships that might compensate for lack of government backing, and other institutional and cultural factors. Countries dominated by social democratic and leftist parties produced welfare systems that were relatively generous, inclusive, and universalistic, where welfare benefits were provided to all citizens. On the other hand, countries dominated by right and center secular parties, in which workers had little collective voice in the labor market through independent unions or other forms of associational power (such as occupations), produced welfare states with relatively weak social and statutory, needs-based protections.

The expansion of the welfare system coincided with the development of the SER. In some countries (especially the United States, but also Germany and Japan) many welfare provisions (such as health insurance in the United States, until very recently with the passage of the Affordable Care Act, and retirement and pension benefits in all three countries) were tied to full-time regular employment.

The social protections provided by the welfare states were designed to counter the primary economic risks of the post-World War II period, which were mainly the economic uncertainties associated with unemployment for male breadwinners (who were the main source of family income at that time), by providing UI to them and thereby taking care of their families. UI schemes were generally predicated on the assumption that periods of joblessness would be relatively short and associated with generally brief business-cycle downturns.

The political dynamics changed about 1985 as it became clear that the era of rapid growth (i.e., the 1945–73 period) would not return, and welfare state reform slowed and even reversed in some countries as the emphasis shifted to austerity (e.g., in the United Kingdom). (Spain is clearly different because of it being under authoritarian rule until the mid-1970s.) The increase in joblessness during this period meant that more people relied on unemployment benefits while tax revenues declined as fewer people were employed. After 1985, welfare state reform and labor market policies shifted from an emphasis on protecting people from the consequences of unemployment to labor market activation policies that emphasized the individualization of responsibility (Van Gerven and Ossewaarde 2012; Huber and Stephens 2015). In Europe, this swing represents a shift from a view of the state as a source of protection to its role in promoting social investments in human capital by underscoring the importance of education and equality of opportunity, among other priorities (Taylor-Gooby 2008), as in the East Asian welfare model (see Holliday 2000).

Many of the same factors that have promoted precarious work have also put pressure on countries (arising from within countries and from the European Union regulations for EU member countries) to liberalize their welfare states.[8] The desire for greater employer and labor market flexibility by reducing the fixed costs associated with "permanent" employment corresponded to political decisions to promote austerity by marketizing welfare provisions, such as creating work requirements for receipt of welfare provision, reducing employment protections, incentivizing unemployed workers to seek new jobs by lowering the amount and duration of UI benefits (as in Denmark, for example), and shifting risks from governments toward workers through policies designed to promote individual responsibility and privatization.

Welfare Generosity

There are a variety of social welfare protection policies. Two important types of social protections are *social insurance*, or contributory schemes that are designed to help people respond to common risks, such as illness, old age, and unemployment (e.g., health insurance, pensions, and UI); and *social assistance*, which refers to unrequited transfers to groups, such as the poor, who cannot qualify for insurance or would receive inadequate benefits from such a source (e.g., cash or in-kind transfers, child welfare, assistance to the elderly, health assistance, disability benefits, and disaster relief).

An overall picture of the generosity of welfare benefits is provided by figure 2.2, which compares the six countries on the overall *generosity* of the social welfare system. I measure this by the share of GDP spent on social welfare policies and the extent to which the population is covered by these policies.[9] In interpreting these figures, we need to keep in mind that public spending is only one way (albeit the most common one) of providing social welfare protections. Social welfare protections result from a mix of public and private spending, as is more often the case in the United States. In addition, welfare

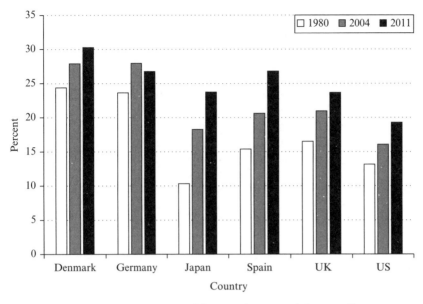

Figure 2.2 Private and public mandatory social expenditures (% of GDP), 1980, 2004, and 2011

Source: OECD data

supports from families (via an emphasis on individual responsibility and personal savings) have historically played a larger role in some countries, such as Japan (Kwon 1997).

The level of social welfare generosity is highest in Denmark, which is Europe's most generous welfare state overall. This is consistent with Denmark's principle that "no citizen should suffer any economic hardship; thus welfare benefits are intended to cover everybody" (Westergaard-Nielsen 2008: 24). This has led to a well-developed social safety net and a generous and inclusive welfare system that produces a low degree of dependence on the labor market to provide a minimum standard of living. Rather, the role of the government is to pay the bills, providing the social safety net (i.e., healthcare and disability pensions and UI benefits for those who are not otherwise covered, though the government-provided UI is means tested and relatively low) and retrain workers who have lost their jobs (Westergaard-Nielsen 2008: 38). To pay for these policies, Denmark has a very high marginal income-tax rate: 56.5 percent on incomes of more than about $80,000 (Daly 2013); the effective tax rate for even low-wage earners is 44 percent (Westergaard-Nielsen 2008: 16).

Despite the overall high level of welfare generosity in Denmark, budget concerns in recent years led the Danish government to adopt a whole host of neoliberal reforms, such as privatizing pensions, cutting benefits, and reducing the time limit for receiving unemployment benefits from four years to two. The requirement for the unemployed (the proportion of which increased during the crisis) to participate in retraining and job placement programs designed to get them back to work intensified. These policies are social investments designed to make workers more mobile and to enable the most vulnerable people in society to obtain and keep good jobs (rather than any job at all).

Overall public social welfare spending in Germany is also relatively high, ranking second behind Denmark (at least until 2011, when the high unemployment rates in Spain led to a big increase in welfare spending). Germany also has comparatively high levels of unemployment replacement, ranking the highest among the six countries. Germany has a social insurance-based welfare system, which historically has been heavily stratified along occupational and class lines. While Germany's dualistic welfare regime provides generous supports for labor market insiders, it provides less support for labor market outsiders (Emmenegger et al. 2012).

In Japan, social rights to welfare are limited and connected to productivity increases, though Japan spends the most on public welfare and social protections of the countries in East Asia and the percentage of GDP spent on social welfare was comparable to that in the UK and greater than that in the US in 2011 (see figure 2.2). Welfare benefits in Japan differ by firm, however. And, once unemployed, Japanese workers have the lowest levels of income replacement of the six countries (Chatani 2008). Instead of a well-developed, publicly financed social safety net, the relatively conservative Japanese welfare system places a "high level of reliance on mutual aid within family and occupational groups. This comes from the effect of Confucianism which places an especially high level of reliance on the family" (Nozaki and Matsuura 2010: 56).

The welfare system in Spain is relatively new compared to other European countries and still has features that are remnants of the Franco-era policies designed to support patriarchal family structures and the authoritarian state by providing relatively small payments to families, thereby encouraging women to stay at home with their children. This system also depended for elder care on unpaid family services. Social expenditures have increased over the past decade, however, rising to a level comparable to Germany's and only slightly less than Denmark's in 2011 (see figure 2.2); as noted earlier, this growth in welfare expenditures reflects mainly the increasing beneficiary base created by high unemployment resulting from the economic crisis.

Welfare generosity is higher in the UK than in the US; levels of public and private mandatory social expenditures in the UK were about the same proportion of GDP in 2011 as Japan, and greater only than those in the US among the six countries. In both the UK and US, conservative government policies made UI and other income transfers both less plentiful and less accessible. In both countries, the main trend since the mid-1990s has been toward labor market activation policies and away from unconditional unemployment benefits (Bonoli 2005). Welfare-to-work has been the orienting principle of many welfare and labor market policies (as in the Jobseeker's Allowance, enacted by the Blair government in 1998; and President Bill Clinton's Temporary Assistance for Needy Families [TANF] program created in the mid-1990s). These policies limited eligibility periods as well as required persons to work in the labor force as a condition of payments. In the UK, an unemployed worker must sign a "claimant commitment" that outlines a specific job search plan to receive benefits, a reflection of neo-conservative attempts to separate the "deserving" from "undeserving" poor (Van Reenen 2004). The overall effect in the UK, as in the US, has been to provide economic incentives to move unemployed workers (often women without marketable skills) into low-wage, precarious jobs.

Unlike the United States, however, the United Kingdom does provide universal health coverage. The Beveridge Report (Beveridge 1942), i.e., the report on *Social Insurance and Allied Services*, written during World War II, provided the outline for the British welfare state that emerged after the war and led to the establishment of the National Health Service in 1948. In Britain, as in Europe generally, it was agreed that governments most effectively organized social security and health benefits to address the evils of "Want, Disease, Ignorance, Squalor, and Idleness" (Davis 2016: 116). Indeed, the US is also the only country among the six without a universal system of health coverage. This was due largely to the government's failure to enact this after World War II; as a result, unions pushed for the adoption of employer-delivered health insurance and, when this was achieved, dropped their insistence that it be provided by the government. The 2010 Affordable Care Act was designed to expand health insurance coverage to most US citizens and legal residents, though coverage for all has not yet been attained.

The welfare state in the United States, however, is not as small as implied by figure 2.2: It operates more via principles such as tax expenditures and public–private partnerships (Howard 2007; Prasad 2016). Thus, there are different types of tax subsidies provided to individuals at both the federal and state levels, though these are often more likely to be tax cuts (which usually favor higher-income persons) and result in a diminishing of state capacity rather than risk pooling and redistribution (Prasad 2016). In addition, American companies are more involved in the provision of welfare than is generally the case in other countries (though the extent of this involvement varies by such things as company size); while private welfare also characterized many other advanced industrial countries, it tended to crowd out public welfare more in the US.

Welfare payments appear to have become more generous in 2011 compared to 2004, though this reflects the increases in unemployment experienced by these countries – and therefore the increase in UI expenditures – due to the economic crisis of 2008–9; there were cutbacks in entitlements in all countries during this period.[10]

Labor Market Institutions

Labor market institutions are the macrostructural, organized patterns and laws that govern the relations between employers and employees, such as unions and collective bargaining arrangements, occupational associations, and minimum wage and equal opportunity laws. Labor market institutions not only regulate how people enter and exit from employment and are trained and retrained, but also define their rights and conditions of employment.

Welfare and social protection regimes are important sources of variation in labor market institutions (Esping-Andersen 1990; Kolberg 1991). The generosity of pension benefits affects retirement decisions, for example, while provision of ample UI impacts decisions regarding labor force participation. In addition, the welfare state has become a major employer in many rich democracies, with the expansion of health, education, and social service jobs.

Moreover, similar macrostructural forces, such as workers' power resources and the nature of production regimes, shape key features of both welfare and labor market institutions. Thus, the strength of labor organization both leads to generous welfare support during periods of unemployment and encourages retraining policies to enable unemployed workers to find new jobs. Also, the kinds of relations among firms, banks, labor, and government emphasized by the VoC theory help to explain why firms can obtain capital that enables them to make investments in research and development, as well as to account for the cooperation among employers that support training and retraining (Soskice 1999; Huber and Stephens 2001).

I focus on three major sets of labor market institutions: employment systems, which shape the employment relations that form the core of precarious work; skill formation systems, which provide workers with the skills needed to participate in the labor market; and labor market policies related to re-employment and employment protections.

Employment Systems

The employment system encompasses the institutional and cultural aspects of hiring, training, retaining, and promoting employees in employment relationships (Marsden 1999). Employment systems are "cultural and social constructions that reflect a societal tendency of important actors toward enforcing certain forms of careers and social organization" (Fligstein and Byrkjeflot 1996: 12). Fligstein and Byrkjeflot argue that employment systems are institutional projects that are shaped by the political interactions among employers, workers, and the state, and involve the construction of cultural rules that legitimize and stabilize these interrelations through labor markets and the interaction between employers and employees in firms, and the educational system. In these ways, macro-level employment systems shape meso- and micro-level employment relations in a society.

Employment systems differ systematically across countries due to dissimilarities in the relative power of employers and workers and in the nature and scope of their educational and skill formation systems. These characteristics reflect the extent of competition between different unions and other sources of worker power (such as occupational associations), the role of workers in workplace representation and social policy, the extent and nature of gaps in collective regulation, principles underlying employment policy, the role of the public sector, salience of work–life programs, support provided to balancing work and family lives, and the level of welfare protection offered to the unemployed (Estevez-Abe, Iversen, and Soskice 2001).

Duncan Gallie (2007a) builds on the PRT and VoC and distinguishes among countries on the basis of their "employment regimes" or underlying employment systems and industrial relations policies. Paralleling key differences among welfare and production regimes, he identifies three main models of employment regimes that differ in their degree of inclusiveness of social protections (such as those offered to the unemployed), skill formation systems, and principles governing employment policy: inclusive, dualist, and market regimes.

- *Inclusive employment regimes* (such as Denmark) extend employment rights and social protections to all workers.
- *Dualist employment regimes* (such as Germany, Spain, and Japan) offer social rights and employment protections to a skilled, long-term core workforce often at the expense of those in the periphery, such as those on temporary and other nonstandard contracts. For core workers, such regimes tend to have more robust vocational education and training systems that transmit skills that are more specific to firms and industries, and there are stronger employment protections that tend to discourage inter-firm mobility and lead to longer tenures with employers (Thelen 2014: 2).
- *Market employment regimes* (such as the United Kingdom and United States) are largely governed by market mechanisms. Education and training systems are highly stratified and emphasize the formation of general skills that are transferable across firms and are developed in formal and vocational educational institutions.

Education and Skill Formation Systems

Employment systems differ in their skill formation (education and training) schemes. Skills are developed in formal education systems (such as primary, secondary, and tertiary schools) in vocational training systems that teach skills that are relevant to jobs (and may be located either within the formal educational system, within separate vocational schools, or in dual systems that combine work and training); and within firms or occupational schools (such as medical or law schools).

Different skill formation systems provide different opportunities for acquiring and transferring skills. We can distinguish between models of skill formation that emphasize general skills that are transferable across employers, on the one hand, and on the other those that focus on firm- or industry-specific skills that are useful primarily in particular firms and industries, and are generally linked to systems of vocational training. A dual system that combines work and school vocational training, for example, is widespread only in Germany and Denmark; the other countries maintain a school-based vocational education system.

Denmark has a dual vocational training system, with a high level of apprenticeship training that is actively promoted and financed by the government. Unlike in Germany, apprenticeships in Denmark are heavily geared toward adults, in keeping with that country's emphasis on active labor market policies. The dual system in Denmark is relatively closed, as in Germany, and it is difficult to change in to or out of the vocational training track, though the system in Denmark is more flexible and provides greater access to training opportunities at various life stages. Also unlike in Germany, the Danish vocational training system is more decentralized and the colleges exert more control over designing curricula (Eichhorst et al. 2015). Denmark also has a high public expenditure on tertiary education and institutions of higher education are free of charge to students.

Germany represents a system of *vocationalism*, which results from the actions by strong workers' associations that exert considerable control over the supply of workers to occupations, and relies on a dual apprenticeship system in which skills are formed both in schools and in employing organizations. The dual system is fairly closed and it is difficult to change in to or out of the vocational training track, and so the system is marked by a commitment to one occupation or a group of occupations within an industry. Germany's well-developed vocational and apprenticeship systems helped it create the world's most skilled manual labor force and were facilitated by: strong labor–management cooperation and relations with banks that did not require dependence on the market for financing; coordination among businesses; and a social welfare system that provided workers with the security to invest in their long-term skill development. The dual vocational system has a long history, going back to the regulations established for the skilled trades by the German guilds in the Middle Ages. The system became more formalized and regulated by the state in the 1800s as vocational schools were established to provide skilled and loyal workers for the chemical and machinery industries (Thelen 2004). The dual vocational system originated in manufacturing but has been extended to services as well.[11]

Japan illustrates *managerialism*, where the relatively greater power of employers and firms enables them to use firm-internal labor markets to: exert control over workers; create primary and secondary labor markets within firms; provide specific training to core employees over the course of their careers; and govern the recruitment, training, and allocation of labor to tasks and positions (see Koike 1983; Kalleberg and Lincoln 1988; Lincoln and Kalleberg 1990). Lifetime employment, promotion (based on seniority), abundant welfare services, internal training, and a strong corporate culture combine with broader societal norms and values to evoke from employees a strong commitment to and identification with their employers. Enterprise unions and a penchant for mixing personal life with company affairs round out a picture of organizational affiliations that form a structural attachment critical for the life chances of the Japanese.

The importance of company-based training in the core sector in Japan is reflected in the relatively low proportion (about one-third in 2003) of Japanese high school students who are in vocational tracks. Primary and secondary educational systems focus more on providing students with broader, general skills, presuming that more specific skills will be taught on the job. The lack of emphasis on providing portable skills is reflected in the relatively small amounts of public monies spent on skill training and other active labor market policies, again ranking only ahead of the United States (Brinton 2011).

In *Spain*, the employment system is heavily influenced by the state and its regulations, given the relatively weak capacity of labor and the fragmentation of employers (see Lucio et al. 2007). Unlike Germany's, Spain's system of vocational education and training does not involve apprenticeship but takes place in separate vocational schools and in distinct vocational tracks in upper secondary schools; only 4 percent of those in vocational upper secondary education combine school and work-based training, compared to 74 percent in Germany (Zimmerman et al. 2013). Graduates of vocational secondary schools have an easier time transitioning from school to work than those without vocational training (Field, Kis, and Kuczera 2012). However, the status of vocational training in Spain is relatively low, reflecting Spain's past reliance on low labor costs to maintain competitive advantages, and so there were few incentives for the skill formation system to provide highly skilled workers; before the economic crisis, for example, Spain's economic model was based on cheap labor and a runaway property market. Spain also invests relatively little in research and development and in information technology (Aguilera 2005) and its public investment in tertiary education is below the OECD average (OECD 2014a), though it did expand its education system after joining the European Union in 1986.

The *United Kingdom*, unlike Germany and Denmark (but like the US), has a mainly school-based vocational training system. A major objective of vocational training is to produce workers with general and hence flexible skills and qualifications who are able to move within external labor markets. There is also an emphasis on lifelong learning to adapt to changing job skill requirements. Also in contrast to Germany (but also like the US), there is less of a role for the social partners, and employers are expected to provide the specific skills needed within the firm (Euler 2013). Public spending on tertiary education in the UK is at the OECD average, though expenditure on lower secondary education is relatively high (OECD 2014a).

The *United States* exemplifies a hybrid employment system that combines the managerialism characteristic of Japan with the associational power of occupations typical of Germany. Large employers use firm-internal labor markets to train workers and to provide them with career opportunities, as was historically the case in Japan. In addition, the US exhibits a system of *professionalism,* whereby strong professional associations (usually associated with white-collar occupations) obtain the compliance of the state to create licenses and credentials that enable occupations to exert control over the entry and practice of the occupation, and use universities or professional schools (such as law or medical schools) to produce the kind of expert knowledge that provides the profession with a claim to exclusive jurisdiction. In the US, professional associations obtain the legitimacy from the government to provide credentials and maintain autonomy over the occupation by claiming that only the association is knowledgeable enough to certify entrants.[12] The system of professionalism in the US is similar to that of traditional blue-collar occupations in Germany, in the sense that it results from the associational power of occupations to obtain social closure over the supply, training, and evaluation of workers.

Like Japan, the United States has a weak, school-based vocational training system. The US spends the most on tertiary education, but this is largely due to its relatively high level of private, not public, spending. The emphasis on tertiary education is consistent with the weight placed in the US on the formation of general skills that are portable among firms, and the prominent roles played by open competitive and occupational internal labor markets in pricing and allocating labor within and between firms.

Labor Market Policies

I focus here on two main types of labor market policies: active labor market policies and employment protection legislation.

Active Labor Market Policies Active labor market policies are designed to help working age people obtain jobs and transition from unemployment to employment. Active labor market policies provide workers with greater opportunities for lifelong learning and employability (Viebrock and Clasen 2009). These include chances for retraining, job counseling, and help in finding new jobs through placement services and job search assistance, benefit administration, recruitment incentives, employment maintenance incentives that give workers security as they move from one job to another, sheltered and supported employment and rehabilitation, direct job creation, and start-up incentives. Receipt of these benefits usually requires engagement on the part of individuals, who must take personal responsibility to search for jobs, participate in retraining, and visit job counselors to take advantage of the opportunities available through active labor market policies.

Active labor market policies are a type of social investment strategy (as are investments in education and family policy – see Hemerijck's 2013 review). They include both positive incentives – such as investing in skills and enabling people to move to better jobs – and negative restrictions, such as requiring people to work in the labor force as a condition of receiving welfare benefits ("workfare," as in the LMEs of the US and UK) and limiting benefit times (see Gautié, Westergaard-Nielsen, and Schmitt with Mayhew 2010: 170–5; Van Vliet and Koster 2011; Bonoli 2013).

The measure of active labor market policies used here is the share of GDP spent on labor market policies targeting re-entry into employment. This includes:

> all social expenditure (other than education) which is aimed at the improvement of the beneficiaries' prospect of finding gainful employment or to otherwise increase their earnings capacity. This category includes spending on public employment services and administration, labour market training, special programmes for youth when in transition from school to work, labour market programmes to provide or promote employment for unemployed and other persons (excluding young and disabled persons) and special programmes for the disabled. (OECD 2007: 15)

Figure 2.3 presents the percentage of GDP spent on active labor market policies in the six countries. These include public employment services, training schemes, and employment subsidies. Denmark ranks highest by far among the six countries in the proportion of GDP spent on active labor market policies. Unemployed workers are given a great deal of help in the form of income compensation, education, and job training to find new jobs. The idea behind the Danish model of flexicurity is to protect individual workers (through

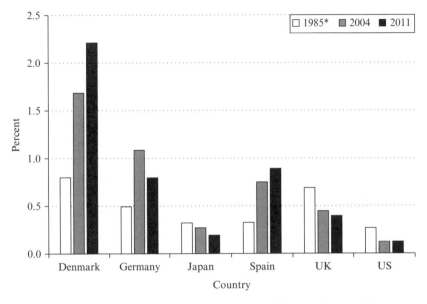

Figure 2.3   Public expenditures on active labor market policies
(% of GDP), 1985, 2004, and 2011
*Denmark 1986; Japan 1990
Source: OECD data

mechanisms such as opportunities for retraining) rather than to try
to protect existing jobs. This gives Danish employers a great deal
of numerical flexibility while giving workers greater employment or
labor market security.

Germany and Spain also spend a relatively high proportion of their
GDP on active labor market policies. The increase in this proportion
is especially great in Spain, so that it now ranks second (to Denmark)
in such expenditures. In Spain, state policies have supported labor
market outsiders through substantial unemployment benefits rather
than through active labor market policies (Aguilera 2005). The average unemployment income replacement rate in Spain is high, ranking
second only to Germany among the six countries.

By contrast, the UK spends less on active labor market policies,
though the proportion of GDP spent on such policies exceeds that
of Japan and the US. Active labor market policies received a boost
at the turn of the twenty-first century from the New Labour government headed by Tony Blair, which reversed some of the Conservative
government's policies by strengthening unions and adopting a series

of "New Deals" especially for young unemployed and long-term unemployed adults that placed greater responsibility on these groups to actively pursue employment opportunities.

The US spends the lowest proportion of its GDP on active labor market policies among the six countries, so unemployed persons are more often on their own when it comes to finding new jobs.

Employment Protection Legislation   EPL refers to a set of norms and procedures that regulate hiring and firing practices in labor markets. The OECD compiles two measures of employment protections, one for regular workers and another for temporary workers. EPL for regular workers refers to protections against firing these workers, while EPL for temporary workers denotes the restrictions on hiring such workers. Both types of EPL are used to compare countries in terms of their amount of labor market rigidity (see Boeri and Van Ours 2008; Venn 2009).

The OECD's scale of employment protection for regular workers includes laws and regulations related to: defense against procedural inconveniences due to dismissal; provision of a notice period and severance pay; and difficulty of dismissal. Such rules serve to protect regular employees against the abusive behavior of employers and help to limit dismissals and thereby reduce transaction costs of employment, among other benefits. The OECD measure of protections for temporary workers includes rules about the types of work allowed with fixed-term contracts, their renewal and duration, as well as regulations on agency work (high EPL for temporary workers denotes stricter rules on the use of temporaries).

EPL can increase the power of permanent workers since it is harder for employers to fire them. But high EPL for regular workers can create incentives for employers to hire temporary workers, thus leading to dualism and more unprotected (and often low-wage) jobs. In this way, tough job-protection laws for regular workers combined with relatively weak restrictions on the use of temporary workers help to create dual labor markets. Indeed, the gap between EPL for regular and temporary workers has been used as an indicator of the degree of labor market dualism (Barbieri and Cutuli 2016), as big gaps denote that there are strict regulations against firing permanent employees but relatively low constraints on hiring temporary workers.

Figure 2.4 presents comparative information on employment protections for regular and temporary workers in the six countries. Employment protections for regular workers were the strictest in Spain and Germany in 1985. These restrictions were reduced dra-

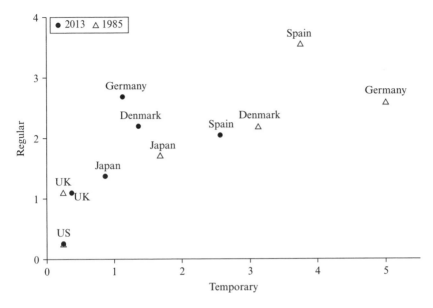

Figure 2.4 Employment protections: regular and temporary workers,
1985 and 2013

Source: OECD data

matically between 1985 and 2013 in Spain. The Franco regime was characterized by a paternalistic stance of the state and management toward employees that was reflected in the strongest employment protections for regular workers among the six countries in 1985, protections that increased substantially as a concession to trade unions during the political transition. Pressures on the post-Franco regime to enhance job creation and address high levels of unemployment, especially after the economic crisis of the 2008–9 period, have led to a weakening of these employment protections for regular workers, though these are still higher than in Japan, the UK, and US.[13]

There was much less of a loosening of EPL for regular workers in Germany, which had the strongest employment protections for regular workers among the six countries in 2013.[14] EPL for regular workers is moderate in Denmark, ranking below Germany (and Spain in 1985) but higher than in Japan, the UK, and US, and did not change much during this period. There is a functional fit between the Danish industrial system (with its small and medium-sized enterprises [SMEs]) and high turnover. The SMEs can't afford to keep people on during slow times, so they are able to lay them off, give them generous

UI for six months, and then hire them back into the same firm. This is one of the reasons for the adoption of flexicurity in Denmark.

The strictness of employment protections for regular workers in Japan overall is moderate, reflecting the dual nature of its economy. It is the large-firm sector where the distinctive features of the Japanese employment system appear in high relief: permanent employment, whereby (overwhelmingly male) school graduates are recruited by a highly selective screening process to work in "tenured" job positions until retirement at age 55–60; the *nenko* system tying promotion and compensation to age, length of service, and family need; and the heavy investment by companies in internal training, welfare services, social programs, and cultural symbolism. By contrast, small firms pay lower wages, provide fewer welfare services, job guarantees, and promotion opportunities, and are less likely to practice *nenko* (Koike 1983). Small Japanese companies are often satellites and subcontractors of larger firms, obligated to take on the latter's surplus labor when demand is slack or, when it tightens, to supply the parent firm with temporary workers (Yamaguchi 1983).

By contrast, employment protections for regular workers (as well as restrictions on the use of temporary workers) are the lowest in the two LMEs of the UK and US. While the UK's labor market, like that in the US, was never highly regulated, the Conservative government's supply-side revolution weakened unions and further loosened legal provisions such as unfair dismissal and redundancy legislation (Mason, Mayhew, and Osborne 2008: 28). The relatively weak employment protections for regular workers and few restrictions on the use of temporary workers in the UK rank only above those in the US on both indicators among the six countries. The greater ease with which employers can discharge regular workers in the UK has made it less necessary for employers to use temporary workers, despite the relatively few restrictions on their use, as we will see in the low levels of temporary work in that country (see chapter 3).

The very low employment protections enjoyed by regular workers in the United States reflects the fact that except for (the relatively few) union members and some well-paid professionals with individual employment contracts (and academics with tenure), most employees are "at will" and can be discharged for any (non-discriminatory) reason and without warning.

Consistent with my discussion of the liberalization of labor markets, restrictions on the use of temporary workers were eased in all countries except the United Kingdom (where these restrictions increased slightly) and United States (where limitations on hiring temporary workers are the lowest of all the countries and there was no change over the period 1985–2013). The strictness of regulations for hiring temporary workers decreased the most in Germany, reflecting the liberalization produced by the Hartz reforms (see chapter 3). However, the relaxation of restrictions on temporary workers was also substantial in Denmark, Japan, and Spain.

EPL promotes dualism in the labor market, as it creates different conditions for permanent as opposed to not-permanent statuses in the employment relationship. Figure 2.4 indicates that the EPL gap (i.e., the strictness about firing permanent workers minus the strictness about using temporary workers) is relatively high in Germany and Japan (in 2013), two countries with highly developed dual labor markets. In Spain, there are asymmetric laws providing differential protections to primary and secondary segment workers, though there have been attempts to reduce this asymmetry by substantially reducing employment protections for permanent workers (see figure 2.4).

Summary and Conclusions

Country differences in labor market and social protection institutions shape reactions to precarious work and its consequences for insecurity and well-being. The six countries studied here illustrate different models of capitalism: Denmark represents the social democratic model with an inclusive employment regime; Germany, Japan, and Spain exemplify the various types of CMEs that are associated with dualist employment regimes consisting of a protected group of core workers and a more precarious periphery; and the United Kingdom and United States illustrate LMEs.

This chapter provides the theoretical foundations for examining country differences among these countries. Drawing upon neo-institutional theories rooted in the VoC and PRT approaches, I have argued that these six countries differ in important social welfare protections and labor market institutions and policies. Nevertheless, all these countries have encountered pressures to liberalize their economies and labor markets and all have adopted some form of neoliberalism. Union density and worker power generally declined in all the countries, as power shifted toward employers. However, the institutional structures and the balance of class power in these countries have produced varying responses and outcomes: a greater collectivization of risk in Denmark; labor market dualization in Germany, Japan, and Spain between a protected group of insiders and vulnerable outsiders; and the shifting of the risks of work to individuals in the United Kingdom and the United States.

The evidence presented in this chapter shows that the generosity of public spending on welfare benefits and active labor market policies is relatively high in Denmark, Germany, and Spain, and relatively low in Japan, the UK, and US. Employment protections for regular workers is higher in Germany, Denmark, and Spain compared to Japan, the UK, and US. Relatively high employment protections for regular workers coupled with low restrictions on the use of temporary workers underscore the dual nature of labor markets in Germany and Japan. In Spain, pressures to loosen protections for regular workers and restrictions on the use of temporary workers have reduced the duality of labor markets in that country since the 1980s.

I will show in subsequent chapters how these labor market and social welfare institutions and policies affect the ways in which precarious work impacts individuals' economic insecurity, transitions to adulthood and family formation, and subjective well-being. Some institutions are likely to be more relevant than others for different outcomes: Active labor market and employment protection policies are apt to have especially strong impacts on job insecurity, while social insurance and social assistance should affect mainly economic insecurity.

Part II

Manifestations of Precarious Work

3
Nonstandard Employment Relations

Social scientists usually identify types of precarious work as various forms of *nonstandard work arrangements*. The most commonly used indicator of nonstandard work is temporary work, which includes those who are hired on temporary labor contracts for fixed or limited terms or tasks as well as those who are hired through temporary employment agencies, labor brokers, or dispatch agencies. Temporary work does not exhaust all the types of nonstandard work, however. Others include: contract work (comprising employees of contract companies and independent contractors); "own account" self-employed persons who do not have any employees; irregular and casual employment; informal economy work; short-term work; and part-time work, especially involuntary part-time work. I will use the term "nonstandard work arrangements" to refer to these types of work in this book, though the terminology for them differs among countries, such as "non-regular work" in Japan or "atypical or alternative work arrangements" in other countries.

Some nonstandard forms of work are precarious because they are uncertain and insecure and, more importantly, lack the social and statutory protections that came to be associated with regular, standard employment relations in the early post-World War II period. Categorizing nonstandard work arrangements as precarious assumes that classifications such as temporary jobs capture the features associated with the three dimensions of precarious work (i.e., as insecure/uncertain; having limited economic and social benefits; and with restricted statutory entitlements) sufficiently to serve as a good proxy for them. By definition, temporary jobs are of course insecure and uncertain. But countries differ in the chances that temporary jobs will lead to more permanent careers, and in the degree to which temporary and other nonstandard workers have social and statutory protections. In some cases (such as Denmark), social protections tend to be universal and based on citizenship, while in other countries, workers must work a certain number of hours or have minimum contribution periods to qualify for protections such as UI or (as in the United States) health insurance and pension coverage.

I elaborate on nonstandard work arrangements and their relationship to precarious work in this chapter. I first provide an overview of the incidence and trends in key nonstandard work arrangements in the six countries. I then discuss how an important form of nonstandard work – temporary work – differs in its degree of precarity among countries. In some countries, temporary jobs are stepping-stones to more standard employment – and so working in them does not matter all that much for economic security and well-being – while in other countries, temporary jobs are dead-end jobs. Before doing this, it is necessary to elaborate on the idea of employment relations and the distinction between standard and nonstandard work arrangements.

Employment Relations

The basic units of employment systems are *employment relationships*, which are implicit or explicit contractual arrangements between employers and employees that involve reciprocal expectations and obligations.[1] These relations encompass a wide range of phenomena, such as how work is organized, governed, evaluated, and rewarded. By linking individuals to their employing organizations, the concept of employment relations provides a theoretical framework that connects phenomena at multiple levels of analysis: macrostructures such as economic, political and social institutions; mezzoscopic aspects of firms and organizations; and microscopic characteristics associated with individuals' experiences of work. Moreover, the intrinsically contextual nature of employment relations makes it necessary to study them comparatively.

Employment relations differ along a continuum anchored by transactional exchange on one side and relational exchange on the other. Transactional employment relations involve little commitment on the part of either employers or employees to each other and are usually instrumental in nature, involving the exchange of money for work with no necessary expectation of training, continued employment, or welfare provision. By contrast, relational employment relations involve close linkages between organizations and their employees that reflect their mutual commitment and are represented by the notion of a SER (see Kalleberg and Marsden 2015 for a discussion of types of employment relations).

As I discussed in chapter 1, SERs were the normative form of employment relations in industrial nations for much of the twentieth century, blossoming in the first three decades after World War II as part of the social accords in many of these countries that accompanied the spread of Fordist mass production and the ascendancy of large organizations. SERs involve considerable fixed costs because of the range and duration of their open-ended commitments, and so are most likely to be an efficient form of organizing work during periods of high economic growth such as those that characterized the early post-World War II period. Although the SER was normative in many countries during this period, it was far from universal; it was found mainly in larger organizations and concentrated among white-collar employees (usually men) in managerial occupations and blue-collar workers in certain organized industries. Indeed, the viability of the SER depended on a model of the family having a full-time, primary-breadwinner husband, and a wife who cared for children and the home. The lifetime employment regime in Japan – also generally limited to men working in large organizations – closely resembles the ideal-typical model of the SER.

SERs are characterized by: the exchange of work for monetary compensation; performance of work on a pre-set schedule at the employer's place of business and under the employer's control and direction; and jobs having well-defined boundaries and descriptions. SERs often, but not always, involved full-time employment. They were typically associated with a psychological contract in which employers' pledges of job security were exchanged for employees' loyalty, and there was a shared expectation of continued employment that was contingent on satisfactory employee performance. In the ideal-typical model of the SER, much training took place within the firm, as the long-term and open-ended nature of the employment relationship provided incentives for employers to invest in transmitting firm-specific skills, as well as for employees to learn them to advance their careers by moving up job ladders within the firm. SERs were also the normative foundation of the framework within which labor law, collective bargaining, social security systems, and other features of welfare regimes developed in many industrial countries.

Nonstandard employment relations (such as temporary or contract work) depart from standard employment in one or more ways (Kalleberg 2000). First, in some cases the employer–employee relationship is mediated via a third party such as a temporary help agency or contract company. In these tripartite employment relations, the worker's *de jure* employer is an intermediary organization rather than the *de facto* employer that pays for and makes use of the employee's labor. Second, some nonstandard work carries no assumption of continued employment, in contrast to the SER in which the expectation is that employment will be at least open-ended with an indefinite future. Third, still other nonstandard work arrangements, including self-employment and independent contracting, collapse the employer–employee distinction altogether (see Kalleberg and Marsden 2015 for a discussion of the transformation of employment relations).

While many nonstandard work arrangements are often regarded as precarious, so too are many standard employment relations in recent years. Reductions in social and legal protections, as well as increased chances of layoffs due to downsizing or offshoring, for example, have rendered *all* forms of employment relations more precarious to some degree.

Nonstandard Work Arrangements

There is a paucity of systematic data about trends in the various types of nonstandard work arrangements in different countries that span a relatively long period, and so information limitations constrain our ability to study them historically. In the United States, for example, nationally representative data on nonstandard work (such as temporary work or independent contractors) were not collected systematically until the mid-1990s and comparative information from sources such as the OECD are sparse before the 1980s. Since the recent rise of nonstandard work arrangements in industrial countries began in the mid-1970s to 1980s (see chapter 1), the lack of information on these types of work from these earlier periods makes it difficult to assess long-term trends (see Green 2006 for a discussion of this problem). In addition, studies of nonstandard work arrangements in different countries often focus on specific occupations or industries and measure them in distinctive ways, making comparisons among countries difficult. Nevertheless, some more recent information on the types of nonstandard work arrangements is available and provides partial glimpses of the scope and trajectories of this phenomenon.

We can get a general picture of the rise of nonstandard work arrangements by contrasting regular, full-time employment with a global indicator that combines workers on temporary contracts, part-time jobs, and own-account self-employed persons (who are classified as self-employed and who do not have any employees). A recent study of twenty-six European OECD countries using such a global indicator showed that over half of all jobs created in these countries between 1995 and 2013 were in these nonstandard work arrangements, as were about 60 percent of those created between 2007 and 2013 (OECD 2015a). Further, in 2013, about one-third of all jobs in these countries were in nonstandard work arrangements, divided about equally among temporary jobs, permanent part-time jobs, and self-employment.

The expansion of nonstandard work differs among the six countries. Between 1995 and 2007, 22.7 percent of the jobs created in Spain were in nonstandard jobs, compared to 12.7 percent in Germany. The percentage of nonstandard jobs declined by 0.5 percent in Great Britain and 7.45 percent in Denmark. By contrast, the percentage of jobs created between 2007 and 2013 that were nonstandard jobs increased slightly in Great Britain (3.2 percent) and Germany (2 percent), but declined in Spain (8.9 percent) and Denmark (0.5 percent).

In Japan, the proportion of non-regular workers increased from about 27 percent in 2001 to slightly over a third of Japanese workers in 2010 (Osawa, Kim, and Kingston 2013). Non-regular workers are called *furita* or *freeter* (i.e., "free" + *arubaito*, a Japanese translation of the German word for worker, *arbeiter*) and have defined terms of employment and no explicit job security between fixed-term contracts. These *furita* include: part-time workers (*pato*); side jobs held by students or those working in other full-time positions (*arubaito*); temporary workers whose commitments vary greatly with regard to work terms and durations (*rinjikoyo*); and various other dispatch and temporary employees (e.g., *haken, keiyaku, shokutaku*) that work on fixed short-term contracts that are exempt from firm subsidies and fringe benefits. The dominant form of non-regular employment is part-time work (*pato*), which refers to a status rather than to the number of work hours, and is distinguished by the type of personnel policies applied to such workers (e.g., the absence of seniority-based policies) (Houseman and Osawa 1995).

In the United States, the percentage of employed persons who worked in alternative work arrangements (defined as independent contractors, on-call workers, temporary help agency workers, and workers provided by contract firms) increased from 10 percent in 1995 to 10.7 percent in 2005 and rose to 17.2 percent in 2015. By far the largest such alternative work arrangement was that of independent contractors, which grew from 6.3 percent in 1995 to 6.9 percent in 2005 and 9.6 percent in 2015. Indeed, almost all the growth represented by the nine million new jobs created in the US in the past decade were in these alternative work arrangements, with no net increase in regular, full-time employment (Katz and Krueger 2016).

However, grouping the various types of nonstandard work arrangements together into a single indicator obscures important differences among them, and so is tantamount to comparing apples to oranges. For example, part-time work in some countries can be stable and associated with social and statutory protections akin to those enjoyed by regular, full-time workers, and so is less likely to be precarious than short-term and irregular jobs, for example. For this reason, most studies of nonstandard work eschew comprehensive, overall indicators and focus instead on the various types of such arrangements. I follow this convention and so concentrate in the rest of this chapter on two of the most prominent types of nonstandard work: temporary work and involuntary part-time work.

Temporary Work

Figure 3.1 shows the trends in the proportion of employed persons who were in temporary employment in each of the six countries from

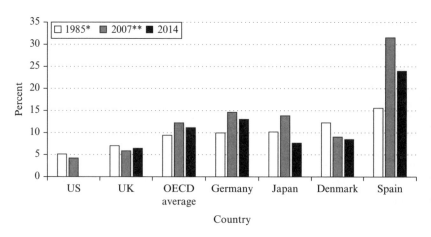

Figure 3.1   Percentage of workers in temporary employment, 1985, 2007, and 2014

*Spain 1987; US 1995; **US 2005

Source: OECD Employment database 2015

the mid-1980s to 2014. Here, temporary work is defined as wage-and-salaried employment that has a predetermined ending date.

Countries with relatively high employment protections – such as Spain and Germany – have relatively high levels of temporary work. Spain has one of the highest rates of temporary employment in Europe and the world, reaching about a third of the labor force in the mid-2000s, though it has decreased since the economic crisis. The high level of temporary work in Spain reflects the impact of high employment protections that made it difficult for employers to discharge regular workers, creating a disincentive for them to hire regular workers, as well as the effect of the policy reforms introduced in 1984 that were designed to increase employment (especially among young workers) by allowing the use of fixed-term contracts for any type of work. These laws were initially directed at younger workers but were extended to other categories of workers (ILO 2016: 56–7). The decline in the proportion of temporary workers since the economic crisis reflects temporary workers being laid off at much higher rates than regular workers, as the use of temporary contracts in the two decades before the crisis led Spanish companies to rely on them and so the companies were unable to respond to the crisis by mechanisms to create internal flexibility (as in Germany).

Despite the high levels of temporary employment, Spain also provides some of the strongest employment protections for temporary workers (Grimshaw et al. 2016). In addition, the high overall levels of temporary employment in Spain mask considerable diversity among industrial sectors and in the reasons for their use. Temporary employment is highest in construction, where skilled temporary workers change employers frequently as they move from one project to another. Hospitality also uses a high number of temporaries, but here this is due to the seasonality of demand (Banyuls and Recio 2017).

In Germany, there was an increase in the proportion of temporary workers from 1985 to 2007 (to about 15 percent of the labor force) before it declined after the crisis. The earlier increase in temporary workers reflects the policy reforms that facilitated the use of fixed-term contracts in the 1980s through 2000s that sought to increase the flexibility in labor markets to counteract negative effects of recessions and increase employment, especially among young workers. Named after Peter Hartz (who was the chair of the commission that developed them), the Hartz reforms were part of a package of tax, regulatory, and labor reforms in 2003, introduced by the Social Democratic Party led by Gerhard Schröder (who called his plan "Agenda 2010"), that made it easier to hire and fire workers and to use temporary work (fixed-term contracts were prohibited until 1972); workers from temporary help agencies can now be used without limit in Germany. The 2003 Hartz Act also reduced UI payments, tightened restrictions on benefit receipt, increased eligibility requirements, reduced the duration of benefits, and broadened the definition of an acceptable job to encompass work that does not use a worker's existing skills or training (Eichhorst and Marx 2011). This made unemployment more painful for those without jobs but made it easier for those without jobs to get them.

Japan also experienced an increase in the proportion of temporary workers from 1985 to 2007 before a larger decline since 2007. Denmark, on the other hand, has experienced a rather steady decline in the proportion of the labor force in temporary work since the mid-1980s. This might reflect the transition of temporary workers to permanent jobs (see next subsection) or out of the labor force entirely.

By contrast, the percentage of temporary workers is much lower in the United States and the United Kingdom than in the other four countries, as well as compared to the OECD countries overall. There has also been relatively little change in the proportion of temporary workers in the UK and US (though, as I have mentioned, national data on temporary workers were unavailable in the US before the mid-1990s, well after the period when temporary work is assumed to have increased markedly).

A major reason for the low levels of temporary work in these two LMEs is the weak employment protections in these countries, so employers can more easily lay off or fire permanent workers "at will" without the need for the flexibility that comes with temporary work. As shown in figure 2.4, the US and the UK rank lowest among the six countries in terms of the employment protections for regular workers and have the fewest restrictions on the use of temporary employees. The low levels of job protections in the US and UK imply that all jobs are characterized to some extent by uncertainty and insecurity. Since both regular jobs and non-regular jobs are insecure (albeit perhaps in different degrees), it has become increasingly difficult to distinguish good and bad jobs by their degree of security (Kalleberg 2011).

Is Temporary Work Precarious?

The risks associated with temporary employment depend on how social protections are tied to the employment relationship. Whether we consider a nonstandard work arrangement to be precarious is contingent on the nature of the labor market and social welfare protection institutions, as well as the labor laws and statutes covering work and employment. Some countries have sought to make nonstandard work arrangements less precarious, for example, by extending social protections to nonstandard work and using collective bargaining and active labor market policies to regulate and enhance the quality of nonstandard work (Adams and Deakin 2014). Some people also *prefer* temporary jobs – especially if they are associated with some social protections – to obtain greater flexibility in their working lives to be able to give greater attention to caregiving and other family obligations. In addition, temporary jobs can give highly skilled workers (such as nurses) more flexible career prospects and greater remuneration.

Whether a work arrangement or employment relation is classified as standard or nonstandard is less relevant for defining them as precarious, then, than the kinds of social and legal protections associated with them. Social protections and labor laws in industrial countries often assumed that workers had standard employment relations, with full-time and relatively stable work. But while people in regular (i.e., non-temporary, full-time) jobs may be relatively secure compared to temporary workers, such regular jobs may now have fewer social protections than they once did (Vosko, MacDonald, and Campbell 2009). The decline of unions, for example, has weakened the institutional protections formerly associated with jobs in countries such as the United States; combined with the paucity of protections against dismissal in that country (where employment tends to be at the "will" of the employer), this has made regular jobs more precarious. In Spain, the deterioration of protections for standard workers and the improvement of protections for temporary workers have reduced the protection gaps between these forms of employment (Grimshaw et al. 2016).

While temporary work is generally insecure and uncertain, there are pessimistic and optimistic scenarios about the eventual destinations of those who are employed temporarily. The pessimistic, "dead-end" perspective argues that working in temporary jobs does not promote the acquisition of skills that are transferable to more permanent jobs. Temporary workers are thus unable to develop their human capital to advance to more rewarding jobs. Thus, Autor and Houseman (2010) found that there was considerable churning of temporary workers, rather than their moving to permanent jobs, in the United States (but see Andersson, Holzer, and Lane 2007).

More optimistically, some temporary jobs do promote the acquisition of skills that can be transferred to other occupations, resulting in upward mobility to regular employment. According to this view, temporary jobs are "stepping-stones" where work experience results in skill growth and mobility opportunities for workers in the occupation generally, not just a handpicked few. Such temporary jobs may provide opportunities to acquire skills (both firm-specific and general technical skills, as well as "soft skills" such as an acceptable work ethic), expand social and professional networks, become familiarized with the labor market, and try out different kinds of jobs. From the employers' point of view, temporary jobs may be used to screen and evaluate people for regular positions and to assess a person's fit with the organization. In these cases, temporary work may represent bridges that lead to stable career progressions as opposed to traps that forestall opportunities for upward mobility during one's career.

One indicator of the degree to which temporary jobs might lead to more permanent positions is whether the employer provides them with training, either organized or paid for by the employer. This is an essential feature of firm-internal labor markets, and such training provides the worker with skills that can be utilized on other jobs, usually within the firm, but potentially in other firms in the industry and even more generally.

Figure 3.2 shows the estimated percentage effect of temporary contract status on the probability of a worker receiving employer-sponsored training in 2012 in each of the six countries.[2] These figures suggest that temporary workers receive relatively little employer-sponsored training in all the countries. However, employers in the US are the most likely to provide their temporary workers with some training relative to their permanent workers, though the gap between temporary and permanent workers is not very large (about 6 percent) and the amount of training they provide to their permanent employees is not very sizable.

By contrast, temporary workers in Spain have the lowest probabilities of receiving employer-sponsored training relative to permanent employees. This underscores the precariousness of temporary work in Spain, where a sharp divide separates temporary and permanent workers (despite the improvement in protections for temporary workers in that country). It also reflects the school-based nature of the Spanish vocational system, along with the paucity of training provided by employers. Similarly, the relatively low chances of temporary workers receiving employer-sponsored or organized training in Japan point to the dualistic structure of the Japanese employment

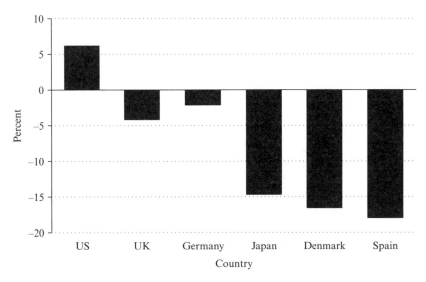

Figure 3.2 Percentage difference between temporary workers and permanent workers in the probability of having received employer-sponsored training, 2012

Source: OECD 2014a, 2014b data

system, where regular workers are given on-the-job training in firm-internal labor markets while temporary workers are not. Temporary workers in Denmark are also relatively less likely to receive employer-sponsored or organized training, which might be explained by the Danish dual vocational educational system in which the state pays much of the training costs. This explanation would not, however, account for the lack of differences between temporary and permanent workers in employer-provided training in Germany.

Another indicator of whether temporary jobs are stepping-stones to more permanent jobs or traps that constitute dead ends is the probability that temporary workers move into permanent positions. I would expect that temporary workers have greater opportunities to use temporary jobs as stepping-stones to more permanent jobs in countries where the temporary workers receive more employer-provided training. Figure 3.3 suggests that this is the case: it displays transition rates from temporary to permanent jobs in 2007, 2012, and 2013 for the four European countries (Denmark, Germany, Spain, and the United Kingdom), and compares these with averages from the eighteen Euro Area countries[3] and the twenty-seven European

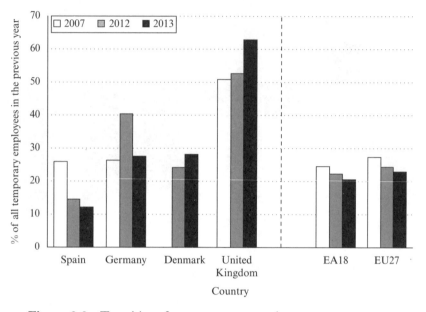

Figure 3.3 Transitions from temporary employment to permanent employment: share of temporary employees in year t who transit to a permanent job in year t+1, 2007, 2012, and 2013
Source: OECD 2014b data

Union countries (see European Commission 2016a: 88). The bars represent the proportion of all temporary workers in the previous year that moved to a permanent job in the years shown on the graph. In general, this study found that countries with higher proportions of temporary workers were also those who had a smaller share of temporary workers moving to permanent employment.

Figure 3.3 shows that temporary workers in the United Kingdom are the most likely to have transitioned from temporary to permanent jobs: over 50 percent of temporary workers in 2006 moved to permanent jobs in 2007, and over 60 percent by 2013. This indicates the greater mobility associated with this LME and the role of temporary work in providing access to more permanent jobs. This is consistent with an analysis by the OECD (2014b) that showed that 48.8 percent of workers on temporary contracts in Great Britain in 2008 were employed as full-time permanent employees in 2011.

By contrast, relatively low proportions of temporary workers in Spain were able to transition to a permanent job in the following year: this percentage declined from about a quarter in 2007 to 14.4

percent in 2012 and 12 percent in 2013, undoubtedly a reflection of the difficult labor market situation in Spain after the economic crisis. (The OECD study [OECD 2014b] found that only 20.6 percent of workers on temporary contracts in Spain in 2008 were employed as full-time permanent employees in 2011.) These relatively low chances of transition from temporary to permanent jobs also underline the dualistic nature of the Spanish labor market, whereby temporary jobs are generally "dead ends" and provide neither much training nor career opportunities. Indeed, people in Spain are more likely to obtain permanent positions when they are unemployed than if they are a temporary worker.

About a quarter of the temporary workers in Germany transitioned to permanent jobs in 2007 and 2013 (compared to about 40 percent in 2012). This is consistent with the (relative) lack of disadvantages that temporary workers have in Germany (see figure 3.2). It is also similar to the results from Eichhorst and Tobsch's (2013) analysis of the German Socio-Economic Panel survey, which showed that about a third of temporary fixed-term workers moved to an open-ended contract (here, open-ended contracts included vocational training and self-employment), as did about 30 percent of temporary agency workers in the 2007–11 period. Similarly, about a quarter of the temporary workers in Denmark in 2012 and 2013 moved to permanent jobs in the subsequent year (no data were available for Denmark in 2007).

Involuntary Part-Time Work

The quality and nature of part-time work vary considerably among countries (see Fagan et al. 2014).[4] Many less-than-full-time jobs incorporate all other features of the SER, particularly in countries such as the Netherlands where part-time workers receive many of the same protections as full-time workers. In those cases, part-time work is not nonstandard at all, as when it represents employer accommodations to employee preferences for reduced hours and more flexible schedules, for example. In other countries (notably in the United States and United Kingdom), part-time jobs are often highly insecure, lacking enhancements such as benefits, training opportunities, and the expectation of continuity. Countries also differ considerably in their regulation of part-time work, though the ILO (2015) reports that there have been increases in protections regarding equal treatment and equal dismissal rights in both OECD and emerging countries (but not in developing countries) since the early 1990s.

In considering the desirability of part-time work, it is important to take into account workers' preferences and needs. Part-time work does not mean the same thing for traditional male breadwinners as it does to women or younger workers or those using them as an extra job to supplement income. A common indicator of preferences for part-time work is whether people work in these jobs voluntarily or involuntarily. Part-time work is classified as involuntary if workers say that they would prefer full-time work but cannot find such work due to lack of demand for full-time work or cutbacks in hours (involuntary part-time work is also called working part-time for economic reasons). Such part-time jobs are often nonstandard and more likely to be precarious. By contrast, those who are working part-time voluntarily are classified as doing so for personal, non-economic or supply-side reasons such as family obligations, school, or partial retirement. Here, part-time jobs may have some of the features of regular full-time work, such as set schedules and relative stability of employment. Most part-time workers in advanced countries are classified as doing the jobs for voluntary reasons, though such "voluntary" choices may be constrained by lack of adequate childcare or inability to afford to retire completely.

The precarious and thus most problematic type of part-time work is thus working part-time involuntarily. Figure 3.4 shows trends in involuntary part-time work from 2000 to 2014 in the six countries.

Spain has the highest proportion of involuntary part-time workers, and the percentage of such workers has increased steadily since 2000, especially after the economic crisis. (Note that part-time jobs account for only 15 percent of Spanish jobs compared to almost 50 percent in the Netherlands, however.) The United States has the smallest percentage of involuntary part-time workers but here too the proportion of such workers has increased monotonically throughout from 2000 to 2014 (especially after the Great Recession). The growth in the percentage of involuntary part-time workers after the economic crisis is also observed in Denmark and the United Kingdom.

In Germany, however, the percentage of involuntary part-time workers decreased (as did the unemployment rate; see chapter 4) following the economic crisis, after having risen during the period 2000–7. An explanation may be found in the German legislation that has sought to encourage part-time work (especially among women) by mandating equal treatment for part-time and full-time workers; this tends to make part-time work more attractive and hence make it easier for workers to accept such jobs voluntarily to enable them to balance work with family and other aspects of their lives (Bosch and Kalina 2008: 80–5).

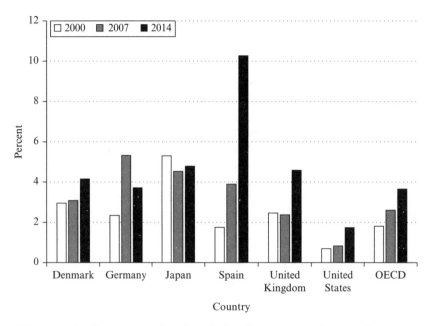

Figure 3.4 Percentage of workers in involuntary part-time employment, 2000, 2007, and 2014

Source: OECD Involuntary Part-Time Employment database 2015 data

In Germany, Denmark, and the UK, more than 40 percent of establishments employ at least some of their workforce for fewer than 15 hours per week (ILO 2016: 82). A prominent example of such marginal part-time jobs is the German "mini-job," defined as an employment relationship with monthly earnings of not more than 400 euros per month, regardless of working time, though the vast majority of those working in such jobs earn low wages. These jobs have the same protections against dismissal as standard employment contracts, though in practice those in them are treated more as temporary workers. Mini-jobs are concentrated in service activities, especially in retailing, cleaning services, and catering, and among women (the share of women in mini-jobs is 64.4 percent), where they have been attractive to housewives (Bosch and Kalina 2008).

Finally, involuntary part-time work in Japan (where working part-time is a status within the firm reflecting the absence of the benefits and privileges accorded to regular workers, not an indicator of hours worked) has declined somewhat since 2000, with a slight uptick since 2007.

Temporary and part-time employment relations are often related.

In Europe, part-time employment is also more often associated with temporary work: 25 percent of workers with a fixed-term contract and 37 percent of temporary agency workers worked part-time in the EU27 countries in 2007 (ILO 2016: 76); by contrast, only 14 percent of workers on indefinite term contracts worked part-time.

The use of "zero-hours" arrangements in the UK illustrates the linkage between part-time and temporary jobs. Here, workers agree to be "on call" or available to work when needed but are not assured of a fixed number of hours per day, week, or month. About 40 percent of workers on such contracts average about 16 hours per week. There was a sharp increase in zero-hours contracts in the UK between 2012 and 2015 (reaching 800,000 or 2.5 percent of all employees in the fourth quarter of 2015). This is the most notorious form of nonstandard work in the UK, especially in certain sectors such as care work, higher education, retail, and hospitality. Many people don't realize that they are on such contracts, however, and so their substantial rise may reflect greater awareness of them generated by media attention and statistical clarifications.

A similar concept in the US is that of on-call workers used by major retail businesses and food services as well the more traditional substitute teachers. This is a form of direct-hire temporary work that generally involves part-time work. Related to this is the notion of precarious scheduling, in which workers' schedules are not set in advance and often change in unpredictable ways, causing considerable stress for workers and their families.

Summary and Conclusions

Nonstandard work arrangements include temporary and part-time work, as well as non-employment relations such as those involving independent contractors and self-employed persons. Such nonstandard work arrangements – especially temporary and involuntary part-time work – are often used as proxies for precarious work. I have argued in this chapter that while nonstandard work arrangements are generally insecure and uncertain, the degree to which they are associated with the other features of precarious work, namely lack of social and statutory protections, differs among countries depending on their employment, labor market, and social welfare protection systems. Thus, temporary work may be quite precarious in countries where such jobs are associated with few protections and do not provide much opportunity to advancement to more permanent jobs, but may be rather desirable if they provide workers with the flexibility they want and/or provide training or experience that is likely to lead to more attractive permanent jobs.

The incidence of temporary jobs varies among countries depending on their labor market institutions. In countries with high levels of employment protections for regular workers (such as Spain), employers are incentivized to create temporary jobs to maintain their flexibility over the employment relationship, while the relaxation of laws regarding the use of temporary contracts led to their increased use.

Moreover, the degree to which temporary jobs can be considered precarious depends on the nature of the social protection systems in a country, such as whether temporary workers are afforded the same kinds of welfare entitlements as those who are working in regular jobs. In addition, some temporary jobs provide stepping-stones to more permanent jobs while others represent dead ends. In Spain, temporary workers receive relatively little employer-provided training compared to permanent workers, and small proportions of temporary workers subsequently move to permanent jobs. By contrast, temporary workers in the LMEs of the US and UK are more likely to be able to transition to permanent jobs, as temporary jobs provide workers with opportunities to develop skills and try out different kinds of work, while employers use temporary jobs to screen and evaluate potential regular employees.

4

Job Insecurity

It has emerged clearly that job insecurity is now everywhere: in the private sector, but also in the public sector, which has greatly increased the number of temporary, part-time or casual positions; in industry, but also in the institutions of cultural production and diffusion – education, journalism, the media, etc. In all these areas it produces more or less identical effects, which become particularly visible in the extreme case of the unemployed: the destructuring of existence, which is deprived among other things of its temporal structures, and the ensuing deterioration of the whole relationship to the world, time and space ... Objective reality gives rise to a generalized subjective insecurity which is now affecting all workers in our highly developed economy. (Pierre Bourdieu 1998: 82–3)

Job insecurity is the new norm. (Guy Standing 2011: 37)

The feeling of insecurity is inimical to our sense of wellbeing, as it causes anxiety and stress, which harms our physical and mental health. It is no surprise then that, according to some surveys, workers across the world value job security more highly than wages. (Ha-Joon Chang 2013)

These quotations illustrate the profound importance of job insecurity for a host of individual and organizational outcomes. Numerous studies have shown that people who are insecure about their jobs have lower mental and physical health and work performance (e.g., Burgard, Brand, and House 2009; Tegund 2014). Job insecurity also lowers one's trust and commitment to the employing organization, which negatively affects work-related behaviors such as performance (see the reviews by De Witte 1999; Sverke, Hellgren, and Näswall 2002).

These passages also underscore the fact that job insecurity is spreading and becoming more of a problem, largely due to the dynamics of precarious work that I have discussed previously. While this is generally becoming the new normal situation of work in contemporary capitalism, though, the degree to which people perceive their jobs are insecure and the consequences of this will differ among countries depending on their social welfare protection and labor market institutions.

Job insecurity is a multidimensional concept (see Greenhalgh and Rosenblatt 1984; De Witte 1999; Sverke and Hellgren 2002) and refers to at least two kinds of instability and uncertainty: (1) *job* insecurity, which denotes the degree to which a person is likely to lose the current job; and (2) *employment* (or labor market) insecurity, which refers to how easy or hard it will be to find a new, generally comparable job. The empirical relationship between these two conceptually distinct types of job insecurity varies among countries as well as within different types of occupations and industries within countries. For example, in countries with very active labor market policies but weak employment protections, job insecurity may be high but employment insecurity could be relatively low. This conceptual distinction is important to keep in mind, as these dimensions speak to the efficacy of different policies for reducing job-related insecurity, with job insecurity more related to employment protections, and employment insecurity more closely linked to active labor market policies that enable unemployed persons to transition to new jobs.

As dimensions of precarious work, job and labor market or employment insecurity are *objective* states that exist independently of the perceptions and opinions of workers. As such, these forms of insecurity can in principle be measured objectively, in terms of indicators such as the probabilities that one will lose one's job within a period and the likelihood of being able to find a new, at least comparable job. But the extent to which precarious work produces *perceived* job insecurity also varies – perhaps more than the objective realities – among countries. It is people's perceptions of insecurity that directly affect their attitudes, feelings, and behaviors. Indeed, perceived insecurity is what psychologists have shown to be strongly related to poor mental and physical health, job dissatisfaction, and a host of other outcomes. There is also considerable evidence that the anticipation of a negative event can be worse than experiencing the actual event itself: the dread and uncertainty of losing one's job can be worse than losing it, since insecurity constitutes an unknown that people are unsure how to deal with.

This chapter presents evidence on country differences in both objective and subjective aspects of job and employment insecurity.

Social welfare protection and labor market institutions affect the extent to which jobs are insecure (the objective aspect of insecurity, which is a dimension of precarious work) as well as the degree to which people perceive that their jobs are insecure and the degree to which they are worried about this (subjective aspects of insecurity, which are important outcomes of precarious work).

Objective Job Insecurity

Job insecurity refers to the likelihood that a person will lose their job within a period of time. The most commonly used objective indicator of job insecurity is the degree of *job stability*, which is usually measured by *employer tenure*, or the length of time a person has worked for a given employer. Employment or labor market insecurity denotes the likelihood that a person can find a new, at least comparable job. This is usually represented by measures of the amount and costs of *unemployment.*

Job Stability

Employer tenure[1] indicates the likelihood that a person will remain with an employer for a given period of time: stable, long-term jobs are assumed to be more secure than unstable, short-term jobs.

Debates about whether there have been changes – and the extent of any change – in the stability of employment relations usually focus on measures of employer tenure. In the United States, early studies often found that employer tenure had remained relatively constant since the early 1970s. This was a surprising result, since speculation about the consequences of the growth of nonstandard work arrangements and the use of downsizing and layoffs as business strategies suggested a decline in job stability. Thus, Diebold, Neumark, and Polsky (1997), using data from the Current Population Survey, found that job retention rates were stable over the 1980s and early 1990s, and the exchange between Diebold, Neumark, and Polsky (1996) and Swinnerton and Wial (1996) seemed to support the view that there was not a decrease in job stability during the period 1979–91. Similarly, Auer and Cazes (2003), in a study of the US, the European Union, and Japan, found that there was a relatively high level of stability in rates of employer tenure in these countries. Some writers have interpreted the relative stability of employer tenure, especially in the United Kingdom, as indicating that much of the discussion about the rise of precarious work and insecurity has been overblown (e.g., McGovern et al. 2004; Fevre 2007; Doogan 2009).

More recent studies of this topic have concluded that there has indeed been a general decline in the average length of time a person spends with his or her employer, however. These studies have shown that different groups display varied patterns of job instability: in particular, women's employer tenure has generally increased, while men's has decreased (though tenure levels for women remain substantially lower than those for men in the private sector). The decline in employer tenure is especially pronounced among older white men, the group that had been most protected by internal labor markets in the past (Cappelli 2008; Farber 2008). A more recent study by Auer (2006) also found that the average employer tenure in the US declined over the 1990s, and employer tenure was less in the US than in the other countries studied.

It is thus important to specify carefully the sub-group within which to assess levels and trends in employer tenure. For the purposes of assessing whether there have been changes in job stability, it's most useful to focus on the group of workers who are most likely to be at their prime working ages and therefore apt to be most highly committed and dependent on full-time, career-oriented work, which in most countries would be men aged 30–50. Figure 4.1 presents results for the average employer tenures for this labor force group in the six countries in 1992 and 2014; this time frame includes periods of economic expansion (in the 1990s) and economic recession (in the late 2000s), and thereby provides insights into relatively long-term trends in job stability in these countries for these men.

Figure 4.1 shows that there has been a general decline in the length of employer tenure for prime working-age men from 1992 to 2014 in all the countries. This is consistent with the argument that there has generally been a decline in job stability in the new age of precarious work. Despite the overall decline in job stability as measured by employer tenure, levels of tenure differ among countries depending on labor market and welfare protection institutions, as well as on the state of the economy in terms of economic growth and the relative supply of and demand for labor, among other factors.

Average job tenure is highest in Japan in both time periods. Japan has long been recognized as characterized by having lifetime employment (at least for Japanese men, up until their mid-fifties) that is rooted in firm-based employment systems in which highly developed firm-internal labor markets bind workers to their employers for a relatively long period of time. This stability of employment with a firm facilitates the acquisition of firm-specific skills and engenders strong

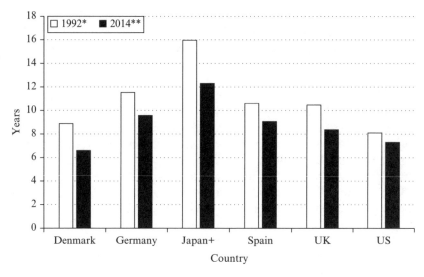

Figure 4.1 Average job tenure for men aged 30–50, 1992 and 2014
*US 1996; **US and Japan 2012; +Based on men aged 35–44
Source: OECD Firm Tenure database; US Current Population Survey (author's calculation); Japan Employment Status Survey

commitment to the employer (see Lincoln and Kalleberg 1990). Japan has not been immune from the general liberalization of labor markets prompted by pressures for greater flexibility and cost cutting, however, resulting in a weakening of the lifetime employment system and a gradual decline of firm-internal labor markets. Consequently, the average employer tenure in Japan for men aged 30–50 declined from sixteen years in 1992 to about twelve years in 2014, which was the most dramatic decrease in any of the six countries.

Job tenure in Germany was also relatively high in 1992, as Germany is another country with dual labor markets in which a protected core of workers remain with their employers for a considerable amount of time. Germany's hybrid employment system, which combines firm- and occupation-internal labor markets that are shaped by its strong system of vocational education, tends to encourage inter-firm mobility more than in Japan, however (Bosch and Kalina 2008: 78–80). In Germany, too, the average tenure declined over the period, from nearly twelve years to nearly ten years, though this decline in tenure was tempered by German firms' adoption of mechanisms of internal and working-time flexibility rather than numerical flexibility.

In Spain, the decline of employer tenure for prime-age men was more moderate than in Japan and Germany, though the relaxation of Spain's strict employment protection laws in response to pressures to liberalize the labor market also led to a decrease in job stability in that country. Levels of tenure in the UK were fairly similar to those in Spain.

The two countries with the lowest levels of average employer tenure for prime-age men are Denmark and the United States. Employer tenure declined substantially in Denmark over the period, so that it had the lowest average tenure among the six countries in 2014. This underscores the high levels of flexibility for employers in the Danish labor market, where turnover is rather high among its numerous SMEs and where active labor market institutions, weak employment protections, and an extensive social safety net promote employment and labor market insecurity rather than security in any specific job. Employer flexibility is relatively high in the United States as well, given its low employment protections and pervasiveness of the principle of employment at will that governs large numbers of employment relations.

OECD Labor Market Insecurity Index

A second objective indicator of country differences in job insecurity is the OECD's scale of labor market insecurity. This measures the likelihood and costs of job loss on a scale based on two main dimensions related to job loss: (1) the risk of unemployment and (2) the quality of UI, or the amount of income support received once unemployed (see Hijzen and Menyhert 2016).

The first dimension measures the objective risk that an employed person will become unemployed during a given period along with the average length of time that the person will be unemployed; this measure is closely related to the unemployment rate. Here, job and employment or labor market insecurity are somewhat conflated as the risk of unemployment combines the probability of losing one's job and that of re-employment.

The risk of unemployment is calculated based on inflow and outflow probabilities. The inflow probability (risk of unemployment) is the proportion of employed persons at a given point in time that becomes unemployed during the following month, while the unemployment outflow probability (expected duration of unemployment) is defined as "one minus the share of unemployed persons at a given point in time that remains unemployed for at least another month" (Hijzen and Menyhert 2016: 11).

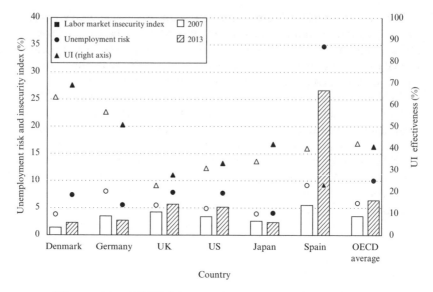

Figure 4.2   OECD labor market insecurity, 2007 and 2013
Source: OECD data

The second dimension speaks to the expected cost of unemployment, defined as a composite of both the coverage and generosity of UI. Combining indicators of coverage rates and replacement rates by benefit category yields a measure of "effective unemployment insurance [that] represents the share of earnings that employed workers can reasonably expect to retain during their eventual unemployment spell on average" (Hijzen and Menyhert 2016: 16).

These two dimensions might offset each other somewhat in terms of insecurity: high unemployment might produce less insecurity if income replacement is high. Similarly, high costs of unemployment (low income replacement) may create greater insecurity even if the actual chances of becoming unemployed are relatively low.

Figure 4.2 shows these OECD labor market insecurity scores for our six countries in 2007 and 2013, thus permitting a comparison of objective insecurity before and after the economic crisis. The vertical height of the bars represents the combined index, the circles indicate the unemployment risk (first component, on the left axis, where high values indicate greater risk), and the triangles show the quality of UI (second component, on the right axis: note that high values indicate greater UI effectiveness).

Labor market insecurity generally was relatively low in Denmark,

Germany, and Japan as compared to Spain, the UK, and the US. Differences among countries in the provision of UI appear to be greater than the probabilities of becoming unemployed: the generosity of UI was highest in Denmark and lowest in the United Kingdom and the United States, reflecting the differences in social welfare protection policies in these countries.

Insecurity is highest in Spain in both periods, but especially after the economic crisis (2013), when insecurity increased dramatically compared to 2007. The large growth in insecurity in Spain was due mainly to the elevated risk of unemployment during the period, which was markedly higher than in any of the other countries. (The risk of unemployment was also highest in Spain in 2007, but the gap between Spain and the other countries was not nearly as great as it was after the economic crisis.) The increase in unemployment after the economic crisis has been blamed largely on the bursting of the real estate bubble in that country, which created a great deal of joblessness in industries related to construction, for example. Spain is unusual among these countries also in that the generosity and coverage of UI declined at the same time as the risk of unemployment rose; in the other five countries, there was a positive relationship between changes in unemployment risk and UI.

Labor market insecurity also increased during this period in both the United Kingdom and the United States; these countries had the next highest levels of insecurity after the economic crisis. There was also a slight increase in labor market insecurity in Denmark, though the level of insecurity was low relative to that in the other countries. In all three of these countries, the growth in the labor market insecurity index was due mainly to the elevated risk of becoming unemployed, though in all three cases the greater unemployment risk was somewhat offset by the increased effectiveness of UI. Hence, in these countries, the coverage and generosity of UI were expanded in response to the growth in unemployment.

By contrast, labor market insecurity declined somewhat in Germany and Japan after the economic crisis. In Germany, the reduction in insecurity was due primarily to the reduced risk of becoming unemployed since the effectiveness of UI there also decreased. The decline in unemployment in Germany during the economic crisis was rooted in labor market policies such as the creation of mini-jobs and job-sharing practices, which reduced the hours that people worked rather than forcing them to become unemployed. In Japan, the slight decline in insecurity was due to the greater effectiveness of UI, as there was little change in the risk of becoming unemployed.

Perceived Job Insecurity

There are also two dimensions of perceived job insecurity (see Anderson and Pontusson 2007). First, people differ in their perceptions of the likelihood that they will lose their job as well as in their confidence of getting a new, at least comparable job. This is a *cognitive* condition in which people presumably evaluate the likelihood that an event will happen (e.g., losing one's job or finding a new one). Cognitive measures are most closely linked to policies such as employment protections or active labor market policies and are likely to be strongly related to business cycles and fluctuations in unemployment.

Measures of objective job insecurity may not always correspond to indicators of cognitive job insecurity, however. The correspondence between objective and subjective job insecurities depends on a variety of psychological mechanisms that may color one's perceptions, such as: whether people are optimistic or pessimistic; have sufficient information about the objective probabilities to form accurate opinions; feel that they have a high degree of control over what happens to them as opposed to being more fatalistic; the opinions of those they interact with; and so on. Moreover, subjective perceptions of insecurity also depend on economic conditions such that high levels of unemployment may enhance perceptions of job insecurity for people with similar levels of employer tenure compared to situations where unemployment is lower (Auer 2006).

Moreover, Doogan (2009) argues that perceptions of job insecurity might be high even if there is high employment stability due to the pervasiveness of precarious work as an ideology of domination (cf. Bourdieu 1998).

Nevertheless, subjective assessments of the chances of losing one's job are strongly related to actual job loss rates[2] (Manski and Straub 2000; Dickerson and Green 2012). Green (2009) finds that measures of perceived job insecurity closely track the unemployment rate for a wide variety of industrial countries in data collected by the International Social Survey Programme (ISSP) in 1997 and 2005. And the research reviewed by Dixon, Fullerton, and Robertson (2013) generally concluded that unemployment was consistently the most significant predictor of perceived insecurity (they also found this in their analysis of 2006 Eurobarometer data on twenty-seven European Union countries).[3] It would be surprising if indicators of other objective conditions were not mirrored in subjective perceptions too, though possible divergences between them might reveal notable discrepancies that warrant closer investigation. While perceptions are arguably less useful for comparing countries on levels of job security due to perceptual differences among individuals, they are nevertheless helpful in filling out the story.

Second, people also differ in the degree to which they worry about losing their job or finding a new one. This is an *affective* rather than cognitive aspect of perceived job insecurity that relates more directly to moods, feelings, and attitudes and is likely to be directly linked to stress, depression, and other negative mental and physical health outcomes. People who perceive cognitively that their job is insecure may not necessarily be worried about this, if they are confident that they will have opportunities to be retrained for new jobs, help in getting placed in a comparable job, or economic and social supports while they are unemployed. On the other hand, affective job insecurity is apt to be high if these labor market and social welfare institutions are not in place, since the consequences of job loss are then greater.

Perceived Cognitive Job Insecurity

Perceived cognitive job insecurity is usually measured by asking survey respondents about their chances of losing their jobs and of finding comparable new ones. The assessment of employment insecurity is apt to be rather hypothetical for individuals who believe their jobs are secure, and so measures of perceived cognitive job insecurity often combine the two aspects of this concept: the degree to which a person perceives she or he will lose the job; and one's perception of how easy or hard it will be to find a new, generally comparable job.

A typical composite measure of perceived cognitive job insecurity thus consists of two items, such as: "My current job is secure" (1 = Very true, 2 = Quite true, 3 = A little true, 4 = Not at all true); and "How difficult or easy would it be for you to get a similar or better job with another employer if you had to leave your current job?" (0 = Extremely easy; 10 = Extremely difficult). These two items can be combined into a single variable, coding those as being insecure (= 1) who say their jobs are insecure (scoring 3 or 4 on the first item) and also that they would find it difficult to get a similar or better job if they left their current job (scoring 6 and above on the second item).

Figure 4.3 presents information on perceived job insecurity measured in this way for four European countries (i.e., Denmark, Germany, Spain, and the United Kingdom) from the European Social Survey (ESS), a research program that is co-funded by the

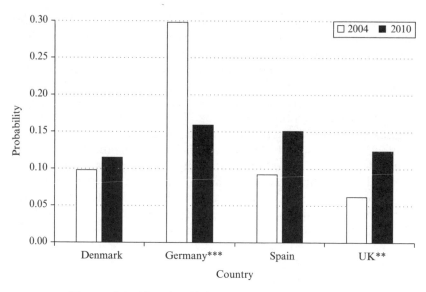

Figure 4.3　Perceived job insecurity, 2004 and 2010
Significant difference between years: *** p<0.001, ** p<0.01
Source: ESS 2004 and 2010 data

European Commission, European Science Foundation, and national research funding bodies.

The most striking feature of figure 4.3 is the substantial decline in perceived cognitive job insecurity in Germany between 2004 and 2010: The percentage of Germans who said that they were likely to lose their jobs and be unable to find a comparable new one declined from about 30 percent in 2004 to slightly more than 15 percent in 2010, after the economic crisis. Indeed, this was the only one of the four countries that reported a decline in perceived insecurity. This result for Germany is consistent with figure 4.2, which showed a decline in the risk of unemployment in Germany (and overall labor market insecurity) between 2007 and 2013. As discussed in chapter 3, the labor market reforms designed to preserve employment at the expense of hours worked in Germany during this period lowered both the objective chances of job loss and the extent to which workers perceived that their jobs were insecure. Nevertheless, even in 2010, Germans reported the highest levels of job insecurity, comparable to the Spanish.[4]

Workers in the other three countries reported an increase in perceived cognitive job insecurity between 2004 and 2010, though only in the United Kingdom was this difference statistically significant;

this is also a country in which the resources allocated to active labor market policies declined during this period (see figure 2.3). The gap in Denmark was especially small, consistent with the expansion of active labor market policies in that country (see figure 2.3). Not surprisingly, given the large increases in unemployment risks in Spain, there was an increase in perceived job insecurity during this period (though this increase was not statistically significant when individual differences within Spain are controlled for), despite the rise in resources allocated to active labor market policies.

To assess the impacts of these institutions on job insecurity more directly, my colleague Hande Inanc and I used the 2004 and 2010 ESSs to estimate differences among seventeen European countries in the extent to which labor market policies (active labor market policies and employment protections) and social welfare protections (generosity of welfare spending and UI) affect how insecure people feel about their jobs, using a measure of job insecurity that is the same as that utilized in figure 4.3 (see Inanc and Kalleberg 2016).[5]

We found that differences among the seventeen countries accounted for 14 percent of the variation in job insecurity among individuals, after controlling for differences in perceived job insecurity as well as the yearly country unemployment rate and degree of income inequality. People in countries with higher levels of active labor market policies reported less job insecurity. Similarly, Lübke and Erlinghagen's (2014) analyses of the 2004 and 2010 ESSs from nineteen European countries found that an increase in expenditure on active labor market policies lowered the perception of job loss.

In addition, we found that there was less perceived job insecurity in countries with more generous UI benefits. This is consistent with the results by Anderson and Pontusson (2007), who used data on fifteen countries from the 1997 ISSP and found that spending on unemployment compensation is negatively related to affective job insecurity (see also Clark and Postel-Vinay 2009). Moreover, we found that there was less perceived job insecurity in countries with higher union density, a result that is consistent with Dixon, Fullerton, and Robertson's (2013) analysis of the 2006 Eurobarometer data on twenty-seven EU countries, which showed that there is lower average cognitive job insecurity in countries with higher union density. Higher unemployment in a country also increased perceived job insecurity, as we would expect (see also Dixon, Fullerton, and Robertson, 2013). Lübke and Erlinghagen's (2014) analysis also showed that cognitive job insecurity increased in countries facing economic crisis but decreased in countries with more prosperous economic conditions.

Our results for employment protections and job insecurity were complex: for regular workers, having strong employment protections increased their perceptions of job insecurity, presumably because they were concerned that if they lost their present job, they would have difficulty obtaining a new one due to the protections enjoyed by those who are still working. On the other hand, strong restrictions on the use of temporary workers were associated with temporary workers' lower perceived job insecurity.

This complexity is consistent with much of the literature, which has found either a negative or no relationship between employment protections and job insecurity. Thus, Anderson and Pontusson (2007) found that employment protections in a country were negatively related to cognitive job insecurity in fifteen countries in the 1997 ISSP, while Clark and Postel-Vinay (2009) used data for twelve European countries from the European Community Household Panel study and found workers perceive that they are less secure in their jobs in countries with higher employment protections. Moreover, Erlinghagen (2008) found no effect of employment protection on job insecurity in seventeen European countries. Chung and van Oorschot (2011) used the fourth wave of the ESS (2008/9) for twenty-two European countries and showed that active and passive labor market policies are more important for employment security than employment protections. Finally, Lübke and Erlinghagen's (2014) analysis of the 2004 and 2010 ESS data for nineteen countries found no significant relationship between employment protections or changes in employment protections and perceived job insecurity.

Temporary Work and Perceived Cognitive Job Insecurity

Temporary jobs are objectively insecure and unstable by definition, since they are short term in duration. And the evidence indicates that temporary workers are more likely to become unemployed or leave the labor force compared to regular workers (ILO 2016: table A5.1). But whether people who hold temporary jobs perceive these jobs to be insecure differs among individuals. Some people may have a relatively easy time moving from one temporary job to another or even moving from temporary to more permanent jobs, whether because they have skills that are in high demand or they live in countries in which temporary work serves as a bridge to permanent employment (such as Denmark or the United States; see chapter 3, and ILO 2016).

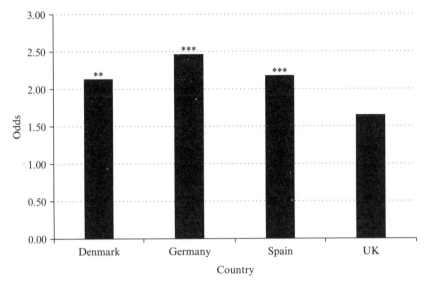

Figure 4.4   Effect of temporary employment on perceived job insecurity,
2004 and 2010

Significance: *** p<0.001, ** p<0.01

Source: ESS 2004 and 2010 data

Figure 4.4 presents information that speaks to this question, again based on the analysis of the 2004 and 2010 ESS data. Here, I show how the chances of perceiving jobs as insecure differ for temporary workers as opposed to those who have regular, open-ended contracts, in the four European countries.[6] The values on the Y-axis represent the odds that temporary workers will perceive their jobs as more insecure than non-temporary workers.

Temporary workers in all four countries perceive their jobs to be more insecure when compared to regular workers. Temporary workers in Germany and Spain are the most likely to perceive that their jobs are insecure relative to regular workers, which is consistent with the high levels of dualism that characterize these countries. The well-developed distinctions between objectively more secure "insider" core workers and less secure "outsider" peripheral and temporary workers in Germany and Spain are reflected in the gaps in perceived job insecurity between temporary and regular workers.

The odds that temporary workers in the United Kingdom perceive their jobs to be more insecure are not statistically significantly different from non-temporary workers, though temporary workers in the

UK still report greater insecurity with their jobs than non-temporary workers. The relatively low levels of employment protections in LMEs such as the UK imply that there is not all that much difference in the risk of unemployment between temporary and non-temporary workers on open-ended contracts. We would expect to find similar results for temporary workers in the US.[7]

Affective Job Insecurity

Affective job insecurity, or the extent to which people are worried about losing their jobs, results from two main sets of factors: the individual's assessment of the likelihood of losing the job (i.e., the cognitive job insecurity discussed in the previous section); and the person's evaluation of the consequences or costs of losing the job. These dynamics are related to institutional factors such as the generosity of welfare protections, the extent of active labor market policies and employment protections, and the state of the economy in terms of the level and length of unemployment.

Figure 4.5 presents information on affective insecurity for each of the six countries from the 2005 and 2015 Work Orientations Modules of the ISSP. The measure of affective insecurity is the percentage of workers in these countries who say that they worry "a great deal" or "to some extent" about losing their jobs; I also present the unemployment rates in these countries in these years.

Figure 4.5 indicates that the Danes were not very worried about

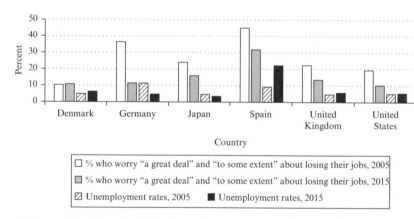

Figure 4.5   Perceived job insecurity concerns and unemployment rates, 2005 and 2015

Source: ISSP Work Orientations Modules 2005 and 2015 data

losing their jobs in either year, which is consistent with Denmark's high active labor market policies and generous welfare benefits (see also Böckerman 2004).

Workers in the other countries experienced a decline in affective job insecurity in 2015 compared to 2005. The sharp decline in affective insecurity in Germany mirrors the reduction in perceived cognitive insecurity between 2004 and 2010 shown in figure 4.3, as well as the reduction in the unemployment rate during this period. In Spain, however, the decline in affective job insecurity is not consistent with the rise in cognitive job insecurity shown in figure 4.3 or with the rise in unemployment between 2005 and 2015. Rather, the reduction in worry about losing one's job likely reflects the reduction in EPL in Spain during this period, which might make it easier for persons to find a new job once unemployed. Workers in Japan, the United Kingdom, and the United States also were less worried about losing their jobs after the economic crisis (2015) than before (2005); these countries are also characterized by relatively low unemployment rates.

Summary and Conclusions

Job insecurity is both an objective dimension of precarious work and a subjective perception on the part of individuals about the level and consequences of such objective insecurity. This chapter has unpacked the concept of job insecurity into its objective and subjective components. I also differentiated between insecurity associated with the loss of the job itself and that related to the chances of finding a new, comparable job.

Length of employer tenure declined in all six countries from the early 1990s for prime-age working men, indicating that there has been a general rise in job instability. This is consistent with my arguments presented in chapter 1 about the general decline in long-term attachments to employers associated with the transformation of work arrangements away from standard employment relations.

The data presented in this chapter also show that job insecurity is relatively low in Denmark, whether this is measured objectively by the risk and economic consequences of unemployment or as perceived cognitive and affective job insecurity. The Danes scored lowest among the six countries on the OECD labor market insecurity index, though this was due more to the relatively generous UI provisions in Denmark than to the actual risk of job loss. That the risk of unemployment is not particularly low in Denmark is consistent both with the relatively low employer tenure (figure 4.1) and the prominent role played by flexicurity policies in that country. Denmark's active labor market policies provide support to those who lose their jobs to help them receive additional job-related training and placement services that facilitate their re-entry into the workforce; and generous labor market policies offer an economic cushion that enables the unemployed to maintain a reasonable standard of living while searching for a new job. The results for Denmark also reiterate the importance of workers' institutional and associational power, such as the higher union density and collective bargaining coverage we observed in figure 2.1, which in conjunction with the policies of Social Democratic political parties led to the social welfare protection and labor market policies that reduce job insecurity.

Spain has by far the highest level of labor market insecurity (measured objectively by the OECD index in figure 4.2) and this is reflected in relatively high perceived cognitive job insecurity, which increased after the crisis. The Spanish are also the most worried about losing their jobs (figure 4.5). The reasons for the high levels of perceived job insecurity in Spain are not so clear-cut as for Denmark, since the Spanish scored fairly high on labor market activation policies (figure 2.3) as well as on the generosity of income replacement and welfare spending policies (figure 2.2). It is likely that the changes in social welfare protection and labor market institutions discussed in chapter 2 were instituted in response to the very high unemployment rates resulting from the economic crisis in Spain. For example, figure 2.3 shows that the Spanish markedly increased their expenditures on active labor market policies after the economic crisis, like Denmark but unlike the other countries. Moreover, the proportion of GDP spent on social expenditures also increased considerably after the crisis, like the other countries except for Germany (see figure 2.2).

Job insecurity appears to be relatively low and declining in Germany, as shown by the lower unemployment risk after the economic crisis (figure 4.2) and the sharp reductions in both perceived cognitive and affective insecurity. In Japan, there was little change in unemployment risk, though there was an increase in UI support (figure 4.2), which is consistent with the decline in affective job insecurity in Japan. In the UK and US, there were slight increases in unemployment risk and decreases in affective job insecurity, which is also in line with the slight increase in UI support in those countries.

Taken as a whole, this chapter has highlighted that there are differences in both objective and subjective forms of job insecurity, and that these dissimilarities are consistent with the arguments developed in the previous chapters about the importance of labor market and social welfare protection institutions and policies in shaping both the degree of precarious work (in this, case, the dimension of job insecurity) and the extent to which job insecurity is problematic for workers.

Part III

Dimensions of Well-Being

5

Economic Insecurity

It is normal to be anxious if you are living a precariat existence, in and out of unemployment, worried about having enough money to buy food or where you will be sleeping next month. (Guy Standing 2011: 142)

Economic insecurity has become the rule, not the exception, for many Americans – even in good times. (Jacob S. Hacker et al. 2010: 3)

These quotations highlight the difficulties for people that are caused by economic insecurity. Precarious jobs usually provide low economic rewards as well as create greater volatility and instability in earnings from one year to the next. This results in greater economic insecurity, which refers to the extent to which a person has *sufficient* and reasonably *stable* income[1] and assets to be able to pay expenses and to maintain at least a minimum standard of living (Western et al. 2012; Osberg and Sharpe 2014).

The spread of precarious work has contributed to the risk factors that have made it increasingly difficult for many people and their families to attain economic security, even in the rich democracies. The problematic nature of economic insecurity has been central to European debates about economic exclusion, a term commonly used to refer to those subjected to poverty due to the economic restructuring that occurred in the 1970s and 1980s (Rodgers, Gore, and Figueiredo 1995). The factors promoting economic exclusion and economic insecurity are similar to those responsible for the growth of precarious work and job insecurity discussed in earlier chapters, such as globalization, technological change, deregulation of markets, and the decline of unions.

Economic insecurity is particularly pervasive and problematic for non-regular workers and immigrants, who are often outside systems of social protection and excluded from participation in many of the social and economic opportunities available to insiders and legal residents. In general, economic insecurity is likely to be more common now than in the period from the 1940s to the 1970s due to the widespread implementation of austerity policies that have led to restructuring of social welfare spending in most industrial countries, in addition to the rise of precarious work.

Jobs that pay low wages are more likely to be economically insecure, and there has been an increase in the number and proportion of low-wage jobs in many of the rich democracies, such as Germany (Brady and Biegert 2018). Low-wage jobs that provide few prospects for advancing to better jobs and lead to flat earnings trajectories are especially problematic. As is the case with temporary work, the extent to which people are stuck in low-wage jobs may differ among countries depending on their labor market institutions, as well as vary among occupations and industries within countries.

The relationship between low-wage work and economic insecurity depends on the social welfare protection institutions that provide persons with economic supports of various kinds to help them cope with periods of unemployment and suboptimal employment. This again underscores a basic theme in this book, namely that the extent and consequences of precarious work depend on social contexts such as a country's social, legal, and welfare social protections. Thus, in countries where the receipt of social protections is not dependent on working in certain kinds of employment relations, low-wage work is less likely to engender economic insecurity than in cases (such as the United States) where the delivery of benefits tends to be tied to regular, full-time jobs.

It is the responsibility of governments to provide basic human rights such as economic security. Article 25 (paragraph 1) of the Universal Declaration of Human Rights states that everyone has the right to have a standard of living that is sufficient for their health and well-being, "including food, clothing, housing and medical care and necessary social services, and the right to security in the event of unemployment, sickness, disability, widowhood, old age or other lack of livelihood in circumstances beyond his control" (United Nations, Department of Economic and Social Affairs 2008: iii). In the US, the government's obligation to provide economic insecurity was the impetus for President Franklin Roosevelt's creation of the Committee on Economic Security in 1934 and his proposal in 1944 to implement a second "bill of rights" that guaranteed Americans security with regard to income, medical care, social security, education, and employment, among other things; while some of these rights were ultimately provided (such as social security), others (such as economic and job security) have yet to be realized (see Sunstein 2004).

This chapter will link country differences in social welfare protections to variations in economic insecurity. As with job insecurity, I examine objective as well as subjective aspects of economic insecurity. I first discuss country differences in earnings quality, which includes the average level of earnings and the degree of inequality. Second, I assess differences in the proportion of persons who are in low-wage jobs and below the poverty level in the various countries. I next consider differences in the social wage or overall economic well-being in the countries. Finally, I examine variations in persons' subjective perceptions of economic insecurity, i.e., whether the person feels that his or her economic resources are sufficient to meet his or her needs and the needs of the family.

Earnings Quality and Inequality

The rise of economic inequality in a society is problematic for many reasons. These social and economic problems range from its links with poor mental and physical health to violence, disintegration of community life, political polarization and malaise, and subjective well-being, as is documented by Wilkinson and Pickett (2010) and Therborn (2013), among many others. What is especially concerning about the increase in economic inequality from the point of view of precarious work is that this growth has been accompanied by the expansion of low-wage jobs, thereby creating a group of people who are increasingly economically marginal and insecure. Indeed, it may well be that the spread of low-wage work is more problematic than the actual growth in economic inequality for many people's economic security and quality of life.

Countries differ in their *average levels of earnings* as well as in their amount of *earnings inequality*, or how evenly earnings are distributed among individuals. Both of these two objective aspects of earnings are important for individuals' economic security and well-being. The OECD has constructed an index of objective earnings quality that combines the level of and inequality in earnings. The first dimension, level of earnings, is measured as the arithmetic (simple) mean of gross hourly wages (i.e., before deductions of employee taxes and social security contributions) over all workers. The second dimension,

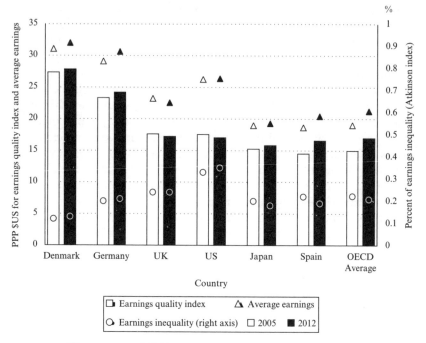

Figure 5.1   OECD earnings quality, 2005* and 2012
*Denmark 2008
Source: OECD data

earnings inequality, refers to how hourly wages are distributed among workers (Cazes, Hijzen, and Saint-Martin 2015).

Figure 5.1 shows these OECD earnings quality scores for the six countries in 2005 and 2012, thus enabling comparisons to be made before and after the economic crisis of 2008–9. The vertical heights of the bars represent the combined index, the triangles indicate the average earnings (first component, on the left axis) and the circles show the level of inequality in earnings (second component, on the right axis) in each of the time periods.

Earnings quality is highest in Denmark, which has the highest level of average earnings and the lowest amount of earnings inequality of these six countries and indeed of any Western nation. Earnings quality increased slightly in Denmark from 2008 to 2012, due mainly to the rise in average earnings. Denmark's high earnings quality results to a great extent from the high degree of worker power exercised by unions and supportive political parties. Its high earnings quality also reflects

Denmark's strong societal commitment to equality among individuals overall as well as between men and women, resulting in the country having one of the lowest gender gaps in earnings in the world.

Germany also has a relatively high level of earnings quality (second only to Denmark), with the second highest average level of earnings and the next lowest amount of earnings inequality. Wage compression in Germany is rooted in a deep preference for wage equality, which tends to limit the wages of high-skilled workers (and encourages them to emigrate) and to forestall the creation of a low-wage service sector, though as we will see, low-wage work has increased in Germany in recent years. Germany had low levels of income inequality up to the 1990s, at which point inequality increased substantially with the decline of industry-wide collective agreements (Brady and Biegert 2018). The Hartz reforms also increased income inequality in Germany, as they provided tax cuts for high earners and led to stagnating wages and a reduction in the middle class. Unlike the US, where the top 1 percent drove income inequality, there was not much increase in the top 1 percent in Germany. As in Denmark, earnings quality in Germany grew slightly over the period, mainly due to rises in average levels of earnings.

At the other extreme, earnings quality is relatively low in Japan and Spain, which have similar levels of average earnings and earnings inequality (and levels that correspond closely to the OECD average). In both countries, the low level of earnings quality is due mainly to the relatively low levels of average earnings, which are substantially below the averages in Denmark and Germany as well as the UK and US. Earnings equality increased somewhat during the period in Japan and Spain, with small declines in earnings inequality and modest increases in levels of earnings.

The two LMEs, the United Kingdom and the United States, had similar levels of earnings quality in both periods, though the components of earnings quality differed in the two countries. Average earnings were considerably higher in the US (which had the third highest level of average earnings, behind Denmark and Germany), while earnings inequality was lower in the UK. In both countries, earnings quality declined slightly over the period. In the UK this was due to a decline in average earnings, as multi-employer agreements have declined and there is no negotiation regarding pay and working conditions in over 70 percent of workplaces (Mason et al. 2008).

In general, the changes shown in figure 5.1 are relatively modest and in some cases (such as in Japan and Spain) earnings inequality has declined. This contrasts with the picture for income inequality (which includes both earnings and non-labor forms of income), which has increased markedly in all these rich democracies as well as around the world more generally.

Low-Wage Jobs

Denmark has the smallest incidence of low-wage work (Gautié and Schmitt 2010: xix); in 2005, the incidence of low-wage work was 8.5 percent in Denmark (and it has remained consistently low over time), compared to 25 percent in the US, 22.1 percent in the UK, and 20.8 percent in Germany (Solow 2008: 6). While Denmark has no minimum wage, it does have a minimum tariff that is negotiated by the social partners and to which most firms adhere. This again highlights the role played by Denmark's strong unions and collective bargaining arrangements: agreements among the social partners (employers via the Danish Employers' Federation and employees through the trade unions), over issues such as working hours and conditions as well as wage scales and minimum wages, are more important than government actions or legislation as regulatory mechanisms.

The Danish policy has been to set incomes in the labor market (based on the value of production) and then to provide economic assistance to those who are unable to obtain a decent level of living by working. Westergaard-Nielsen (2008: 29) describes the situation regarding low-wage work in Denmark by observing: "Overall, we might say that the low-skilled tend to be jobless in Denmark but not penniless, whereas in the United States the low-skilled tend to have a job but to be penniless."

The proportion of low-wage workers in Germany has grown: the low-wage share of employment in 2005, at over 20 percent of the labor force, was an unprecedented high, about the same as in the UK and not much lower than in the US (Appelbaum et al. 2010: 11). Germany has recently introduced a national minimum wage, which was designed to counteract the large group of working poor and labor market outsiders (though all low-paid workers are entitled to health and old-age insurance, which enhances the social wage, as I discuss later) (see Bosch and Weinkopf 2008: 292). The Hartz reforms led German unions and the Social Democrats to push for minimum wage laws; before, the unions had no need for such laws due to Germany's more extensive collective bargaining coverage. The government also subsidizes the pay of underused employees, who are put on short-time schedules, which we have seen in the last chapter reduced the unemployment rate. This labor market policy of sustained employment also enabled workers to keep their skills up to date, a strategy that is used especially in the auto and capital goods industries. Despite these advantages, this policy has been criticized for putting off needed economic restructuring in these industries by propping up demand for cars and auto workers.

The rise of low-wage jobs since the mid-1990s reflects Germany becoming a more individualistic system, with labor laws permitting mini-jobs (the low-paying part-time jobs that are excused from social security taxes), thus increasing the number of low-wage jobs in the 1990s and 2000s. Around three-quarters of low-paid workers had a vocational degree (Bosch and Weinkopf 2008), whereas in the United States, for example, low skill and low pay are highly correlated: 70 percent of low-wage workers in the US have no qualifications or only graduated from high school.

Low-wage jobs are likely to be marginal part-time and temporary jobs and result from outsourcing (Bosch and Weinkopf 2008: 289) as well as the other drivers of precarious work that I outlined in chapter 1. Low-wage jobs in Germany are concentrated among women (Gautié, Westergaard-Nielsen, and Schmitt with Mayhew 2010). Low-wage work in Germany also used to be more evenly distributed through the economy, though now it is moving from the core to the periphery of the labor market and is apt to be concentrated in smaller firms and service industries, which are areas with weak collective bargaining and few works councils.

In the UK the proportion of low-paying jobs appears to have stabilized at a historically high level (Mason, Mayhew, and Osborne 2008: 33). The expansion of such low-paying jobs is due in no small part to policies advanced by former Prime Minister Tony Blair's workfare program, which, like the welfare reforms in the United States in the mid-1990s (TANF), forced people (especially single women with children) often to take low-quality jobs to qualify for social benefits. Not surprisingly, low-wage jobs are also more concentrated among women in the United Kingdom (Gautié, Westergaard-Nielsen, and Schmitt with Mayhew 2010).

Workers in the United States are more likely to be in a low-paid job no matter what sociodemographic group they fall in; for example, low-wage work is much more common among older workers than in other countries. The US also had the highest level of low-paying jobs in the 1970s, but this has changed little since then, while the proportion of low-wage jobs in the UK and Germany has moved closer to the US level (Mason and Salverda 2010: 36–9).

The evidence suggests that low-wage work is a sticky state in the sense that low-wage workers are often apt to remain in such jobs and more liable to become unemployed than those in higher-wage jobs. For example, about half or more low-wage workers in Denmark, Germany, the United Kingdom, and the United States remained in low-wage work while between 8 and 23 percent left the labor force from one year to the next (Schmitt 2012).

Nonstandard jobs have contributed to earnings inequality. Thus, despite policies such as EU directives designed to provide them with social protections (e.g., European Commission 2008), the evidence suggests that workers in nonstandard jobs tend to earn less than comparable workers in regular jobs. In 2012, for example, the wage penalty for working in a temporary job in Germany was nearly 20 percent, while it was about 15 percent in Spain and about 10 percent in the United Kingdom (ILO 2016: fig. 5.2).

Theories of occupational polarization have sought to explain the growth of earnings inequality among occupations and have considerable relevance for accounting for the increase in low-wage jobs. Goos, Manning, and Salomons (2009), for example, have attributed the increase in the bottom and top tiers of the occupational structure in European countries to technological developments that have routinized and automated middle-level, semi-skilled jobs, both in white-collar occupations such as clerical work and in blue-collar manufacturing jobs. As these jobs have become more routinized, fewer workers are needed in them. By contrast, highly skilled jobs have been more difficult to routinize since they are more apt to involve complex cognitive tasks; and low-skilled service and sales jobs are often paid so little that it doesn't make economic sense to replace them with machines, or these jobs may require human involvement that machines have difficulty with (such as moving furniture). Autor, Katz, and Kearney (2006) also find such patterns of occupational polarization in the United States, and also attribute this growth at the top and the bottom of the occupational structure to the effects of routinization resulting from technological changes or "skill-biased technological change."

However, Fernández-Macías (2012) shows that the picture is a bit more complex. He uses differences in wages and education among occupations to examine polarization in fifteen European countries from 1995 to 2007. He finds that only some countries (Continental countries such as Germany) fit the polarization pattern of increases in both good and bad jobs, while others were more consistent with patterns of general structural upgrading and increases in good jobs

(Denmark) and the relative expansion of middle-quality occupations (Southern European countries such as Spain, which saw an increase in construction jobs, for example). He also finds that LMEs such as the United Kingdom were characterized by a pattern somewhere between polarization and upgrading.

While the skill-biased technological change story is compelling in many ways, then, it is not sufficient to account for the growth of occupational polarization and low-wage jobs, as evidenced by the differential patterns observed among countries, all of which are subject to similar technological forces. Indeed, a substantial amount of occupation-level wage inequality remains even after controlling for measures of human capital skills such as education and experience and other labor force characteristics such as gender, which also vary by occupation, as Mouw and Kalleberg (2010) demonstrate for the United States. This is also consistent with the view that while skills are a major determinant of wages, the correlation between the two is not perfect. Low-wage jobs are not always low-skilled jobs: some low-skill jobs pay well (as was the case with some relatively low-skilled unionized manufacturing jobs); on the other hand, some high-skill jobs pay poorly, such as those of caregivers or teachers in the United States or the high proportion of skilled, low-wage German workers. Moreover, differences in skill levels do not account very well for variations in low pay across advanced industrial economies: the US is relatively highly ranked on skill indicators (e.g., average years of formal schooling, proportion of population holding qualifications above the upper secondary level), but has the highest incidence of low pay (Gautié, Westergaard-Nielsen, and Schmitt with Mayhew 2010: 149).

The extent to which a country has a relatively large low-wage population depends principally on the inclusiveness of national wage-setting institutions (Appelbaum et al. 2010: 11). Inclusive labor market institutions refer to mechanisms (such as centralized and solidaristic collective bargaining and strong minimum wage laws, benefit systems designed to support unemployed and low-income households, and the enforcement of national labor laws; see Schmitt 2012) that extend the gains made by workers with relatively high power to those with relatively little power (Appelbaum et al. 2010: 7). In countries with less inclusive labor market institutions (such as the US and UK, and increasingly in Germany), it is more likely that individual differences in bargaining power (due to skills and human capital and ability to move among jobs) have forced those with less power (women, young people, older workers, less educated workers, immigrants) to take low-wage jobs. Note that while Denmark is generally inclusive, there are outsiders who are often in low-wage jobs: refugees are in the periphery and their benefits were recently cut by 45 percent (Eakin 2016).

The degree of low-wage work in a country also depends on the prevalence of exit options that may provide loopholes that allow employers to avoid the terms of collective bargaining agreements. Examples of such exit options include the choices made by many SMEs in Germany to withdraw from collective bargaining agreements, setting wages below minimum levels for youth (as in the UK and in the retail sector in Denmark), and using employees of foreign firms who are not subject to the laws of the country within which they work (Applebaum et al. 2010). These exit options helped fuel the growth of low-wage work in Germany in the 1990s (Gautié and Schmitt 2010).

Inequality in earnings and precarious work more generally is also generated by differences in worker power, as I argued in chapter 2. The role of worker power in enhancing earnings was also seen in figure 5.1, which showed that countries such as Denmark and Germany, where unions and bargaining are comparatively strong (though declining somewhat), had the highest levels of earnings coupled with relatively low earnings inequality.

Poverty

Unlike low-wage jobs, poverty is a household-level concept: Someone can be working in a low-wage job and still not be considered poor if there are other family members (such as a spouse) who are working and whose earnings may help to compensate for the low wages. Brady, Fullerton, and Cross (2010), for example, show that not having multiple earners in the household makes it more likely that the household will be poor.[2] Hence, the income that is available to a household is likely to be more salient for a worker's and her or his family's degree of economic insecurity than working in a low-wage job.

The OECD defines the poverty rate as the percentage of people whose household income is below 50 percent of the median household income of the total population. Figure 5.2 shows the poverty rates for the six countries for two time periods (2000 and 2011), obtained from OECD statistics and based on this definition. The rates presented here refer to the proportions who are considered poor after taking into consideration the taxes people in the various

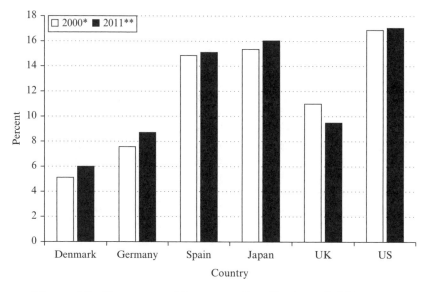

Figure 5.2   Poverty rate (50 percent of median household income,
post-taxes and transfers), 2000 and 2011
* Spain 2004 ** Japan 2014
Source: OECD data

countries pay on their income and any transfers (such as welfare payments) that might help to supplement their incomes. These figures
thus take into consideration not only differences among countries in
earnings quality (as in figure 5.1), but also the number of earners in a
household as well as the generosity of welfare payments.

Denmark has the lowest proportion of people in poverty among
the six countries, with just about 5 percent of households classified
as poor in 2000. This percentage increased slightly during the first
decade of the twenty-first century, though Denmark still has one of
the lowest poverty rates of any Western nation.

Germany has the second lowest proportion of persons in poverty
among the six countries. While Germany has lots of low-wage jobs
(see previous section), this does not necessarily translate into high
poverty since the latter is a household concept, not a labor market
one: low-wage workers (who are often women working part-time)
may be married to higher-wage men, for example. The relatively
low poverty rate in Germany is consistent with the patterns earlier
for earnings quality (figure 5.1); as in Denmark, the poverty rate
increased slightly in Germany between 2000 and 2011.

Spain has a relatively high degree of poverty, below only the US and Japan among these six countries. The deep recession and austerity hit Spain particularly hard, resulting in lower incomes per person, though it did not seem to result in a marked increase in the poverty rate.

The in-work poverty rates in the four European countries (see note 2, this chapter) mirror the poverty rates shown in figure 5.2. Thus, Denmark has the lowest in-work poverty risks while Spain has the highest; rates of in-work poverty in the UK are higher than in Germany. In all these countries, households with temporary workers have higher in-work poverty rates than households with permanent workers (European Commission 2016b).

Japan also has relatively high levels of poverty, second only to the United States among these countries, and only slightly more than Spain. Allison (2013: 5) reports that Japan has the second-highest poverty levels in the OECD, despite being the third strongest economy in the world. This situation is rooted in the spread of non-regular work in Japan along with the economic crises the country has endured in the last several decades and the associated austerity policies. With low wages and limited social support, the working poor in Japan are becoming entrenched in poverty. The desperate man described in the opening pages of this book reflects the anger and hopelessness that this situation has created, leading to horrific events such as random killings.

The US has the highest proportion of people in poverty. These results are consistent with the view that the key to explaining poverty is the generosity of the welfare state; the role of the welfare state is to manage risk and organize the distribution of economic resources to enhance equality (Brady 2009).

Social Wages

Earnings and income are only part of the story about economic insecurity. The extent to which average earnings levels and earnings inequality – and the extent of low-wage work and poverty – translate into economic insecurity differs among countries depending on the depth and breadth of social protections that make people less dependent on the labor market to maintain their way of life. The type of social welfare protection system is fundamental to the long-term costs of experiences of precarious work and inequality (Barbieri 2009).

Hence, we need to consider differences in the social wage (which includes not only earnings but non-income sources of social and economic protections such as statutory and negotiated benefits including healthcare, annual leave, sickness leave, and retirement benefits) when thinking about the standard of living and economic insecurity in comparative perspective. There is apt to be less economic insecurity in countries with more generous welfare and social assistance programs, regardless of levels of earnings quality or incidence of low-wage work. This is especially true when welfare support is not linked closely to social insurance schemes that depend on working full-time in regular employment. In countries with generous and widespread social and economic assistance, workers are not as dependent on the labor market for maintaining a minimal level of income and so are likely to be less economically insecure even when they are employed in precarious jobs.

A useful way of comparing social wages is by using Osberg and Sharpe's (2014) Index of Economic Well-Being (IEWB). These authors computed these for a cross-section of seventy rich and poor nations for 2007/2008 that includes five of those I consider here. Osberg and Sharpe measure four of the risks identified in Article 25 of the UN Universal Declaration of Human Rights: livelihood security (i.e., greater UI benefits); security from cost of illness (i.e., the extent to which people are reimbursed for the cost of medically necessary medical expenses); security from widowhood (which protects a non-employed spouse from the death of the family breadwinner); and security in old age (i.e., the risk of poverty in old age). These authors computed an index that enables them to compare levels and trends in economic insecurity across countries by combining the various sub-indices into a composite IEWB that weights each risk by the relative size of the populations most affected in each of the countries (e.g., the working age population – aged 15–64 – is most affected by unemployment; retirement and old age issues are more of a concern to those aged 45–64; illness risk affects everyone). Figure 5.3 compares five of the six countries on their overall measures on the IEWB as well as information on the specific sub-components of the overall index.[3] Each index varies between 0 and 1.

Figure 5.3 indicates that Denmark has the highest level of overall economic well-being (0.92) among these five countries – as well as the highest among all seventy of the countries analyzed. Denmark also scores highest on all four components of the index except the measure of security resulting from illness, on which the UK and Germany score slightly higher. The Danish advantage in economic

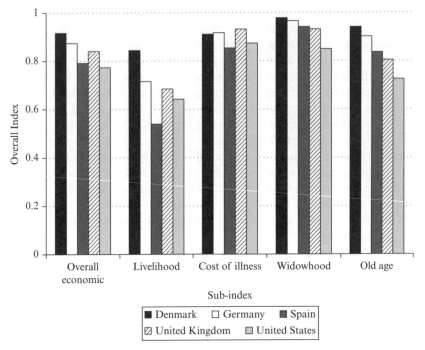

Figure 5.3   Economic well-being indices, 2007–2008
Source: Osberg and Sharpe 2014 data

well-being is consistent with my description in chapter 2 of the relatively generous welfare protections in Denmark and further underscores the role played by its powerful unions and collective bargaining mechanisms, coupled with strong government support for equality and economic security in that country.

Germany (0.87) has the second highest score on the overall well-being index. The relative ranking of Denmark and Germany is consistent with the ranking on earnings quality shown in figure 5.1. By contrast, the US has the lowest level of overall economic well-being (0.77), though it scores higher than Spain on livelihood security (which is related to unemployment compensation) and slightly higher on security resulting from illness.

Osberg and Sharpe (2014) also present trend information for Demark, Germany, and the US for the period from 1980 to 2008. They find that Denmark and Germany had similar levels of economic well-being in 1980, though the level of economic security in Germany decreased in the early 1980s and has remained below Denmark's ever since. The relative decline in economic well-being in Germany reflects weakening worker power in that country, evidenced by the diminished union density and collective bargaining, increasing liberalization of labor markets, and waning of welfare protections. The level of economic well-being in the US was considerably below that of Denmark and Germany throughout the period.

The UK had the third highest level of overall economic well-being (0.84) and had the highest score of all five countries on the index of security from the cost of illness. The comparison between the UK and US – the two LMEs – starkly demonstrates the importance of social and welfare protections for well-being. Despite the higher average earnings in the United States (figure 5.1), overall economic security is greater in the United Kingdom due to that country's more extensive social protections: The UK has higher scores on all four components of the index of overall well-being; unemployment, sickness, widowhood, and old age. Therefore, despite having similar levels of overall earnings quality, the social wage in the UK is higher than in the US due to the greater social protections in the UK. The lower social wage in the US is especially problematic for workers in low-wage jobs, given the relatively weak benefits in that country for access to healthcare, paid sick days, paid family leave, and other protections.

Perhaps the most dramatic example of social protections in the UK is the comprehensive National Health Service, which provides public financing for most medically necessary healthcare (which is also true in most affluent countries except the US) and offers greater security from the costs of illness than the more piecemeal and less inclusive system of health insurance found in the United States, which has traditionally has been delivered through employers. While the Affordable Care Act passed during President Obama's tenure sought to provide universal coverage, there are still major gaps and difficulties in doing this. That one may lose health insurance if one loses the job is a major source of anxiety and stress in the United States.

Economic Instability

The degree of instability and volatility of earnings is an additional objective aspect of economic insecurity. Economic instability is particularly problematic as it makes it difficult for individuals and families to plan and to protect themselves from unexpected events such as illness or the death of a breadwinner. The political scientist

Jacob Hacker (2006) argues that there has been a rise in economic instability and that this represents a "great risk shift" away from the government and employers toward individuals and their families. This shift has affected not only those who are poor, but also those middle-class (and even upper-class) people who were the main beneficiaries of the economic growth and stability during the three decades after World War II in the United States and many of the other countries. Using data from the US Panel Study of Income Dynamics, Hacker shows that American family incomes have become increasingly volatile since the mid-1970s, a period that corresponds to the beginning of the "new age of precarious work" that I discussed in chapter 1. Indeed, he argues that American families' economic instability has grown faster than economic inequality.

While Hacker makes his argument specifically for the United States, which in addition to income volatility has also experienced marked erosion in guaranteed pensions (i.e., away from defined benefit toward defined contribution plans), weakening health benefits, growing layoffs, and extended periods of unemployment. But his theme of a risk shift also aptly describes the impacts of the growth of precarious work and the adoption of austerity principles associated with the liberalization of labor market and social welfare protection policies in all the countries.

Perceived Economic Insecurity

Economic insecurity has a substantial subjective and psychological component that reflects the anxiety and uncertainty that people face when confronted with personal circumstances such as unemployment and other life events. These subjective perceptions of economic insecurity are apt to affect individual stress and health as well as organizational outcomes. A person's level and stability of earnings are important of course, but whether the person sees this as a problem may well be more salient for their physical and psychological well-being.

Information on perceived economic insecurity was also collected in the 2004 and 2010 ESSs discussed in the previous chapter. Figure 5.4 shows the percentages of respondents in the four European countries who said that they found it "difficult" or "very difficult" to live on their present incomes (as opposed to "living comfortably" or "coping" on their present incomes).[4] There was no difference in the level of perceived economic insecurity in 2004 as compared to 2010 in any of the four countries, so I combine the information from these two surveys.

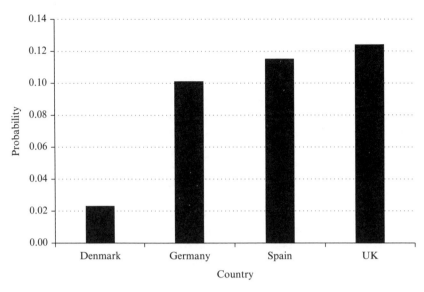

Figure 5.4   Perceived economic insecurity, 2004 and 2010
Source: ESS 2004 and 2010 data

The results for this subjective measure of economic insecurity are broadly consistent with the evidence obtained from the objective measures of economic insecurity presented earlier in this chapter. The most dramatic difference is between Denmark and the other three countries, as the Danes are much more likely to perceive themselves as economically secure. This is consistent with the higher levels of earnings quality (figure 5.1) and other social protections (figure 5.3) enjoyed by the Danes, as well as the lower proportions of low-wage jobs and people living in poverty (figure 5.2) in Denmark.

The relatively high earnings quality, low proportions in poverty, and social protections enjoyed by the Germans do not appear to translate directly into lower perceived economic insecurity, as this does not differ from that of Spain. The Germans perceived themselves as less economically insecure than workers in the United Kingdom after the economic crisis (2010) but there was no difference between these countries in 2004.

To assess more systematically the impacts of labor market and social welfare institutions on perceived economic insecurity, I again turn to the 2004 and 2010 ESSs to estimate differences among seventeen European countries in the extent to which the labor market and welfare institutions affect perceived economic insecurity (see

Inanc and Kalleberg 2016).[5] We find that 22 percent of the variation in perceived economic insecurity lies among countries, even when controlling for the yearly country unemployment rate, degree of income inequality in the country, and individual-level predictors. Moreover, individuals in countries with higher levels of active labor market policies, more generous welfare and unemployment replacement benefits, and more extensive collective bargaining coverage are less likely to perceive themselves to be economically insecure. This reiterates the role of these labor market and welfare institutions in shaping perceptions of economic inequality, even when considering a person's earnings, family situation, demographic profile, and characteristics of the job.

We also find that people are more likely to perceive that they are economically insecure in countries where the unemployment rate is higher, though the degree of income inequality in a country had no significant effect on perceived economic insecurity after taking into consideration a person's earnings and the other individual characteristics listed earlier.

Summary and Conclusions

This chapter has examined country differences in economic insecurity. As with job insecurity, economic insecurity has objective and subjective aspects. Objectively, we can compare countries in their levels of earnings and degree of earnings inequality, incidence of low-wage jobs and extent of the population living in poverty, the non-income components of the social wage, and the stability of earnings. Subjectively, countries differ in the degree to which people perceive that their economic situations enable them to live comfortably and maintain a minimum standard of living as opposed to having economic difficulties.

In general, the evidence presented in this chapter reinforces the importance of social welfare protection policies and institutions in shaping the consequences of precarious work for both objective and perceived economic insecurity. The data tell a consistent and coherent story: Economic insecurity is lowest in Denmark and Germany, and highest in the LMEs of the UK and US.

The lower levels of economic insecurity in Denmark – reflected in the high levels of earnings and low earnings inequality, low proportions of people working in low-wage jobs and in poverty, high economic and social protections, and low perceived economic insecurity – are all in line with the greater inclusiveness of Danish labor market institutions, which extend the gains made by unions and those with more power to those with less power. The relatively low economic insecurity in Denmark also follows from the generous system of social protections in that country that I have discussed in chapter 2, a system based on high levels of public spending on welfare programs and income replacement when one becomes unemployed. This is also the case to a lesser extent in Germany, which also has high earnings quality, low proportions in poverty, and high social protections, but has a substantial number of low-wage jobs as well.

People in the two LMEs – the United Kingdom and the United States – have higher levels of economic insecurity, in terms of lower earnings quality, higher proportions of people living in poverty, and lower social wages, than the Danes or Germans. Those in the UK are also more apt to feel economically insecure compared to the other three European countries. But there are important differences between the US and the UK. While earnings quality is lower in both countries than Denmark and Germany, this is mainly due to relatively high earnings inequality in the United States while it results primarily from lower average earnings in the UK. Moreover, the proportion living in poverty is considerably lower in the UK than in the US.

More dramatic, though, are the differences in the social wage between these two: LMEs that result from the greater availability of economic and social supports in the United Kingdom that help people to mitigate various types of life course risks. The advantages for economic security provided by the universal system of health insurance in the UK is perhaps the most familiar, though the gaps in supports for widows and for older people are also stark. These differences between the UK and US – which are similar in many of their labor market institutions – illustrate vividly the importance of social protections for diminishing the impacts of precarious work on economic insecurity.

6

Transition to Adulthood and Family Formation

> Throughout the developed world, we are seeing young people falter in their entry into the labor market as they confront weaker job prospects, less security in employment, greater demands for educational credentials, and creeping underemployment . . . Everywhere, this is producing a rocky road for not-so-young workers, making it harder for them to leave home. Yet what these trends mean, whether they are defined as a social problem, a welcome change, or an unremarkable mutation, depends on the surrounding historical and cultural context. (Katherine Newman 2012: 84)

The rise of precarious employment and the associated increase in uncertainty and risk for workers have been especially severe, as Katherine Newman makes clear, for young people, who disproportionately make up the ranks of the unemployed, the underemployed, and the non-regular and low-wage workforce. The young face considerable hurdles in gaining a foothold in the labor market and launching their work careers in many industrial countries: The growth of precarious work has also made the quality of jobs available to young people problematic, especially as these jobs are less likely to offer prospects of establishing career narratives and regular sources of income, as well as limited chances of advancing to better jobs in the future.

This chapter looks at country differences in two key transitions to adulthood: the school-to-work transition and entry into the labor force; and family formation, especially marriage. Failing to make these transitions successfully represents important forms of social exclusion that stem from both job and economic insecurity and often lead to political exclusion as well. I present quantitative data on youth unemployment in these countries as well as on the extent to which young people are in neither school nor training as well as not in the labor force. I also examine in detail the case of marriage formation in

Japan, where the effects of precarious work on family formation are especially pronounced.

Transitions to Adulthood

The transition to adulthood has traditionally been conceived and measured as the successful completion of five life course events or markers: leaving school; starting a full-time job; leaving the home of origin; getting married or forming a first union; and becoming a parent for the first time (Shanahan 2000). Countries differ in the rigidity of the timing and sequencing of these events: In Japan, for example, marriage almost always precedes becoming a parent, while in the United States, these two events are more loosely connected; and children are more apt to leave the parents' home in Denmark and live independently before finishing school or obtaining a full-time job than in countries such as Spain.

The timing and sequencing of these life course transitions depend on the opportunities available to individuals to move from one stage to another. These prospects in turn depend on young persons' economic and non-economic (e.g., social capital) resources, the kinds of jobs available to them at the time they are ready to enter the labor force, and the ability of families to provide private safety nets. Moreover, societal and cultural age-related informal and legal norms define with varying degrees of precision and flexibility what are normal life course progressions, when one is expected to move from one life course event to another (Buchmann and Kreisi 2011).

These pathways to adulthood are being reshaped by social and economic changes such as: the growth of precarious work and its drivers (such as global competition, rapid technological change, political changes, and rising unemployment in some countries); changing patterns of migration (such as from rural to urban areas); rising costs of housing; differences in who pays for education and the extent to which this generates individual debt; and cultural changes that have enhanced the opportunities for work careers for women and others. These economic and social changes have made it more problematic for young people to gain a firm foothold in the labor market and be able to: afford to leave their parents' home; complete their education; find a marriage partner; and feel comfortable having children and starting families. As a result, the completion of these stages often departs from traditional time schedules and sequences in the current age of precarious work.

The social and economic changes that present challenges to these standard pathways to adulthood and family formation are similar in the six countries. However, the impact of these economic and social changes on persons and the responses by governments and others to them depend on the historical and cultural context, as suggested by the quotation at the beginning of this chapter.

Thus, the kinds of social welfare protection and labor market institutions I have discussed in previous chapters shape the opportunities youth have for obtaining jobs and supporting themselves. Countries differ in their likelihood of launching youth into stable jobs, leading to the emergence of "accordion families" in which adult children live with their parents for an extended period and have few resources of their own (Newman 2012). The transition to adulthood and family formation is likely to be especially extended in countries that have a male breadwinner model coupled with a social welfare system that depends heavily on the family rather than the state, such as Japan or Spain, where about 50 percent of men aged 18–34 still live with their parents. Families in Spain represent a private safety net based on owner-occupied housing that compensates partly for the relatively weak public safety net. This has created a large generational divide in Spain as well as in Japan. By contrast, less than 30 percent of men aged 18–34 in Denmark – where the public welfare system and residential independence of youth compensate for the weak family safety net – and Germany and the UK live with their parents, according to a survey conducted in 2007 (Newman 2012: 41).

Transitions to adulthood are also particularly difficult in countries such as Japan that are traditionally characterized by well-defined, rigid progressions to adulthood that involve strong attachments to work organizations (see Brinton 2011; Allison 2013). Here, the absence of opportunities for regular jobs constitutes a major impediment to one's ability to find a suitable marriage partner and to have children. This is especially true for young men, who have been highly impacted by the disruption in life plans caused by the breakdown of orderly transitions from school to work and the paucity of opportunities for orderly career lines in regular full-time employment.

The traditional view of adulthood as achieving these well-defined life events or markers is also changing: Definitions of adulthood based on achieving status transitions are giving way to a more psychological, developmental view in which one is considered to become an adult by acquiring social skills, identity, and a sense of agency and autonomy (Shanahan 2000; Buchmann and Kreisi 2011). The shift from status transitions to a more psychological perspective means "you are an adult when you feel like one" (Newman 2012: 5), rather than when you get married, obtain a full-time job, or leave your parents' home. In this sense, earning money and working in the labor force are not the only factors that determine whether one is regarded as an adult (Newman 2012). The nature of these psychological aspects of adulthood too differs among countries. For example, Europeans more often emphasize social and psychological features such as taking on responsibilities toward oneself and others, while Americans are more apt to stress self-discovery and searching out one's passion and interests. Attaining these psychological states is of course more ambiguous than achieving traditional markers such as having a steady job, marriage, or one's own home, and this also creates insecurity and anxiety as people may struggle with familial and personal problems for extended periods of time.

The contextual nature of precarious work implies that it is likely to be experienced differently for those for whom it is a sudden, new experience as opposed to those for whom it is more normalized; the key is the difference between expected and actual life plans. People adapt to uncertainty and have for a long time. What is new is that the period of uncertainty comes after a long period of stability and order.

The group that is likely to be most affected by the recent rise of precarious work is non-minority men (such as white semi-skilled workers in industries such as auto manufacturing) who were the main beneficiaries of the relatively secure, high-paying career jobs associated with the standard employment relations of the early post-World War II period. By contrast, work has always been more precarious for women, immigrants, and members of various minority groups who have generally held the worst jobs in the economy. The young men profiled by MacLeod (2009) in the US, for example, were always aware that they were only likely to get precarious work, so their attainment of such jobs was not surprising to them. The setting of expectations in Germany is illustrated by Shavit and Müller (2000), who argue that lower-class young persons and their parents often choose to forgo a chance of making it into the middle and upper middle classes (via attending a university) in exchange for a stable lower-class job obtained via vocational training. By contrast, middle-class parents who want their children to achieve the same status as them have more to lose for their children (in terms of downward mobility) if they don't make it to university or a high-end apprenticeship.

A person's birth cohort and the historical period in which one grows up and enters adulthood and the labor force thus have important impacts on reactions to the rise of precarious work. Karl Mannheim described this as the "problem of generations," wherein persons who are born in a certain period or year shared ways of thinking and experiences (Mannheim 1952 [1927]). Young people are particularly disposed to develop worldviews that reflect the historical and social contexts to which they are initially exposed. Bourdieu described this as an individual's *habitus*, which comes from growing up in a particular socioeconomic environment. In the case of precarious work, people coming of age in an era of sustained economic growth (such as the early post-World War II period) and with career narratives defined by standard employment relations are likely to be especially subject to upheaval when the cultural logics underlying the nature of work and employment relations change suddenly and dramatically. This is likely true for those whose careers unfolded during the early postwar period, but is also apt to affect those who closely observed their parents' careers, since people tend to make relative judgments about economic progress they have made in their own lifetimes compared to the progress made by the previous generation (Friedman 2015).

While changes in cultural logics are dynamic and people will adapt to changing conditions, these adaptations are likely to occur slowly, creating cultural lags, an idea suggested by William F. Ogburn (1950) in 1922 to refer to situations when changes in non-material culture (e.g., norms and attitudes toward family formation) do not keep up with changes in material culture (e.g., technology, availability of opportunities for stable and regular work careers). Social disruptions produced by such cultural lags result in stress and hence pressures to change either structures and/or expectations so as to create better fits between people and institutions.

Gaining a Foothold in the Labor Force

The ability of young people to gain a stable foothold in the labor market depends on their economic and non-economic resources as well as their society's educational, labor market, and welfare state institutions. Educational systems differ in their degree of access (for example, whether the responsibility for higher education rests with the individual and her or his family, as in the US and increasingly in the UK, or with the government, as in Denmark) as well as in the availability of vocational training that prepares people for specific types of work such as the trades and other skilled occupations (as is the case in the well-developed vocational training systems in Germany and Denmark).

Labor market institutions such as active labor market policies help to provide youth with job training opportunities and information about available jobs, among other ways of facilitating entry (and re-entry) into jobs. And welfare institutions such as unemployment benefits (which in some countries, such as Denmark, are provided to youth even before they have begun to work in the labor force) enable young people to support themselves as they search for a stable job.

Youth Unemployment

A common indicator of the opportunities available to young people is the youth unemployment rate (Eurostat 2015), which is typically double or triple the rates for workers who are in their thirties or forties (ILO 2016). Young people in countries with high youth unemployment are likely to have a more difficult time making the transition to adulthood by embarking upon a career and establishing an independent household. Figure 6.1 shows the percentage of youth unemployment in the six countries in three years, using data from the OECD: the earliest period for which data are available,[1] 2007 (just

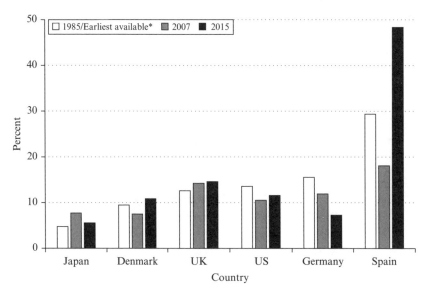

Figure 6.1   Percentage of young workers (15–24) unemployed, 1985, 2007, and 2015

*Denmark and Spain 1999; UK 2000; Germany 2005

Source: OECD data

before the start of the Great Recession in the United States and the economic crisis in Europe), and 2015.

Youth unemployment is by far the highest in Spain and increased sharply in that country after the economic crisis, reaching nearly 50 percent of workers aged 15–24 in 2015. As we have seen in chapter 4, Spain was hit very hard by the economic crisis, resulting in high levels of unemployment, a situation that was even more extreme among youth, who bore the brunt of this downturn and were the group hardest hit by the crisis. Due to the rigidities of the Spanish labor market, big companies (such as Telefónica, the telecommunications monopoly) have expanded abroad rather than in Spain (*The Economist* 2011). This has reduced opportunities for young Spaniards, contributing to Spain having the highest youth unemployment rates in Europe (and fueling the anger of the Spanish "indignants" (*los indignados*), as I discuss in chapter 8).

Youth unemployment in Spain is high despite the current generation being the best-educated Spain has ever produced (Sills 2012): Spaniards in their twenties and thirties have a high school graduation rate of 86 percent, as opposed to 50 percent of those in their fifties and sixties. Spanish youth are of course very concerned about their difficulties in securing regular jobs, as are their parents. The situation of José Garcia, a doorman who lost his job two years before and who, at 62, has expended his UI and is not optimistic about finding work before he claims his pension at 65, illustrates the concerns of Spanish parents about their children. His main worry is his 16-year-old son:

> Spain's strict school system ejects pupils whom other European countries keep teaching. A quarter leave at 16 without qualifications. They once found jobs on building sites. But precious few of these are left – hence the present hype over plans by an American billionaire for hotels, casinos and conference centres outside Madrid. Mr Garcia just hopes that his son will pass his exams next month, so that he can stay for two more years at school and keep off the unemployment register. But then what? In today's market the young often lose out most. (*The Economist* 2013a: 52)

There was also an increase in youth unemployment after the economic crisis in Denmark, resulting in a rate of about 10 percent, which resembles that in the United States. The UK has seen consistent but rather moderate growth in youth unemployment since the 1980s and had the second highest proportion of youth unemployment among the six countries in 2015. By contrast, youth unemployment is lowest in Japan and Germany in 2015. Moreover, there was a decline in both countries in the percentage of youth who were unemployed in 2015 compared to before the economic crisis. In Germany, the decline is linked to the changes in employment policies that I have discussed in chapter 3, which led to the creation of mini-jobs and job sharing and thereby led to reductions in unemployment.

O'Reilly et al. (2015) identify a variety of programs designed to address the problem of youth unemployment, most of them associated with Europe 2020, a ten-year strategy proposed by the European Commission in 2010 to guide the economic advancement of the European Union. These include several flagship initiatives designed to enhance the quality of education and training as well as to promote the mobility of workers and the matching of young workers to jobs (see also Newman and Winston 2016). The successful implementation of these initiatives presents challenges, however, such as the legacies of previous recessions resulting in workless families and the higher probability of their children also being unemployed, as well as the massive change in youth migration, which brings with it other sets of problems both at home and abroad.

Youth in Temporary Jobs

Youth unemployment rates, however, provide only a partial picture of the difficulties young people in these countries have in obtaining a foothold in the labor market. Those who find jobs often are forced to take temporary or other nonstandard jobs that are often of poor quality, as young people generally lack the skills and experience of older workers. Therefore, young people are generally over-represented in temporary jobs, and the proportion of people aged 15–24 in temporary jobs typically exceeds that of older workers.

The reasons for the greater incidence of young people in temporary jobs – and the extent to which they lead to more stable, permanent jobs – vary among these countries, however. In most European countries, the main reason why young people work in temporary jobs is because they are unable to find permanent ones. This is especially the case in Spain, where more than 80 percent of young temporary workers in 2014 have taken such jobs because they were unable to find a permanent job. The inability of young people to gain access to permanent jobs has much to do with the employment protections that tend to restrict such jobs to older workers, as I have discussed earlier. By contrast, in Denmark and Germany, the main reasons why people aged 15–24 are in temporary jobs is because they are involved in apprenticeship and internship programs that often lead to regular jobs and stable employment relationships: Slightly over half of the young workers in Denmark and about 90 percent of those in Germany are working in temporary jobs with such education or training arrangements. In the UK, 40 percent of young workers are in temporary jobs because they couldn't find a permanent job, while about another third did not want a permanent job, and less than 20 percent were in education or training (ILO 2016: fig. 3.14).

In addition to temporary work, young workers are also over-represented in part-time work. Young people are six times more likely than prime-age workers to have part-time jobs in Denmark, more than three times as likely in the United States, more than twice as likely in Spain, and higher in the United Kingdom. An exception is Germany, where part-time work is more prevalent among prime-age workers, though not statistically significantly so (ILO 2016: fig. 3.17).

NEET: Not in Education, Employment, or Training

Young people who cannot find jobs might choose to stay in school or otherwise pursue training opportunities that delay their entry into the labor market until they perceive their chances of finding a suitable job have improved. The decision to forgo labor force entry could also reflect young people's decision to wait until a "good" job comes along rather than to take a job that they regard as a "bad" one. This is especially likely if parents are willing to subsidize their children living at home for an extended period and there is little stigma attached to such arrangements. In Spain, for example, continuing to live with one's parents has come to be recognized as a reasonable adjustment to difficult economic times and there is less of a stigma attached to doing this than in the past. By contrast, the Japanese are more critical of young people who do not become independent financially and leave the home of origin (Newman 2012).

A more expansive indicator of the degree of marginalization and exclusion of youth from the labor market and other major societal institutions, as well as an indication of their self-sufficiency, is the "NEET rate" or the proportion of youth who are not in education, employment, or training (see ILO 2012a). This relatively new indicator is gaining in prominence among international organizations and the media as a barometer of the degree to which youth are socially excluded and disconnected from major institutions in society, such as education and work.

Figure 6.2 presents NEET rates for the six countries for two time periods, both before (2007) and after (2012) the economic crisis.

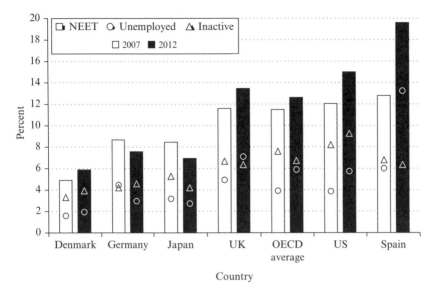

Figure 6.2 Percentage of young people (15–24) not in employment, education, or training (NEET), 2007 and 2012

Source: OECD 2014a data

The height of the bars represents the total NEET rate for the country in a given time period. The circles denote the unemployment rates while the triangles represent those that are neither employed, nor registered as unemployed (i.e., inactive or out of the labor force), nor received any education or in training in the four weeks preceding the survey.[2]

Spain again had the highest percentage of youth (defined here as those who were aged 15–24) who were not employed or in education and training. The major reason for this is the high level of youth unemployment in Spain,[3] which, as we have seen in chapter 4, increased greatly after the economic crisis (see also figure 6.1). For those who find jobs, a large proportion of the jobs are temporary, which young people most likely are forced to take because they are unable to obtain permanent ones (see previous subsection). Once employed in these temporary jobs, their chances of moving to more permanent jobs are relatively small, as they tend to churn between short employment spells and unemployment, making it hard for them to acquire the "insider" status that is associated with more permanent jobs (Golsch 2003); fewer than 30 percent of temporary employees in Spain had moved to permanent jobs three years later

(O'Connor 2015; see also chapter 3). These disadvantages associated with temporary work create incentives for young workers to remain unemployed, often continuing to live with their parents, as a way of making ends meet in the hopes of eventually getting a permanent job.

The United States and the United Kingdom have the second highest proportions of youth classified as NEET, and these rates also increased after the economic crisis. These rises in NEETs are also due mainly to the increase in youth unemployment, which was a bit higher in the UK than in the US. The United States also had the highest percentage of youth who are inactive, i.e., not working or in school but also not in the labor force. An important reason for the high levels of inactivity in these LMEs is their limited options for vocational education at the upper secondary level, apart from apprenticeship programs. Like Japan, the United States has no real vocational training system. The United Kingdom, like Spain, mainly has a school-based vocational training system (Euler 2013). Eichhorst et al.'s (2015) review of the literature on vocational training in industrial societies concludes that vocational education and training are both valid alternatives to general education and that apprenticeships are more effective when combined with institutional learning rather than when it is based in schools.

The overall percentage of young people who are NEET was the lowest in Denmark among the six countries (less than 6 percent in 2012), though the rate also increased in Denmark after the economic crisis. Youth unemployment in Denmark is relatively low in part because of the country's extensive youth apprenticeship system, which employs about 40 percent of Danish youth (people in apprenticeships are regarded as employed) (Westergaard-Nielsen 2008: 35). These apprenticeship programs last between three and four years, are organized by the Ministry of Education in collaboration with the social partners, and are financed by a fund to which all employers contribute and which helps to provide part of the salary of apprentices (ILO 2012b).

By contrast, the NEET rates declined in Germany and Japan after the economic crisis. The proportion of both unemployed and inactive Japanese youth waned as the Japanese government created programs in schools that gave young people a more realistic picture of future jobs and established relationships between universities and workplaces that enabled students to obtain internships that provided them with experience to help them obtain jobs. Still, youth in Japan suffered the brunt of the economic downturn, as Japan has the worst generational inequality in the world (Newman 2012: 47). As in

Spain, the older generation in Japan has been reluctant to step aside and allow younger persons to replace them in the labor market, and the dualistic structure of the labor market has enabled older workers to do this.

In Germany, the reduction in NEETs reflects mainly a decline in youth unemployment (see also figure 6.1), which results in part from the labor market policies that emphasized continued employment at reduced hours to stave off higher unemployment. In addition, the vocational system in Germany has facilitated the employment of youth. Like Denmark, Germany has a dual vocational training system that combines schooling and training with working (see chapter 2), which, while effective in facilitating the movement of young people into the labor force, tends to reduce the proportion of highly educated people in these countries. Also like Denmark, Germany has a closed vocational system, making it difficult to change into or out of the vocational training track.

The dual system of vocational training and apprenticeship in Germany has become increasingly important as a source of skilled workers given the labor shortages of native-born German youth. About half of high school students go on to dual training in one of 344 trades. These are three-year programs that combine learning in the classroom with practical work experiences within companies, rely heavily on voluntary efforts by firms, and are geared toward youth apprenticeships (Shavit and Müller 2000; Thelen 2014). Germany invests a great deal in training its master teachers and equipping its schools, as it produces a skilled group of young people with good job prospects, contributing to the very low youth unemployment rate in Germany (Newman and Winston 2016).

There is some question as to whether this system of vocational education in Germany will continue to be viable or whether it is outdated (*The Economist* 2010b). It is rigid and discriminatory, and highly specialized, which makes it difficult to transfer to other, even related, fields. The numbers of applicants are fewer than the number of available jobs, as many young people opt for a transitional system that is designed to prepare students for either the dual system or another qualification, though this system is often a blind alley, especially for male immigrants. It should be noted, further, that the German apprenticeship system puts minorities (such as Turks) at a disadvantage relative to German natives. This is due to anti-immigrant prejudice, as well as difficulties that immigrants have in learning the German language and the associated problems with school performance. While some big German companies (such as

Volkswagen) have made deliberate efforts to diversify their apprenticeships, small firms and those owned and operated by immigrants are less likely to participate in the dual-education system in Germany (Newman and Winston 2016).

Family Formation

> The breakdown in school–work institutions and in employers' guarantee of secure employment to large numbers of new graduates produced a "lost generation" [in Japan] in the 1990s, a cohort of young people unable to gain a stable economic toehold from which to embark on their adult lives ... [The] idealized process whereby Japanese young people move out of the status of full-time student and into the status of worker or adult has been heavily predicated on the availability of full-time jobs in *shokuba* or workplaces. (Mary Brinton 2011: 1–2)

The changes in employment relations associated with the rise of precarious work have had a profound effect on families. As Pugh (2015) shows, the growth of job insecurity and the associated "tumbleweed society" have deep implications for family stability and diversity as well as the nature of, and meanings associated with, caregiving. Job and economic insecurity has made futures more uncertain, making people wary of, and less able to afford, making major commitments such as getting married and having children. The average age at first marriage has increased by as much as seven years in the US, Europe, and Japan, and the number of children born has declined in all six countries (Newman 2012), though the reasons for these changes in family formation reflect a wide variety of demographic, social, and economic trends in addition to the growth of precarious work.

Precarious work is apt to be more problematic for family formation in some countries than in others. In countries where the dominant family structure consists of a male breadwinner and female homemaker – such as Japan and Spain – the inability of men to obtain regular, permanent jobs is likely to create difficulties in their getting married and having children, as men in these situations are expected to have stable work careers prior to marriage. By contrast, we would expect easier transitions to adulthood in countries with higher proportions of dual-earner families, whether they are comprised of two full-time workers (as in the United States) or a full-time male and part-time female worker (as in Germany). Easier transitions are also likely in countries with extensive state provisions, such as Denmark, which has made large investments in enabling youth to be independent by providing relatively inexpensive public housing, substantial student stipends for higher education, and unemployment benefits even for those who have never had paid employment (Newman 2012).

Japan exemplifies a country where the impact of precarious work on family formation has been especially severe. Young men are most likely to have been highly impacted by the disruption in life plans caused by the breakdown of orderly transitions from school to work and the paucity of organized career lines in regular full-time employment that have historically been the basis of strong attachments to work organizations. Well-established institutional arrangements underlying normative expectations of life course transitions by which men attend school, establish careers, and then form families are being disrupted by the increasing difficulty in obtaining regular jobs. Brinton (2011) underscores the importance in Japan of social locations (or *ba*) that provide people with an identity and sense of security, and argues that being attached to a stable workplace was essential to the psychological as well as economic well-being of Japanese men in the postwar period.

Moreover, in Japan, gender norms related to the male breadwinner–female homemaker model of marriage have changed quite slowly – as this is strongly linked to conservative institutions such as religion and traditional culture – despite the reality that young men cannot easily find the regular and stable employment needed to be the primary provider, while women enjoy greater opportunities for education and employment, allowing them to forgo marriage altogether (Piotrowski, Kalleberg, and Rindfuss 2015). The cultural disruption engendered by the rise of precarious work has made it more difficult to adjust to the new realities in Japan than in countries such as the US, UK, and Denmark. Hence, in Japan "the new abnormal takes on the quality of a crisis" (Newman 2012: 83).

Young men who cannot find regular employment are unable to learn new skills or to earn enough money to get their own place to live. Lacking such jobs, young men, now increasingly marginalized as non-regular workers, are less able to get settled, often living with parents until their late twenties or early thirties (nearly four in ten Japanese men aged 30–4 still live with their mothers; Newman 2012: 39) and putting off getting married and having children.

Research confirms the changes that have occurred in patterns of family formation in Japan. The ratio of never-married men to married men has risen sharply since the second half of the 1980s. The percentage of men who will not marry during their lives in 2005 (16 percent) exceeded that of women (7.3 percent), reversing patterns that had held since 1955. This rise in the percentage of men who never marry is not easily reversed (if it is reversible at all) since it depends on sex ratios. As the number of single men increases, this will put great pressure on the Japanese welfare system, which is heavily dependent on mutual aid within family groups (Nozaki and Matsuura 2010).

In addition to the increase in those who never marry in Japan, there has also been a rise in the age at which Japanese men marry, from 20 in 1970 to 30 in 2008 (Japanese women, too, are marrying later than previously). This increase in age of marriage is also observed in the US, from age 23.2 in 1970 to 28 in 2009. What makes the situation especially problematic in Japan is that marriage and childbearing are strongly related there, with only about 2 percent of all births in 2010 registered to unmarried women (National Institute of Population and Social Security Research 2011). By contrast, nearly 40 percent of births are to unmarried women in the US (Hamilton et al. 2015). Moreover, virtually all children in Japan are planned, whereas about 50 percent of all pregnancies in the United States are unintended (Finer and Henshaw 2006). It is likely that precarious work would modify the fertility behavior more of people who are more apt to plan their families, such as in Japan as opposed to the US. Given the very low fertility rate in Japan, the country's reluctance to rely on immigration to supplement its labor force, and the aging of the population (which is taking place in all these countries), this does not bode well for Japan's future economic vitality, as government social policies relying on a supportive family (which was formerly the *de facto* welfare system in Japan) are at odds with emerging social realities. With low wages and limited social support, the working poor in Japan are becoming more entrenched in poverty.

The dramatic consequences of working in non-regular jobs for marriage formation in Japan are illustrated by a study of Japanese men and women workers that included data from retrospective life histories covering the twenty-one-year period from 1988 to 2009 (Piotrowski, Kalleberg, and Rindfuss 2015). Figure 6.3 shows the main results from that study, i.e., the probability of marriage for men and women in different combinations of work–school categories. Men who have non-regular employment positions are significantly less likely to marry than men in regular employment. This finding is consistent with our theoretical expectations for a country with a strong male breadwinner–female homemaker model and a gendered division of household labor. Further, being in school also diminishes the chance of marriage, but, as anticipated, this effect fades the longer the lag separating school attendance and actual marriage year.

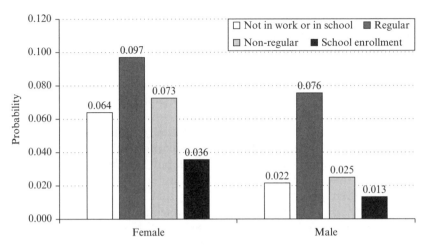

Figure 6.3   Predicted probability of marriage by work–school measures, Japanese men and women

Model also contains controls for school attainment, age, cohabitation, cohort, migration, and data wave. N = 5,485 males and 4,924 females.

Source: Piotrowski, Kalleberg, and Rindfuss 2015

For women, having a non-regular job has a negative effect on marriage, but the effect is significantly lower than the comparable effect for men. This is not surprising in a strong male breadwinner–female homemaker society. A woman, when she marries, is expected to bear and raise children and maintain the household. Her prior labor force experience is not as critical, as women in Japan are often expected to leave the labor force altogether when they marry and have children. Raymo and Lim (2011) describe an M-shaped employment trajectory followed by some Japanese women over their life course: Following an initial increase in labor force participation after the completion of schooling, women leave the labor force for a few years to raise children, returning years later (mostly to non-regular positions) once children are older, and ultimately dropping out of the labor force in their retirement years.

In Spain too, the inability of young men to secure insider status in the labor market through regular employment has contributed to a postponement of marriage. Spain also has a male breadwinner–female homemaker family model coupled with a social welfare system that depends heavily on the family rather than the government. However, living at home for an extended period does not carry much of a stigma in Spain (unlike in Japan) since it is understood that while it is not a desirable situation, it is an adaptation to economic and structural conditions for which individuals are not responsible and over which they have little control. The Spanish thus tend to blame the government (as well as business and the global economy) for their economic insecurity, criticizing the "rubbish contracts" that remove employment protections, and following a political tradition in Spain of protesting against the government.

By contrast, the Japanese, in view of their emphasis on individual agency and responsibility, tend not to denounce the government or business for the rise of non-regular work but to explain the deviation from the standard paths to adulthood as due to their fault or the faults of their parents, especially their mothers, who were mainly responsible for bringing up children (Newman 2012). This stigmatizes Japanese men living with their parents, though the stigma of not being married has lessened considerably for women. By comparison to Spain and Japan, American parents view the accordion family in more conditional terms, depending on why the youth has returned home. It is considered fine in the United States to come home to obtain more schooling or to search for a job that permits fulfillment or self-discovery (which, as I have noted, is increasingly seen as a marker of adulthood), for example, but not to be idle and hang around the house playing video games (Newman 2012).

All the six countries are experiencing demographic challenges, which have profound implications for the future of work. A problem in all the countries, for example, is declining fertility rates, which are linked to the delay in having children. In both Japan and Spain, the disruption in family formation has contributed to the low fertility rates in these countries (total fertility rates in 2013 of 1.4 and 1.3 in Japan and Spain, respectively), which are among the lowest in the world (World Bank 2014). These low fertility rates, coupled with the aging of the populations in these countries, raise alarms about their future economic vitality. This is especially true of Japan, in view of its low rate of immigration. Fertility is declining in Denmark too, which also has a problem with the aging of the population (18 percent are over 65, compared to 13 percent in the US) and those not working in 2013 outnumbered those with jobs in an estimated ninety-five of ninety-eight regions of the country (compared to thirty-nine in 2009; this comparison includes everyone in the region, including children).

Germany is also facing demographic decline. It has the oldest population in Europe (and the world's second oldest population, after Japan) and the number of people who are of working age will shrink sharply, by an estimated 6.5 million between 2013 and 2025

(*The Economist* 2013b). While the number of children per woman dropped below the replacement rate (2.1) in the 1970s, Germany made up for this in immigration until 2002, when the influx started to slow. In 2008, net migration was negative for the first time in twenty-five years. In 2009, the number of people of working age declined for the first time. With a declining labor force, the number and quality of workers are likely to be more important than the number of jobs (*The Economist* 2010a).

These labor shortages have led to pressures to increase immigration, especially for skilled workers. Immigration as a solution to labor shortages in Germany is hampered by the country's apprenticeship system, however, which creates a closed shop and does not provide employment opportunities to large numbers of skilled immigrants, who are consequently overqualified for their job, as they lack the requisite credentials. Other immigrants lack education and skills. A growing share of Germany's aging population is either of non-German origin or poorly educated, or both. Additional strategies to increase the size of the labor force in Germany include encouraging older people and more women to work (about half work part-time), though the paucity of suitable childcare is a disincentive to their working (*The Economist* 2010a).

In the United States, there are "diverging destinies" in the second demographic transition (when fertility has begun to decline), a period that began around 1960 and was associated with delays in marriage and fertility and increases in cohabitation, divorce, and non-marital childbearing. This has produced two different trajectories for women, with the most educated gaining resources (and delaying childbirth and increasing maternal employment) and the least educated experiencing losses associated with divorce, marital instability, and non-marital childbearing (McLanahan 2004). Silva (2013), for example, shows that greater economic insecurity and uncertainty about marriage and family have made the transition to adulthood and family formation increasingly problematic for members of the working class in the United States.

Summary and Conclusions

Precarious work has made it especially difficult in some countries to make life course transitions such as gaining a firm foothold in the labor force, moving out of the home of one's origin, and marrying and having children. Moving from one of these stages to another has been the traditional way of identifying when one has become an adult, though the definition of adulthood is now shifting away from these concrete events toward a psychological sense where one "feels" like an adult. This kind of psychological state is difficult to pin down, however, and is likely to vary among countries on the basis of cultural norms and perceptions as well as within countries due to gender roles, education levels, and class differences. Thus, gaining a foothold in the labor market, getting married, and establishing a family remain central aspects of becoming an adult.

Precarious work affects these life course transitions because the job and economic insecurities it engenders have made it difficult for young people to establish career narratives that lead to orderly and stable life plans. These forms of insecurity also affect the degree to which people's economic resources are sufficient and stable enough to create confidence that they will be able to live on their own or to form and support families.

The ability to gain a solid foothold in the labor market is especially important for moving on to the other life course stages, such as moving out of the parents' home and establishing a household. This is shown most dramatically in countries such as Spain and Japan, where young adults are taking longer to leave home due to not being able to find regular employment, and young men (especially in Japan) are having difficulty finding suitable marriage partners because they have been unable to obtain a regular job that provides the promise of future advancement and economic security. In both Japan and Spain, there is a wide generational divide produced by a dual labor market system that favors older workers at the expense of the young. Older workers enjoy considerable employment protections (more legal in the case of Spain, more cultural in Japan) and so younger workers have difficulty in obtaining regular jobs, and thus must settle for (often a series of) non-regular positions that often do not lead to permanent ones. In Japan, for example, it is estimated that only about 2 percent of non-regular workers transition to regular employment each year (Devine 2013), since Japanese employers prefer to hire recent high school or college graduates, depending on the educational requirements of the job.

The failure to launch careers in the labor force tends to delay marriage and family formation. The impact of marriage on fertility varies among countries, with having children outside of marriage being much more common in countries such as the United States than in Japan, where almost all births are to women who are married. Here again the example of Japan clearly underscores the negative consequences of precarious work for family formation, as young men without regular jobs have difficulty not only in finding a marriage partner, but in having children.

The country differences in the consequences of precarious work on life course transitions that I have described in this chapter underscore the pervasive effects of labor market and social welfare protection institutions. Labor market institutions and policies that enable young people to gain access to regular jobs as opposed to forcing them to take temporary, often dead-end jobs are critical for helping them obtain a foothold in the labor market. Vocational and training institutions that ease the move into permanent positions are key aspects of employment systems that help workers make the transition from school and home of origin to secure footholds in the labor market. Social welfare protection systems that rely on family supports rather than public welfare provisions encourage young people to remain with their parents until they can enter jobs that they are relatively happy with. Moreover, cultural norms and values affect the rigidity of the transitions between life course events, as does whether "failing to launch" is viewed as a stigma or a reasonable adaption to difficult economic times.

The linkages between precarious work and life course transitions also underscore vividly the salience of work experiences for people's lives more broadly, such as the shaping of identities and forming and perpetuating of families. These, in turn, have profound effects on communities and societies more generally.

7
Subjective Well-Being

> John Rawls, while not viewing the possession of virtue or of religious belief as required for happiness, nevertheless includes one outside standard – that of possessing a rational life plan – as part of his very definition of happiness. Like Aristotle and many other philosophers, Rawls takes for granted that happiness requires such a plan. (Sissela Bok 2010: 42)

A rational life plan plays an important role in Rawls's theory of justice, as made clear in this quotation from Sissela Bok, and involves establishing goals for what one hopes to accomplish during life and a strategy for attaining them. Rawls's idea is that people will be happy when they are able to carry out their life plan successfully, as it indicates that the person is able to satisfy his or her rational desires.

Unfortunately, the growth of precarious work has made constructing a rational life plan or career narrative increasingly difficult to achieve for many people in the rich democratic countries. Richard Sennett (2000) vividly described the "corrosion of character" resulting from the transformations associated with precarious work, which have made it difficult to achieve coherence and continuity in one's work experiences and reduced the ability of people to think in terms of a long-term plan. Linear and well-defined career trajectories involving transitions from education to stable jobs are fast becoming a thing of the past as both the young and old struggle to make sense of their working lives in countries characterized by rapidly changing work, family, and political environments. The insecurity associated with precarious work, as well as the uncertainty associated with transitions to adulthood and family formation, result in physical and psychological distress, as well as lower objective[1] and subjective well-being (e.g., Scherer 2009).

Younger workers who are considering their educational and occupational options are especially impacted by the rapid changes in work, as they are likely to have considerable difficulty establishing a foothold in the labor market, as I discussed in the previous chapter. Older workers also often have trouble maintaining the career narratives and life plans that they may have established during an earlier period of greater stability and certainty, as these plans are likely to have been disrupted by the disappearance of stable jobs and the obsolescence of their skills; they have thus been forced to scramble to find new work (and life) identities and to learn new skills.

In this chapter, I examine differences among the six countries in their overall levels of subjective well-being, a concept that has gained in popularity in recent years as a way of evaluating one's overall quality of life. In particular, I focus on the external determinants of subjective well-being, such as the kinds of labor market and social protections institutions that I have discussed in previous chapters, along with other institutional, cultural, and historical factors that may be only marginally linked to precarious work, such as the degree of trust and quality of social relations, levels of and degree of inequality in education and income, and so on. While these sources of subjective well-being account for a relatively small portion of the overall individual differences in happiness and life satisfaction, they are important because many of them are amenable to public policies and interventions.

Measuring Subjective Well-Being

The concept of subjective well-being is closely related to people's assessments of how satisfied they are with their lives or how happy they are generally, and as such is an apt notion by which we can assess the extent to which various life events – such as those associated with precarious work and its attendant insecurities and exclusions – affect people's emotional and cognitive judgments of their overall well-being.

While psychologists have long studied the role played by subjective well-being in mental health and psychological functioning, the notion is now being increasingly used by economists, sociologists, political scientists, epidemiologists, and management scientists to assess the contributions of both non-economic work rewards (such as challenge or meaning) and economic work rewards to promoting one's overall welfare, as well as to evaluate how characteristics of a society (such as income inequality or the degree to which political systems are democratic) affect the social well-being of its citizens.

There are a variety of definitions of subjective well-being. A well-known definition suggested by the psychologist Edward Diener and his colleagues (Diener, Oishi, and Lucas 2003: 404) links the concept to related notions of happiness and life satisfaction: "These evaluations [of happiness or life satisfaction] include people's emotional reactions to events, their moods, and judgments they form about their life satisfaction, fulfillment, and satisfaction with domains such as marriage and work. Thus, subjective well-being concerns the study of what lay people might call happiness or satisfaction" (see also Pichler 2006). I will for simplicity use the concepts of happiness and life satisfaction interchangeably in referring to subjective well-being in this chapter. Nevertheless, there are important distinctions between the concepts of happiness and life satisfaction. Happiness denotes a positive feeling or state of well-being and is often tied to specific situations and events. As defined by Layard (2005: 12), happiness means "feeling good – enjoying life and wanting the feeling to be maintained." Similarly, as Radcliff (2013: 78) defines it, happiness is "nothing more – and nothing less – than the degree to which people enjoy their lives." On the other hand, life satisfaction refers to a longer time horizon, and to people's evaluation of how well they have managed to achieve their goals and thus how content they are with their lives.

The distinction between happiness and life satisfaction has a long history. Jeremy Bentham viewed subjective well-being in terms of happiness, which he evaluated as hedonic utility, or the maximization of pleasure and contentment. This is what people generally report when they are asked about their happiness, and it is consistent with the view adopted by Adam Smith and other economists in their theories of utility as preferences for goods or services. By contrast, the concept of life satisfaction is more in line with Aristotle's notion of *eudaemonia*, which translates roughly into the idea of well-being or flourishing and refers to the degree to which one has lived a life of virtue. This is reflected in the way people live their lives more generally and can be measured objectively, often by a third party, as opposed to persons' subjective perceptions about themselves at certain moments. The philosopher John Rawls, represented in the quotation at the beginning of this chapter, viewed subjective well-being as living a purposeful and fulfilling life, a perspective more in line with that of Aristotle's (see Graham 2011 for a discussion of various conceptions of subjective well-being and happiness).

The measures of subjective well-being I use in this chapter encompass both the happiness and life satisfaction views (see OECD 2013 for a discussion of issues involved in the measurement of subjective well-being). The first is an indicator of life satisfaction, which assesses how people evaluate their life as a whole as opposed to particular aspects of it. A frequently used indicator of this is the "Cantril ladder" measure (Cantril 1965), which asks people to rate their general satisfaction with their lives on a 0–10 scale. The scale is used by several research initiatives including the OECD Gallup surveys and serves as the basis for the OECD 2016 Better Life Index (OECD 2016).[2] The reliability of this life satisfaction measure is "generally well above the required threshold for acceptable reliability" (OECD 2013: 13).

I also construct a second measure of subjective well-being from the ESS data discussed in chapters 4 and 5. This is based on a combination of indicators of happiness and life satisfaction:

Taking all things together, how happy would you say you are? (0 = Extremely unhappy, 10 = Extremely happy)

All things considered, how satisfied are you with your life as a whole nowadays? (0 = Extremely dissatisfied, 10 = Extremely satisfied)

Here, the measure of subjective well-being is a scale constructed as the sum of these two questions (divided by 2); the scale has an internal consistency reliability (Chronbach's alpha) of 0.82, indicating that these two dimensions of subjective well-being are highly correlated.

It is generally accepted among social scientists that one can measure subjective well-being or happiness validly and reliably[3] on the basis of people's responses to survey questions such as these. Ruut Veenhoven (1996), a Dutch scholar who is a pioneer in the scientific study of happiness and life satisfaction, provides convincing evidence of the validity of these subjective measures. For example, he finds that there does not appear to be a tendency for people to over-report their feelings of happiness, nor that social desirability effects seem to distort them. He also observed that there is considerable temporal stability in reports of satisfaction, though they do vary in theoretically expected ways with respect to negative events such as unemployment or divorce.

Veenhoven (1996) also shows that measures of life satisfaction and happiness can be usefully compared across different countries and thereby serve to assess societal progress and well-being. He finds that linguistic differences in words such as "happiness" or "satisfaction," for example, do not affect the ranking of countries on these measures when compared to alternative ways of asking questions about these concepts. His work helped to inspire the United Nations to adopt subjective measures of happiness as holistic indicators of how well public policies contribute to people's social and economic well-being, thereby overcoming some of the limitations of a narrow focus on economic development that are represented by traditional measures of GDP (see Ban 2013).

Country Differences in Subjective Well-Being

It is now well known that indicators of subjective well-being differ among countries (e.g., Blanchflower and Oswald 2011). Diener et al. (1995) argue that differences among countries in subjective well-being reflect dissimilarities in living conditions (e.g., income) in addition to psychological factors such as values or aspirations and cultural factors such as norms governing emotional experience or social desirability. Veenhoven (1995) also found strong evidence that "livability theory" (which holds that people are happier in countries that have better absolute living conditions, regardless of whether they perceive that others have better living conditions than they do) explains country differences in happiness better than alternative theories.

I have established in previous chapters that there are differences among the six rich democracies in many external sources of subjective well-being, such as the differences in job insecurity reported in chapter 4, the dissimilarities in earnings quality and economic insecurity discussed in chapter 5, and the variations in the ability of young people to gain a solid footing in permanent jobs discussed in chapter 6. I attributed these country differences in part to the variations in the social welfare protection and labor market institutions and policies that influence the levels of insecurity and exclusion in a country and may mitigate the impacts of precarious work on perceived job and economic insecurity. At the same time, country differences in subjective well-being are only one source of dissimilarity in this concept. Within countries, there is likely to be a great deal of variation in subjective well-being produced by people's personalities and genetic make-up (which influence their set points of well-being) as well as voluntary actions that people might engage

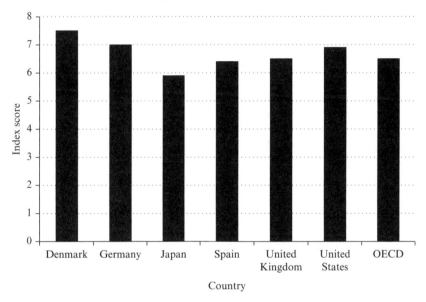

Figure 7.1   Life satisfaction, 2016
Source: OECD 2016 data

in (such as attending religious services or helping others) that might enhance their well-being.[4]

Figure 7.1 presents recent estimates of life satisfaction, based on the OECD 2016 Better Life Index, for the six countries (OECD 2016). As is typical of this kind of subjective measure, the overall mean scores tend to be relatively high, as the overall mean for the OECD is 6.5/10. Moreover, as these are all relatively successful, rich democracies, it is unsurprising that levels of life satisfaction are fairly high.

Figure 7.1 shows that the Danes have the highest level of life satisfaction (7.5), followed closely by the Germans (7) and the Americans (6.9). The life satisfaction in the UK was at the OECD average, while the Japanese scored the lowest on the life satisfaction measure (5.9). The Spanish also score slightly below the OECD average (6.4).

These patterns are broadly consistent with the differences among countries in job and economic insecurity that I have presented in previous chapters. The high levels of reported life satisfaction in (especially) Denmark and to some degree Germany reflect in part the greater objective and perceived job and economic security in these countries, along with the labor market and social protection institutions and policies that contribute to such securities. The relatively high level of life satisfaction reported in the United States departs somewhat from what we have observed earlier for job and economic insecurity, however. To some degree, this reflects the general optimism associated with Americans, who tend to score relatively highly on satisfaction measures due to cultural tendencies to be hopeful and upbeat.

The lower level of life satisfaction expressed by the Japanese also appears somewhat inconsistent with the relatively low levels of job and economic insecurity in Japan observed in chapters 4 and 5 respectively, though it is in line with my discussion in the last chapter about the profound impacts of precarious work on young people (especially young men) in Japan. Again, there may be a cultural explanation for the relatively low scores for Japan, which may partly reflect culture-based definitions of happiness in Buddhist, collectivist Japan, which places less of a premium on individual happiness. It might also be due to higher aspirations and expectations in Japan, which tend to dampen expressions of satisfaction. Moreover, there is also the well-known tendency of the Japanese to score low on measures of satisfaction, which has been linked to cultural disposi-tions to assume an excessively modest, self-denigrating posture in describing themselves and their accomplishments (Lincoln and Kalleberg 1990). Diener et al. (1995) also found that people in the US scored higher than those in Japan on subjective well-being even when controlling for differences in income, but there was no evidence that general response style differences between persons in these two countries were responsible for this. Similarly, Veenhoven's (1996) analyses found that social pressures to over- or understate happiness levels in Japan did not unduly affect conclusions regarding cross-national differences in happiness.

These patterns of country differences are also generally consist-ent with the results of a report by Deutsche Bank (Deutsche Bank Research 2007), which distinguished among different varieties of capitalism on the basis of their ratings of happiness. They found that Denmark, the UK, and US illustrated a "happy" variety of capitalism in which institutions are organized so as to promote happiness (i.e., high degree of trust in fellow citizens, low amount of corruption, low unemployment, high level of education, high income, high employment rate of older people, small shadow economy, extensive economic freedom, low employment protection, and high birthrate). On the other hand, Germany and Spain were regarded as the "less happy" variety, in which institutions trailed on several dimensions.

This observation does not seem borne out by the relatively high satisfaction scores observed in figure 7.1 for Germany, though the lower life satisfaction expressed by the Spanish may also be traced to the high levels of job insecurity and difficult economic times faced by that country. Japan scored well on some happiness-relevant criteria (small shadow economy, high employment rate among older people) but relatively poorly on others (birthrate, lower incomes) though its population was characterized as relatively unhappy in figure 7.1.

The country averages presented in figure 7.1 are suggestive, but such cross-sectional, aggregate data cannot tell us whether the observed differences are due to labor market and other social, economic, and political characteristics, or whether they reflect differences among countries in characteristics of the jobs and persons in these countries. For example, persons in these countries may differ in their reported levels of life satisfaction because they have different levels of education, income, marital status, age, and other characteristics that are known to influence differences in perceived subjective well-being (see note 4, this chapter). While I am unable with the available data to carry out a systematic and rigorous analysis of the mechanisms that produced the differences among the six countries observed in figure 7.1, it is possible to carry out a more refined analysis for four of the countries using information on these concepts from the same ESS data sets that I've discussed in chapters 4 and 5.

Figure 7.2 presents results for levels of predicted subjective well-being in the four European countries for 2004 and 2010, using the two-item scale of subjective well-being described earlier in this chapter. These predicted levels control for a variety of individual-level demographic and job characteristics that have been shown by previous studies to be related to subjective well-being. The models producing the estimates in figure 7.2 thus take into account respondents' age, education, gender, marital status, disability status, size of employing establishment, and three indicators of objective job insecurity (i.e., whether the person has a temporary job, length of employer tenure, and recent unemployment experience).

Subjective well-being is again the highest in Denmark in both time periods, which is in line with the lower perceived job and economic insecurity observed in that country, as well as with the active labor market policies and generous welfare provisions that contribute to these lower levels of insecurity. While the level of subjective well-being in Denmark was a bit lower in 2010 than 2004 (reflecting, perhaps, the impacts of the 2008–9 economic crisis), the difference between the two years is not statistically significant.

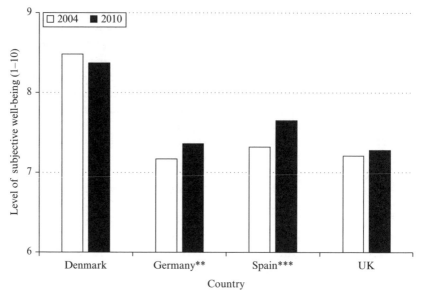

Figure 7.2   Perceived subjective well-being, 2004 and 2010
Significant difference between years: *** p<0.001, ** p<0.01
Source: ESS 2004 and 2010 data

Subjective well-being increased in the other three countries during the period, though the increase in the UK was not statistically significant. In Germany and Spain, however, the levels of subjective well-being were significantly greater after the economic crisis than before, when differences in the composition of jobs and persons within the samples were considered. Why subjective well-being should increase in these countries after the economic crisis is not immediately obvious. We might speculate that persons in these countries, having experienced difficult economic times in the period leading up to the crisis, might be more hopeful about the future in 2010 when the economic crisis had subsided. This underscores the importance of expectations and psychological adaptation mechanisms in shaping people's assessments of their happiness and life satisfaction.

The 2004 and 2010 ESSs also permit me to assess more directly the extent to which perceived job and economic insecurity help to explain country differences in subjective well-being. To assess this, I added the perceived indicators of job and economic insecurity discussed in chapters 4 and 5 to models containing the predictors of subjective well-being that were used to construct the predicted levels

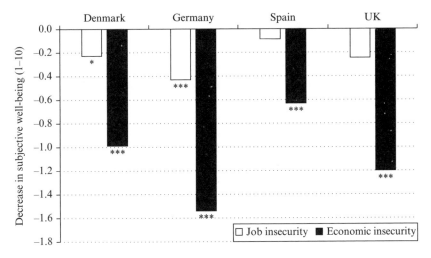

Figure 7.3   Effect of job insecurity and economic insecurity
on subjective well-being, 2004 and 2010

Significance: *** p<0.001, * p<0.05

Source: ESS 2004 and 2010 data

in figure 7.2. The results of this analysis, presented in figure 7.3, show the effects of perceived job and economic insecurity on subjective well-being in the four countries, after controlling for the other predictors.[5] The sizes of the bars indicate the degree to which levels of subjective well-being shown in figure 7.2 are reduced when measures of job and economic insecurity are added to the equations. The fact that the bars are below 0 indicates that the effects of perceived job and economic insecurity on subjective well-being are consistently negative, as I would expect since both types of perceived insecurity lower well-being; when indicators of job and economic insecurity are taken into consideration, people report lower levels of subjective well-being than if their levels of insecurity are not considered.[6]

Figure 7.3 shows that perceived economic insecurity has a stronger negative impact on subjective well-being than perceived job insecurity in all four countries, as the sizes of the bars indicating reductions in well-being are much larger for perceived economic insecurity. Perceived economic insecurity reduces subjective well-being most in Germany, followed by the UK and Denmark. Taking into account economic insecurity reduced subjective well-being the least in Spain. It might well be that the Spanish may report higher levels of subjective well-being than might be expected from their levels of insecurity due to their strong family ties and social relationships, pleasant weather, good food, and so on. On the other hand, this might reflect the fact that the downturn in the Spanish economy was so salient that its structural nature was apparent, hence less stigmatizing to the individual; this explanation is consistent with the tendency of the Spanish to blame economic hard times rather than young people for "failures to launch" that was discussed in chapter 6.

The only statistically significant difference among the countries in the degree to which economic insecurity reduced subjective well-being is between Germany and Spain: Economic insecurity reduced subjective well-being more in Germany than in Spain. The effect of economic insecurity in Germany is only marginally larger than in the UK, while the effect is significantly larger in the UK than Spain. The role of economic insecurity in reducing subjective well-being in Denmark is not significantly different from that in the other three countries.

By contrast, perceived job insecurity does not appear all that strongly related to subjective well-being, especially in Spain and the United Kingdom, where including the measure of perceived job insecurity does not reduce significantly the level of subjective well-being. Perceived job insecurity significantly reduced subjective well-being only in Denmark and Germany (and there is not a statistically significant difference in the effect of job insecurity in Denmark as opposed to Germany). We should keep in mind, though, that these equations control for three indicators of objective job insecurity (temporary work, tenure with the employer, unemployment experience), all of which affect both perceived job insecurity and subjective well-being.

Country differences in subjective well-being result not only from differences in perceived insecurity, however. The kinds of labor market and social protection institutions that I have discussed in earlier chapters also shape people's well-being. To assess the impacts of labor market and welfare protection institutions on subjective well-being more directly, I again turn to the 2004 and 2010 ESSs to estimate differences among seventeen European countries in the extent to which the labor market and social welfare protection institutions affect the degree of insecurity that people feel about their jobs and economic situations, as well as country differences in subjective well-being (see Inanc and Kalleberg 2016).[7] We found substantial country-level variation in subjective well-being; country differences accounted for nearly 20 percent of the variation in subjective well-being observed among individuals in these countries. We also found that perceived job and economic insecurity are negatively related to subjective well-being and help to account for the observed country differences in subjective well-being (as suggested by figure 7.3 for the four countries examined there).

Our results also provide robust evidence that labor market and social welfare protection institutions have substantial effects on subjective well-being, even after individual-level characteristics are taken into account: The level of active labor market policies strongly enhances subjective well-being, as do the levels of unemployment income replacement and the generosity of welfare spending.[8] Moreover, and consistent with previous research, the extent of collective bargaining coverage increases subjective well-being and the degree of income inequality decreases it. Similarly, Di Tella and MacCulloch (2008) show that differences in happiness among OECD countries between 1975 and 1997 were positively related to country differences in income and the level of welfare protections, and negatively related to inflation, unemployment, and average number of hours worked, among other variables.

On the other hand, changes in income per se seem to be weakly related to changes in happiness, as predicted by Easterlin's (e.g., 1995) argument that economic growth does not produce greater happiness once a country reaches a certain level of economic growth, due to people's adaptations to higher income levels. Greve (2012), for example, used data from the 2008 and 2010 ESS surveys (among others) and found that change in income (as measured by GDP per capita) was not significantly related to changes in happiness. He argues that one reason for this might be due to expectations, as people might have assumed that their income would be reduced as a result of the economic crisis. In addition, the ILO's (2004) major report on economic security, based on data for over ninety countries (covering 86 percent of the world's population), found that the most important determinant of national happiness was income security (measured in terms of income protection and low levels of income inequality) rather than the income level itself. And Arampatzi, Burger, and Veenhoven's (2015) analysis of data for twenty-eight European countries (from the Eurobarometer Survey Series) for the period from 2008 to 2012 found that employed people who are relatively economically secure were not affected by rising unemployment and inflation, while those who were in financial distress were negatively affected.

We also found the unemployment rate in a country decreased subjective well-being, at least in most of our models. This finding is consistent with Wulfgramm's (2014) results of her analysis of twenty-one countries using the ESSs from 2002 to 2009. She also found that the effect of unemployment on subjective well-being depends a great deal on the generosity of unemployment benefits in a country: The unfavorable effects of unemployment on subjective well-being are almost twice as large if unemployment benefits are scanty. In addition, Sjöberg's (2010) analysis of twenty-one countries using the 2004/5 ESS found that the generosity of unemployment benefits lessens the effects of job insecurity on the subjective well-being of both unemployed and employed persons by reducing their concerns about future financial security.

The extent of active labor market policies in a country can also help to ameliorate somewhat the negative effects of unemployment on subjective well-being, but this effect disappears once unemployment benefit generosity is controlled. Carr and Chung's (2014) analysis of twenty-two countries using the 2010 ESS found that the negative impact of perceived job insecurity on life satisfaction was weaker in countries with more generous active labor market policies and unemployment benefits.[9]

These results are broadly consistent with previous studies of country differences in subjective well-being as summarized by Radcliff's (2013) comprehensive review and analysis. He used data from five waves of the World Values Survey (WVS) between 1981 and 2007 to examine the determinants of life satisfaction[10] for twenty-one core member states of the OECD (including the six countries studied here). He then merged these data with information for these countries from other sources to include indicators of: GDP per capita growth; unemployment rates; decommodification (based on an updated version of Esping-Andersen's index, which includes the extent of social insurance for pensions, income maintenance for the ill or disabled, and unemployment benefits); welfare generosity; taxation and size of the government; and employment protection, among others. In assessing the effects of these country characteristics on life satisfaction, he also controlled for the key individual-level determinants that have been emphasized by previous research.

He reached the following conclusions. First, he finds that: "[T]he single most powerful individual- or national-level determinant of the degree to which people positively evaluate the quality of their lives is the extent to which they live in a generous and universalistic welfare state" (Radcliff 2013: 7). Second, labor market institutions and policies that offer strong social protections for employees enhance their life satisfaction. These include: labor laws that protect employees from arbitrary dismissal and unsafe working conditions; the rigidity of working time policies; minimum wage laws; and restrictions on the use of temporary work. In addition, he finds strong evidence that life satisfaction is boosted for both unionized and unorganized workers in countries with strong labor movements, and larger shares of workers who are covered by collective bargaining agreements.

Surveys such as the ESS, WVS surveys, or the Gallup surveys for the OECD do not contain the information needed to assess differences in subjective well-being that reflect individual genetic or personality predispositions, or those due to a host of group-level factors such as the quality of certain kinds of social relationships. We should also keep in mind that subjective well-being is due to many factors in addition to precarious work and insecurity (see note 4, this chapter). These include characteristics of the person (such as health and social participation) as well as more group-level attributes such as the degree of democracy, social protections, and levels of social relationships in a country (e.g., Pichler 2006). Nevertheless, Radcliff's (2013: 8–9) overall conclusion is that:

> the extent to which individuals find life rewarding is largely the result of political factors [which] ... dwarfs conventional individual-level indicators such as income, social connectedness (e.g., marriage or cohabitation), and even unemployment. As the most powerful causes of happiness are things that governments are entirely capable of control-ling, we can follow Thomas Jefferson and Jeremy Bentham in believing that happiness is something that is politically produced and distributed. Happiness, then, is a function of public policy.

Summary and Conclusions

Subjective well-being is a useful concept that provides a summary evaluation of a person's overall perceived quality of life. It enables an assessment of how particular life events – such as those associated with precarious work and its attendant perceived job and economic insecurities – affect people's current emotional state and their sense of how well their life goals are being met.

The results presented in this chapter are consistent with the argu-ment I have offered in earlier chapters that precarious work tends to reduce one's subjective well-being because it leads to greater objec-tive and perceived job and economic insecurity. Not all the country differences in subjective well-being can be attributed to differences in precarious work and perceived job and economic insecurity, however. Labor market and social protection institutions also matter, because they affect subjective well-being directly by contributing to the overall social, economic, and political contexts that shape many of the external conditions (such as the extent of economic inequality and the degree and duration of unemployment), as well as by ameliorating or enhancing the impacts of these external conditions on subjective well-being. These differences in subjective well-being among countries and among those who differ in their experiences of objective and perceived job insecurity and economic insecurity are not attributable to individual differences such as income, gender, age, or many of the other individual characteristics that are typically used to explain life satisfaction and happiness, since these have been considered in the analysis.

But the labor market and social protection institutions considered here are not the only macrostructural factors that produce differences among countries. While the number of countries studied here is too small to conduct systematic analyses of the sources of country differences, it is undoubtedly the case that these are also affected by dissimilarities among countries in characteristics such as: political governance mechanisms; the degree of trust that people have in their governments and other institutions; the extent of worker power, such as the amount and strength of unions; a high standard of living and opportunities for mobility; good social relations with friends and family; and cultural factors such as religion and the degree of optimism prevalent in the country.

Many of these country differences – especially those related to the labor market and social welfare institutions discussed in this book – not only matter for subjective well-being, but are amenable to public policy intervention. Labor market institutions such as active labor market policies and social welfare protections associated with such things as illness or retirement are within the purview of governments and social and political actors, who can take steps to reduce the impacts of precarious work on individuals' psychological as well as economic well-being. Hence, addressing precarious work becomes a matter of concern for public policy, as I will discuss in the next chapter.

Part IV

Responses to Precarious Work and Lives

8

Politics and Policies of
Precarious Work

The precariat hovers on the borderline, exposed to circumstances that
could turn them from strugglers into deviants and loose cannons prone
to listen to populist politicians and demagogues. (Guy Standing 2011:
132)

Casualization profoundly affects the person who suffers it: by making
the whole future uncertain, it prevents all rational anticipation and,
in particular, the basic belief and hope in the future that one needs in
order to rebel, especially collectively, against present conditions, even
the most intolerable. (Pierre Bourdieu 1998: 82)

The new social question is: democracy or the rule of the financial
markets. We are currently witnessing the end of an era. The neoliberal ideology has failed worldwide. The U.S. movement Occupy Wall
Street is a good example of this. (Sigmar Gabriel, Vice-Chancellor of
Germany 2011)

The free market utopia is not the solution but a major cause of the
problem. (Ulrich Beck 2000: 5)

Precarious workers share experiences of anger (due to frustration
over blocked aspirations), anomie (a passivity resulting from despair
about not finding meaningful work), anxiety (due to chronic insecurity), and alienation (due to lack of purpose and social disapproval).
These mutual understandings make the precariat a potentially dangerous class, capable of being mobilized by different groups for various ends, to provide democratically based solutions – as in the New
Deal in the United States in the 1930s – or authoritarian movements
that blame immigrants and the poor for the precariat's insecurity
(Standing 2011). The latter was what Polanyi (1957 [1944]) was
most concerned about, and his fears were realized with the adoption

of totalitarian governments in Germany and Italy in the build-up to World War II (see also Harvey 2005). The quotations here illustrate both the dangers and challenges involved in addressing precarious work and its consequences.

The rise of precarious work after long periods of economic and social development after World War II has raised apprehensions that hard-won gains by workers during this period may be lost. The growth of precarious work is not only about the need to adapt to change (as I discussed in chapter 6), but also about real structural disadvantage. While there have always been poor people in rich societies, now precarious work has become widespread, as the middle class has been hollowed out in many countries and insecurity characterizes all workers to some extent. Precarity has become a discursive practice that serves as an action framework for political organizing by emergent social movements as well as more established unions. Just as union struggles were an important part of the emergence of the SER in the first half of the twentieth century, the rise of precarious work is provoking vigorous political and workplace struggles today.

I elaborate in this chapter on some key political and policy challenges posed by the recent rise of precarious work. I first discuss social movements and electoral politics stimulated by precarious work. These include both "bottom-up" attempts by workers to acquire power resources through social movements, and "top-down" efforts by organized unions and political parties to enact laws and politics designed to address the negative consequences of precarious work. I then summarize the new risks for workers and their families that are raised by the changes in employment relations and reconfiguration of social welfare protection systems discussed in previous chapters. I next identify the main elements of a new social and political contract that has the potential to collectivize the risks associated with precarious work, thereby helping individuals and their families cope with the upheavals they are facing in the labor market. I finally discuss some of the dynamics among workers, employers, and governments involved in the implementation of this new social and political contract. These involve actions by state, employers, and workers as they struggle to confront the challenges presented by precarious work.

Protests and Politics

Protests against policies that have fueled the rise of precarious work have erupted in all of the countries being studied and have led to pressures on their governments to "do something" to reduce social and economic distress. Protests grew after the economic crisis of 2008–9, underscoring their strong association with economic performance (Quaranta 2016). Precarious work thus creates a challenge for governments as well as business and labor as they strive to develop institutional structures capable of alleviating current conditions of insecurity and inequality. The responses to precarious work are fundamentally couched in these actors' political and economic interests: "This is an 'age of insecurity,' to quote the *Guardian* journalists Atkinson and Elliot, in which anxiety and uncertainty are to some extent 'manufactured' for both political ends and economic advantage" (Doogan 2009: 10).

Albert O. Hirschman (1970) identified three different ways that people might respond to economic declines such as those represented by precarious work: exit, loyalty, and voice (see Kalleberg and Vallas 2018 for a discussion). Exit and loyalty are primarily individual-level responses. *Exit* is likely to characterize workers with limited educational and social capital resources in regions with declining economies that resign themselves to their marginalized economic positions. These workers are likely to be disengaged from formal social and political institutions and cynical about the likelihood of escaping precarious work.

Loyalty is also an individual-level response that is more likely to typify workers whose skills enable them to take advantage of the greater openness of labor markets and better opportunities for moving among employers in the new age of precarity. Some of these persons are likely to commit wholeheartedly to market logics, complying with the cultural injunction to market themselves, often by adopting career management ideologies such as "packing their own parachute" by being "Me, Inc."

The final response, *voice*, is the most promising reaction to precarious work from the point of view of generating social change, as it is most likely to lead to collective actions. This kind of response can take forms from sporadic expressions on the left to ethno-nationalist political movements on the right.

Social Movements

The anxiety, anger, anomie, and alienation produced by the spread of uncertainty, insecurity, and inequality have motivated workers in the United States, Europe, and many Asian countries to adopt protective strategies to defend themselves against the insecurity and commodification generated by recent globalization and deregulation policies and unregulated markets. Collective protests against precarious work include sudden mass mobilizations (as in the case of the Occupy movements) as well as confrontations with governments and businesses by more traditional unions and other social movements.

While Polanyi (1957 [1944]) described the organizing principles of industrial society in the nineteenth and twentieth centuries as a double movement that represented a struggle between unfettered markets and social protections, he did not provide a theory of power that would enable us to understand how societies were able to swing back to the security side of the double movement. Nevertheless, he did suggest elements of such power dynamics by identifying the emergence of a cross-class countermovement among the various groups that were threatened by insecurity produced by the operation of unfettered markets (Lee and Kofman 2012). The contours and strategies of these emerging cross-class coalitions are not yet fully clarified, though they appear to characterize anti-precarity movements in several European countries, including Denmark, Germany, Spain, and the United Kingdom. In the United States, such mass mobilizations were represented by the Occupy movement that began on September 17, 2011, with the occupation of Zuccotti Park near Wall Street.

The potential of precarious work for prompting mass protests was vividly illustrated by the self-immolation of the Tunisian fruit seller Mohammed Bouazizi in December 2010 as an act of desperation after the police seized his produce cart. This act resonated with the feelings of large groups of people and sparked the protests against insecurity and precarity known as the Arab Spring that spread to Egypt, Libya, and Yemen, among other places in the Middle East and Northern Africa (Lee and Kofman 2012).

Occupy and similar social movements have provided a way for diverse groups of people to display publicly their fears of and outrage at uncertainty and insecurity. As such, these worker movements have contributed to the conversation in these six countries about how (and whether) to restructure the economy and adopt policies to collectivize the individual risks that are created by the spread of precarious work.

Not all of the current wave of protests were directed specifically at precarious work, of course; some were targeted at related developments such as the austerity imposed by governments in the aftermath of the economic crisis of the latter part of the first decade of the twenty-first century, with its cuts in public spending and weakened unemployment provisions and other social protections. Still, a big reason for these protests was the widespread insecurity experienced by workers, especially young, educated persons, who had grown increasingly frustrated at being unable to obtain non-precarious jobs and to establish coherent career narratives and life plans.

The characters of these anti-precarity, anti-austerity protests were also not homogenous: some were episodic mass mobilizations such as the globalized Occupy movement, *los indignados* in Spain, *freeters* in Japan, and the annual EuroMayDay demonstrations; others were more traditional social movements such as those organized by trade unions and political parties in Spain during 2010–12 (Peterson, Wahlström, and Wennerhag 2015).

In Spain, the movement of May 15, 2011 (15-M), called the *indignados* by the media, was mobilized by *¡Democracia real Ya!* (Real Democracy Now!), a digital platform that rallied thousands of people in fifty Spanish cities; the core constituency of this episodic, non-hierarchical mass movement was younger and more educated than those involved in movements organized by traditional unions. The 15-M movement had its roots in other movements too, such as the *Precarios en movimiento*, a loose network of groups struggling against the lack of certainty (*precariedad*) in employment, housing, pensions, health, and education. Spain's radical leftist groups and unions associated with autonomist and anarchist traditions also led large protests that were often much more confrontational than those of the *indignados*.

Peterson, Wahlström, and Wennerhag's (2015) study of the motivations and attitudes of participants in the various types of anti-precarity protests found that those involved in the *indignados*/Occupy protests in Spain and the UK tended to identify with the middle class rather than the working class, as cutbacks in public spending had undermined the economic insecurity of large parts of the middle class. This is consistent with the notion that those protesting precarity can be characterized as representing a cross-class coalition. By contrast, those involved in protests conducted by traditional unions were more apt to identify with the working class.

Anti-precarity resistance movements have been embraced by diverse groups in the population whose lives are threatened by the consequences of market deregulation, not just members of a class whose jobs are endangered. For example, the globalized Occupy movement was comprised of many highly educated, over-qualified, and younger workers who were protesting the impacts on other people and on societal institutions more generally if not always their own experience of precarity. The precariat, as described by Standing (2011), is a much larger group than those involved in the Occupy movements, consisting of cross-class clusters such as the poor and working class as well as the downwardly mobile middle class (who have lost well-paying blue-collar and white-collar jobs) and professionals whose livelihoods and futures are increasingly vulnerable. A key portion of the precariat is what Standing calls "denizens," which comprise any worker, immigrant or not, who has limited civil, social, economic, legal, or political rights and is thereby excluded from the social, economic, and political institutions of society.

In the United Kingdom, anti-precarity movements were exemplified by Occupy London, which, while relatively small, was the main offshoot in Europe of the US Occupy Wall Street movement. Like Occupy Wall Street, Occupy London was organized along a non-hierarchical principle that made it skeptical about collaborating with more established trade unions or political parties.

Protests against precarious work also occurred in Japan. Here, union membership had declined from a historic high of 12.7 million in 1994 to 10.04 million in 2006, but the decline was arrested in 2007 as enterprise unions began to organize nonstandard workers (by redefining their criteria for membership), and new types of unions – regional general unions (known as community unions) – emerged that organized workers in multiple small companies on a regional (as opposed to enterprise) basis (Nakamura and Nitta 2013). These community unions include the Precariat, representing nonstandard workers, and the Tokyo Youth Union of Contingent Workers (Gottfried 2015). In addition to union activity, dissatisfied youth are gravitating toward right-wing organizations such as the Net Right. Moreover, the emergence of tent cities populated by homeless and unemployed persons has raised people's awareness of the negative consequences of precarious work, as I discussed in the introduction to this book.

All these protest movements underscore the concerns felt by people in these countries about the social and economic consequences of recent transformations in labor markets and social welfare protection systems. While the notion of precarious work is emphasized more clearly in some of these movements than others, they all reflect people's fears and frustrations at the shifting of risks away from the state and employers toward workers, and the uncertainty and insecurity this has created. Grasso and Giugni (2016) show that participants in anti-austerity protests in Europe had more organizational memberships and were less likely to be unemployed, but believed that their situation had worsened over the past five years. People who felt relatively deprived were also more likely to protest in countries with high levels of unemployment and greater social spending, conditions these authors argue are associated with greater political opportunities for protests. While these protest and political movements often lack a cohesive agenda and their goals are often murky (such as "giving power back to the people") and unstated, there is a common feeling that the new risks associated with the growth of precarious work need to be addressed collectively.

At the moment, these protest movements have lacked a concrete political agenda and strategy and have yet to link up with unions or civic organizations. As a result, their potential remains unrealized. By raising issues of precarious work and inequality that are not being addressed by the political system, however, such social movements are often a prelude to more concrete political actions in electoral politics (Piven and Cloward 1979).

Electoral Politics

Dramatic political challenges to precarious work have been slow to develop in these countries, especially from the left. Part of the reason is that the most precarious workers are often relatively powerless: being on the periphery of the labor force, they are often also on the margins of politics and hence not very hopeful that electoral political change will improve their situation. Moreover, the dominance of neoliberal political-economic policies has weakened unions and other sources of worker power that could serve as agents to promote political change.

Nonetheless, there are signs in all of these countries of political entrepreneurs on the left as well as the right being able to mobilize voters in response to real or perceived risks to workers and their communities and to challenge dominant political parties. Much of this political activity has come from right-wing movements in Denmark, Germany, the United Kingdom, and the United States. Former middle-class workers whose standard of living has been eroded by the transformation of employment relations and retrenchment of social welfare protections powered these movements. There has also been growing opposition from the left, however, and left-wing movements have appeared in Spain and Japan.

In Denmark, politics have moved to the right with the Social Democrats being defeated and the Liberal Party receiving support from the anti-immigrant Dansk Folkeparti or Danish People's Party (DPP) (Eakin 2016). The founder of the DPP in 1995, Pia Kjærsgaard, has been the speaker of the Danish Parliament since 2015, though at present the DPP is not a force in the Parliament.

In Germany, a far-right party, the Alternative for Germany (Alternative für Deutschland or AfD), has gained traction due largely to discontent over Chancellor Merkel's immigration policies, and is now Germany's fastest growing party. The AfD became Germany's third largest party after the 2017 federal election, marking the first time it had won any seats in the Bundestag.

In Japan, the post-World War II hegemony of the conservative LDP was interrupted by the election of the Democratic Party of Japan (DPJ) in 2009. The DPJ's administration was short-lived, as it was cut short by the March 11, 2011, nuclear accident at the Fukushima power plant. While the DPJ managed to enact some protections while it was in power, it is too soon to know their longer-term influence over the future direction of policy and politics.

The 15-M movements in Spain have so far not evolved into effective political programs. This has been a source of consternation to older Spaniards, who see the dependence of grown children on their parents as a sign of political apathy. This appears odd to the generation of people who previously chafed against Franco's authoritarian rule, and who grew up in an era where mass protests against the government were common, unlike the case in the US or Japan (Newman 2012). Recently, though, Spain, like Greece, saw the rise of Podemos as a new left-wing political party, a left-wing populism that needs to be understood in terms of its fear of right-wing Fascism stemming from Franco's rule.

A variety of concerns, including fears of immigration and worries about insecurity, motivated the appearance of the United Kingdom Independence Party, which was a major voice behind the Brexit vote to leave the European Union, and inspired the far right British National Party and the English Defence League. But the UK has also seen growing strength on the left, as shown by the Labour Party's increased vote share (particularly among younger voters) in the 2017 national election under the leadership of left-wing Jeremy Corbyn.

In the United States, the Tea Party emerged in 2009 as a conservative movement within the Republican Party. Tea Party members generally advocate a reduction in government involvement in the economy and the national debt as well as opposing tax increases, among other economic goals. Its members are often fairly well-to-do persons who own their own homes, not necessarily those experiencing precarious work directly. Tea Partiers often fear losing what they have, however, and their opposition to big government is rooted in their views that their taxes are used to help undeserving "freeloaders" such as immigrants, non-whites, and low-wage earners (Skocpol and Williamson 2011).

Tea Partiers, like many supporters of Brexit, the AfD, and the DPP, tend to blame immigrants for threatening their standard of living.

The Tea Party helped create the discontent that was seized upon by Donald Trump in the 2016 US Presidential election, which clearly demonstrated the extent and depth of anger and frustration felt by large segments of the US population at the insecurity engendered by globalization, technological change, and the other economic, social, and political forces discussed in earlier chapters.

It is unclear at this writing if the social and political movements described in this chapter will be able to deliver the social welfare protections and labor market institutions that would alleviate the most negative consequences of precarious work, such as job and economic insecurity, and thereby enable workers to navigate rapidly changing labor markets. To do this effectively, these movements must respond to the new risks of work that are created by the transformation of employment relations.

New Employment Relations, New Risks

Existing welfare regimes and labor laws were based on models of relatively stable work and families comprised of a male breadwinner and female homemaker. Hence, welfare policies were directed at addressing problems associated with unemployment, which was the major job-related risk during the postwar period. It was assumed that providing income replacement to the unemployed breadwinner would protect families during spells of joblessness. Moreover, educational systems were designed to provide workers with the skills needed to gain a foothold in the labor force, as it was assumed that companies would then provide additional firm-specific skills that might be required for jobs.

These assumptions are no longer viable due to the emergence of precarious work as the normative form of the relations between employers and workers in the contemporary world. Unemployment now, as opposed to the recent past, often has more to do with business strategies of profit maximization than company survival, reflecting the changing norms associated with the employment relationship that have weakened the ties between employers and their employees. In the United States, for example, downsizing and layoffs have become an employer strategy for restructuring as well as increasing short-term profits by holding down the price and quantity of labor, thereby transferring income from labor to capital.

Changes in employment relations have made careers now less continuous, and long-term employment with a single company is much less frequent due to the decline of firm-internal labor markets. Rather, moving from one job and firm to another is more common, as is the likelihood that people will change the types of work they do; the rapidity of social changes makes some jobs obsolete and creates opportunities for new ones. This underscores the necessity of lifelong learning and retraining as one's career unfolds. Accompanying these transformations in employment relations has been the shifting of the risks of work from employers and governments to workers, one of the major hallmarks of precarious work.

Moreover, there have been major changes in family structures in the rich democracies. Families in which both partners work have become more common, making it more necessary to help families reconcile the needs and demands of work and family life through better provision of childcare, parental leave policies, flextime, and other forms of flexible scheduling. In addition, the growth of single parenthood in the United States and other countries raises questions as to the continued viability of workfare programs that require single mothers to work in the labor force as a condition of receiving social assistance.

Finally, demographic trends such as the aging of the population – coupled with declining fertility – in virtually all these advanced capitalist countries will put increasing pressure on the pension system, as there will be fewer workers to support a growing retired population (as I discussed in chapter 2).

In view of these new risks associated with employment and social welfare, a new political and social contract is needed to alleviate and collectivize the new major risks to individuals and families that have been triggered by the rise of precarious work.

Elements of a New Social and Political Employment Accord

All countries are faced with the basic problem of balancing flexibility for employers and security for workers. Governments need to reconcile two often conflicting agendas to obtain political legitimacy and secure economic growth: an economic agenda related to the requirements of competitiveness and growth (emphasized by economic elites); and a social agenda linked to social protection, employment stability, and economic security (emphasized by workers). As Deyo (2012: 4) puts it: "It is the problematic and seeming incompatibility of these two agendas – making markets work, and protecting society and ensuring social order – that drives the continuing and incessant change in trajectories of social and economic regulation." Neilson and Rossiter (2005: 7–8) suggest that "precariousness meets precarity" in cases when the workings of capital in global markets (such as the desire for deregulated financial markets that are associated with neoliberalism) conflict with the desire of state actors for greater security (such as blocking the flow of money that finances terror networks). The challenges of reconciling agendas of flexibility and security are magnified by the slowdown in economic growth in the past three decades in the rich democracies.

In order to tackle these issues, policies in three general areas are necessary to maintain flexibility for employers yet still provide individuals with ways to cope with the negative consequences produced by such flexibility. These include: (1) a safety net and various kinds of social protections to collectivize risk and help individuals cope with the uncertainty and insecurity associated with the growth of precarious work; (2) greater access to early childhood and formal education as well as lifelong education and retraining in order to prepare people for changes that will occur in jobs; and (3) labor regulations and laws to protect those in both regular and non-regular employment.

Expanding and Strengthening the Safety Net

The social safety nets in all these countries need to be able to provide portable social protections that are not tied to employment with an employer, and basic coverage to all. Such a safety net must be constructed *outside* of the labor market, as part of the social welfare system, to protect people from the negative consequences of uncertainty and insecurity that will certainly continue to characterize the world economy for the foreseeable future.

Social insurance is a common solution to problems of high risk (Mandel 1996; Hacker 2006). Since people are very loss-averse, uncertainty has a big impact on their lives and so insurance is needed to socialize risks, help people cope with losses, and compensate people for bad events. Such insurance is also needed to give people the self-confidence to take entrepreneurial risks. Most countries provide three types of social insurance: portable health insurance benefits; retirement benefits; and unemployment benefits and other wage supports (including assistance with acquiring new skills and relocation) to help people navigate the transitions between jobs and employers. The US lags in many of these basic protections compared to the other countries discussed here, as we have seen in chapter 2.

A major challenge for all the countries is to extend these basic forms of social insurance to all workers, regardless of their employment status. This is particularly problematic in countries with high levels of labor market dualism, especially Germany and Japan, in which systems of social insurance rely largely on contributions by employers and workers and are more commonly available to regular workers in core firms than those in the periphery and nonstandard workers.

There has been increased attention to welfare in several Asian states since the financial crises of 1997–8, which can be seen as an attempt to maintain order and regulate labor, much like Bismarck's introduction of welfare policies in Germany in the late nineteenth century. Governments have recognized that there is a need to provide workers with greater protections due to the pressures on employers to be more flexible. Thus, Kwon (2007: 3) asserts that Bismarck's interest in social welfare was "to facilitate industrialization . . . and at the same time to undermine support for the socialist movement." Kwon (2007: 4) then notes that welfare regimes in Japan and other advanced East Asian countries "conceived as instrumental to economic and political objectives . . . are clearly in line with the Bismarckian concept."

The kinds of political pressures generated by various forms of activism and democratization that I discussed earlier have led to an expansion of social spending and a deepening of welfare programs in Japan and East Asia, particularly in healthcare.[1] Indeed, Haggard (2005: 46) notes that many of the countries of East Asia "are no longer the minimal welfare states that earlier literature had suggested. To the contrary, in several policy areas, most notably healthcare, these middle-income countries have leapfrogged more liberal welfare systems. . . [including] the United States." For example, the increases in state social expenditures in Japan have been significant (OECD 2013), reflecting pressures for some of the previously narrow welfare programs to be expanded and for some new programs to be introduced, especially following the 1997–8 financial crisis. Once in place, these programs are often difficult to wind back and became institutionalized as a more-or-less permanent and expanded social safety net in some countries (see also Huber and Stephens 2001).

A prominent idea for enhancing the safety net is that of a universal (or unconditional) basic income (UBI). The idea behind this policy is the provision of a universal, unconditional, regular, government-funded basic income that would supplant the current assortment of means-tested, conditional welfare state benefits that characterizes many industrial countries. This is not a new idea, as those at both ends of the political spectrum have previously suggested it for many years. The principle behind it is to provide everyone who is a legal resident of a country with regular, unconditional payments that would provide a basic level of economic security, but not so high as to discourage people from participating in paid work to supplement their incomes to achieve a higher standard of living.

The UBI is controversial and objections to it range from cultural concerns on the right over people "free riding" and not making contributions to society[2] to fears among Social Democrats that it would eventually undermine public provision of healthcare, child-care, and other social services. Guy Standing has been prominent in promoting the notion of a UBI and has long played a key role in the Basic Income Earth Network, which advocates for basic income policies in a score of countries. Standing proposes funding the basic income from, among other things, taxes on financial transactions and financial assets. But it is debatable whether a UBI is economically feasible: much of the debate about this centers on assumptions as to the nature of the incentives associated with a UBI (e.g., whether they would encourage people to work or remain unemployed), as well as the level of incomes provided.

Proposals to institute a UBI have thus far had mixed success. In a public referendum in Switzerland in June 2016, only 23 percent of voters were in favor (*BBC News* 2016). But there seems to be increasing interest in the idea of a UBI. Finland, for example, has launched an experiment involving some 2,000 randomly selected unemployed people who will be given unconditional grants of about $580 a month for two years, in place of other social benefits. They will receive these grants regardless of whether they work during the period. In the US, Y Combinator, a Silicon Valley startup incubator, is conducting a pilot project in Oakland, California, in which 100 families will receive unconditional grants of $1,000–2,000 a month. UBI experiments in India have reported outcomes such as better financial integration, health, and education, less debt, an increase in labor hours worked, and the greater economic independence of women (UNICEF 2014). And a recent study by the Roosevelt Institute in the US estimated that giving each American adult $12,000 would grow the US economy by roughly $2.5 trillion over eight years (Nikiforos, Steinbaum, and Zezza 2017).

Much of the motivation behind the growing attention to a UBI in the rich democracies is driven by the concern that technological innovations and changes in work arrangements will result in a paucity of full-time jobs (Goodman 2016). If it becomes clear that there will not be enough jobs for everyone, then a UBI might receive support from both the right and left. In that event, a looming question is the form a UBI would take: whether it would be tied to work (as is the Earned Income Tax Credit in the US), which is a bit limiting, or the kind of foundational grant advocated by the UBI's most ardent supporters.

Education and Skill Acquisition

A second essential feature of a new social and political contract is the need for greater access to education at all life stages to help people obtain the skills needed to compete successfully in the new world of work and to manage labor market transitions from one job to the next. The macrostructural forces of globalization and technology that underlie the transformation of employment relations have placed a greater premium on workers having the skills needed to participate in the new economy, and reinforced growing gaps between high-skilled and low-skilled jobs and workers. Mid-level skilled jobs, once the backbone of the middle class in industrial countries, are increasingly being routinized as employers have used technology to replace people by machines whenever possible (Ford 2015), driving a growing polarization between high- and low-skilled jobs. The increasing importance of education as a differentiating factor within the labor force is consistent with this greater emphasis on skills.

Early Education and Childcare   Early childhood education is vital for providing the foundational skills and abilities that are crucial for the acquisition of additional skills later in life. The importance of early childhood education was demonstrated dramatically by a recent study led by James Heckman that followed children from birth until age 35, and found that high-quality care during the earliest years enabled both mothers and children born into disadvantage to be more engaged in the workforce, have higher skills, and be more active participants in society (Garcia et al. 2016). Additional advantages of an emphasis on early childhood education are that it provides jobs (mainly for women) and frees people (again mainly women) to work, or to work more hours a week.

Continuing Education and Managing Labor Market Transitions   Workers need to find ways to remain employable in fast-changing economic environments in which skills become rapidly obsolete. Unlike workers of the 1950s and 1960s, workers now are more likely to need to engage in lifelong learning and to return to school again and again to retool their skills as they shift careers.

General, portable skills that can be used in a variety of settings have become especially important in the new economy due to the rapidity of technological change, while firm-specific knowledge and skills have arguably become less valuable. As I discussed in chapter 2, country models of skill formation differ in the degree to which they emphasize general skills that are transferable across employers, as opposed to those who focus on firm- or industry-specific skills that are useful primarily in particular firms and industries. Here, the kinds of strong credentialism promoted by the German vocational system can hamper the flexibility of workers to move from one occupation to another; while workers might well have the skills to do these jobs, they may lack the needed credentials, making leaving the occupation one has trained for much riskier (see Protsch and Solga 2016).

Active labor market policies are important for helping workers manage transitions from unemployment to employment. As I have shown earlier, these policies have important effects on reducing job and economic insecurity, as well as enhancing subjective well-being. Denmark's active labor market policies illustrate the effectiveness of providing additional job-related training and placement services to those who have lost their jobs, so as to facilitate their re-entry into the workforce.

Updating Labor and Employment Laws and Regulations

The SER was the basis of most labor laws and labor market regulations that were enacted in industrial nations in the middle of the twentieth century. The assumption of a male breadwinner who worked full-time, full-year in a standard employment relation coupled with a female homemaker was also the model for many welfare systems in the postwar period, such as in Germany, Japan, Spain, and the LMEs. The rise of non-regular and precarious work has led to pressure on governments to update these laws and re-regulate labor markets and social welfare protection systems so as to extend protections to those who do not have standard employment relations.

Various labor market regulatory reforms are needed. Regulatory gaps must be closed to assure equality of treatment of people in different kinds of employment relations. Moreover, employment misclassification is currently a big issue in these countries – especially in the LMEs – as employers seek to classify employees as independent contractors to avoid making contributions to health insurance and pension plans that they are obligated to provide to employees, as well as to avoid liability for the accidents and other actions incurred while these workers are in their employ. In addition, laws governing collective bargaining must be strengthened and adapted to the changing nature of employment relations, to provide unions with the ability to organize non-regular workers.

Japan, for example, has sought to extend protections to non-regular workers: It has adopted a new individual labor tribunal system for resolving the rights disputes that have increased since the early 1990s due to the rise in non-regular workers. This new system operates outside of the workplace and traditional Japanese enterprise unions (see Araki 2013). The question remains as to how effective these efforts have been, however. Policies have sometimes reflected the kind of path dependence discussed earlier: In Japan, for example, policies (such as the *paato* law of 2008) that prohibit discriminatory treatment of non-regular workers (such as part-timers) only apply to workers who display ideals of company citizenship, are as committed to firms as are regular workers, and perform similar work (see Imai 2015). This reinforces the social investment logic of the East Asian welfare system (and, increasingly, of other welfare systems as well) of basing social protections on making contributions to business success and economic growth.

Flexicurity

The idea of flexicurity offers a general way of conceptualizing the needed risk structures by involving both employers and workers in a cooperative effort (European Commission 2007). Flexicurity is an appealing concept in that it offers a narrative about how employers and labor markets can have greater flexibility and workers can still be protected from the insecurity created by employers' search for such flexibility. A key design feature of flexicurity is that it takes different forms in different settings and can be adapted to the characteristics of different countries. Various countries have adopted – or are in the process of adopting – some version of flexicurity systems. These principles need to be tailored to their national contexts, however.

The system of Danish flexicurity offers an exemplar of best practices for such a new political and social contract. This model combines generous social welfare benefits (such as relatively high unemployment income replacement rates, paid for by high taxes rather than employers), with reduced unemployment scar effects and high active labor market policies, associated with low employment protections for regular workers but higher levels of employment security (Wilthagen and Tros 2004; Westergaard-Nielsen 2008).[3]

In the Netherlands, employers achieve flexibility through atypical, flexible types of jobs, such as part-time work, but workers in these nonstandard jobs have similar social security rights to those on standard employment contracts. The Dutch system emphasizes employment (as opposed to job) security and social security especially for weaker groups (such as those on nonstandard employment relations) inside and outside the labor market.

By contrast, the Japanese system of flexicurity has traditionally provided employers with high levels of internal, functional flexibility, as broad job classifications permitted them to move workers among tasks and departments in response to organizational needs. High levels of employment protection in the past facilitated such flexibility for workers, especially males below a certain age in large organizations, who enjoyed "lifetime" employment. Once unemployed, however, Japanese workers had relatively low levels of social protection due to a weak social welfare system. Hence, the company-level system of flexicurity in Japan differs from the societal-level systems in countries such as Denmark or the Netherlands, which are linked to these countries' active labor market policies. The challenge for Japan is to provide more active labor market policies to help workers transition among jobs and to provide greater social security protection for non-regular workers to compensate for their low level of employment protection (Chatani 2008).

The flexicurity strategy raises several challenges, however. One is whether it is realistic and acceptable to deregulate job protection laws (to increase flexibility) in countries when social security systems are not yet fully developed. Expanding social protections is also likely to require increased taxes at a time when nations are competing by *lowering* taxes. Moreover, flexicurity strategies require social dialogue, which is especially difficult in countries where capital–labor tensions are high, such as in Japan. Moreover, the idea of flexicurity has often been used as a means of reducing employment protections, dubbed "flex-insecurity" (e.g., Murphy 2017). The criticism is that while policies underlying this idea may increase flexibility for employers, it does little to reduce insecurity experienced by workers.

It is also the case that the economic crisis of 2008–9 has threatened aspects of the Danish flexicurity system. Thus, the pressures produced by growing unemployment and declining employment have led to reductions in the unemployment replacement benefit period (from four to two years), a drop in the level of unemployment benefits, and hence an increase in the numbers of people who have exhausted their unemployment benefits. This has also resulted in an escalation in the number of Danes who are worried about losing their jobs and finding new ones. Nevertheless, recent reforms making unemployment benefits more generous, and providing unemployment benefits to less skilled workers while they are pursuing formal education to enhance their skills, have eased concerns somewhat about the crisis in the flexicurity system.

While the Danish example of flexicurity and embedded liberalization is attractive in many ways, we need to keep in mind that while we can borrow insights from successful examples, labor market and social welfare systems are complex configurations that adhere together and cannot be simply added piecemeal. Davis (2016) argues that it is difficult to transfer institutions or practices from one country to another because they require a supporting ecosystem to be effective. For example, the strong German vocational system requires robust labor–management cooperation, private ownership, relations with banks that do not require dependence on the market for financing, coordination among businesses, and a social welfare system that provides workers with the security to invest in their long-term skill development. So each country will need to adopt ways of addressing precarious work that are consistent with its own history and institutions.

Hence, to tackle the new risk structures, countries are likely to adopt institutions that are not fundamentally different from the previous ones, since "'postindustrial' transformation is institutionally path-dependent" (Esping-Andersen 1999: 4). Despite an expansion of healthcare benefits, for example, there are still gaps in health insurance coverage in many countries for regular as opposed to non-regular workers, since the former are more apt to participate in contributory social insurance schemes that provide higher quality healthcare.

Implementing a New Social and Political Accord

Differences among countries in their labor market and social welfare protection institutions, along with the balance of power among the state, business, and labor that underlie these institutions, have molded the public dialogues and collective responses to precarious work in these rich democracies. The challenges of implementing the elements of the political and social contract I have outlined are vast, given the aging of the population and other demographic changes, and the speed of technological innovation and the other forces behind the growth of precarious work discussed in chapter 1 (Levinson 2016). Moreover, despite the slowdown in economic growth under neoliberal political-economic policies, it remains to be seen whether alternative models such as flexicurity can lead to economic growth along with greater security.

Realizing a new political and social contract thus requires coordinated efforts among several key actors, such as the state, capital, and labor, supplemented by the activities of civic society groups such as NGOs. It is important here to identify the institutional conditions that offer the promise of re-instituting social protections and improving employment conditions. To what degree is this dependent on the strategies of unions and other forms of worker power? How can we best create more encompassing institutions at the national and sub-national levels to ameliorate the negative consequences of precarious work and the growth of dualism?

Addressing the consequences of precarious employment systems requires global as well as national solutions. The downward pressure on wages exerted by the existence of unregulated low-wage production in some countries highlights the need for local solutions to be linked to transnational unions, international labor standards, and other global efforts (Silver 2003; Webster, Lambert, and Bezuidenhout 2008). Greater international cooperation is needed among governments and multinational agencies for setting standards to avoid a "race to the bottom." Professional organizations and unions must also cooperate more fully across borders, rather than being divided by them. Implementing the new social contract is necessarily incomplete without a fuller elaboration of a global agenda to supplement national and local initiatives.

My discussion in the remainder of this chapter is more modest, as I focus on national solutions to the concerns raised by precarious work. National solutions are a first, but necessary, step toward wider implementation, as countries are where governments, business, and workers interact and social welfare protection and labor market policies are enacted.

The State

The politics of modern capitalism are focused on the struggle between the pressures toward free markets and those toward social protections. The state and markets are intimately related political and social constructs ("the market society") as economic activity is embedded within social and political contexts (Polanyi 1957 [1944]). Polanyi felt that explanations of economic concerns that were based solely on the market or state were overly simplistic, as was the idea that the struggle is a zero-sum game with winners and losers. Marx assumed that the state serves to promote capital accumulation as well as political legitimacy and is the vehicle by which the ruling class obtains and maintains its control of society. Hence, Marx believed that capital and labor are engaged in a struggle for control of the state.

The government is essential as a vehicle of the good society and as an instrument to be used in the public interest. Looking after the common good is the job of the government; the state exists not only to preserve freedom, but also to protect the weak and the vulnerable and to manage uncertainty and collectivize risk. The government also needs to provide economic security, a strong infrastructure for job creation, and opportunities for people to succeed, as well as to foster social integration and solidarity through work.

All the six countries have liberalized their social welfare protection and labor market institutions to adapt to the demands of a rapidly changing international economy, as I discussed in chapter 2. These liberalizations have contributed to the recent rise of precarious work and many of its negative consequences. To address the outcomes of these politically driven policies, the government needs to create or solidify a safety net that provides *all* its citizens with basic protections such as health insurance and retirement benefits. Workers should have access to a safety net and basic social protections whether or not they work for a minimum number of hours for an employer who is willing and able to pay for various benefits. The government is also responsible for setting labor market standards for wages, hours, and working conditions, as well as for establishing policies for the treatment of non-regular workers. In addition, it plays a big role in providing support for education in the primary, secondary, and tertiary systems as well as through vocational training.

Another key role of the state is to broker and sustain coalitions between employers and workers, using both positive and negative incentives. To address issues of precarious work, for example, the state needs to balance the interests of employers and workers through policies such as flexicurity that are based on a logic of social investment, whereby the state enacts policies that actively promote growth (as opposed to passively providing for social welfare) while also giving protections to the vulnerable parts of the population who are not otherwise included in the safety net (Thelen 2014: 198–9).

The state needs sufficient capacity to broker deals between employers and workers, however. In Denmark, for example, the state has had relatively strong capacity in labor relations in recent years: Since the Danish Confederation of Labor Unions and the Danish employers' federation repeatedly failed to come to an agreement that would control wage costs, the state was forced to intervene and impose a settlement. The German state has less power to negotiate deals between employers and workers as coordination among employers depends a lot on voluntarism (Thelen 2014: 23–4). Similarly, the state is relatively weak in deregulated liberal economies such as the United States and the United Kingdom, where business reduced the power of government as well as labor beginning with the Reagan and Thatcher revolutions in the 1980s. Unfortunately, trust in government is low across the rich democracies, especially in countries such as Japan and the US. Thus, there is little reason for optimism that the government will initiate policies to address the negative consequences of precarious work.

The role of the state needs to be theorized more completely, however, to be able to assess the likelihood of it pursuing progressive policies such as the implementation of the new political and social contract. Recall that it is the actions of the state that are largely responsible for the recent rise of precarious work through deregulation of labor markets and policies that have reconfigured or reduced social welfare protections. And to date, the state has often acted in contradictory ways in addressing the consequences of precarious work: In the United Kingdom, for example, while the state steps in to support low-wage workers via conditional benefits and strong sanctions, it also pushes people into low-wage work via workfare and in-work benefits. It is thus imperative that we address questions such as whether the state can support capitalism and neoliberalism and still act in a benevolent way toward workers and their families by enacting a new political and social contract.

Employers

Employers are key actors in any efforts to create high-quality employment relationships. Precarious work puts a greater burden on the social welfare and social reproduction systems at a time when states cannot afford to provide the needed social protections, given the aging of populations and reductions in states' power through the imposition of austerity and tax cuts. So we need employers to step in and take up part of the burden. Doing so would also be beneficial to employers, who have much to gain from implementing the social and political contract discussed earlier in this chapter, as this would help to create workforce stability and facilitate social reproduction.

The ability of employers to act collectively to achieve such goals is limited. Mizruchi (2013) shows that after launching an offensive against labor in the US in the post-1975 period, employers began to feel that organized collective action within the business community was no longer needed and the corporate elite started to fragment, with its cohesion beginning to disappear by the late 1980s. He argues further that one possible factor for the recent retrenchment of welfare policies among Western European nations is, as in the US, a disintegration of their corporate elites (Mizruchi 2013: 274–5), such as the declining network density among businesses in Germany. A fragmented employer class is often problematic; as Thelen notes: "from labor's perspective, the only thing worse than a strong and organized business class is a weak and disorganized one" (Thelen 2014: 203).

A new social contract requires models of corporate governance that include social factors (a "stakeholder" model) as opposed to the prevailing economic logic in some of the rich democracies that focuses mainly on shareholder value in designing and rewarding jobs. The norms that govern business behavior are shaped heavily by societal and community values, and by pressures from consumers and workers. Hence, the impetus to provide solutions to concerns raised by precarious work must come from workers themselves, who need sufficient collective power to enforce their claims against employers and the state.

Worker Power

Worker power is necessary to motivate governments and businesses to act on a new political and social contract and to provide workers with protections from precarious work. Employers and states are more likely to adopt protective labor market and welfare institutions if they are prodded into doing this by strong progressive unions or other forms of worker power. A high degree of solidarity among organized labor is essential for establishing labor market and social protection institutions that address issues of precarious work. Such solidarity is threatened as unions now tend to be more numerous and often stronger in public as opposed to private sectors, which often pits union members' bargaining demands against concerns by taxpayers over the expansion of government budgets. The power resources available to labor depend on national institutions as well as on sectoral and workplace structures, along with the structure of the labor movement. Workplace arrangements depend on local unions' capacity to strategically complement institutional and organizational power resources so as to protect the working conditions of different groups of workers, thereby responding to distinctive management strategies of externalization and outsourcing as well as of internal segmentation.

In Europe, unions have often been traditionally strong, which has tended to crowd out other forms of organization, though Germany, with its strong occupational associations and vocational system of skill formation, is a notable exception. Unions were also key actors behind efforts to institute welfare systems. Thus, it is not surprising that the establishment of active labor market policies and flexicurity is especially prominent in Denmark, which has a history of strong unions and extensive collective bargaining coverage. In Southern Europe, such as in Spain, unions have historically sought to protect job security, unlike in Northern Europe, which has more of a flexicurity emphasis. The decline of unions in LMEs such as the US represents a major challenge for changing the balance of power from capital to labor. Unfortunately, market reforms and the growth of precarious work have decreased the power of workers to push for progressive social policies, and unions have become less influential in all six countries.

The growth of the service sector presents new challenges for labor. Establishments tend to be smaller and more spatially dispersed (both within and between countries) than the manufacturing plants of yesteryear, making it more difficult to organize workers. Service industries also change the standard management–labor story by bringing into focus the autonomous consumer, enhancing the potential for consumer–worker coalitions, often in local communities, to influence work and its consequences. By contrast, in the manufacturing economy, there was often a split between consumers and producers, and the key social relations were primarily defined as those among workers (i.e., forms of labor solidarity) or between labor and management (i.e., class conflict). The historically strong manufacturing cross-class coalitions in countries such as Germany, for example, are less able to exercise political leadership in the emerging service economy. Here, the Ver.di (Vereinte Dienstleistungsgewerkschaft or United Services Trade Union), which represents 2 million members, as compared to the dominant metalworkers' union IG Metall with 2.27 million members, is an increasingly important actor shaping employment relations, though it does not yet have the institutional power of IG Metall. More generally, as welfare states are increasingly privatizing personal services – among the lowest paid and the least secure types of work – service workers are mobilizing at local, national, and transnational levels; their associational modalities range from joining traditional unions to organizing worker cooperatives.

A key question is what *kinds* of worker power are best suited to meeting the challenges created by the transformations in work in the twenty-first century. To be successful, unions must adapt to and match up with changes in the structure of the economy and the organization of work. Therefore, the next generation of worker organizations needs to experiment with a variety of new forms to meet the challenges posed by the changing nature of employment relations (e.g., Clawson 2003). The specific mechanisms by which the collective actions of workers are exercised are less important than the ability of workers to exert countervailing power to influence government policy makers and businesses. The introduction of works-council-type legislation and the encouragement of cooperative efforts between workers and employers (and not just in the private sector) illustrate alternative strategies for enhancing worker power. This underscores the centrality of labor laws in promoting worker power. Canada, for example, did not experience the drastic union decline that the US did because of its more favorable labor laws. This is, however, a chicken-and-egg situation: How do you change laws without pressure from unions; and how do you get more pressure from unions without updating labor laws?

Unions are not the only vehicles for employee voice, however. An alternative form of worker power is associational power in these precarious, post-bureaucratic times that is exercised via occupations. Workers can organize around sets of skills and, with the support of the state, establish licensing and certification practices that lead to social closure mechanisms that enable them to control the supply of persons to the occupation and thereby to maximize their rewards and advantages. This is reflected in the vocational-based employment system in Germany, which enabled some occupational groups to obtain social protections through social insurance arrangements that were not available to others. This is also a common model among professional occupations, which use mandates from the state to establish control over skills. Like the transition from craft to industrial unionism in the past, there may well be a post-bureaucratic, guild-like unionism emerging in place of the bureaucratic, corporate-era unions.

Unions have also collaborated with other kinds of social movements to better position themselves to help these groups – and all workers – to enhance the quality of jobs (Clawson 2003). Such non-union worker strategies are especially important in countries such as the United States, where unions are especially weak due to reasons ranging from employer opposition to the Taft–Hartley law that restricts what unions can do. Non-union social movements include: worker advocacy groups (such as immigrant alliances, women's groups, racial and ethnic movements, community organizations, and social movements concerned with global justice or with providing more support for working families); worker centers (i.e., non-profit organizations that organize immigrant and low-wage workers) (see Fine 2006); and living wage campaigns. The recent success of the Service Employees International Union-sponsored "Fight for 15" movement to increase wages for fast food workers in the US illustrates the potential of efforts by people who are most vulnerable in the labor market to enhance their market power.

A major challenge for unions and other forms of worker power is to reconcile the interests of regular and non-regular workers. Unions in some of these countries (such as Germany, Japan, and the United States) have begun to organize non-regular workers. Given that collective bargaining strives for standardization, it is often difficult for unions to represent the interests of both groups simultaneously, however. This also raises the question of the extent to which the precariat is really a cross-class movement that represents those in nonstandard jobs as well as those in regular jobs in core sectors of the economy whose employment relations are becoming increasingly insecure. There are various issues that the two groups have in common, though, such as their mutual interests in maintaining principles of meritocracy, gender equality, and sustainable work–family relations, as well as economic goals of human capital development and social protections.

Civil Society

With the state-built and state-serviced defences against existential tremors progressively dismantled, and the arrangements for collective self-defence, such as trade unions and other instruments for collective bargaining, increasingly disempowered by the pressures of market competition that erode the solidarities of the weak – it is now left to individuals to seek, find and practise individual solutions to socially produced troubles, and to try all that through individual, solitary actions, while being equipped with tools and resources that are blatantly inadequate to the task. (Zygmunt Bauman 2007: 14)

Civil society organizations, including NGOs, are another vehicle for achieving change in labor market policies and welfare policies. Precarious workers are difficult to organize in some countries where company unionism prevails and in countries with a large informal sector. Precarious workers are also less likely to have access to formal and institutional politics, and so new forms of organization are more likely to be successful. Some of these movements and organizations overlap with union–social movements, such as NGOs organized around particular identities (such as gender, race, and immigration). Two particularly important demographic groups to organize are millennials (i.e., those born in the early 1980s to the late 1990s) and members of "Generation Z" (i.e., those born in the mid-1990s to mid-2000s). These young people offer hope for social movements, as they have been in the forefront of Occupy movements and are likely to be especially frustrated by the lack of opportunity to develop career narratives and life plans.

Summary and Conclusions

This chapter has discussed some of the main political and policy challenges posed by the recent rise of precarious work. All six countries have gone through periods of liberalizing their labor markets in response to developments in the global economy as well as technological changes that have altered the standard employment relations of the mid-twentieth century. As I have documented in previous chapters, this has resulted in a rise in precarious work, with its attendant insecurity and negative impacts on individuals' well-being.

Workers have sought to counter this rise in precarious work and its consequences through both social movements and actions by organized unions and political parties. These efforts have sought to address the new risks for workers and their families that are raised by the changes in employment relations and reconfiguration of social welfare protection systems. A new political and social accord that has the potential to collectivize the risks associated with precarious work has three basic elements: strengthening and expanding the safety net; providing access to both early and continuing education and training;

and updating labor and employment laws and regulations. The notion of flexicurity offers a model for the contours of such a political and social contract.

I finally discussed some of the political dynamics among the state, employers, and workers that are involved in the implementation of this new political and social contract. These dynamics have focused both on policies designed to help people adapt to precarious work through social insurance and skill acquisition, and on ways of reducing precarious work (what Hacker [2011] has called "pre-distribution") such as those related to changes in labor and employment laws.

There are various criteria by which one can assess the success of the policies and strategies of addressing precarious work. These include: slowing the expansion of precarious work; re-regulating precarious work by bringing work back in-house as opposed to being outsourced; improving conditions for precarious groups; organizing collectively for better working conditions; and maintaining/ improving working conditions for both core and peripheral workers. Some of these goals are more realistic than others. There are likely to be continued pressures on governments and businesses to remain flexible in a rapidly changing world economy with a heavy emphasis on services rather than manufacturing, for example, which suggests there will continue to be needs for temporary and part-time work. Thus, balancing the needs of business for flexibility with those of labor for greater security, especially those who are most vulnerable to precarious work, will remain important challenges and goals for public policy.

Conclusion

The transformation of employment relations represented by the recent rise of precarious work presents important challenges for individuals, families, businesses, and societies. The growth of insecure, uncertain jobs that have few social and legal protections departs from the more stable, standard employment relations of the three decades after World War II. We must be careful not to glamorize this earlier era of relative stability and high economic growth, as it was much more beneficial to white men than to women and minorities. Nevertheless, we are now in a different era, a new age of precarious work that represents a fundamental shift toward widespread uncertainty and insecurity. People who have the skills and resources to successfully navigate rapidly changing labor markets have welcomed this new era as an opportunity to achieve their market potential by moving between organizations. Others, perhaps the majority, are more economically insecure, often have difficulties in forming families, and experience low well-being.

I began the book by posing several puzzles: Why has there been a rise in precarious work in rich democracies, with their high standards of living and privileged positions in the world economy? And how and why do people experience precarious work differently in countries with dissimilar institutions and cultures? I sought to answer these puzzles by studying six countries – Denmark, Germany, Japan, Spain, the United Kingdom, and the United States – that differ in their social welfare protection and labor market institutions and hence illustrate the variation among rich democratic countries in the incidence and consequences of precarious work.

There are common trends among the six countries. All have had to respond to similar political and economic forces unleashed by an increasingly global and technology-driven economy, as well as constraints on state budgets produced by slowdowns in economic growth coupled with the aging of labor forces and more diversity in what labor forces need to be productive. In all six countries, there has been a decline in long-term employment among prime-age men. And all countries have liberalized their labor markets and restructured their social welfare protections to cope with the growth of precarious work. While precarious work is universal, it is cross-nationally variable, as the nature of this liberalization has differed, depending on a country's political situation and the strength of workers, from a general deregulation of markets and social protection institutions (the UK and US), to dualism (Germany, Japan, Spain), to a more collective sharing of risk (Denmark).

I have sought in this book to provide an overview of how differences among these countries in their social welfare protection and labor market institutions and policies affect both precarious work and its consequences for well-being. Some countries have been able to address the concerns raised by precarious work more successfully than others by re-establishing and expanding social safety nets, managing labor market transitions more effectively, and implementing social and economic reforms that are targeted at the needs and choices of increasingly diverse labor forces. The empirical evidence I have presented is intended to lend credence to my arguments, not to provide the kind of detailed analysis found in many of the sources I have cited. This evidence suggests the following five conclusions.

First, the generosity of public spending on social welfare benefits and active labor market policies is relatively high in Denmark, Germany, and Spain, and relatively low in Japan, the UK, and US. Differences in these policies can be traced to variations in the power of workers and political dynamics in these countries.

Second, labor market institutions affect the incidence of precarious work. Temporary work is less common in the LMEs of the United Kingdom and United States and relatively high in Spain. These differences are associated with the low levels of employment protections in the UK and US and the high employment protections in Spain. Moreover, the degree to which temporary jobs can be considered precarious depends on the nature of the social protection systems in a country, such as whether temporary workers are afforded the same kinds of welfare entitlements as those who are working in regular jobs.

Third, generous social welfare benefits are linked to lower economic insecurity, which is lowest in Denmark and Germany and highest in the LMEs of the UK and US. The latter countries differ, however, in the social wage due to the greater availability of economic and social supports in the UK that help people to mitigate various types of life course risks.

Fourth, young persons have difficulty gaining a solid foothold in the labor market especially in Spain, with its high levels of employment protection that relegates young workers to temporary jobs. Trouble establishing families is especially pronounced for young males in Japan, with its rigid markers of the transition to adulthood.

Fifth, the generosity of social welfare protections, along with high levels of active labor market policies, is associated with greater subjective well-being in a country.

In sum, then, the evidence presented in previous chapters underscores the importance of country differences in social welfare protection and labor market institutions in shaping how precarious work affects individuals and their families. And cultural factors such as the nature of the gendered division of labor have important impacts on family formation.

Nevertheless, while institutional and cultural factors may modify the basic thrust toward the rise of precarious work, the underlying political, economic, and social trends responsible for precarious work are intimately linked to the dominance of neoliberalism, which "has become a machine that moves of its own accord. It is the accepted logic of our time" (Schram 2015: 173–4). The desirability of market-oriented solutions to economic, political, and social problems has become an article of faith accepted by governments and businesses alike, who regard the current situation as the "new normal" in a new era of capitalism characterized by a global, technologically driven economy.

Across the political spectrum, leaders yearn nostalgically for years past, such as the three decades after World War II, with its high levels of economic growth and equality. Those on the left harken back to the social protections of the New Deal and Keynesian welfare states, while those on the right pine for the periods of high growth in the early part of the neoliberal era. There is no return to the past, however, as the conditions that made that era possible have now disappeared; we must find new ways to adapt to the changing nature of work and employment relations.

I have outlined the elements of a new political and social contract that offers the potential for addressing some of the major challenges raised by the current rise of precarious work. The implementation of such a new social contract – with its expanded and portable safety net, better-managed labor market transitions, and appreciation for the needs of a diverse labor force – ultimately requires, of course, an associated political contract among the state, business, and labor that seeks to balance the needs for flexibility and security. Achieving such a new social-political contract constitutes one of the great challenges of the first part of the twenty-first century. The kinds of policies, neoliberal or otherwise, that will come to dominate in these countries are of course uncertain. I can imagine both dystopian and more utopian futures.

Plausible Futures

It is relatively easy to envision a variety of dystopian futures, as here one must only extrapolate from current trends. The confluence of forces related to globalization, technological change, the financialization of firms' organization of work, and weak worker power may well continue and perhaps extend trends such as: expansion of low-wage jobs; outsourcing and subcontracting of the production of goods and services to lower-wage firms; growing polarization between good and bad jobs and increasing inequality; expansion of digital platforms creating short-term and poorly protected jobs (the "Uberization" of the economy); and so on. Moreover, the implications of the automation of jobs are unclear and many fear that it will reduce drastically the need for workers.

It is more difficult to imagine utopian possibilities, given the priorities of current political and economic debates in these countries. Necessary conditions for any optimism require strengthening and expanding social welfare protections and providing active labor market policies to facilitate job mobility. But more comprehensive and long-term solutions require more basic changes.

One optimistic scenario is Beck's (2000) notion of an emerging "post-full-employment society" or "multi-activity work society" that defines work as something beyond market work, an idea which is similar to Standing's (2011) vision of work as going beyond paid labor. My focus in this book was on market work, but the idea of work is broader than that and includes many activities that produce non-economic value as well. Beck envisions a multi-activity society wherein people are able to shift their actions over the course of their lives among formal employment (albeit perhaps working fewer hours), parental labor, and civil labor (i.e., labor in the arts, culture, and politics, which helps the general welfare). The latter activity could be rewarded with "civic money" that is not a handout from the state or community but a return for engaging in these activities. Each person would control her or his own time-capital that she or he could allocate to different activities over time. Beck advocates that paid work and civil labor should complement each other and calls for greater equality of housework and outside care work with artistic, cultural, and political civic labor in the voluntary sector, which he believes will help create a gender-neutral division of labor.

Vosko's (2010) vision is similar to Beck's. She recognizes the low chances that there will ever be a return to the standard employment relations that characterized the post-World War II period and thus suggests possible alternatives that include: a new gender contract that places greater value on caregiving; and a "beyond employment" approach (see also Supiot 2001) that decouples social protection from labor force status and adjusts types of work to diverse stages in the life cycle.

If we are to formally define work as something beyond paid market work, it is essential to decouple economic security from market work. One increasingly popular option, a UBI, is very controversial for economic, political, and cultural reasons, and it is unclear how this would work on a large scale. A major objection to the UBI is that it redistributes value that has already been created in society. Its viability depends largely on how much economic growth there will be in the future, since as economic growth slows, the contests over the distribution of a shrinking economic pie become very fraught. Some influential economists feel the period of growth is over (e.g., Gordon 2016), while others are more optimistic. We really do not know what is possible with respect to economic growth, however, since austerity policies in the rich democracies have stalled social investments in innovation, research, and development in recent years. It is critical to ramp up such investments if we hope to stimulate economic growth.

We may also need to reconceptualize not only the meaning of work but also our understanding of what constitutes value in a society. The commonly used economic indicator of value, the GDP, is increasingly unable to capture developments in the service economy such as widening inequality and the rise of precarious work. Alternative, "beyond GDP" indicators of well-being are needed that shift the emphasis from measuring economic production to assessing the multiple dimensions of people's well-being, as argued forcefully by Stiglitz, Sen, and Fitoussi (2009).

The recent rise of precarious work represents a dramatic change in relations among workers, employers, and governments from the standard employment relations that characterized rich democracies in the three decades after World War II. Upheavals such as those created by precarious work generate anxiety and uncertainty as people, organizations, and governments scramble to adapt to a new reality. The challenge is to respond to these changes with policies and practices that promote *both* economic growth *and* workers' well-being.

Notes

Chapter 1   The New Age of Precarious Work

1 Another aspect of precarious work that is important but not emphasized here is work that exposes workers to *dangerous and hazardous* conditions and does not provide much protection against accidents and illness at work.

2 While work in rich democracies has become more precarious in the past three decades than in the first three decades after World War II, such work is much less insecure and unstable than it is in developing and less industrial societies, especially for those who work in the informal sector of the economy. About 90 percent of workers in India, for example, are in the informal sector and this is the case in much of the developing world. Moreover, large numbers of people in these countries live on less than $2 a day, thus experiencing a very precarious existence. Furthermore, life in general is generally less precarious now than in the past, as we have conquered many diseases and life expectancies have generally increased. We must keep in mind the relatively privileged situation of workers in these relatively rich democracies when considering the nature and consequences of precarious work in this book.

3 Polanyi's notion of the double movement suggests that history is not linear but rather characterized by cycles and structural changes from one condition to another. These swings occurred at different points in time in different countries. Scholars differ as to the length of these cycles, with some social scientists maintaining that they should be equated with relatively short business cycles and others proposing that they reflect "long" waves. My view is closer to the latter in that the most recent growth of precarious work reflects a more fundamental structural change than simply shifts in the business cycle.

4 Neoliberalism can be measured by indicators such as the degree of "economic freedom" or market openness as to: ease of starting a business,

lack of tariffs on trade, fiscal policy, size of government, monetary policy, openness to foreign investment, openness of banking and financial systems, private property rights, political corruption, and labor regulations. However, not all countries adopted neoliberal ideologies at the same time or in the same way. Mijs, Bakhtiari, and Lamont (2016) show that there is considerable local, national, and regional variation in neoliberal ideologies and policies in Europe, for example.

5 In social democratic nations, the implementation of progressive social policies (such as parental leave or childcare) – rather than the desire to cut costs – also led to the need for more temporary workers to fill in for regular workers while on leave.

6 In some cases, as in Germany, women did not necessarily prefer working part-time, but ended up in part-time work because of the difficulty of combining work and family given problems in securing acceptable childcare, for example.

7 The power of VoC is its wide-ranging implications for diverse phenomena including corporate governance, wage setting, skill formation systems, and the quality of work, among others (Gallie 2007b). Consequently, it is not surprising that the dualist VoC framework rapidly spawned a large literature and soon "achieved a level of theoretical sophistication, explanatory scope, and predictive ambition that has rapidly made it close to hegemonic in the field" (Howell 2003: 103).

8 There are almost no limits on the degree to which geographical units can be disaggregated (see Amable 2003); studying differences in employment systems and social protections across nation-states is still a reasonable focus.

Chapter 2   Social Welfare Protection and Labor Market Institutions

1 As I mentioned in chapter 1, precarious work also characterizes less industrial countries and is represented by the vast informal economies associated with them. However, precarious work in less developed countries is beyond the scope of this book.

2 VoC is an example of a dualist theory that contrasts the market model emphasized by neoclassical economics (i.e., the LMEs) with one or a small number of other models (see Crouch 2005 for a review).

3 Esping-Andersen (1990) recognized that these three welfare regimes were not pure types. Denmark, for example, has features of both liberal and conservative regimes. Moreover, the typologies do not always differentiate countries adequately in their welfare services. For example, the LME of the United Kingdom has a much more socialized healthcare system than Christian Democratic Germany.

4 Source of 2017 population figures for the six countries: http://www.worldometers.info/world-population/population-by-country.

5 German companies sought greater flexibility through mechanisms such

as outsourcing production to Eastern Europe. Other sources of stress to the German system included: growth of the service sector (which was less amenable than manufacturing companies to co-determination [see next note] and hence associated with lower wages); decline in union power; shift of collective bargaining from national to local levels; greater international competition, especially from Eastern Europe (which made it easy to outsource); decline in corporatist ideas; and immigration from the European Union.

6 Co-determination involves workers' representatives on half the seats of firms' supervisory boards; a separate management board or *Vorstand* runs the day-to-day business (a dual-board system of corporate governance was created by an 1884 law, and became mandatory in the twentieth century) (*The Economist* 2012). Germany's corporatist *Mitbestimmung* model gives workers a say in management.

7 The paucity of childcare has been attributed to reactions to the Nazi regime but also to developments in the GDR, where "raising children was considered a matter purely for the family, and any state intervention was rejected as an unwarranted intrusion into the private sphere" (Bosch and Kalina 2008: 85).

8 Of the six countries I am discussing, the three (at least as of this writing) that belong to the European Union have been affected by EU supra-national apparatuses that have encouraged or even required austerity, if only because budget caps place limits on Keynesian policies as well as via technocratic interpretations of debt. The fiscal limits that the EU has established for members of the eurozone ensure a politics of austerity that have tended to encourage member countries to prioritize economic over social dimensions of work: as the EU social policy agenda (labor protection, welfare benefits, social insurance, etc.) is weakly developed, it tends to be supplanted by the fiscal and monetary policy objectives of budget consolidation and austerity economics (Daly 2012).

9 The OECD defines social expenditure as the "provision by public (and private) institutions of benefits to, and financial contributions targeted at, households and individuals in order to provide support during circumstances which adversely affect their welfare, provided that the provision of the benefits and financial contributions constitutes neither a direct payment for a particular good or service nor an individual contract or transfer" (OECD 2007: 724–5). Esping-Andersen (1990) based his welfare state typology on social expenditures related to: unemployment benefits, sickness benefits, healthcare, and pensions. Other types of welfare benefits include: publicly funded social services (such as healthcare, education, cultural institutions such as libraries, recreational facilities such as parks); social work and personal social services (child and elder care, social work); and economic governance (large-scale government controls such as labor market institutions, training programs, industrial policies, minimum wage laws) (Garland 2016: 46–52).

10 Huber and Stephens (2001) point out that despite austerity pressures, political differences in the 1980s narrowed and partisan politics mattered less, since conservatives were reluctant to cut programs and liberals couldn't raise taxes due to economic difficulty. Hence, there were only relatively modest reductions in welfare benefits. There were larger cuts – driven by ideological factors rather than unemployment – in the UK (in healthcare, sick and disability pay, and UI) and somewhat less so in the US (mainly in social assistance programs) (e.g., Kenworthy 2014).

11 While there is a great deal of interest in adopting the German dual vocational and educational system in other countries, the bases of that system in historical and cultural forces make such transferability difficult. See Euler (2013) for a discussion of the issues involved in exporting the German system of dual vocational training to other countries.

12 By contrast, France typifies a form of professionalism where the state plays a major role in constructing the professional system, often via a system of exams for entry into professional schools. In both cases, careers unfold within and are focused on an occupation, not a firm or industry.

13 The rigid labor rules and costly regulation during the 2000s hindered the growth of companies (Spain ranks forty-fourth on the World Bank's ease of doing business index, between Puerto Rico and Rwanda) (see Sills 2012).

14 Employment protections are both individual and collective (see Bosch and Kalina 2008: 78–80). These vary by size of firms; there are considerable differences depending on company size, seniority, and the economic situation of the company (there are exceptions for hardship).

Chapter 3 Nonstandard Employment Relations

1 Precarious work is a broader concept than precarious employment, as there are self-employed persons (such as independent contractors) whose work is still insecure, uncertain, and risky, and who lack social and legal protections. Nevertheless, I focus here mainly on precarious forms of *employment*, since most persons in these rich democracies work for others.

2 Figure 3.2 represents the estimated percentage difference between temporary and permanent workers in the probability of having received training paid for or organized by the employer in the year preceding the survey, obtained by controlling for literacy and numeracy scores and including dummy variables for gender, nativity status, nine age classifications, nine occupational groups, nine tenure categories, and five size categories (http://dx.doi.org/10.1787/empl_outlook-2014-graph60-en).

3 These are: Austria, Belgium, Finland, France, Germany, Ireland, Italy, Luxembourg, the Netherlands, Portugal, Spain, Greece, Slovenia, Cyprus, Malta, Slovakia, Estonia, and Latvia.

4 Legislation in different countries varies in what is defined as part-time work, but with the notable exception of Japan (where part-time work

refs to a status, not hours worked), the threshold for part-time work is usually set at 30–5 hours per week. Comparative analyses by the ILO (2016), for example, use the 35-hour threshold.

Chapter 4 Job Insecurity

1 Employer tenure is measured by the actual length of time a person is employed by the organization. This can in principle be measured from administrative personnel records. However, it is more commonly measured by asking workers to report on the length of time they have worked for an employer. As is the case with many such questions, there may be some bias in workers' reports due to faulty recall or other reasons.

2 Anderson and Pontusson (2007) distinguish job loss from job insecurity, defining the latter as reflecting people's interpretations of environmental signals.

3 The chapters in Bermeo and Pontusson (2012) underscore the importance of institutional factors by providing evidence that government policies affect the unemployment rate as well as subjective job and employment insecurity.

4 In figure 4.3 as well as the other graphs that are based on data from the ESSs, the results presented control for individual differences within countries in age, gender, disability status, marital status, education, and the size of the firm.

5 We first estimated multi-level models in which data on individuals are nested within countries, and information on countries is nested within the two data points before and after the economic crisis. This enabled us to assess the extent to which variation in individual-level measures of job insecurity is due to differences between countries as opposed to variability within countries. We also assessed differences in the effects of country-level variables on individual outcomes in 2004 and 2010 by means of interaction effects.

6 The effects of having a temporary contract on perceived insecurity did not differ in 2004 compared to 2010, so I pooled the data for the two periods to simplify the presentation.

7 Gash and Inanc (2013) found that permanent female part-timers in the different parts of Europe had either the same job insecurity as permanent male full-timers (as in the UK), or less, and there was no evidence that their relative position deteriorated with the crisis. This is further evidence that how insecure part-time work is perceived to be (as well as how secure it is objectively) depends on institutional context.

Chapter 5 Economic Insecurity

1 Earnings and wages refer to the economic rewards associated with jobs, while income includes both job- and non-job-related economic rewards

(such as welfare payments and economic returns on investments).

2 Brady, Fullerton, and Cross (2010) measure working poverty (or "in-work" poverty) as households with less than 50 percent of the median household income *and* at least one household member who is employed.

3 Lars Osberg, in a personal communication, explained that Japan was not included in these computations because it was not part of the Luxembourg Income Study data set that was originally used to construct the measures of poverty incidence and poverty gap for single-parent female and elderly households; these were needed for the sub-indices of security in the event of widowhood and old age (using the one half median equivalent income criterion for international comparability).

4 As with the figures from the ESSs presented in the previous chapter, the results presented here control for individual differences within countries in age, gender, disability status, marital status, education, and the size of the firm.

5 Economic insecurity is measured in the same way as in figure 5.3. See note 5, chapter 4, for details on the estimation of this model.

Chapter 6   Transition to Adulthood and Family Formation

1 This date is 1999 for Denmark and Spain, 2000 for the UK, 2005 for Germany, and 1985 for Japan and the US.

2 While there is no international standard for defining NEETs, the ILO, Eurostat, and other organizations have defined it as "the percentage of the population of a given age group and sex who is not employed and not involved in further education or training" (ILO 2012a: 1).

3 The differences between the youth unemployment rates presented in figure 6.1 and those in figure 6.2 reflect differences in the denominators used to calculate them: The denominators of the rates in figure 6.1 are the number of youth who are in the labor force (i.e., employed and unemployed), while those in figure 6.2 are the total population aged 15–24. The latter percentage will always be smaller than the former (see Eurostat 2015).

Chapter 7   Subjective Well-Being

1 Economic insecurity has been raised as a possible explanation for the alarming increase in mortality among middle-aged white non-Hispanic men and women in the United States between 1999 and 2013, as observed by Case and Deaton (2015). This highlights the likelihood that aspects of precarious work negatively impact physical health. However, these authors did not observe this increase in mortality for the other rich countries they studied.

2 This question is asked in the following way: "Please imagine a ladder with steps numbered from zero at the bottom to 10 at the top. The top

of the ladder represents the best possible life for you and the bottom of the ladder represents the worst possible life for you. On which step of the ladder would you say you personally feel you stand at this time?"

3 Validity denotes the degree to which a question measures the concept it is intended to measure. Thus, a question about happiness or life satisfaction is valid to the extent that people's responses truly reflect their feelings about how happy or satisfied with their lives they really are. Reliability refers to whether people respond to a question similarly when asked repeatedly. Hence, people who say that they are satisfied with their lives at one point in time are apt to give a similar response when asked again (and again). An internal consistency reliability coefficient (such as Chronbach's alpha) refers to the chances that a person responding in one way to one item will also respond similarly to another item; hence, the two items can be assumed to be measuring the same construct (in this case, life satisfaction).

4 Social scientists' theories about differences in a person's subjective well-being can be grouped into those emphasizing mechanisms internal to individuals – in their genetic make-up, personalities, and psychological characteristics – and those that focus on external events and conditions, such as position in the stratification system, social relations with family and friends, job and working conditions, environmental characteristics (e.g., cold, heat, pollution, noise), features of the political economy (such as the nature of governance structures in a society and its labor market and welfare institutions), along with circumstances and experiences associated with one's age, race, or gender. The latter include relatively immutable attributes – such as gender, age, and race or ethnicity – as well as achieved characteristics such as income, education, social relationships, and intentional activities. These psychological and socioeconomic explanations are not competing, however, but are rather complementary.

5 I pool the results for 2004 and 2010 since there are no significant differences between these years for Germany, Spain, and the UK. For Denmark, the effects shown are found in 2010 and not 2004 (results not shown).

6 I am of course not able to establish definitively with such cross-sectional data that perceptions of job and economic insecurity *cause* subjective well-being.

7 Subjective well-being is measured in the same way as in figures 7.2 and 7.3. See note 5, chapter 4, for details on the estimation of these models.

8 We assessed the impact of institutions by seeing how much of the differences in subjective well-being among countries are reduced when variables measuring the institutions are added to the model. Collective bargaining coverage rate and active labor market policies reduce the cross-country variation (i.e., explain country differences) by almost a third (from 13.6 percent to 8.6 percent and 9.5 percent respectively) and

social spending by a fifth (from 13.6 percent to 10.6 percent).

9 On the other hand, Burchell (2009), using data from the 2005 and 2006 European Working Conditions Surveys, found that measures associated with flexicurity (such as active labor market policies and unemployment benefits) did not reduce the impacts of perceived job insecurity on subjective reports of work-related health problems. While subjective well-being is presumed to be positively related to reported health issues, the correlation between these two is not perfect, which might account for the apparent discrepancies in these results.

10 The measure of life satisfaction in the WVS is: "All things considered, how satisfied are you with your life these days?" (coded 1–10).

Chapter 8 Politics and Policies of Precarious Work

1 By contrast, in the already developed countries of Western Europe, North America, and Australia and New Zealand, there has been a stagnation of state social expenditures, seeing an upward bump following the 2008 economic crisis, but generally staying about the same percentage of GDP through the 1990s and 2000s (OECD 2013).

2 The Earned Income Tax Credit, one of the few very successful anti-poverty measures in the United States, gained acceptance in large part because it was labeled as something that was "earned."

3 Among other benefits to flexicurity, it helps to create an environment that promotes entrepreneurial activity. For example, Peer Hull Kristensen (cited in Davis 2016: 125) found that every year 250,000 businesses fail in Denmark but 260,000 new ones are started, due to the ability of people to explore risky business ventures since they are not worried about losing health insurance and other employment benefits.

References

Adams, Zoe and Simon Deakin. 2014. "Institutional Solutions to Precariousness and Inequality in Labour Markets." *British Journal of Industrial Relations* 52: 779–809.

Aguilera, Ruth V. 2005. "Corporate Governance and Employment Relations: Spain in the Context of Western Europe." Pp. 197–225 in Howard Gospel and Andrew Pendleton (eds.), *Corporate Governance and Labour Management: An International Comparison*. Oxford, UK: Oxford University Press.

Alderman, Liz. 2017. "Feeling 'Pressure All the Time' on Europe's Treadmill of Temporary Work." *New York Times*, February 9, https://www.nytimes.com/2017/02/09/business/europe-jobs-economy-youth-unemployment-millenials.html

Allison, Anne. 2013. *Precarious Japan*. Durham, NC: Duke University Press.

Amable, Bruno. 2003. *The Diversity of Modern Capitalism*. Oxford, UK: Oxford University Press.

Anderson, Christopher J. and Jonas Pontusson. 2007. "Workers, Worries and Welfare States: Social Protection and Job Insecurity in 15 OECD Countries." *European Journal of Political Research* 46: 211–35.

Andersson, Fredrik, Harry J. Holzer, and Julia Lane. 2007. "Temporary Help Agencies and the Advancement Prospects of Low Earners." NBER Working Paper No. 13434. Cambridge, MA: National Bureau of Economic Research.

Appelbaum, Eileen, Gerhard Bosch, Jérôme Gautié, Geoff Mason, Ken Mayhew, Wiemer Salverda, John Schmitt, and Niels Westergaard-Nielsen. 2010. "Introduction and Overview." Pp. 1–32 in Jérôme Gautié and John Schmitt (eds.), *Low-Wage Work in the Wealthy World*. New York, NY: Russell Sage Foundation.

Araki, Takashi. 2013. "New Forms of Dispute Resolution: Japan's Labor Tribunal System." Pp. 174–93 in Katherine V. W. Stone and Harry

Arthurs (eds.), *Rethinking Workplace Regulation: Beyond the Standard Contract of Employment*. New York, NY: Russell Sage Foundation.

Arampatzi, Efstratia, Martijn J. Burger, and Ruut Veenhoven. 2015. "Financial Distress and Happiness of Employees During Times of Economic Crisis." *Applied Economics Letters* 22: 173–9.

Auer, Peter. 2006. "Protected Mobility for Employment and Decent Work: Labour Market Security in a Globalized World." *Journal of Industrial Relations* 48: 21–40.

Auer, Peter and Sandrine Cazes. 2000. "The Resilience of the Long-Term Employment Relationship: Evidence from the Industrialized Countries." *International Labour Review* 139: 379–408.

Auer, Peter and Sandrine Cazes (eds.). 2003. *Employment Stability in an Age of Flexibility*. Geneva, Switzerland: International Labour Organization.

Autor, David H. and Susan N. Houseman. 2010. "Do Temporary-Help Jobs Improve Labor Market Outcomes for Low-Skilled Workers? Evidence from 'Work First'." *American Economic Journal: Applied Economics* 2: 96–128.

Autor, David H., Lawrence F. Katz, and Melissa S. Kearney. 2006. "The Polarization of the U.S. Labor Market." *American Economic Review* 96: 189–94.

Ban Ki-moon. 2013. "Happiness: Towards a Holistic Approach to Development." *Sixty-Seventh Session Agenda Item 14*. New York, NY: United Nations, http://www.un.org/ga/search/view_doc.asp?symbol=A/67/697

Banyuls, Josep and Albert Recio. 2017. "Labour Segmentation and Precariousness in Spain: Theories and Evidence." Pp. 129–49 in Damian Grimshaw, Colette Fagan, Gail Hebson, and Isabel Tavora (eds.), *Making Work More Equal: A New Labour Market Segmentation Approach*. Manchester, UK: Manchester University Press.

Barbieri, Paolo. 2009. "Flexible Employment and Inequality in Europe." *European Sociological Review* 25: 621–8.

Barbieri, Paolo and Giorgio Cutuli. 2016. "Employment Protection Legislation, Labour Market Dualism, and Inequality in Europe." *European Sociological Review* 32: 501–16.

Bauman, Zygmunt. 2000. *Liquid Modernity*. Cambridge, UK: Polity.

Bauman, Zygmunt. 2007. *Liquid Times: Living in an Age of Uncertainty*. Cambridge, UK: Polity.

BBC News. 2016. "Switzerland's Voters Reject Basic Income Plan." June 5, http://www.bbc.com/news/world-europe-36454060

Beck, Ulrich. 1992. *Risk Society: Toward a New Modernity*. Thousand Oaks, CA: Sage.

Beck, Ulrich. 2000. *The Brave New World of Work* (trans. Patrick Camiller). Cambridge, UK: Polity.

Bell, Daniel. 1973. *The Coming of Post-Industrial Society: A Venture in Social Forecasting*. New York, NY: Basic Books.

Bermeo, Nancy and Jonas Pontusson (eds.). 2012. *Coping with Crisis:*

Government Reactions to the Great Recession. New York, NY: Russell Sage Foundation.

Beveridge, Sir William. 1942. *Beveridge Report*, http://www.sochealth.co.uk/national-health-service/public-health-and-wellbeing/beveridge-report

Blanchflower, David G. and Andrew J. Oswald. 2011. "International Happiness: A New View on the Measure of Performance." *Academy of Management Perspectives* 25: 6–22.

Blau, Francine D. and Lawrence M. Kahn. 2013. "Female Labor Supply: Why is the U.S. Falling Behind?" NBER Working Paper No. 18702. Cambridge, MA: National Bureau of Economic Research.

Böckerman, Petri. 2004. "Perception of Job Instability in Europe." *Social Indicators Research* 67: 283–314.

Boeri, Tito and Jan van Ours. 2008. *The Economics of Imperfect Labor Markets*. Princeton, NJ: Princeton University Press.

Bok, Sissela. 2010. *Exploring Happiness: From Aristotle to Brain Science*. New Haven, CT: Yale University Press.

Bonoli, Giuliano. 2005. "The Politics of the New Social Policies: Providing Coverage Against New Social Risks in Mature Welfare States." *Policy and Politics* 33: 431–49.

Bonoli, Giuliano. 2013. *The Origins of Active Social Policy: Labour Market and Childcare Policies in a Comparative Perspective*. Oxford, UK: Oxford University Press.

Bosch, Gerhard and Thorsten Kalina. 2008. "Low-Wage Work in Germany: An Overview." Pp. 19–112 in Gerhard Bosch and Claudia Weinkopf (eds.), *Low-Wage Work in Germany*. New York, NY: Russell Sage Foundation.

Bosch, Gerhard, Ken Mayhew, and Jérôme Gautié. 2010. "Industrial Relations, Legal Regulations, and Wage Setting." Pp. 91–146 in Jérôme Gautié and John Schmitt (eds.), *Low-Wage Work in the Wealthy World*. New York, NY: Russell Sage Foundation.

Bosch, Gerhard and Claudia Weinkopf (eds.). 2008. *Low-Wage Work in Germany*. New York, NY: Russell Sage Foundation.

Bourdieu, Pierre. 1998. "La précarité est aujourd'hui partout." Pp. 95–101 in *Acts of Resistance: Against the New Myths of Our Time* (trans. Richard Nice). Cambridge, UK: Polity. (Originally published as *Contre-feux*, Paris, France: Editions Liber-Raisons d'Agir.)

Brady, David. 2009. *Rich Democracies, Poor People: How Politics Explain Poverty*. New York, NY: Oxford University Press.

Brady, David and Thomas Biegert. 2018. "The Rise of Precarious Employment in Germany." Pp. 245–72 in Arne L. Kalleberg and Steven P. Vallas (eds.), *Precarious Work: Causes, Characteristics, and Consequences (Research in the Sociology of Work, Vol. 31)*. Bingley, UK: Emerald.

Brady, David, Andrew S. Fullerton, and Jennifer Moren Cross. 2010. "More Than Just Nickels and Dimes: A Cross-National Analysis of Working Poverty in Affluent Democracies." *Social Problems* 57: 559–85.

Braverman, Harry. 1974. *Labor and Monopoly Capital: The Degradation of Work in the Twentieth Century.* New York, NY: Monthly Review Press.

Breman, Jan and Marcel van der Linden. 2014. "Informalizing the Economy: The Return of the Social Question at a Global Level." *Development and Change* 45: 920–40.

Brinton, Mary C. 2011. *Lost in Transition: Youth, Work, and Instability in Postindustrial Japan.* New York, NY: Cambridge University Press.

Buchmann, Marlis C. and Irene Kreisi. 2011. "Transition to Adulthood in Europe." *Annual Review of Sociology* 37: 481–503.

Burchell, Brendan. 2009. "Flexicurity as a Moderator of the Relationship Between Job Insecurity and Psychological Well-Being." *Cambridge Journal of Regions, Economy and Society* 2: 365–78.

Burgard, Sarah A., Jennie E. Brand, and James S. House. 2009. "Perceived Job Insecurity and Worker Health in the United States." *Social Science and Medicine* 69: 777–85.

Butler, Judith. 2004. *Precarious Life: The Powers of Mourning and Violence.* New York, NY: Verso.

Butler, Judith. 2015. "Foreword." Pp. vii–xi in Isabell Lorey, *State of Insecurity: Government of the Precarious.* London, UK: Verso.

Cantril, Hadley. 1965. *The Pattern of Human Concerns.* New Brunswick, NJ: Rutgers University Press.

Cappelli, Peter. 2008. *Employment Relationships: New Models of White-Collar Work.* New York, NY: Cambridge University Press.

Carr, Ewan and Heejung Chung. 2014. "Employment Insecurity and Life Satisfaction: The Moderating Influence of Labour Market Policies Across Europe." *Journal of European Social Policy* 24: 383–99.

Casas-Cortés, Maribel. 2009. "A Genealogy of Precarity: A Toolbox for Rearticulating Fragmented Social Realities in and Out of the Workplace." *Rethinking Marxism* 26: 206–26.

Case, Anne and Angus Deaton. 2015. "Rising Morbidity and Mortality in Midlife Among White Non-Hispanic Americans in the 21st Century." *Proceedings of the National Academy of Sciences* 112: 15078–15083.

Cazes, Sandrine, Alexander Hijzen, and Anne Saint-Martin. 2015. "Measuring and Assessing Job Quality: The OECD Job Quality Framework." OECD Social, Employment and Migration Working Papers No. 174. Paris, France: OECD, http://dx.doi.org/10.1787/5jrp02kjw1mr-en

Chang, Ha-Joon. 2013. "There's a New Jobs Crisis – We Need to Focus on the Quality of Life at Work." *The Guardian*, December 22, https://www.the guardian.com/commentisfree/2013/dec/22/jobs-crisis-quality-of-life-at-work

Chatani, Kazutoshi. 2008. "From Corporate-Centred Security to Flexicurity in Japan." Employment Working Paper No. 17. Geneva: International Labour Office, Employment Sector.

Chung, Heejung and Wim van Oorschot. 2011. "Institutions versus Market Forces: Explaining the Employment Insecurity of European Individuals

During (the Beginning of) the Financial Crisis." *Journal of European Social Policy* 21: 287–301.

Clark, Andrew and Fabien Postel-Vinay. 2009. "Job Security and Job Protection." *Oxford Economic Papers* 61: 207–39.

Clawson, Dan. 2003. *The Next Upsurge: Labor and the New Social Movements*. Ithaca, NY: ILR Press.

Crouch, Colin. 2005. "Models of Capitalism." *New Political Economy* 10: 439–56.

Daily Mail. 2010. "Rise of the 'Bamboccioni' (Big Babies): Why More Young Italians Than Ever Before are Choosing to Live at Home." June 24, http://www.dailymail.co.uk/news/article-1289005/Rise-bamboccioni-big-babies--Why-young-Italians-choosing-live-home.html

Daly, Mary. 2012. "Paradigms in EU Social Policy: a Critical Account of Europe 2020." *Transfer* 18: 273–84.

Daly, Suzanne. 2013. "Danes Rethink a Welfare State Ample to a Fault." *New York Times*, April 21, http://www.nytimes.com/2013/04/21/world/europe/danes-rethink-a-welfare-state-ample-to-a-fault.html

Davis, Gerald F. 2016. *The Vanishing American Corporation: Navigating the Hazards of a New Economy*. Oakland, CA: Berrett-Koehler.

Deutsche Bank Research. 2007. "The Happy Variety of Capitalism." April 25, https://www.scribd.com/document/326082058/DBank-The-happy-variety-of-capitalism-pdf

Devine, Ethan. 2013. "The Slacker Trap." *The Atlantic*, May, https://www.theatlantic.com/magazine/archive/2013/05/the-slacker-trap/309285

De Witte, Hans. 1999. "Job Insecurity and Psychological Well-Being: Review of the Literature and Exploration of Some Unresolved Issues." *European Journal of Work and Organizational Psychology* 8: 155–77.

Deyo, Frederic C. 2012. *Reforming Asian Labor Systems: Economic Tensions and Worker Dissent*. Ithaca, NY: Cornell University Press.

Dickerson, Andrew and Francis Green. 2012. "Fears and Realisations of Employment Insecurity." *Labour Economics* 19: 198–210.

Diebold, Francis X., David Neumark, and Daniel Polsky. 1996. "Is Job Stability Declining in the U.S. Economy? Comment." *Industrial and Labor Relations Review* 49: 348–52.

Diebold, Francis X., David Neumark, and Daniel Polsky. 1997. "Job Stability in the United States." *Journal of Labor Economics* 15: 206–33.

Diener, Ed, Shigehiro Oishi, and Richard E. Lucas. 2003. "Personality, Culture and Subjective Well-Being: Emotional and Cognitive Evaluations of Life." *Annual Review of Psychology* 54: 403–25.

Diener, Ed, Eunkook M. Suh, Heidi Smith, and Liang Shao. 1995. "National Differences in Reported Subjective Well-Being: Why Do They Occur?" *Social Indicators Research* 34: 7–32.

Di Tella, Rafael and Robert J. MacCulloch. 2008. "Gross National Happiness as an Answer to the Easterlin Paradox?" *Journal of Development Economics* 86: 22–42.

Dixon, Jeffrey C., Andrew S. Fullerton, and Deanna L. Robertson. 2013. "Cross-National Differences in Workers' Perceived Job, Labour Market, and Employment Insecurity in Europe: Empirical Tests and Theoretical Extensions." *European Sociological Review* 29: 1053–67.

Doogan, Kevin. 2009. *New Capitalism? The Transformation of Work.* Cambridge, UK: Polity.

Eakin, Hugh. 2016. "Liberal, Harsh Denmark." *New York Review of Books,* March 10: 34–36.

Easterlin, Richard. 1995. "Will Raising the Incomes of All Increase the Happiness of All?" *Journal of Economic Behavior and Organization* 27: 35–47.

Edwards, Richard. 1979. *Contested Terrain: The Transformation of the Workplace in the Twentieth Century.* New York, NY: Basic Books.

Eichhorst, Werner and Paul Marx. 2011. "Reforming German Labour Market Institutions: A Dual Path to Flexibility." *Journal of European Social Policy* 21: 73–87.

Eichhorst, Werner, Núria Rodríguez-Planas, Ricarda Schmidl, and Klaus F. Zimmermann. 2015. "A Roadmap to Vocational Education and Training Systems in Industrialized Countries." *ILR Review* 68: 314–37.

Eichhorst, Werner and Verena Tobsch. 2013. "Has Atypical Work Become Typical in Germany? Country Case Study on Labour Market Segmentation." IZA Discussion Paper No. 7609. Bonn, Germany: IZA, http://ftp.iza.org/dp7609.pdf

Emmenegger, Patrick, Silja Häusermann, Bruno Palier, and Martin Seeleib-Kaiser (eds.). 2012. *The Age of Dualization: The Changing Face of Inequality in Deindustrializing Societies.* New York, NY: Oxford University Press.

Erlinghagen, Marcel. 2008. "Self-Perceived Job Insecurity and Social Context: A Multi-level Analysis of 17 European Countries." *European Sociological Review* 24: 183–97.

Esping-Andersen, Gøsta. 1990. *The Three Worlds of Welfare Capitalism.* Princeton, NJ: Princeton University Press.

Esping-Andersen, Gøsta. 1999. *Social Foundations of Postindustrial Economies.* Oxford, UK: Oxford University Press.

Estevez-Abe, Margarita, Torben Iversen, and David Soskice. 2001. "Social Protection and the Formation of Skills: A Reinterpretation of the Welfare State." Pp. 145–83 in Peter A. Hall and David Soskice (eds.), *Varieties of Capitalism: The Institutional Foundations of Comparative Advantage.* New York, NY: Oxford University Press.

Euler, Dieter. 2013. "Germany's Dual Vocational Training System: A Model for Other Countries?" Gütersloh, Germany: Bertelsmann Stiftung, http://www.bertelsmann-stiftung.de/fileadmin/files/BSt/Publikationen/GrauePublikationen/GP_Germanys_dual_vocational_training_system.pdf

European Commission. 2007. *Towards Common Principles of Flexicurity: More and Better Jobs through Flexibility and Security.* Brussels, Belgium: Directorate-General for Employment, Social Affairs and Equal

Opportunities, http://eur-lex.europa.eu/LexUriServ/LexUriServ.do?uri=COM:2007:0359:FIN:EN:PDF

European Commission. 2008. Directive on Temporary Agency Work (2008/104/EC), http://eur-lex.europa.eu/legal-content/EN/TXT/HTML/?uri=CELEX:32008L0104&from=EN

European Commission. 2016a. *Employment and Social Developments in Europe 2015*. Brussels, Belgium: Directorate-General for Employment, Social Affairs and Inclusion, http://ec.europa.eu/social/main.jsp?catId738&publd=7859

European Commission. 2016b. "Precarious Employment in Europe: Patterns, Trends and Policy Strategies." Brussels, Belgium: Employment and Social Affairs, http://www.europarl.europa.eu/RegData/etudes/BRIE/2016/587303/IPOL_BRI(2016)587303_EN.pdf

Eurostat. 2015. "Youth Unemployment: Statistics Explained," http://ec.europa.eu/eurostat/statistics-explained/index.php/Youth_unemployment

Fagan, Colette, Helen Norman, Mark Smith, and María González Menéndez. 2014. *In Search of Good Quality Part-time Employment*. Geneva: International Labour Office, http://www.ilo.org/travail/whatwedo/publications/WCMS_237781/lang--en/index.htm

Farber, Henry S. 2008. "Short(er) Shrift: The Decline in Worker–Firm Attachment in the United States." Pp. 10–37 in Katherine S. Newman (ed.), *Laid Off, Laid Low: Political and Economic Consequences of Employment Insecurity*. New York, NY: Columbia University Press.

Fernández-Macías, Enrique. 2012. "Job Polarization in Europe? Changes in the Employment Structure and Job Quality, 1995–2007." *Work and Occupations* 39: 157–82.

Fevre, Ralph. 2007. "Employment Security and Social Theory: The Power of Nightmares." *Work, Employment and Society* 21: 517–35.

Field, Simon, Viktória Kis, and Malgorzata Kuczera. 2012. "A Skills Beyond School Commentary on Spain." Paris, France: OECD Reviews of Vocational Education and Training, https://www.oecd.org/edu/skills-beyond-school/OECD%20Reviews%20of%20Vocational%20Education%20and%20Training%20-%20A%20Skills%20Beyond%20School%20Commentary%20on%20Spain.pdf

Fine, Janice. 2006. *Worker Centers: Organizing Communities at the Edge of the Dream*. Ithaca, NY: ILR Press.

Finer, Lawrence B. and Stanley K. Henshaw. 2006. "Disparities in Rates of Unintended Pregnancy in the United States, 1994 and 2001." *Perspectives in Sexual and Reproductive Health* 38: 90–6.

Fligstein, Neil and Haldor Byrkjeflot. 1996. "The Logic of Employment Systems." Pp. 11–35 in James Baron, David Grusky, and Donald Treiman (eds.), *Social Differentiation and Social Inequality*. Boulder, CO: Westview Press.

Ford, Martin. 2015. *Rise of the Robots: Technology and the Threat of a Jobless Future*. New York, NY: Basic Books.

Fraser, Steve. 2015. *The Age of Acquiescence: The Life and Death of American Resistance to Organized Wealth and Power*. New York, NY: Little, Brown.

Freeman, Richard B. 1995. "The Limits of Wage Flexibility for Curing Unemployment." *Oxford Review of Economic Policy* 11: 63–72.

Freeman, Richard B. 2007. "The Great Doubling: The Challenge of the New Global Labor Market." Pp. 55–65 in John Edwards, Marion Crain, and Arne L. Kalleberg (eds.), *Ending Poverty in America: How to Restore the American Dream*. New York, NY: New Press.

Friedman, Benjamin M. 2015. *The Moral Consequences of Economic Growth*. New York, NY: Knopf.

Gabriel, Sigmar. 2011. Spiegel Online: "Interview with German Opposition Leader: Commercial Banking Should Be Split From Investment Banking," http://www.spiegel.de/international/germany/interview-with-german-opposition-leader-commercial-banking-should-be-split-from-investment-banking-a-792223.html

Galbraith, John Kenneth. 1952. *American Capitalism: The Concept of Countervailing Power*. Boston, MA: Houghton Mifflin.

Gallie, Duncan. 2007a. "Production Regimes, Employment Regimes and the Quality of Work." Pp. 1–45 in Duncan Gallie (ed.), *Employment Regimes and the Quality of Work*. Oxford, UK: Oxford University Press.

Gallie, Duncan. 2007b. "Production Regimes and the Quality of Employment in Europe." *Annual Review of Sociology* 33: 85–104.

Garcia, Jorge Luis, James J. Heckman, Duncan Ermini Leaf, and María José Prados. 2016. "The Life-Cycle Benefits of an Influential Early Childhood Program." Working Group Paper 2016–35. University of Chicago, Human Capital and Economic Opportunity Global Working Group.

Garland, David. 2016. *The Welfare State: A Very Short Introduction*. Oxford, UK: Oxford University Press.

Gash, Vanessa and Hande Inanc. 2013. "Insecurity and the Peripheral Workforce." Pp. 142–68 in Duncan Gallie (ed.), *Economic Crisis, Quality of Work, and Social Integration: The European Experience*. Oxford, UK: Oxford University Press.

Gautié, Jérôme and John Schmitt (eds.). 2010. *Low-Wage Work in the Wealthy World*. New York, NY: Russell Sage Foundation.

Gautié, Jérôme, Niels Westergaard-Nielsen, and John Schmitt, with Ken Mayhew. 2010. "The Impact of Institutions on the Supply Side of the Low-Wage Labor Market." Pp. 147–82 in Jérôme Gautié and John Schmitt (eds.), *Low-Wage Work in the Wealthy World*. New York, NY: Russell Sage Foundation.

Giddens, Anthony. 1991. *Modernity and Self-Identity: Self and Society in the Late Modern Age*. Stanford, CA: Stanford University Press.

Golsch, Katrin. 2003. "Employment Flexibility in Spain and its Impact on Transitions to Adulthood." *Work, Employment and Society* 17: 691–718.

Goodman, Peter S. 2016. "Free Cash in Finland: Must be Jobless." *New*

York Times, December 17, https://www.nytimes.com/2016/12/17/business/economy/universal-basic-income-finland.html

Goos, Maarten, Alan Manning, and Anna Salomons. 2009. "Job Polarization in Europe." *American Economic Review: Papers and Proceedings* 99: 58–63.

Gordon, Robert J. 2016. *The Rise and Fall of American Growth: The U.S. Standard of Living since the Civil War*. Princeton, NJ: Princeton University Press.

Gottfried, Heidi. 2015. *The Reproductive Bargain: Deciphering the Enigma of Japanese Capitalism*. Leiden, Netherlands: Brill.

Graham, Carol. 2011. *The Pursuit of Happiness: An Economy of Well-Being*. Washington, DC: Brookings.

Grasso, Maria T. and Marco Giugni. 2016. "Protest Participation and Economic Crisis: The Conditioning Role of Political Opportunities." *European Journal of Political Research* 55: 663–80.

Green, Francis. 2006. *Demanding Work: The Paradox of Job Quality in the Affluent Economy*. Princeton, NJ: Princeton University Press.

Green, Francis. 2009. "Subjective Employment Insecurity Around the World." *Cambridge Journal of Regions, Economy and Society* 2: 343–63.

Greenhalgh, Leonard and Zehava Rosenblatt. 1984. "Job Insecurity: Towards Conceptual Clarity." *Academy of Management Review* 9: 438–48.

Greve, Bent. 2012. "The Impact of the Financial Crisis on Happiness in Affluent European Countries." *Journal of Comparative Social Welfare* 28: 183–93.

Grimshaw, Damian, Mat Johnson, Jill Rubery, and Arjan Keizer. 2016. *Reducing Precarious Work: Protective Gaps and the Role of Social Dialogue in Europe*. Manchester, UK: European Work and Employment Research Centre, University of Manchester, http://www.research.mbs.ac.uk/ewerc/Portals/0/Documents/Comparative-Report-Reducing-Precarious-Work-v2.pdf

Hacker, Jacob S. 2006. *The Great Risk Shift: The New Economic Insecurity and the Decline of the American Dream*. New York, NY: Oxford University Press.

Hacker, Jacob S. 2011. "The Institutional Foundations of Middle-Class Democracy." Presented at Progressive Governance Conference, Oslo, May 12–13, http://www.policy-network.net/pno_detail.aspx?ID=3998&title=The+institutional+foundations+of+middle-class+democracy

Hacker, Jacob S., Philipp Rehm, and Mark Schlesinger. 2010. "Standing on Shaky Ground: Americans' Experiences with Economic Insecurity." The Rockefeller Foundation and Yale University, http://www.economicsecurityindex.org/upload/media/ESI%20report%20final_12%2013.pdf

Haggard, Stephan. 2005. "Globalization, Democracy, and the Evolution of Social Contracts in East Asia." *Taiwan Journal of Democracy* 1: 21–47.

Hall, Peter A. and David Soskice (eds.). 2001. *Varieties of Capitalism: The Institutional Foundations of Comparative Advantage*. Oxford, UK: Oxford University Press.

Hamilton, Brady E., Joyce Martin, Michelle J. K. Osterman, and Sally C. Curtin. 2015. "Births: Preliminary Data for 2014." *National Vital Statistics Reports* 64: 1–18.

Hardt, Michael and Antonio Negri. 2000. *Empire.* Cambridge, MA: Harvard University Press.

Harvey, David. 2005. *A Brief History of Neoliberalism.* Oxford, UK: Oxford University Press.

Haynie, Devon. 2016. "Countries Where the Most Young Adults Live With Their Parents." *U.S. News and World Report,* October 5, https://www. usnews.com/news/best-countries/articles/2016-10-05/countries-where-the-most-young-adults-live-with-their-parents

Hemerijck, Anton. 2013. *Changing Welfare States.* Oxford, UK: Oxford University Press.

Hewison, Kevin. 2016. "Precarious Work." Pp. 428–43 in Stephen Edgell, Heidi Gottfried, and Edward Granter (eds.), *The Sage Handbook of the Sociology of Work and Employment.* Thousand Oaks, CA: Sage.

Hijzen, Alexander and Balint Menyhert. 2016. "Measuring Labour Market Security and Assessing its Implications for Individual Well-Being," OECD Social, Employment and Migration Working Papers No. 175. Paris, France: OECD,, http://dx.doi.org/10.1787/5jm58qvzd6s4-en

Hirschman, Albert O. 1970. *Exit, Voice, and Loyalty: Responses to Decline in Firms, Organizations, and States.* Cambridge, MA: Harvard University Press.

Holliday, Ian. 2000. "Productivist Welfare Capitalism: Social Policy in East Asia." *Political Studies* 48: 706–23.

Horning, Rob. 2012. "Precarity and Affective Resistance." *The New Inquiry,* February 14, https://thenewinquiry.com/blog/precarity-and-affec tive-resistance/

Houseman, Susan N. and Machiko Osawa. 1995. "Part-Time and Temporary Employment in Japan." *Monthly Labor Review* 118: 10–18.

Howard, Christopher. 2007. *The Welfare State Nobody Knows.* Princeton, NJ: Princeton University Press.

Howell, Chris. 2003. "Varieties of Capitalism: And Then There Was One?" *Comparative Politics* 36: 103–24.

Huber, Evelyne and John D. Stephens. 2001. *Development and Crisis of the Welfare State: Parties and Policies in Global Markets.* Chicago, IL: University of Chicago Press.

Huber, Evelyne and John D. Stephens. 2015. "Postindustrial Social Policy." Pp. 259–81 in Pablo Beramendi, Silja Häusermann, Herbert Kitschelt, and Hanspeter Kriesi (eds.), *The Politics of Advanced Capitalism.* New York, NY: Cambridge University Press.

ILO (International Labour Organization). 2004. *Economic Security for a Better World.* Geneva, Switzerland: ILO Press.

ILO (International Labour Organization). 2012a. "What Does NEETs Mean and Why is the Concept So Easily Misinterpreted?" Work4Youth Technical Brief No. 1. Geneva, Switzerland: International Labour Office, http://www.ilo.org/wcmsp5/groups/public/@dgreports/@dcomm/docu ments/publication/wcms_343153.pdf

ILO (International Labour Organization). 2012b. "Overview of Apprenticeship Systems and Issues." ILO contribution to the G20 Task Force on Employment. Geneva, Switzerland: International Labour Office, http:// www.ilo.org/wcmsp5/groups/public/@ed_emp/@ifp_skills/documents/ genericdocument/wcms_190188.pdf

ILO (International Labour Organization). 2015. *World Employment Social Outlook 2015*. Geneva, Switzerland: International Labour Office.

ILO (International Labour Organization). 2016. *Nonstandard Employment Around the World: Understanding Challenges, Shaping Prospects*. Geneva, Switzerland: International Labour Office.

Imai, Jun. 2011. *The Transformation of Japanese Employment Relations: Reform Without Labour*. Basingstoke, UK: Palgrave Macmillan.

Imai, Jun. 2015. "Policy Responses to the Precarity of Non-Regular Employment in Japan." Pp. 49–80 in Hsin-Huang Michael Hsiao, Arne L. Kalleberg, and Kevin Hewison (eds.), *Policy Responses to Precarious Work in Asia*. Taipei, Taiwan: Academia Sinica.

Inanc, Hande and Arne L. Kalleberg. 2016. "Institutions and Changing Employment Relations: Country Differences in Insecurity and Subjective Well-Being in Europe." Presented at Annual Meetings of the American Sociological Association, Seattle, WA.

Kalleberg, Arne L. 2000. "Nonstandard Employment Relations: Part-time, Temporary, and Contract Work." *Annual Review of Sociology* 26: 341–65.

Kalleberg, Arne L. 2009. "Precarious Work, Insecure Workers: Employment Relations in Transition." *American Sociological Review* 74: 1–22.

Kalleberg, Arne L. 2011. *Good Jobs, Bad Jobs: The Rise of Polarized and Precarious Employment Systems in the United States, 1970s to 2000s*. New York, NY: Russell Sage Foundation.

Kalleberg, Arne L. and Kevin Hewison. 2013. "Precarious Work and the Challenge for Asia." *American Behavioral Scientist* 57: 271–88.

Kalleberg, Arne L. and James R. Lincoln. 1988. "The Structure of Earnings Inequality in the U.S. and Japan." *American Journal of Sociology* 94 (Supplement on Organizations and Institutions): S121–S153.

Kalleberg, Arne L. and Peter V. Marsden. 2015. "Transformation of the Employment Relationship." In Robert Scott, Marlis Buchmann, and Stephen Kosslyn (eds.), *Emerging Trends in the Social and Behavioral Sciences*. Hoboken, NJ: John Wiley and Sons.

Kalleberg, Arne L. and Steven P. Vallas. 2018. "Probing Precarious Work: Theory, Research, and Politics." Pp. 1–30 in Arne L. Kalleberg and Steven P. Vallas (eds.). *Precarious Work: Causes, Characteristics, and Consequences. (Research in the Sociology of Organizations, Vol. 31)*. Bingley, UK: Emerald.

Katz, Lawrence F. and Alan B. Krueger. 2016. "The Rise and Nature of Alternative Work Arrangements in the United States, 1995–2015."

NBER Working Paper No. 22667. Cambridge, MA: National Bureau of Economic Research, http://www.nber.org/papers/w22667

Kenworthy, Lane. 2014. *Social Democratic America*. New York, NY: Oxford University Press.

Kerr, Clark, John T. Dunlop, Frederick H. Harbison, and Charles A. Myers. 1960. *Industrialism and Industrial Man*. Cambridge, MA: Harvard University Press.

Koike, Kazuo. 1983. "Internal Labor Markets: Workers in Large Firms." Pp. 29–62 in Taishiro Shirai (ed.), *Contemporary Industrial Relations in Japan*. Madison, WI: University of Wisconsin Press.

Kolberg, Jon Eivind (ed.). 1991. *The Welfare State as Employer*. New York, NY: M. E. Sharpe.

Korpi, Walter. 1983. *The Democratic Class Struggle*. London, UK: Routledge and Kegan Paul.

Korpi, Walter. 1985. "Developments in the Theory of Power and Exchange." *Sociological Theory* 3: 31–45.

Krippner, Greta R. 2005. "The Financialization of the American Economy." *SocioEconomic Review* 3: 173–208.

Kwon, Huck-Ju. 1997. "Beyond European Welfare Regimes: Comparative Perspectives on East Asian Welfare Systems." *Journal of Social Policy* 26: 467–84.

Kwon, Huck-Ju. 2007. "Transforming the Developmental Welfare States in East Asia." Working Paper No. 40 ST/ESA/2007/DWP/40. New York, NY: United Nations Department of Economic and Social Affairs.

Lash, Scott and John Urry. 1987. *The End of Organized Capitalism*. Cambridge, UK: Polity.

Layard, Richard. 2005. *Happiness: Lessons from a New Science*. New York, NY: Penguin.

Lee, Ching Kwan and Yelizavetta Kofman. 2012. "The Politics of Precarity: Views Beyond the United States." *Work and Occupations* 39: 388–408.

Levinson, Marc. 2016. *An Extraordinary Time: The End of the Postwar Boom and the Return of the Ordinary Economy*. New York, NY: Basic Books.

Lincoln, James R. and Arne L. Kalleberg. 1990. *Culture, Control, and Commitment: A Study of Work Organization and Work Attitudes in the United States and Japan*. New York, NY: Cambridge University Press. (New edition, with updated prologue, Percheron Press, Clinton Corners, NY, 2003.)

Lübke, Christiane and Marcel Erlinghagen. 2014. "Self-Perceived Job Insecurity Across Europe Over Time: Does Changing Context Matter?" *Journal of European Social Policy* 24: 319–36.

Lucio, Miguel Martínez, Sveinung Skule, Wilfried Kruse, and Vera Trappmann. 2007. "Regulating Skill Formation in Europe: German, Norwegian and Spanish Policies on Transferable Skills." *European Journal of Industrial Relations* 13: 323–40.

Lukes, Steven. 1977. *Essays in Social Theory*. New York, NY: Columbia University Press.

MacInnes, John. 2009. "Spain: Continuity and Change in Precarious Employment." Pp. 159–76 in Leah F. Vosko, Martha MacDonald, and Iain Campbell (eds.), *Gender and the Contours of Precarious Employment*. Abingdon, UK: Routledge.

MacLeod, Jay. 2009. *Ain't No Making It: Aspirations and Attainment in a Low-Income Neighborhood*, 3rd edition. Boulder, CO: Westview Press.

Mandel, Michael J. 1996. *The High Risk Society: Peril and Promise in the New Economy*. New York, NY: Times Business Books.

Mannheim, Karl. 1952 (1927). "The Problem of Generations." Pp. 276–322 in Paul Kecskemeti (ed. and trans.), *Essays on the Sociology of Knowledge*. London, UK: Routledge and Kegan Paul.

Manski, Charles F. and John D. Straub. 2000. "Worker Perceptions of Job Insecurity in the Mid-1990s: Evidence from the Survey of Economic Expectations." *Journal of Human Resources* 35: 447–79.

Marsden, David. 1999. *A Theory of Employment Systems: Micro-Foundations of Societal Diversity*. Oxford, UK: Oxford University Press.

Marks, Gary. 1989. *Unions in Politics: Britain, Germany, and the United States in the Nineteenth and Early Twentieth Centuries*. Princeton, NJ: Princeton University Press.

Mason, Geoff, Ken Mayhew, and Mathew Osborne. 2008. "Low-Paid Work in the United Kingdom: An Overview." Pp. 15–40 in Caroline Lloyd, Geoff Mason, and Ken Mayhew (eds.), *Low-Wage Work in the United Kingdom*. New York, NY: Russell Sage Foundation.

Mason, Geoff, Ken Mayhew, Mathew Osborne, and Philip Stevens. 2008. "Low Pay, Labor Market Institutions, and Job Quality in the United Kingdom." Pp. 14–95 in Caroline Lloyd, Geoff Mason, and Ken Mayhew (eds.), *Low-Wage Work in the United Kingdom*. New York, NY: Russell Sage Foundation.

Mason, Geoff and Wiemer Salverda. 2010. "Low Pay, Working Conditions, and Living Standards." Pp. 35–90 in Jérôme Gautié and John Schmitt (eds.), *Low-Wage Work in the Wealthy World*. New York, NY: Russell Sage Foundation.

McGovern, Patrick, Deborah Smeaton, and Stephen Hill. 2004. "Bad Jobs in Britain." *Work and Occupations* 31: 225–49.

McLanahan, Sara. 2004. "Diverging Destinies: How Children are Faring Under the Second Demographic Transition." *Demography* 41: 607–27.

Mijs, Jonathan J. B., Elyas Bakhtiari, and Michèle Lamont. 2016. "Neoliberalism and Symbolic Boundaries in Europe: Global Diffusion, Local Context, Regional Variation." *Socius: Sociological Research for a Dynamic World* 2: 1–8.

Mitropoulos, Angela. 2005. "Precari-Us?" EIPCP: European Institute for Progressive Cultural Policies, March, http://eipcp.net/transversal/0704/mitropoulos/en

Mizruchi, Mark S. 2013. *The Fracturing of the American Corporate Elite*. Cambridge, MA: Harvard University Press.

Mouw, Ted and Arne L. Kalleberg. 2010. "Occupations and the Structure of Wage Inequality in the United States, 1980s–2000s." *American Sociological Review* 75: 402–31.

Murphy, Mary P. 2017. "Irish Flex-Insecurity: The Post-Crisis Reality for Vulnerable Workers in Ireland." *Social Policy and Administration* 51: 308–27.

Nakamura, Keisuke and Michio Nitta. 2013. "Organizing Nonstandard Workers in Japan: Old Players and New Players." Pp. 253–70 in Katherine V. W. Stone and Harry Arthurs (eds.), *Rethinking Workplace Regulation: Beyond the Standard Contract of Employment*. New York, NY: Russell Sage Foundation.

National Institute of Population and Social Security Research. 2011. *Marriage Process and Fertility of Japanese Married Couples: Overview of the Results of the Fourteenth Japanese National Fertility Survey in 2010*. Tokyo: National Institute of Population and Social Security Research http://www.ipss.go.jp/ps-doukou/e/doukou14/Nfs14_Couples_Eng.pdf

Neilson, Brett and Ned Rossiter. 2005. "From Precarity to Precariousness and Back Again: Labour, Life and Unstable Networks." *The Fibreculture Journal* 5, http://five.fibreculturejournal.org/fcj-022-from-precarity-to-precariousness-and-back-again-labour-life-and-unstable-networks

Newman, Katherine S. 2012. *The Accordion Family: Boomerang Kids, Anxious Parents, and the Private Toll of Global Competition*. Boston, MA: Beacon Press.

Newman, Katherine S. and Hella Winston. 2016. *Reskilling America: Learning to Labor in the Twenty-First Century*. New York, NY: Metropolitan Books.

Nikiforos, Michalis, Marshall Steinbaum, and Gennaro Zezza. 2017. "Modeling the Macroeconomic Effects of a Universal Basic Income." New York, NY: Roosevelt Institute, August, http://rooseveltinstitute.org/modeling-macroeconomic-effects-ubi

Nozaki, Yuko and Katsumi Matsuura. 2010. "The Increasingly High Sex Ratio and Lifelong Unmarried Rate in Japan." *Journal of Population Research* 27: 43–57.

O'Connor, Sarah. 2015. "The New World of Work: Recovery Driven by Rise in Temp Jobs." *Financial Times*, August 4, https://www.ft.com/content/b2171222-31e4-11e5-8873-775ba7c2ea3d

OECD (Organisation for Economic Co-operation and Development). 1994. *The OECD Jobs Study*. Paris, France: OECD.

OECD (Organisation for Economic Co-operation and Development). 2007. "Glossary of Statistical Terms." Paris, France: https://stats.oecd.org/glossary/alpha.asp?Let=A

OECD (Organisation for Economic Co-operation and Development). 2011. "Employment in General Government and Public Corporations." *Government at a Glance 2011*. Paris, France: OECD, http://www.oecd-ilibrary.org/governance/government-at-a-glance-2011/employment-in-general-government-and-public-corporations_gov_glance-2011-27-en

OECD (Organisation for Economic Co-operation and Development). 2013. *OECD Guidelines on Measuring Subjective Well-being.* Paris, France: OECD, http://dx.doi.org/10.1787/9789264191655-en

OECD (Organisation for Economic Co-operation and Development). 2014a. *Education at a Glance 2014: OECD Indicators.* Paris, France: OECD, http://dx.doi.org/10.1787/eag-2014-en

OECD (Organisation for Economic Co-operation and Development). 2014b. *OECD Employment Outlook 2014.* Paris, France: OECD.

OECD (Organisation for Economic Co-operation and Development). 2015a. *In It Together: Why Less Inequality Benefits All.* Paris, France: OECD, http://www.oecd.org/social/in-it-together-why-less-inequality-benefits-all-9789264235120-en.htm

OECD (Organisation for Economic Co-operation and Development). 2015b. "Employment in the Public Sector." *Government at a Glance 2015.* Paris, France: OECD, http://dx.doi.org/10.1787/gov_glance-2015-22-en

OECD (Organisation for Economic Co-operation and Development). 2016. *OECD Better Life Index,* oecdbetterlifeindex.org

Ogburn, William F. 1950. *Social Change with Respect to Cultural and Original Nature.* New York, NY: Viking Press.

O'Reilly, Jacqueline, Werner Eichhorst, András Gábos, Kari Hadjivassiliou, David Lain, Janine Leschke, Seamus McGuinness, Lucia Mýtna Kureková, Tiziana Nazio, Renate Ortlieb, Helen Russell, and Paola Villa. 2015. "Five Characteristics of Youth Unemployment in Europe: Flexibility, Education, Migration, Family Legacies, and EU Policy." *Sage Open* 5: 1–19.

Osawa, Machiko, Myoung Jung Kim, and Jeff Kingston. 2013. "Precarious Work in Japan." *American Behavioral Scientist* 57: 309–34.

Osberg, Lars and Andrew Sharpe. 2014. "Measuring Economic Insecurity in Rich and Poor Nations." *Review of Income and Wealth,* Series 60, Supplement Issue, May, http://dx.doi.org/10.1111/roiw.12114

Parramore, Lynn Stuart. 2012. "Job Insecurity: It's the Disease of the 21st Century – And It's Killing Us." *AlterNet,* http://www.alternet.org/story/156104/job_insecurity%3A_it's_the_disease_of_the_21st_century_--_and_it's_killing_us

Peng, Ito. 2012. "Economic Dualization in Japan and South Korea." Pp. 226–49 in Patrick Emmenegger, Silja Häusermann, Bruno Palier, and Martin Seeleib-Kaiser (eds.), *The Age of Dualization: The Changing Face of Inequality in Deindustrializing Societies.* New York, NY: Oxford University Press.

Peterson, Abby, Mattias Wahlström, and Magnus Wennerhag. 2015. "European Anti-Austerity Protests: Beyond 'Old' and 'New' Social Movements." *Acta Sociologica* 58: 293–310.

Pichler, Florian. 2006. "Subjective Quality of Life Among Young Europeans: Feeling Happy But Who Knows Why?" *Social Indicators Research* 75: 419–44.

Pierson, Paul. 2000. "Three Worlds of Welfare State Research." *Comparative Political Studies* 33: 791–821.

Piore, Michael J. and Charles Sabel. 1984. *The Second Industrial Divide: Possibilities for Prosperity.* New York, NY: Basic Books.

Piotrowski, Martin, Arne L. Kalleberg, and Ronald R. Rindfuss. 2015. "Contingent Work Rising: Implications for the Timing of Marriage in Japan." *Journal of Marriage and the Family* 77: 1039–56.

Piven, Francis Fox and Richard A. Cloward. 1979. *Poor People's Movements: Why They Succeed, How They Fail.* New York, NY: Vintage Books.

Polanyi, Karl. 1957 (1944). *The Great Transformation: The Political and Economic Origins of Our Time.* New York, NY: Beacon Press. (Originally published New York, NY: Farrar and Rinehart.)

Prasad, Monica. 2016. "American Exceptionalism and the Welfare State: The Revisionist Literature." *Annual Review of Political Science* 19: 187–203.

Protsch, Paula and Heike Solga. 2016. "The Social Stratification of the German VET System." *Journal of Education and Work* 29: 637–61.

Pugh, Allison. 2015. *The Tumbleweed Society: Working and Caring in an Age of Insecurity.* New York, NY: Oxford University Press.

Quaranta, Mario. 2016. "Protesting in 'Hard Times': Evidence from a Comparative Analysis of Europe, 2000–2014." *Current Sociology* 64: 736–56.

Radcliff, Benjamin. 2013. *The Political Economy of Human Happiness: How Voters' Choices Determine the Quality of Life.* New York, NY: Cambridge University Press.

Rampell, Catherine. 2017. "Uncertainty is Sweeping the Globe: That's Very Bad for Business." *Washington Post,* February 6, https://www.washingtonpost.com/opinions/uncertainty-is-sweeping-the-globe-thats-very-bad-for-business/2017/02/06/707516ea-ecb2-11e6-b4ff-ac2cf509efe5_story.html?utm_term=.c030be783e34

Raymo, James M. and So-Jung Lim. 2011. "A New Look at Married Women's Labor Force Transitions in Japan." *Social Science Research* 40: 460–72.

Rich, Motoko. 2011. "Economic Insecurity." *New York Times,* November 22, https://economix.blogs.nytimes.com/2011/11/22/economic-insecurity

Rodgers, Gerry. 1989. "Precarious Work in Europe: The State of the Debate." Pp. 1–16 in Gerry Rodgers and Janine Rodgers (eds.), *Precarious Jobs in Labour Market Regulation.* Geneva, Switzerland: International Institute for Labour Studies, International Labour Organization.

Rodgers, Gerry, Charles Gore, and José B. Figueiredo (eds.). 1995. *Social Exclusion: Rhetoric, Reality, Response*s. Geneva, Switzerland: International Institute for Labour Studies, International Labour Organization.

Saad, Lydia. 2013. "U.S. Workers Still Haven't Shaken the Job Worries of 2009," http://www.gallup.com/poll/164222/workers-haven-shaken-job-worries-2009.aspx

Sabel, Charles F. 1982. *Work and Politics: The Division of Labor in Industry.* New York, NY: Cambridge University Press.

Scherer, Stefani. 2009. "The Social Consequences of Insecure Jobs." *Social Indicators Research* 93: 527–47.

Schmitt, John. 2012. "Low-Wage Lessons." Washington, DC: Center for Economic and Policy Research, http://cepr.net/publications/reports/low-wage-lessons

Schram, Sanford F. 2013. "Occupy Precarity." *Theory and Event* 16, http://muse.jhu.edu/journals/theory_and_event

Schram, Sanford F. 2015. *The Return of Ordinary Capitalism: Neoliberalism, Precarity, Occupy.* New York, NY: Oxford University Press.

Schröder, Martin. 2009. "Integrating Welfare and Production Typologies: How Refinements of the Varieties of Capitalism Approach Call for a Combination of Welfare Typologies." *Journal of Social Policy* 38: 19–43.

Sennett, Richard. 2000. *The Corrosion of Character: The Personal Consequences of Work in the New Capitalism.* New York, NY: W. W. Norton.

Shanahan, Michael J. 2000. "Pathways to Adulthood in Changing Societies: Variability and Mechanisms in Life Course Perspective." *Annual Review of Sociology* 26: 667–92.

Shavit, Yossi and Walter Müller. 2000. "Vocational Secondary Education." *European Societies* 2: 29–50.

Shin, Kwang-Yeong. 2013. "Economic Crisis, Neoliberal Reforms, and the Rise of Precarious Work in South Korea." *American Behavioral Scientist* 57: 335–53.

Shirai, Taishiro. 1983. "A Theory of Enterprise Unionism." Pp. 117–44 in Taishiro Shirai (ed.), *Contemporary Industrial Relations in Japan.* Madison, WI: University of Wisconsin Press.

Sills, Ben. 2012. "Spain's Lost Generation Looks Abroad." *Bloomberg Businessweek*, March 29, https://www.bloomberg.com/news/articles/2012-03-29/spains-lost-generation-looks-abroad

Silva, Jennifer. 2013. *Coming Up Short: Working-Class Adulthood in an Age of Uncertainty.* New York, NY: Oxford University Press.

Silver, Beverly J. 2003. *Forces of Labor: Workers' Movements and Globalization since 1870.* Cambridge, UK: Cambridge University Press.

Sjöberg, Ola. 2010. "Social Insurance as a Collective Resource: Unemployment Benefits, Job Insecurity and Subjective Well-Being in a Comparative Perspective." *Social Forces* 88: 1281–1304.

Skocpol, Theda and Vanessa Williamson. 2011. *The Tea Party and the Remaking of Republican Conservatism.* New York, NY: Oxford University Press.

Solow, Robert M. 2008. "The German Story." Pp. 1–14 in Gerhard Bosch and Claudia Weinkopf (eds.), *Low-Wage Work in Germany.* New York, NY: Russell Sage Foundation.

Soskice, David. 1999. "Divergent Production Regimes: Coordinated and Uncoordinated Market Economies in the 1980s and 1990s." Pp. 101–34 in Herbert Kitschelt, Peter Lange, Gary Marks, and John D. Stephens (eds.), *Continuity and Change in Contemporary Capitalism*. Cambridge, UK: Cambridge University Press.

Standing, Guy. 2011. *The Precariat: The New Dangerous Class*. New York, NY: Bloomsbury.

Stephens, John D. 1979. *The Transition from Capitalism to Socialism*. London, UK: Macmillan.

Stiglitz, Joseph E., Amartya Sen, and Jean-Paul Fitoussi. 2009. *Report by the Commission on the Measurement of Economic Performance and Social Progress*. Commission on the Measurement of Economic Performance and Social Progress, http://ec.europa.eu/eurostat/documents/118025/118123/Fitoussi+Commission+report

Stone, Katherine V.W. 2012. "The Decline in the Standard Employment Contract: Evidence from Ten Advanced Industrial Countries." Institute for Research on Labor and Employment Working Paper 2012–11. Los Angeles, CA: UCLA, http://papers.ssrn.com/sol3/papers.cfm?abstract_id=2181082

Sunstein, Cass. 2004. *The Second Bill of Rights: FDR's Unfinished Revolution – And Why We Need It More Than Ever*. New York, NY: Basic Books.

Supiot, Alain. 2001. *Beyond Employment: Changes in Work and the Future of Labour Law in Europe*. Oxford, UK: Oxford University Press.

Sverke, Magnus and Johnny Hellgren. 2002. "The Nature of Job Insecurity: Understanding Employment Uncertainty on the Brink of a New Millennium." *Applied Psychology: An International Review* 5: 23–42.

Sverke, Magnus, Johnny Hellgren, and Katharine Näswall. 2002. "No Security: A Meta-Analysis and Review of Job Insecurity and its Consequences." *Journal of Occupational Health Psychology* 7: 242–64.

Swinnerton, Kenneth A., and Howard Wial. 1996. "Is Job Stability Declining in the U.S. Economy? Reply to Diebold, Neumark, and Polsky." *Industrial and Labor Relations Review* 49: 352–5.

Taylor-Gooby, Peter. 2008. "The New Welfare State Settlement in Europe." *European Societies* 10: 3–24.

Tegund, Alina. 2014. "Uncertainty about Jobs Has a Ripple Effect." *New York Times*, May 16, https://www.nytimes.com/2014/05/17/your-money/uncertainty-about-jobs-has-a-ripple-effect.html?_r=0

The Economist. 2010a. "Older and Wiser." March 13: 3–5.

The Economist. 2010b. "Inside the Miracle: How Germany Weathered the Recession." March 13: 5–7.

The Economist. 2011. "Split Personality." July 9: 72–3.

The Economist. 2012. "What Germany Offers the World." April 14, www.economist.com/node/21552567/print

The Economist. 2013a. "Indignant, Undignified." May 25, https://www.economist.com/news/europe/21578415-it-young-who-suffer-most-high-unemployment-indignant-undignified

The Economist. 2013b. "Erasmus Generation: Labour." June 15: 13–15.

Thelen, Kathleen. 2004. *How Institutions Evolve: The Political Economy of*

Skills in Germany, Britain, the United States and Japan. New York, NY: Cambridge University Press.

Thelen, Kathleen. 2014. *Varieties of Liberalization and the New Politics of Social Solidarity*. New York, NY: University Press.

The Local.es. 2016. "80% of Spaniards Under Thirty Still Live at Home with Parents." March 1, https://www.thelocal.es/20160301/80-of-spanish-young-adults-live-at-home-with-parents

Therborn, Göran. 2013. *The Killing Fields of Inequality*. Cambridge, UK: Polity.

Thesing, Gabi, Jana Randow, and Aaron Kirchfield. 2010. "Germany's Growth: New Rules, Old Companies." *Bloomberg Businessweek*, September 30, https://www.bloomberg.com/news/articles/2010-09-30/germanys-growth-new-rules-old-companiesbusinessweek-business-news-stock-market-and-financial-advice

UNICEF. 2014. "A Little More, How Much It Is . . . Piloting Basic Income Transfers in Madhya Pradesh, India." SEWA Bharat, UNICEF India Office, January, http://sewabharat.org/wp-content/uploads/2015/07/Report-on-Unconditional-Cash-Transfer-Pilot-Project-in-Madhya-Pradesh.pdf

United Nations, Department of Economic and Social Affairs. 2008. *World Economic and Social Survey 2008: Overcoming Economic Insecurity*, www.un.org/en/development/desa/policy/wess/wess_archive/2008wess.pdf

Van Gerven, Minna and Marinus Ossewaarde. 2012. "The Welfare State's Making of Cosmopolitan Europe." *European Societies* 14: 35–55.

Van Reenen, John. 2004. "Active Labor Market Policies and the British New Deal for the Young Unemployed in Context." Pp. 461–96 in David Card, Richard Blundell, and Richard B. Freeman (eds.), *Seeking a Premier Economy: The Economic Effects of British Economic Reforms, 1980–2000*. Chicago, IL: University of Chicago Press.

Van Vliet, Olaf and Ferry Koster. 2011. "Europeanization and the Political Economy of Active Labour Market Policies." *European Union Politics* 12: 217–39.

Veenhoven, Ruut. 1995. "The Cross-National Pattern of Happiness: Test of Predictions Implied in Three Theories of Happiness." *Social Indicators Research* 34: 33–68.

Veenhoven, Ruut. 1996. "Developments in Satisfaction Research." *Social Indicators Research* 37: 1–46.

Venn, Danielle. 2009. "Legislation, Collective Bargaining and Enforcement: Updating the OECD Employment Protection Indicators." Paris, France: OECD, http://www.oecd.org/employment/emp/43116624.pdf

Viebrock, Elke and Jochen Clasen. 2009. "Flexicurity and Welfare Reform: A Review." *Socio-Economic Review* 7: 305–31.

Vosko, Leah F. 2010. *Managing the Margins: Gender, Citizenship, and the International Regulation of Precarious Employment*. Oxford, UK: Oxford University Press.

Vosko, Leah F., Martha MacDonald, and Iain Campbell (eds.). 2009. *Gender and the Contours of Precarious Employment*. Abingdon, UK: Routledge

Waldinger, Roger and Michael I. Lichter 2003. *How the Other Half Works: Immigration and the Social Organization of Labor*. Berkeley, CA: University of California Press.

Wallace, Michael and David Brady. 2001. "The Next Long Swing: Spatialization, Technocratic Control, and the Restructuring of Work at the Turn of the Century." Pp. 101–33 in Ivar Berg and Arne L. Kalleberg (eds.), *Sourcebook of Labor Markets: Evolving Structures and Processes*. New York, NY: Kluwer Academic/Plenum.

Webster, Edward, Rob Lambert, and Andries Bezuidenhout. 2008. *Grounding Globalization: Labour in the Age of Insecurity*. Oxford, UK: Blackwell.

Westergaard-Nielsen, Niels. 2008. *Low-Wage Work in Denmark*. New York, NY: Russell Sage Foundation.

Western, Bruce, Deirdre Bloome, Benjamin Sosnaud, and Laura Tach. 2012. "Economic Insecurity and Social Stratification." *Annual Review of Sociology* 38: 341–59.

Wilkinson, Richard and Kate Pickett. 2010. *The Spirit Level: Why Greater Equality Makes Societies Stronger*. New York, NY: Bloomsbury.

Wilthagen, Ton and Frank Tros. 2004. "The Concept of 'Flexicurity': A New Approach to Regulating Employment and Labor Markets." *Transfer* 10: 166–86.

Wood, Stewart. 2001. "Business, Government, and Patterns of Labor Market Policy in Britain and the Federal Republic of Germany." Pp. 247–74 in Peter A. Hall and David Soskice (eds.), *Varieties of Capitalism: The Institutional Foundations of Comparative Advantage*. Oxford, UK: Oxford University Press.

World Bank. 2014. Fertility Rate, Total (Births Per Woman), http://data.worldbank.org/indicator/SP.DYN.TFRT.IN

Wright, Erik Olin. 2000. "Working-Class Power, Capitalist-Class Interests, and Class Compromise." *American Journal of Sociology* 105: 957–1002.

Wulfgramm, Melike. 2014. "Life Satisfaction Effects of Unemployment in Europe: The Moderating Influence of Labour Market Policy." *Journal of European Social Policy* 24: 258–72.

Yamaguchi, Koichiro. 1983. "Employment Adjustment and the System of 'Loaned Employees.'" Pp. 8–10 in Japan Institute of Labour, *Highlights in Japanese Industrial Relations*. Tokyo, Japan: Japan Institute of Labour.

Zimmerman, Klaus F., Costanza Biavaschi, Werner Eichhorst, Corrado Giulietti, Michael J. Kendzia, Alexander Muravyev, Janneke Pieters, Núria Rodríguez-Planas, and Ricarda Schmidl. 2013. "Youth Unemployment and Vocational Training." *Foundations and Trends in Microeconomics* 9: 1–157.

Index

Notes: Abbreviations used within the index are explained on p. xi.
Page numbers in *italics* refer to figures.

Vimana Aircraft
of
Ancient India
&
Atlantis

Special thanks to Bangalor Sanskrit professor G.R. Josyer, Ivan T. Sanderson, Desmond Leslie, Harry Osoff, John Tyson, Bob Richardson, Bill Clendenon, Carole Gerardo, Howard Zitko, Robert D. Stelle & others! Without their help, it never would have been possible.

Vimana Aircraft of Ancient India & Atlantis

**Vimana Aircraft of
Ancient India & Atlantis**

Copyright 1991, 2004
by
David Hatcher Childress and Adventures Unlimited Press

Printed in the United States of America
Ninth Printing August 2004

ISBN 0-932813-12-7

Published by Adventures Unlimited Press
One Adventure Place, Kempton, Illinois 60946 USA

email: auphq@frontiernet.net
www.adventuresunlimitedpress.com

Write for our free catalog of unusual books & videos

TABLE OF CONTENTS

Legendary flying chariot of a Chinese prince.

One of the Gopurams (gateways) in the Temple of Madurai in southern India. Carved into rock are scenes from India's great Epic, *The Ramayana.* Detailed friezes depict the well-known and incredible tale of Rama, Sita, Hanuman and the flights between Ayodha and Lanka.

The spiral nebula in Coma Berenices, a distant island universe seen on edge. Its similarity to flying saucer shapes is significant, showing that the forces and that the vortex mechanics of the universe are operational from the smallest scale to the largest. Photo courtesy of Mount Wilson Observatory.

INTRODUCTION
by
IVAN T. SANDERSON

THE ANCIENT INDIAN VIMANAS

§§§

There is a tremendous volume of published material in almost all western languages on a subject that somewhere along the line and about a century ago was tabbed "the Ancient Writings." About 99 percent of this is not only drivel but pure fabrication. It has become the bible of the mystics, psuedoscientists, and crackpots and it—or specific parts of it, such as "The Tibetan Mysteries," the "Atlantean Texts," and so forth—are now quoted as a sort of gospel. However, if you ask any Orientalist, historian, or librarian in any of the great museums of the world, you will encounter a wry smile. No such works have ever been known to exist outside the imagination of the mystics. Nonetheless, there are some truly ancient and authenticated texts, notably of Indian origin, which is to say from various parts of that great subcontinent, and handed down from various of its cultures from various dates.

It is, moreover, from these authenticated texts, mostly in poetic form, that some truly astonishing concepts have been derived. Poetic they may be; and nothing more than myth, legend, or folklore may they purport to record; but they make statements that are more than just surprising. Several are, what is more, couched in perfectly straight-forward terms and are, time and time again, stated to be not legendary but technological, and thus called *Manusa*. These are said by the writers to explain how certain devices were constructed for aerial flight, but not *how* to so construct them because the inventors and the establishment did not want such things to be mass-produced and get into the hands of any other than the rulers, commonly called "kings" and "princes." What is more, among the non-technical works devoted to the more poetic stories, and known as *Daiva*, there would appear to be more than ample suggestion, if not evidence, that such airships could be and were put to the most gruesome and devastating use in wartime.

These texts make most fascinating reading, but being unable to read the originals or copies of them in the language in which they were written, I appealed to friends who were either Orientals themselves or students of Oriental literature. Among these was the late Dr. Ranjee Shahani, who at the time of his death was Professor of English Literature at Seton Hall University. Dr. Shahani had published considerably on these texts, and I derive most of the following from his works. At the same time, I quote certain passages as published (in translated form) by the British author, Desmond Leslie,[1] by kind permission of the author and publishers. From these sources we are told that:

In the *Manusa*, the most elaborate details for building (such aerial machines) are set down. The *Samarangana Sutradhara* says that they were made of light material, with a strong, well-shaped body. Iron, copper, and lead were used in their construction. They could fly to great distances and were propelled by air. This text, according to Leslie, devotes 230 stanzas to the building of these machines, and their uses in peace and war. This author then goes on to state that this same text says:

"Strong and durable must the body be made, like a great flying bird, of light material. Inside it one must place the *Mercury-engine* with its iron heating apparatus beneath.

10

By means of the *power latent in the mercury* which sets the driving *whirlwind* in motion, a man sitting inside may travel a great distance in the sky in a most marvelous manner.

"Similarly by using the prescribed processes one can build a vimana as large as the temple of the God-in-motion. Four strong *mercury* containers must be built into the interior structure. When these have been heated by controlled fire from iron containers, the vimana develops thunder-power through the mercury. And at once it becomes a pearl in the sky.

Moreover, if this iron engine with properly welded joints be filled with mercury, and the fire be conducted to the upper part it develops power with the roar of a lion."

Leslie and several others who at least tried to take a serious view of these odd statements subsequently indulged in some perfectly valid speculations as to just what the significance of mercury might be. These are both sensible and permissible but lead off into matters that do not concern us here. Needless to say, they did not encompass the basic observation that a circular dish of mercury revolves in a contrary manner to a naked flame circulated below it, and that it gathers speed until it exceeds the speed of revolution of said flame. I fancy that Mr. Leslie will be enchanted with this new observation.

Here is the projection of energy by an exceedingly simple process. Should the ancients have stumbled across this process—though how in the dickens they might have done so is almost beyond comprehension—they might well have followed up the lead and ended up by finding out how to tap and channel such energy. Take this lead far enough and one can suggest the development of an "engine" employing it and being put to use to do (as the engineers say) work.

Desmond Leslie's theme is that this was one type of engine developed for aerial flight, and he extrapolates therefrom to the suggestion that it may have been developed far enough for space travel, and that something on this principle powers some UFOs.

Herr Theodor Schwenk on Vortices

Vortices, or in more popular parlance whirlpools, constitute a subject of considerable complexity. They are individual entities being born due to a particular set of circumstances, having a life span that, given precise knowledge of enough factors, is predictable, and eventually dying through slow disintegration or accident. They form in gases—including, of course, air—liquids of all kinds, and even in solids when they are in a plastic state. The vortex as a structure liked at the very core of existence, as in the atom and apparently down to the behavior of quanta.

The origin of vortices, their structure, and their behavior constitute a somewhat complex subject calling for mental visualization of three-dimensional movement. They are whirligigs, the centers of which have been pulled either downward or upward, and mostly downward in the case of air and water. As a geometric form they permeate the whole of life as well as mere matter. The best exposition of vortices, and one that is couched in terms that are understandable to anybody, may be found in a book entitled *Sensitive Chaos,* by Theodor Schwenk.[2] Therein there is a passage on p. 39 which succinctly describes the causes of vortices as follows: "Wherever any qualitative differences in a flowing medium come together, these isolated formations (vortices) occur. Such differences may be: slow and fast, solid and liquid; liquid and gaseous. We could extend the list: warm and cold; denser and more tenuous; heavy and light (for instance, salt and fresh) viscous and fluid; alkaline and acid...At the surfaces of contact there is always a tendency for one layer to roll in upon the other. In short, wherever the finest differentiations are present the water acts as a delicate 'sense organ' which as it were perceives the differentiations and then in a rhythmical processes causes them to even out and to merge."

It should be noted that in vortices in a liquid such as

water, objects are sucked inward and downward, whereas in a gas such as air they go upward and outward, as in tornadoes. Our Vile Vortices would appear to coincide with larger vortices in the surface layers of the oceans, but we are not presuming to suggest that these ever form gigantic maelstroms that have a hold going down the middle into which ships could be sunk. Rather, the alleged action of the VVs would seem to be in the atmosphere above these vast, comparatively placid whirligigs. In this medium, things would be sucked up and then tossed out over the upper rim of the vortex. Considering the power of tornadoes or twisters over the sea, it is just conceivable that lighter planes might be so whirled upward and tossed far away where search parties would never think of looking for them. However, the idea is neither proven nor altogether tenable from a purely physical point of view. While the VVs do appear to be associated with natural vortices, the mysterious effects that have been described as occurring within them do not seem to be purely mechanical, and we have to investigate a number of other factors.

In the same book named above, there is another most pertinent passage which applies to the centers of vortices and which provides a very neat and simple explanation of what is called suction-pressure. This states:

"Imagine we have some kind of filled space—we will call it A and place a plus sign in front of it (+A). Now we can make the space emptier and emptier, whereby A gets smaller and smaller; but there is still something in the space, therefore we still use the + sign. We can imagine that it could be possible to create a space which is entirely empty of air, although this is not possible under earthly conditions because a space can only be made approximately empty. Were it possible, however, to make a space entirely void, it would contain nothing but space. Let us call it nought; the space has zero contents. Now we can do with the space as you can do with your purse. When you have filled it you can take out more and more, until at last there is nothing left in it. If then you still want to go on spending money, you cannot take out any more, but you can incur debts. But if you have made debts there is less than nothing in your purse. This, then is how you can imagine the space—not only empty, but one might say sucked out, filled with less than nothing (- A)."

Just how you borrow against a nothingness, vacuum, or space I leave to the cosmologists; but I am wondering if this is not where anti-matter, counter-matter, and things like Gravity II might not come in. Vortices generated great energies the origin of which has not yet been sufficiently explained. From, in what, and from what fields are they generated? Do purely mechanical vortices stimulate others in other fields such as the electromagnetic, magnetic, gravitic, and other?

1. Leslie, Desmond, and Adamski, George. *Flying Saucers Have Landed.* New York: The British Book Centre, 1953, pp. 90-94.

2. London: Rudolph Steiner Press, 1965.

From *Invisible Residents,*
1970, World Publishing, Cleveland.
Many thanks to Ivan T. Sanderson, a great scientist.

BOOK

1

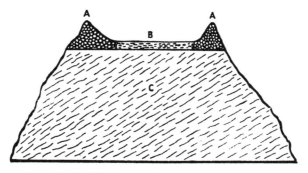

Cross section of a vitrified stone fort in Scotland. The stones were literally fused together by intense heat thousands of years ago.

The March, 1910 cover of *AIRCRAFT* magazine, with a large boat shaped aircraft taking into the skies. This elongated airship design became popular at the turn of the century, along with the concept of ancient powered flight.

1

SECRET LIBRARIES
&
ANCIENT SCIENCE

§§§

*In these dusty books, which the student
doesn't bother to consult until the eve
of the exam, there are marvels, miracles!*
— H.G.Wells, *The Invisible Man*

The subject of ancient Indian aircraft, called *Vimanas* by
the ancient "Indians" themselves, is no doubt one of the
most fascinating subjects of both modern and ancient
science!

For the skeptic, this book hopes to cancel all doubt
that the subject of *Vimanas* is a genuine one, though
various interpretations of the texts can be assumed. That
ancient man was capable of building flying machines there
seems no doubt. After all, the human beings of ten, twenty
or a hundred thousand years ago were of the same brain
size and mental capability as today's modern man.
Therefore any mechanical or scientific achievement that

modern man was capable of, ancient man was capable of as well. However, the question that the skeptic may ask is, "Did ancient man actually achieve the goal of flight and mechanical motive power?"

A large part of esoteric information, including some material on *Vimanas* and ancient technology, allegedly comes from secret libraries supposedly kept in various places around the world. These secret libraries are often underground beneath ancient monasteries or temples, or sometimes walled up in caves until they can be found later.

To many critics of the belief in advanced ancient civilizations, the notion of secret libraries in Tibet, India or elsewhere and tablets with ancient, unintelligible symbols on them was just as absurd. Yet, if these critics bother to check their history, they would know that such libraries are a fact.

In the year 1900 at Dunhuang, a small desert town on the border of northern Tibet, a Taoist monk found a hidden library inside a cliff honeycombed with caves. The room had been walled up with bricks in the eleventh century to keep it from falling into the hands of invading barbarians. For eight hundred years the books had lain there, preserved by the dry desert air and maintained in excellent condition. Then the famous explorer and archaeologist Sir Aurel Stein passed through Dunhuang in 1907 and persuaded the monk to allow him to view the treasure, which was, at that time, still kept in the secret cave.

He found Buddhist texts in many languages—Chinese, Tibetan, Sanskrit— and some in languages that were completely unknown! Just how old some of the texts were was impossible to tell, but they had probably already been copied over several times from earlier texts. The originals had been written hundreds and in most cases, thousands of years ago. [12,13,14]

Throughout history huge archives and libraries have

been purposely destroyed. According to the famous astronomer Carl Sagan, a book entitled *The True History of Mankind Over the Last 100,000 Years* once existed and was housed in the great library in Alexandria, Egypt. Unfortunately, this book, along with thousands of others, was burned by fanatical Christians in the third century A.D. Any volumes which they might have missed were burned by the Moslems to heat baths a few hundred years later.

All ancient Chinese texts, especially those of Lao Tzu and Confucius, as well as the I Ching , speak of the ancients and the glory of their civilization. They were presumably speaking about the people living at least at the time of the "Five Monarchs" and probably before. Possibly, they are really referring to the people of the "Motherland, Mu."

Unfortunately, not much is known about the early part of Chinese history, from the first millennia B.C. and before. Just before he died, in 212 B.C., Emperor Chi Huang Ti ordered that all the books and literature relating to ancient China be destroyed. Vast amounts of ancient texts—virtually everything pertaining to history, astronomy, philosophy, and science—were seized and burnt. Whole libraries, including the royal library, were destroyed. Some of the works of Confucius and Mencius were included in this destruction of knowledge.

Fortunately, some books survived because people hid them in various underground caves, and many works were hidden in Taoist temples where they are even now religiously kept and preserved. They are on no account shown to anyone, but kept hidden away as they have been for thousands of years. The recent persecution and closing of religious temples by the Red Chinese Government indicates that the lamas still have cause to keep their ancient books hidden. It is known that the Russians have suppressed a great many religious texts that have been discovered in

Soviet Union, because they are afraid these would give the churches a boost.

Doubtless, there was a great deal of history relating to the early days of ancient China lost. What caused the emperor Chin to want to destroy any record of the past just prior to his death? Was he such a megalomaniac that he wanted history to start with him, or was he influenced by the same evil forces that inspired Genghis Khan and Hitler to the same sort of book burning?

The Spanish conquistadors had every Mayan codex that they found destroyed. Out of many thousands of Mayan books found by the Spanish, only three are known to exist today. Like the fanatical Christians of the third century and Emperor Chin in the second century B.C., they wanted to erase all knowledge of the past and the knowledge that it contained.

While despots, fanatics and cruel conquerors have been busy throughout history trying to destroy knowledge and erase the memory of the dim past, others have been attempting, like those who walled the library of Dunhuang up inside a cave, to save this precious knowledge.

When the patriarch of Constantinople, Nestorius, was deposed at the Council of Ephesus in 431 A.D. for the heresy of believing that Christ was in fact two persons, the Archangel Melchizedek and the human Jesus of Nazareth, son of Joseph and Mary, he was banished to the Libyan Desert. The followers of Nestorius were then persecuted for their Christian beliefs which ran against the newly created Catholic Church. They moved eastward from Constantinople, first to Edessa (the modern Urfa) in Mesopotamia, and later to Baghdad, India and Central Asia. There was a medical school in Edessa, and in this scientific community they translated into Syriac—which had become the common language of western Asia—the works of Aristotle, Plato, Euclid, Archimedes, Heron, and Ptolemy and many other books of philosophy and science. These Syrian books were then later translated into Arabic in Baghdad and other places.

These Syrian books then formed the basis for Arabian science and philosophy which flowered during the dark ages of Europe when the Catholic church had imposed ignorance and superstition on the people, and destroyed those books as heresy. In the course of time, the Syriac works, now in Arabic, were then translated into Latin, Hebrew, and modern western languages. Ancient science reached us in a round about way, and were it not for the Nestorian Christian refugees and their libraries, we would not have these books today![28]

Even in modern times knowledge has been purposely destroyed, even in the United States! While we all know that the Nazis destroyed books, it is less well known that the U.S. government ordered all of the works of the Austrian psychologist Wilhelm Reich's destroyed by court order in 1954. His works, curiously, had a great deal to do with free energy devices and "strange" technology.

To any student of ancient history and lover of ancient knowledge, I think that it is painfully obvious why secret libraries and the preservation of books is actually necessary if ancient wisdom and technology were to be preserved!

Something else which lends credibility to the belief that these secret libraries exist is the fact that many references are made to them in Central Asian literature. It is said that they can be found in many temples in India, Nepal and Tibet. They probably can also be found in China and Mongolia as well.

About forty years ago, a Chinese representative of the Rosicrucian Brotherhood visited the Rosicrucian Fraternity in San Jose, California. He brought with him a manuscript which had been kept in a secret Asian archive for thousands of years. It was said to have been authored by the Egyptian

Pharaoh Akhnaton, historically the founder of monotheism. The Rosicrucians translated this book and published it under the title *Unto Thee I Grant.* [22,25] The appearance of this book would seem to illustrate that such archives do in fact exist, and that knowledge is occasionally disseminated from them. Furthermore, the Rosicrucians claim to have access to a number of secret libraries in Tibet.

§§§

Extant Chinese texts state that the first of the dynasties was that of the "Five Monarchs," in which there were, confusingly, nine rulers whose combined reigns lasted from 2,852 to 2,206 B.C., which is just after the time at which the archeologists date the Ban Po Neolithic Site. Confucius ascribed to one king, Yao, whose reign started around 2,357 B.C., "...kindliness, wisdom, and sense of duty." He was succeeded by Shon, who built a vast network of roads, bridges, and passes through the enormous land, and many scholars attribute the building of the Silk Road to him.

One of the great proponents of ancient civilizations and advanced technology of the past was James Churchward, an Anglo-American who spent a great deal of his life in India. Here he was initiated into certain eastern esoteric "truths," being shown, supposedly, some ancient tablets in an Indian/Tibetan monastery. (There have been many Tibetan monasteries in India for hundreds, if not thousands of years.) He was taught how to read the tablets and was told many fascinating things about ancient history. Then, after traveling all over the world, he wrote a series of very popular books. These were *The Lost Continent of Mu, The Children of Mu, The Sacred Symbols of Mu, The Cosmic Forces of Mu,* and *The Second Book of the Cosmic Forces of Mu.* He died just as the last book was being published in 1935.

22

In the late eighteen hundreds, there was a French traveler and writer by the name of Louis Jacolliot (1837-1890) who collected a great many Sanskrit myths on his travels to India. According to him, the Hindu classics told of a former continent in the Pacific which they called Rutas. This continent was where civilization had begun, and it had sunken into the ocean in remote antiquity, leaving only a bunch of small islands.[57]

Jacolliot's tales are remarkably similar to Churchward's, and he is one of the few sources that back up Churchward's tales of stone tablets which say pretty much the same things about ancient Indian sources and a lost continent in the Pacific. The Ring of Fire is certainly the most active earthquake zone in the world, and there is some archeological evidence of an advanced civilization in the Pacific, such as the gigantic megalithic stone city of Metalanim (Nan Modal) on small, sparsely populated Ponape Island not to mention evidence on mysterious Easter Island and other islands scattered throughout the Pacific.

The great Chinese philosopher, Lao Tzu, often talked of the "Ancient Ones" in his writings, much as Confucius did. They were wise and knowledgeable, human beings that were as Gods — powerful, good, loving, and all-knowing. Born around 604 B.C., Lao Tzu wrote the book which is still perhaps the most famous Chinese classic of all time, the Tao Te Ching. When he finally left China, at the close of his very long life, he journeyed to the west, to the legendary land of *Hsi Wang Mu,* which may have been the headquarters of the "Ancient Ones," the *Great White Brotherhood.* It was as he was leaving at one of the border posts of China that a guard persuaded him to write down the *Tao Te Ching,* so that Lao Tzu's wisdom would not be lost. No one ever heard of Lao Tzu again, though it is presumed that he made it to the Land of Hsi Wang Mu.

> The Ancient Masters were subtle,
> mysterious, profound, responsive.
> The depth of their knowledge is unfathomable.
> Because it is unfathomable,
> all we can do it so describe their appearance.
> Watchful, like men crossing a winter stream.
> Alert, like men aware of danger.
> Courteous, like visiting guests.
> Yielding, like ice about to melt.
> Simple, like uncarved blocks of wood.
> —*Lao Tzu, Tao te Ching (Chapter 15)*

Hsi Wang Mu is also another name for the popular Chinese Goddess Kuan Yin, the "Merciful Guardian" and "Queen Mother of the West." Therefore, this land, traditionally located in the Kun Lun mountains, was known as the "Abode of the Immortals" and "The Western Paradise." Other ancient Chinese also went off to the "Abode of the Immortals;" the Chou-dynasty emperor "Mu" (1001-946 B. C.) journeyed to the Kun Lun mountains to find the land, and is said to have actually had an audience with "Goddess Hsi Wang Mu" on the bank of Jasper Lake in the Kun Lun range. Over the years of Chinese history, expeditions were sent out to the Kun Lun mountains, the "Mount Olympus" of ancient China, in order to contact the "Ancient Ones."[38]

A secret library was possibly underground, and it has been said by many to be near Lhasa, possibly connected to the underground tunnels beneath the Potala, the Dalai Lama's fabulous skyscraper. The tunnels, however, being reportedly quite extensive, would be very difficult to explore, and certainly such a library would be ingeniously hidden. The prolific occult writer T. Lobsang Rampa tells an interesting story of the exploration of these underground tunnels beneath the Potala in his fascinating books, *The Third Eye* and *Cave of the Ancients.*

While the story is somewhat dubious, it does at least indicate that there is a great deal of myth about the existence of such tunnels. Rampa reports them as very extensive, and including a large underground lake. Nicholas Roerich also mentions tales of the tunnels and lake beneath the Potala, perhaps it is from here that Rampa learned of such things, if not from actual experience.[69]

Just north of the Kun Lun mountains, in Sinkiang, the famous Russian artist, explorer and mystic, Nicholas Roerich heard of the "Valley of the Immortals" just over the mountains. "Behind that mountain live holy men who are saving humanity through wisdom; many tried to see them but failed — somehow as soon as they go over the ridge, they lose their way," he was told. A native guide told him of huge vaults inside the mountains where treasures had been stored from the beginning of history. He also indicated that tall white people had been disappearing into those rock galleries.[93]

Nicholas Roerich at one time was in the possession of a fragment of "a magical stone from another world," called in sanskrit the Chintamani Stone. Alleged to come from the star system of Sirius, ancient Asian chronicles claim that a divine messenger from the heavens gave a fragment of the stone to *Emperor Tazlavoo of Atlantis*[94] A fragment of this stone was supposedly sent to Europe to help aid in the establishment of the League of Nations.

With the failure of the League of Nations, Nicholas Roerich then had the stone in his possession. On one of his expeditions in the 1920's he returned the fragment of the stone to its rightful owners, whoever they were. The stone has been described as being the size of a small finger in the shape of a fruit or heart, shiny gray in color with four unknown hieroglyphs inscribed on it. It has certain magical properties, and can be used for divination. [94]

Roerich may have taken the stone to the "Valley of the Immortals" in the Kun Lun Range, or possibly to Lhasa, where it is also said that the Thirteenth Dalai Lama was also in possession of a fragment of the stone (perhaps this was the one sent to Europe). The Thirteenth Dalai Lama was a man of certain mystery. Tibetan tradition had it that would be but one more Dalai Lama after him who is the Dalai Lama of today.

The Potala Palace is a fairly recent structure, built by the fifth Dalai Lama, Ngwang Lobsang Gyatso who was born in 1617. It was he who persuaded the Mongol king and the Chinese emperor to recognize his suzerainty over Tibet. The Potala, the most famous building in Tibet, is a tall, massive, imposing mud-and-brick skyscraper, now turned into a museum by the Chinese.

Recently, Sanskrit documents discovered by the Chinese in Lhasa were sent to India to be studied by experts there. Dr. Ruth Reyna of the University of Chandigarh said that the manuscripts contain directions for building interplanetary spaceships!

In any case, Dr. Reyna explained that the document stated that the method of propulsion was "anti-gravitational." On board these machines, which were called "astras," the builders of these crafts could have sent a detachment of men to any planet. The manuscripts do not say that any interplanetary communication was achieved, but do mention a trip from the earth to the moon, though it is not clear whether the trip was just planned or actually carried out.

Indian scientists were at first extremely reserved about the value of these documents, but became less so when the Chinese announced that certain parts of the data were being studied for inclusion in their space program![14]

These "Astras" of Dr. Reyna's manuscript are no doubt what other Indian texts describe as *vimanas*. It is also interesting to note that the Great White Brotherhood is said to be in possession of a number of such airships, similar to these "astras" or the vimanas and vailxi of the Rama Empire and Atlantis. These airships, perhaps powered by "anti-gravity," as the document found by the Chinese suggests, are theoretically kept in secret bases. These airships, virtual UFO's, may actually be the cause of some UFO sightings, especially those in Central Asia. Interestingly, the Kun Lun mountains and the Lop Nor desert nearby are the center for Central Asia's main UFO mystery!

§§§

Of a more recent date, historically speaking, are the ancient books and library of Asoka, the great Indian emperor who lived circa 274-232 B.C. and is well known for his *Edicts* which was an early code of ethics, moral law and a "Bill of Rights." According to the French authors of the well known book, *Morning of the Magicians*, [29] Asoka formed a secret society of scientists known as the *Nine Unknown Men*. There were nine books, one written by each of the scientists in the employ of Asoka. Book number six was a treatise on the Secrets of Gravitation!

One wonders if this book was perhaps the *Vaimanika Shastra* of Maharishi Bharadwaja? It is also interesting to note here that Asoka's empire in India was immediately after the attempted invasion of the Indian subcontinent by Alexander the Great, whose army retreated and all attempts were given up to subdue India, after his army was "attacked" by what Greek historians later called, "fiery, flying shields"![19,21]

The idea of a secret society keeping secret knowledge is

hardly very fantastic. Dr. J. Allen Hynek, the American astronomer who served for over twenty years as the Air Force's scientific consultant on UFOs, explained his term The Invisible College in an article called "The UFO Mystery" published in the *FBI Bulletin* (February 1975):

"Way back in the *'dark ages'* of science, when scientists themselves were suspected of being in league with the Devil, they had to work privately. They often met clandestinely to exchange views and the results of their various experiments. For this reason, they called themselves the *Invisible College*. And it remained invisible until the scientists of that day gained respectability when the Royal Society was chartered by Charles II in the early 1660s." [25]

§§§

To let understanding stop at what cannot be understood,
is a high attainment.
Those who cannot do it
will be destroyed on the lathe of heaven.
—*Chuang Tzu*

One alleged possessor of ancient aircraft (vimana, as the ancients called it) was the noted Biblical king, Solomon. Some researchers point out that there is some evidence of a strong connection between Kashmir and ancient Israel, indicating that it was Kashmir that was the "Promised Land" rather than Palestine. Today in Kashmir, there are ancient places with names like, "The Tomb of Moses," the "Throne of Solomon" (which is a mountain), the last resting place of Mother Mary, just near Rawalpindi a few miles away in Pakistan, and the *Garden of Solomon.*

Most Kashmiris genuinely believe that Moses is buried in Kashmir, and that the forty years of wandering and

28

hostile tribes were not in the Sinai, but across Asia to Kashmir. After all, forty years is a long time to wander around the Sinai Peninsula, which could be walked across in a few days, and is virtually uninhabited, with no hostile tribes to be found, then or today. [56]

One of the most interesting features concerns the mountain known as the "Throne of Solomon." There is at least one other "Throne of Solomon" mountain in Central Asia and it is in Iran. Why should a mountain be called "The Throne of Solomon?" According to an ancient Ethiopian text, the *Kebra Nagast*, Solomon had some kind of airship with which he would fly great distances, probably landing on top of mountains. The ancient kingdom of Ethiopia was founded by the son of Solomon, born to him and the Queen of Sheba. The *Kebra Nagast* says that Solomon had a "heavenly car" which he inherited from his forefather (King David, I suppose) and used frequently. "The King...and all who obeyed his word, flew on the wagon without pain and suffering, and without sweat or exhaustion, and traveled in one day a distance which took three months to traverse (on foot)," says the *Kebra Nagast*. [34]

Could it be that Solomon possessed a vimana airship, left over from the days of the Rama Empire and Atlantis, some several thousand years before? Did he use his "heavenly car" to fly to "Solomon's Throne" in Iran and Kashmir?

According to Nicholas Roerich, other "Thrones of Solomon" can be found elsewhere in Tibet and Central Asia. That Solomon flew there in his airship is a popular belief throughout Central Asia. [69] Perhaps the mountain in Iran, which, like the one in Kashmir, is flat-topped, was a landing pad between Israel and Kashmir. If so, are some of these airships still around today, and is someone operating them from a secret base in some remote hinterland of Central Asia, South America, a remote Pacific Island, or somewhere else? Could they be responsible for some of the UFO sightings? The thought is mind-boggling!

Kashmir is also connected with the fantastic war in ancient times that destroyed the Rama Empire. The massive ruins of a temple called Parshaspur can be found just outside Srinagar. It is a seen of total destruction, huge blocks of stone are scattered about a wide area giving the impression of explosive destruction. The large dressed blocks of stone are reminiscent of the massive stone slabs at Puma Punku, near Tiahuanaco on the Altiplano of Bolivia.[81]

Was Parshaspur destroyed by some fantastic weapon during one of the horrendous battles detailed in the *Mahabharata?*

In this ancient Assyrian Cylinder Seal from the British Museum, a winged disc-shaped object, without occupants (at least visibly) can be seen to the left. A rocket-shaped object can be seen to the right of the horseman.

One of the scrolls written in an unknown language, found in the secret library in a cave in Dunhuang, China in 1910 by Sir Aurel Stein. They are now in the British Museum.

An alchemist confers with an "Ancient Master" on alchemical matters. Notice the triangular pyramid, symbolizing knowledge, superimposed on the head of the "Master."

Two alchemists, possibly preparing mercury from cinnabar are depicted in this woodcut from a 16th-century translation of *Summa Perfectionis*, an 8th century work by the alchemist Geber.

2

VIMANAS IN
ANCIENT
INDIAN TEXTS

§§§

Kill, therefore, with the Sword of Wisdom, the doubt born of ignorance that lies in thy heart. Be one in self harmony, in yoga,—and arise, great warrior, arise!
Krishna to Arjuna in the Bhagavad Gita (4:42)

Throughout history there have been many common myths and legends of flying machines or devices—the familiar flying carpets of ancient Arabia; Biblical figures such as Ezekial and Solomon flying from place to place and the "magical chariots," or *Vimanas,* of ancient India and China.

There are many Chinese legends of flight, including a legendary flying chariot belonging to an ancient Chinese prince and the more recent Wan Hoo-of the 15th century A.D. or so. He allegedly built a sturdy wooden framework around a comfortable chair and attached 47 skyrockets to the back of the seat. Atop it he fastened two large kites.

After strapping himself to the chair, he raised his hand and servants carrying blazing torches advanced toward the vehicle and ignited the skyrockets. A moment later there was a mighty blast, followed by an impressive cloud of black smoke. Wan Hoo vanished, leaving nothing behind but a legend.[88]

A UPI report by Tony Samstag originating in Oslo, Norway in the early 1980s was entitled *Hunt for 1633 Rocket* and was a brief article about how Norwegian and Turkish scientists hope to collaborate "history's first manned rocket" from beneath the Bosphorus Straits of Turkey. According to the story, the rocket, fueled by gun powder, was fired in 1633, according to records in the Topkapi Museum with a pilot named Hasan Celebi aboard. The 10 foot long projectile had a central fuel-driven motor with six smaller engines fastened on the outside.

Said Norwegian engineer Tore Thoerud "It is not immediately clear where the pilot sat as he flew 300 metres (980 feet) over the Bosphorus before launching himself in the world's first hang-glider."

Yet it is apparent that the *Vimanas* of ancient times were not powered by rocket technology.

The best place to begin a discussion of *Vimanas* is to discuss the ancient texts themselves.

Among the more famous ancient texts that mention aerial cars (Vimanas) are the *Ramayana* and *Mahabharata.* Other lesser known texts include the *Samarangana Sutradhara,* the *Yuktikalpataru of Bhoja* (12th century A.D.) the *Mayamatam* (attributed to the architect Maya celebrated in the Mahabharata), the *Rg Veda,* the *Yajurveda* and the *Ataharvaveda.*

According to the Indian historian Ramachandra Dikshitar who wrote the still classic text on ancient Indian warfare,[5] other texts which mention aerial vehicles and travels are the *Satapathya Brahmanas;* the *Rg Veda*

34

Samhita; the *Harivamsa;* the *Makandeya Purana;* the *Visnu Purana;* the *Vikramaurvasiya;* the *Uttararamacarita;* the *Harsacarita;* the Tamil text *Jivakacintamani;* and the *Samaranganasutradhara..*[5] The complete text of Dikshitar's discussion on aerial warfare and Vimanas, with some passages in Sanskrit can be found in Appendix A of this book.

§§§

In the *Manusa,* the most elaborate details for building aerial machines are set down. The *Samarangana Sutradhara* says that they were made of light material, with a strong, well-shaped body. Iron, copper, mercury and lead were used in their construction. They could fly to great distances and were propelled by air by motors. The *Samarangana Sutradhara* text devotes 230 stanzas to the building of these machines, and their uses in peace and war:

"Strong and durable must the body be made, like a great flying bird, of light material. Inside it one must place the *Mercury-engine* with its iron heating apparatus beneath. By means of the *power latent in the mercury* which sets the driving *whirlwind* in motion, a man sitting inside may travel a great distance in the sky in a most marvelous manner.

"Similarly by using the prescribed processes one can build a vimana as large as the temple of the God-in-motion. Four strong *mercury* containers must be built into the interior structure. When these have been heated by controlled fire from iron containers, the vimana develops thunder-power through the mercury. And at once it becomes a pearl in the sky.

"Moreover, if this iron engine with properly welded joints be filled with mercury, and the fire be conducted to the upper part it develops power with the roar of a lion."[1]

35

The *Ramayana* describes a vimana as a double-deck, circular (cylindrical) aircraft with portholes and a dome. It flew with the "speed of the wind" and gave forth a "melodious sound" (a humming noise?). Ancient Indian texts on *Vimanas* are so numerous it would take several books to relate what they have to say. The ancient Indians themselves wrote entire flight manuals on the control of various types of Vimanas, of which there were basically four: the Shakuna Vimana, the Sundara Vimana, the Rukma Vimana and the Tripura Vimana.

At the *World Space Conference* on October 11, 1988 in Bangalore, India, as reported in the local newspaper called *The Hindu,* an Italian by the name of Dr. Roberto Pinotti addressed the delegates and spoke on ancient Indian Vimanas. After briefly telling them what Vimanas were, he went on to say that the *Tripura Vimana* was powered by motive power generated by solar rays and had an elongated form similar to a modern blimp.

He went on to say that the "ancient Aryans knew the use of the element 'fire' as could be seen from their 'Astra' weapons that included *soposamhara* (a flame belching missile), *Prasvapna* (which caused sleep) and four kinds of *Agni Astras* that traveled in sheets of flame and produced thunder."

While Dr. Pinotti concluded his talk by telling the delegates that they should take the subject of Vimanas seriously, he was really speaking to the foreign delegates, as most Indians, especially Hindus or those of religions derived from Hinduism such as Buddhism or Jainism, already believe that their ancestors had such a technology.

Pinotti also mentioned (as does Desmond Leslie[1]) the the *Samara Sutradhara* is a scientific treaty dealing with every possible angle of air travel in a *Vimana*. There are 230 stanzas dealing with construction, take-off, cruising for thousands of miles, normal and forced landings, and even possible collisions with birds.

The *Vaimanika Sastra,* (sometimes spelled *Vimanika Shastra* or *Vymaanika-Shaastra*) perhaps the most important ancient text on Vimanas (reprinted in full in this book) was first reported to have been found in 1918 in the Baroda Royal Sanskrit Library. Baroda is located north of Bombay and south of Ahmedabad in Gujerat. No earlier copies have been reported, however, Swami Dayananda Saraswati in his comprehensive treatise on the *Rg Veda* dated 1875 references the *Vaimanaik Sastra* in his commentary, as well as other manuscripts on Vimanas.[3]

The *Vaimanika Sastra* refers to 97 past works and authorities, of which at least 20 works deal with the mechanism of aerial Flying Machines, but none of these works are now traceable.[3] Says Sanskrit literature professor Dileep Kumar Kanjilal, Ph.D. of the West Bengal Senior Educational Service, "Since the transcripts of the work date from early 20th century the authenticity of the Vai. Sastra may be pertinently questioned. On careful analysis it has been found that the work retained some antique features pertaining to an old *Sastra.* Like the Sutras of Panini the rules have been laid down in an aphoristic style with the explanation couched in Vrittis and Karikas. The Sutra style is to be found in the earliest works on grammar, Smrti and Philosophy, while the use of Karikas is as old as Batsyayana, Kautilya and others of the early Christian era. Bharadwaja as the author of a Srauta Satra and Smrti work is well-known and a sage Bharadwaja as the seer of the 6th Mandala of the Rg Veda is also well-known. Panini also referred to him in VII. II.63. Kautilya had also shown that Bharadwaja was an ancient author on Politics. The Mbh. (*Mahabharata*, Santiparva Ch. 58.3) refers to Bharadwaja as an author on politics. Authors on politics have very often been found to have written on the technical sciences also. The genuineness, therefore, of any

37

treatise on technical sciences composed by Bharadwaja cannot be ignored.[3]

With the authenticity of the *Vaimanika Sastra* verified, Professor Kanjilal then struggles to ascertain the date in which Bharadwaja assembled the manuscript from earlier sources. According to Kanjilal, only four out of the 97 works and treatises quoted in the *Vaimanika Sastra* are still extant. Says he: "It appears that most of these works were very old and are now lost."[3]

The *Vaimanika Sastra* refers to no less than thirty-six authorities on various technical sciences, all of which date from at least the 8th century B.C. and most, if not all, from much earlier. Chronologically the authorities mentioned in the *Vaimanika Sastra* are: Valmiki, the legendary author of the *Ramayana* (circa 3000 to 1000 B.C.); Apastamba (450 B.C.); Gobhila (4th century B.C.); Usanas (3rd Century B.C.); Vasistha (circa 2nd century B.C.); Atri (before the 3rd century B.C. as cited by the Sanskrit historian Manu); Garga, an astronomer and astrologer cited in the *Mahabharata* (Kanjilal places him prior to 500 B.C., he is more likely from a period much earlier, at least 900 B.C.); Vyasa, the legendary author of the *Mahabharata* (although another Vyasa was a writer on "Smrti" was much later, circa 200 A.D.); Angiras (c. 1st century A.D. according to Kanjilal); Gautama (Buddha? circa 500 B.C.); Jaimini (c. 500 B.C.); Gobhila, author of "Saruta" and "Grhyasutra" (c.500 B.C.); Saunaka, probable author of the *"Saruta"* and *"Grhyasutra"* (c. 500 B.C.); Saunaka (as author of the *"Rkpratisakhya"* he can be placed earlier 500 B.C.); and Sakatayana (before the 5th century B.C.).[3]

Most of the above authorities are from the 5th century B.C. which tends to place the origin of the *Vaimanika Sastra* at the 4th century B.C. However, anomalies such Angiras and other authorities mentioned in

38

the text such as Lalla, Vachaspati Isvara and Samba (not mentioned above) may be from the period of the 6th century A.D. Yet, it seems that none of these persons can be clearly identified, as these names, strange to Westerners, are quite common in Hindi/Sanskrit, and while well known persons having these names may have existed in the 5th, 6th or 9th century A.D., the actual works sited by Bharadwaja are unknown. Therefore, the actual authors being referred to may easily be from the 5th century B.C. or earlier. For instance, Kanjilal says that Samba may be the Samba who is the author of the *"Samba Purana"* of the late 9th A.D. or he may be the Samba who is identified in the Mahabharata as the son of Krishna (or another person entirely).[3] Considering the thrust of Bharadwaja's *Vaimanika Sastra* , the latter identity as Krishna's son is more likely, considering that two other persons from the *Mahabharata* are referenced.

Therefore, it can be concluded that the *Vaimanika Sastra* was written, at the very latest, in the 10th century A.D. and apparently at the very earliest, in the 4th century B.C. It is unquestionably taken entirely from earlier texts, as the author, Bharadwaja, himself says frequently. These ancient texts probably reference still earlier texts, many in Dravidian, the language of the Rama Empire. That India is really the only ancient country in which ancient books have actually survived the ravages of history and purposeful destruction of libraries is discussed in the next chapter.

Says the *Vaimanika Sastra* about itself: "In this book are described in 8 pregnant and captivating chapters, the arts of manufacturing various types of Aeroplanes of smooth and comfortable travel in the sky, as a unifying force for the Universe, contributive to the well-being of mankind.

"That which can go by its own force, like a bird, on earth, or water, or in air, is called *'Vimana.'*

39

"That which can travel in the sky, from place to place, land to land, or globe to globe, is called *'Vimana'* by scientists in Aeronautics."[48]

The ancient manuscript claims to give: "The secret of constructing aeroplanes, which will not break, which cannot be cut, will not catch fire, and cannot be destroyed.

"The secret of making planes motionless.

"The secret of making planes invisible.

"The secret of hearing conversations and other sounds in enemy planes.

"The secret of of receiving photographs of the interior of enemy planes.

"The secret of ascertaining the direction of enemy planes' approach.

"The secret of making persons in enemy planes lose consciousness.

"The secret of destroying enemy planes."[48]

The manuscript is highly detailed and gives such information and advice as: ... "Just as our body, if complete in all its limbs, can achieve all things, so an Aeroplane should be complete in all its parts in order to effective. Commencing from the photographing-mirror underneath, an aeroplane should have 31 parts."

"The pilot should be provided with different materials of clothing according to differences in seasons, as prescribed by Agnimitra."

"Three varieties of food should be given to pilots, varying with the seasons of the year, as Kalpa-Sastra. 25 kind of of poisons which arise in the seasons are destroyed the above changes in diet."

"Food is of five forms, cooked grain, gruel, paste, bread, and essence. All of them are wholesome and body-building."

"Metals suitable for Aeroplanes, light and heat-absorbing, are of sixteen kinds, according to Shaunaka. Great sages have declared that these metals alone are the best for aeroplane construction."[48]

§§§

There are many other ancient texts from India that provide fascinating and incredible information on the highly technological ancient world, of which ancient India was only a part. The *Bhagavad Gita* (known as *Srimad-Bhagavatam* to Hindus) is part of the *Mahabharata.* In text 19 of the Third Canto we read (as translated by Bhaktivedanta Swami Prabhupada, founder of the ISCON movement):

"The elder child, Hiranyakasipu, was unafraid of death from anyone within the three worlds because he received a benediction from Lord *Brahma.* He was proud and puffed up due to this benediction and was able to bring all three planetary systems under his control."

That Hiranyakasipu was in control of three planetary systems is an incredible statement, and one that seems a bit out of line for a supposedly primitive people whose main interest was growing food, hunting and gathering and fending off wild animals. Yet, these "cave-men" were, by their own written records, quite sophisticated and in possession of not only aircraft, but spacecraft as well.

It is interesting to conjecture as to what three planetary systems they are talking about. It may be assumed that earth is one of these systems. Considering the fascinating photos of pyramids and other structures found on Mars by NASA, we may believe Mars to have been a planet worthy of "bringing under control." Perhaps Venus (sometimes referred to as *Hesperus*) is the third planet. Even more interestingly, perhaps this third planet is that of

"Maldek" a planet that supposedly once existed between Mars and Jupiter, where the asteroid belt exists today.

This planet allegedly blew itself up many thousands of years ago, while playing around with some very dangerous and destructive technology — a lesson that our planet at this point in time and space might be well to learn before we repeat such a cosmic disaster.

The idea of the three planetary systems being brought under control would seem to have to be done via physical travel in a space ship, though the fascinating book *Easy Journey To Other Planets*, also written by Bhaktivedanta Swami Prabhupada, founder of the *ISCON* movement. This book is about astral travel, however, and not about visiting other planets in mechanical devices.

One Sanskrit authority who has held to the idea of the Vimanas of ancient India texts as genuine flying machines of the past is Dr. V. Raghavan who wrote the classic book Yantras or Mechanical Contrivances in Ancient India.[96] This book was first published in 1952 by *The Indian Institute of Culture* in Bangalore and republished in 1956 with a second introduction by the author.

The short book, to be used as a school text by students of ancient Indian literature and science, is a reference to all kinds of mechanical contrivances, including robots, war machines and aircraft, in classical Indian literature. Dr. Raghavan (a professor at the University of Madras) answers his critics in the preface to the second edition (1956) by saying: "Regarding these critics I only want to emphasize what I have clearly stated in the opening of my lecture as to my exact intention in presenting this material. In the whole thesis, I have not myself made any claim or argued that aeroplanes were roaring across the skies in ancient India. I have not pressed into service any unpublished manuscript said to exist in secret or private possession and claiming to contain precious information on

42

the construction of *Vimanas* or aerial vehicles. I have, on the contrary, used only the most reputed works, the references to different *yantras* in which have to be explained, if one does not want to close his eyes to them."[96]

Indeed, Dr. Raghavan is possibly referring to such secret libraries as Churchward claimed to have consulted (of dubious value to the scholar, certainly) and discounting his own treatise in such light, as all of his references are from freely available sources. One need not turn to obscure sources on Vimanas when a great deal of material is available. Dr. Raghavan's answer to those critics who object to his discussions of ancient Indian aircraft is "What meaning do the critics propose to attach to the manifold *yantra* references in the epics...?"[96]

Dr. Raghavan quotes many sources and his book if filled with classical stories of people and their flying machines, artisans whose specialty is to construct aircraft, and amusing tales of robots and other strange, exotic "contrivances." He quotes from the *Samaranganasutradhara* attributed to Bhoja at length. This ancient text, "in many ways, a rare treatise in Sanskrit literature" says Raghavan, is particularly revealing because it goes into great detail on the construction, propulsion and uses of aircraft. Bhoja, with Raghavan's commentary, gives certain details on the mercury engine that propelled the craft.

Dr. Raghavan also gives details on how *Vimanas* were used to frightened war elephants (a more common scene usually ascribed to ancient India), and even on mechanical birds that flew, mainly as toys and amusement devices. Apparently some Vimanas were similar to cylindrical airships and "flying saucers" while other *Vimanas* were more typical of an airplane with wings, modeled after nature's own invention of birds and other flying animals.

Ancient artifacts of aircraft with wings have been found. In 1898 a model was found in an Egyptian tomb near Sakkara. It was labeled a "bird" and cataloged object 6347 at the *Egyptian Museum* in Cairo. Then in 1969 Dr. Khalil Messiha was startled to see that the bird not only had straight wings, but also an upright tailfin. To Dr. Messiha, the object appeared to be that of a model airplane.

It is made of wood, weighs 39.12 grams and remains in good condition. The wingspan is 18 cm, the aircraft's nose is 3.2 cm long and the overall length is 14 cm. The extremities of the aircraft and the wingtips are aerodynamically shaped. Apart from a symbolic eye and two short lines under the wings, it has no decorations nor has it any landing legs. Experts have tested the model and found it airworthy.

After this sensational discovery, the Minister for Culture, Mohammed Gamal El Din Moukhtar, commissioned a technical research group to put other birds under the microscope. The team nominated on Dec. 23, 1971 consisted of Dr. Henry Riad, Director of the *Museum of Egyptian Antiquity,* Dr. Abdul Quader Selim, Deputy Director of the Egyptian Museum for Archaeological Research, Dr. Hismat Nessiha, Director of the Department of Antiquities, and Kamal Naguib, President of the Egyptian Aviation Union. On January 12, 1972, the first exhibition of Ancient Egyptian model aircraft was opened in the Hall of the *Egyptian Museum for Antiquities.* Dr. Abdul Quader Hatem, Representative of the Prime Minister, and the Air Minister Ahmed Moh presented fourteen Ancient Egyptian model aircraft to the public.

Another curious exhibit at the Egyptian Museum in Cairo is a large display of boomerangs found in the tomb of King Tutankhamen. While boomerangs may not be models of ancient aircraft, they demonstrate that the Egyptians were highly interested in the mechanics of flight, as few devices operate like a boomerang after being thrown. A number of Egyptian reliefs show Egyptians hunting with boomerangs.

It has long been shown by the pundits of higher learning that ancient texts, legends, traditions and even actual artifacts such as models and frescoes are not sufficient proof of anything, especially when it runs contrary to the established academic dogma.

A relief from the underground chamber in the Temple of Hathor at Dendera, Egypt. It shows priests carrying devices attached by a braided cable to an altar. Supporting the "light bulbs" are Djed columns, associated with the Egyptian god Osiris. Are these ancient electrical devices?

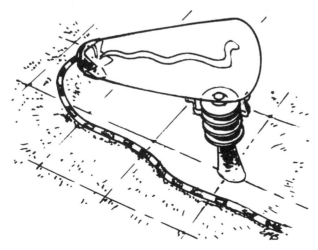

A perspective drawing by artist Eliot Brown of the device at the Temple of at Dendera, Egypt. Was it used to light the temples?

That electricity was known to the ancients is proved by these electric batteries from the first century B.C. now in the Bagdad Museum in Iraq.

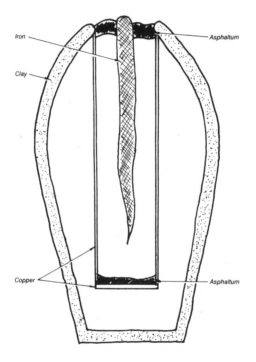

Baghdad Battery. Willard Gray of the General Electric High Voltage Laboratory produced the sketch above based on the specifications of the 2000-year-old Baghdad battery. With the addition of copper sulfate, acetic acid, or even citric acid, this battery will produce an electrical current. In the *Grand Dictionaire Universal du 19th Siecle* the French archaeologist Auguste Mariette writes that while excavating in the area of the Great Pyramid at a depth of 60 feet, he discovered gold jewelry whose thinness and lightness "make one believe they had been produced by electroplating."

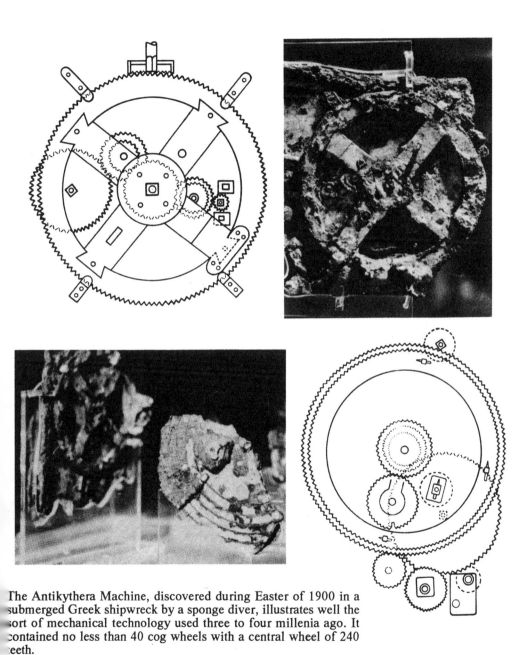

The Antikythera Machine, discovered during Easter of 1900 in a submerged Greek shipwreck by a sponge diver, illustrates well the sort of mechanical technology used three to four millenia ago. It contained no less than 40 cog wheels with a central wheel of 240 teeth.

Three men or "gods" are apparently hovering in a flying machine above a half-moon in this cylinder seal from the British Museum in London. On the left is an unexplained rocket-like object.

A common Assyrian symbol found on cylinder seals and other reliefs. It may show an ancient *Vimana*

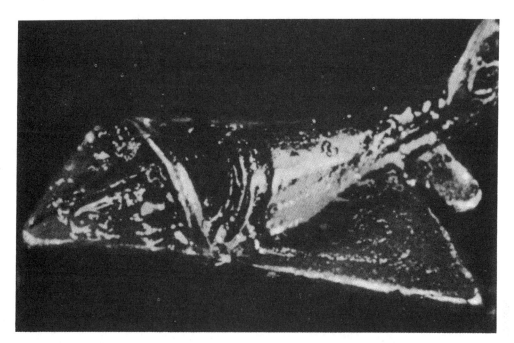

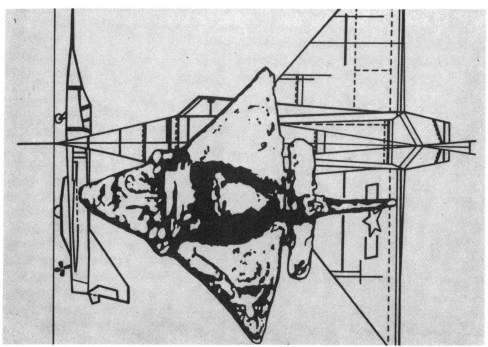

A solid gold model of an aircraft on show at the State Museum in Bogota, Columbia. It, and several others like it have been called religious objects, bees, birds, stingrays and other things. Technical tests prove that it is airworthy.

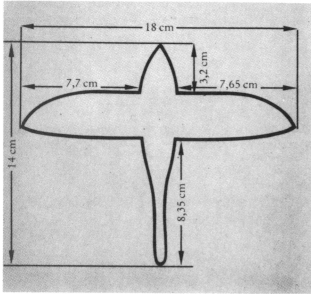

This apparent model of an airplane was found in an Egyptian tomb in 1898 and kept in the Cairo Egyptian Antiquities Museum. In 1969 it was brought to the world's attention by Dr. Khalil Missiha because he noticed that the "bird" (catalogue # 6347) had straight wings and a tail fin.

3

THE ANCIENT RAMA
EMPIRE OF INDIA

Rama ruled the earth for eleven thousand years.
He gave a year-long festival
in this very Naimisha Forest.
All of this land was in his kingdom then;
one age of the world ago;
long, long ago;
long before now, and far in the past.
Rama was King from the center of the world
to the four Oceans' shores.
—The *Ramayana by Valmiki*

§§§

Perhaps the best evidence for advanced civilizations and the use of aircraft in the remote past is the remarkable pre-Aryan Indian Epic of the *Ramayana*.

The *Ramayana* (literally, "Rama's Way") is one of the great Indian Epics, handed down over thousands of years to the twenty-first century. Even the author to which the Ramayana is attributed, the poet Valmiki, has achieved a legendary status. The Ramayana is some 25,000 verses long. It tells a story of romantic courtly intrigue, heroic renunciation, fierce battles and the triumph of good over evil. The hero is Prince Rama of Ayodhya. Born into a family of noble rulers, the treacherous machinations of his stepmother force him to abdicate his claim to the throne of Ayodhya in favor of his half-brother, Bharata. Rama withdraws into the forest for thirteen years accompanied by his faithful wife Sita and devoted half-brother, Lakshmana. Here they battle demons called the Rakshasas, who kidnap the beautiful Sita. The evil demon king Ravana takes her away in his Vimana, or flying machine, to his capital on the island of Lanka (Ceylon). He urges her to yield to him and be his queen, but she remains faithful to her husband, Rama.

Meanwhile, Rama and Lakshamana search frantically for signs of Sita. They go from one witness to another to learn her whereabouts. Finally, they ally themselves with an army of talking monkeys and bears. The army operates under the generalship of the great monkey, Hanuman. The animals discover that the place where Sita is kept prisoner is Ceylon and Hanuman crosses the water to visit her.

After setting fire to the city he returns to Rama who decides he must rescue his wife by force. With the help of thousands upon thousands of monkeys they build a causeway between the mainland and the island. A frightful battle ensues and hosts of monkeys and demons are slaughtered. Both sides use devastatingly powerful weapons which are hurled from their flying machines and which destroy whole cities and disintegrate whole armies at a time. Naturally, Rama and his buddies win, Sita is saved, and they go back to Ayodhya in a flying machine, where Rama is crowned king. Unfortunately, in the end, vicious rumors about Sita's purity are spread, Rama is forced to banish her to the forest where she gives birth to Rama's two children, and the poet Valmiki helps her to raise them. Thus, the story comes full circle back to the story teller, Valmiki.[37]

The *Ramayana,* and its companion The *Mahabharata,* are something like a combination of George Lucas' *Star Wars* and J.R.R Tolkien's *Lord of the Rings.* In texts thousands of years old, the combatants fly around in metallic flying machines that run on some sort of "anti-gravity" mechanism and battle each other with particle beam weapons and horrifying explosive devices.

Many historians discount the Ramayana as being nothing more than the vivid opium dreams of a bunch of stone-age Indians. Fortunately, other more "open-minded" historians discern a thread of authenticity present in these great epics, and indeed, clues to the mysterious and fabulous past of ancient India, Ceylon, and even of Atlantis and "Mu."

According to the Indological Newsletter of Motilal Banarsidass Newsletter (Delhi) of January, 1989, in a 1988 conference in India, historians have claimed that Rama, the son of Dasharatha, ruled over Ayodhya during 5000 B.C. This theory was expounded by Dr. Kunwarlal Jain Vyas "who has tried to establish the date after an in-depth study of puranic sources and literature. Several papers were read regarding dates of the events of Pre-Mahabharata period on the occasion of this conference called "Itihasa Bharati." The papers said that Manu existed 31,000 years ago, Harinya-Kashyap 12,000 B.C.; Indra, Vishnu and Bali lived 11,000 B.C. in the seventh yuga while Parshurama, Rama and Dasharatha belong to the twenty-fourth yuga, i.e. 5,000 B.C. This is proved by the literatures of India and its neighboring countries. On the basis of his study, Dr. Vyas determined the period of a historical cycle to be of 360 years. He told that there is an interval of 71 cycles between Manu and Mahabharata period, which comes out to be 26,000 years. So Manu can be ascribed a period of about 31,000 years from now."

The same newsletter, speaking about the same conference says that the Hindu historian Acharya Ram Dayal exposed the trick played by western historians when discussing Indian history. Although the newsletter does say what this trick is, one can easily guess that the trick is a manipulation of dates to make Indian history much more recent than the ancient epics distinctly proclaim. Certainly 31,000 years of history in India is bound to raise even the most liberal eyebrows of academia!

§§§

It is only by Shiva's grace that my composition can be beautified, as is the night by the moon and her company of stars. Those who will hear and repeat this story with love and understanding will be purged of the defilement of the *Kaliyuga* and, loving the feet of *Rama*, shall enjoy heavenly felicity.

If the grace of Shiva and Parvati be at all truly with me, even in dream, then all the influence I claim for my verses, composed in the vulgar tongue, shall come true.

I reverence the very holy city of *Ayodhya* and the river Sarayu that washes away the impurities of the *Kaliyuga*; and again I do reverence to the inhabitants of that city, who enjoy the affection of the Lord in no small degree.
—The Shriramacharitamanasa
by Tulasidasa, Twelfth Century A.D. Hindu commentary on the Ramayana of Valmiki.

The devastating wars of the Ramayana and particularly of the Mahabharata are said to have been the culmination of the terrible wars of the last Kali Yuga. The dating process is difficult, in that there is no exact way to date the yugas because there are cycles within cycles and yugas within yugas. A greater yuga cycle is said to last 6000 years while a smaller yuga cycle is only 360 years in the theory expounded by Dr. Kunwarlal Jain Vyas. His papers said that Rama belongs to the twenty-fourth small yuga cycle and that there is an interval of 71 cycles between Manu and Mahabharata period, which comes out to be 26,000 years.

In the large yuga cycle as expounded at the Mount Abu Raja Yoga center, we are now at the last few moments of a 6,000 year greater Kali Yuga cycle, ending in the year 2000 or so. The last ending of a greater Kali Yuga cycle was 24,000 years ago, or 22,000 B.C. According to the *Lemurian Fellowship*, an esoteric brotherhood formed in the 1930s, this is the time of a cataclysmic shift in the earth's tectonic plates and the sinking a large continent in the Pacific, generally known as Lemuria or Mu, but sometimes called Pan, Rutas, Hiva or Pacifica.

Other cataclysmic earth shifts were occur later (a natural cyclic occurrence, they and others claim, happening ever seven to ten thousand years, depending on accumulated ice at one or more of the poles, planetary positions and other factors. They place the time of Atlantis and Rama, as well as Osiris (in the Mediterranean and North Africa) and the Uigers of the fertile Gobi Desert area as being of a time after that Kali Yuga, a golden age from approximately 22,000 B.C. to 16,000 B.C. when man lived in peace with his fellow man and in harmony with nature, much as it had been prior to 28,000 B.C. during the height of the so-called Mukullian Empire on the Pacific continent (Mu, or whatever). This was two Treta Yugas ago (34,000 to 28,000 B.C.) The last Treta Yuga 10,000 to 4,000 B.C., which was the period of the decline of Atlantis and Rama and the period when Valmiki probably wrote the ancient Ramayana (circa 4,000 B.C.) in ancient Dravidian, a now extinct language from which Tamil is partially derived.

According to the *Lemurian Fellowship*, Lemuria sank at about 24,000 B.C., which would place it at the end of a Kali Yuga and the beginning of a new Krita Yuga. In Indian cosmology, the Krita Yuga marks a time which is a "Golden Age" of enlightenment. Each Yuga becomes progressively worse, until a cataclysmic destruction at the end of the Kali

Yuga destroys the world. Then a new Golden Age starts again. Auspiciously, we are at the end of a Kali Yuga.

Interestingly, the *Ramayana's* time line fits in well with the occurrence of cataclysmic changes and civilizations outlined by the *Lemurian Fellowship.* Says the *Ramayana.* "We live now in the third age of Time, and Rama lived in the second age of the world." Perhaps the time of Mu, the supposed Mother-Civilization of the World was the first age, the time of Atlantis and Rama the second age, as the Ramayana says; the time after the destruction of Atlantis and Rama, and the time when the great epics were written was the third age, and the fourth age is the time in which we are now living.

The Kali Yuga which is referred to by Tulasidasa, of the Twelfth Century A.D. is therefore a small yuga cycle, lasting 360 years. It is fascinating to think that we are only just now completing a 24,000 year cycle which began approximately 22,000 B.C. Traditionally, Kali Yugas end with a massive and devastating world war in which the combatants virtually wipe each other out, taking most of civilization with them. Who can deny that we are apparently on the verge of such an event ourselves?

It is especially ironic to consider, especially in the light of so-called free energy motors, anti-gravity, gyroscopes, magnets, crystals and vortex technology as apparently used in Vimanas and other craft, that our current "war of Armageddon" is largely due to oil, energy cartels, and maintaining a certain amount of out-dated technology, coupled with religious and political fanaticism! One wonders if the fantastic wars of the past were fought for similar purposes?

Another fascinating thought along those same lines is that even the combatants in these wars, the leaders and common soldiers being sent to the sudden and violent termination of their current incarnations, may be the reincarnated souls from previous wars, working out their collective and personal karma for better or for worse.

It is a well known fact that the famous American WWII General George Patton believed himself to be the reincarnation of a Roman General, and believed many Nazi German Generals and leaders to have been the reincarnations of the Huns and Vandals who had destroyed Rome.

Similarly, it has been reported that Saddam Hussein, the Military Dictator of Iraq believes himself to be the reincarnation of the Babylonian king Nebucaneezer whose army destroyed Jerusalem, the Temple, and took the Israelites into captivity in Babylon, present day Iraq!

According to adepts of Raja Yoga, the man of violence and war will reincarnate during the periods of Kali Yuga (and other times as well). Each a chance to change their way of thinking and therefore their entire life, and so improve their karma. However, many are sucked deeper into negative karmic situations by participating in violence and destruction for what they believe to be a justifiable cause.

Perhaps this is why Christ told his disciples that "the meek shall inherit the earth," because the man of violence and war will be removed from incarnation in the next Yuga, the Krita Yuga.

§§§

One way to unravel the tangled web of the *Ramayana* is to go back to *The Lemurian Fellowship* lessons' accounts of ancient Mukulia and see what sense can be made out of the Ramayana story.

According to their lesson material, the non-citizens of Mukulia divided into two opposing factions, which had grown to be poles apart in philosophy. The first group, the "Phrees" prized practicality. Generally they worked in the

Empire as highly skilled laborers and professionals. The second group, the "Katholis", prized spirituality and were more interested in "artistic" pursuits. The Citizenry of the Empire by contrast were "balanced" mentally; they could see the value of both sides. As open conflict manifested between the two groups, the government encouraged the emigration of these peoples to hitherto uninhabited lands. The main colony of the Phrees was established upon an island group in the Atlantic Ocean called Poseid, while the main colony of the Katholis was established in India.[60]

Even today, Indians, especially the women, prize spirituality above all things. Throwing oneself on the funeral pyre of one's husband is still customary in many parts of India today. Atlantis, by many reports (all rather difficult to verify, unfortunately) developed a technology which was described as being extremely advanced and rather war-like.

The *Lemurian Fellowship* lessons state that the destruction of Lemuria occurred circa 24,000 B.C. The civilization which developed in ancient India afterwards was known as the Rama Empire, and was ruled by Priest-Kings called "Rishis" who were "Adepts". Rishi is a Sanskrit term meaning "Master" or "Great Teacher." The Rishis were wise and kind and possessed considerable "yogic" powers. The Rama Empire spread out to include most of the Indian sub-continent. It probably extended as far west as Iran or so, and as far east as Burma. There were seven capital cities known as "The Seven Rishi Cities of the Rama Empire." The Lemurian Fellowship does not say which cities these were, but my guess is that they included Ayodhya, Nagpur, Mathura, Mohenjo Daro, Lothal, Kot Diji, Kalibangan, Dwarka and Harappa. It is also probable that both Benares (Varanasi) and Madurai (in southern India) were inhabited cities during the Rama Empire. This would probably make them the oldest inhabited cities in the world!

§§§

During the heyday of Atlantis and Rama, both the Ramayana and the *Lemurian Fellowship* agree that other advanced civilizations were also in existence. According to the *Lemurian Fellowship* the Osiris Civilization existed in what is today North Africa and the Mediterranean Basin, and the Uiger Empire ruled over what is today the Gobi Desert. Yet of all of the civilizations, Atlantis and Rama were supposedly the two most developed.

These two cultures had developed advanced technology, which they shared between themselves and the rest of the world. It had been mainly developed in Atlantis and would seem like science fiction to us today, just as the *Ramayana* and *Mahabharata* seem like science fiction. Not only did they have aircraft such as vimanas and vailxi (as the Atlantean craft was called), they had weapons such as fireballs that could destroy a whole city, "Kapilla's Glance" which could burn fifty thousand men to ashes in seconds and flying spears that could ruin whole "cities full of forts."[37,58,46,47,49]

According to The Lemurian Fellowship, as Atlantis and Rama each reached the height of civilization, war broke out between them. The Atlanteans, a highly technical, patriarchal and war-like culture were bent on conquering the world. Subjugating the Rama Empire was an important step in their plan.

Although both sides had airships, Atlantis had developed military applications for its technology, while the Rama Empire had always applied its technology towards peaceful purposes. The main vehicles for both nations during their war were airships, called Vimanas in Indian Epics, and Vailxi by the Atlanteans.

An interesting episode in Atlantean history as related by The Lemurian Fellowship involves the Atlanteans sending a well-equipped army to India in order to subjugate the Rama Empire and bring it under the sovereignty of Atlantis. Equipped with "a formidable array of weapons," the Atlanteans landed their vailxi outside one of the Rishi cities. They got their troops in order and sent a message to the ruling Priest-King of the city that they should surrender. The Priest-King sent word back to the Atlantean general: "We of India have no quarrel with you of Atlantis. We ask only that we be permitted to follow our own way of life."

The Atlanteans regarded the Rishi's mild request as a confession of weakness. Expecting an easy victory, as the Rama Empire did not possess the technology of war nor the aggressiveness of the Atlanteans, the general sent another message: "We shall not destroy your land with the mighty weapons at our command provided you pay sufficient tribute and accept the rulership of Atlantis."

The Priest-King of the city responded humbly again, seeking to avert war: "We of India do not believe in war and strife, peace being our ideal. Neither would we destroy you or your soldiers who but follow orders. However, if you persist in your determination to attack us without cause and merely for the purpose of conquest, you will leave us no recourse but to destroy you and all of your leaders. Depart, and leave us in peace."

Arrogantly, the Atlanteans did not believe that the Indians had the power to stop them; certainly not by technical means. At dawn, the Atlantean army began their march on the city. Sadly, the Priest-King watched the army advance from a high point of view. He raised his arms heavenward and, using a mental technique supposedly known to certain yogis in the Himalayas today, he caused the general and each officer in descending order of rank to drop dead in their tracks, apparently of a heart attack. Without leaders, the panicked Atlantean force fled to the waiting airships, and retreated back to Atlantis! Of the siege of the Rishi City, not one man from the Rama Empire was lost!19

The Indian Epics, especially the Mahabharata, pick up the thread of the tale from here and go on to tell the rest of the horrible story; a story of devastation and destruction. Apparently Atlantis, rather displeased at its humiliating defeat, decided that they were no longer interested in subjugating the Rama Empire, and decided instead to annihilate the major cities using weapons so destructive that Sanskrit scholars could not comprehend what was being described in the Epics until the first dropping of atomic bombs on Japan.

These are authentic verses from the Indian Epics:

"Gurkha, flying a swift and powerful vimana,
hurled a single projectile
charged with all the power of the Universe.
An incandescent column of smoke and flame,
as bright as ten thousand suns,
rose with all its splendor.

It was an unknown weapon,
an iron thunderbolt,
a gigantic messenger of death,
which reduced to ashes
the entire race of the Vrishnis and the Andhakas.

The corpses were so burned
as to be unrecognizable.
Hair and nails fell out;
Pottery broke without apparent cause,
and the birds turned white.

. . .After a few hours
all foodstuffs were infected. . .
. . .to escape from this fire
the soldiers threw themselves in streams

to wash themselves and their equipment."
—The Mahabharata

"(It was a weapon) so powerful
that it could destroy the earth in an instant—
A great soaring sound in smoke and flames—
And on it sits death. . ."
—*The Ramayana*

"Dense arrows of flame,
like a great shower,
issued forth upon creation,
encompassing the enemy. . . .
A thick gloom swiftly settled upon the Pandava hosts.
All points of the compass were lost in darkness.
Fierce winds began to blow.
Clouds roared upward,
showering dust and gravel.

Birds croaked madly . . .
the very elements seemed disturbed.
The sun seemed to waver in the heavens.
The earth shook,
scorched by the terrible violent heat of this weapon.
Elephants burst into flame
and ran to and fro in a frenzy . . .
over a vast area,
other animals crumpled to the ground and died.
From all points of the compass
the arrows of flame rained continuously and fiercely."
—*The Mahabharata*

§§§

THE QUEST FOR ANCIENT LANKA

Sri Lanka (formerly Ceylon) is about the size of Indiana, and is made up of low, rolling hills which culminate in a mountain range and jungle in the south central part of the island. Its history extends far back into the world of myth and legend; Sri Lanka plays a major part in the ancient Indian Epic of the Ramayana.

The earliest recorded history of Ceylon only goes as far back as the sixth century B.C. These records tell of a Prince Vijaya who was banished from India by his father, and who embarked on ships with seven hundred companions in search of a new home. Most scholars believe that Prince Vijaya was of Aryan stock, and came from northwestern India. Vijaya landed in Ceylon, and the reports he sent back home must have been encouraging, for soon he was joined by other princes and their followers. The new arrivals subdued the "savage inhabitants": the Yakkhas and Nagas, who already existed on the island.

The descendants of these ancient people can still be found in remote parts of the island. They are called Veddas, which in their own, obscure language means "hunter." Standing about five feet tall, with dark skin and frizzy hair, they wear clothes made of bark cloth. They live a nomadic existence sleeping in caves or crude huts. With bows, arrows, stone axes and hunting dogs, they hunt and gather fruit, wild yams, honey, truffles and fish.[41]

The prehistory of Ceylon is rather mysterious. It is generally believed that prior to Prince Vijaya, nothing more than stone-age men lived in Ceylon, yet there is a certain amount of evidence to indicate that this is not the case.

Modern history on the island begins with the advent of Buddhism in the third century B.C. Mahinda, son of the converted Buddhist Emperor Asoka, came from India to the court of the Devanampiya Tissa, who was a Sinhalese descendant of Prince Vijaya. After a series of sermons delivered at Anuradhapura, the king and most of the court

63

converted to Buddhism, a religion that stresses good deeds, positive thinking, harmless living and high moral conduct.

Later, Mahinda's sister brought a cutting from the Bodhi Tree to Ceylon; the tree under which the prince Siddhartha, later Gautama Buddha, had become enlightened according to Buddhist tradition. This tree was planted at Anuradhapura, and is still growing today, two and half thousand years later! After Siddhartha's cremation (the term Buddha actually means "wise one" in Sanskrit), his remains had been divided into eight main parts and then subdivided into more. When Mahinda's sister came she also brought Buddha's right collar bone and begging bowl and she enshrined them in a dagoba, or stupa. In the fourth century A.D. the left eyetooth of the Buddha was brought to Anuradhapura and preserved in a noble shrine; it was exhibited once a year. This tooth is now kept in the Temple of the Tooth in Kandy.

Anuradhapura has some of the most magnificent structures in the world! The largest is carved out of solid rock, covered with brass, and is larger in size than the Great Pyramid of Egypt. The Ruwanweli Pagoda, built in 144 B.C. is constructed on a base of solid silver. The silver is over 500 square feet in area and is seven inches thick. The value of the metal used in the foundation alone is estimated to equal over three million dollars![42]

In the late 19th century when the British excavated the ancient city which had been abandoned in the 11th century because of an invasion from Southern India, they uncovered an extremely sophisticated irrigation system. An engineer called Parker, who worked for the Irrigation Department of Ceylon was astounded at the skill of his ancient Ceylonese counterparts. Not only had they successfully created large reservoirs as early as the 4th century B.C., but by the 3rd century B.C., they were using a highly sophisticated discharge system: the valve-pit.

This involved a stone-lined sluice which had a gate that

could be raised or lowered to control the discharge of water from the reservoir. Its stones were finely worked to create a completely smooth internal face. Probably it had been originally lined with wood to make the sluice completely watertight. Parker marveled at the competent way in which the prehistoric engineers had coped with the problems of gravity and flow speed. The system fed three large man-made lakes that served as reservoirs.[39]

The British and other western archaeologists had been impressed at how a bunch of islanders had accomplished fairly modern engineering feats, though such an irrigation system would have been necessary for the prosperity of the culture since the northern part of Sri Lanka is quite arid. Also, the existence of modern technology in ancient cultures of India, including cultures that are far older than Anuradhapura, has been already been proven many times. What amazes the academics is that their findings consistently push the beginnings of technology and civilization farther and farther back in time. Suddenly, the mystics who have insisted that civilization hadn't started in Sumeria five thousand years ago, and that ancient peoples in India were quite sophisticated, have become correct.

§§§

From Paradise to Taprobane
is forty leagues:
There may be heard the sound of
The Fountains of Paradise.
—Traditional
Reported by the Friar Marignolli, A.D. 1335

In 1893, a young British officer named Percy Fawcett was stationed in Ceylon. Operating out of Trincomalee and keenly interested in archaeology, history and Buddhism, he would often take long walks, sometimes lasting for days, into the remote jungle areas of the island. On one such trek, he was overtaken by a storm, which forced him to seek shelter beneath some trees for the night. As dawn broke into a new, sunny day, he found himself near an immense rock, covered with strange inscriptions of unknown character and meaning.

He made a copy of the inscriptions, and later showed them to a local Buddhist priest. This priest said the writing was similar to that used by the old Asoka-Buddhists, and was in a cypher which only those ancient priests could understand. His assertion was confirmed ten years later by a Ceylonese Oriental scholar at Oxford University, who claimed that he was the only man alive who could read the script.[54,55]

Young Percy Fawcett, later to become a respected Colonel and one of the most famous South American explorers of all time, believed that the letters which he had seen on the ancient, vine covered wall in Ceylon, had been taken from the ancient Sansar alphabet. This alphabet was first discovered by the French traveler and missionary, Abbe Huc, in 1845 while visiting a lamasery on the frontier of Tibet and China. The lamasery, known as the monastery of Sinfau or Sifau, or more popularly, the Kumbum Monastery, contained the "mystic Kounboum tree"; upon each leaf of this tree a Sansar character was allegedly written. Kunbum or Kounboum means "ten thousand images" referring to the images on the leaves of the tree.

According to the report given to Huc, the tree and alphabet came from the drowned land of Rutas, which in central Asian mythology, is identical with Mu, Lemuria, or a lost Pacific continent. The tree itself was a white sandal tree of some sort, and was located in a great brick-walled court-yard of the Buddhist temple at the foot of a mountain. Each leaf of the tree bore a different character of Sansar, or ancient Sanskrit, the "language of the sun in the drowned land of sun-worshippers of Rutas." Other legend has it that the tree sprang from the Tibetan saint Tsong Khapa's hair. Given these two choices, the idea that tree came from a lost continent seems all the more likely (though probably both are equally false)!

Huc said the sweat mounted to his forehead in his effort to detect any lamaic fraud about the tree, which he added, "is very old, about eight feet high, with brilliant scarlet flowers, and nowhere else exists, and cannot be propagated from seeds or cuttings."[54] It is said that sometimes the tree will hold images of Buddha on its leaves, as well.

While legends in Central Asian monasteries do include stories of Rutas and Sansar, the "magical" Kounboun tree appears to have been a fraud. The Prussian traveler, Kreitner, visited the same lamasery in 1880 and saw neither letters nor Buddhas on the leaves of its trees. He says he did detect, however, an ironic smile on the corner of the mouth of the lama guide when asked about such images, and he suspected trickery with acids. Other travelers who visited the monastery at the turn of the century saw no images on the leaves. Robert Ripley, of the famed *Ripley's Believe It or Not* claimed he saw the images, or at least he included them in his feature, and an article appeared on them in a well known London Sunday paper in 1940.[54]

Lamas have been known to pull tricks to impress visitors, and it seems probable that the Kounboun tree may have been dressed up for important visitors. But even if the lamas had used acids to inscribe characters on leaves, what were these unknown characters? Were they truly Sansar, an ancient language from Mu?

A number of events were set into motion by young Percy Fawcett's finding of these strange characters on a rock wall in Ceylon, some involving mysteries still to be worked out. Colonel Fawcett set off from Cuyaba in the Mato Grosso in Brazil in 1925 to find a lost city in the jungle. He believed there was a connection between the city and the letters he had found in Ceylon. Neither he nor his two companions were ever seen again, and their expedition became the archetypical "lost expedition" (for more information on the fascinating story of Colonel Fawcett and his lost city, see my book, *Lost Cities & Ancient Mysteries of South America*).

If it is true, as Colonel Fawcett and certain Ceylonese scholars believed, that an ancient and vanished civilization once existed in Sri Lanka, where are the ruins of that civilization's cities? In the ancient Tamil literature of southern India there is a flood myth which tells of a destructive cataclysm and of two lost cities named Tenmaturai and Kapatapuram. These cities were two of three sites on which literary academies had been established. The third was at "Maturai," which is apparently the present day city of Madurai, near the southern tip of India. According to ancient tradition, there were forty-four rulers at Maturai before the great flood. Many cities were lost, but Maturai was reestablished afterward.[36]

Some sense of the time scale we are are dealing with when looking at myths from Indian literature can be gleaned by recognizing that the length of time that each of the literary academies existed were 4440 years for Tenmaturai, 3700 years for Kapatapuram and 1850 years for Maturai.[36] Assuming the existence of these literary academies to be factual (Maturai is a very real place, indeed), it would not be unreasonable to suggest that Tenmaturai and Kapatapuram were lost in a cataclysmic flood that in in all probability took place thousands of years ago. This being the case it would not be difficult to place the dates of these cities back to five or six thousand years B.C. if not earlier. Fantastic? These stories and dates are tame by comparison to other stories in the incredible realm of Indian literature!

According to the Ramayana, the ancient home of

Ravana, evil kidnapper of Rama's wife Sita, was the island of Lanka. Yet if Ceylon, officially named Sri Lanka now, is really the home of Ravana and the bad guys, where are the ancient cities, that were supposedly destroyed by the Vimanas and weapons of Rama? Perhaps they are there waiting to be discovered in the jungle growth. Recently some such megalithic cities in the interior of the island have been found!

The Sri Lankan archaeologist A. D. Fernanado in an article in the Journal of the Sri Lanka Branch of the Royal Asiatic Society (1982)[61] cites what may be one source of information about such a city. The Mahawamsa, the Buddhist "Bible" of the Sri Lankans which portrays the conquest of the island and building of Anuradhapura by Prince Vijaya, says that the early inhabitants of the island, the Yakkhas, had great skill in metallurgy. Reference is made to a temple with "gold images of 4 great kings, 32 maidens, 28 Yakkha chiefs, devas, dancing devetas playing instruments, devas with mirrors in hand and a host of other devas with flowers, lotus, swords and pitchers."[61,44]

Fernando claims that the true hydraulic engineers of Sri Lanka and Anuradhapura were the Yakkhas. According to the Mahawamsa, the Yakkhas were celebrating the marriage of the Yakkha king's daughter in the palace of the great city of Lanka, when Vijaya and his "lion soldiers" struck and conquered them. The official history of the island begins after this point.

Where the ancient Yakkha city of "Lanka" was located, we don't know for certain. It might be the megalithic fortress of Ariththa, presently located at Ritigala, where large prehistoric monoliths in perfect rectangular shapes standing 18 feet high by 6 feet by nearly 2 feet, and bearing a great similarity to Stonehenge in England can be found. Another city which Fernando discovered by air was that of Vijithapura covering 250 acres.

Perhaps the most incredible discovery of all occurred

69

when Sri Lankan engineers wanted to place a dam at Maduru Oya thereby drowning a large valley. As the bulldozers set to work they began to scrape against bricks which already lay in the ground. To everybody's amazement it turned out that prehistoric engineers had made the same calculations and had built a dam at the very same spot![61,44]

The Norwegian archaeologists visited the site and reported that the grandeur of these prehistoric megalithic waterworks would have impressed a Pharaoh. Heyerdahl says that much of the water system was constructed out of 15 ton blocks of stone 33 feet high and arranged in the shape of square tunnels and brick walls. The dams had sluices measuring more than 6 miles in length to control the water flow to a series of artificial lakes. Millions of tons of water had been regulated by this huge and sophisticated dam.[44]

Suddenly we realize that the primitive Yakkhas of Sri Lanka had not been so primitive after all, but instead were highly ingenious, sophisticated builders. Upon their conquest, the society gradually degenerated into a tribe of roving hunters; they probably became hunted themselves by the Sinhalese. Once again our dating for the rise of civilization has been pushed further back in time, and the great epic of the Ramayana is further vindicated. Could the Yakkhas have been the ancestors of the "evil" Ravana and his people who were defeated by Rama?

Another theory suggests that the "Lanka" of the Ramayana was actually located along the west coast of India in lands that are now submerged.

This area today is the Lacadive and Maldive islands. The Lacadive islands are part of India, while the Maldive islands are an independent nation to the south of them. Says James Churchward, author of the popular "Mu" series, "In the Indian Ocean, adjoining the West Coast of India, there exists a large area of submerged lands with structures

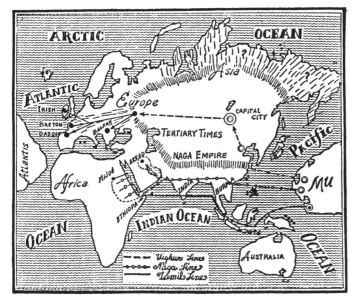

James Churchward's drawing of the dispersion of tribes from the ancient Pacific continent called variously Mu, Lemuria or others. The Naga Empire allegedly founded the Rama Empire.

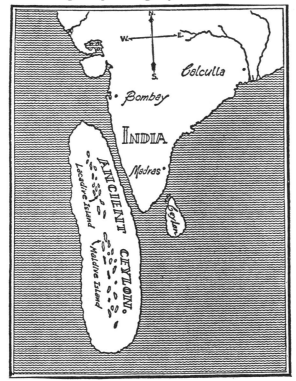

Churchward's drawing of ancient Ceylon, which is instead a large island that includes the Lacadive and Maldive Islands.

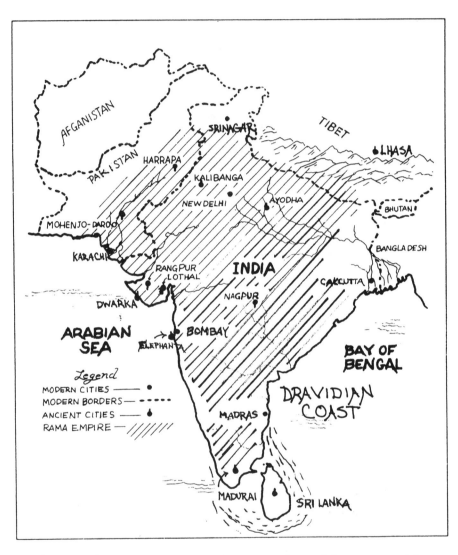

A map of the Rama Empire showing a few of the ancient cities in respect to modern India and Central Asia.

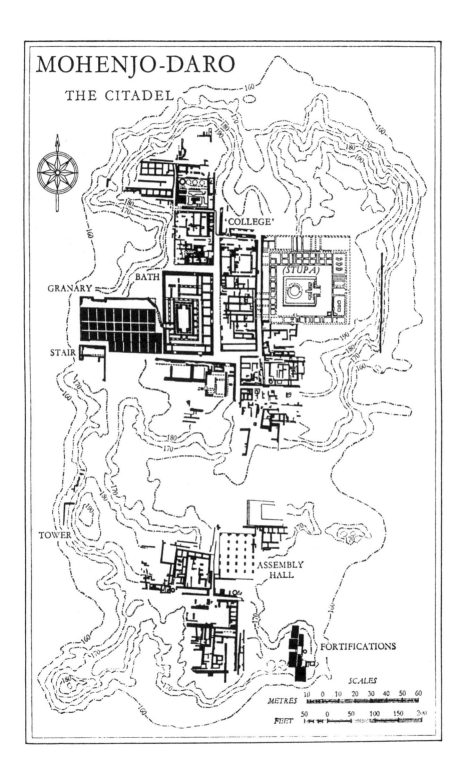

MOHENJO-DARO

THE CITADEL

'COLLEGE'

(STUPA)

GRANARY

BATH

STAIR

TOWER

ASSEMBLY
HALL

FORTIFICATIONS

SCALES

METRES   10   0   10   20   30   40   50   60

FEET   50   0   50   100   150   200

A so-called Priest-King from Mohenjo Daro. Is it possible that he was one of the adepts who ruled the Rama Empire?

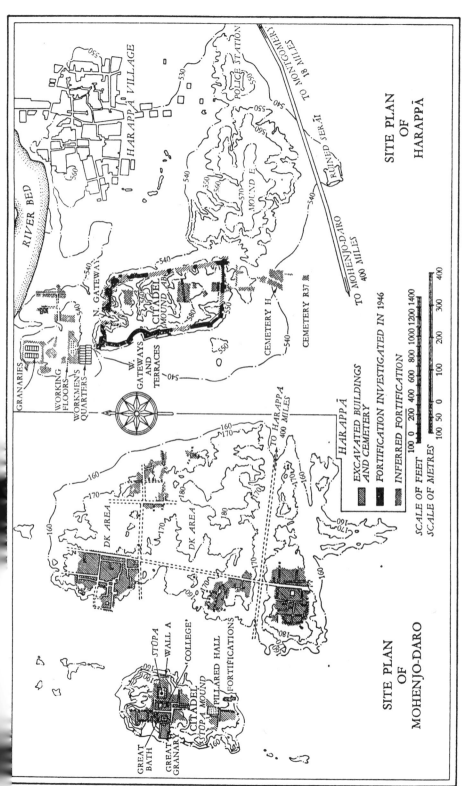

Comparative layout of Mohenjo-daro and Harappā.

Plan of Mohenjo-daro

showing thereon. Like the remains of the South Sea Islands, these structures are prehistoric.These submerged lands commence at about 231 degrees north latitude, or just below the mouth of the river Indus, and extend south to about the equator. These submerged lands are apparently of an elongated oval shape. The Lacadive and Maldive groups of low-lying islands are within the boundaries of this oval.

"Although I have several times passed quite close to them, I have never been on any of them, so I cannot say whether they are parts of the sunken land still above water, or whether they are the subsequent work of coral insects. There is a long stretch of very shallow water both north and south of these islands with various channels of deeper water crossing them, through which ships have to pass going to or from India. This geological phenomenon has never been noted by any geologist or archaeologist as far as I can ascertain or by any historian.

"On days when conditions are favorable—that is, water and sky—imposing remains of ancient structures are clearly to be seen on the shallow water within the oval mentioned. These submerged lands are well known to the fisherman along the coast; as a matter of fact, it was through them that I became aware of this submersion. Hindu scientists also know of them; no one, however, can account for structures being at the bottom of the ocean as the submergence is not spoken of in Hindu history no matter how far one goes back.

"I have never come across any references to the submersion either in India or elsewhere, so the probability remains that it took place during those five to seven thousand years when apparently no history was being written in any part of the world. Yet this submergence is a fact because the submerged structures can be seen. To my mind, there is not the slightest doubt what caused this submergence and that the present island of Ceylon was raised through it."[8]

Whether there are indeed sunken structures in the Lacadives, and possibly the Maldives, remains to be seen. However, Churchward is incorrect when he says that there are no references to a submergence in any Indian texts, as there most certainly are! For instance, we noted earlier that the cities of Tenmaturai and Kapatapuram were lost in a cataclysmic flood thousands of years ago.[36] These cities were located on what is now submerged land, according to legend. Was that land an ancient Ceylon where the Maldives and Lacadives now exist?

§§§

Another possible location and identity of the ancient land of Lanka as portrayed in the *Ramayana* is non other than the land of Poseid, known to us today as Atlantis. In this version of the story, mainly portrayed by the Lemurian Fellowship, the story of the Ramayana is a personified version of the early war between Atlantis and Ancient India.

According to the *Lemurian Fellowship*, the basis for the Ramayana is a actual event which took place about 10,000 B.C. A young prince from Atlantis, essentially a foreign exchange student, fell in love with a young woman, "Sita" of the ancient Rama Empire of India. Probably with her partial permission (this is a main, recurring theme within the *Ramayana,* that of Sita's purity and whether she had any roll in her departure to "Lanka"), the two left India in a *Vimana* and went back to Atlantis. The girl's boyfriend "Rama" (probably not his real name) would not stand by while his girlfriend ran off or was kidnapped by a rival, and gave chase in his *Vimana.*

According to the *Lemurian Fellowship's* version of the story, what then occurred was the equivalent of a teenage hot-rod chase in the super-tech world of *Vimanas* which are capable of not only flying through the air, but of going underwater and even into outer space. The *Vimana* chase was of epic proportions, and

78

the *Lemurian Fellowship* even alleges that a *Vimana* battle took place on the moon! Eventually, Sita's Indian boyfriend managed to recapture her, she returned to India with her reputation slightly tarnished, and life went.

The *Lemurian Fellowship's* version of the story behind the *Ramayana* is a tale of hot-rodding, hot-blooded young adults of royal parentage who use their vimanas to chase each other when a girl friend is stollen or runs-off with with a rival. In any case, she returns to her old boyfriend.

Whether political problems between the two countries developed at this time is not said. Eventually, war did break out between the two countries, and it is probable that portions of this war are described in the *Mahabharata*.

§§§

ARCHAEOLOGICAL EVIDENCE

For a long time, Indian civilization was not believed to go back farther than about 500 B.C. which is only a few hundred years prior to Alexander the Great's invasion of the subcontinent. In the past century, however, the extremely sophisticated cities of Mohenjo Daro ("Mound of the Dead") and Harappa have been discovered in the Indus Valley of what is today Pakistan by British Engineers.

Once called Brahminadad, Harappa was brought to light by two brothers, John and William Brunton, who were engineers for the East Indian Railway. In 1856, they were looking for ballast on which to lay the railway tracks; locals told them that not far away was an ancient ruined city. They looted the ancient city and obtained ninety-three miles of good kiln-fired brick ballast at little expense from the ancient city (This has been the unfortunate fate of many ancient cities; they are often looted of their building materials to

79

build other cities. That is why today many megalithic remains have very little substance to them aside from some megalithic blocks; all of the smaller stones that were movable have been taken!). Eventually, the Director-General of the Indian Archaeological Survey became aware of the site, and began to excavate it.

India's own records of their history claim that their culture has been around for literally tens of thousands of years. Yet, until 1920, all the "experts" agreed that the origins of the Indian civilization should be placed within a few hundred years of Alexander the Great's expedition to the sub-continent in 327 B.C. However that was before another similar city, Mohenjo-Daro (Mound of the Dead), was discovered 350 miles south, and eventually other cities with the same plan were found and excavated, including Kot Diji, near Mohenjo-Daro, Kalibangan, and Lothal, the port in Gujerat, Lothal being discovered just in the past thirty years. [50]

The discoveries of these cities forced archeologists to push the dates for the origin of Indian civilization back thousands of years, just as Indians themselves insisted. A wonder to modern-day researchers, the cities are highly developed and advanced. The way that each city is laid out in regular blocks, with streets crossing each other at right angles, and the entire city laid out in sections, causes archaeologists to believe that the cities were conceived as a whole before they were built: a remarkable early example of city planning. Even more remarkable is that the plumbing-sewage system throughout the large city is so sophisticated, it is superior to that found in Pakistan, India, and most Asian countries today. Sewers were covered, and most homes had private toilets and running water. Furthermore, the water and sewage systems were kept well separated. [50, 51, 43]

This advanced culture had its own writing, never deciphered, and used personalized clay seals, much as the

Chinese still do today, to officialize documents and letters. Some of the seals found contain figures of animals that are unknown to us today.

These cities, which allegedly date back to the Rama Empire, are laid out in regular blocks, with the streets crossing at right angles to one another. Archaeologists who have excavated the cities theorize from this that the cities were planned before they were built, which is highly unusual in the ancient world (and in the modern one also, for that matter). Even more remarkable, is that the plumbing and sewage systems found throughout the " *Indus Valley Culture*" are well laid out and planned. So much so that they are superior to sewage systems found today in Pakistan, India and most Asian countries. Sewers were covered, and most homes had private toilets and running water. Plus water and sewage were kept well separated. [50,43,51,39]

So the cities were sophisticated, but is there any evidence of the devastating wars spoken of in the Indian Epics? Hold onto your seat for a reality-shaking ride to Harappa and Mohenjo Daro! When archaeologists reached the street levels of these two cities during their excavation in the early fifties, they discovered skeletons scattered about the city, many just lying in the streets and some holding hands! It was as if some horrible doom had taken place, annihilating the inhabitants in one fell swoop. These skeletons are among the most radioactive ever found, on a par with those at Nagasaki and Hiroshima. At another site in India, Soviet scholars found a skeleton with a radioactivity level in excess of fifty times that which is normal. [13,39,50,64,31]

Thousands of lumps, christened "black stones", have been found at Mohenjo Daro. These are apparently, fragments of clay vessels that melted together in extreme heat and fused. Other cities have been found in northern

India that indicate explosions of great magnitude. A city was found between the Ganges and the mountains of Rajmahal which seems to have been subjected to intense heat. Huge masses of walls and the foundations of an ancient city were found fused together, literally vitrified![13,39,50,64]

Vitrified structures have been found in Turkey, France, Scotland, Ireland and Peru. No explanations for this fusing of rock has been volunteered, since heat of such an intense nature is not normally generated by natural means. A news item that appeared in the New York Herald Tribune on February 16, 1947 (and repeated by Ivan T. Sanderson in Pursuit, January, 1970) reported that "(archaeologists) have been digging in the ancient Euphrates Valley (Iraq) and have uncovered a layer of agrarian culture 8000 years old, and a layer of herdsman culture much older, and a still older caveman [sic] culture. Recently, they reached another layer. . .of fused green glass."[28]

When the first atomic bomb went off at Alamagordo in New Mexico, it turned the desert sand to green glass! Interestingly, Dr. Oppenhiemer, the "Father of the H-Bomb," was also a Sanskrit scholar. Once when speaking of the first atomic test, he quoted the *Mahabharata* saying, "I have unleashed the power of the Universe. Now I have become the destroyer of worlds." Asked at an interview at Rochester University seven years after the Alamagordo nuclear test whether that was the first atomic bomb to ever be detonated, his reply was: "Well, yes," and added quickly, "in modern history."[9]

Fused glass and stone has often been used as evidence for atomic war in the ancient past, although traditional archaeologist have of course rejected that notion, attributing fused rock to weird, unexplained fires usually in a war situation and fused patches of glass to meteor strikes or bizarre lightening phenomena.

In an article called *Libyan Desert Glass* from *Eos*

magazine (70:379, 1989) and quoted in the Science Frontiers newsletter from the Sourcebook Project in Bethesda, Maryland, the author, A.V. Murall discusses the characteristics of "natural glass fragments" found in the western desert of Egypt. These pieces of glass weigh as much as 16 pounds each and are found in an oval area measuring approximately 130 by 53 kilometers. The clear-to-yellowish-green pieces are concentrated in sand-free corridors between north-south dune ridges.

Says the article, "... We made a systematic study (employing INAA, microprobe and mass spectrometry techniques) of several varieties of LDG (Libyan Desert Glass) and locally associated sand and sandstone to provide insight into the nature and formation of these enigmatic glass fragments.... The gases in the vessels of LDG (N_2, Ar, O_2, CO_2, H_2O and their dissociation products) are present in proportions consistent with derivation from the terrestrial atmosphere. Dark streaks present in some samples of LDG contain significantly higher siderophile element abundances (Ir, ˜0.5 ppb), possibly representing a meteoritic residue.

"Our studies suggest that LDG is the product of meteorite impact into quartz-rich surficial eolion and alluvial sand, and perhaps also into quartz-rich sandstone, of the western desert of Egypt."

Science Frontiers newsletter editor William Corliss comments however "the origin of this immense deposit of glass has been attributed by some to ancient nuclear explosions and alien activities, but investigating scientists have always been satisfied with a meteor-impact hypothesis...although no one has found a crater of suitable size or other supporting evidence."

If we then proceed from the assumption that the ancient Indian Epics are based on real events, related as a kind of mythicized version of the conflicts between India, Atlantis and the rest of the world, Rama himself would then seem to be the personification of the ancient Rama Empire; not necessarily a real person, but rather a combination of persons and events.

The great Indian philosopher, poet and writer Rabinath Tagore (1861-1941) agreed with this view of the hero Rama. Said Tagore in *A Vision of India's History*[70] "As the leading figures of the movement which sought to embrace both Aryan and non-Aryan in a larger synthesis, we find the names of three Kshatriyas (belonging to the second highest caste among Hindus, traditionally warriors) most prominent in the story of the Ramayana: Janaka, Visvamitra and Rama-chandra; they are related not merely by kinship and affection, but by the same ideal. What if, as a matter of historical fact, Janaka, Visvamitra and Rama may not have been contemporaries? That does not diminish their nearness in idea....In the history of an idea, a hero often represents the ideal of his race, and in Aryan history, Janaka and Visvamitra, as well as Rama, have become historical symbols; they are composite pictures of numerous personalities having a common purpose."[70]

Tagore sees the Mahabharata and Ramayana as Aryan epics, though he admits that (speaking of the creation of a modern Indian state, always referred to as female, as in Mother India): When she now tried to know and name herself, she recalled the empire of Bharata, a legendary suzerain of by-gone days, and defining her boundaries accordingly, she called herself Bharata-varsha. In order to restore the fabric of her original civilization, she tried to tie together the lost threads of earlier achievements. Thus, collection and compilation, rather than any new creation, were characteristics of this age. The great sage of this epoch, Vyasa, who is reported to have performed this function, may not have been a real person, but he was, at any rate, the personification of the spirit of the times....Let no one imagine, however, that the non-Aryan contributors were received only because of circumstance, and that they had no value of their own. As a matter of fact, the old Dravidian culture should in no way be underrated; the result of its combination with the Aryan was the Hindu civilization, which acquired both richness and depth from the Dravidians."[70]

An important personality from the *Mahabharata* , Krishna, may well have been a real person as described in the *Bhagavadgita* , a sub-book within the *Mahabharata*. Tagore agrees that Krishna was a real person: "...the fact that the two nonmythical human avatars of Vishnu, Krishna and Ramachandra, were both Kshatriyas, and the Vaishnava religion of love was spread by the teaching of the one the life of the other."[70]

According to the *Motilal Banarsidass Indiological Newsletter* of October, 1990, "There is conclusive evidence that the legendary city of Dwaraka (or Dwarka) did exist until it was submerged in the sea, lending credence to the view that 'underlying the many of myth in the *Mahabharata* there is a nucleus of truth,' said Dr. S.R. Rao of the National Oceanography Institute. In a paper presented at the 33rd International Congress of Asian and North African Studies in Toronto (Canada) Dr. Rao said recent excavations under the sea on the Dwaraka site off the Gujerat coast have yielded scientific evidence which confirm it as the one mentioned in the *Mahabharata*.."

Central India, the site of Churchward's ancient capital of Dravidia, is also loaded with unexcavated ruins. Says a 1958 book published for the British Scientific Book Club, "...[buried cities] waiting for the spade and shovel to reveal their secrets to a civilization remote in time to that which peopled them. There are many such cities in central India, which were buried some time before the Christian era, but which have never since been properly excavated. More than eighty large towns were said to have been covered with a 'shower of earth'. Coins have been found there and various utensils. Pillars of stone and brick walls have also been discovered, as well as fossilized wood of an extraordinary hardness. No doubt a wealth of treasure lies buried there, and a rich harvest awaits the antiquary, for India was a centre of art and learning at that time, when much of the Western world was barely civilized."[79]

Evidence for the former glory of ancient India and its fantastic level of civilization, virtually equivalent to ours today (though probably with a greater understanding of "cosmic law") continues to pile up, and anyone who is aware of the many discoveries and advances in Indian archaeologist will readily admit that ancient India was not a primitive country at all.

§§§

The Mahabharata and the Drona Parva, two ancient Indian epics, speak of the war and of the weapons used: great fireballs that could destroy a whole city, "Kapilla's Glance" which could burn fifty thousand men to ashes in seconds, and flying spears that could ruin whole "cities full of forts." [9, 43, 13]

According to Churchward, the Rama Empire was started by the Nagas (Naacals) who had come into India from Burma and ultimately from "the Motherland to the east" if the tablets that James Churchward claims to have read are correct. After settling in the Deccan Plateau in northern India, they made their capital in the ancient city of Deccan, where today the modern city of Nagpur stands.

The empire of the Nagas apparently began to extend all over northern India to include such cities as Harappa, Mohenjo-Daro, and Kot Diji, now in Pakistan, and Lothal, Kalibanga, Mathura, and possibly other cities such as Benares and Pataliputra. Cities like Dwarka are now

86

underwater, while port cities like Lothal are now several miles inland. The ancient Sumerian City of Ur, and others in Saudi Arabia, are similarly port cities now located many miles from the coast (see my book *Lost Cities & Ancient Mysteries of Africa & Arabia* for more information on port cities in the desolate Arabian interior).

Just exactly which were the seven cities of the Rama Empire is anyone's guess, though it seems fairly certain that Ayodhya and Deccan (Nagpur) was among them, as well as Dwarka, and that Mohenjo-Daro, Harappa, and Lothal were important centers, if not one of the Rishi cities. Probably there were many thriving cities in the Rama Empire and there were seven capitals, which became known as the "Rishi Cities." Rishi is a Sanskrit term meaning "Master" or "Great Teacher."

It was these "Great Teachers, "or "Masters" that were the benevolent aristocracy of the Rama civilization. Today, they are generally called "Priest-Kings" of the Indus Valley civilization, and a number of statues of these so-called "Gods" have been discovered. In reality, apparently their mental-psychic powers were of a degree that seems incredible to most people of today. It was at the height of power for both the Rama Empire and Atlantis that the war broke out, seemingly because of Atlantis' attempt to subjugate Rama.

Evidence of a world-wide influence of the Rama Empire can be found across South-East Asia, into the Pacific and to South & Central America. The plain of Nazca in Peru is very famous for appearing from high altitude as a rather elaborate, if confusing, airfield. Some researchers have theorized that this was some sort of Atlantean outpost. It is also worth noting that the Rama Empire had its outposts: Easter Island, almost diametrically opposite Mohenjo-Daro on the globe, astonishingly developed its own written language, an obscure script lost to the the present inhabitants, but found on tablets and other carvings. This odd script is found in only one other place in the world: Mohenjo-Daro! Could it be that a trade network, operating even across the Pacific Ocean, was used by the Rama Empire and the Atlanteans? It seems incredible. However, it's interesting that pottery found at Nazca has drawings of zeppelin-like airships, much as described in Indian epics. 52, 31

The Rama Empire and the devastating war fought there have even been mentioned several in TIME magazine, a publication note usually noted for reporting on such controversial and esoteric topics.

In an article in TIME on March 26, 1990, entitled *A Digger's Life On a Big Ditch*, the author Edward W. Desmond profiles a ditch digger Tiloka Ram who is working on 587-mile Indira Gandhi Canal which stretches from the northern state of Punjab south into the Thar Desert of Rajasthan. Begins the article: "According to ancient chronicles, it began during a battle among the gods when one of Rama's flaming arrows landed in the heart of Hindustan. The impact made a desert of the land just east of the Indus River, an area known today as the Thar Desert of Rajasthan. There is no record as to whether Rama worried about the environmental impact of his action...."

Desmond goes on to mention in the article that Tiloka Ram is an Oad Rajput, "one of as nomadic caste in Rajathan whose members are, and always have been, diggers. In mythical times, the Oad Rajputs are said to have helped Rama build a bridge to Sri Lanka so that he could finish off an enemy."

While it may seem the stuff of exaggerated mythology, that the Thar Desert of Rajathan was created by a devastating missile during the war described in either the Ramayana or the Mahabharata is hardly so fantastic, especially considering the wealth of written material on the subject, and the archaeological evidence that remains.

It is said in esoteric literature, that Atlantis at the same time, or shortly afterwards, also attempted to subjugate a civilization extant in the area of the Gobi Desert, which was then a fertile plain. By using so-called "Scalar Wave Weaponry" and firing through the center of the earth, they wiped out their adversaries, and, possibly at the same time, did themselves in! Much speculation naturally exists in connection with remote history, we may never actually know the complete truth, though ancient texts are certainly a good start!

The ruins of Kot Diji.

KALIBANGAN : RAJASTHAN
HARAPPAN TOWN

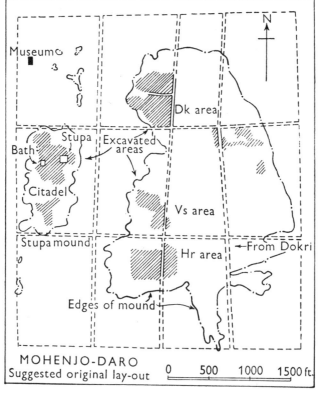

MOHENJO-DARO
Suggested original lay-out

When Mohenjo Daro was first excavated, people were just lying dead in the streets, often holding hands, just like the ancient Indian epics had indicated.

The excavation of the Great Bath at Mohenjo Daro, built out of high quality, kiln fired brick. It and hundreds of other cities flourished many thousands of years ago in the Indian sub-continent.

An inscribed stamp seal found in the ruins of Mohenjo Daro. It depicts an extinct animal, some sort of bull. Possibly a relative of the auroch and the modern brahma bull, it was probably the result of thousands of years of breeding by the "Indus Valley Culture" otherwise known as the Rama Empire. The inscription remains undeciphered.

Indus Valley	Easter Island	Indus Valley	Easter Island	Indus Valley	Easter Island	Indus Valley	Easter Island
I	II	III	IV	V	VI	VII	VIII

Writting from Mohenjo Daro, Harappa, Kot Diji and other ancient cities has never been deciphered. Some linguists point to the similarity between its writing and that of also undeciphered Rongo Rongo writing from Easter Island. Currently, Ancient Dravidian, related to Tamil, is being used to try and decipher the Harappan writing.

Portion of the ancient port of Lothal, now several miles from the coast.

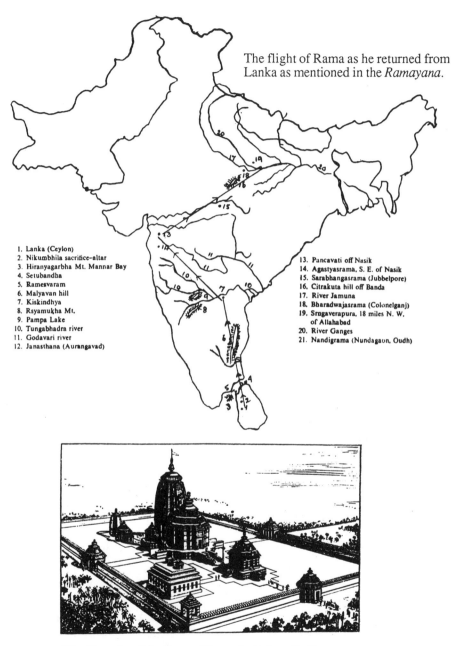

The flight of Rama as he returned from Lanka as mentioned in the *Ramayana*.

1. Lanka (Ceylon)
2. Nikumbhila sacrifice–altar
3. Hiranyagarbha Mt. Mannar Bay
4. Setubandha
5. Ramesvaram
6. Malyavan hill
7. Kiskindhya
8. Rsyamukha Mt.
9. Pampa Lake
10. Tungabhadra river
11. Godavari river
12. Janasthana (Aurangavad)

13. Pancavati off Nasik
14. Agastyasrama, S. E. of Nasik
15. Sarabhangasrama (Jubbelpore)
16. Citrakuta hill off Banda
17. River Jamuna
18. Bharadwajasrama (Colonelganj)
19. Srngaverapura, 18 miles N. W.
   of Allahabad
20. River Ganges
21. Nandigrama (Nundagaon, Oudh)

The Temple of the Sun at Konarak, Orissa, India.
It is built as a model of a huge sun chariot.

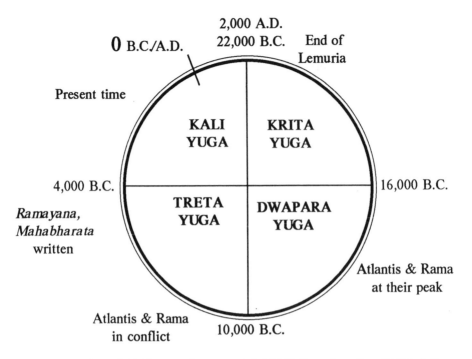

Yuga Cycles of 6000 years begining 22,000 B.C. and ending 2,000 A.D.

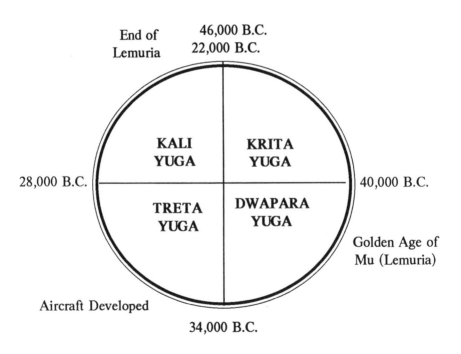

The Great Yuga Cycle starting 48,000 years ago and ending 22,000 B.C.

BOOK

2

THE
VIMAANIKA
SHASTRA

FOREWORD

On 25-8-1952 the Mysore representative of the Press Trust of India, Sri N. N. Sastry, sent up the following report which was published in all the leading dailies of India, and was taken up by Reuter and other World Press News Services :

"Mr. G. R. Josyer, Director of the International Academy of Sanskrit Research in Mysore, in the course of an interview recently, showed some very ancient manuscripts which the Academy had collected. He claimed that the manuscripts were several thousands of years old, compiled by ancient rishis, Bharadwaja, Narada and others, dealing, not with the mysticism of ancient Hindu philosophy of Atman or Brahman, but with more mundane things vital for the existence of man and progress of nations both in times of peace and war.

"Mr. Josyer's manuscripts dealt in elaborate detail about food processing from various indigenous materials like grass, vegetables and leaves for human consumption, particularly during times of famine.

"One manuscript dealt with Aeronautics, construction of various types of aircraft for civil aviation and for warfare. He showed me plans prepared according to directions contained in the manuscript on Aeronautics of three types of aircraft or Vimanas, namely, Rukma, Sundara and Shakuna Vimanas. Five hundred slokas or stanzas dealing with these go into such intricate details about choice and preparation of metals that would be suitable for various parts of vimanas of different types, constructional details, dimensions, designs and weight they could carry, and purposes they could be used for.

"Mr. Josyer showed some types of designs and drawing of a helicopter-type cargo-loading plane, specially meant for carrying combustibles and ammunition, passenger aircraft carrying 400 to 500 persons, double and treble-decked aircraft. Each of these types had been fully described.

"In the section giving about preparation and choice of metals and other materials that should go into such construction of aircraft, details were specified that the aircraft, (these metals are of 16 different alloys), must be "unbreakable, which cannot be cut through, which would not catch fire, and cannot be destroyed by accidents." Details as to how to make these vimanas in flight invisible through smoke screens are given in Vimanasastra of Maharshi Bharadwaja.

"Further description and method of manufacturing aircraft, which will enable pilots not only to spot enemy aircraft, but also to hear what enemy pilots in their planes were speaking, on principles akin to radar, have all been given in elaborate detail with suitable explanatory notes. There are eight chapters in this book which deal with construction of aircraft, which fly in air, go under water, or float on water.

TRAINING OF PILOTS

"A few slokas deal with qualifications and training of pilots to man these aircraft. These ancient types of aircraft are provided with necessary cameras to take pictures of approaching enemy planes. Yet another set of slokas deals with the kind of food and clothing to be provided for pilots to keep them efficient and fit in air flying conditions.

"Mr. Josyer said he was attempting to publish these manuscripts suitably translated in English.

"Another manuscript dealt with ancient Indian architecture, fully illustrated to facilitate construction. This treatise is ascribed to Maharshi Narada, and gives elaborate details about choice of constructional material for various types of buildings, even 15 storeys high. Sectional drawing has also been provided. A few chapters deal with construction of villages, cities and towns, fortresses, palaces and temples. This manuscript is full of plans and engineering constructional details to guide engineers.

"Yet another manuscript from which Mr. G. R. Josyer read out passages referred to preparation of imitation diamonds and pearls. He also showed me another remarkable manuscript which deals in detail about food processing for invalids, for youth and for old and debilitated persons."

A mild avalanche of letters blew towards us during the following days from all over India. One of the first was from James Burke of "Life International", from Delhi asking if he could come and see the Mss. We replied, "Please wire 1000 dollars, and then come." He was taken aback, and wrote that he thought people here felt honoured by being mentioned in "Life Inter-

iii

national," but that we seemed to be different. We did not reply. Now James Burke is dead ; and great "Life International" also is no more! Such is human evanescence !

Miss Jean Lyon, journalist of Toronto and New York, wrote from Delhi that she would visit us. She came and saw the Mss, and recorded her interview with us in her book "Just Half a world Away" in a chapter headed "Science by Sutras", concluding with the charge that we were guilty of a rabid nationalism, seeking to wipe out everything since the Vedas !

That is no way for a journalist to judge persons. We only hold that for Indians, or others, to wipe out the Vedas is absurd ! We are neither rabid, nor national. God has created the Earth like a round ball, all its contents forming one compact unit, not a hundred and odd broken units as in the League of Nations. Only in maps is the earth shown broken into 2 hemi-spheres. If you actually break the Earth into 2 hemi-spheres, you will be having Doomsday !

Ours is not nationalism, rabid or tame, but one world humanism, or world-citizenship. That should not shock Miss Jean Lyon.

Others who wrote to enquire with excited wonder were Governor R. R. Diwakar of Behar, Maharaja of Kashi, Dr. Trivedi of "Searchlight," Patna, Professor Dwivedi of Gorakhpur, Professor Chauhan of Seoni, Professor Theeanee of Madras, Swamy Chaitanya of Mussoorie, H. R. Sharma of Phagwara, Harit Krishna Deb of Calcutta, R. B. Lal of Allahabad, P. S. Bharathi of Ootacamand, Miss McIntyre of Bangalore, M. V. Sharma, Industrialist, Madras, D. V. Potdar of Poona, Raja A. K. N. Singh of Ramnagar, U. P., Rao Bahadur M.A. Rangaswamy, Patna, N. Anandalwar, Bangalore.

S. M. Sharma, editor, wrote in "Searchlight," Patna, "To an eminent Sanskrit scholar, Shri G. R. Josyer, Director of the International Academy of Sanskrit Research, Mysore, we owe the discovery of the manuscript on Vimanas by Maharshi Bharadwaja. Shri Josyer is already more than 70. Many will share my hope and prayer that the Nehru Goverment would lose no time in acquiring the manuscript, which, according to my information, is most unique." Editor Sharma too is no more !

The Mss. came to us by Divine grace ! When on 28-6-1951 we got H. H. the Maharaja of Mysore to inaugurate the International Academy of Sanskrit Research, evidently it was an auspicious occasion. The Academy has truly attained International fame, and has become known from one end of the globe to the other!

One of the guests coming from Bangalore for the ceremony brought a small manuscript in exercise book form containing the beginning of Maharshi Bharadwaja's "Vymanika Sastra." We were struck by it, and exhibited it along with our other Mss. in various stages of decay, to H. H. The Maharaja and Chief Minister K. C. Reddy and others when we took them round.

After the function the Mss. was returned to the guest, who gave it back to the custodian of Pandit Subbaraya Sastry's literary records, Sri Venkatrama Sastry, B.A.,B.L., Advocate of the Bangalore Bar. Subsequently we contacted him, and on our promise of doing our best to publish them, he was good enough to let us have copies of some of the manuscripts. The message of the Press Trust of India was with reference to them. The fan mail resulting therefrom brought enquiries from personages such as Air Commodore Goyal of the Western Command, Bangalore, The Editor of the Kesari and Mahratta, Poona, Major Gadre of Saraswati Mahal, Tanjore, Minister A. G. Ramachandra Rao, Bangalore, Sri Swamy of Bhandarkeri Mutt, M. G. Seth, Bombay, P. D. Padam Chand, Delhi, P. M. Kabali, Bombay, Aeronautical Society of India, Ministry of Scientific and Cultural Affairs, Delhi, the Director General of Civil Aviation, the Hindustan Aircrafts, Ltd.

We then commenced printing the original in Sanskrit, and had made some progress, when suddenly there came a harsh letter from the donor, Sri Venkatrama Sastry, accusing us of exploiting the manuscripts for our personal benefit. Having had no such idea ourselves, it evoked disgust, and we replied that he could take back the manuscripts, and discontinued the printing !

But then letters continued to come from far away, from estimable men avidly interested in the manuscript, and organs of learned Associations and books by scholars of the abstruse began to quote us as intending to bring out the publication. Seigfried Hansch, Deschenes, Canada, Hans krefft, Berlin, Blaes-Gustaf-Nordquist, Stockholm, Sweden, Bjorn Loven, Innsbruck, Austria, Joachim Rothaner, Kellerburg, Austria, Jan Wallgren, Stockholm, P. Salzmann de la Mar, Eskilstuna, Sweden, Hans-Werner-Von Engel, Bad Gadesberg, West Germany, Sten Lindgreu, Stockholm, Lars Eric

Helin, Kalender, Gothenburg, Sweden, WM. Dawson & Sons, London, Charles Danois, Kristianstad, Sweden, James Alves, Sao Paulo, Brazil, Torbjorn Holmquist, Vetlanda, Sweden, Ernest Heinrich, Homburg, Klaus Aarsleff Jorgensen, Skellingsted, Denmark, Gosta Karlsson, Stockholm, Peter Bernin, Malmo, Sweden, Dr. Curtis J Mccall, Lake Worth, Florida, Robert Ashley Falk, Auckland, New Zealand, Terry W. Colvin, Evansville, U.S.A., Sven Bertil Hansson, Malmo, Sweden, Kjell Ericson, Borlonge, Maurice T. Caison, North Carolina, M. A. Gresham, Jr. Atlanta, U.S.A. Alan Y. Wilcox, Lauderdale, Florida, Strubes, Copenhagen, Demmark, Alan D. William, Downey, California, Stuve Sundquist, Uppsala, Bo H. Svensson, Sweden, Karen Kesti, Republic WA, U.S.A., Richard Watson, New South Wales, Australia, Ontario College of Art, Toronto, Canada, Dr. Jacq Eskens, Rotterdam, Netherlands, Bernin Co Moberg, Montmartre, Paris, L.S.U. Rydberg, Stockholm, Chairman, E. A. G. Mackay, British Unidentified Flying Object Research Association, London, Mrs. Annica Foxcraft, Transvaal, Oliver Williams, Weimar, Texas, Jan Swagermann, Ship "Johannra", Amsterdam, Robert B. Young, Jr. Radco Incorporated, Houston, Texas, Sam J. Lundwall, Askild and Karnekull, Stockholm, Dr. Cedric Leonard, Oklahoma, Gwendelholm, Stockholm, Michele Bonamici, Milan, Italy, Jose M. Fernandez, Goteborg, Sweden, President Lennort Lidfoss, Spectrum, Forlags, A. B. Danderyd, Sweden.

The "Clima Astral" of Brazil, "The Mexican News" of Mexico, The "Spectrum" and "Pursuit" of U.S.A. and three Swedish books on ancient and astral research, "Kulturer Fore Istiden" by Ivan Troing, "Forntidens Teknik" by H. Kjellson, and "Flygande Tefat" by Max B. Miller, reproduced our original descriptive leaflet, and announced that we expected to publish the remarkable volume. The Maharaja of Mysore invited us, and after offering Tea, wanted the Manuscript for being shown to Dr. Thacker, the National Scientist of India. We reminded him that Sanskritists were averse to parading knowledge before idle curiosity, and that the manuscript had to be translated into English and tested by research, and then only made available for the public gaze. Four scientist Doctors from the Indian Institute of Science, Bangalore, came with a letter of Introduction from the Head of The Department of Power Engineering, Dr. M.A. Tirunarayanan, and sought clarification from us!

It was as if the orange-shaped Earth had become a porcupine, and was shooting its quills at us from all sides, in order to goad us into the task, which we had been reluctant to take up as being too onerous for us!

We had therefore to gather strength from the cumulative good-will of the world-wide public, and gird ourselves up for the strenuous undertaking.

To be really of value the volume had to include the Sanskrit original, its translation in English as demanded by western readers, and sketches showing the designs of the Vimanas for further clarification. It had to be a beautiful volume commensurate with the magnificence of its subject, and the high expectations of the public awaiting its publication.

Thus, at the age of 81 we had to sit up and translate the technical Sanskrit into readable English, and scrutinise the printing of both the Sanskrit and English, involving the strain of multiple proof-reading. The finance required was considerable, and as no help was forthcoming, we had to scrape together the meagre savings of a life-time, procure needful printing equipment at mounting costs, engage labour at emergency rates, and at long last, with the help of Divine grace, are able to herald the birth of the volume, which has been in gestation for over ninety years !

"Vymaanika Shastra" consists of nearly 6000 lines, or 3000 verses of lucid Sanskrit, dealing with the construction of Vimaanas or Aeroplanes. That the vocabulary of ancient Sanskrit could in simple flowing verse depict the technical details with effortless ease is a tribute to the language, and the greatness of the author.

Maharshi Bharadwaja is an august name in the pantheon of Hindu Sages who recorded Indian civilization, in the spiritual, intellectual, and scientific fields in the hoary past. They transmitted knowledge from mouth to mouth, and from ear to ear, for long eras. Written transmission through birch-backs or palm-leaves, or home-made paper, are from this side of a thousand years. Even they are to be found in mangled forms owing to the depredation of time, weather and insect hordes. There is no written material for the vast volume of Vedas, Upanishads, Shastras, and Puranas, which have come down for over 10000 years as a patrimony, not only for India, but for mankind in general. They remain imbedded in the ether of the sky, to be revealed—like television,— to gifted mediums of occult perception.

Venerable Pandit Subbaraya Sastry, who has left the legacy of manuscript treasures including "Vymanika Shastra", was a simple, orthodox, intellectual Brahmin with spiritual gifts, who was esteemed by all who knew him, Englishmen and anglicised or educated Indians, in various walks of life.

He was a walking lexicon gifted with occult perception. His sole aim was to transmit his knowledge to posterity. He lived a life of poverty, like Socrates, and sought no gains for himself.

In 1885 Mr. B. Suryanarain Rao, B.Sc., M. R. A. S., distinguished Astrologer and Editor, first met him and became his devoted exponent. In 1911 he started a Magazine in Madras named "Bhowthika Kalaa Nidhi," or "Treasure house of physical sciences", and published extracts from the revelations of the venerable scholar. We are in possession of 6 issues of that rare Journal which came to us by Divine grace.

On 1-8-1918 he began to dictate "Vymanika Sastra" to Mr. Venkatachala Sarma, who took down the whole in 23 exercise books up to 23-8-1923.

That gave manuscript shape to Maharshi Bharadwaja's "Vymanika Sastra". Then by a flash of genius he engaged a draughtsman, and got drawings of some varieties of the Vimanas prepared under his instructions, which form an indispensable adjunct to the manuscript proper. That was in 1923. India was then under British rule. Gandhi's Non-co-operation movement was catching fire. And, it is said, Pandit Subbaraya Sastry was arrested ! Yeoman efforts procured his release. But his activities had to remain confined. In 1928 he addressed a letter to the Maharaja of Darbhanga for aid in publication of the manuscripts. But the rich in India have got deaf ears, and warped minds! Then, disappointed and broken-hearted, in the early 30's, venerable Subbaraya Sastry passed out of this world, and left it the poorer thereby !

For some 20 years his literary treasures remained as under frigidaire, guarded by his daughter and young Mr. Venkatrama Sastry. Then the Unseen Powers began to play, and the manuscripts were released to light. And at last it has pleased God to enable us to present Maharshi Bharadwaja's "Vymanika Sastra" to the world's elite, and pay our tribute to the memories of Maharshi Bharadwaja and venerable Subbaraya Sastry.

We thank God for His gracious favour. We thank Mr. Venkatrama Sastry who made the manuscript available to us ; our first son, G. S. Josyer, M.A., B.ED., who contacted Mr. Venkatrama Sastry and brought the Mss., prepared it for the press, and even composed a portion of the Mss., and met an untimely death in the midst of his useful career; our younger son, G. N. Josyer, B.E., who has been helping us in seeing the work through ; and our consultants in the course of the work, Sris. Alwar Tirumaliengar and M. A. Tirunarayan, B.E., M.I.E., M. N. Srinivasan, B.Sc, Hons, LL.B., Professor M. A. Tirunarayanan, D.Sc, and Sris M. C. S. Chari, B.Sc., N. Narasimhan, B.E., R. T. Krishnan, B.E., Pandit K. Ramaswamy Iyengar, and Mr. N. N. Sastry of P.T.I., and other associates and assistants.

Sanskrit and English have been our two eyes since some 75 years, and we are placing the unique volume before the elite of the world as an outstanding contribution to world literature from the ever-living past. We hope they will deem it an invaluable addition to their libraries, and find it an ever interesting companion.

The 20th century may be said to be made historic by 2 achievements, the bringing of Moon-rock from outer space, and the publication of "Vymanika Sastra" from the unknown past. The Moon-rock is just rock, not a cluster of shining pebbles from Kimberley of South Africa. But the "Vymanika Sastra" is a Cornucopia of precious formulas for the manufacture of Aeroplanes, which should make Lindbergh, Rolls, Zeppelin, De Havilland, Tupolev, and Harold Gray of Pan American, gape in astonishment, and if duly worked up, herald a new era of Aeroplane manufacture for the benefit of Mankind !

G. R. JOSYER
Hon. Director, International
Academy of Sanskrit Research,

15-3-1973
Mysore-4, India.

श्रीमहर्षिभरद्वाजप्रणीत
"यन्त्रसर्वस्वा"न्तर्गत

वैमानिकप्रकरणम्

श्री बोधानन्दमुनिवरेण्य प्रणीत
वित्तृत्या समुल्लसितम्

◦•◦•◦

श्री पण्डितवर्यै सुब्बरायशास्त्रिभि:
दैवकृपया समुपलभ्य
हस्तलिखित मातृकारूपेणानुगृहीतम्

◦••◦

उभयभाषाविदुषा
गोमठं रामानुज ज्यौतिषिकेण
यथामति संशोध्यपरिष्कृत्य
आंग्लेय भाषान्तरेणसह

◦•◦◦•

मैसूर कारोनेषन् मुद्रणालये
लोकोपकागय मुद्राप्य प्रकटीकृतम्

॥ ओम् तत् सत् ॥

MAHARSHI BHARADWAAJA'S

VYMAANIKA-SHAASTRA

OR

SCIENCE OF AERONAUTICS

❖❖❖— —❖❖❖

Part of his unknown work

"YANTRA SARVASVA"

or

"ALL ABOUT MACHINES"

as revealed to venerable

Pandit SUBBARAYA SASTRY

and recorded in hand-written
Sanskrit Manuscript Form

translated into English by

G. R. JOSYER, M.A., Hons., F.R.E.S., M.R.S.L.

Founder Director,
INTERNATIONAL ACADEMY OF SANSKRIT RESEARCH.

Printed at the

CORONATION PRESS, MYSORE 4, INDIA.

Original Title Page of Josyer's English translation of the *Vymaanika-Shastra,*
found in 1908 in the Royal Baroda Library.

CONTENTS

Maharshi Bharadwaaja's
VYMAANIKA SHAASTRA

FIRST CHAPTER

Maharshi Bharadwaaja :

I make obeisance to the Divine Being, who is visible on the crest of the Vedas, who is the fountain of eternal bliss, and whose abode is reached by Vimaanas or Aeroplanes. Having studied the Shaastraas or sciences propounded by previous men of science to the best of my ability, for the benefit of mankind, I shall deal with the science of Aeronautics, which is the essence of the Vedas, which will be a source of joy and benefit to humanity, which will facilitate comfortable travel in the sky from world to world, in eight chapters, consisting of 100 topics, in 500 sutras or cryptic pronouncements.

Commentary by Bodhaananda :

I bow to God Mahadeva and His Consort, to Saraswathi Goddess of learning, to Ganapathy guardian of benevolent efforts, and to my venerable preceptor, and I bow to Maharshi Bharadwaaja. In Addition to my own knowledge of Logic, I have five times turned over Vaalmeeki's Mathematics, 'Paribhaashaa Chandrikaa,' and 'Naamaarthhakalpaka,' and aided by their authority, I, Swaamy Bodhaananda, for the easy understanding of the young, have written this 'Bodhananda Vritti,' to elucidate Maharshi Bharadwaaja's concisely worded text on Acronautics.

At the outset Maharshi Bharadwaaja invokes God in the traditional manner for the successful commencement, progress, and completion of his great literary work. Attaining mastery over the Vedas by Divine Grace, and studying the works of earlier Aachaaryaas or preceptors, he has churned the Vedic lore, and extracting the cream, presented it to mankind for reaping untold benefits, in the work named 'Yantrasarvasva.' In the fortieth chapter therein he deals with the science of Aeronautics, explaining the construction and use of many kinds of aeroplanes, in 8 chapters, containing 100 subject heads, comprising 500 sutras or oracular pronouncements.

In the first stanza the reference is to the teaching of the sacred works, "Uttara-taapaneeya," 'Shaibya-prasna,' 'Kaataka,' and 'Maandookya,' that the symbolic letter, 'Om,' leads to the knowledge of God and Salvation. Bharadwaaja implies that the Vimaana or aeroplane constructed according to Vymaanika Shaastra, may enable men to reach God, and enjoy the benefits of His Divine abode.

The previous Aachaaryaas Bharadwaaja refers to are named by Vishwanaatha as,—Naaraayana, Shownaka, Garga, Vaachaspathi, Chaakraayani and Dhundinaatha, venerable authors of "Vimaana–Chandrikaa", "Vyomayaana-Tantra," "Yantra-Kalpa", "Yaana-Bindu," "Kheta-yaana Pradeepikaa," and "Vyomayaana-Arkaprakaasha," respectively.

Bharadwaaja thus defines the word Vimaana :

☞   Vega–Saamyaat Vimaano Andajaanaam.   Sootra 1.

"Owing to similarity of speed with birds, it is named Vimaana."

Bodhaananda   Vritti :

The word "andaja" means "egg–born", and includes eagles and other birds which fly by their own volition. The Vimaana is a vehicle which flies in the sky with speed comparable with birds.

Lallachaarya says, "That which can fly in the sky with speed equal to that of birds, is called Vimaana."

Aachaarya Naaraayana says,

"That which can speed on earth, on water, through air, by its own power, like a bird, is a "Vimaana."

Shankha says, "Experts in the science of aeronautics say, "That which can fly through air from one place to another is a Vimaana"

And Vishwambhara says, "Experts say that that which can fly through air from one country to another country, from one island to another island, and from one world to another world, is a "Vimaana"."

Having thus defined the name of the Vimaana, the sage proceeds to describe its details.

☞   Rahasyagnyodhikaaree.   Sootra 2.

"The pilot is one who knows the secrets."

Bodhaananda : Scientists say that there are 32 secrets of the working of the Vimaana. A pilot should acquaint himself thoroughly with them before he can be deemed competent to handle the aeroplane. He must know the structure of the aeroplane, know the means of its take off and ascent to the sky, know how to drive it and how to halt it when necessary, how to manoeuvre it and make it perform spectacular feats in the sky without crashing. Those secrets are given in "Rahasya–Lahari" and other works, by Lalla and other masters, and are described thus :

"The pilot should have had training in maantrica and taantrica, kritaka and antaraalaka, goodha or hidden, drishya and adrishya or seen and unseen, paroksha and aparoksha, contraction and expansion, changing shape, look frightening, look pleasing, become luminous or enveloped in darkness, deluge or pralaya, vimukha, taara, stun by thunderous din, jump, move zig–zag like serpent, chaapala, face all sides, hear distant sounds, take pictures, know enemy manoeuvres, know direction of enemy approach, stabdhaka or paralyse, and karshana or exercise magnetic pull.

These 32 secrets the pilot should learn from competent preceptors, and only such a person is fit to be entrusted with an aeroplane, and not others.

They are explained thus by Siddhanaatha :

1. **Maantrika** : As prescribed in "Mantraadhikaara," by invoking the mantras of Chhinnamasta, Bhairavee, Veginee, Siadhaamba, acquire the powers of ghutikaa, paadukaa, visible and invisible and other mantraas with potent herbs and efficacious oils, and Bhuvaneswaree Mantra which confers spiritual and mesmeric powers, to construct aeroplanes, which don't break cannot be cut, cannot be burnt, and cannot be destroyed.

2. **Taantrika** : By acquiring Mahaamaaya, Shambara, and other taantric powers, to endow the plane with those powers.

3. **Kritaka** : By study of architects like Vishwakarma, Chhaayaaparusha, Manu, Maya and others, to construct aeroplanes of various patterns.

4. **Antaraala** : In the wind-swept atmospheric region of the sky, in the clash at the borders of mighty currents, an inadvertent plane is likely to be smashed to pieces. But by getting warned of the approach of such danger spots, the plane could be halted and steered with care.

5. **Goodha** : As explained in 'Vaayutatva–Prakarana', by harnessing the powers, Yaasaa, Viyaasaa, Prayaasaa in the 8th atmospheric layer covering the earth, to attract the dark content of the solar ray, and use it to hide the Vimaana from the enemy.

6. **Drishya** : By collision of the electric power and wind power in the atmosphere, a glow is created, whose reflection is to be caught in the Vishwa-Kriyaa-darapana or mirror at the front of the Vimana, and by its manipulation produce a Maaya–Vimaana or camouflaged Vimana.

7. **Adrishya** : According to "Shaktitantra", by means of the Vynara-thya Vikarana and other powers in the heart centre of the solar mass, attract the force of the ethereal flow in the sky, and mingle it with the balaahaa-vikarana shakti in the aerial globe, producing thereby a white cover, which will make the Vimana invisible.

8. **Paroksha** : According to "Meghotpatthi-prakarana," or the science of the birth of clouds, by entering the second of the summer cloud layers, and attracting the power therein with the shaktyaakarshana darpana or force-attraction mirror in the Vimana, and applying it to the parivesha or halo of the Vimaana, a paralysing force is generated, and opposing Vimaanas are paralysed and put out of action.

9. **Aparoksha** : According to 'Shakti-tantra,' by projection of the Rohi-nee beam of light, things in front of the Vimaana are made visible.

10. **Sankocha, or Contraction** : As prescribed in the Yantraango-pasamhaara section, when the Vimaana is flying at speed with fully extended wings, and there is danger ahead, turning the 7th switch in the Vimana, its parts can be made to contract.

11. **Vistrita** : According to 'Akaashatantra', when the Vimana is in the central air flood in the third and first regions of the sky, by turning the switch in the 11th section of plane, it becomes expanded suitably according to "Vaalmeeki Ganita."

12. **Viroopa Karana** : As stated in "Dhooma Prakarana", by produ-cing the 32nd kind of smoke through the mechanism, and charging it with the light of the heat waves in the sky, and projecting it through the padmaka chakra tube to the bhyravee oil–smeared Vyroopya–darpana at the top of the Vimaana, and whirling with 132nd type of speed, a very fierce and terrifying shape of the Vimana will emerge, causing utter fright to onlookers.

13. **Roopaantara** : As stated in "Tylaprakarana," by preparing griddhrajihwaa, kumbhinee, and kaakajangha oils and anointing the distor-ting mirror in the Vimaana with them, applying to it the 19th kind of smoke

and charging with the kuntinee shakti in the Vimana, shapes like lion, tiger, rhinoceros, serpent, mountain, river will appear and amaze observers and confuse them.

14. **Suroopa** : By attracting the 13 kinds of Karaka force mentioned in "Karaka prakarana" applying snow--surcharged air and projecting it through the air conveying tube to the pushpinee–pinjula mirrors in the front right side of the Vimana, and focusing on it the suragha beam, a heavenly damsel bedecked with flowers and jewels will appear to onlookers of the Vimana.

15. **Jyotirbhaava** : As stated in "Amshubodhinee," out of Samgnaana and other 16 digits of the solar glow, by attracting the 12th to the 16th digits and focusing them on the air force in the Mayookha section in the fourth pathway in the sky, and similarly by attracting the force of the etherial glow and mingling it with the glow in the 7th layer of air mass, and then by projecting both these forces through the 5 tubes in the Vimana on to the section of the guhaa–garbha mirror, a rich glow like the morning glow of the sun will be produced.

16. **Tamomaya** : As described in "Darpana Prakarana," by means of the dark force mirror, capture the force of darkness, pass it through the Thamo-Yantra in the north–west side of the Vimana, and by turning a switch produce at noon–day the utter darkness of the night of the new–moon.

17. **Pralaya** : As described in the magic book of destruction, attract the 5 kinds of smoke through the tube of the contracting machine in the front part of the Vimana, and merge it in the cloud-smoke mentioned in "Shadgarbha Viveka", and pushing it by electric force through the five-limbed aerial tube, destroy everything as in a cataclysm.

18. **Vimukha** : As mentioned in "Rig-hridaya", by projecting the force of Kubera, Vimukha and Vyshawaanara poison powder through the third tube of the roudree mirror and turning the switch of the air mechanism, produce wholesale insensibility and coma.

19. **Taara** : By mixing with etherial force 10 parts of air force, 7 parts of water force, and 16 parts of solar glow, and projecting it by means of the star-faced mirror through the frontal tube of the vimana, the appearance of a star-spangled sky is created.

20. **Mahaashabda Vimohana** : By concentrating the air force in the seven tubes of the Vimana, and turning the switch, produce, as stated in "Shabda prakaashikaa" a crescendo of thunderous din, which stuns people, and makes them quake with fear and become insensible.

21. **Langhana** : As stated in "Vaayu tattva prakarana" When crossing from one air stream into another, the Vimana faces the baadaba glow of the sun and catches fire. In order to prevent that, the electric force and air force in the Vimana should be conjoined and centred in the life–centre of the Vimana, and by turning the switch, the Vimana will leap into safety.

22. **Saarpa–Gamana** : By attracting the dandavaktra and other seven forces of air, and joining with solar rays, passing it through the zig–zagging centre of the Vimana, and turning the switch, the Vimana will have a zig–zagging motion like a serpent.

23. **Chaapala** : On sighting an enemy plane, by turning the switch in the force centre in the middle section of the Vimana, a 4087 revolutions an hour atmospheric wave speed will be generated, and shake up the enemy plane.

24. **Sarvatomukha** : When a formation of enemy planes comes to attack one's Vimana, by turning the switch at the crown of the Vimana, make it revolve with agility and face all sides.

25. **Parashabda Graahaka** : As explained in "Sowdaaminee kalaa" or science of electronics, by means of the sound capturing yantra in the Vimana, to hear the talks and sounds in enemy planes flying in the sky.

26. **Roopaakarshana** : By means of the photographic yantra in the Vimana to obtain a television view of things inside an enemy plane.

27. **Kriyaagrahana** : By turning the key at the bottom of the Vimana, a white cloth is made to appear. By electrifying the three acids in the north-east part of the Vimana, and subjecting them to the 7 kinds of solar rays, and passing the resultant force into the tube of the Thrisheersha mirror and making the cloth screen face the mirror, and switching on the upper key, all the activities going on down below on the ground, will be projected on the screen.

28. **Dikpradarshana** : Turning the key at the front of the Vimana the dishaampati yantra will show the direction from which the ememy plane is approaching.

29. **Aakaashaakaara** : According to "Aakaasha-tantra", by mixing black mica solution with neem and bhoonaaga decoctions and smearing the solution on the outer body of the Vimana made of mica plates, and exposing to solar rays, the plane will look like the sky and become indistinguishable.

30. **Jalada roopa** : Mixing pomegranate juice, bilva or bael oil, copper-salt, kitchen smoke, granthika or gugul liquid, mustard powder, and fish scale decoctions, and adding sea-shell and rock-salt powder, and collecting smoke of the same solution and spreading it with solar heat enveloping the cover, the Vimana will have the appearance of a cloud.

31. **Stabdhaka** : By projecting apasmaara poison-fume smoke through the tube on the north side on the Vimana, and discharging it with stambhana-yantra, people in enemy planes will be made unconscious.

32. **Karshana** : When enemy planes come in strength to destory one's Vimana, by setting aflame the Jwaalinee shakit in the Vyshwaanara-naala or pipe located at the navel of the plane, and switching the keys of the two wheels to 87 degrees of heat, the burning shakti will envelope the enemy plane and destroy it.

These are the 32 rahasyaas or secrets which should be known by pilots according to Siddhanaatha.

"Maargaadhikaranam " Aerial Routes :

☞ Panchagnyascha. Sootra 3.
"The pilot should know five things."
Bodhaananda Vritti :

As the secrets of aeronautics are indicated in the second sutra, the five atmospheric regions are referred to in the third sutra. According to Shownaka, the regions of the sky are five, named, Rekhaapathha, Mandala, Kakshya, Shakti, and Kendra.

In these 5 atmospheric regions, there are 5,19,800 air ways traversed by Vimanas of the Seven Lokas or worlds, known as Bhooloka, Bhuvarloka, Suvarloka, Maholoka, Janoloka, Tapoloka and Satyaloka.

Dhundinaatha and "Vaalmeeki Ganita" state that Rekha has 7,03,00,800 air routes, Mandala has 20,08,00200 air routes, Kakshya has 2,09,00,300 air routes, Shakti has 10,01,300 air routes, and Kendra has 30,08,200 air routes.

According to "Vaalmeeki Ganita" in the Rekhaapathha region, sections 1 to 4 are suitable for the passage of the Vimanas of this Bhooloka. In the Mandala region sections 3 to 5 are suitable for Vimanas of Bhuvarloka, Suvarloka, and Maholoka dwellers. For the Janoloka Vimanas sections 2 to 5 in the Kakshya region are suitable. Section 1 to 6 in the Shakti region are suitable for the Vimanas of Tapoloka. For the dwellers of Bramhaloka sections 3 to 11 in the Kendra region are suitable, according to shaastras like "Vaalmeeki Ganita" and others.

Maharashi Bharadwaaja:

☞ Aavartaascha. Sootra 4.

"Whirl-Pools"

Aavartaas or aerial whirlpools are innumerable in the above regions. Of them the whirlpools in the routes of Vimanas are five. In the Rekhapathha there occurs "Shaktyaavarta" or whirlpool of energy. In Mandala-pathha there occurs the whirlpool of winds. In Kakshyaa-pathha there occurs Kiranaavarta or whirpool from solar rays. In Shakti-pathha there occurs shytyaavarta or whirlpool of cold-currents. And in Kendra-pathha there occurs gharshanaavartha or whirl-pool by collision. Such whirlpools are destructive of Vimanas, and have to be guarded against.

The pilot should know these five sources of danger, and learn to steer clear of them to safety.

Maharshi Bharadwaaja:

☞ Angaanyekatrimsat. Sootra 5.

"The parts are thirty one"

Bodhaananda Vritti :

Just as the human body, if it is complete in all its limbs, is best able to accomplish things, the Vimana, if it is complete in all its parts, will be capable of functioning efficiently. From the location of the Vishwakriyaadarpana

31 locations of Vimana components are mentioned.
According to "Chaayaapurusha Shaastra" they are :

1. Vishwakriyaadarpana or mirror of outside views.
2. Shaktyaakarshana or energy attracting mirror.
3. Parivesha mechanism above the hood of the Vimana.
4. Angopasamhaara yantra or folding up yantra at the 7th bindu-keelaka.
5. Vistritakriyaa or opening out yantra location in the middle of the 11th section.
6. Vyroopya darpana and
7. Padmachakramukha at the shirobhaaga or crest of the Vimana.
8. The Kuntinee-shakti mechanism is to be in the neck of the Vimana.
9. Pushpinee and Pinjulaa Mirrors are to be in the right side of the centre.
10. At the front of the left side are to be located the Naalapanchaka or 5 pipes.
11. Guhaagarbha mirror yantra is to be in the front part of the stomach of the plane.
12. Thamoyantra at the north western side.
13. Pancha-vaataskandha-naala on the western centre.
14. Rowdree mirror.
15. Vaataskandha keelaka at the bottom centre.
16. Shaktisthaana at the front and right sides.
17. Shabda-kendra-mukha at the left side.
18. Vidyuddwaadashaka at the north-east side.
19. Praanakundala at the moola of the Vimana.
20. Shaktyudgama at the navel of the Vimana.
21. Vakraprasaarana at the side of Vimanaadhaara.
22. Shaktipanjara in the central portion.
23. Shirahkeelaka at the head of the Vimana.
24. Shabdaakarshaka yantra at the shoulder.
25. Pata-prasaarana at the bottom centre.
26. Dishaampati yantra at the left front.
27. Pattikaabhraka at the centre of the hood of the Vimana.
28. Solar power attractor at the top of the Vimana.

29. Apasmaara or poison gas at the sandhi-naala mukha or junction tube front.
30. Sthambhana yantra at the bottom.
31. Vyshwaanara-naala at the navel centre.

This is the placing of the 31 components of the Vimana.

"Vasthraadhikaranam": On Clothing

Maharashi Bharadwaaja:

☞ "Yantu-praavaraneeyow prithak prithak ritubhedaat." Sootra 6.

"The clothing should be different for different seasons."

The sootra defines the clothing which is to be provided to the pilot in accordance with different seasonal conditions. The impact of the sun's myriad rays on the revolving earth causes seasonal climatic changes. Their effects on human life are either wholesome or unwholesome, as the case may be. The latter cause cramps, drain blood, and denude the body of fat, flesh, and other ingredients. The evil forces of the seasons are reckoned as 25, and affect the skin, bone, flesh, fat, muscles, nerves, joints and other parts of the pilots' body. The clothing provided to them should be such as to safeguard against such effects, and maintain their efficiency.

According to "Pata-samskaara Ratnaakara", silk, cotton, moss, hair, mica, leather, are to be purified by 25 processes, washed with mica-saturated water, and spun into yarn as prescribed by Gaalava. Then fibres from the ketaki flower palm, arka or swallow wort or madar, sun flower tree, cocoanut and jute, should each be purified 8 times as prescribed and by 19 processes, spun into yarn, and woven into cloth. Then the cloth should be soaked in the oils of linseed, tulasi or basil, goose-berry, shamee or acacia suma, bael, and mustard, and dried in the sun 5 times daily for 7 days. Then yellow ochre, lac, tamarind, honey and gingelly manure aud mica in equal parts and yena-kshaara salt, put in a crucible vessel, placed in koorma furnace, and boiled with the aid of 3 faced bellows. 8 seers of linseed juice should be added to it. Bees wax, mica, shinjeera, vajra, borax, and ashoka fruit should be boiled, and their oil mixed with the other composition, and boiled in garbhataapana yantra. Then the cloth should be soaked in that decoction and dried 5 times. With this material, fashioning the apparel and clothes of the pilots handsomely, according to the types of the cloth and requirements the crew, as prescribed by Agnimitra, and handing it to them to wear, they should be conferred benediction, given a protective amulet and then sent out with cheers. It will ward off evils, promote fitness of body and health of mind, and improve their strength, energy, and competence.

Aahaaraadhikaranam : On Food

Maharshi Bharadwaaja :

☞ "Aahaarah Kalpabhedaat"   Sootra 7.

"Food according to Seasons."

Bodhaananda Vritti :

As stated in Kalpa Sootra, the food of the pilots is of three kinds, according to the seasons. "Ashana–Kalpa" or "Principles of Diet", says–"During the spring and summer months, the pilot's food should consist of buffalo–milk among liquids, among grains aadhaka or tuvar–dhal, and among flesh, the flesh of sheep.

In the 4 months of rains and autumn, cow's milk among liquids, wheat and black–gram among grains, and flesh of cocks and hens.

In the 4 months of winter and snow, goat's–milk, yava and black–gram among grains, and flesh of sparrows.

For pilots belonging to the three Dwija castes of Braahmin, Kshatriya and Vyshya, the food will not include flesh.

Maharshi Bharadwaaja :

☞ "Visha Naashas Tribhyaha"   Sootra 8.

"The three Varieties ward off seasonal evil effects"

Bodhaananda Vritti :

The 25 kinds of poisonous effects of the seasons are warded off by alteration in the food so as to suit the seasonal conditions.

"Vishanirnaya–adhikara" states, –

The seasons are each differently conditioned by the changes in the watery forces in the sky. The 101 forces in the aerial atmosphere, colliding with the 1/16th force in the watery sky in the seventh region, at the sineevaalee and kuhoo yogas or full–moon and new–moon conjunctions, produce maleficent and beneficent effects. The beneficent forces are 7,58,00,700 in number, and the maleficent forces also are of the same number, according to "Vaalmeeki Ganita". The beneficent effects are during the full moon period, and the maleficent effects during the new–moon period. 25 maleficent poisonous forces known as Bhedinee, tend to paralyse the pilots' physical effeciency. That is avoided by altering their food according to seasons. So says Sage Shaataatapa.

By such adjustment the pilots' physical fitness will be maintained.

Maharashi Bharadwaaja:

☞ "Tat Kaalaanusaaraat iti"   Sootra 9.

"That at set times"

Bodhaananda Vritti :

Having defined the seasonal types of food, the meal times are now defined. According to Shownaka, the times for taking meals are prescribed as follows : Family men should take food twice a day, or once a day. Ascetics should take food once a day. Others can take food four times a day. Air pilots should take food 5 times a day. And yogis may take as many times as they like.

According to "Lalla–kaarika" or "Diet Rules" by Lalla,

Food should be taken at the end of the 2nd yaama–(yaama = 3 hours) in the day time, and at the end of the 1st yaama in the night. That is for family men. If they take only one meal a day, it should be during the 3rd and 4th yaamas. Sanyaasis or ascetics who eat only once a day should dine as above. For the labouring classes the times are thrice during day time, and once in the night. For pilots of Vimanas the meals are thrice during day time, and twice at night.

Maharshi Bharadwaaja:

☞ "Tadabhaavay Sathva-Golovaa" Sootra 10.

"If unavailable, then vitamin pills or food-balls"

Bodhaananda Vritti :

If the prescribed food-stuffs are not available for use during their flights, then essence extracts made by proper cooking with admixture of spices and condiments into potable and eatable form, or food balls–made out of them should be supplied to the pilots for consumption on flights.

Says "**Ashana kalpa**" or "Food manual",

"There are 5 kinds of food, that are nutritious and wholesome ; cooked rice or grain, gruel, cooked flour, baked flat bread, and preparations made out of essence-extracts from food materials. The last named are superior to all the others".

"Paakasarvasva" or "Art of cooking" observes,

"Removing the husk and other non-food parts from it by machines, the grain should be made into flour and cooked in a suitable vessel and when it has reached the 8th degree of reduction, add essences, sweets, condiments, and ghee, and prepare food–balls, having nice flavour and delicious taste, and being nourishing to the body.

Maharshi Bharadwaaja :

☞ "Phala Moola Kanda Saarovaa." Sootra 11.

"Or essence of fruits, roots, and bulbs."

Bodhaananda Vritti :

In this sootra it is stated that preparations made from edible roots, potato and other bulbous vegetables, and from fruits are also suitable as food.

"Ashana-Kalpa" says,

If food made of grains is not available, that from roots, bulbs, and fruits may by used as food, in the form of flour, sugarcandy, manjoosha or jaggery, honey, milk, ghee, oily–products, and roots and berries which contain sweet, salt, pungent, acrid, and alkaline tastes. Such roots are said to be 56 in number. They should be purified, powdered, and duly cooked, and made into balls, and given out for use as food.

Similarly the bulbous vegetables which are of 16 kinds, and fruits which are of 32 kinds, and food prepared out of them are excellent food, Food from roots develops brain, nourishes the body, strengthens the bones, and gives virility. Food from bulbs promotes brilliance, and bodily vigour, and strengthens the life current. Food from fruits nourishes mind, intelligence, blood, flesh, and vital liquids. Therefore these alternatives are rcommended for pilots of Vimanas.

Maharshi Bharadwaaja :

☞   "Apicha Trinaadeenam."   Sootra 12.

"Even grasses, herbs and shrubs."

Bodhaananda Vritti :

This sootra indicates that even grasses, herbage, and creepers, could be made to yield food.

Says "Ashana-Kalpa",

Like roots, bulbs and fruits, grasses, shrubs and herbs, provide good food for men. Six kinds of doorva grass, 6 kinds of munja hemp, 6 kinds of darbha or long grass, 6 kinds of shoundeera, and 6 kinds of Ashwakarna or sal, or mimordica charantia, Shatamoolee of 3 kinds, Kaaruvellee, Chandravellee, Madhuvellee, Varchulee, Makutee vellee, sugandhaa, and sooryavellee may be made to yield good food, nutritious and bracing.

Selected by men who know them well, these vegetation, including their flowers, shoots, and leaves, by proper cleaning and cooking, may be made to yield solid or liquid food, which will serve as satisfactory substitute food for pilots of Vimanas. And Somavallee or moon-plant, Chakrikaa, Rasavallikaa, Kooshmandavallee, Ikshuvallee, Pishtavallaree, Sooryakaanta, Chandrakaanta, Meghanaada, Punarnava, Avantee, Vaastu, Matsyaakshee, and Rukma and others, provide good bases for lasting food, duly mixed with sweets and condiments.

Lohaadhikaranam : Metals

Maharshi Bharadwaaja:

"Athha Yaana Lohaani."   Sootra 13.

"Next, the Metals for aeroplanes"

Bodhaananda Vritti :

Having dealt with clothing and food for pilots, now the metals suitable for aeroplanes are being dealt with.

Says Shounaka :

There are 3 kinds of metals named somaka, soundaalika, and mourthwika. By mixing them, 16 kinds of heat-absorbing metals are produced.

Their names are ushnambhara, ushnapaa, ushnahana, raajaamlatrit, veerahaa, panchaghna, agnitrit, bhaarahana, sheetahana, garalaghna, amlahana, vishambhara, vishalyakrit, vijamitra and Vaatamitra etc.

"Maanibhadra Kaarika," or "Dictas of Manibhadra," Says, "Metals which are light, and are suitable for producing aeroplanes are 16. They are heat absorbing, and should be used in the manufacture of aeroplanes."

Saamba also says that the 16 metals formed by mixing the root metals, soma, soundaala and mourthwika, are non-heat-conductors and are useful for Vimanas. Their characteristics are now examined.

In the 7th layer of the earth, in the third mine therein, metals of the Soma series are found. They are of 38 kinds. Among them there are three from which Ooshmalohas or heat resisting metals are to be extracted. "Lohatantra" or "Science of Metals" also says that in the 3rd section of the 7th layer of the earth, Metals of Souma class, possessed of 5 special qualities, are called "beejalohas" or "root-metals".

There are 3000 metal bearing layers within the earth. Of them 1300 layers contain the better quality. In the 7th layer metals are of 27 types. The 3rd type of metals are of five-fold qualities, and are known as root metals. The origin of metals of the Soma class is thus described in "Lohakalpa." :

"The gravity of the centre of the earth, the gravity of global earth, the solar flood, the air force, the force emanating from the planets and stars, the sun's and moon's gravitational forces, and the gravitational force of the Universe, all together enter the layers of the earth in the proportion of 3, 8, 11, 5, 2, 6, 4, 9, and, aided by the heat and moisture therein, cause the origin of metals, of various varieties, grades and qualities."

The Souma group of metals are named, as per sage Atri, in "Naamaartha Kalpa". "Souma, Sowmyaka, Soundaasya, Soma, Panchaanana, Praanana, Shankha, Kapila are the names of the Souma metals, with distinct qualities indicated by their names."

The name "Souma" consists of sounds, s, ou, ma, and ha. "Paribhaasha· Chandrika" and "Vishwambhara Kaarikaa" state, "The oceanic force and solar force instil 4 kinds of forces into root metals. The sum total of the forces are said, according to "Vaalmeeki Ganitha" to number 1, 67, 768. Some of these forces are indicated by the sound "s" Some of the forces emanating from the sun and the elements are indicated by the sound "ou". Similarly other concerned forces are indicated by the letters "ma" and "ha".

The Varuna and Soorya force contents of all root metals are of four groups. In each group the force content is said to be 1, 67, 768. Of the Koorma and Kashyapa forces of Vaaruna group, the 67th from Ooshaa koorma, and the 85th Kaashyapa force, called "Kaala", are indicated by the letter "Sa".

Of the solar group of forces, maartaanda and bhoota 71st, and the ruchika force 160 are indicated by the sound "ra". Similarly, of the forces of sun and stars in aditi, the 9th called "Sundaa", and the stellar force 101 called "Bhowma" are indicated by the letter "Ma". And in the dhruva varga, soma and baadaba forces, 109 and 14 respectively, are indicated by the visarga sound "ha".

The four forces working inside the earth, by flux of time mature into the Souma type metal.

In Soundaala metal, the 11th force, dhanadaa, in Koorma is indicated by letter "sa". The 110th Kaashyapee force, rook, is indicated by the sound "ow". The sun's 100 powered dravamukhee shakti, and bhoota-shakti known as anvee 700 powered, are together indicated by the anuswaara sound "m". The sun's kaantaa shakti 49, and the stars' 25 shaktis, varchaa, are indicated by the letter "da". Similarly the soma forces in dhruva varga, is indicated by the long "aa" in "daa". The moon's 364 ujwalaa and baadabaa's 500 known as kaala are indicated by the letter "la".

That is "Soundaala".

Regarding the third, "Mourtwika", Koormashakti, paarthiva 1300, is indicated by the letter "ma". Kaasyapa shakti, kaalima 2001, is indicated by the sound "ow". Maartaanda shakti, laaghava 260, is indicated by the sound "r" : bhootashakti, vaarchulee 37, by the letter "tha" : stellar force, rukshmaka 1063, is indicated by the letter "va". Arkashakti, varuna 113, is indicated by the sound "e" : soma force rijukaa 8009, and pooshnikaa 1012, are indicated by the letter, "ka".

Lohashuddhyadhikaranam : Purification of Metals.

Maharshi Bharadwaaja :

☞   "Tatchhuddhir yathaa shodhanaadhikaaray."   Sootra 14.

"Their purification is as per shodhanaadhikaara".

Bodhaananda Vritti :

Taking soma metal first, it should be filled in a wide-brimmed vessel and adding jambeera or citron juice, likucha or lime juice, vyaaghra or castor, chinchaa or tamarind, and jamboo or rose apple juices, it should be boiled to 27th degree of heat for a day. Then taking it out and washing it, it should be boiled in 5 kinds of oils, 4 kinds of acids, and 7 kinds of decoctions.

They are named in "Samskaara Darpana" :
Gunjaa or wild liquorice, Kanjala, castor, kunjara, and karanja or Indian beach oils, praana-kshara, viranchi, kanchuki, and khura acids, and hingoo or asafoetida, parpata, ghontikaaa, jataa-maamsee or spikenard, white gourd or Vidaaraanginee, and matsyaakshee decoctions.

That is the process of purification of soma metal.

The purification of soundaala metal is like that of soma with regard to boiling in the cauldron, but the process of purification is with 6 acids, 7 oils, and 5 decoctions. They are, according to Samskaara Darpana."—

18

Ingaala or, ingudee, gouree or reddish herb, couries, grapes, rata, aapya, and ulbana oils, ankola, mushti, shankha, bhallaataka, kaakola, and virancha acids, and kuluththa or horsegram, nishpaava, sarshapa or mustard, aadhaka, and wheat decoctions or gruels.

Mourthweeka metal also should be baked like soundaala, and then should be boiled with shivaari oil, kudupa acid and vishambharee leather decoction.

Having defined the root-metals and their purification, we next consider the casting of Ooshmapaa loha.

SECOND CHAPTER

Maharshi Bharadwaaja:

☞ "Ooshmapaastriloha Mayaaha." Sootra 1.

"Ooshmapaa metals are made up of 3 metals."

Bodhaananda Vritti :

The heat-proof metals are made out of the three, Souma, Soundaala, and Morthweeka mentioned in the previous chapter. It is said in "Loha Ratnaakara" that each of the three yields varieties of seed metals. Their names are, in souma group,—souma, soumyaka, sundaasya, soma, panchaanana, ooshmapa, shaktigarbha, jaangalika, praanana, shankha, and laaghava; The names of the metals of soundeera origin, are viranchi, souryapa, shanku, ushna, soorana, shinjikaa, kanku, ranjika, soundeera, mugdha, and ghundaaraka. In the mourthweeka group, the 11 are anuka, dvyanuka, kanka, tryanuka, shvetaambara, mridambara, baalagarbha, kuvarcha, kantaka, kshvinka and laghvika.

Maharshi Bharadwaaja :

        ☞   "Melanaath"   Sootra 2.

            "By Mixing"

Bodhaananda Vritti :

The said metals are to be mixed in requisite proportions and melted. It is said in " Lohatantra " that ushnambhara metal is produced by mixing numbers 10, 5, 8 of soma, soundala, mourthweeka groups of metals respectively in the proportion of 1, 3, 7, and mixing with one third the quantity of tankana or borax and melting in the crucible. Similarly taking metals no, 3, 5, and 7 respectively in the three groups in the proportion of 4, 1, and 8, and mixing with tankana, and melting in crucible, the metal ooshma is obtained. Metal ooshmahana is produced by melting metals 2, 5, and 9 from the three groups in the proportion of 6, 3, and 7, with tankana. Metal Raaja is produced by melting nos. 3, 8, and 2 of the three groups as before. Similarly metal Aamlatrit is produced by taking numbers 9, 7, 1 in the three metal groups, in the proportion of 10, 7, 8 and mixing with tankana and melting as prescribed.

Similarly metals 6, 4, 5, respectively in the proportion of 5, 5, 12, melted with tankana or borax, will yield the metal veerahaa. The metal panchaghna is got by taking numbers 8, 6, and 4 of the three groups in the proportion of 20, 18, 26, and mixing with tankana or borax and melting.

The metal agnitrit is produced by mixing numbers 5, 2, 10, in the proportion of 30, 20, and 10, and melting with borax in the crucible. The metal bhaarahana is produced by mixing numbers 7, 11, and 6 in the three groups in the proportion of 5, 12, and 7, mixing with borax, and melting in the crucible.

To produce metal sheetahana, metals 10, 9, and 3 in the three groups respectively, in the proportion of 22, 8, and 10, should be mixed with borax and melted in the crucible. Garalaghna is produced by taking numbers 11, 10, and 11 in the three groups in the proportion of 20, 30, and 8, and melting with borax in the crucible.

Similarly Aamlahana is produced by taking numbers 11, 8, and 4 in the three groups in the proportion of 20, 12, 36, and melting with borax in the crucible. Metal Vishambhara is produced by taking numbers 19, 8, and 10 in the three Ooshmapa groups respectively in the proportion of 20, 12, and 6, and melting with borax in the crucible.

Metal vishalyakrit is produced by taking numbers 3, 5, and 11, in the proportion of 20, 12, and 6, and melting in the crucible with borax. Dwijamitra is produced by taking numbers 8, 3, and 9 in the proportion 5, 8, 10, and melting with borax in the crucible. And metal Vaatamitra is produced by taking numbers 8, 6, and 5 in the three groups of Ooshmapa metals, in the proportion of 22, 8, and 10, and adding borax and melting in the crucible.

Mooshaadhikaranam : The Crucible.

Maharshi Bharadwaaja :

☞ " Panchamaad dwitheeyay " Sootra 3.

"From the 5th variety in the 2nd group."

Bodhaananda Vritti :

According to " Nirnayaadhikaara ", the melting of the superior, medium, and inferior kinds of metals is to be done in 407 different kinds of crucibles. They are divided into 12 groups. For the melting of the root–metals the second group of crucibles is considered the best.

Lallacharya also states that metallurgists mention 12 kinds of metals : kritaka or artificial, apabhramshaka or corrupted, sthalaja or mud-born, khanija or found in mines, jalaja or aquatic, dhaatuja or mineral–born, oshadhivargaja or vegetation-born, krimija or evolved from vermin, maamsaja or flesh–born, kshaaraja or grown from salts, baalaja or hairborn, and andaja or resultant from eggs. Different classes of crucibles are to be used for melting different kinds of metals. In the second class of crucibles there are said to be 40 varieties. Of them, number 5, known as antarmukha or inward-mouthed, is prescribed for melting the root–metals.

It is described in " Mooshaakalpa " or art of making crucibles. 8 parts of gingelly manure or black–gram flour, 4 parts of metal rust, 3 parts of metal, 3 parts of laangalee or jussieuea repens or gloriosa superba, 6 parts of gum arabic, 2 parts of ruruka, 3 parts of salt-petre, 5 parts of creepers, 6 parts of charcoal, 5 parts of 5 kinds of grasses, 4 parts of paddy husk ashes, 2 parts of red arsenic, 2 parts of naagakesara, 5 parts of varolika flower, 5 parts of borax, 2 parts of black laamancha or scented grass or andropogon muricatus, 5 parts of sindoora or red ochre, 2 parts of gunja seeds or wild liquorice, 4 parts of sea-foam, all these are to be ground and made into fine flour, to which are added equal quantity of gum and 5 parts of earth and dust, and the whole is baked in a vessel with shivaaree oil for 3 yaamaas or 9 hours. When the contents have unified and become properly fluid, it should be poured through the nozzle into the crucible mould, and allowed to rest. The resultant crucible, known as "antarmukha," would be best suited to melt the metals required for producing a Vimaana.

Athha Vyaasatikaadhikaranam : The Fire-place.

Maharshi Bharadwaaja:

☞ "Athha Kundas-Saptamay-Nava". Sootra 4.

"Then fire-place, number 9 in class 7."

Bodhaananda Vritti :

Having dealt with crucible in the last sootra, we now consider the fire-place.

Experts mention 532 varieties of vyaasatikaas or fire-places. Of them Koorma-vyaasatika, or tortoise-shaped fire-place is best suited for melting the seed-metals for the Vimaana.

Kunda-kalpa or the art of furnace construction mentions 532 kinds of furnaces. They are divided into seven classes, each including 76 varieties. Furnace no. 9 in the 7th class, is best suited for melting the requisite metals of the vimaana, and its name is koorma-vyaasatikaa, or tortoise-shaped furnace.

It is said in " Kunda-nirnaya ", that on a prepared ground, a quadri-lateral or circular shaped furnace 10 feet wide should be constructed, shaped like a tortoise. In order to place the bellows, there should be constructed a pedestal shaped like a tortoise, and with five faces. In the middle of the furnace arrangements should be made for placing the crucible. On either side of the furnace there should be an enclosure for stocking charcoal. And on either side there should be a mechanism for receiving the molten metal.

Athha Bhastrikaadhikaranam : The Bellows.

Maharshi Bharadwaaja :

        "Syaad-bhastrikaashtame Shodashee"   Sootra 5.

"The bellows should be number 16 in the 8th class."

Bodhaananda Vritti :

    The making of bellows is referred to in this sootra. It is said in "Bhastrikaa Nibandhana," that as there are 532 kinds of furnaces, there are 532 kinds of bellows. Narayana also says that there are 532 varieties of bellows used in melting metals. They are divided into 8 classes. In the eighth class, the variety numbered 16 is the one suited for the tortoise-shaped furnace. The construction of bellows is described in the work " Bhastrikaa-Nibandhana ", as follows :

    The barks of suitable trees, leather, thick cloth made from milk cream, bark of areca-nut palm tree, and trinetra (bael ? Bengal Quince ?), shundeera, suranji, silk-cotton, sheneera, munjaakara, and jute by due processing yield suitable cloth of 605 varieties with which pretty and attractive bellows could be made, with fittings of wood or copper.

THIRD CHAPTER

Darpanaadhikaranam : Mirrors & Lenses.

Maharshi Bharadwaaja :

        "Darpanaashcha"   Sootra 1.

                "Mirrors".

Bodhaananda Vritti :

    This chapter deals with the mirrors and lenses which are required to be installed in the vimaana. They are seven different ones. Their names are given by Lalla in " Mukura-kalpa " as Vishwakriyaadarpana, or television mirror, Shaktyaakarshana darpana or power-capturing mirror, Vyroopya darpana or appearance changing mirror, Kuntinee darpana, Pinjulaa darpana, Guhaagarbha darpana, and Rowdree darpana or terrifying darpana.

Vishwakriyaa darpana is to be fixed on a revolving stand near the pilot so that he could observe whatever is happening outside on all sides. Its manufacture is thus described in Kriyaasaara :

Two parts of satva, 2 parts of shundilaka, one part of eagle bone, 5 parts of mercury, 2 parts of the foot-nails of sinchoranee, 6 parts of mica, 5 parts of red lead, 8 parts of pearl dust, 18 parts of the eyeballs of sowmyaka fish, one part burning coal, 8 parts of snake's slough, 3 parts of eye pigment, 6 parts of maatrunna, 10 parts of granite sand, 8 parts of salts, 4 of lead, 2 parts of sea foam, 3 parts of white throated eagle's skin, 7 parts of bamboo salt, 5 parts of vyraajya or white keg tree bark, these ingredients should be purified, and weighed, and filled in a beaked crucible and placed in the furnace called chandodara and subjected to a 800 degree heat, and when duly liquified, should be poured into the funnel of the kara-darpana yantra or hand-mirror mould. The result will be an excellent mirror in which will be reproduced minute details of the phenomena outside.

Next Shaktyaakarshana darpana :

As the vimaana flies through the regions of the sky, three classes of destructive forces tend to overcome it. This mirror is capable of neutralising and overcoming their effects.

Dhundinaathaachaarya also says : The wind, solar rays, and fire are known as trivargas. Each of the three has 122 evil effects on the plane's pilot. Those evil forces this mirror will absorb and nullify.

Paraankusha also says : There are certain crucial regions in the air routes of the vimaana, at which the wind, solar heat and fire have 366 malefic influences, and shaktyaakarshana mirror is meant to safeguard against them. It is to be prepared as follows :

5 parts of haritaala or yellow orpiment, 5 parts of virinchi, 8 parts of salts, 4 parts of gingelly husk, 6 parts of diamond, 1 of red mica, 8 parts of burning coal, 3 parts of sand, 2 parts of tortoise egg, 3 parts of bhaarani, 3 parts of kanda, 5 parts of powshkala, 5 of coral, 2 of pearl, 6 of sea-shell,

8 of borax, 3 parts of Bengal quince seed, and 5 of shankha or conch, cleaned, powdered, filled in swan crucible, placed in mandooka furnace and boiled to 500 degrees and poured slowly into vistritaa–mirror yantra will yield a fine shaktyaakarshana mirror.

The Vyroopya–darpana Mirror :

When enemy planes with men intent on intercepting and destroying your vimaana attack you with all the means at their disposal, the viroopya-darpana will frighten them into retreat or render them unconscious and leave you free to destroy or rout them. The darpana, like a magician, will change the appearance of your vimaana into such frightening shapes that the attacker will be dismayed or paralysed. There are 27 such different shapes that are said to be possible. Sammohana–kriyaa–kaanda, or the work dealing with the methods causing insensibility, mentions 17 of them. They are fire, water, wind, thunder, lightning, fumes, scorpion, bear, lion, tiger, and giant–sized frightful birds.

The manufacture of this mirror is thus given in Darpana–prakarana :

5 parts of bone salt, 3 parts zinc, 3 of lac, 8 of iron, 3 parts of shashabola, 2 of raajakurantika, 8 parts of charcoal ashes, 3 of borax, 8 parts of nakhaa, 7 of sand, 6 of matrunna, 2 of sun-crystal, 3 parts of poora or lime, 25 of mercury, 3 of yellow orpiment, 4 parts of silver, 6 of kravyaada, 8 of garada, 3 of pishta, 4 parts of arshoghna root, 3 parts of vaaraaha pittha, 3 of ammonium chloride, 25 of liquorice oil, taking these and 7 times purifying, filling in crucible, and placing in furnace and boiling it to 800 degrees and pouring into Darpanaasya yantra, will yield an excellent Vyraajaka mirror.

The Kuntinee Mirror :

We now consider the Kuntinee mirror. The wise say that the mirror by the glare of whose rays people's minds get deranged is Kuntinee mirror. Paraankusha says that in the region of the solar electric heat waves of the sky, seven streams of poisonous whirl-winds derange the mind. Scientists have discovered the Kuntinee mirror as a protection aginst that evil effect.

In "Sammohana-kriyaa-kaanda," the evil forces are described as follows :

Fat, blood, flesh, marrow, bone, skin, intelligence are adversely affected by the evil wind currents known as gaalinee, kuntinee, kaalee, pinjulaa, ulbanaa, maraa, in the electric heat wave regions of the upper sky.

The manufacture of this mirror is thus explained in "Darpana–prakarana" :

5 parts of sowraashtra earth, 7 parts of snake's slough, 3 of sea-foam, 5 of shanmukha seeds, 8 of zinc, 3 parts of rhinoceros' nails, 8 of salts, 7 of sand, 8 of mercury, 4 of conch, 6 parts of matrunna, 3 parts of yellow orpiment, 4 of elephant and camel salts, 7 parts of suranghrikaa, 5 of gingelly oil, 8 of pearl-shells, 3 of sea–shells, 4 parts of camphor, purified and filled in shinjikaa crucible, and placed in shinjeera furnace and boiled to 700 degrees, the fluid poured into the Darpanaasya yantra, will form into a morning sun-like kuntinee mirror.

The Pinjulaa mirror :

The conflicting inter-action of the solar rays is called pinjulaa. It has deleterious effect on the black eye-balls of the pilots. The pinjulaa mirror, by intervening will prevent the eye-balls being blinded by the evil rays.

It is said in " Amsubodhinee ", or the work on solar rays, " There are four directions, east, west, north and south, and four corner directions, south-east, south-west, north-east and north-west. The solar force of each direction has got its own intensity, owing to different fire-force, different seasonal force, the effect of the five winds, combined with the vaarunee or liquid force of the clouds, and the resulting tension gives rise to four evil forces, andha, andhakaara, pinjoosha, and taarapaa, whose glows, known as rakta, jaathara, taaraagra, and prabha, striking the eye-balls result in blindness of both eyes. "

The manufacture of this mirror is thus described in " Darpana prakarana " :

6 parts of goat's milk, 5 parts of red-lead, 8 parts of salts, 7 parts of sand, 5 parts of tree-gum, 8 parts of borax, 2 parts of dambholi essence, 8 parts of mercury, 2 parts of copper and 2 of lead, 4 parts of surolika essence, 8 parts of twak, 3 parts of vaardhyushika, 3 of kanda, 4 parts of pishta or gingelly husk, 3 parts of orpiment, 7 parts of Tinnevelli senna, 4 parts of vrikodaree seeds, these 18 to be purified, powdered, and filled in crucible, and placed in furnace and boiled to 700 degrees, and poured into Darpana yantra, will yield an excellent pinjulaa mirror.

Next Guhaa–garbha darpana :

"The conflict between the electricity in the clouds, wind, and rays, generates forces harmful to pilots. The guhaa–garbha darpana, by attracting them and projecting them by electric force against enemy planes, renders the persons inside them physically disabled and incapable of fighting."

"Prapanchasaara" also says :

"In the Middle of the two shells above kashyapa, there is vaarunee force. Between the shell and vaarunee force 5000 wind currents subsist. Similarly there are disease causing rays numbering 80 millions. The various winds and rays by mutual action result in flows and counter flows. When the cloud force, wind force, and solar force interplay they give rise to various harmful forces like bubbles."

Lallaacharya also avers, "In accordance with the 110 th principle, when the cloud–power, wind–power and sun–power meet with force and collide, they produce poisonous effects which are dangerous to mankind."

Vasishtha says in "Swatassiddha–Nyaaya" or "self-evident truth", that when alien forces cross one another, a poisonous flow will result naturally as an egg comes out of a tortoise.

"Sammohana kriyaa–kaanda" explains :

"By the conflict of cloud force, wind force and solar forces, 305105 poisonous waves known as guha and others emanate, and cause, kushtha, apasmaara, grihinee, khaasa, and shoola. Chief among them are five, known as gridhnee, godhaa, kunjaa, roudree, and guhaa. By accelerating them and directing them against the enemy, the guhaa-garbha mirror disables them."

" Darpana prakarana " describes its manufacture thus :

7 parts of couries, 3 parts of manjula or madder root, 6 parts of sea-foam, 8 parts of ranjaka or phosphorous, 6 parts of mandoora or rust, 8 parts of mercury, 3 parts of orpiment, 7 parts of brahmika, 2 parts of lead, 8 parts of eye pigment, 6 parts of matrunnna, 8 parts of sand, 6 parts of kishora, 5 of muchukunda, 2 parts of gingelly oil, 25 of lohika, 5 parts of mridaani garbha essence, 8 of sowraashtra earth, 5 parts of sphatika, 3 of bones, 15 of indusatva or moonstone ?, and 5 of dambholi taakaa dwaya satva,

taking these 22, purifying and powdering them and filling crucible, and placing in furnace and boiling to 700 degrees, and cooled in yantra, guhaa garbha darpana is produced.

Rowdree-darpana is a mirror or lens which liquefies everything that it flashes against.

Paraankusha says that where Rudraanyosharaa and abhralinga come into contact, a fierce force called roudree comes into being. Mingling with solar rays it melts everything. " Sammohana kriyaa kaanda " says :

" By the mixing of roudree and solar rays an evil force called maarikaa is generated, and impelled by the solar electricity, it destroys the enemy planes."

Darpanaa prakarana describes its manufacture :

8 parts of lead, 3 parts of shaalmali, 7 of durvaara, 8 parts kudupinjara, 21 parts of droonee, 8 parts sun-crystal, 27 parts of rudraanee-graavoshara, 6 parts betel leaves, 8 parts of kowtila, 30 of veeraabhra linga, 8 parts of salts, 7 of sand, 6 parts of matrunna, 3 of dimbhika, 8 of zinc, 13 of ant-hill earth, 6 of gum, 3 of kumbhinee, 3 parts sweet oil, 27 of Tinnevelly senna, 6 of godhaamla, 8 of silk cotton, 8 parts of virinchi satva, 5 parts of kanda, 3 parts of yellow orpimet, 7 parts of kaarmukha, or brown barked acacia ?, these 26, powdered, purified, and filled in crucible and placed in furnace and boiled to 800 degrees, and poured into Darpana yantra, will yield a fine roudrikaa-darpana.

28

FOURTH CHAPTER

Shaktyadhikaranam : The Power.

Maharshi Bharadwaaja :

☞ "Shaktayassapta"   Sootra 1.

"The power sources are seven."

Bodhaananda Vritti :

In this chapter the motive power of the vimaana is explained. In the functioning of the vimaana, there are 7 distinct operating forces. They are named udgamaa, panjaraa, sooryashaktyapa-karshinee or that which extracts solar power, parashaktyaakarshinee or that which extracts opposite forces, a set of 12 shaktis or forces, kuntinee, and moolashakti or primary force. At set spots in the vimaana, the motors which produce these 7 powers should be installed, duly wired and equipped with springs and wheels, as prescribed.

It is said in "Yantra-sarvasva :"

"The seven kinds of powers which are required for the Vimaana are produced by 7 motors which are named tundila, panjara, amshupa, apakarshaka, saandhaanika, daarpanika, and shaktiprasavaka. Each of these produces its specific power. Thus tundilaa produces udgamaa shakti, panjaraa produces the panjaraa shakti, shaktipaa produces the power which sucks solar power, apakarshaka produces the power which plucks the power of alien planes, sandhaana yantra produces the group of 12 forces, daarpa-nikaa produces kuntinee shakti, and shakti-prasava yantra produces the main motive power.

Shownaka-sootra also says :

"There are seven sources of power of the vimaana : fire, earth, air, sun, moon, water and sky. The seven kinds of powers are named udgamaa, panjaraa, solar heat absorber, alien force absorber, solar electric dozen, kuntinee, and primary force."

"Soudaaminee-kalaa" says :

Ma, la, ya, ra, sa, va, na constitute the seven vimanic forces. Ma is udgamaa, la is panjaraa, ya is solar heat absorber, ra is the solar dozen, sa is alien force absorber, va is kuntinee, and na is primary force.

Their actions are thus defined in "Kriyaa-saara" :

"The ascent of the vimana is by udgamaa shakti. Its descent is by panjaraa-shakti. Solar heat absorbing is by shaktyapakarshinee. Alien force restraining is by parashakty snatcher. Spectacular motion of the vimaana is by the vidyud-dwaadashaka-shakti. All these various activities are by the prime force of the vimana."

Vidyuddwaadashaka is thus explained in "Soudaaminee-kalaa" :

"The spectacular motions of the vimaana are of 12 kinds. Their motive forces are also 12. The motions and the forces are, proceeding, shuddering, mounting, descending, circling, speeding, circumambulating, side-wise motion, receding, anti-clockwise motion, remaining motionless, and performing miscellaneous motions."

Maharshi Bharadwaaja :

☞ "Shaktayah-pancha -iti-Narayanaha."   Sootra 2.

"Narayana holds that the forces are five only, and not twelve."

Bodhaananda Vritti :

Five forces are generated by the yantra or dynamo called Sadyojaata, and they produce all the spectacular motions of the vimana.

Says "Shakti sarvasva" :

"The motions of a vimaana are five, Chaalana, Gaalana, Panjaraprerana, Vakraapasarpana, and Spectacular manoeuvring."

Maharshi Bharadwaaja:

☞ "Chitrinyeveti sphotaayanah."   Sootra 3.

Sphotaayana holds that chitrinee is the sole shakti.

Bodhaananda Vritti :

Sphotaayana declares that the force called chitrinee shakti is the one which enables the vimana to perform spectacular manoeuvres.

"Shakti-sarvasva" says that both from experience and scientific knowledge Sphotaayana propounds the view that 32 various kinds of motions of the vimaana are solely by the power of Chitrinee-shakti.

" Kriyaa-saara " also states that Chitrinee force of the 17th quality is solely responsible for the 32 types of aeronautical motions.

Maharshi Bharadwaaja:

☞　　 " Tadantarbhaaavaat Saptaiveti "　　　Sootra 4.

"The shaktis are 7 only, and include all others"

Bodhaananda Vritti :

Out of the five forces produced dy the sadyojaata mechanism, panjaraa shakti is the most important. The other shaktis are incidental to it, just as sparks are incidental to fire. Chaalana and other motions may therefore be said to result from panjaraa shakti.

Says " Shaktibeeja " : " It is by the panjaraa shakti generated by sadyojaata yantra that the chalana and other shaktis branch out. "

" Shakti kousthubha " also says, "From the panjaraa shakti produced by sadyojaata, emanate the chaalana and other 4 shaktis."

Thus since the other shaktis branch out from panjaraa shakti, they may be said to be in essence identical with it. That panjaraa and chitrinee are included in the seven shaktis which have been enumerated by Maharshi Bharadwaaja. Hence there cannot be said to be any conflict of opinions. Some even hold the view that each one of the seven shaktis is capable of producing all the 32 motions of the vimaana. But since each of the several motions of the plane is definitely ascribed to a particular kind of force, it would be incorrect to hold that one force could be responsible for the whole gamut of motions. Any attempt to give practical effect to such a theory would prove disastrous. Therefore the right conclusion is that the seven forces are the true cause of the 32 kinds of aerial activities of the vimaana.

FIFTH CHAPTER

Yantraadhikaranam : Yantras : Machinery.

Maharshi Bharadwaaja:

☞ "Athha Upayantraani."   Sootra 1·

"The Mechanical Contrivances."

Bodhaananda Vritti :

Having described the forces or energies required for the various functions of the vimaana, now the mechanisms necessary for these activities are described.

"Kriyaa–saara" says :

"As stated by the eminent Bharadwaaja in "Yantrasarvasva", the mechanical equipments necessary for the vimaana are 32. They are vishwakriyaadarsa or universal reflecting mirror, shaktyaakarshana yantra or force absorbing machine, pariveshakriyaayantra or halo-producing machine, angopasamhara yantra or machine for folding up or contracting its parts, vistrutakriyaa yantra, or expanding yantra, vyroopyadarpana or fantastic mirror, padmachakra-mukha, kuntinee shakti yantra and pushpinee shakti yantra, pinjula mirror, naalapanchaka and guhaa-garbhabhidha yantras, tamo–yantra or darkness spreading machine, pancha vaataskandhanaala, roudree mirror, vaataskandha naalakcelaka, vidyudyantra or electric generator, and shabdakendra mukha, vidyuddwaadashaka, praanakundalinee, shaktyudgama, vakraprasaarana, and shaktipanjara keelaka, shirah-keelaka and shabdaakarshana, pataprasaaranayantra, dishaampati yantra, pattikaabhraka yantra, suryashaktyapakarshana yantra or collector of solar energy, apasmaaradhooma prasaarana or ejector of poisonous fumes, stambhana yantra, and vyshwaanara naalayantra."

They are thus described in "yantrasarvasva," chapter 7, by the illustrious Maharshi Bharadwaaja.

32

Maharshi Bharadwaaja:

    "Athopayantraani."   Sootra 1.

"Subsidiary Yantras."

Bodhaananda Vritti:

Prepare a square or circular base of 9 inches width with wood and glass, mark its centre, and from about an inch and half thereof draw lines to the edge in the 8 directions, fix 2 hinges in each of the lines in order to open and shut. In the centre erect a 6 inch pivot and four tubes, made of vishvodara metal, equipped with hinges and bands of iron, copper, brass or lead, and attach to the pegs in the lines in the several directions. The whole is to be covered.

Prepare a mirror of perfect finish and fix it to the danda or pivot. At the base of the pivot an electric yantra should be fixed. Crystal or glass beads should be fixed at the base, middle, and end of the pivot or by its side. The circular or goblet shaped mirror for attracting solar rays should be fixed at the foot of the pivot. To the west of it the image-reflector should be placed. Its operation is as follows :

First the pivot or pole should be stretched by moving the keelee or switch. The observation mirror should be fixed at its base. A vessel with mercury should be fixed at its bottom. In it a crystal bead with hole should be placed. Through the hole in the chemically purified bead, sensitive wires should be passed and attached to the end beads in various directions. At the middle of the pole, mustard cleaned solar mirror should be fixed. At the foot of the pole a vessel should be placed with liquid ruchaka salt. A crystal should be fixed in it with hinge and wiring. In the bottom centre should be placed a goblet-like circular mirror for attracting solar rays. To the west of it a reflecting mechanism should be placed. To the east of the liquid salt vessel, the electric generator should be placed and the wiring of the crystal attached to it. The current from both the yantras should be passed to the crystal in the liquid ruchaka salt vessel. Eight parts of sun-power in the solar reflector and 12 parts of electric power should be passed through the crystal into the mercury and on to the universal reflecting mirror. And then that mirror should be focussed in the direction of the region which has to be photographed. The image which appears in the facing lens will then be reflected through the crystal in the liquid salt solution. The picture which will appear in the mirror will be true to life, and enable the pilot to realise the conditions of the concerned region, and he can take appropriate action to ward off danger and inflict damage on the enemy.

Next Shaktyaakarshana yantra :

"Yantra sarvasva" says, "Owing to the etherial waves and raging winds of the upper regions in accordance with the seasons, evil forces are generated which tend to destroy the vimaana. The Shaktyaakarshana yantra in the vimaana is meant to subdue those forces and render them harmless."

Narayana also says :

"Three fierce forces arise from the fierce winds and ethereal waves, and cause destruction of the plane. The shaktyaakarshana yantra by its superior force subdues them and ensures safety of the vimaana."

Its construction is as follows :

The base is to be 3 feet long and 2 feet wide, and made of krouncha metal. A 12 inch tall 3 inch wide pole or peg made of 27th kind of glass should be fixed in its middle. To the east of it, as also to the west, 3 centres should be marked on each side. To the north and south also 2 centres should be marked on each side. At each centre screw–bolts should be fixed. Then tubes made of the 107th glass, with cleaned wiring should be fixed. A goblet shaped 15 inch sized glass vessel should be fixed on the base of the central peg. A 1 foot circular glass ball with three holes should be fixed in the main centre. A triangular shaped 1 foot sized mirror made of Aadarsha glass should be fixed on the 3rd kendra. Two circular rods made of magnetic metal and copper should be fixed on the glass ball so as to cause friction when they revolve. To the west of it a globular ball made of vaatapaa glass with a wide open mouth should be fixed. Then a vessel made of shaktipaa glass, narrow at bottom, round in the middle, with narrow neck, and open mouth with 5 beaks should be fixed on the middle bolt. Similarly on the end bolt should be placed a vessel with sulphuric acid (bhraajaswad-draavaka). On the pegs on southern side 3 interlocked wheels should be fixed. On the north side liquefied mixture of load-stone, mercury, mica, and serpent-slough should be placed· And crystals should be placed at the requisite centres.

" Maniratnaakara " says that the shaktyaakarshana yantra should be equipped with 6 crystals known as Bhaaradwaaja, Sanjanika, Sourrya, Pingalaka, Shaktipanjaraka, and Pancha-jyotirgarbha.

The same work mentions where the crystals are to be located. The sourrya mani is to be placed in the vessel at the foot of the central pole. Sanjanika mani should be fixed at the middle of the triangular wall. Pingalaka mani is to be fixed in the wide mouthed glass globe. Bhaaradwaaja mani should be fixed in the opening in the naala-danda. Pancha-jyotirgarbha mani should be fixed in the sulphuric acid vessel, and Shakti-panjaraka mani should be placed in the mixture of magnet, mercury, mica, and serpent-slough. All the five crystals should be equipped with wires passing throuh glass tubes.

Wires should be passed from the centre in all directions. Then the triple wheels should be set in revolving motion, which will cause the two glass balls inside the glass case, to turn with increasing speed rubbing each other, the resulting friction generating a 100 degree power. That power should be conveyed through wires to the sanjanika mani. Mingling with the force existing therein, that force issues out and should be transmitted through wires to the sourrya mani. On contact of the power therein the force will split into 5 streams. Each of the five power streams should be connected with one of the manis, Bhaaradwaja, Sourrya, Pingala, Pancha-jyotirmani, and Shakti-panjara mani. Mingling with the force in each mani, they form five forces, which are named by Atri maharshi as Raja, Mourtvica, Chundeera, Shoonya, and Garbha-vishodara. These should be passed by wires to the sulphuric acid vessel. They then form 3 forces, named marthanda, rowhinee, and bhadra. Marthanda shakti should be passed into the load-stone, mercury, mica, and serpent slough liquids. The resulting current should then be passed through wires to the wide mouthed glass globular vessel. Solar force pregnant with etherial force should be passed into the Naaladanda, and thence to the vessel with marthanda shakti. The power of the solar rays entering that vessel mingles with the marthanda shakti inside, and the resultant force has to be focussed towards the adverse force of the etherial current which will be thereby nullified and the vimaana will be protected.

Then the Rohinee shakti should be passed through wires into the vessel containing the fivefold loadstone, mercury, mica, serpent slough acid, and the resulting current passed to the Bhrajasvaddraavaka or luminous acid vessel at the foot of the central pole. Then from the air-route collect the wind-force impregnated solar rays and pass them also into the above vessel. Mingling with the rowhinee shakti therein a super-force will be created which should be passed through the northern pivot, into the rowhinee power vessel. The united force should then be directed against the malefic wind force in the air-route, so that it will tame the evil force and protect the Vimaana.

Then from the suragha tube Bhadraa shakti should be passed into five fold acid vessel. The resulting force should be passed through wired tubes to the foot of the triangular wall, and thence to the pivot on the southern side. The force should then be directed against the evil roudree force in the air-route. Neutralising that third destructive force in the sky, the vimaana will be allowed smooth passage in the sky.

The Parivesha-kriya yantra :

According to Yantra-sarvasva, by manipulating the five forces a halo is formed around the vimaana, and by drawing the solar rays into contact with it, the rays will speed the aeroplane along the rekhaamaarga or safety line. This is achieved by the operation of the above said yantra.

Narayanacharya also says :

"The mechanism which will manipulate the five forces so as to create a halo round the plane, and attracting the solar rays and contacting them with the plane, make them draw the plane smoothly and speedily along the air route without swerving into danger, is called parivesha-kriyaa yantra or halo-forming mechanism."

Soudaaminee kalaa says, "The forces of ksha, ja, la, bha, and ha, when united attract solar rays. "

According to " Gopatha-kaarika, " the forces in shireesha or Indra or lightning, clouds, earth, stars, and sky, are indicated by the letters ksha, ja, la, bha, and ha. By combining these five forces a halo, like that around the solar orb, will be created, and it will have the power or attracting solar rays.

Kriyaa-saara says Shireesha has 2 parts, Clouds have 8 parts, Earth has 5, Stars have 7, and Aakaasha or Sky or Ether has 10. The Aakarshana yantra should attract these forces and unify them. Then through the mirror above the vimaana attract solar rays, and apply them to the unified forces.

A halo will be created, and that halo, in combination with the solar rays, will draw the plane through a safe course like a bird held by a string. Its formation is thus explained in Yantra-sarvasva :

" Athha Yantraangaani "

We now deal with the parts of the yantra :

A foot-plate : 23 main centres to be marked on it, with lines connecting the centres. Similar number of revolving screws, wired tubes, pole with three wheels, eight liquids, eight crystals, eight liquid containers, mirror to attract the forces of shireesha, cloud, earth, stars, and aakaasha, five electric mechanism, five barks of trees, copper coated wires, five leathers, hollow screws, revolving screw with wire, vessels for storing the energies, vessel for mixing the energies, smoke-spreading yantra, air-fanning yantra, halo-creating tube made of milky-leather, solar ray attracting mirror tube, tube for collecting the solar rays reflected in the mirror at the top portion of the vimaana, crest-crystal, screw for connecting the solar rays to the vimaana. These are the 23 parts of halo producing yantra.

Its construction is now explained : A wooden base 23 feet square, made of black pippala or holy fig tree. 23 centres enclosed in a case made of 35th type of glass. 23 lines to the centres. Revolving keys to be fixed at the 23 centres. Wired glass tubes should connect one centre with another. A glass pole made of the 37th type of glass, 5 feet long, 1 foot thick in the middle, 18 inches thick at the neck, with a 10 feet wide top, should be fixed as the central pillar, with 3 revolving wheels. Eight acids should be placed in the eight directions from the north-east side. Their names are rubnaka, kraantaja, taarkshya, naaga, gowree, vishandhaya, khadyota and jwalana.

The rubnaka acid is to be placed in the north-east centre, kraantaja in the centre, naaga at the southern centre, gowree at the south-west corner, vishandhaya in the western centre, khadyota at the north-west centre, and jwalana at the northern centre in 8 glass vessels.

The names of the vessels are also given by Shaarikaanaatha: shila, abhra, paara, vyrinchika, vaaluka, asuragranthika, sphutika, and pancha—mrith,

The 8 vessels are made out of these 8 elements by process defined in "Darpana-prakarana."

The rubnaka acid should be filled in shila–darpana vessel ; kaarshnya– acid in abhrakaadarsha ; kraantaja acid in paaraadarsha vessel ; naagadraava in vyrinchi–aadarsha vessel ; khadyota acid in sphutikaadarsha ; gowree acid should be filled in vaalukaadarsha vessel ; vishandhaya acid should be filled in suragrathika vessel ; and jwalana acid in panchamrid vessel.

In the 8 acid filled vessels 8 crystals are to be inserted. As mentioned in " M˄niprakarana " their names are dhoomaasya, ghanagarbha, shalyaaka, shaaˀ tushaasya, somaka, shankha, and amshupa.

Having mentioned their names, we now explain their disposal. Dhoomaasya mani is to be placed in rubna acid vessel. Ghanagarbha mani should be placed in kraantaja acid vessel. Shalyaaka in kaarshni acid vessel. Shaarika in naaga acid vessel. Tushaasya is to be placed in gowree acid, Shankha in jwalana acid ; Somaka in vishandhaya acid; and Amshupa mani is to be placed in khadyota acid vessel.

In front of these manis, eight shaktyaakarshana, or energy-imbibing mirrors are to be fixed. Their names according to Bharadwaja are taaraasya, pavanaasya, dhoomaasya, vaarunaasya, jalagarbha, agnimitra, chhaayaasya, and bhanukantaka. Their location is as follows : Six inches in front of dhoomasya mani the taaraasya mirror with an iron rod with a switch attached to it should be fixed. Pavanaasya mirror should be fixed similarly in front of ghanagarbha mani. Dhoomaasya mirror should be fixed 6 inches in front of shalyaaka mani. Vaarunaasya mirror should be fixed in front of shaarikaa mani. Jalagarbha mirror should be fixed in front of somaka mani. Agnimitra mirror should be fixed in front of tushaasya mani. Chhayaasya mirror should be fixed in front of shankha mani. And Bhanukantaka mirror should be fixed in front of amshupaa mani.

Then in the western centre should be installed the electric generator with switch. Copper-coated wires covered with five kinds of skins, should be spread all-round, proceeding from the shakti-yantra or electric generator. The names of the five skins, according to " Kriyaa-saara, " are rhinoceros, tortoise, dog, rat or hare, and crocodile.

According to " Twangnirnaya-adhikaara, " or chapter on skins, for seats in vimaanas, and, for containing acids, and covering wires, five kinds of skins are mentioned by the learned ; skins of rhinoceros, tortoise, dog, rat or hare, and crocodile. These five are to be used for the purposes of covering, and seating. Wires covered with these skins are good conductors of electricity. The bhraamanee keela, or central revolving pole should be fixed in the centre so that when it revolves all the other pivotal centres also revolve. Eight energy storing vessels should be placed in the 9th, 8th, 10th, 12th, 13th, 15th 16th and 11th centres. The sammelana vessel or coordinating vessel should be placed in the front of the 23rd centre. To the south of it at the 21st centre the wind blowing mechanism should be fixed.

The Vaata-prasaarana or wind-blowing yantra is thus described : In the central pivot there are to be 5 wheels which will turn with 100 linka revolutions by contact with electric wires : in the east and west two bellows on pivots : two air-containers with 3 mouths or openings : 6 wheels which prevent air-motion : two tubes with switches which will cause spreading : wheels with keys that will induce speed, or full speed, slow, very slow or stop, shaped like a tortoise, having two bharas or parts?, and having a wheel fixed at the top. That is a vaata-prasaarana yantra.

The dhooma—prasaarana yantra or smoke-spreading yantra is as follows : with three openings, 5 satchels inside, 8 wheels, three keelakas or switches, encircled by electric tube, provided with smoke-generating mani or crystal, and equipped with 5 acids, with two churning wheels with keys, with two smoke containers attached to the bellows tube, with smoke-spreading yantra, and it is to be fixed at the 20th centre.

The parivesha-kriyaa naala or halo-creating tube is thus explained. Out of 5 milks from 5 kinds of milk trees, 6 barks of trees, and 2 valkalas (hemp, jute), cloth is fashioned. And that cloth should be used in preparing the parivesha-kriya or halo-forming tube.

It is stated in "Ksheeree-pata kalpa" :

In the realm of milk-yielding trees, dugdha-pranaalee, patapaadapa, payodharee, panchavatee, and virinchi are the 5 most suitable for manufacture of milk-cloth useful for vimaanas.

"Patapradeepikaa" also says, "Among the milk–trees, the best for producing milk–cloth are the following five, payodharee, panchavatee, viranchi, patapaadapa and dugdhapranaalika.

The six bark–trees are godaakanda, kurangaka-niryaasa, aandolikaaviyatsaara, lavika, prishatka, and kshmaamala. In conjunction with the milk from milk–trees these barks produce cloth which is flawless, strong, and soft.

For the two valkalas, according to "Agatatva–nirnaya" out of 5000 kinds of valkalas from shaarikaa to panchamukhee, the two named simhikaa and panchaanga are said to be excellent for producing the milk–cloth required for vimaanas.

The composition of the cloth is as follows :

Dudgdhapranaalika milk 8 parts, 10 parts of the milk juice of the patavriksha, 7 parts of payodaree or cocoanut milk, 18 parts of the milk of the 5 vata or ficus trees, and 12 parts of virancha tree.

The ambikaa–shatka composition is 10 parts of godaa–kanda, 17 parts of gum from kurangaka, 15 parts of aandolikaa viyatsaara, 12 parts lavika, 20 parts of prishatka, and 15 parts of kshmaamala.

The two jute cloth proportions are given in "Shana–nirnaya chandrikaa," as 28 parts of simhikaa jute, and 18 parts of panchaangavalkala jute.

These proportions of 5 ksheera or milk, 6 ambika or barks, and 2 valkalas or jutes, should be mixed together and unified, and boiled in paakaadhaana yantra and churned a number of times, and processing with acids 12 times, should be filled in pata–garbha kriya or cloth–making yantra, and milk–cloth of excellent quality obtained. The parivesha kriyaa–tube made out of this cloth will, by manipulation of the concerned switch, expel smoke from the vimaana, and by quick advancing and reverse revolutions of the wheel will spread the smoke all round so as to envelope the vimaana by means of the smoke–screen.

The Kiranaakarsha-Naala :

16 parts of the 305th variety of glass, 5 parts of kaancholikaabharana, 6 parts of nagakesara or merua ferrea,—aletris hyacinthoides, 4 parts of

couries, sunflower, and Indian spikenard, 8 parts of pure borax, iron dross, onion juice, cuscus grass powder, ruby glass, the three varieties of salt–petre, sand, essence of suranjikaa, viranchi flour, essence of black–mica, essence of bael fruit, and juice of flower buds, these twelve ingredients, in the propor- tion of 27, 5, 7, 3, 8, 7, 3, 11, 8, and 12, are to be filled in the frog–shaped crucible, and placed in the frog–shaped furnace, and melted with 300 degrees of heat with the help of two–winged bellows. The resulting liquid is to be poured into the darpana yantra or glass–making machine, so as to produce the kiranaakarshana or rays–attracting yantra.

The tube made of this glass should be fixed at the top of the concerned yantra.

Next the pratibimba–arka–kiranaakarshana naala, or tube for attrac- ting the reflection of the solar says :

According to "Naalikaa–nirnaya," the essence of squash gourd, juice of momardica, 2 parts of the salt of the two wheeled root vegetable, 3 parts of salt of simhamoola, 122nd type of glass, essence of white mica, jelly stone, borax, root of Bengal–madder, thorn at the root of bamboo, lead, mercury, these 15 ingredients are to be mixed in the proportion of 5, 12, 4, 3, 7, 3, 11, 4, 9, 12, 20, 18, 12, 5, 20. The mixture should be filled in the crucible known as samavargika, and heated in the furnace of the same name, and heated to the degree of 315, with the aid of bellows called suraghaa. The resulting liquid should be poured into the mirror–making machine. The resulting product will be a fine bimbaarka–kiranaadarsha, or reflected solar ray attracting mirror. This should be fixed in the central portion of the vimaana and in the 10th kendra, with five circled screws.

Now we deal with the crest crystal of the vimaana. The crest–crystals are of 103 kinds. They are named in "Mani–kalpa–pradeepika" as belonging to the 12th class of 32 groups of crystals. Their names are shankara, shaan- taka, kharva, bhaaskara, Mandana, kalaantaka, deeptaka, nandaka, chakra- kantha, panchanetra, Rajamukha, Raakaasya, kaalabhyrava, chintamani, koushika, chitraka, bhaskara, uduraaja, viraaja, kalpaka, kaamikodbhava, panchasheershna, paarvanika, panchaaksha, paaribhadraka, isheeka, kaasha- bhrit, kaala, kanjaasya, kowtika, kalaakara, kaarmika, vishaghna, pancha- paavaka, symhikeya, roudramukha, manjeera, dimbhika, pingala, karnika, krodha, kravyaada, kaala–kowlika, vinaayaka, vishwamukha, paavakaasya, kapaalaka, vijaya, viplava, praanajanghika, kaarmukha, prithu, shinjcera, shibika, chanda, jambaala, kutilormika, jrimbhaka, shaakamitra, vishalya, kanka–gowrabha, suragha, suryamitra, shashaka, shaakala, shaktyaakara, shaambhavika, shibika, shuka, bherunda, mundaka, kaarshnya, puruhoota, puranjaya, jambaalika, sharngika, jambcera, ghanavarshmaka, chanchvaaka, chaapaka, ananga, pishanga, vaarshika. Raajaraaja, naagamukha, sudhaakara, vibhakara, trinetra, bhoorjaka, kumuda, koorma, kaarmuka, kapila, granthika, paashadhara, damaruga, ravi, munjaka, bhadraka.

These are the 103 crystals suitable for being fixed as crest–jewels of the vimaana. One of them is to be fitted to the central pinnacle at the top of the vimaana, and the wires from the electric dynamo should be connected to it, so that it might be supplied with power. On the upper side should be attached wires for collecting solar rays, so that the two forces might act in combination.

The switch-gear for connecting the vimaana with the solar energy is explained in "Brihath–kaandika." Sandhaana–keelakaas are of 25 kinds. Their names are pinjuleeka, keeranaka, dimbhaka, paarvateeyaka, kachchapa, gaaruda, uddanda, shaktipa, govidaaraka, pavanaasya, panchavaktra, vajraka, kankana, ahirbudhnya, kundalika, naakula, oornanaabhika, trimukha, sapta–sheershanya, panchaavartha, paraavatha, aavarta, naabhika, oordhvaasya, shilaavarta.

Amongst these the 9th, govidaaraka, is best suited to connect the vimaana with the solar beams for safe navigation. This is Pariveshakriyaa-yantra.

Next Angopasamhaara yantra :

During the passage of sun and other planets in the 12 houses of the zodiac, owing to the varying speeds of their progressive and retrogressive motions, conflicting forces are generated in the zodiacal regions, and their collisions will let loose floods of fierce forces which will reduce to ashes the parts of the plane which get involved with them. The pilot should get warned by the ushna–pramaapaka yantra, or heat–measuring instrument, and quickly fold the concerned parts and ensure their safety.

It is described in "Yantrasarvasva" as follows:

Purifying the metal sumrileeka mixed with manjeera, a pedestal should be cast, 12 feet long, 18 inches thick, and shaped as a square or circle. Then mixing the magnetic stone and dimbika, after purifying them with acids, cast a pole 3 feet thick and 30 feet tall, with springs, as in an umbrella, at the foot, in the middle and at the upper end, and fix it in the centre of the pedestal. Rods made of mixed metal like umbrella rods, provided with 5 springs, should connect the springs in the pole with the several limb mechanisms of the vimaana. Two revolving wheel springs with two tubes with 3 faces and 3 wheeled springs should be fixed at the bottom of the pole, near the spring. Above there should be fixed an oiling tube which will keep all the springs well-oiled. When a particular limb of the plane has to be contracted the spring at the foot of the pole should be turned so as to induce the spring of the part to operate so as to contract or open up the part as need be so that the danger to the part will be prevented. By the operation of the angopasamhaara yantra, any part of the plane can be folded up to avoid danger and opened out subsequently.

Vistritaasyaa kriyaa yantra or wide-opening mechanism:

When the various powers, subterranean, eight cardinal points, earth, cloud, electricity, and oceanic, consemble in padma-mukha, a power called vishambharee is generated. It breaks through the earth, emitting great heat, mounts with a 300 linka spead to the upper sky regions, and reaching the aerial routes, envolopes the vimaana, and affects the personnel inside causing grave physical disabilities, and paralysing the brain. For the purpose of curbing it and nullifying it, the vistritaasyakriyaa yantra is to be installed in the vimaana.

According to "Yantrasarvasva," a foot-plate, of an arm's length, and 22 inches thick, and round-shaped, is to be made of the wood of the sacred peepul tree. A pole of an arm's thickness, and 32 inches high, is to be fixed in the middle of it. Reversible wheeled double-switches should be fixed along its height, connecting each of the sectional mechanisms in the vimaana, through tubes reaching to the bhastrikaa naala or bellows tube attached to the mechanisms. At the foot of the pole three revolving wheels, and at its back the contracting switches, have to be fixed.

First peetha or footplate, then pillar, then revolving springs, jointure tubes, two-wheeled keelakas, two-winged bellows, three wheel moving mechanism, contracting mechanism, are eight constituent parts of this machine.

First the triple wheeled mechanism should be switched on. That will set the double wheels in motion. That will make all the springs attached to the pillar begin to operate. The two winged bellows attached to the double-wheels will open up. Wind will rush out and force through all the sandhi-naalas or jointure tubes. That will set the the bellows in the central operating ; thereby the bellows of the sectional mechanisms will come into play, and air will flow out in a flood, and taking hold of the vishambharaa shakti expel it to the aerial regions where it will get lost. Thus the personnel inside the vimaana will be saved from disabilities and restored to normalcy.

Vyroopya mirror :   Says "Yantrasarvasva",

When enemy planes come intent on destroying the vimaana, the vyroopya mirror is intended to frustrate them. Its parts are, peetha or stand, central switch-gear, electric pole, smoke tube, betel–nut oil, triple–wheeled spring, three satchels, smoke light, and contraction tube.

The peetha or seat should be 2 feet wide and 2 feet tall, and circular, and made of bael tree wood. 12 centres are to be marked therein. At each centre revolving joints should be fixed. Jyotistambha or electric pole, 24 inches thick and 24 inches tall and made of vyroopya darpana glass, is to be fixed in the centre. In front of it the electric machine should be fixed in the 2nd kendra. In the 3rd kendra should be fixed the turning smoke tubes with winding wires. The oil vessel should be fixed in the 5th kendra. The 3 satchels, with 3 mouths, one foot high and made of milk-leather should be fixed in the 6th 7th, 8th and 9th kendras, up to the smoke tube. In the tenth kendra should be fixed the smoke–extinguishing tube mechanism, and the light–extinguishing tube in the eleventh kendra. The winding wire tube should be fixed in the 12th kendra.

The operation of the mechanism is as follows :

Drawing the electrical energy from the dynamo, it must be applied to the triple–wheeled mechanism. That will be set in motion. The wires proceeding from there will convey the power to all the other mechanisms and set them in motion. Kendras 3, 4, and 5, will become active. When kendra 9 is switched on the koshas attached thereto will become active. From the 5th kendra the current should be passed to the oil vessel. The oil will then convert itself into poisonous ·gas. The gas should be filled in the 3 satchels and the 3 tubes. The fumes from two of the tubes should then be discharged towards the enemy planes. They will encircle the enemy planes and envelope them with a smoke-screen. Then the betelnut oil should be lighted, and fiixed in the jyoti stambha or light-pillar. The light within the pillar will suffuse it with red glow like a china rose; and pervade the sky. Then the electric glow should be applied to that glow. The resulting glow will be multi-coloured like a rain-bow, with violet, indigo, blue, green, yellow, orange, and red. Then the poison-fumes from the 3rd tube should be drawn through the air tube, and let into the multicolour-glowing light-pillar. The fume will burst into light, and then should be passed through tube into the vyroopya-darpana. The light glow will pervade the mirror and attain 3000 degree intensity, causing a blinding glare and paralising the enemy. Then the gas in the three satchels should be projected with 25 linka speed towards the smoke screen enveloping the enemy. Then the smoke from the tubes should be projected with 28 linka speed into that screen. Then the smoke filled glow will flood over the enemy personnel and affect their body joints, organs, mind, vision, and induce inertness, and make them all fall down senseless. Then the pilot could change his air-route and proceed forward safely.

Then Padmachakra mukha yantra :

According to "Yantra sarvasva," its parts are, peetha or pedestal, pillar, tubular pole, electric wiring, glass lotus petals, lotus formation process, places where the lotuses are to be located, wind inhaling and leather-bellows mechanism, contracting and expanding switches, triple-wheel fixing arrangement, air flow outlets, folding up mechanism. These are the 12 parts of the padmachakra mukha yantra.

The peetha or seat should be made of the wood of pippala or the holy fig tree, 8 feet and 3 feet high, and square or circular. Mark 12 fixing centres on it. From the central pillar draw lines towards the 12 spots. The central pole, two tubular posts on either side of it, electric wire in eastern centre, lotus petals in the north, formation of lotus in the northern and southern centres, fixing of the lotuses from the north-east to the south-east corner, to the east air-filling bellows. In the north west corner the contracting switch, and the expansion switch in the south-west corner, triple-wheel revolving mechanism on the eastern side, air flow outlets underneath each lotus. To its south, the contraction switch.

These are the 12 parts to be fixed in the 12 centres.

The production of the parts is as follows :

The central pivot should be made of abhra-mrid-darpana, or mica-sand glass. According to "Darpana-prakarana"—

5 parts of rambhasatva (plantain stem ?), 8 of manjoosha (madder root ?), 5 parts of kaanta (ayaskaanta ? sooryakaanta ?), 8 parts of kravyaada (jataa-maamsi), 3 parts of aadhaka essence, 7 parts of tortoise shell essence, 18 of bhalyatvak, 3 essence of kudmala or flower buds, 8 of bamboo salt, 3 of hooves, 28 parts of shoonya-mrid or mica ash, 4 of trivikrama kshaara, 2 of conch, 5 of mercury, 8 of salts, 1 of creepers, 3 of silver, 3 of eye-ointment, these 18 ingredients, purified, filled in crucible, placed in varaatakunda furnace and boiled to 200 degrees, and slowly filled in darpana yantra, will yield an excellent abhra-mrid darpana.

Two tubular poles of the size of an arm, made of this glass, should be placed on either side of the pivot. From the central pole electrical wiring should be connected to the 12 centres. In the centre of the switch tubes should be placed the lotus petals, and 150 finely made glass lotus petals should be spread on the northern side electric wires.

The petals are to be made, according to Lalla, by mixing 15 parts of the mica glass, with 4 parts of sourika salt, duly mixed and finely powdered and melted in pattikaa machine, when like onion-skin layers, petals will take shape. Then the wires attached to the petals should be brought together from the several centres, and attached to the lotus forming mechanism. By turning the concerned wheel the petals will move towards the centre and form a lotus. Each petal will then become a tube, and by their juggling each tube will form 2 petals. The air–attracting mechanism should be placed in front and set to work. With a shrieking noise the air will be sucked in by each tube and the petals will shoot the air far into the outer air.

It is said in "sandhaana–patala—"

The scattering of a blizzard which may obstruct the progress of the vimaana is only possible by means of the padma–sandhaana and not otherwise. Therefore the spots where the lotuses are to be inserted are now indicated. On the eastern side from the north east to the south east the lotuses are to be erected in seven places in close order. Beneath the seven lotuses should be fixed seven leathern bellows capable of deep draughts of air. On the north west corner should be fixed the double–wheeled contracting mechanism.

According to "Kriyaa saara," by turning the main wheel in right motion, and the upper wheel in reverse motion at full speed, the yantra will suffer contraction. This machine is composed of 6 wheels spread out, 5 naalaas or tubes, 12 wires and 12 openings, and 12 keys which will cause contraction of the 12 parts, with widened mouth at the upper and lower parts, and provided with 2 revolving keys. By placing such a contracting machine in the north–west corner, the machine could be contracted when desired.

Now we shall deal with the expanding mechanism. It is round like a water pot, with 12 wheels and mouths, having 12 tubes with rods inside with 12 revolving springs for ascending motion, and with a central spring for filling with air. With such a mechanism the yantra can be made to stretch its parts. This should be fixed in the south west corner.

Then at the eastern face the triple–wheeled revolving spring, called "bhraamanee–keelaka", should be fixed.

It has 3 ivory wheels, consists of 3 poles, wooden top shaped like shimshumaara, with wheels with spring on top. By its operation the several parts of the yantra are set in motion, and by the operation of the concerned springs, the yantra will expand. Therefore the 3 wheeled bhraamanee mechanism should be properly fixed at the eastern kendra with 5 bolts.

Underneath the lotuses air flow routes should be provided. There should be openings 12 inches wide, 2 inches high, be leather–covered, made of pippala wood, with 7 tubes for the flow of wind. Seven such tubes should be fixed beneath the seven lotu‚es, and provided with keys.

In the southern centre the contracting mechanism or upasamhaara keela, with 12 outlets, should be fixed.

Owing to the seasonal changes forces will generate in the joints of the outer space, and combining with the oceanic forces will reach the realm of air and cause a commotion which will spread out with fierce force into the farthest air pockets, and let loose typhoons which reach the vimaana, and produce a dusty excrescence which will induce chicken–pox–like skin eruptions on the pilots and other occupants, and also break up the vimaana. In order to suck up that foul wind–flow, and expel it out of the vimaana, the padma–patra–mukha yantra is prescribed.

Next Kuntinee–shakti–yantra :

Now we shall deal with kuntinee–shakti yantra. In mid–summer, out of the myriad heat rays of the sun, by the union of the 3, 5, and 10th class of rays, a fierce force of blazing heat named kulakaa is generated.

It is said in "Ritukalpa",

From the solar heat generative source 3 Mahaakshoni and 21 crores 500 lakhs 16 thousand and nineteen heat rays emanate. They are classified into 5 crores 8 thousand and 107 groups in Vaalmeeki ganita. Each group is divisible into 100 sub-groups. Of these when the rays of sub–groups 3, 5, 10 from the second group get mixed up in the heart of summer, a force called Kulakaa with fiery intensity is generated ; and when it moves into the path of the flying vimaana, the plane will be reduced to ashes. To protect against that the kuntinee–shakti yantra should be installed in the neck portion of the vimaana.

Sage Narayana also says :

Amongst the divisions of the heat rays of the summer sun, the second group has 85000 rays. Out of them those numbered 8, 3, and 10 are specially intense, and they attract the pramlochana shakti from koorma portion of the universe, and produce a fierce heat-wave called kulikaa. If a vimaana happens to encounter it in its course, it will be burnt to ashes. To safeguard against that the kuntinee-shakti yantra should be installed in the neck section of the vimaana.

Lallaachaarya also confirms :

Out of the many groups of the heat-rays of summer, numbers 3, 5, and 10 in the 32nd division of the 2nd group of rays' tend to contact the pramlochana shakti in koorma and produce a fierce force called kulakaa which will destroy the vimaana. The erection of the kuntinee-shakti yantra in the vimaana will prevent it from such destruction.

According to "Yantra Sarvasva",

Among the constituent yantras of the vimaana, the kuntinee-shakti yantra is required to protect it from the combustible heat waves known as kulikaa in summer. Its parts are ground-plate, central switch-board, acid vessel cloth, with folds, chakradanti naala, milk cloth, tube covering switches, revolving wheel equipped with electric wiring, and contracting mechanism.

The peetha or ground-plate should be 3 feet wide and ½ foot high, and round like a drinking bowl, seven kendras or centres commencing from the eastern side, turning switches in the seven centres, the acid vessel in the central kendra.

"Kriyaasaara" Says :

For capturing kulikaa the oil from gunja or the seeds of the shrub abrus and tobacco leaves, and mercury and shanaka crystal are recommended for use. The oils or acids of the seeds and tobacco leaves are to be filled in goblet like cup made of glass made of naaga, crownchika, and sowrambha metal, add purified mercury, and fix in the central kendra. Then apply the solar rays to the vessel. By the action of the rays on the acids the crystal in the vessel will become charged with a cold frigid force called krownchinee. Then when the kulikaa force enters the vessel with its fierce heat, it will be sucked in by the cold-storage crystal.

In the left kendra the cloth with folds should be fixed. Says "Patakalpa.—"

In order to confine in the crystal the fierce heat of kulikaa it should be wrapped in the folds of a cloth of fine and strong texture made of spikenard and jute yarn, with 5 folds and 3 openings. From the openings 3 glass tubes should be projected with downward bends into 3 wide mouthed vessels. To the north-east must be fixed the chakradanti naala for attracting the kulikaa force. Snake-skin, gum of srini, woollen yarn, soft grass, should be boiled together and lac-coloured cloth-like glass prepared, and purified with sundikaa wood oil. It should be rolled in coils just as a snake circles up in coils and sleeps. The tiny glass tubes should be attached at the bottom of the chakradanti as directed.

Then ksheeree-pata naala, or milk-cloth tube is to be fixed. Made of milk-cloth with wide-opening, strong, soft, a tube should be inserted in the mouth of the chakradanti, and its end should be made to reach the hole in the peetha. Through that the kulikaa force makes its exit. After placing ksheeree pata naala like this with key, the electric wire connected central operating switch should be placed in the west. And to the north-east of it the vistritaasya or opening out switch should be fixed.

Says "Kriyaasaara" :

It should have two satchels, two openings, two right-revolving and reverse-revolving wheels. In the eastern opening should be fixed the 2 right-revolving wheels. And in the northern mouth should be fixed the 2 reverse motion wheels. And as in an umbrella, sticks connecting all the parts with the centre, for the purpose of expansion and contraction by turning a switch. By operating the switch in the eastern opening all parts will open out or expand. By operation of the northern switch all parts will close up. This is the upasamhaara keelakaa.

Having enumerated the parts of the yantra, their operation is now given. First the electric switch. By putting it on, the Bhraamanee chakra or pivotal wheel will revolve setting in motion individual parts as and when desired by turning their respective switches. Then electric current should be passed to the acid containing the crystal. Solar rays also should then be passed into it. Thereby, in the acid there will be generated a female shakti of 5 nyankas called sowlikaa. Similarly in the crystal there will be generated a male shakti of 8 nyankas called chulikaa. By operation of the electric current the two shaktis will get unified and produce an extremely cold shakti called "crownchinee," capable of attracting the kulikaa. That crownchinee force should be projected through naala or tube towards the kulikaa, like imbedding a gunja pea in a lump of lac. Thereby the crownchinee will drag the kulikaa inside the yantra through the tube and drop it into the acid vessel where it will be imbibed by the crystal.

Then the patormikaa key should be turned, whereby the patormikaa will become wide open preventing any air from entering the crystal by covering it completely. Then the chakradanti key should be turned slowly, so that its mouth opens out and sucks the hot kulikaa from the crystal, and stores it inside itself. Then the key of the sookshmaadarsa naala, fine mirror tubes, should be operated. The kulikaa in chakradanti will emerge through the 3 tubes. Then the vistritaasya key should be operated quickly so that all the parts will open out, and the kulikaa shakti will get out and disappear, and the danger to the pilot will have passed. Then by operating the upasamhaara keelaka, the expanded parts will close up and the yantra will return to normalcy.

Now we shall deal with Pushpinee yantra. When the pilot has to travel during spring and summer months, the pushpinee yantra is intended to provide him with necessary comforts.

According to "Khetavilaasa" :

In spring a force called sowrikaa emanates from the south-east. And in summer a force called panchashikhaa arises in the north-west and is intensified by the sun's rays. Panchashikhaa contains two kinds of poisons. Sowrikaa having fire and moon contents is cold and hot, cold internally, and hot externally. It generates warmth in all creations, making the human kind perspire, and the trees and vegetation bring out their milk and gums. Thereby their bodies are relieved of harmful materials likely to lead to diseases.

By its cold effect and attracting the spring effect from the solar rays, it permeates all things, and brings out shoots, tendrils, flowers and a glow in all trees and creepers. Similarly it effects the 7 physiological components of the human body and increases their vigour, strength, growth, and glow.

Panchashikhaa shakti or force effects movable and immovable life adver-sely by its stultifying influence, shrinks and dries up the growth process of both vegetable and animal life and causes deterioration. To counteract this harmful effect of the season on the personnel of the vimaana, the pushpinee yantra is commended as one of the constituents of the aeroplane.

Its parts are, the base, the cold processing mirror, keelaka or key, cold generating crystal, acid vessel, electric wheel with 100 spokes.

The sunda–mud made glass is prepared, according to "Paarthiva-paaka Kalpa" as follows. Take salt, shinjeera, bone, and betel-nut salt, durona, kuruvinda grass (cyperus rotundus), gum, sowraashtra mud, virinchi vatika or banyan bark, silk cotton tree bark, and coir salt, these ingredients are to be taken in the proportion of 5, 12, 2, 3, 8, 3, 30, and 6, purified, filled in the crucible, and placed in the tortoise shaped furnace, boiled 32 times in 100 degree heat with the help of two faced bellows, and the resulting fluid poured into the cooling yantra. A pure and fine sunda–mud–glass will be formed.

With the glass thus produced by boiling 32 times, a base is to be formed 12 inches wide, 3 inches high, four-square or circular. From the centre of it 4 kendras or centres are to be marked. In the centre an arm-sized pivot made of the said glass should be fixed. On top of it is to be fixed the cold-processing mirror key. At its centre should be fixed the cold producing crystal. At the eastern centre should be placed the acid vessel.

Dravapaatra or acid vessel is described in "Kriyaasaara." It should be 12 inches wide and 12 inches high, shaped like a tumbler, circular, and hard like a cocoanut shell, and be made of the sheeta–ranjikaa glass.

The glass is described in "Darpana Prakarana". Shasha-piththa, udupiththa, borax, kutmala, jyotsnaa saara, rasonta kanda flour, kudupa–salt, mica salt, shoundeera jangha shalya flour, vaatohara, white niryaasa earth salt, and uragha.

These 12 ingredients should be taken in the proportion of 5, 3, 5, 1, 10, 10, 11, 8, 7, 2, 20, and 6, and after properly purifying them, fill them in lotus–shaped crucible, and placing it in the lotus shaped furnace filled with burning charcoal, and with the aid of the five-mouthed bellows blow the heat to 323 degrees temperature, and pour the liquid into the yantra. The resulting glass is called sheeta-ranjikaadarsa or cold-receptacle glass.

Cold-producing crystal is described in "Maniprakarana": 5 parts of couries and manjula powder, 4 parts udumbara salt, 3 of rubhna, 8 parts of varchulaka, 7 of sheeta ranjikaadarsha, 3 of vatu, 28 of shaalmali, 3 of salts, 7 of mercury, 8 of white mica, 8 of karkataanghri salt, 5 of chowlika satva, 15 of niryaasa earth, 25 of sampaathi bird kneebone—

These 14 ingredients, in the named proportions are to be purified and filled in mritkundala-moosha or earthen crucible, and placed in kulakundika furnace, and with the aid of tryambaka bellows blown into 300 degree temperature. Fill the boiled liquid into the mani-prasoothika, or crystal forming yantra. The crystal produced will be pure, hard, and intensely cold.

In front of it should be fixed the electric panka wheel, with 100 spokes and electric wiring, and purified by 3 acids.

As per "Kriyaasaara," 12 parts of copper, 3 of collyrium, 8 of zinc, should be mixed and melted with 100 degree heat. It will become pure like gold, yellow, fine, soft, and strong. It is called pancha-loha or five-in-one metal by those who know. 100 leaves like those of lotus should be formed out of them. Then 3 navels, three navel keys, and 3 wires, and a sounding keelaka or key, or switch, or wheel.

First the navel wheels with hinged rods should be fixed so that the 100 petals will be made to revolve with due speed on the four sides of the wheel. Similarly by the side of the wheel in front of it, another 100 petals should be properly fixed for revolving in reverse direction. And electric wires should be fixed on both sides of the centre of the western wheel, for operating the 100 spoked electric panka or fan. Then the vessel should be filled with the cold generating acid. And encircling the cold-generating mani or crystal, it should be placed in another vessel in the centre. And copper wiring enclosed in milk-cloth should be attached to the wire in the acid vessel. Two wires from there with switches should be connected with the cold ranjikaa glass or mirror in right-turning fashion. Then current should be switched into the electric wiring in the crystal and acid. Then by the contact of the electric current the forces within the crystal and the acid will get active and their combined cooling and comforting quality will enter the cold ranjanikaa mirror and concentrate in it. On operating the switch attached to it, the cold effect will spread out all over the interior of the vimaana, and overcoming the scorching seasonal effect, make it comfortable and pleasant for the pilot, and restore his efficiency. Similarly the 100 spoked panka (fan ?) should be switched on, when a breeze will be generated and air-condition the atmosphere of the pilots. Thus by the use of the crystal, acid, and panka, a state of pleasant comfort will be induced, and vigour, exhilaration, and competence will be injected into all the limbs of the body. Therefore this Pushpinee yantra should be installed in the southern section of the vimaana.

Next Pinjula Aadarsha or Pinjulaa Mirror :

By the collision of two winds giving rise to a whirlwind, and the fierce solar ray dashing against it, a lightning bolt erupts and strikes the unwary vimaana. To protect against such an event, the pinjula mirror is to be installed. An eight petalled lotus is to be made of the pinjula glass. Where the petals join, a circular dandaakaara should be made. At the back two hinged bolts should be fixed. They should be wound round by wires from the cold mirror. The back should be covered with a coir-made cloth covering. It should be fixed in the southern side of the vimaana, at an arm's height, facing the sun. The lightning will be absorbed by the projecting rods coiled with wires from the cold aadarsha mirror, and no evil effect will occur, and the pilot can proceed in safety.

And Naalapanchaka or Five tubes :

If the smoke from the kitchen over of the vimaana spreads, it will cause discomfort for people inside. Therefore the five tubes or pipes should be inserted for the smoke to go out and the air become clear. The pipes are to be manufactured as follows. Magnetic iron, pinjula mica, ghontaara metal, dhoomapaasya metal, and tortoise shell, are to be taken in the proportion of 1, 7, 5, 5, 8, purified, filled in crucible, and melted with 100 degree heat, and when ultimately cooled, a fine metal called vaataayanee metal, or window metal will result shining like gold.

With that metal 5 tubular outlets, 12 inches in diameter and 12 inches in length, should be fashioned. At one end of each of the tubes should be fixed a smoke–abosrbing crystal. The tubes should be inserted in the 4 sides of the vimaana, forming outlets. One tube should be fixed at the ceiling. The dhoomapa crystals will attract the smoke and pass it to the outside, and clear the vimaana of its discomfort. Hence the necessity for the naalapanchaka, or five tubes.

Then Guhaa–garbha aadarsha yantra, or hidden mine descovering mechanism :

According to "Yantra Sarvasva" enemies would have placed mines and bombs underground for the destruction of the vimaana, unless they are discovered and de-fused in time there would be danger. Therefore the mine–finder yantra has to be installed in the vimaana.

Says kriyaasaara, out of the 72nd type of glass, make a triangular, a circular, and a quadrangular shaped glass mirrors. These are to be fixed as follows with bolts made of pancha–dhaaraa metal in a frame made of the wood of the anjishtha tree. The circular mirror should be fixed at the bottom facing downwards. The quadrangular mirror should be fixed facing upwards. The triangular mirror should be fixed to the west of these two, with a pancha–mukha keelee or 5 faced hinge. From the main pivot of the quadrangular mirror to the foot of the bolt at the south–east corner of the yantra, wires made of copper, tiles, and panchaasya metal should be drawn and connect them, and then the wire ends and chumbaka crystal should be placed in the mercuric–sulphur acid vessel. Four other wires should be made to circle the triangular mirror, pass through the mirror facing upwards, and fixed to the centre of the down–ward facing mirror. Then solar rays should be let in from the western side. A screen cloth coated with mirror–like gum should be placed opposite to the triangular mirror. Then the solar rays and electric current should be passed into the acid vessel containing the crystal. When the electrified rays from the crystal are passed on to the downward facing mirror, they will explore the ground over which the vimaana is to pass, and discover mines and bombs like mahagola and agni–garbha, which may have been inserted there and reflect their complete picture in the crysta in the acid vessel. The picture will then be projected to the scree opposite in clear detail, and by washing with chemicals present a perfec photograph of the buried mines and bombs, which could then be destroye by due safety measures. Therefore the guhaa–garbha aadarsha yantra o mine–discovering yantra is essential for a vimaana.

Its parts are as follows :

First the 72nd type of mirror, known as suranjitaadarsha. "Darpana Prakarana" says :

Madder-root, live coal, ox-gall, snake-gourd, mercury, karanja or gale-dupia arborea, copper, 3 kinds of sharkara (sugar or sand?), borax, sulphur, chaaru or silk-cotton bark, lac, kuranga, rouhinee, iron-rust, panchaanana, liquid amber, shiva or brionia laciniosa, vishwa, mica, paarvanija, vydoorya gem stone, in the proportion of 11, 27, 5, 7, 7, 3, 7, 5, 20, 3, 7, 3, 1, 32, 30, 38, 8, 7, 3, 9, 30, duly pulverised and filling in a beaked crucible, placed in a vaaraaha furnace, and heated to the 100th degree with the aid of the tortoise-shaped bellows. When the finely boiled liquid is poured in the cooling yantra, suranjika glass of exquisite quality will result, out of which three mirrors have to be fashioned for the guhaa-garbha-aadarsha yantra.

Aanjishtha Tree

Kriyaasaara says, "Many kinds of trees are suitable for use in making yantras. Of them all the tree called aanjishtha is the finest." "The trees having 5 qualities are 87 in number. The best among them all is aanjishtha," says "Udbhijya tatva saaraayanee."

Agatatvalaharee also says, the five qualities such as the capacity to capture reflections, and others, are found inherent in the Aanjishtha (or madder root) tree. Therefore out of all woods the wood of that tree is most suitable for use in this yantra.

Pancha-dhaara-loha

In making yantras, pivots of various metals are being used. But for use in connection with the guhaa-garbha-aadarsha, or hidden mine discovering instrument, the shankus or pivots made of pancha-dhaaraa-loha or five alloy metal are the best.

Kshvinkaa, iron-pyrites, copper, indra, and ruruka, purified, powdered, and filled in mrugendra moosha crucible and boiled to 300 degree heat with beaked bellows, will yield a 5 alloy metal, strong and heavy.

Paara-granthika acid for insertion of the crystal, is described in " Moolikaarka prakaashikaa. " Mercury, bamboo salt, Indian spikenard joint, paarvanika or clerodendrum phlomides, svarna seeds or Indian labernum seeds ? or yellow thistle seeds ?, and ghatotkaja or American aloe, in equal quantities, should be filled in a big bellied earthen pot, heated to yield a golden hued shining liquid, which is very useful for capturing reflections.

Chumbaka crystal is the one most suited for use in capturing reflections of objects. It is manufactured as per "Manipradeepikaa," with the following ingredients. Magnet, sand, borax, ivory, shoundika or long pepper, mercury, paarvana or clerodendrum phlomoides, copper, vermillion, iron-pyrites, grudhnika, souri or marking nut, buffalo hoop, vishwakapaala, cleaned and powdered, and filled in karpala crucible and baked in a furnace with the aid of owl-nosed bellows to 100 degrees, will yield a fine image producing crystal.

Pigment for coating the screen so as to present a clear picture, is called "Roopaakarshana-niryaasa," or image reproducing niryaasa or varnish. Out of 360 such varnishes that is the best.

Says "Niryaasa kalpa" :

Moonstone, crownchaka, bamboo rice, five milks from banyan, fig, keg etc., trees, magnet, udusaara, mercury, mica, pearl, earth from ant-hill, saarasvata oil, and nakha or nail ? these 16 articles to be taken in equal parts, purified, should be ground for a period of 30 days in the juice of the peacock's egg, then mixed with bilva oil and boiled for four yaamaas or twelve hours until it becomes a perfect gum or varnish. Some call it reflector varnish. Some call it virinchi-varnish.

The varnish is to be evenly spread on the special cloth called pata-darpana, so that it may present as on a cinematograph screen, the pictures reflecting the location of anti-aircraft mines discovered by the roopaakarshana yantra.

The production of Pata-darpana is described in "Darpana-prakarana" :

Gum, cotton, pratolikaa, kuranga or pallatory root, maatanga or keg tree bark, cowries, kshoneeraka, gholikachaapa, granite sand, parotikaa, sea-foam, priyangava, ghanjhotikaa, sugar-cane, rukma or argemone mexicana, kesara or mesua ferraa gum, earthen salt, suvarchala, urugha, bydaara oil, muchukunda flour, sinjaanu, anchaalika, turmeric, kaarmuka or acacia catechu, these ingredients in the proportion of 100, 58, 25, 28, 4, 12, 5, 3, 1, 30, 10, 5, 8, 12, 3, 13, 22, 27, 28, 3, 24, 7, 3, 13, should be cleansed, powdered, filled in a vessel, and boiled in the furnace with 100 degree heat, and the unified fluid should be poured on a flat surface so as to form an even surfaced sheet. After drying, the photographic niryaasa varnish is to be used to coat this sheet, for use in the Guhaa-garbha aadarsha-yantra.

Thamo yantra or Darkness creating yantra :

Vimaanaas are liable to be attacked by enemies with poison fumes of Rouhinee or krakachaarimani rays. As a protection against it the thamo yantra has to be installed in the vimaana. Out of 132 types of thamo–yantras, the 62nd variety is said to be the best for safe–guarding against poison fume and ray attacks by the enemy.

Black lead, aanjanika (collyrium ?), vajra-tunda are to be powdered and mixed in equal quantities, filled in fish-shaped crucible and placed in crow shaped furnace, heated to 100 degrees, and poured into the cooling receptacle will yield a fine, light, strong thamo–garbha–loha, or darkness impregnated alloy metal, useful for making Thamo–yantra.

The peetha or stand is to be 3 feet wide and ½ foot high, square or round. In the centre of it is to be fixed the pivot. At its front should be placed the vessel of the acid of guggala or Indian dellium. To the west should be fixed the mirror for enhancing darkness, and in the east should be fixed the solar ray attracting tube. In the centre should be fixed the wire operating wheel, and to its south should be fixed the main operating wheel or switch.

Its working is as follows. On turning the wheel in the south east, the two faced mirror fixed to the tube will revolve and collect the solar rays. By operating the wheel in the north west, the acid in the vessel will begin functioning. By slightly moving the wheel in the south-east, the solar rays will enter the crystal in the acid vessel. By turning the wheel in the west, the darkness intensifying mirror will begin to function. By turning the central wheel the rays attracted by the mirror will reach the crystal and envelop it. Then the main wheel should be revolved with great speed, when the darkness will be produced enveloping the vimaana and making it invisible, and the efforts of the enemies to attack it with poison gas and rays will miss their target and become ineffective. This yantra should be placed in the north-west sector of the Vimaana Panchavaataskandha-Naala.

Iron rust, shaarana, copper, suvarchala salt, in equal parts, to be filled in mayookha crucible, placed in jumboo-mukha furnace, and using kaaka-mukha bellows boiled to 102 degrees and cast in the yantra, will yield a pure, light, soft, strong, nice cool metal known as vaatadhaarana loha.

4 tubes, each 2 yards long and 1 yard high, should be prepared. Like the circular opening in the top of the vimaana two openings on each and one at the bottom should be prepared. Each tube should be inserted in the said openings. Another tube 12 feet long and 3 feet high should be fixed on the western side in the opening at the top. To each tube should be attached bellows' mouth operated by wheels. By turning the wheels of the 5 tubes the 5 poisonous winds will be sucked in and passed into the tubes to make their exit, without causing harm to the plane.

Lohasarvasva says :

There are 13 air layers known as Vrishni and others. By the force of the Panktiraadhasa Kendra, they tend to jostle each other, and generate fierce forces which will be destructive to the unwary vimaana which may get involved in them. Therefore the Pancha-Vaata-Skandha-Naala Yantra is to be inserted in the back portion of the vimaana, to safeguard against evil consequences.

Roudree Darpana Mirror.

From the south-eastern side of the earth-sun axis solar rays touch the turbulent forces in the etherial regions, and burst into flames, and vimaanas which may be out on their course may be destroyed by the flames. To prevent such a happening the roudree-darpana yantra should be installed in the bottom of the vimaana.

Says "Yantrasarvasva", "At the time when spring passes into summer, the forces in the junctional regions of the sky, on contact by fierce solar rays, burst into tumultuous flames, and destroy all things that pass through. Therefore the roudree darpana should be fitted in the vimaana as a safe-guard against that."

According to "Darpana Prakarana," iron rust, magnet, veera iron, borax, panchaanana metal, mica, honey, red castor bark, banyan, surya-varchula or sweet-salt, gold, alika, shaarkara or benzoin tree bark, pancha tikta or 5 sours, snake gourd, and paaduka, are to be powdered, cleaned, and in equal quantities filled in padmaasya crucible, and placed in vishvodara furnace and heated to 200 degrees. The molten liquid poured into the mould will yield excellent flame-proof roudree-darpana glass.

With this roudree-darpana glass a plank of 16 feet in dimension should be prepared. A pivot 25 inches thick should be fixed at the centre of the plank. At the edge of the pivot, two wheels should be fixed revolving with right motion and reverse motion for expanding and contracting. A wheel equipped with rods for spokes should be fixed, the spokes being 15 inches from each other. Sheets made of roudree glass, washed with linseed, drona or lucas aspera, liquid amber, and madder root oils should be fixed to the rods with hinges. Similarly crystals made of roudree-darpana glass, with 5 facets, cleaned with the oils should be fixed at the end of the rods. Between each rod 18 leaves like lotus leaves with revolving keys should be fixed. The instrument is to be shaped like an umbrella. The leaves should be fixed at the pivot top with 8 keys.

When the burning flames are imminent, the pilot should turn the expansion wheel vigorously, and the umbrella will open up and provide a shielding cover for the vimaana. The lotus petals, the crystals, and the enveloping cover will protect the vimaana from the threatened danger.

Next, the Vaata-skandhana-naala.

According to "Gati-nirnaya-adhyaaya"

In the Aavaha and other giant wind spheres there are 122 kinds of different motions of the wind. In the summer season the 79th kind of motion occurs mostly. When the vimaana travels in the 4th region of the sky, it tends to zig-zag owing to the wind currents, and cause hardship to pilots and other occupants. Therefore as a safe-guard against it, the Vaatastambhana-naala-yantra should be installed in the bottom section of the vimaana.

Says "Yantra Sarvasva",

The vaatastambhana naala yantra should be manufactured with the vaatastambhana metal only. According to "Lohatatva prakarana," dantee or croton seeds, suvarchala or sun-flower salt, mayoora or sulphur, loha-panchaka or copper, brass, tin, lead, and iron, bhrisundika, suranjika or sulphate of mercury, varaahaanghri loha, virohina or creya arboria, kuberaka, muraarikaanghri metal, ranjika or phosphorus, suhamsanetraka, dala or folia malabathy, courie sea-shell, mrinaalikaa or lotus stalk, to be powdered, cleaned, and in equal quanties filled in matsya or fish-shaped crucible, and placed in maaghima furnace, and with the aid of vijrimbhana bellows duly melted, will yield a molten liquid which when poured into the mould and cooled will yield an excellent vaatastambhana loha.

With that metal 6 naalas or tubes of 15 inches diameter, with wide openings should be prepared and fixed in the tail and centre and front of the vimaana 10 inches deep, east to west and north to south, and held together with hoop iron binders. At the mouth of each tube a vaatapaa or air imbibing crystal should be fixed by wires. Between the tubes flags or pennants made of cotton-cloth duly processed, should be tied. And wheels made of the special metal should be fixed above each pennant. When the vaataayanee wind blast blows, the pennants will flutter noisily, and the wheels fixed underneath them will also revolve as also the crystals. The fluttering pennants pass the blowing wind to the wheels which pass them on to the crystals, which will pass them into the tubes from which they will be ejected through openings to the outside. That will protect the vimaana from their interference.

Next Vidyuddarpana Yantra.

Sowdaaminee kalaa explains it as follows :

During the rainy season, when rain clouds gather in the sky, lightnings of five kinds begin to play. They are named vaaruni, agnimukha, danda, mahat, raavanika. Of them, vaaruni and agnimukha are very active and fearful and are likely to be attracted by the roudree-darpana and other mirrors and cause fires which destroy the vimaana. In order to prevent that the vidyud-yantras should be installed in the front and the right side of the aeroplane.

According to Yantra-Sarvasva :

In order to protect the plane from lightning, vaaruni and agni, the vidyuddarpana should be installed in the vimaana.

Darpana Prakarana explains its structure :

Kuranga or pallatory root, panchaasya metal, virinchi, shonaja or red lead, sand, alum, kutbha or hellebore, pearl, sundaaliga, mercury, yavakshaara or salt-petre, borax, bidouja salt, pingaaksha or terminalia chebula (?), cowries, and karbura or hedychum specatum, powdered and purified, in the proportion of 10, 7, 4, 3, 12, 2, 3, 7, 11, 27, 14, 3, 22, 18, 5, and 11, filled in padmaasya crucible, placed in vishvodara furnace, and with the aid of the 5 mouthed bellows heated to 500 degrees, the molten liquid will yield in the cooling mould a glass which is impregnated with 300 shaktis or forces, and can overpower the lightning blasts from the vaaruni and agni forces, shining with wonderful rays, and capable of spreading its own lighting force within 2 kshanas or a few seconds to a distance of 5 yojanas or 15 miles.

With that lightning darpana glass should be constructed the Vidyuddarpana yantra. A plank, 20 feet in diameter and 1 foot high, square or circular in shape should be prepared, 4 glass tubes of crescent moon shape should be fixed around the peetha or plank. In the centre should be fixed a cage made of chumbuka glass, fitted with wires and 5 faced switches at each face, and 5 goblets made of vidyuddarpana. In the centre should be fixed a spire made of the same glass with 7 cross spokes and tubes, 8 faced and 10 angled. By turning the key inside, the spire is to revolve with speed. That will attract and contain the lightning emitted by the clouds. The rays will expel it to the outer air region, and incapacitate it. Then a snow-like cool temperature will render the interior of the vimaana safe and pleasant for the pilot and other occupants. Therefore this vidyuddarpana yantra should be installed duly in the vimaana.

Shabda-Kendra Mukha Yantra.

"Kriyaasaara" says—

The spots from which sounds emanate in the sky are called shabda-kendras or sound centres. The different directions from which the sounds are projected are called shabda-kendra mukhas. The yantra which is meant to control the sounds so projected is called shabda-kendra mukha yantra.

Out of 304 classified sounds the sounds of water-laden clouds, wind, and lightning are said to be fiercest. In the 8th region of the sky these three sounds unify in the shishira Ritu or February–March period, and produce ear-splitting thunders. They would deafen pilots and others in the vimaana. As protection against that the shabda-kendra mukha yantra is to be installed.

It is said in Shabda-nibandhana, "By the combination of water, fire, air, and sky, sound is generated both among living and life-less objects. The sounds in the word "Shabdaha," i. e., sha, b, d, and ha, indicate water, fire air, and sky symbolically."

"Naamarthha-kalpa" says,

We shall deal with the nature of sound or "shabdaha". The word consisting of sounds sha, ba, da, and ha, stands for water, fire, air, and sky. By the combination of these four forces in various proportions, 304 different kinds of sounds are generated.

The Braahmana bhaaga of the Veda also says shabdaas are of 304 kinds, such as sphota or embryo, very feeble sound, feeble sound, manda or soft, very soft, fast, very fast, medium, very medium, great sound, thunder sound, and thunder-bolt sound.

It is said in Yantra-Sarvasva,

In the 8th region of the sky, by the concatenation of water–cloud, wind and fire, an extremely fearful thunder clap will occur which will blast the ears of pilots who may enter the region. To safeguard against that the vaatas-kandha mukha yantra is to be installed in the vimaana.

In the 8th region of the sky there are 307 centres of sound. From the 70th centre a fierce sound proceeds by the force of water. From the 312th centre a fierce sound produced by wind will emanate. Similarly from the 82nd centre a fierce sound generated by lightning will emanate. By collision of the three a terrible sound will result which will deafen the pilots of the vimaana. Therefore facing each sound emanation centre the shabdopasam-haara yantra is to be established.

The construction of the yantra is as follows :

Gavyaarika, monkey's skin, duck-weed, shana-kosha or jute product, crounchika or lotus stalk, vaaripishtaka or shag, roonthaaka, flesh, elephant trunk, and tin, are to be purified, and the nine elements, other than the skin, in equal parts, filled in niryaasa yantra and baked for 3 days with buffalo bile, will yield a decoction of fine scarlet colour. Seven times this decoction should be spread on the skin, and left to dry in the sun. The skin will then acquire the capacity to suppress sound.

A box 2 feet long and 1 foot high made of badhira or deaf metal is to be made. Two pipes made of the same metal shaped like crane's beak, should be fixed inside it. Above it should be fixed an umbrella made of shabdapaa darpana, or sound-drinking glass. A crystal washed with tulasee or basil seed oil should be placed inside the monkey skin and sealed with rhinoceros gum. The sealed skin with crystal should be placed in the central pipe inside the box. Monkey skin alone should be placed in the pipe on the left side. Thin wires should connect them all and be fitted with hinges and switches. Above the canopy of the box a monkey skin shaped like lion's mouth should be connected by wire through a pipe to the crystal in the tube inside the box. The top of the box should be covered, securely.

Badhira loha or deaf-proof metal is explained in Lohatantra-Prakarana ; lime fruit, laguda or sweet-scented oleander, virinchi, rishika or water-calteop, maaloora or Bengal quince, panchaanana metal, luntaaka, varasimhika or solenum xunthokurpum, kuravaka or gigantic swallow-wort, sarpaasya or mesua ferrea, vaakula or surinam medlar, jack-fruit, camphor and vatika or salvinia cusullata, in equal parts, purified, and filled in tryutee crucible, and heated in the furnace, will when cast produce a metal, cold, dark, sound-proof, powerful, able to control bleeding, and draw out missile parts from the war wounds of soldiers and healing them, and capable of reducing the effect of thunder claps.

The simhaasya bellows is to collect the fierce sound and transmit it to the crystal inside the metal box so that the monkey skin will absorb it and stifle its intensity. Therefore shabda-kendra mukha yantra should be installed in the vimaana.

Vidyud-dwaadashaka Yantra, or Yantra of 12 lightnings is explained in Kriyaasaara.

In the realm of the comets and shooting stars in the sky, at the 8th region there are 30703221 shooting stars. 8000 of them are prone to lightnings, and 12 of them known as mahaakaala etc., are of importance.

Shakti-tantra says, "The 12 lightnings which form the eyes of the shooting stars are named, rochishee, daahakaa, simhee, patanga, kaalanemikaa, lataa, vrindaa, rataa, chandee, mahormee, paarvanee, mridaa."

Kheta-sarvasva Says:

Mahaakaala, mahaagraasa, mahaajwaalaamukha, visphulinga mukha, deerghavaala, khanja, mahormika, sphulinga-vamana, ganda, deergha-jihva, duronaka, and sarpaasya are 12 comets with 12 lightning eyes.

The lightning effects of the comets are extremely severe in the period of sharat or autumn, October and November, and vasanta or spring, March and April. By the collision of the solar rays and the lightnings a force called ajagara is created. When the vimaana reaches the 20th region of the sky, that force paralyses the plane. To protect against such happenings the vidyuddwaadasha yantra is to be installed.

Yantra Sarvasva also Says:

Vidyuddwaadasa yantra is excellent in protecting against the lightning effect of comets. Its details are as follow. First duly coated jataghana should be prepared. It should have 22 folds so as to cover the vimaana. Poundraka and other crystals should be fixed in each of the folds. Then mahorna acid should be placed inside in the north-east side of the vimaana. 8 rods, each of 6 arms length, made of anti-lightning glass should be fixed in the 8 directions over the cover of the vimaana. At the begining, middle, and end of the vimaana canopy, spring wheels made of dambholee metal, 5 faced and interconnected should be fixed with revolving bolts. Cages made of wire should enclose the poundraka crystals, and the wire terminals should be attached to the spring wheels. The wire ends from 4 of the cages should have a common switch.

On the main wheel being put in speedy motion the 12 crystal cages will revolve, the enveloping cloth cover will spread out, and the lightning absorbing power of the cloth will be activated. The crystals will attract the ajagara lightning, bifurcate the comet lightning from the solar rays, and transmit it to the 8 rods. The rods will absorb and then transfer the lightning power to the folds of the power proof cloth. By operating the central switch in the enclosure, a force called vidyut–kuthaarika, or lightning–axe, will be generated in the acid, and it will attract the comet force from the cloth, and submerge it in the acid. Then by operating the end switch in the enclosure, the ajagara force in the acid will dart towards the pataghana cloth–cover and take refuge, where upon the blowing wind will evaporate it and nullify its effects, and the vimaana will be out of danger.

According to Darpana Prakarana,

Shundaala metal, mridakaantaka or mountain ebony, ghanodara, budilaakara or tamarind, vatsanaabha poison, pankaja or eclipta prostrala, kutilaraga, naga or mesua ferrea, white sand, vara or syndhava salt, garada, mica, garala, or honey product, mukha, shringa, sphatika crystal, avara, muktaaphala or pearl? guggulu or boswellia glabra, kaanta or steel, kuranja or Indian beach, natron, salt–petre, borax, copper, snake scale, udupa, barren tree, sonamukhee or Tinnevelly senna, brown barked acacia, jaambalika or citrus grass? lemongrass? kusha grass, kudmala or flower bud, gold, these 26 ingredients, purified and filled in crucible and placed in padmaakara furnace, and with the aid of simhaasya or lion–faced bellows heated to 300 degrees, and poured into the mould, will yield a fine anti–lightning glass.

Dambhola loha or thunderbolt metal is thus described in
Lohatantra–Prakarana :

Urvaaraka, kaaravika, kuranga, shundaalika, chandramukha, virancha, kraantodara, yaalika, simhavaktra, jyotsnaakara, kshwinka, pancha–mourtwika, metals should be purified and placed in mandooka–or frog-crucible, placed in the five faced furnace, and with the aid panchamukha or 5 mouthed bellows heated to 500 degrees, will yield the dambholi alloy.

Poundrika crystals are described in Maniprakarana which describes the poundrika crystal.

Poundrika, jrimbhaka, shibira, apalochana, chapalaghna, amshupa-mani, veeragha, gajatundika, taaraa mukha, maandalika, panchaasya, amrita sechaka, these 12 crystals are destroyers of ajigara.

Draavaka prakarana explains mahorna acid : pynaaka, panchamukha, ammonium chloride, wild liquorice, iron–pyrites, kudupa, vajrakanda, budila, mercury, steel, charcoal, mica, these in equal parts purified and boiled in acid boiler, will yield mahorna acid.

Praana–Kundalinee Yantra.

According to "Kheta–Sarvasva," where the contact of smoke, lightning and wind courses in the sky occurs is the praanakundalee position. The yantra which can control, restrain, and set in motion the forces of these three in their several courses, is called praana–kundalee yantra.

According to Kriyaasaara, the yantra which is installed in the praana–kundalee kendra of the vimaana in order to control the forces of lightning, wind, and smoke, and adjusts their movements is called praana–kundalinee yantra.

Says Yantra–sarvasva, "In order to control the movements of the forces of smoke, electricity and wind, and make them disperse, move, halt, or make stunt move or reverse move, the praana–kundalinee yantra is installed in the vimaana. A peetha or stand 3 feet in diametre and 3 feet high, square or circular, should be made of vrishala metal, with 8 kendras or central spots. In each central spot, two wheels with revolving hinges ; small peethaas or plates with 3 holes, 4 teeth, 3 pivots, in their middle a central pivot, three red–coloured tubes or pipes with opening and closing wheels, and switches for right motion, and reverse motion, with a shabda–naala in the centre, with wheels (with hinges and rods) which will flap the wings ; from the north–east and south–east kendras and the middle–kendra in the west up to the middle of the course of the yaana kundalinee revolving wheels with pivots. Motions are by means of hand wheels. By the operation of the several wheels the plane will be set in motion. From the central pivot of the 8 kendras strong wires should pass the eastern peetha or footboard through randhras or holes and reach the tops of the 3 tubes at the window. The 3 forces should be made to aid the motion of the vimaana, and the remnant of the force should be passed through the 8 tubes and get lost in the sky, leaving the vimaana unperturbed."

Shaktyudgama Yantra

The eight powers of the planets and stars, at the time of full moon in the month of kaartika,—i.e., November–December, are pulled forcefully by mahaa-vaarunee shakti or great cold force. In the 137th route in the sky there is a jala-pinjooshikaa shakti which will attract and spread them all over, and there will be a fierce outburst of dew and snow. Then 3 currents will be generated : one will be a damp cold air flow ; the second will be a wet dewy flow; and the third will be a cold air flow. When the vimaana approaches that region, the first force will divest it of all power. The second force will benumb the pilots and operators. The third force will envelop the vimaana and make it invisible. Thus overcome, the vimaana will crash. As protection against such a happening the shaktyudgama yantra should be fixed in the navel spot of the vimaana.

"Khetasangraha" says,

"Eight planets are, Mars, Sun, Saturn, Venus, Mercury, Moon, Jupiter, and Ruru. And krittikaa, shatabhisha, makha, mrigashiras, chitra, shravana, pushya, and ashvinee are eight luminous stars. In the course of their transit through space the planets and stars approach each other in the period of sharat or autumn generating eight forces."

"Chaara-nibandhana" also says, "According to the science of astronomy, planets and stars in the course of their perambulations happen to approach one-another. Then conflict arises between the magnetic and electric forces of planet and star, and eight cold forces are generated in consequence."

"Shakti-sarvasva" says, "When the star krittika comes near planet Mars, a force called shaktyudgamaa is generated. Similarly, by the star shatabhisha coming near the planet, Sun, a cold force called jwaalaamukhee is generated. By the nearness of mrigashiraa and Venus a damp cold windy force called mahojjwalaa is generated. By the approach of star makhaa to planet Saturn a force called shytya–damshtraa is generated. By the approach of chitta to Mercury a force called shytya–hymaa is generated. By the approach of shravana to Moon a cold wave force called sphoranee is generated. By the nearness of pushya to Ruru a force called mahormilaa in generated. And by the approach of ashwinee towards Jupiter a force called mandookinee is generated.

68

These eight forces, shytyodgamaa, sheeta jwaalaa–mukhee, shytya–damshtraa, sheetarasa–jwaalaa, shytya hemaa, sphoranee, sheetarasaghanaatmikaa, and shytya–mandookinee, by mutual inter-play according to the seasons, will become six new forces."

Says "Ritukalpa,"—"In spring the differing forces will be 5, in summer 7, in the rainy season 8, in autumn 3, in hemanta or cold season 10, and in winter 2.

The 3 forces during autumn are as follows. The planet–star forces by contact with the sun's rays, assume 3 forms. Sheeta–jwaala, shytya–damshtraa, and shytyodgamaa, coalesce and become sheetarasa–vaata shakti. Shytya–rasa-jwaalaa, shytya hymaa, and sphoranee coalesce and become vaari sheetasheekaraa shakti. Shytya–ghanarasaa and shytya mandookinee become sheeta–vaata–rasa–praavaahika shakti."

Yantra Sarvasva Says,

"To protect the vimaana from the effects of these three forces the shaktyudgama yantra should be installed.

First with the shytyagraahaka loha or cold–absorbing metal, protective hoods should be prepared both for the pilot and for the plane. At the front and tail portion of the aeroplane cover should be fitted switches for contraction and expansion. In the front or elbow hinge of the supporting beam of the covers the two sandhi–keelie should be fitted. Three tubes should be prepared out of the cold-proof glass, and should be fitted in front and on either side of the pilot's cock–pit. Bhraamanee chakra or wheel should be fitted at the front. When the three shaktis or forces attack the vimaana, the expansion wheel should be revolved vigorously, It will first cover the pilots and then cover the entire plane also. By operating the bhraamanee wheel the attacking forces will be slowly absorbed, and the shaktis will be forced through the cold air tubes. By operating the main switch of the naala tantries, or wires, the forces will be made to go through the tubes into the outside air, and vanish therein. The pilot and the vimaana will both be saved from danger.

"Loha-tantra" describes the shytya–graahaka loha, or cold absorbing metal as follows :

Blue lotus, crowdika or rhinoceros horn or vaaraahi root, somakanda, vishwaavasu, crownchika alloy, chandrakaanta or moon-stone, vaardhyashvaka alloy, varuna tree, 5 kudmalas, simhaasya, shankhalavaa, and goose-berry, to be purified and in equal quantities filled in shundaalaka crucible, placed in chanchoomukha kunda, and with panchaanana bellows heated will yield a fine cold-capturing alloy.

"Darpana prakarana" describes cold-proof glass: lead, kapaalee, moonstone, castor, margosa seed, trinaanga or cus–cus grass, kshaara-traya or natron, salt–petre, and borax, suvarchalaa or sun–flower?, fine sand, bhaarika, collyrium or eye–black, kuranga or pallatory root, panchormikaa, chandrarasa, and shivarika, purified and in equal quantities filled in simhika crucible, placed in padmaakara furnace, and with the aid of shoorpodara bellows heated to 300 degrees, and poured into mould and cooled, will yield an excellent sheetaghna darpana or cold–proof glass.

Vakra–prasaarana Yantra :

Enemies attempt to destroy one's vimaana by missiles and dambholi and other mechanisms. The pilot should discover them by means of mukura and other yantras and immediately change course and avoid the trouble. Therefore the Vakraprasaarana yantra, or diversion enabling mechanism should be installed in the vimaana.

Yantra Sarvasva says,

"When there is danger from dambholi and 8 other kinds of destructive mechanisms contrived by enemies, in order to escape that danger the vakra–prasaarana yantra is prescribed :

Sulphate of iron, sacred peepul gum, and copper 16 parts, krishnaaguru or black sandalwood 3 parts, zinc 5 parts, collyrium 1 part, should be purified and mixed and boiled with 100 degree heat. Aaraara copper alloy will be formed, goldish and light and hard. A wheel 3 feet wide and 3 feet high should be made out of it. It should have a pivot, and be installed in the bottom of the eeshaadanda axle moola of the vimaana. Four inches thick and of arm's length, with 16 wheels having band-saw toothed edges attached to two pivots, oil-cleaned, with 3 joints, with oil–cleaned rods attached to the saw-toothed wheels, with keys; in the middle should be fixed 2 keys which will eject smoke, and 2 keys which will shut off smoke. Proper wiring should connect the several parts. This will enable the vimaana to zigzag like a serpent, to reverse, and to divert so as to avoid the danger zone, and get out safely."

Shakti Panjarakeela Yantra :

In order to provide electric force to all parts of the vimaana and make them operate smoothly the shakti–panjara–keela yantra is to be installed.

According to Yantrasarvasva, "As a means of charging all parts of the vimaana with electric current the shakti-panjara–keela is prescribed. It is made as follows :

Steel, crownchika alloy, and iron, in the proportion of 10, 8, and 9, to be powdered and filled in crucible, and placed in aatapa furnace and heated to 100 degrees and charged with 10 degrees of electric current, will yield Shakti–garbha metal with which the yantra is to be made.

A peetha or plank of arm's length and equal height, should be made out of above metal. In the middle and at either end of the peetha three pivots with half moon shaped hinges should be fixed. A flat bar made of copper should be fixed and tightened with bolts. Pipes with holes are to be made out of the metal and equipped with rods fixed in the holes, and connected all round with wires, forming a strong caged globe. The cage should be fixed at the top of the copper band. For the rods and wires in the cage to receive electric current a switch should be duly fixed at the bottom of the cage. And switches should be provided for all the 32 parts of the vimaana for electric connection and disconnection. This enables the plane to career through the sky in any desired direction."

Shirah–Keelaka Yantra.

It is said in Kriyaa–saara, "When the plane is passing through a region of overhanging clouds, there is possibility of lightning striking and destroying the plane. As protection against that the shirah–keelaka yantra should be installed at the crest of the vimaana."

The Yantra is described in Yantra Sarvasva :

"When there is danger of lightning striking the plane, the shirah–keelaka yantra is to protect it. Therefore it is explained below. An umbrella, of the same size as the top of the vimaana, with ribs and metal covering should be made out of vishakantha metal. The umbrella stick, of arm's length, and peetha or stand, circular in shape, should be made out of the same metal. Then out of baka-tundila metal three wheeled keelakaas or hinges should be fixed at the front, back, and middle of the vimaana. The umbrella rod should be fixed in the middle of two keelakas.

The agnikuthaara crystal with metal cage should be fixed at the top like a crown. A three wheel switch revolving key should be fixed by the side of the pilot. Then wires made of kulishadhwamsa metal should be run from the crystal to the three wheeled revolving keelaka. In front of it shabda-naala tube with switch should be fixed. The yantra should be enclosed in a cover made of suranjikaa glass. When there is anticipatory thunder in the clouds, the glass covering cracks, and the tube of the wiring will emit sounds, and the wires will be severely shaken. When the pilot notices these signs, he should quickly set in motion the three-wheel keelee, which will revolve the umbrella with 100 linka speed. Then the crystal switch should also be turned, where-upon the crystal will also revolve with intense speed. By the speed of the revolution of the umbrella, the force of lightning will be stemmed, and the danger will be passed, leaving the vimaana and the pilot safe. That is the use of the shirah-keela yantra."

Shabdaakarshana yantra :

In order to tap or discover the sounds in the 8 directions of the vimaana, wired or wireless, up to 12 krosas or 27 miles, caused by birds or quadrupeds or by men, with 8 mechanisms, the shabdaakarshana yantra is prescribed to be fixed in the shoulder of the vimaana. A peetha or foot-plate four-cornered or round should be made out of bidaala metal, with a pivot in the centre. On either side should be fitted machines which will attract any kind of sound and repeat it. With the soft leather of roruva or grinjinee bird two ball-shaped domes should be fixed. Between them in a suraghaadarsa vessel katana-drava acid should be filled and the vessel should be installed. Above the acid vessel and between the two globes should be fixed sound spotting rod made of sound capturing ghantaara metal, fitted with a bunch of wires. It should be enclosed in a cover made of kwanaka glass. In the corner three thumb size wheeled knots should be fixed. From them to the rod fine strong wires should be connected. Enclosing the wires a karanda or container made by kwanaadarsa glass, with small holes should be placed. A vessel made of the same glass, shaped like a drona or grain measurer, should be placed on top of it. In the east and west and north and south 4 crystals named rudantee-ratikaa should be arranged with wires. Above it shabda-phenaka covering, with small shankus or screws fixed, should be placed. It should be covered by a covering made of kwanaadarsa glass, with 8 small holes. Wires starting from the screws and passing through the holes should reach the top of the covering. In the centre of it in an inch size hole simhaasya-danda-naala or tube should be fixed. In front of it a vaataapaa-karshana chakra or wind wheel with 16 spokes with wires should be fixed. The wheels should be fixed in all 8 directions. In the simhaasya mukha naala or lion–faced tube on 8 sides revolving wheels should be fixed. 8 goblet like vessels made of pure vajeemukha metal should be fixed. Wires from the 8 holes of the covering should be placed in them. Similarly from the wind wheel wires should be connected to 8 screws in the 8 goblets on the simhaasya. Then from the 8 screws in shabda–phena, wires should be connected to the crystal in the acid vessel.

By the flow of wind the wheel turns with speedy right and left motion, and will set in motion the shabda–phena wheel. Then the wheels on the 8 screws also will turn. Then the sound detection rod made of sound–capturing ghantaara metal will be set in motion. Thereupon the two globes made of roruva–grinjinee skin will attract all sounds clearly and store inside them-selves. By moving the central switch there the sounds will pass through the simhaasya tube and enter the dronaasya vessel, and make the sounds clearly audible to the hearer. The pilot will listen to the voices and direct the plane away from the vicinity of danger. Hence the shabdaakarshana yantra is prescribed.

This yantra is in 32 varieties. And it is distinct from the 32 parts constituting the vimaana.

Of the materials required for this yantra,—Byndaala Metal, according to Lohasarvasva, is made as follows :

Zinc, sharkara or quartz powder ?, kaanta or steel, mica, shilaarasa, kamatha or benzoin, dimbhaari, areca–nut, karagrathinee, copper, virinchi, karna or sal tree, patalee or long blue cucumber, gumbhalee, dumbholika alloy, kshaara or chloride, kraantika, simha, panja or momordika, dalinee, mercury, eye–black powder or surma ?, kshonika, veera or red–lead, yellow thistle, madder–root, mridarutee, brass, iron, these articles should be pow‑ dered, and purified in equal quantities, filled in shashamoosha crucible, placed in mandooka furnace, and with five–mouthed bellows heated to 200 degrees and melted to eye–level, when cast will yield a fine, light, blue, bydaala alloy.

Rutana acid is explained in "Moolikaarka prakaasikaa" as follows :

Yellow thistle, karanda or iron pyrites, wild liquorice, paarvani or chlorodendrum phlomaides, chanchooli or red castor, bhantikaa or madder root, kaarambha, vishwesha, chandikaa or sesbenia grandiflora, amara or Indian turnsole ?, shundaalika, barbaraasya, sowrambha or tooth–ache tree ?, praana–kshaara or ammonium chloride, virinchi, borax, arka or calotropis gigantia, surubhee or basil, these in the proportion of 4, 3, 3, 5, 7, 12, 15, 1, 3, 10, 24, 25, 30, 12, 20, 8, purified and filled in vessel and boiled to 108 degrees, will become a fine yellow rutana–draavaka acid.

Ghantaarava metal is explained in Lohatantra :

Bell–metal, aaraara, ruchaka or natron ?, gaaruda or emerald stone ?, shalyakrintana, panchaasya, veerana, rukma or gold–metal, shukatunda, and sulochana, these 10 metals purified and powdered in the proportion of 5, 3, 12, 2, 3, 7, 5, 30, 4, 24, should be filled in shukti crucible, wrapped all round with earth, placed in alaabu shaped furnace, and boiled to 500 degrees up to eye level, should be poured into the mould. A fine, light, scarlet metal which will record all sounds will result.

Kwanadarpana mirror is explained in Darpana Prakarana :

Wild liquorice seeds, red catechu, false catechu, white catechu, garadaka or a poison, 8 kinds of salt, salyaaka, vara or sodium chloride, sharkaraa or granite powder, budilaka salt, jwaalaamukha or wolf's bane ?, tundila or kayidonda, bydaala or arsenic ?. shukatunda, ravimukha or magnifying glass, chancholika or red castor seed, arjuna or tin, luntaaka, varataala or yellow orpiment ?, kuravaka or crimson thorny amaranth, kambodara, kaamuka or punnaaga or Alxandrian laurel or pinnay oil tree, these ingredients, after triple cleaning, are to be filled in padma crucible, placed in padmaakara furnace, and heated to 700 degrees, and poured in mould, will yield an excellent kwanadarpana glass.

Rudantee-mani is explained in "Mani Prakarana" :

Kshaaratraya or natron, salt-petre, borax, aanjanika or eye-black powder, kaanta or sun crystal, sajjecka, vara or sodium chloride, karna or oxide of arsenic, cowrie shells, maakshika or iron pyrites, sharkara or granite grains, sphaatika or alum, kaamsya or bell-metal, mercury, taalaka-satva or yellow orpiment, gyra or marking nut, ruruka, rouchyaka, kudupa, garada or aconite, panchamukha metal, shingara or iron dross, and shundolika or great leaved caledium, these 21 articles, purified, and filled in aanika crucible, placed in shouktika furnace and boiled to 103 degrees, and cast into maniyantra mould, becomes a fine rudantee crystal.

Ruchika mani also is explained in Maniprakarana :

Sea-foam, chamaree cat's nail and mouth bones, steel, paarthiva, granite grains, shilaarasa or liquid amber, mercury, praana-kshaara or ammonium chloride, alum, naaga, cowrie, maakshika or iron pyrites, shundaala or great-leaved caledium, rundaka or eagle wood, kudupa, suvarchala or natron, jambaalika, musk-cat's tooth, or yellow orpiment ?, ranjaka, manjishtha or madder root, paarvani or stag-horn, rukma or gold quartz, yellow thistle, owl's nails, vara or ammonium chloride, oyster shell, these ingredients, purified and filled in equal proportion in nakhamukha crucible, placed in mahodara furnace and heated with the aid of six-faced bellows to eye-level, and poured into mould will yield a strong, dark, heavy rutikaa crystal.

Shabda phena mani is described in " Shabda-Mahodadhi " :

"Take badaba sound from the sky, life-giving trait from water, the fire of air from the atmosphere, the echoing quality from boulder, the splitting quality from solar-rays, moss layer, sea-foam, bamboo, conch, manjishtha or madder root, kusha grass, gribhdnaka, rudra-shalya, gokarna or sal ?, and musali or curculigo orchioides, in the proportion of 7, 22, 45, 13, 32, 19, 38, 14, 22, 38, 42, 13, 25, 9, and 23. These purified and boiled will yield shabdaphena."

From moss-layer to musali the ingredients should be purified, and in the said proportions should be filled in phenaakara yantra, should be baked for 3 days, and for a week the sankalana key-wheel of the yantra should be turned in full speed for half a ghatika daily, when foam will be formed. The foam should be filled in shakti-sammelana yantra. Then through 6 tubes the 6 shaktis or powers from praanana to sphotana should be injected into the foam patiently. On either side of the yantra switches should turn the mixing or churning wheel inside the yantra. Then moderate heat should be applied from praanana to sphotana power infusion. Then keeping it in the sun, electric power should be applied to the foam up to 85 degrees. This electric cooking should be done for 6 days. Then carefully extracting the foam from the yantra, it should be stored in the vaajeemukha metal box. That shabda–phena would be able to attract and record all kinds of sounds.

Vaajeemukha metal is described in "Lohatantra" :

Copper 3 parts, sonamukhee or iron pyrites 2 parts, zinc 8 parts, veera or black metal 2 parts, kaanta or steel 3 parts, bambhaarika 1 part, kamsaarika 3 parts, panchaanana 6 parts, gowreemukha or mica ? 2 parts, shundaalaka 6 parts, these 10 articles to be purified and filled in shundaalaka crucible, placed in shoorpaasya furnace and heated with vajraanana bellows and poured in vajraanana yantra and churned energetically for proper cohesion of the liquid, will yield vaajeemukha loha of light reddish brown colour.

Pataprasaarana yantra is described in Kriyaasaara :

In order to realise dangers to the vimaana en route, and shift directions towards safety, pataprasaarana yantra is prescribed. Says Patakalpa :

"Munja grass, lac, sal, red brinjal, shaambaree or arjuna tree bark, jute, raajaavarta or sphatikaari or hydrorgirum sulphuratum, darbha grass, kravyaada or Indian spikenard, with triple purification, and thrice exposing to soorya–puta or sun–baking, placing them in the cooking vessel, and baking for 3 days. Then the product should be filled in kuttinee yantra, and churned for 3 yaamaas or ⅜ of a day, then placed in cooking vessel and rebaked for 3 days. Then it must be poured into patakriyaa yantra or cloth–forming machine and churned, so as to form an even emulsion, and that will form a fine artificial cloth. It should then be coloured with seven colours. It should be rolled round a long pole, and the pole fixed in thrimukhee–naala yantra, and equipped with a key should be installed in the shoulder of the vimaana.

When the flag–like contraption shows red indicating danger ahead the pilot should loose height and reach safety. When favourable colours are shown, the pilot should note their significance and move the vimaana in the favourable direction.

Dishaampati Yantra : says "Kriyaasaara,"

"In its passage in the sky in the eight directions, the vimaana is likely to meet 15 fierce hurricanes called kowbera by the effects of the planetary forces with solar rays and unfavourable seasonal conditions. They will cause baneful skin effects on the occupants of planes and throat and lung troubles. To protect against that the Disaampti yantra is to be installed in the left shoulder of the vimaana."

The yantra is described in "Yantra Prakarana" :

"In order to act as antidote to the poisonous effects of the kowbera winds, I shall describe the disaampati yantra. A peetha or foot plate, quadran-gular or circular, should be made of paarvanee wood cured three times with requisite acids."

Paarvanee wood is described in "Agatatwa Laharee" :

"Parvanee wood is wood which has very close joints as in sugarcane. It is red coloured, long leaved, decked with red flowers. It has small thorns, is antidote for snake-poison, is acrid in taste, and is used in driving away demons and other evil forces. It blooms in the dark half of the month."

In the centre of the peetha, a tube or pivot made of the 19th type of glass, with 9 holes, 9 switches, and 9 wires, and of arm's length, should be fixed. Eight kendras or centres should be spotted in its 8 directions. 8 naalas, pipes, or tubes, should be made 2 feet long, 6 feet high and 3 feet wide, and round in the middle. A lotus with 8 petals should be prepared and fixed on the top of the pivot. The whole should be covered with hare-skin. Manchoolika linen should cover its mukha or entrance. The wires in the tubes should be taken to the petals above the lotus and fixed in the joints.

Manchoolikaa linen is explained in "Pata-pradeepikaa" :

Vaasantee or gaertnera racemosa creeper, mrida, ranjikaa or betel or madder root, ruchikaa or citron or castor, samvartakee or myrabalan belliriki, phaalgunee or sepistan plum, chanchora or red castor, arunakaanta or sun-flower, kudalinee, mandoorika or iron dross, maarikaa or cubed pepper, lankaari, kapivallaree or elephant pepper, vishadharaa, samvaalikaa, manjaree or ashoka, rukmaangaa or cassia fistula, dhundikaa or acacia sirisa, arka or gigantic swallow wort or madar, garudaa or coculus cordifolious, gunjaa or wild liquorice, and janjharaa.

Taking the twigs, shoots, leaves, buds, tendrils and barks of the above ingredients, and putting them in the baking vessel, they should be well cooked. Then add crowncha acid and boil again for 3 days. That will produce a soft white, pure, strong, fine manjoolikaa linen cloth.

Vaatapaa crystal should be placed in it. Amshupaa mirror should be placed at its front. When the Kowbera whirlwind contacts solar rays, then the amshupaa mirror will show a red and blue tinge. Then the keys of the nine tubes should be turned with great speed. By this a force will be generated in each tube, and passing to the hare-skin, a strong force called sammarshtikaa will be generated. The manjoolika cloth will receive that force and pass it to the lotus petals, and the petals by means of wires will transmit the force to vaatapaa crystal. The crystal, will, with the aid of sammarshtika force, absorb the Kowbera evil wind and throw it out through the lotus petal tube to merge in the outside atmosphere, and no harm will be caused to the occupants of the vimaana. Therefore disaampati yantra should be installed in the vimaana.

19th type mirror is described in Darpana prakarana :

Uraga-twak or snake-scales, pancha-mukha, vyaaghradanta or tiger's tooth, sand, salt, mercury, lead, white gum or shweta-niryaasa, mrittikaa, sphaatika or alum, ruruka, veera or red lead ? mrinala or lotus tendril, ravi-karpata, chanchola or red castor, vaalaja, panchapraanasaara or urinal salt of man, horse, ass, ox, and sheep, or ammonium chloride, shashodupa or benzoin shoot. These 18 ingredients in the proportion of 3, 7, 5, 22, 4, 15, 2, 5, 20, 7, 30, 15, 40, 23, 27, 13, 19, 18, purified thrice, filled in matsya moosha crucible, placed in nalikaa furnace, and with the aid of gomukhee bellows boiled to 99th degree, and poured into the mould, will yield pingala mirror.

Pattikaabhraka Yantra :
Says Kriyaasaara,

"In order to safeguard against the fires generated by the juxta-position of planets during its course, the pattikaabhraka yantra is to be installed in the centre of the vimaana."

It is said in "Yantrasarvasva,"

In the course of its planetary motions, two planets sometimes get too near each other, when by the conflict of their giant forces, fires will burst out. They are known as jwaalaamukhee or flame-tongued, and will destroy the vimaana and those inside it. As protection against it, pattikaabhraka yantra should be installed in the vimaana.

The yantra should be made out of the 3rd type of mica amongst the 3rd group of its classification.

It is said in "Shownakeeya,"

"The names of mica belonging to the 3rd group are shaarada, pankila, soma, maarjaalika, rakta mukha, and vinaashaka. The yantra should be made of soma variety."

Somaabhra is described in Loha-tantra :

"It is sky-coloured, fine, strong, absorbent, cure for eye diseases. Its touch is cooling to the body. It has diamond content, and is cure for urinal trouble. It exhibits scarlet lines with whorls. These are the qualities of somaabhraka."

The mica should be purified twice with brinjal and mataa seed oil and melted, and a pattika two feet wide and of arm's length high should be fashioned. A koorma peetha or tortoise-shaped foot-plate 16 inches wide and arm's length high should be made with vaari vriksha. A shanku or pivot should be made like the pattika. Revolving wheels with keys and shoundeerya manis or crystals should be fixed. From the main centre wires should be attached to it to the end of the pattika. On the other side an ivory vessel should be fixed. and filled with shyvaala acid, and adding mercury ravichumbaka mani or crystal should be placed in it. The wires should be connected to the inside of the vessel containing these things. From the pivot it should be covered with shringinee. The root of the naala or pivot should be fixed to face the sky. The mica shanku with five revolving wheel key attachments should be fixed in the centre of the peetha, and the acid purified pattika should be fixed on top of it in the centre of the vimaana covering.

When the jwaalaamukhee erupts from the planetary contact and reaches the direction of the vimaana, the main switch of the pivot should be operated, a cold wave will arise through the wires from the acid vessel, and passing through the five wheels reach the pattika, and contacting the jwaalaamukhee force will draw it and push it to the crystal in the centre of the enclosure, and the crystal will thrust it through the naala or pipe to the outside atmosphere where the flame force will get extinguished.

Soorya Shaktyapakarshana Yantra

or Solar heat extracting Yantra :

In order to relieve the excessive cold of the winter months, the soorya shaktyapakarshana yantra should be installed on the vimaana.

Says Yantra Sarvasva,

"In order to protect from the cold of the 4 winter months the solar heat storing machine is now explained. The 27th kind of mirror capable of capturing solar heat is to be used in its making."

It is said in Darpana prakarana :

Sphatika or alum, manjula or madder root, sea-foam, sarja salt or natron, sand, mercury, garada or aconite, kishora or wild liquorice, gandhaka or sulphur brimstone, karbura or yellow orpiment, praanakshaara or ammonium chloride, in the proportion of 12, 1, 5, 1, 13, 12, 8, 10, 27, 4, 3, 7, 8, 5, 1, 5, 8, 3, 9, 2, purified, to be filled in antarmukha crucible, placing it in shuka-mukha furnace, and boiled. Then pour it into antarmukha yantra or vessel and turn the churning key. When cooled in the mould a fine, light, strong, golden coloured, solar heat collecting glass will be formed.

From this glass prepare a pattika or plank, 80 inches long, 20 inches wide, and 1 inch thick. Three spots are to be marked on it. Two naalas or pipes, of arm's size, with a 10 inch mouth, crescent shaped peetha should be prepared. Another peetha, 2 feet long, and 6 feet high, should be prepared. The crescent shaped peetha should be fixed in it. On its two sides the 2 naalaas should be fixed. Between them a pivot 88 inches long and 3 inches wide should be fixed. The other pattika should be fixed on its top. At its 3 marked spots, lotus shapes with petals made of the above glass with two faces with goblets on them should be fixed. The two naalaas or pipes should be filled with shyvaala or moss acid and shrini acid. Chhaayaamukha crystal should be placed in them. At the foot of the shanku jyotsnaa acid should be placed. Cold absorbing wires with key switches with ball bearings should be fixed in the jyotsnaa acid. The wires should be taken between the neighbouring naalas, taken round the two lotus positions on the sides of the pattika, and then made to surround the central lotus, and lead on and placed inside the jyotsna acid. Then the other naala should be made to cover the acid vessel, and fixed so as to have its opening through the bottom of the vimaana.

On the approach of winter cold into the vimaana, the main wheel at the foot of the shanku should be turned at high speed. That will energise the head wires of the pattika, making the lotus petals active, and the wind will draw the cold and pass to the central acid vessel through the wires, and the acids in the 2 naalas will draw in the cold and pass to the chaayaamukha mani, which by its own force will pass the cold force to the jyotsnaadravaka, which will eject it through the naala to the atmosphere outside for being dissolved. The vimaana will thus be saved from the cold force through the soorya-shaktyapakarshana yantra.

Apasmaara dhooma prasaarana yantra

or poison-gas fume spreading machine :

Says Kriyaasaara,

"When the enemy plane is trying to destroy your vimaana, Apasmaara dhooma prasaarana yantra should be provided in the vimaana to combat it."

Yantra Sarvasva Says :

"Apasmaara dhooma prasaarana yantra is prescribed for protection of vimaana from enemy planes. It should be manufactured with kshoundeera metal only, and not with anything else."

Kshoundeera loha is described in Lohatantra :

8 parts of kshwinka or zinc, 5 parts of mercury, 7 parts of krowncha alloy, 3 parts of kaanta or steel, 4 parts of hamsa or metallic silver, 1 part of maadhweeka, and 5 parts of ruru, these ingredients to be purified and filled in crucible, placed in chhatreemukha furnace, and with the acid of surasa bellows heated to 100 degrees heat, and cast· in mould will yield excellent kshoundeera alloy.

Filling this loha in pattikaayantra, applying 300 degree heat and churning, a fine strong pattikaa will be formed. With that, a shape like bellows, 5 arm's length high, and 3 arm's wide should be formed. It should be provided with a mukha–naala or nozzle 6 feet in size. Its mouth should be like that of peshanee yantra. The opening should be covered and keyed. Three satchels should be attached at its bottom. In the middle an aavarana or covering with hare–skin, circular and provided with switch. Smoke or gas filling switch should be provided at its base. Above it a choorna paatra or powder vessel should be fixed. The switch key should be beneath the middle of the vessel. Thus four bellows should be prepared.

When the enemy plane's attack is expected, the aavaaraka bhastrika or enveloping bellows should shield the vimaana, and the 4 bellows should be fixed on the dikpeethaas or side seats above the aavarana or covering, and electricity should be applied to the choorna–paatra or powder keg. Immediately the powder becomes smoke. The bellows' mouth should be opened and the key turned. The emerging smoke fumes will enter the 4 small bellows, and from them reach the central kunda and spread all around and reach the bellows' mouth. Then on turning that key, the fumes will be emitted from all the bhastrikaas or bellows, and encompass the enemy plane and disable its occupants. That plane will be destroyed and the danger to one's vimaana overcome.

Stambhana Yantra
or Halting machine :
Kriyaasaara says,

When power is generated by conflicting forces in the water–charged regions, shrieking hurricanes and whirl–winds will arise and set out in a mad career of destruction. To safeguard against their onslaughts, the Stambhana yantra should be installed in the bottom of the vimaana.

Yantra sarvasva says,

In order to protect the plane from the attacks of giant wind blasts, vimaana stambhana yantra is described as follows :

A peetha, one fourth the size of the vimaana floor, quadrangular, should be made out of vakratunda metal, three feet in thickness. In its 8 quarters spots should be marked for fixtures. An enclosure with openings, revolving toothed wheels made of the same metal, wheel rods with revolving keys, a metal band which is to encircle it thrice, toothed wheels, pivots, and switches and hinges, and three–stranded wire ropes, should also be of the same metal. In the 8 selected spots naalaas or pivots with wheels and wiring should be fixed. Through the naala or pipe at the contraction switch of the vimaana, wires should be passed through the other naalas to the central pivot, and tied at the foot of the revolving wheel. When the dreaded wind current is observed the switch or wheel for the contraction or folding of the expanded vimaana parts should be turned, as also the 8 side wheel turning switches. That will reduce the speed of the vimaana. Then the switches of the 8 pivots on the peetha or foot-plate should be turned. The entire speed of the vimaana will be extinguished thereby. The wheel at the central pivot of the peetha should then be turned, so that the vimaana will be halted completely. Then the switch of the plane-wings should be turned. The flapping of the wings will produce winds which will encircle the vimaana and form a globe protecting it. Then by turning the switch of the brake-rod, the vimaana becomes motionless. Therefore the Yaana-sthambhana yantra should be fixed at the bottom centre of the vimaana.

Vyshvaanara-naala yantra :

Kriyaasaara says,

For the purpose of providing fire for passengers to perform agnihotra or daily fire rituals, and for the purpose of cooking food, Vyshwaanara naala yantra is to be fitted up at the navel centre of the vimaana.

Yantra-sarvasva says,

To provide fire for travellers in vimaanas, vyshwaanara naala yantra is now described. A 2 feet long and 12 inches wide peetha or foot-plate should be made out of naaga metal, quadrangular or circular in shape. Three kendras or spots should be marked thereon. Three vessels should be made of copper and karpara or (black jack ?) zinc blended metal. One vessel should be filled with sulphur-brimstone acid. Another should be filled with rookshaka bdellium acid, or croton seed acid? And manjishta or madder root acid should be filled in another vessel. The three vessels should be placed on the 3 kendra spots on the peetha.

In the sulphur acid vessel the prajwaalaka mani or flame producing crystal should be placed. In the rookshaka acid vessel the dhoomaasya mani or smoke crystal should be placed. In the manjishtha acid vessel the mahoshnika mani, or heat producing crystal should be placed.

In the places in the vimaana where kitchens are located, and where sacred agnihotra fires are needed by passengers, keelaka sthambhas or pivots should be fixed. The acid vessels should be connected with power wires from the central pivot. The wires should be attached to the manis or crystals in the acid vessels. At the top of the central pole jwaalaamukhee mani should be fixed in the centre of chumbakee keela with glass covering. On either side of it sinjeeraka mani and dridhikaa mani should be fixed. From each mani a wire should be stretched from the top of the central pole and fixed at the granthikeela at the foot of the pole. From there up to the cooking spots and agnihotra spots, a circle should be formed like a kulya, and metal tubes should be fixed therein. Wires should be drawn through the tubes to the fire places and fixed to the kharpara metallic pattikas therein.

First the bhadramushti keelaka should be revolved. The acid in the vessel will become heated. The heat generated in the rookshna acid will pass into the manjishtha mani, and generate smoke in the mahoshnika mani. By the force of that acid intense heat will be generated. And by the heat generated in the sulphuric acid vessel flames will erupt in the prajwaalika mani. The smoke, heat and flames will pass through the wires to the sinjeeraka, dridhikaa and jwaalaa–mukhee manis. Then the chumbaka wheel should be turned vigorously, whereupon the smoke, heat, and flames will reach the key at the top of the central pole. And on that keelee being turned, they will reach the central switchboard keelee at the foot of the pole. When that switch is put on, the heat and flames will reach the metal bands of the cooking ovens and religious fire places, and generate fires. Therefore vyshwaanara naala yantra should be fixed at the navel centre of vimaana.

We have so far dealt with anga yantras or constituent machines of the vimaana. We proceed next to deal with Vyoma–yaanas or Aeroplanes.

SIXTH CHAPTER

Atha Jaatyadhikaranam: Varieties of Vimaanas.

Maharshi Bharadwaaja:

☞ Jaati tryvidhyam Yugabhedaad Vimaanaanaam.   Sootra 1.

"Three types according to changing Yugas."

Bodhaananda Vritti:

According to the differences in yugas, there are three different types of planes:

Having dealt with the constituent mechanical parts of the Vimaana, we shall now deal with the Vimaanas according to their different classes.

The sootra indicates that there are different types of planes, and that they are of 3 types.

In the Krita Yuga, Dharma or Righteousness was four-footed, that is, it was four-square, fully established, all paramount, and it was adhered to implicitly by men. The men were inherently noble-born and were possessed of remarkable powers. Without needing to go through yogic discipline to attain special powers, or practise mantras which secured extraordinary results, the men of that yuga, merely by their devotion to dharma, became Siddha-purushaas or gifted with superhuman powers. They were virtuous men and men of learning and wisdom. Going in the sky with the speed of wind by their own volition was natural to them. The eight super-sensory, and now superhuman, attainments, known as animaa, mahimaa, garimaa, laghimaa, praaptih, praakaamya, eeshatwa, and vashitwa, were all possessed by them. That is, animaa is assumption of infinitesimal shape; mahimaa is growing into gigantic shape; garimaa is becoming astonishingly heavy; laghimaa is becoming weightless; praaptih is securing any desired thing; praakaamyam is becoming rid of desires; eeshatwa is attaining paramountcy; and vashitwa is becoming extremely pliant.

*   *   *   *

I.   Krita yuga–1728000 years.   II.   Threthaa yuga–1296000 years.
III. Dwaapara yuga–864000 years.   Kaliyuga–432000 years.

Therefore in Krita Yuga, or first epoch, the ancients say, there were none of the three classes of Vimaanas.

Krita Yuga passed ; and Tretaa Yuga commenced. Dharma then became limp of one foot. It served with 3 feet only, and grew gradually less efficient. So men's minds became dense, and the conception of Vedic truths, and anima and other super-sensory powers, became scarcer. Therefore, by the corrosion of Dharma or righteousness, men lost the power of flying in the sky with the speed of wind.

Perceiving this, God Mahadeva, desiring to confer the power of understanding the Vedas properly on the Dwijas, or brahmins, kshatriyas, and vysyas, graciously descended on earth in the form of Dakshinaamurthy, and through the instrumentality of Sanaka and other anointed sages, classified the Veda mantras, and then bestowing his benedictory glance on the worshipping Munis or ascetics, he blessed them with the gift of Vedic perception. And then to ensure that they were properly receptive, he embraced them and entered their hearts and illuminated their memories. The munis, overwhelmed by the Divine grace, aglow with horripulation, with voice choked with emotion, praised the Supreme with shata–rudreeya and other hymns, and manifested profound devotion.

Pleased with their receptiveness, divine Dakshinaamurthy, favouring them with a benign glance, and with smile on his face, said to them, "Till now you have been known as "Munis" or ascetics. Henceforth, having by my grace attained insight into the Vedas, you shall be known as "Rishis" or seers. You will cultivate the Vedic mantras, and practising celebacy, you will adore the divine Goddess of the Vedas, and winning her favour, and approaching the Great God Easwara by Yogic Samadhi, ascertain His mind, and by His and my grace, rising to the pinnacle of intellectual vision, become adepts in the meaning and purport of the Vedas ; and confirming by them our own experiences and meditative introspection, you will create the Dharmashaastras or moral codes, Puranas and Itihaasas, and physical and material sciences, in conformity to the truths of the Vedas, for the benefit of mankind. And for travelling in the sky, propagate the art of manufacturing Vimaanas, and for attaining wind–speed, evolve Ghutica and Paadukaa methods through Kalpashaastras or scientific treatises."

Then those munis or seers, enshrining in their hearts God Mahadeva in the form of Dakshinaamurthy, produced the Dharmashaastras or ethical codes, epics, chronicles, manuals on rituals, treatises on the arts and sciences, ritualistic and sacrificial codes, in conformity to the Vedas, and propagated them among men. Amongst them it is said that there are six treatises bearing on the manufacture of Vimaanas produced by the ancient seers. In them are described three classes of vimaanas, known as maantrikaas, taantrikaas, and kritakaas, capable of flying everywhere.

It is said in Vimaana Chandrika,

"I shall indicate the different kinds of vimaanas. In Tretaa yuga as men were adepts in mantras or potent hymns, the vimaanas used to be produced by means of maantric knowledge. In Dwaapara yuga as men had developed considerable tantric knowledge, vimaanas were manufactured by means of tantric knowledge. As, both mantra and tantra are deficient in Kaliyuga, the vimaanas are known as kritaka or artificial. Thus, owing to changes in dharma during the yugas, the ancient seers have classified the vimaanas of the 3 yugas as of 3 different types."

"Vyomayaana Tantra" also says,

"By the influence of mantras in Tretaa, vimaanas are of maantrika type. Owing to the prevalence of tantras in Dwaapara, the vimaanas are of taantrika type. Owing to decadence of both mantra and tantra in Kaliyuga, the vimaanas are of artificial type." Thus 3 classes of vimaanas are mentioned in shaastras by ancient seers.

In "Yantra Kalpa" also,

"Vimaanas are classified into mantra and other varieties by experts according to differences in yugas. They are defined as maantrika, taantrika, and kritaka."

The same is expressed in "Kheta yaana pradeepika," and also "Vyoma Yaana Arkaprakaashikaa."

Thus according to shaastras vimaanas are divided into 3 classes, on the basis of differences in the modes of their manufacture.

Maharshi Bharadwaaja:

☞ "Pancha-vimshan Maantrikaaha Pushpakaadi Prabhedena"   Sootra 2.

"Maantrika Vimaanas are of Pushpaka and other 25 Varieties."

Bodhaananda Vritti:

In the previous sootra vimaanas were specified as of 3 types owing to differences in the 3 yugas. In this sootra maantrika vimaanas or vimaanas flying by maantrik power are said to be 25.

Shounaka Sootra says,

Maantrika vimaanas in Tretaayuga are 25. Their names are pushpaka, ajamukha, bhraajasvat, jyotirmukha, kowshika, bheeshma, shesha, vajraanga, dyvata, ujvala, kolaahala, archisha, bhooshnu, somaanka, panchavarna, shanmukha, panchabaana, mayoora, shankara, tripura, vasuhaara, panchaanana, ambareesha, trinetra and bherunda.

In Maanibhadrakaarikaa,

The vimaanas of Tretaayuga are 32 of the maantrika type. Their names as given by Maharshi Gowtama are Pushpaka, ajamukha, bhraaja, swayamjyoti, kowshika, bheeshmaka, shesha, vajraanga, dyvata, ujvala, kolaahala, archisha, bhooshnu, somaanka, varnapanchaka, shanmukha, panchabaana, mayoora, shankara priya, tripura, vasuhaara, panchaanana, ambareesha, trinetra, and bherunda, etc.

Maharshi Bharadwaaja:

☞ "Bhyravaadi Bhedaat Tantrikaa-shshat-panchaashat." Sootra 3.

"Taantrika Vimaanas are of Bhyrava and other 56 varieties."

Bodhaananda Vritti:

In previous sootra the names of maantrika vimaanas were mentioned. In this sootra the names of taantrika vimaanas of Dwaapara yuga are mentioned.

In shape, movement and speed there is no difference between maantrika and taantrika vimaanas. There is however one difference in taantrika vimaanas, that is, the way in which the shakti or power at the junction of sky and earth is incorporated.

Lalla also says,

There is only one difference between taantrika vimaanas and maantrika vimaanas : the adaptation of the power of sky and earth. In shape, and movement. variations, they are identical. The taantrika vimaanas are of 56 varieties.

In Shounaka Sootra,

In Dwaapara taantrika vimaanas are 56. Their names are, bhyrava, nandaka, vatuka, virinchi, vynateya, bherunda, makaradwaja, shringaataka, ambareesha, sheshaasya, saimtuka, maatrika, bhraaja, paingala, tittibha, pramatha, bhoorshni, champaka, drownika, rukmapunkha, bhraamani, kakubha, kaalabhyrava, jambuka, garudaasya, gajaasya, vasudeva, shoorasena, veerabaahu, bhusunda, gandaka, shukatunda, kumuda, krownchika, ajagara, panchadala, chumbuka, dundubhi, ambaraasya, maayooraka, bheerunalika, kaamapaala, gandarksha, paariyaatra, shakunta, ravimandana, vyaaghra-mukha, vishnuratha, sowarnika, mruda, dambholi, brihathkunja, mahaanata, etc.

In Maanibhadrakaarikaa :—

In Dwaapara yuga taantrika vimaanas are said to be 56. Their names according to sage Gowtama, are bhyrava, nandaka, vatuka, virinchika, tumbara, vynateya, bherunda, makaradhwaja, shringaataka, ambareesha, sheshaasya, symhika, maatruka, bhraajaka, pyngala, tittibha, pramatha, bhoorshnika, champaka, drownika, rukmapunkha, bhraamanika, kakubha, kaalabhyirava, jambuka, gireesha, garudaasya, gajaasya, vasudeva, shoorasena, veerabaahu, bhusundaka, gandaka, shukatunda, kumuda, krownchika, ajagara, panchadala, chumbaka, dundubhi, ambaraasya, mayoora, bheeru, nalikaa, kaamapaala, gandarksha, paariyaatra, shakuntaka, ravimandana, vyaaghramukha, vishnu ratha, souvarnika, mruda, dambholee, bruhatkunja, mahaanata.

These 56 are taantrika vimaanas of Dwaaparayuga.

Maharshi Bharadwaaja:

☞ "Shakunaadyaah Panchavimshat Kritakaah." Sootra 4.

"Shakuna and other 25 types of Vimaanas are Kritakaah."

Bodhaananda Vritti:

In shape and movements there is no difference in the vimaanas, except in the matter of the use of mantraas and tantraas. The kritaka or artificial vimaanas are of 25 varieties.

According to Shownaka sootra:

"Tishyay kritaka bhedaah panchavigamshatih! teshaam naamaanyanu-kramishyaamah: shakuna sundararukma mandala vakratunda bhadraka ruchaka vyraaja bhaaskara gajaavarta powshkala virinchi nandaka kumuda mandara hamsa shukaasya somaka krownchaka padmaka symhika pancha-baana owryaayana pushkara kodandaa iti."

Says "Maanibhadra Kaarikaa":

In Kaliyuga, the kritaka or artificial vimaanas are said to be 25. Their names are given below as indicated by sage Gowtama: shakuna, sundara, rukmaka, mandala, vakratunda, bhadraka, ruchaka, viraajaka, bhaaskara, gajaavarta, powshkala, viranchika, nandaka, kumuda, mandara, hamsa, shukaasya, sowmyaka, krownchaka, padmaka, symhika, panchabaana, owryaayana, pushkara, and kodanda.

Maharshi Bharadwaaja:

☞ "Raaja-lohaadeteshaam Aakaara Rachanaa." Sootra .5.

"These should be built out of Raajaloha."

Bodhaananda Vritti:

These 25 kinds of vimaanas are to be made of Raajaloha metal only.

Says Kriyaasaara,

In manufacturing artificial aeroplanes the best of metals are those known as Ooshmapaa or heat-imbibing or heat resisting metals. Out of them the variety known as Raajaloha or king of metals is most suited to Shakuna and other vimaanas.

Three kinds of metals, soma, soundaala, and maardweeka, in the proportion of 3, 8, and 2, adding borax, to be filled in crucible or smelter, and placed in furnace, and heated to 272 degrees, and melted thoroughly, and churned, will result in the alloy Raajaloha.

Vishwambhara also says,

"In the science of metals, for the manufacture of aeroplanes, 16 types of Ooshmapaa or heat-sucking lohas or metals are the very best. The fourth in that series, is called Raajaloha. Out of that alone should shakuna vimaana be constructed."

The parts of shakuna vimaana are :

.Peetha or floor board ; hollow mast ; three wheeled keelakas with holes ; 4 heaters, air-suction pipes, water-jacket, oil tank, air heater, chhullee or heater, steam boiler, vidyud-yantra or electric generator, air propelling yantra, vaatapaa yantra or air-suction pipe, dikpradarsha dhwaja or direction indicating banner, shakuna yantra, two wings, tail portion for helping vimaana to rise, owshmyaka yantra or engine, kiranaakarshana mani or sun-ray attracting bead. These 28 are parts of Shakuna vimaana.

The construction of the vimaana :

The floor-board or base should be made of levelled Rajaloha sheet, shaped quadrangular, circular, or cradle shaped. The weight of the peetha should be one-hundredth of that of the plane, and its width should be half the height of the vimaana. In the centre of the peetha the hollow mast should be fixed with screw joints.

Lalla defines the mast in "Yantra kalpataru". The stambha or mast should be made of haatakaasya metal and not otherwise.

Haatakaasya metal is described in "Lohatantra" : 8 parts of suvarchala or natron, 16 parts of laghu-kshwinka or light zinc, 18 parts of laghu bambhaari, and 100 parts of copper, filled in smelter, placed in koorma vyaasatika furnace, and with .the aid of mahormi bellows boiled to 307 degrees, will yield haatakaasya metal.

The Peetha :

The height of the peetha should be 80 feet. It should be 56 feet in length and breadth, 70 feet high on the north and south sides. The tip should be three-cornered. This is for shakuna vimaana.

Naalastambha or Hollow Mast :

At the bottom the mast should be of 35 feet diameter outside, and 30 feet inside. At the middle the mast should be of 25 feet diameter outsioe and 20 feet inside. Higher up it should be of 20 feet diameter outside and 15 feet diameter inside; The height of the mast should be 80 feet. It should be made of Raajaloha. In order to fix the mast in the peetha screw joint should be made. And in order to adjust the air-speed as required, 6 wheels should be inserted inside the mast.

The Wheels :

Inside the mast at the height of 4 feet above the peetha, three wheels should be provided, of 15½ feet diameter, with holes. The wheels above and below should be fixed with bolts, and unmoving. In order to revolve the middle wheel keys should be fixed outside on the mast, As there are holes in the wheels, as two wheels do not move, and as the middle wheel revolves in a group with the other two wheels, movement of air is allowed or stopped by the turning of the key outside.

Similarly at the height of 44 feet above the peetha three wheels corresponding to those below should be fixed and operated similarly.

Window dome :

The window dome should be of 15½ feet outside circumference. Its inside should be five feet wide and it should be 2 feet high. It should be fixed on the top of the mast.

Sun-crystal :

A sun crystal 7 feet round, and 2 feet wide and 2 feet in height should be fixed so as to crown the window dome.

10 feet above the bottom peetha, on a floor-board 3 inches thick, three floors or tiers should be built, each 14 feet high, with 3 inch

floor-boards, the upper two floors being supported by pillars fixed at 10 feet intervals with screw joints and strong bolts. In the four corners 4 heating yantras should be fixed, 10 feet in circumference and 8 feet high. On the ground floor along the supporting pillars accommodation for passengers should be provided in the form of individual boxes.

On the second floor booths should be constructed to accommodate the anga-yantras, or the various mechanisms recommended for the safety of the vimaana. It should be 60 feet wide and 14 feet high with 3 inch thick ceiling board.

The third floor should be 40 feet wide and 14 feet high.

The partitioning boxes for passengers as well as the booths of the various machines should be divided off by railings starting from the hollow mast to the side walls in all the four directions.

Beneath the ground-floor board a 7 feet high cellar should be constructed. In it the several necessary yantras should be located. In the centre is the foot of the hollow mast. On the four directions from it 4 air pumping machines should be fixed. In order to stimulate them 4 steam engines also should be installed. On the two sides of the vimaana two air expelling machines, and an air heater machine, and 2 machines to keep the heater supplied with air from outside, should be erected.

In order to enable the wings on either side to spread and flap, proper hinges and keys should be provided for, safely fixing them to the sides of the vimaana, and for enabling them to fold and open easily.

The revolving tractor blades in the front should be duly fixed to the heating engine with rods so that they could dispel the wind in front and facilitate the passage of the vimaana.

The wings are two, one on each side, very strongly fixed to the vimaana with bolts and hinges. Each wing should be fixed in a 1½ foot scabbard up to 20 feet length, where it would be 10 feet wide, widening further up to 40 feet at the end of its 60 feet length, besides its first 20 feet of scabbard length.

The tail should be 20 feet long, and 3½ feet wide at the start, and 20 feet wide at the end.

The air-blower and heater :

The length of the air-blower should be 15 feet, and width 3 feet. The naalaas or pipes should be 3 feet wide, and their outer circumference should be 4 feet. The rods and hinges and other equipment should be suitably prepared.

The vaatapaa yantra or air blower should be 12 feet long and 9½ feet wide. Inside it should be covered with circling wires. A pipe should be fixed inside, for air flow. By the hot oil fumes from the heated tank, the air becomes heated and should be passed into the owshmya yantra or heater, while the cold air from outside should also be let in. Tubes and fixings should be provided in the yantra. In order to emit the fumes of the oil flames to the outside, a 6 inches pipe should be fixed from the yantra to the foot of the mast. Air blowers should be installed with 10 feet wheels to pump in fresh cold air from outside.

To the east of the air machine should be placed a light burner in order to aid combustion of the oil. An electric generator provided with switches should light the burner. When the light is off the oil should be kept duly sealed. A rope should be tied to the tail joint, for the pilot to manipulate the fluttering of the tail to help the ascent or descent of the vimaana. Similarly ropes should be tied to the hinges of the two wings, and passed to the pilot like reins, so that he might spread them out or close them as needed.

Ten feet beneath the passenger floor of the vimaana, to a height of 2½ feet from the bottom plate there should be a cellar-like enclosure. The bottom of the vaatanaala mast should be fixed in its centre with firm screw joints. In this cellar should be located two oil tanks 15 feet by 9½ feet by 4 feet, with water jackets.

Four bellows of 15 feet by 2½ feet by 6½ feet, should be provided for storing the air pumped in by the air-blowers, and letting it out as required.

And underneath, on all the four sides wheels of 7 feet circumference should be fixed for the movement of the vimaana on the ground.

This vimaana is named **SHAKUNA VIMAANA.**

SUNDARA VIMAANA

Maharshi Bharadwaaja:

☞   "Sundarothha."   Sootra 6.

"Next Sundara."

Bodhaananda Vritti :

Next Sundara vimaana will be described. It has got 8 constituent parts.

First peetha or ground plate, smoke chimney, 5 gas-engines, bhujya metal pipe, wind blower, electricity generator, and four-faced heater, and vimaana nirnaya, or outer cover.

The Peetha or ground plate :

It should be made of Raajaloha metal only. It should be square or round, and of 100 feet in circumference, or any other desired size. It should be 8 feet thick. Seven times the peetha has to be heated with manchuka or madder root oil. Then spots should be marked in it at 10 feet distance from each other, totalling 24. The size of each kendra or centre is 15 feet. In the centre a dhooma-prasaarana or fume distributing naala or pipe 12 feet high should be erected.

Naalastambha, hollow mast :

The naalastambha should be 56 feet high, and 4 feet in diametre. For storing gas, at its base, a 8 feet long, circular, and 4 feet high vessel should be provided. A six feet size water vessel should be arranged. A 4 feet size oil tank should be fixed at its centre. At its foot an electric storing crystal of 1 foot size should be fixed with necessary hinges and keys.

The vessel should be filled with 12 parts of dhoomanjana oil, and 20 parts of shukatundika or bignonia Indica ? (egg-plant ?) oil, and 9 parts of kulakee or red-arsenic oil. To conduct electricity, two wires should be passed through the pipe and fixed to the crystal. In the middle of the naalastambha or mast, for the smoke fumes to be restrained or speeded out, triple wheels with holes should be fixed. In order to work the wheels from outside, two right turning and left turning wheels should be attached outside the pole, and connected to the wheels inside. Three wires should be drawn inside the naala and fixed at the foot, the middle, and at the top.

Dhoomodgama Yantra :

Because it ejects smoke fumes with speed it is called Dhoomodgama yantra.

Hima samvardhaka, soma, and sundaala, in the proportion of 32, 25, and 38, should be filled in pipe crucible, placed in chakra–mukha furnace, and with the help of ajaamukha bellows heated to 712 degrees and properly churned. It will yield excellent dhooma–garbha alloy. With that alloy the dhoomodgama yantra should be constructed.

Underneath the centre of the 15 feet long peetha, for the control of the gas fumes a 10 feet high pipe with right revolving wheel should be fixed. On its 2 sides, to south and north, 2 water steam pipes should be erected. At the foot of the 2 pipes 4 feet long 3 feet high pots should be formed for containing the fumes. Two pipes shaped like goblets, 1 foot by 8 feet by 3 feet, should be fixed at the top of the fume container. A water vessel at its foot, and an oil–vessel at its centre, and in front of it the switches of the electric ray crystals, as in the dhooma prasaarana naala stambha.

On either side of the heat tube, two water jackets should be placed. A pipe with wires should be taken from the electric generator and connected to the hinges of the crystals. Electric current of 80 linkas should be passed to the crystals, whose motion will cause friction and generate heat of 100 degrees (kakshyas). Thereby the oil in the vessel will get heated and boil and emit fumes.

The electric power should then be passed through the smoke pipe between the two water jackets. By this the water will be converted into hot steam. The oil fumes should be filled in the oil fume pipe and the steam in the steam pipe. Then by operating the switches, both the fumes will fly up at 500 degree temperature. The switches should restrain the fumes or pump them out as needed. 40 such yantras should be prepared and should be fixed on the peetha in groups on the four sides. Then connected with the bases of the dhooma–naalas, sundaalas or elephant trunks, one foot wide and 12 feet high should be erected on the four sides, to enable the vimaana to fly with speed.

Sundaala is descibed by Lallachaarya :

The sundaala should be installed for using the oil fumes and steam fumes for the motion of the vimaana. There are. varieties of ksheera vrikshaas or milk–trees according to shaastraas. Vata or banyans, manjoosha or madder root, maatanga or citron ?, panchashaakhee (five branched), shikhaavalee (crested), taamra sheershnee (copper–crested), brihatkumbhee (big bellied), mahishee, ksheeravallaree, shona parnee (crimson–leaved), vajramukhee, and ksheerinee (milky). From these the ooze or milk should be collected, and in the proportion of 3, 5, 7, 10, 11, 8, 7, 4, 7, 30, 12, filled in a vessel. Then granthi metal, naaga or lead, vajra, bambhaarika, vynateya, kanduru, kudapa, and kundalotpala, these in equal parts should be filled in the vessel in equal proportion to the milk contents, and boiled with 92 degree heat. Then the molten liquid should be filled in the milk–cloth machine, and churned. When cooled and put through the levelling machine, it will yield a strong, soft, cool, heat proof, and uncuttable ash–coloured cloth sheet.

This cloth should be boiled in rouhinee taila or oil of black hellebore for 3 yaamaas or 9 hours, and then washed with water. Then it should be boiled in atasee or linseed oil as before. Then it should be kept in ajaa–mootra or goat's urine for one day and kept in the sun. Then it should be dried and painted with kanakaanjana paint and dried. Then the cloth will glow with a golden hue. With this cloth should be made the shundaala or elephant trunk, 12 feet high, 1 foot round, and with pipe–like opening inside.

Two mechanisms for rolling it and unrolling it should be properly attached to it. By the rolling switch the shundaala will coil round like a snake and remain on the floor. By the unrolling switch it will uncoil and stand erect like a raised arm. From the fume generating yantra connecting links to the shundaala should be provided for the fumes to pass through it to the outside air. And to attract outside air into the sundaala a pump–like arrangement should be provided as in an inflator.

Three switches should be provided as in the water tapping yantra. By revolution of its wheel the fumes will go out through the shundaala and 82 linka of fresh air will come in. The direction in which the fumes will emerge from the shundaala will be the direction of the course of the vimaana. The 3 wheels in the shundaala will cause the vimaana to wheel around or make ascent, or to drop height.

At the foot of each dhoomodgama yantra 2 shundaalas should be duly fixed. And on the 4 sides of the dhoomaprasaarana–naala–stambha 4 shundaalas should be erected.

In order to protect against the intense heat from fire and sun inside and outside the vimaana, it should be provided a covering made of the 6th type of Ooshmapaa loha or heat–proof metal. At the top and bottom and on the sides keys should be provided for the movement of the fumes. 40 such dhoomodgama yantras should be properly fixed in the selected spots of the peetha with screw fittings. The vimaana will be enabled to fly smoothly by so doing.

ELECTRIC DYNAMO

Says Yantra Sarvasva :

There are 32 kinds of yantras for generating electricity, such as by friction, by heating, by waterfall, by combination, by solar rays, etc. Out of these, saamyojaka or production by combination is the one most suitable for vimaanas. Its manufacture is explained by Sage Agastya in Shaktitantra :

The peetha or foot–plate should be made of saamyojaka metal, 35 feet in diametre. 5 spots should be marked in it in a circle, 5 feet in diametre, with a spot in the centre. Vessels should be prepared for each kendra, 4 feet wide, 2 feet high, shaped like a pot. On each a cylindrical pipe 1 foot wide and 1 foot high, should be fixed. The top of the cylinder should be 4 feet wide and round.

Then get a Jyotirmukha or flame–faced lion's skin, duly cleaned, add salt, and placing in the vessel containing spike–grass acid, boil for 5 yaamas or 15 hours. Then wash it with cold water. Then take oils from the seeds of jyothirmukhee, or staff-tree, momordica charantia, and pot herb, in the proportion of 3, 7, and 16, and mix them in a vessel, add $\frac{1}{64}$ part of salt. The skin should be immersed in this oil and kept for 24 days in solar heat. It will get a scarlet sheen. The skin should be cut to the size of the top opening of the vessel cylinder, with 5 openings in it. Cover the cylinder with the skin with bolts. All the 5 vessels should be similarly covered, and placed in the 5 selected centres on the peetha. Then 16 drona measures of asses' urine, 16 linka measures of mined charcoal, 3 linkas of salt, 2 linkas of snake–poison, and 2 linkas of copper, should be filled in the vessel on the eastern side.

Then in the vessel on the western side, 7 vidyudgama mani or load–stone, 13 praana–kshaara or ammonium chloride, 22 hare–dung, should be filled. and made into a decoction. Two parts of camel urine should be mixed with one part of the above. Then 50 linkas of rhinoceros bones, 30 linkas of sulphur, and 16 linkas of tamarind tree salt, and 28 linkas of steel should be added to that. And 117 tatin–mitra manis should be placed in the centre of the vessel.

Next the following materials should be filled in the northern vessel :

Eleven parts of oil of apaamaarga or achyranthus aspera seeds, 32 parts of oil seeds of sarpaasya or mesua ferrea, 40 parts of ayaskaantha or oil of steel, in 83 parts of elephant's urine, all these to be put in the northern vessel and mixed together properly. Then add mercury, symhika salt, and paarvanika or bamboo rice, 30, 20, and 25 palas respectively, or 120, 80, and 100 tolas. Sun–crystal of the 800th type, mentioned in Maniprakarana, cleaned in oil, should be put in the vessel.

Next in the vessel on the southern side, put in grandhika draavaka or long-pepper decoction, panchamukhee draavaka, and shveta–punja or white liquorice decoctions, in proportion of 12, 21, and 16, and mix together, add cows' urine 5 parts more than the above liquids, 47 parts of jyotirmayookha root, 28 linkas of kaanta metal, 28th and 10th kind of kudupa 32 parts. 92 jyotirmanis purified in milk should be placed in it, according to Chaakraayani. This is the southern vessel.

Then in the central vessel electric current should be stored. That vessel should be made of chapala–graahaka metal only.

Chapala-graahaka metal is explained in Lohatantra :

Quick-lime, marble stone, lac, sowraashtra earth, glass, root of the elephant trunk tree, bark of karkata tree, cowries, cubeb pepper gum, in the proportion of 8, 11, 7, 27, 8, 5, 3, 7, and 12 parts of tankana or borax, to be filled in urana crucible, placed in kundodara furnace, and with 3 faced bellows, boiled to 427 degrees, will yield, when poured into the cooler and cooled, chapalagraahaka metal.

The electricity storage vessel should be manufactured as follows : A foot-plate 5 feet long, 8 feet high, 1 foot thick, half-moon shaped, should be made of above metal. The vessel should be shaped like a big pot, with a cylindrical top. It should have a glass covering. 2 pipes 3 feet wide 6 feet high should be fixed in the vessel in the nothern and southern sides. They should also be covered with glass. Between the two pipes two wheels with hinges and switches etc. should be fixed. When the switches are put on or turned, causing the two wheels to revolve, electricity will flow from the bottom of the 4 vessels into the two pipes and ascend. Two tubes, 6 inches long, should be prepared, wound round with deer skin, tied with silk thread or silk cloth. The Vajramukhee copper wires cleaned with acids, should be passed through each tube, and taken to the two pipes in the vessel and be fixed with glass cups. 8 palas or 32 tolas of mercury should be placed in the energy container vessel. 391st vidyunmukha mani, wound round with copper wiring with mixing switch, should also be inserted. Then taking the wires in the pipes they should be connected with the wiring of the mani through the kaachakanku hole. In each of the vessels, excepting the middle one, two churning rods should be fixed in the centre. The rods should be made of steel or shakti skandha. They should be 3 feet high and 1 foot thick. Keys should be fixed in them for obverse and reverse churning. To the east of the churning machine wheels should be fixed for raising and lowering. An 8 inches high naala or tube should be fixed. On either side of it should be fixed 5 wheels of 5 inches height, like the wheel of the water lifting machine. 2 inches wide flat pattis made of shakti skandha metal should be passed from the wheels inside the Aavritta-naala to the keys of the wheels in the churning yantra. Then revolving wheels should be attached to the naalas or tubes of the stambha or big pipe. By the turning of these' keys, it will operate like the turning of the churning rod back and forth as in churning curds by drawing and relaxing the rope ends.

Then according to Darpana-shaastra, four vessels, shaped like the bamboo cylinder used on the pounding mortar, should be made out of ghrinyaakarshana glass or solar-heat absorbing glass and fixed on the mouth of the 4 vessels.

The vessel is described by Lallaacharya: 8 inches wide and 1 foot high, and then 2 feet wide and 6 feet high, and at the top a 6 feet wide mouth.

25 palas or 100 tolas of bamboo salt, should be put in it. Then amsupaa mani or solar-ray crystal of the 325th kind, duly cleaned in acid, should be put in it with rice salt. Then rice hay should be spread over it tightly, and facing the sun. The rays from all sides are imbibed by them, and will enter the vessel daily to 105 degrees' strength. If kept thus in the sun for 12 days, 1080 linkas of electric power will be accumulated in each vessel.

In order to store this power in the storage vessel six inches long steel tubes should connect the bottom of the vessel with the storage vessel. They should be covered by deer skin and wound round with silk cloth or yarn. Two copper wires should be passed through the tubes and connected to the storage vessel. 100 palas of mercury should be put in the vessel. And a 391th type of sun crystal duly wired should be placed in the mercury, and the wires coming from the tubes should be connected to it.

The well-oiled keys in the 4 vessels should be revolved with speed, to 200 degrees heat, when the liquids in the vessels will be boiled by the heat rays. Then the keys should be hastened up to 2000 degrees. By the liquids in each vessel 800 linkas of electricity will be generated. The power should be conveyed by the wires in the kaanta metal tubes to the storage vessel. The crystal will absorb and fill the vessel with the power. In front of the storage vessel a five feet long, 3 feet high circular vessel should be installed. It should be covered all round with the bark of vaari-vriksha.

Always water will be flowing in it. So instead of water, water skin is indicated. It will give the vessel the effect of water-immersion. Then in that vessel glass cups containing the decoction of shikhaavalee or lead-wort? or achyranthes aspera ?, 18 parts of ayaskaanta or loadstone? or steel acid?, and 12 parts of vajrachumbaka acid, should be placed. Then power should be drawn from the storage vessel through the wires inside the glass-covered tube, and 4 wires with glass wheel key be let into the acid vessels. Then from the bottom of the vessels 2 wires fitted with keys should be taken in a right circle to the front of the smoke-outlet stambha or pipe, and attached to the wires inside the bhujyu metal tube. The wires should also be connected to the keys of the electric friction crystals in the dhoomodgama stambha or pillar, as also to the key in the stambha. Thereby electricity will be spread in all parts of the vimaana. Therefore the vidyud-yantra or electrical machine should be installed in the left side of the vimaana.

Vaata-prasaarana Yantra
Air Spreading Machine.

Kriyaasaara says:

In order to enable the vimaana to ascend, vaataprasaarana yantra is necessary.

Therefore it is now being described. It should be made out of vaatamitra metal only.

Lohatantra describes vaatamitra loha. 13 parts of rasaanjanika or extract of Indian berbery, 27 parts of prabhanjana, and 37 parts of paraankusha, should be filled in sarpaasya or serpent-faced crucible, placed in chakramukha furnace, and with the aid of vaaranaasya bhastrika or bellows, heated to 216 degrees. Then filled in the sameekarana yantra or churner, and next poured out and cooled, it will yield vaata-mitra loha, or air-companion metal.

First the foot plate, then the naala-stambha or tubular pole, air pumping wheel with keys, air attracting bellows-like mechanism, and mechanism for contracting and expanding the mouth, out-flow and inflow tubes with keys, covering for the yantras, wind pipes, vaatodgama pipe, bhastrikonmukha, vaatapoorakeelakas, vaata nirasana pankha keelaakas, or air–expelling fan keys, these 12 are the organs of the yantra.

The Peetha or foot plate.

The peetha should be 6 feet long, 1 foot thick, square or round, with two spots on the northern and southern side of it for erecting three–wheeled tubular poles.

The 3 weeled naala stambha is described in "Yaana bindu" :

Three feet long and 8 feet high tubular poles should be fixed on 2 sides of the peetha or foot–plate. At the foot and the middle and the top of the pole three openings should be provided for fixing 3 wheels.

In the pole should be fixed tubes, one foot wide and 2 feet long, for drawing in air, and wheels 1 foot wide with teeth as in hack–saw, revolving both ways, be fitted to the tubes. The vaata–pooraka or air–filling naala should be fixed in the middle of the wheel. By turning the fly wheel, the wheel will turn, making the naala move up and down sucking in air. The air pumping wheel keys should be thus fixed in the two poles. The keys at the mouth of the bellows should be connected to these keys.

Bhastrikaa-Mukha-Yantra

Bellows' mouth mechanism

Taking pig–skin, duly cleaning it with putrajeevi or wild olive oil, boil it for 3 days, wash it with clean water. Smear it with gajadantika oil frequently exposing to sun for 5 days, and fashion out of it a 6 foot bellows, three feet wide at bottom, 4 feet wide in the middle, and 1 foot wide at the mouth. Two keys working conversely to each other should be fixed at the mouth. A stick should be inserted between them. The two keys should be capable of being put into quick motion, or left at rest. By turning the keelakas the piston rod is moved, and from its speed, the bellows' mouth also will start in motion, and also the vaataakarshana naala. By putting the naala at the mouth of the bhastrika or bellows, quick air entry from inside the mouth will occur. By starting all the keelakaas in all the centres there will be airflow in the three wheel tubular stambhas. By turning the keelakas with 20 heat-degree force, in the naala stambhas air will rush out with 100 shaker speed. From the bellows' mouth also air will blow with 2000 prenkhana or shaker speed. And these air flows will speed the motion of the vimaana. Therefore in front of the vaatodgama yantra 12 such yantras should be installed on the four sides, 3 on each side. And aavarana or covering should be provided for them according to their measurements. And 12 naala stambhas, 3 feet wide and 12 feet high, should be prepared, and fixed on the top covering of the yantras, for the air to flow out. From each stambha air will blow with 2600 prenkhana speed. The yantras are individually prescribed so that some may rest when not required. The high flight will be helped by these machines. Having thus described the individual sources of air supply for the vimaana, we shall now describe the Brihat-stambha or main mast.

It should be 4 feet wide and 30 feet high, and called vaatodgama naala stambha. It should be erected centrally amidst all the yantras. The bhastrikonmukha yantras should be fixed at the foot of the stambha so that the air flows from the yantras could pass into the stambha. The wind-naalaas or pipes should be connected to the stambha-moola fitted with keys. At the opening of the naala-stambha at the top on the 8 inch wide opening a vessel one foot high and 3 feet wide should be fixed. The wind from the stambha or tunnel will pass out through it in wavy billows. The dhoomodgama yantra or smoke pipe should, be provided with triple keys or fixtures, for the expulsion of smoke and blowing in of air. By operating those keelakas the supply of smoke and air could be controlled according to need. Wind expelling fan wheels should be put in, so that by their quick motion the motion of the vimaana could be facilitated.

Vimaana-aavarana-nirnaya
Covering of the Vimaana

Covering the dhoomodgama yantras and kudyaas or side walls, as in the case of the Shakuna Vimaana, the covering of the Sundara vimaana should be done by raajaloha only. The covering should accommodate the number of partitions or booths required as in Shakuna Vimaana. The location of the 32 component yantras should be determined.

In the centre of the booths for locating the four-faced heat machinery, a thirty feet square area should be set apart. There the four-faced heat yantra should be erected.

Says Yantrasarvasva :

The chaatur-mukha owshnya yantra should be made out of kundo-dara metal only. Kundodara metal is defined in Lohasarvasva.

Soma, Kanchuka, and shundaala metals in the proportion of 30, 45, and 20 to be taken, cleaned and filled in padma crucible, placed in chhatramukha furnace, and with vaasukee bellows heated to 716 degrees, aa-netraanta, and poured into the yantra for cooling. A blue, fine, light, alloy, capable of bearing 2000 degree heat, and which cannot be blasted even by shataghnee and sahasraghnee canons, and very cold, is kundodara alloy. With this alloy the owshnyaka yantra should be fashioned.

Yantraangas or parts of the Machine.

Peetha or foot-plate, smoke container kunda or vessel, water container, fire oven, turret covering, covering of water container, twin wheels for projecting and restraining smoke, window rods, padmachakras or wheels, aavritta chakra keela, heat indicator, speedometer, time clock, ravaprasaarana keelaka naala or sound transmitting instrument, antar-dandaaghaata naala, air-bellows, long sundaala pipes, twin copper pipes, air dividing wheel keys, these 18 parts constitute the ooshmyaka yantra.

The peetha, tortoise-shaped, should be 25 feet long and wide. At peethaadi or starting end should be fixed the agni-kosha or fire place, the water vessel in the middle, and the smoke-container should be fixed at the other end.

The 3 koshaas are explained by Budila :

Ravi or copper, manchoulika, and tigma in equal parts should be mixed with kundodara metal, and be made into 3 inches thick pattika or flats. One pattika should be fixed on the peetha. In the fire place kendra on the peetha a 4 feet long 6 feet high fire-place should be made. For stocking coal or wooden billets, a sort of walled table should be formed. Next a triangular fire-place should be formed, with rods at the bottom for the ashes to fall down. In between the 2 parts the flat sheet should be fixed, fitted with keelakas or hinges for moving the peetha as desired. Three keelakas should be fixed at the fire place, one to fan the flames and straighten them, one to moderate or stimulate the flames, and one to distribute the flames evenly. A naala or pipe should be fixed on the fire kosa. Another pipe with wiring, is to be fixed at the end of the fire-kosa pattika with a smoke transmitting pipe which will convey the smoke of the fire-place to the jalakosa or water container. From the fire kosa to the covering of the water kosa water pipes should be adjusted. In the water kosa enclosure the heat will rise to 5000 linkas in these tubes. The heated water will then give out hot smoke.

The size of the jalakosa or water container is 8 feet. Three triple-wheeled naalas or pipes should be fixed in the jalakosa: one to restrain the heated smoke from the water, one to amass the smoke, and one to lead the smoke into the dhoomakosa or smoke-container. The Dhoomakosa should be 6 feet wide and 4 feet high. In order to fill the kosha with smoke, necessary fittings should be provided. Above the jalakosa a dome-like covering should be erected. It should be provided with fittings, for folding up and opening out. To the front of the smoke container, two pattikaa wheels with holes should be fixed in order to let out the smoke or to restrain it. In order to operate the wheels two bhraamanee keelakaas or revolving switches should be provided. To the east of the Dhooma-kunda, 8 inches long window bars should be fixed with one inch spacings. Then in front of the yantra, in the middle, at top, at bottom, and on both sides, twin padmachakra keelakas should be fixed for spreading the smoke or restraining it. For storing the wood or coal a hole 1½ feet wide should be arranged. The door covering it should be provided with needful fittings. To the north and south of the keelaka the heat-measure and speedometer should be fixed. Above them the timepiece. To the south, a telephonic device called ravaprasaarana or sound ringer, which will give alarm with 1212 sound wave speed, and which gives warnings for the plane's moving, halting, speeding, overspeeding, and danger imminence. An equipment with 5 holes giving 5 different sounds to indicate the above should be installed. On either side of the above, two 6 inches wide, 26 feet tall, Aaghaatha-naalas or pipes should be fixed. Between them two 5 inches thick metal rods are to be adjusted. At the foot, middle, and top of the naalas revolving wheel keelakas should be fitted. By their revolving, the rods will strike each other. That will increase the speed of the plane. On the top of the naala pipes, air bellows with fittings should be fixed. Thereby the air force in the naalas will shoot up, and the speed of the vimaana will double. Then on the four sides of the heated smoke kosha or container, shundaalas or elephant–trunk–like pipes should be fixed with wheeled keys as in vaatodgama yantra. By filling the shundaalas with the smoke and turning the keys as required, the movement of the vimaana in one direction or another, its gaining height and speeding out or halting, will be facilitated. Keys should be adjusted so as to make the shundaalas coil down like a water hose or keep erect. Two pipes made of 3rd division copper should be wound round the agnikosa, water kosa, and smoke kosa, or fire, water and smoke koshas, in order to absorb the excessive heat in them.

In order to part the wind in front of the vimaana, vaata–vibhajana chakra keela or wind-dividing–wheel fittings should be fixed.

Having thus prepared the chaaturmukhoshmyaka yantra, or four–faced heating machine, it should be installed in the centre of the vimaana. By the air, smoke, and heat of the yantras below, the ascent and flight of the vimaana will be facilitated.

Regarding the speed of the vimaana, we have to consider the speed of smoke and other accessories mathematically, and conclude the possibility of the speed of the vimaana. The speed of the smoke from dhooma yantra is 2113 linkas. The speed of wind from the air blowing machine 2500 linkas. Wind from the naala-stambha blows at the speed of 600 linkas. This is the speed of the forces from the 3 machines on the peetha. Of the forces from the upper portion of the vimaana, from the chatur–mukhoshmyaka yantra, heat force of 3400 linkas emanates. By the four–faced heat yantra, and by operating the keys of the shundaalas, and the force of the wind, smoke and heat machines, the vimaana would be capable of a speed of 400 yojanas or 3600 miles.

This is Sundara Vimaana, and it has been described after consulting ancient works, and according to my humble capacity, says Maharshi Bharadwaaja.

RUKMA VIMAANA

"Atha Rukma Vimaana Nirnayaha"

Next the principles of Rukma Vimaana.

Maharshi Bharadwaaja:

☞ "Rukmascha" Sootra 1.
"Rukma too"

Bodhaananda Vritti:

This vimaana is of golden colour. Therefore it is called Rukma vima.. Rukma meaning gold. The Rukma should be made out of Raajaloha only. By duly processing, Raajaloha can be made to assume golden colour. That metal should be used for the vimaana.

"Yaana–Bindu" says,

"After first producing golden colour for Raajaloha, the vimaana should be formed."

"Varna-sarvasva" mentions the colouring process:

Praana–kshaara or ammonium chloride 4 parts, wild Bengal gram 32 parts, shashakanda (or lodhra?) benzoin? 18 parts, naaga or lead 20 parts, sea–foam 16 parts, maakshika or iron pyrites 6 parts, panchaanana or iron 20 parts, paara or mercury 15 parts, kshaara–traya or 3 kinds of salt: natron, salt-petre, borax, 28 parts, panchaanana or mica 20 parts, hamsa or silver 17 parts, garada or aconite 8 parts, and panchaamrita or 5 sweets—curds, milk, ghee, sugar, honey, these should be filled in· the melter, and after boiling, and drawing the liquid through two outlets, fill in the crucible and place in furnace, and blow to 800 degrees' heat, and then transfer it to the cooler.

That will be Raajaloha, pure, golden–coloured, tensile, and mild. The vimaana, made out of this loha or alloy, will be very beautiful and delightful.

The Peetha

The peetha or ground plate of the Rukma vimaana should be tortoise–shaped, 1000 feet long, and 1 foot thick, or any other desired size. On its eight sides, 20 feet long spaces should be fixed underneath the peetha. At each centre fixtures like birds' beaks should be attached with revolving keelakas. Then double iron–balls or wheels, in couples, should be fixed in each of the 8 centres.

Ayas–chakra

Lalla gives the form of ayaschakra–pinda :

12 feet long and wide, and 8 kankushtas in weight, they should be made round like a grind–stone. They should be inserted in the beaks at the 8 centres. From each chakra–pinda up to the electrical generator chain wires should be connected with switches.

Batinikaa-Stambha

Or Button–switch pole

One foot wide and 4 feet high poles should be fixed. They should have switches wired up to the electric pole. 8 inches wide wheels should be fixed in the middle of the pole, on either side, with wires. From the electric pole chain wires should enclose the wheels and be fixed in another pole with inside hinges. On the top of the poles should be fixed goblet shaped cups with button–switches like half–blooms with wheels and keys, so that on pressing the button with the thumb the wheels in the other pole will revolve from electric contact. Then the wheels in the electric pole will also revolve, producing 5000 linkas of speed.

Flying

Due to this electrical force, the ayah-pinda wheels beneath the peetha will beat against it and make it rise and move upwards. And by moving the switches of the wheeled poles above the peetha, the poles will revolve with speed, and accelerate the speed of the vimaana. By the concussion of the wheels underneath, and the action of the poles above, the vimaana will move upwards and gain height and fly with dignity.

Electric tube wheels aiding flight :

Above the peetha, naalas or tubes should be fixed at 1 foot intervals. On both sides of each naala toothed wheels 2 feet wide and 1 foot high should be fixed with proper keelakas. Taking electric wires through the keelakas, and passing over the wheels and reaching the foot of each naala, they should be attached to wheels 3 feet wide and 3 feet high. In the midst of 20 naalas a pole should be fixed in the centre.

Narayana says :

Preparing a pillar 4 feet wide and 4 feet high, and making a 2 feet opening in its middle, fix keelakas at the top, middle, and lower end of the opening. Two keelakas with 6 wheels, with glass coverings, with wires, and naala and leather covering should be fixed at the lower end for attracting electricity. In the middle part of the opening, for transmitting the current, a five-faced keelaka should be fixed, with 5 wheels, glass covering, 2 naala tubes, two wires, attached to 3 rods, and vessel containing veginee oil. By the flow of the current the wheels in the upper end should be made to whirl by properly adjusting keys. In front of the opening a big wheel should be fixed with gum-bha keelakas. Similarly wheels should be fixed at the foot of each pillar. On top of them a four inch wide pattika or flat band should be adjusted commencing from the samsarga key chakra up to the front of the electric yantra. By operating that key, power will flow through the wires, and entering the key at the foot of the pillar set the wheels in motion. On the motion of the big wheel the sandhi-wheels in the naala-dandas will also revolve with speed, and the current will enter the 5 faced keelaka, and entering the oil vessel it will gather force, and passing through the 2 naalas, set all the wheels in the pillar in forceful motion, generating 25000 linkas speed, which will give the vimaana 105 krosa or nearly 250 miles speed per ghatika, or 24 minutes.

Having dealt with the mechanism for setting the vimaana in motion, we now consider the mechanism for giving direction to the vimaana in its course. In the 8 diks or directions of the peetha, pillars made of mica and shining like panchakantha, 2 feet thick and 15 feet high should be fixed at intervals of 10 feet. On the pillars should be built the passenger seating arrangements, and booths or locations for the machinery, as in the case of the Sundara Vimaana. The pillars should be made of mica only.

Its production is given in Kriyaasaara :

Shaara-graava or lime 25 parts, kshwinkaasatva or iron-sulphate 30 parts, gunja or wild-liquorice 28 parts, tankana or borax 12 parts, roudree moola 8 parts, chaandree or kantakaari....solanum xanthocarpum flower salt 1 part, purified shoonya or mica 100 parts, to be filled in koorma crucible, and heated in paadma furnace with blower to 800 degrees, and then poured into the cooler, will yield mica alloy most useful and attractive. Fashioning the pillars or walls or partitions and booths, and fixing the mechanisms for turning, circling, diving, and manoeuvring, in the fore and middle and aft of the vimaana, it could be moved in any direction as desired.

Lallaacharya says :

In order to make the vimaana change its course from one path to another or one direction to another, revolving keelakas should be fixed on the eight sides of the vimaana. Two keelakas should be made, purva and apara, or right side and left side. They should be fitted together.

By operating it, the vimaana could be made to change its course one way or another. In order to operate the keelaka, at the peetha moola, on the 4 sides crescent shaped naalaas or tubes, 2 feet wide and 2 feet high should be fixed. 4 inches long metal rods should be fixed inside the naalaas on either side. One foot wide and 1 foot high wheels should be fixed in them. They should be wired all around. Such crescent naalas should be fixed on the 4 sides of the peetha. In order to set the wheels in the naalas in motion big wheels should be fixed at the beginning, middle, and end of the naalas. By turning the top wheel with speed the wheels inside the naalas will revolve. That will force the keela-shankus to twist round so as to force the vimaana to change its course in the required direction.

TRIPURA VIMAANA

Maharshi Bharadwaaja:

☞ "Tripurothha." Sootra 2.

"Next Tripura."

Bodhaananda Vritti:

Having explained the vimaanas commencing from Shakuna to Simhikaa, Tripura vimaana will now be dealt with.

This vimaana has 3 enclosures, or aavaranas or tiers. Each aavarana is called "Pura." As it consists of 3 aavaranas it is called "Tripura" vimaana. It is operated by the motive power generated by solar rays.

Narayana also says:

The vimaana which naturally can travel on land, sea, and in the sky by alteration of its structure is called Tripura Vimaana.

It has got 3 parts. The first part can travel on land. The second part can travel under and over water. The 3rd part travels in the sky. By uniting the 3 parts by means of keelakas, the plane can be made to travel in the sky. The plane is divisible into 3 parts so that it might travel on land, sea, or air. The construction of the 1st part is now explained. Tripura vimaana should be made out of Trinetra metal only.

Trinetra loha is explained by Shaakataayana:

Jyotishmatee loha 10 parts, kaanta–mitra 8 parts, vajramukha loha 16 parts, these 3 to be filled in crucible, then adding tankana or borax 5 parts, trynika 7 parts, shrapanikaa 11 parts, maandalika 5 parts, ruchaka or natron 3 parts, mercury 3 parts, then filled in crucible in padma-mukha furnace and heated to 631 degrees with trimukhee bellows, the resulting liquid, if poured into cooler, will yield a metal, shining like peacock feather, unburnable, unbreakable, weightless, impregnable by water, fire, air and heat, and indestructible.

With that metal the peetha should be prepared, of any desired size. The following is given as an example. It may be 100 feet wide and 3 feet thick, round or square. Leaving 20 feet on the western side, at intervals of 10 feet 80 spots should be marked for wheeled boats. 80 feet long, 3 feet wide, 5 feet high boat shaped dronies or containers should be fixed on the marked lines. Three feet wide openings should be made in the top of the dronies, so as to raise the wheel inside them quickly and cover them underneath. There should be fittings which enable the wheels to be lowered on land, and raised and covered underneath when going in water. The wheels should have axle rods with fittings to attract electric power. The axle rods should be $2\frac{1}{2}$ feet long and 1 foot thick. The wheels should be 3 feet wide and 1 foot thick, have, 5, 6, or 7 spokes, fixed in the rims, and covered with musheeka up to 4 inches from the edge. Holes with glass coverings should be made in all the wheels. These 12 wheels, or 8, or 6, or 4, should be fixed inside the boat–like structure. For transmitting power wires made of somakaanta loha should be fixed in the holes made in the wheels. In the middle of each wheel electric aaghaata keelakaas should be fixed, and in them chhidraprasaarana keelakas. Over all the chakradronee boats, copper wire pairs should be fixed on both sides, and in the joints of the wheels. Rods should be attached to the wires so that power could be drawn from the wires and passed to the top of the wheels. And power should be passed to the wires underneath the wheels. In climbing hills, and going down slopes, by adjusting the power at the top or the bottom of the wheels, smooth progress is made possible. By adjusting the necessary keelakas it is possible to accelerate the speed, or in going down, to restrain the flow of the current, and put brake on excess speed.

For attracting power from the generator a naala or pipe with wires should be fixed at the front of the peetha through 5 faced wheel keelakas, and the wires should be connected to the fittings at the top and bottom of the wheels, with glass cups.

In order to put covering over the boat formations, pillars should be fixed between each boat line, and covered with mica sheets, as per architectural rules.

Maharshi Bharadwaaja:

☞ " Shuddhhaambaraattadhhi." Sootra 3.

"Out of pure mica alone"
Bodhaananda Vritti :

The vimaana should be made out of pure mica alone.

Mica is described in " Dhatu sarvasva ". There are four kinds of mica, white mica, red mica, yellow mica, and black mica. The white mica has 16 varieties. Red mica has 12 varieties. The yellow mica has 7 varieties. And the black mica has 15 varieties. Thus there are 50 varieties in all.

Shownakeeya also says :

We shall now describe the nature of abhraka or mica. They are of 4 castes, like brahmin, kshatriya, vysya, and sudra. They are of 50 varieties. The brahmin mica has 16 varieties. The kshatriya mica has 12 varieties. The vysya mica has 7 varieties. And the sudra mica has 15 varieties, totalling 50 in all. Their names are as follows. The brahmin mica varieties are ravi, ambara, bhraajaka, rochishmaka, pundareeka, virinchika, vajragarbha, koshambara, sowvarchala, somaka, amritanetra, shytyamukha, kuranda, rudraasya, panchodara and rukmagarbha. The kshatriya varieties are shundeeraka, shambara, rekhaasya, owdumbara, bhadraka, panchaasya, amshumukha, raktanetra, manigarbha, rohinika, somaamshaka, and kourmika. The vysya varieties are krishnamukha, shyaamarekha, garalakosha, panchadhaara, ambareeshaka, manigarbha, and krownchaasya. The shoodra varieties are gomukha, kanduraka, showndika, mugdhaasya, vishagarbha, mandooka, thailagarbha, rekhaasya, parvanika, raakaamsuka, praanada, drownika, raktabandhaka, rasagraahaka, vranahaarika.

Out of these, pundareeka from the 1st class, rohinika from the second, panchadhaara from the third, and drownika from the 4th class are good for use in constructing the vimaana. These should first be purified as per rules.

The process of purification is given in "Samskaara Ratnaakara": kandhaaraka or salt of roitleria tinctoria?, shaaranika or rubus salt ?, anjulee or yellow orpiment ?, cowries, borax, kaakajanghaa or wild liquorice?, moss, rowdrikaa, salt-petre, douvaarika, shambara or benzoin, and phosphorus. These should be separately filled in the smelter. The decoctions should be filled in glass vessels. The mica is to be purified with each one of these.

The mica is to be powdered, put in skandhaavaara acid in smelting vessel. It should be boiled for 3 days in fire, and for 3 days in electric heat. Then take the liquid and put it in a bronze vessel, pour in shaaranika acid and keep it in sun for 3 days. Then add pinjulee acid and keep buried in earth for 5 days. Afterwards add cowri acid, and boil in bhoodhara yantra for one day. Then add mustard, and adding borax acid and burning arjuna, myrabolan wood, place it in brown-barked acacia cinders for 3 days. Then add wild liquorice acid and expose it to the full moon rays on the 14th and 15 days. The mica is to be then taken out and washed in hot water. Then add wild corn, and pouring in moss acid place it under earth for 6 days. Then take out the mica, add roudri acid, place the vessel in a big fire-place, and burn in 64 feet of dried cowdung. Next taking out the mica put it in sesamum oil for 1½ days, and expose to the sun from morning to sundown. Then take out the mica, wash it clean, put in bronze vessel with salt-petre solution with dattoori or yellow thistle seeds, place it in a heap of burning kundalee or mollugo stricta leaves. Then take out the mica, add dourvaarika acid and bake for a day with hay-fire. Then put the mica in benzoin acid for 3 days. Next add one-fourth as much of camphor, and placing it in the churning machine, churn for a day. Then placing it in Simhaasya crucible cook with boiling water. Add ranjaka or phosphorus acid, 3 palas or 12 tolas of tankana or borax, 12 tolas of lime, 4 tolas of soorana root or tacca, karkotaka 20 tolas, vrishala or onion 28 tolas, koorma-tankanaka 8 palas or 32 tolas, rouhinaka or red sandal 40 tolas, shambara 80 tolas, muchukunda 12 tolas. These cleaned and filled in the crucible, and placed in simha-mukha furnace filled with charcoal, and melted with 800 degrees heat will yield a metal shining like a precious stone, very light, unbreakable, unburnable and indestructible.

With that the vimaana is to be constructed.

We shall now consider the parts of the vimaana : 2 feet thick and 3 feet high pillars, painted in different colours and adorned with pictures, should be prepared, and 80 of them should be fixed in the spaces between the boats. On the pillars 10 feet wide pattikas or sheets, and of the same length as the boats, should be fitted with screws, and two-faced hinges.

In order to accommodate crew and passengers of the vimaana, and store luggage, rooms and partitions should be constructed with decorations. In order to provide secrecy, doors should be provided as also ventilators. Revolving wheels with necessary fittings and switches should be fixed so that by putting on a switch the rooms would revolve. Wheels should be fixed in the lanes between the boats. Air–pipes with wheels should be fixed. In order to ensure supply of air, tubes with wheels, and bellows with wide mouths, leaving 20 junctional centres, should be fixed. In the front, two faced tubular wheels should be fixed to dispel the air downwards or upwards or side ways, at 30 feet intervals from the aavrutta or enclosed pradesha of the vimaana. At the bottom of the vimaana metal balls with chain–wirings should be fixed for operations in the course of flight.

The 1st floor will be 7 feet high, with the roofing duly fixed with nalikaa-keelakas with 10 feet intervals. With 20 feet interval in the middle, wires with beaked ends should be attached to each keela. The fittings should be such as to enable opening and shutting like an umbrella. The cloth covering like a tent top should cover the entire floor.

The second aavarana should be made of trinetra metal.

Maharshi Bharadwaaja:

☞ "Taduparichaanyaha." Sootra 4.

"Another above it."

Bodhaananda Vritti:

Having described the first floor above, now the second floor is being described. The second floor should be slightly smaller than the first floor. If the first floor is 100 feet wide, the second should be 80 feet wide. The floor should be 80 feet wide, and 3 feet thick, and made of trinetra metal. Its fittings should be like those on the first floor, and be duly connected with electric wiring from the generator.

In order to take the vimaana through water, first the wheels at the bottom used for land route should be drawn up, and in order to prevent water coming up, the bottom should be completely covered up with ksheeree-pata or milk cloth. Four inches thick metal rods, 12 inches long, to which wheels 1 foot wide and ½ foot thick, and shaped like frog claws, are fixed, should be adjusted on both sides of the dronee or boat lines. Similarly in the front portion of the vimaana, on both sides two such wheeled rods should be fixed in order to divert water. By switching on power the main wheels will revolve, making all the wheels revolve, and expelling water, and aiding the progress of the vimaana forward.

For the supply of air inside, on the sides of the 2nd floor, should be fixed, air pipes 6 inches wide and made of ksheeree pata or milk cloth, cleaned with acid, from the partitions in the 1st floor up-to the top of the vimaana, their tops being covered with revolving metal covers, with air sucking pumps worked by power. The air so pumped into the pipes will fill both the second and 1st floors, and provide air comfort for the crew and passengers of the vimaana.

Above the roofing of the two floors all round, spreading out and closing up keelakas should be fixed. So as to separate the floors, foldable chain fittings should be fixed at 10 feet intervals. Wires from the electrical generator should be connected to the fittings, so that by their operation the floors will be separated, and the separated floors simultaneously move on land and in the air.

In the 2nd floor also cabins, partitions and seating and doors and windows should be constructed as attractively as in the first floor. The enclosing walls of the floor should be 7 feet high from its peetha, and half a foot thick. In order to draw electric current from the third floor two poles should be erected in the back room with trans-mitter from which wires will pass the current to the various fixtures on the floor.

At the front of the vimaana a mast should be erected. At its foot two bells made of bronze should be fixed in order to indicate time to the crew and passengers. In every room on the floor alarm chains, as in railways, should be fixed so that the occupants may call for help in times of danger. On hearing the call the crew will rush to the room and attend to the requirements of the passengers. Sound transmitter, image transmitter, direction indicator, time-piece, and cold and heat gauges should be installed on either side of the floor, with necessary cable connections.

Then in order to protect against excessive wind currents, storms, and heat-waves, three machines should be installed at the back, on either side, and on both sides of the turret.

They are described in "Yantra Sarvasva" as three-faced air protection yantra, solar-blaze conditioning yantra, and rain storm protection yantra. Their construction is given here as per shaastras.

First, three-faced air force reducing yantra.
It must be made of Vaaruna Metal:

Vaaripanka, vishaari, borax, jaalikaa, mango, vishodara, vaaripanchaka, kshaarasaptaka, kshona, manjula or madder root, godhara, vaarunaasyaka, paarvana or chlorodendrum phlomoides, aruna, kaakatunda, bhoodhara, vaarunaabhraka, natron, kundaaleemukha, lodhra or benzoin, varikudmala or water flower, shaarikaarasa, panchabaanasahodara, lead ? parts, soorana or tacca, honey 8 parts, vaata, kankanikodara, sunda, njana or eye-black, kukkutaandaka, khaadira or brown-barked acacia, oddhruka, simhikaa-mukha, koormajangha, and masoorika .or lentil, all these to be cleaned, and filled in crucible, placed in padmamukha furnace, and heated to 700 degrees with 5 faced bellows, poured into liquifying yantra and churned, will yield a light, smoke-coloured, impre\nable vaaruna metal.

Then it is to be purified, according to "Kriyaasaara." First, place it in shundeera acid (great-leaved laburnum?) and boil for 3 days, and then with kuttinee yantra beat it into flat pattis, make thick decoction of soorana root or tacca, and smear it to 1 inch thickness it and heat it for 3 yaamaas or 9 hours. Then mritsaara, vaagura, ium, should be boiled together for a day. The concoctions will come red like lac. The metal patti should be smeared with it and ted in the taapana yantra for a yaama or 3 hours. Then keep it in the sun for a day. Then kantaka or small caltrap, heranda, dhavalo-dara, and chaaraka, and gingelly should be mixed together, and the oil extracted. The metal should be smeared with it and kept in the sun for 3 days, and then heated in the sun for a day. Then paste the gum of kankola or cubeb pepper 1 inch thick, and stick into it thumb-sized vaatakuthaaraka manis, place in furnace of brown-barked acacia and cool for 9 hours. The metal will become like diamond.

Out of this a cover should be made for the vimaana, with necessary fittings for spreading over and folding up, connected with electric wires drawn from inside the vimaana. The charge of electricity will permeate all over, as well as the manis on the pattika. Three serpent-faced keelakas should be fixed. These will suck in the fierce wind as it blows, and belch it out to the upper regions, so that the wind force on the vimaana will be curbed, and danger therefrom averted.

The rain storm protection yantra should be made of crowncha metal. Says "Kriyaasaara", The metal that can destroy the drava-praanana force of water is krowncha loha. Therefore the varshopa-samhaara yantra should be made out of that alone.

Krowncha loha is described in "Yantra Sarvasva" as follows: Jyotirmukha or rose-coloured red-wort 8 parts, tryambaka or copper 11 parts, humsa-tunda 12 parts, camphor 7 parts, tankana or borax 8 parts, sand 4 parts, choorna or lime 12 parts, owrwaara or cucumber?, ruruka 5 parts, patola or snake-gourd 27 parts, and vaardhyushika or sea-foam 1 part, these to be cleaned and placed in crucible, and heated in padma-furnace to 512 degrees with 3 faced bellows, poured into churning yantra, and then cooled, will yield, a metal, honey-coloured, light, strong, rain-storm antidote, and heat-impregnated. Extracting oil from the seeds of basil, rukma or yellow thistle, punkha, red wort, trijataa or bael, and pancha-kantaki or 5 thorny trees, the metal should be smeared and heated. The metal is to be made into pattis with kuttinee yantra, make pipes out of them 3 feet wide of the same height as the vimaana, and fix them properly all around. In front of the vimaana-aavarana also 3 feet high pipes should be fixed with keelakas or hinges. The pipes should be smeared with chana or gram decoction 1 inch thick. On that vajragarbha decoction or triangular spurge milk should be smeared thrice, which will make it hard as diamond. On the pipes, at 12 inches intervals, sinjeera vajra should be smeared and heated by fire. Then thumb-size panchaasya manis which will counteract the effects of water, should be imbedded on the smeared pipes. Then the pipes with proper fittings at both ends should be fixed on the 8 sides of the vimaana. Wires proceeding from the electric generator should be taken through glass tube and connected to the pipes. When the current passes through them to the panchaasya mani, the concentrated force in it blending with the electric force will fiercely oppose the forces of the rain storm and disturb the atmosphere so as to dilute and weaken the storm, and render it ineffective. Therefore the varshopahaaraka yantra should be fixed on the vimaana.

Sooryaathapopasamhaara yantra or the burning-sun protection machine:

It is to be made out of the aathapaashana loha. It is explained in Kriyaasaara: Aatapaashana loha protects against burning sun. Therefore Aatapa samhaara yantra should be made with that metal. "Loha-tantra" describes that metal. Owrvaarika, kowshika, gaaruda, soubhadraka, chaandrika, sarpanetra, sringaataka, sowmyaka, chitraloha, vishvodara, panchamukha, virinchi, these twelve metals should be put in equal parts in padma-moosha crucible. Borax 7 parts, chowlika 5 parts, cowree salt 6 parts, kunjara 12 parts, sand 9 parts, camphor 4 parts, cardamom 6 parts, powshnika 10 parts, should be added to them, and placing it in nalikaa furnace heated to 725 degrees with mooshakaasya bhastrika bellows. Then the liquid should be put in the mixing machine, and afterwards poured into the cooler. The resulting alloy will be light, orange coloured, heat proof, and unbreakable, for the making of sooryaathapopasamhaara yantra, after being duly purified, says Yantra-sarvasva.

Kriyaasaara explains its purification:

Ashwaththa or sacred fig tree, mango, plantain, aala or banyan, nadava or peepul, trimukhee, trijata or bael, gunja or wild liquorice, serinee, patolika or snake gourd, the bark of these trees should be powdered, should be filled in vessel with 10 times as much water, and boiled down to one-tenth measure.

Then taking the 11 kinds of salts, bidaa-lavana or table-salt, syndhava rock-salt, oushara or saline earth, budila salt, maacheepatra salt or solanum indicum?, praanakshaara panchaka, or 5 urine salts or ammonium chloride? and saamudra or sea-salt, these eleven salts, should be placed in dravaakarshana yantra or dehydration machine and boiled. Taking the previous decoction, add half as much this decoction, put the aatapaashana metal in it and boil for 5 days, then wash with water, and anoint with honey, and place in hot sun for 3 days, then wash it, and use it for producing the yantra.

First pattikas should be made from the metal with kuttinee yantra, 2 feet square, or circle, and 3 feet thick. On that 3 pipes, 1 foot wide and 5 feet high, should be fixed. Three triangular glass bowls should be placed underneath the pipes. In each of them one prastha or seer of somadraavaka or white acacia juice should be filled. In each vessel a heat proof crystal of the 121st class should be cleaned with acid and placed. Then an umbrella shape 10 feet wide should be made out of the metal, and fixed so as to cover the 3 pipes, with revolving keelakas fixed half-a-foot underneath the umbrella cover. Above that 3 kalasas, 3 feet wide and shaped like cooking vessel, should be fixed. At their centre circular chaalapattikas should be fixed. Upon that three cold-diffusing crystals of the 185th number, should be fixed. On them three black mica wheels should be fixed. They should be covered with chandrikaa toolikaa or white silk cotton. On that should be placed a vessel with acid of manjoosha or madder root, in which a heat-resisting crystal is immersed. In the front part the toothed mica wheels fitted with bhraamanee-danda keelakas should be fixed. And in order to revolve that keelaka 3 wheeled keelaka should be fixed. By its motion the umbrella will revolve disturbing the heat wave. Then the heat-absorbing mica wheels will absorb the heat, which, passing down to the madder-root acid, will become cold and get extinguished. And the crew and passengers will be saved from its evil effects.

The Third Floor :

In erecting the 3rd floor of the vimaana, the same procedure as was followed in erecting the second floor should be followed. Like the fixtures in the flooring of the 2nd aavarana and roofing of the 1st aavarana, fixtures should be put in connecting the roofing of the 2nd aavarana and the peetha of the 3rd aavarana. The peetha of the 3rd floor should be 5 feet less than the peetha of the 2nd floor, and be square or circular like it. The cabins, doors, walls, and furniture on the 3rd floor should be on the same lines as in the 2nd floor. In the north eastern part of the 3rd floor, a cabin should be prepared for housing the electric generator. It should be made out of somaanka loha.

Somaanka loha is explained in "Lohatantra" as follows: Lead, panchaasya, and copper, 7 parts each, Chumbaka or loadstone 9 parts, nalikaa or Indian spikenard bark, sharaanika or rubus salt?, and borax, in equal parts, to be filled in sarpamukha crucible, and placed in naaga-kunda furnace, filled with coal, and heated to 353 degrees with shasha-mukha bellows. After melting the liquid should be filled in the mixer, and after churning be poured out to cool. The resulting metal will be a fine, light, electricity-impregnated somaanka loha. Out of that metal pattikas should be made with kuttinee yantra, or hammering yantra.

A cradle-like vessel, 3 feet wide and 8 feet high, should be made out of it, and be covered with a pattika with hinges. On the eastern and northern part of the cover two holes $1\frac{1}{2}$ feet wide should be made. The cradle should be fixed in the electric cabin. Below the holes, two peethas should be fixed in the cradle. Two vessels 2 feet wide and 4 feet high should be prepared. Eight goblets 6 inches wide and 1 foot high should be made, and 4 each should be placed in the two vessels, in their four corners. In the middle of the 4 goblets, a big goblet should be placed so as to contact all the four. 2 vessels covered with patties having 5 holes should be placed inside the 2 holes in the cradle cover. Teethed churners 5 inches in size, 8 inches in height, like those of sugarcane machines, 8 in number, should be placed in the 8 goblets in the two vessels in the cradle. 2 churners, bigger than these should be placed in the two central goblets beneath the two holes. Fixtures should be fixed on the central churner so that by their turning all the other churners will turn.

The procedure for extracting electricity out of solar rays is as follows. 8 naalas or tubes should be prepared out of the 192nd kind of amshupa glass. The naalas should be fixed on the 4 corners of each vessel. Panchamukhi karnikaas should be placed on them, filled with sukmapunkhaa shana, and with electric crystals in them. Covering them with the amshupaa glass cover, 5 spires should be formed on it. The top of each spire should be like an open beak, and in it should be inserted sinjeeraka crystal and amshupaa crystal. On the central spire amshu-mitra mani should be fixed. Above the 4 crystals should be fixed 4 glass tubes made of kiranaakarshana glass, 6 inches wide and 3 feet high. On them should be carefully fixed 4 feet-wide-mouthed vessels, acid cleaned. They should be filled with Rudrajataa-vaala or aristolochia indica linn. Revolving ghutikas should be placed in their centre. The ghutikaas will attract the solar rays and send them through the tubes. The crystals in the spire beaks will suck them in. So does the shinjeera crystal inside, as also the amshu-mitra crystal. The power will be absorbed by the glass-covering, and sent to the electric crystal. Then the karnikas inside will receive it and send down to the central tube with force. When the central churner revolves the other churners also revolve. The power will enter the acid, and the crystals in it will whirl with great speed, intensifying the power force to the extent of 1080 linkas. That force should be collected by the ganapa-yantra in front of the cradle, and stored in the central storage.

The Ganapa-yantra is a machine shaped like Vighneshwara, 1 foot broad, and 3 feet high. From its head a tubular projection like

Vighneshwara

elephant's trunk, covered with glass and with wires inside should be fixed at the front of the cradle, and connected to the Ganapa image from the neck to the navel. Three-inch toothed wheels should be so fixed that a big wheel at the neck of the image, by force of the current coming through the trunk or proboscis will whirl, setting the other wheels in motion. A coil of wire should be placed in the centre. On it a sapta-shashthi shankha or conch called simhikaa should be placed, with covering made of kravyaada metal. 5 spoonfuls of jeevaa-vaka acid (ditamine?) should be filled in the conch, and 217

bhaamukha graamukha manis or beads should be placed inside.
5 umbrellas, 2 inches wide, should be made, and 5 sun-crystals of the size
of big liquorice, should be stuck on them. The umbrellas should be
fixed on the conch, with amshupa glass covering. This should attract
the force of the sun rays, and pass to the crystals on the umbrellas,
making the crystals and the umbrellas whirl with fierce force of 1000
linkas, and the force passing to the acid in the conch and the crystal
inside, will thence pass westwards, and could be transmitted through
wires for any desired use. To measure its exact force a meter should
be fixed in, along with thermometer and other needful equipments.

THE GROUND WHEELS

When the vimaana has to move on the ground, the electric current
is switched on the electric motor in the hub of each wheel, thus causing
the rim to revolve and move the vimaana.

But when entering water the wheels are drawn in by the movements of toothed segment and the pinion, the latter being revolved by
an electric motor attached to the shaft. The openings in the bottom
of the vimaana are closed by the sliding covers moved by the rack
and pinion arrangement, the pinion being worked by an electric motor.

The movements of the hinged joints of the folding links will
raise or lower the second floor over the first floor.

ELECTRIC GENERATOR

Two jars are placed on the peetha or stand. Each jar contains
five cups filled with acids. Each cup has a churning rod with gear-
wheels connected together. The wheels are revolved by hand while
starting, and by the generated electric power afterwards. A darpana
or mirror and gharshana manis are fixed above the gear wheels. The
darpana and the manis absorb the sun's energy and transmit it to the
acid cups. The acids, being churned, convert the absorbed energy into
electric current, which will pass through the pancha-mukhee naala, or
five-way-switch, to different points, and work the machines there.

THE ELECTRIC MOTOR

The electric motor consists of a loop of fine wire coil, with a fine wire cage in the centre. The current from the generator is brought to the wire coil through a glass tube. Suitable wheels are attached to the wire cage to connect to the churning gears of the generator or the shaft of the pinion.

The Simhika shankha on the top of the motor contains an acid and the bhaamukha-graahinee mani or crystal. Five rods with amshupaa-mitra manis are fitted to the top of the shankha, and toothed wheels are fitted to these rods to revolve together and rub against the inner surface of amshupaa mirror at the top. The solar power absorbed by the mirror is stored in the shankha, and given out by the bhaamukha graahinee mani to the various motors in the vimaana.

Thus concludes the description of Tripura Vimaana.

And that brings us to the end of the

WONDER MANUSCRIPT

left behind for the edification of Mankind

by the venerable mystic

ANEKAL SUBRAAYA SASTRI

whose occult powers visualised this much from the

"VYMAANIKA SHAASTRA"

section of the giant

"ENCYCLOPAEDIA OF MACHINES"

or

"YANTRA SARVASVA"

of divine sage

MAHARSHI BHARADWAAJA

RUKMA VIMANA

PROFILE

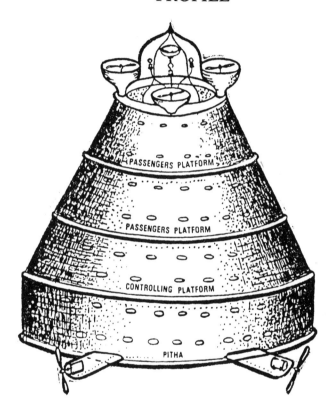

A 1923 drawing by T.K. Ellappa of Bangalore, India
of a Vimana (Vimaana) prepared under instruction
from Pandit Subbaraya Sastry of Anckal, Bangalore.

SHAKUNA VIMANA

HORIZONTAL SECTION

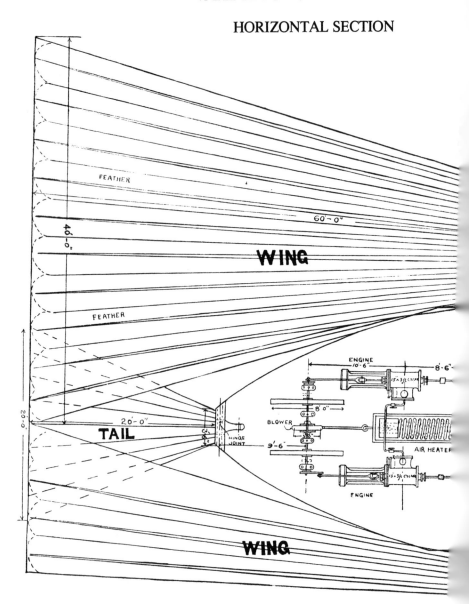

. 1923 drawing by T.K. Ellappa of Bangalore, India of a Vimana (Vimaana) prepared under instruction from Pandit Subbaraya Sastry of Anckal, Bangalore. This early drawing was based on their own turn-of-the-century ideas of flight and the Vimanyka Shastra text.

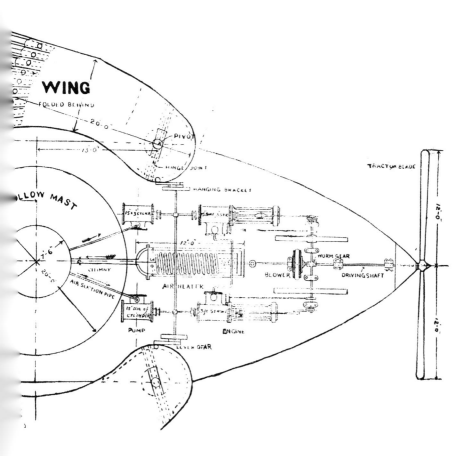

Location of Yantras

1. Vishvakriyaa Mirror.
2. Roopaakarshana yantra.
3. Parivesha kriyaa yantra.
4. Angopasamhaaraka yantra.
5. Vistrita kriyaa yantra.
6. Vyroopya Darpana yantra.
7. Padmachakramukha yantra.
8. Kuntinee Shakthi yantra.
9. Pushpinee yantra.
10. Pinjulaadarsa yantra.
11. Naalapanchaka yantra.
12. Guhaagarbha yantra.
13. Thamo yantra.
14. Panchavaataskandhanaala yantra.
15. Roudree Darpana yantra.
16. Vaathaskandha naala keelaka yantra.
17. Vidyudyantra.
18. Shabda Kendra mukha yantra.
19. Vidyuddwaadashaka yantra.
20. Praana Kundalinee yantra.
21. Shaktyudgama yantra.
22. Vakra prasaarana yantra.
23. Shakthi panjara keelaka yantra.
24. Shirah keelaka yantra.
25. Shabdaakarshana yantra.
26. Pataprasaarana yantra.
27. Dishaampathi yantra.
28. Pattikaabhraka yantra.
29. Soorvarashmyapakarshana yantra.
30. Apasmaaradhooma prasaarana yantra.
31. Sthambhana yantra.
32. Vyshwaanara Naala yantra.

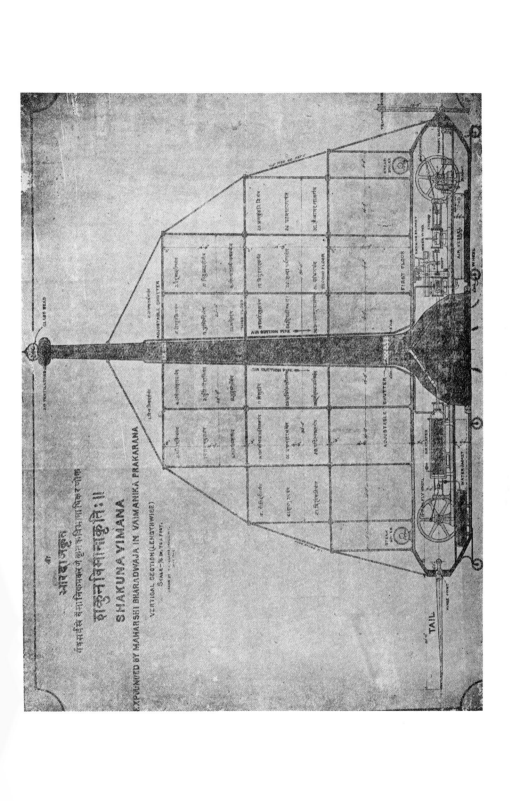

ओम् श्री जगदम्बायै नमः

श्री सद्गुरु वेंकटसुब्बराय जी गुरुभ्यो नमः ॥

हंस विद्या विमान शकुनि ॥

SHAKUNA VIMANA

EXPOUNDED BY MAHARSHI BHARADWAJA IN VAIMANIKA PRAKARANA

VERTICAL SECTION (LENGTHWISE)
SCALE — ⅜ IN. TO 1 FOOT.

RUKMA VIMANA

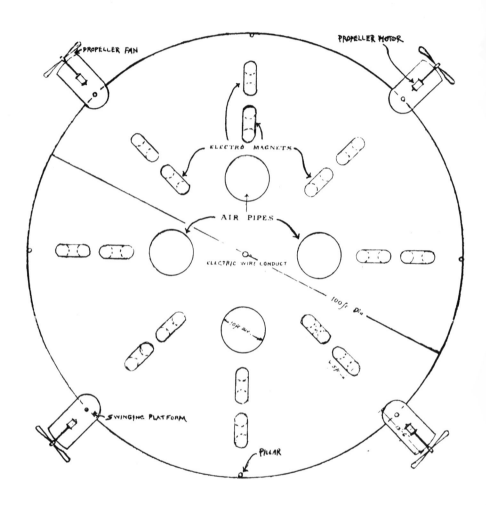

PLAN OF BASE OR PITHA

A 1923 drawing by T.K. Ellappa of Bangalore, India of a Vimana (Vimaana) prepared under instruction from Pandit Subbaraya Sastry of Anckal, Bangalore.

RUKMA VIMANA

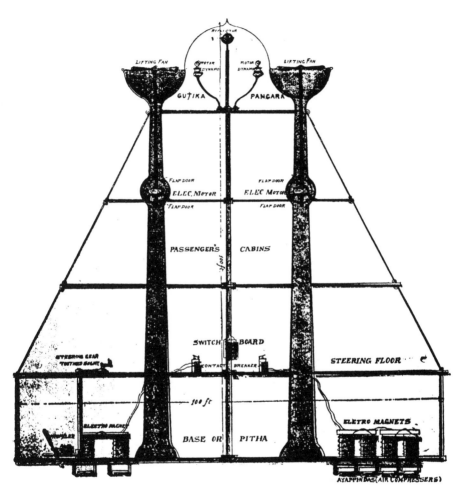

A 1923 drawing by T.K. Ellappa of Bangalore, India of a Vimana (Vimaana) prepared under instruction from Pandit Subbaraya Sastry of Anckal, Bangalore.

TRIPURA VIMANA

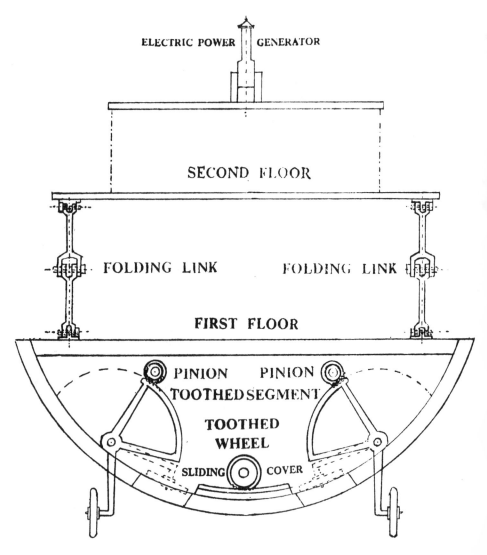

A 1923 drawing by T.K. Ellappa of Bangalore, India of a Vimana (Vimaana) prepared under instruction from Pandit Subbaraya Sastry of Anckal, Bangalore.

SUNDARA VIMANA

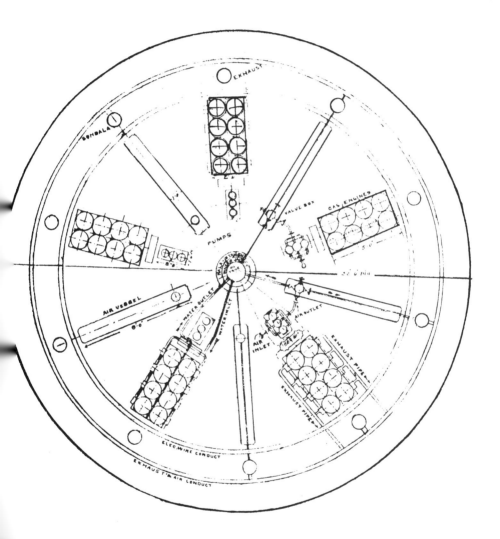

A 1923 drawing by T.K. Ellappa of Bangalore, India of a Vimana (Vimaana) prepared under instruction from Pandit Subbaraya Sastry of Anckal, Bangalore.

SUNDARA VIMANA

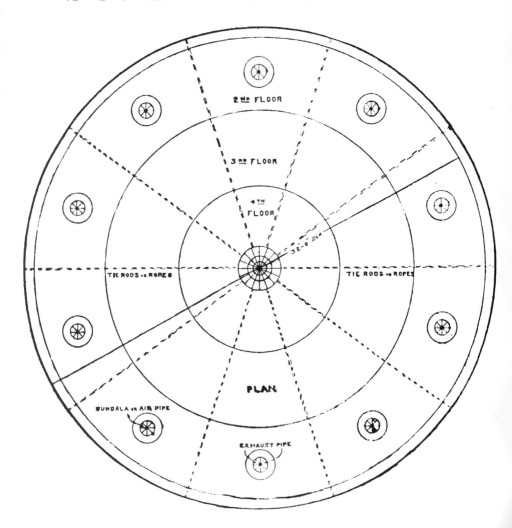

A 1923 drawing by T.K. Ellappa of Bangalore, India of a Vimana (Vimaana prepared under instruction from Pandit Subbaraya Sastry of Anckal, Bangalore.

TRIPURA VIMANA

PERSPECTIVE VIEW

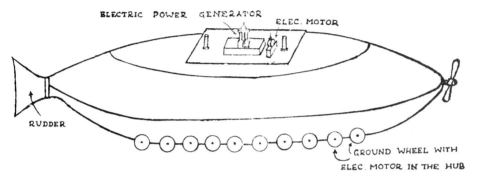

ELECTRIC POWER GENERATOR   ELEC. MOTOR

RUDDER

GROUND WHEEL WITH
ELEC. MOTOR IN THE HUB

VERTICAL SECTION

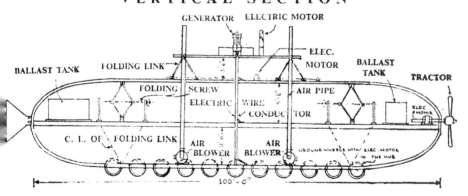

GENERATOR   ELECTRIC MOTOR

ELEC.
MOTOR

BALLAST TANK   FOLDING LINK

BALLAST
TANK

TRACTOR

FOLDING   SCREW

ELECTRIC   WIRE

CONDUCTOR

AIR PIPE

ELEC
& MOTOR

C. L. OF FOLDING LINK   AIR
BLOWER

AIR
BLOWER

GROUND WHEELS WITH/ ELEC. MOTOR
IN THE HUB

100'- 0"

A 1923 drawing by T.K. Ellappa of Bangalore, India of a Vimana (Vimaana)
prepared under instruction from Pandit Subbaraya Sastry of Anckal, Bangalore.

ELECTRIC POWER GENERATOR
TOP VIEW

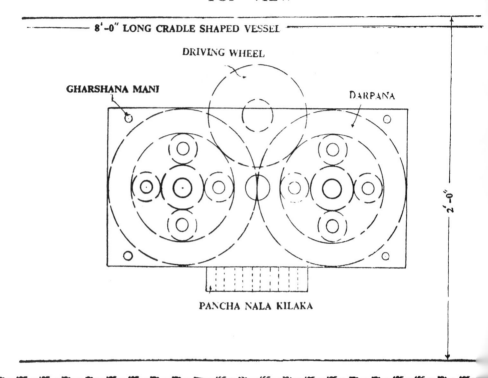

8'-0" LONG CRADLE SHAPED VESSEL

DRIVING WHEEL

GHARSHANA MANI

DARPANA

2'-0"

PANCHA NALA KILAKA

ELECTRIC MOTOR

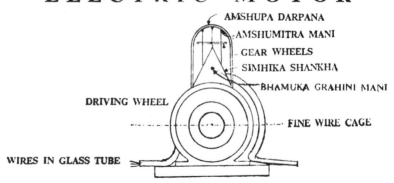

AMSHUPA DARPANA

AMSHUMITRA MANI

GEAR WHEELS

SIMHIKA SHANKHA

BHAMUKA GRAHINI MANI

DRIVING WHEEL

FINE WIRE CAGE

WIRES IN GLASS TUBE

A 1923 drawing by T.K. Ellappa of Bangalore, India of a Vimana (Vimaan prepared under instruction from Pandit Subbaraya Sastry of Anckal, Bangalor

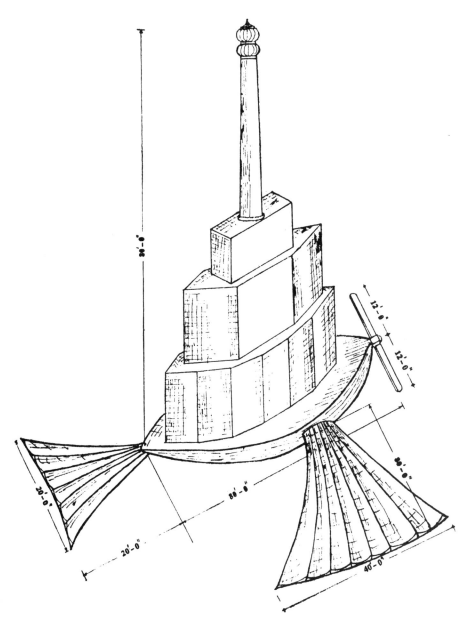

A 1923 drawing by T.K. Ellappa of Bangalore, India of a Vimana (Vimaana) prepared under instruction from Pandit Subbaraya Sastry of Anckal, Bangalore.

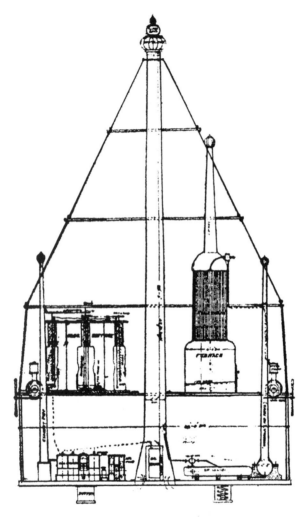

A 1923 drawing by T.K. Ellappa of Bangalore, India of a Vimana (Vimaana) prepared under instruction from Pandit Subbaraya Sastry of Anckal, Bangalore.

BOOK

3

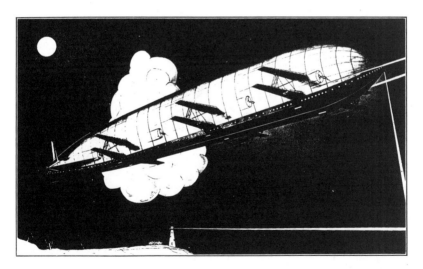

The concept of airflight in 1922 was often geared toward zeppelin
and cyclindrical vimana designs.

The Caduceus, Magic Wand of Mercury, Messenger of the Gods, is an ancient symbol of electromagnetic flight and cosmic energy.

According to Clendenon, the Caduceus is a simplified diagram of a Mercury Vortex Engine:
A. Air is the flight propellant/propeller/wings
B. Expansion of vortex coils/cooling
C. Compression of vortex coils/heating

1. Liquid metal mercury, the bearer of electro-magnetic energy.
2. Mercury boiler
3. Antenna/starter/core
4. Closed circuit serpentine heat exchanger/condenser coils
6. Poisonous mercury vapor reservoir

6

MERCURY VORTEX
ENGINES

§§§

Perhaps the most valuable information that has been gotten
from the *Vimaanika Shastra* of Bharadwaaja is the description
of what are known today as *Mercury Vortex Engines.*

In chapter five of the *Vimaanika Shastra,* Bharadwaaja
describes from the ancient texts which are his reference, how
to create a mercury vortex engine.

"Prepare a square or circular base of 9 inches width with
wood and glass, mark its centre, and from about an inch and
half thereof draw lines to edge in the 8 directions, fix 2 hinges
in each of the lines in order to open shut. In the centre erect a
6 inch pivot and four tubes, made of *vishvodara* metal,
equipped with hinges and bands of iron, copper, brass or lead,
and attach to the pegs in the lines in the several directions. The
whole is to be covered.

"Prepare a mirror of perfect finish and fix it to the *danda*
or pivot. At the base of the pivot an electric *yantra* should be
fixed. Crystal and glass beads should be fixed at the base,
middle, and end of the pivot or by its side. The circular or
goblet shaped mirror for attracting solar rays should be fixed
at the foot of the pivot. To the west of it the image-reflector
should be placed. Its operation is as follows:

"First the pivot or pole should be stretched by moving the

keelee or switch. The observation mirror should be fixed at its base. A vessel with mercury should be fixed at its bottom. In it a crystal bead with hole should be placed. Through the hole in the chemically purified bead, sensitive wires should be passed and attached to the end beads in various directions. At the middle of the pole, mustard cleaned solar mirror should be fixed. At the foot of the pole a vessel should be placed with liquid *ruchaka* salt. A crystal should be fixed in it with hinge and wiring. In the bottom centre should be placed a goblet-like circular mirror for attracting solar rays. To the west of it a reflecting mechanism should be placed. To the east of the liquid salt vessel, the electric generator should be placed and the wiring of the crystal attached to it. The current from both the *yantras* should be passed to the crystal in the liquid *ruchaka* salt vessel. Eight parts of sun-power in the solar reflector and 12 parts of electric power should be passed through the crystal into the mercury and on to the universal reflecting mirror. And the that mirror should be focussed in the direction of the region which has to be photographed. The image which appears in the facing lens will then be reflected through the crystal in the liquid salt solution. The picture which will appear in the mirror will be true to life, and enable the pilot to realize the conditions of the concerned region, and he can take appropriate action to ward off danger and inflict damage on the enemy." [48]

Two paragraphs later Bharadwaaja says, "... Two circular rods made of magnetic metal and copper should be fixed on the glass ball so as to cause friction when they revolve. To the west of it a globular ball made of *vaatapaa* glass with a wide open mouth should be fixed. Then a vessel made of *shaktipaa* glass, narrow at bottom, round in the middle, with narrow neck, and open mouth with 5 beaks should be fixed. Then a vessel made of *shaktipaa* glass, narrow at bottom, round in the middle, with narrow neck, and open mouth with 5 beaks should be fixed on the middle bolt. Similarly on the the end bolt should be paced a vessel sulfuric acid (*bhraajaswad-draavada*). On the pegs on southern side 3 interlocked wheels should be fixed. On the north side liquefied mixture of load-stone, mercury, mica, and serpent-slough should be placed. And crystals should be placed at the requisite centres.

" '*Maniratnaakara*' (here Bharadwaaja is referring to an ancient authority, now lost, -ed.) says that the *shaktyaakarshana* yantra should be equipped with 6 crystals known as *Bhaaradwaaja* , *Sanjanika* , *Sourrya* , *Pingalaka* , *Shaktipanjaraka*, and *Pancha-jyotirgarbha*.

"The same work work mentions where the crystals are to be located. The *sourrya* mani is to be placed in the vessel at the foot of the central pole. *Sanjanika mani* should be fixed at the foot of the central pole. *Sanjanika mani* should be fixed at the middle of the triangular wall. *Pingalaka mani* is to be fixed in the opening in the *naala-danda* . *Pancha-jyotirgarbha* mani should be fixed in the sulfuric acid vessel, and *Shakti-panjaraka mani* should be placed in the mixture of magnet, mercury, mica, and serpent-slough. All the five crystals should be equipped with wires passing through glass tubes.

"Wires should be passed from the centre in all directions. Then the triple wheels should be set in revolving motion, which will cause the two glass balls inside the glass case, to turn with increasing speed rubbing each other the resulting friction generating a 100 degree power...."[48]

From the text of the *Vimaanika Shastra* it is apparent that mercury, copper, magnets, electricity, crystals, gyros (?) and other pivots, plus antennas, are all part of at least one kind of *Vimana* The recent resurgence in the esoteric and scientific use of crystals is interesting in the context of the *Vimaanika Shastra*. Crystals, *mani* in Sanskrit, are apparently as integral a part of *vimanas* as they are today in a digital watch. It is interesting to note here that the familiar Tibetan prayer Om Mani Padme Om, is an invocation to the "Crystal (or jewel) inside the Lotus (of the mind)".

While crystals are no doubt wondrous and important technological tools, it is mercury that concerns us here. Mercury is an element and a metal. According to the *Concise Columbia Encyclopedia,* Mercury is a "metallic element, known to the ancient Chinese, Hindus, and Egyptians." The chief source of Mercury is cinnabar HgS, a mineral. According to *Van Nostrand's Scientific Encyclopedia,*[15] Mercury was mined as early a 500 B.C. out of cinnabar crystals which are usually "small and often highly modified hexagonal crystals, usually of rhombohedral or tabular habit. Its name is supposed to be of Hindu origin."[15]

Mercury was most certainly mined and used earlier than 500 B.C., though scientific encyclopedias and such are usually overly conservative. The metal was named after the messenger of the Gods in Roman mythology. It is a heavy, silver white liquid with the symbol *Hg*. The symbol for Mercury is derived from the Greek word *Hydrargos* meaning water, silver or liquid gyro. It is a liquid at ordinary temperatures and expands and contracts evenly when heated or cooled.

The liquid metal mercury when heated by any means gives forth a hot vapor that is deadly. Mercury is generally kept or confined to glass tubes or containers that are sealed, and therefore harmless to the user. Present day *Mercury Vapor Turbine Engines* use large quantities of mercury but little is required renewal because of its closed circuit systems. Mercury and its vapor conducts electricity, its vapor is also a source of heat for power usage. Mercury amplifies sound waves and doesn't lose timber in quality. Ultrasonics can be used for dispersing a metallic catalyst such as mercury in a reaction vessel or a boiler. High frequency sound waves produce bubbles in the liquid mercury when the frequency of the bubbles grow to match that of the sound waves the bubbles implode, releasing a sudden burst of heat.

According to William Clendenon, well-known UFO investigator and the author of the book *Mercury: UFO Messenger of the Gods*[16] a mercury-filled flywheel can be used

252

for stabilization and propulsion in discoid aircraft/spacecraft. *Liquid Mercury Proton Gyroscopes,* according to Clendenon, can be used as direction sensing gyros if placed 120 degrees apart on the rotating stabilizer flywheel of a discoid craft.

Liquid Mercury Proton Gyroscopes have several advantages, says Clendenon. Firstly, the heavy protons found in mercury atoms are the very stable. Secondly, such gyros do not require a warm-up period as mechanical gyros do. Thirdly, the gyro using stable mercury protons is not affected by vibrations and shock. Fourthly, the Liquid Mercury Proton Gyroscope has no moving parts and can run forever. And lastly, the mercury atom offers the most stable gyro device in nature and has the additional advantages of saving space and weight. This is particularly valuable on long distance flights where all space and weight must be very carefully calculated and conserved.[16]

DIRECTIONAL GYROS

Clendenon's version of mercury directional gyros is that three *Liquid Mercury Proton Gyroscopes* are mounted on and rotate with the rotating stabilizer flywheel of the craft. The three sensing cells are rigidly attached 120 degrees apart on the rotating flywheel of the discoid craft. The three movable coils of the sensing cells are constantly moving in and out or back and forth each in turn as chosen by the computer when the craft flies on a straight course and is rotating. Signals will be generated by the three mercury proton gyros resistance to the three coils movements. The signals can then be measured by computer to determine the speed and direction of the craft.

Further information on Mercury Engines used in vimanas can be found in the ancient Indian text called the *Samarangana Sutradhara.* The *Samarangana Sutradhara,* as quoted by Ivan T. Sanderson,[17] and Desmond Leslie [1] says that they were made of light material, with a strong, well-shaped body. Iron, copper, and lead were used in their construction. They could fly to great distances and were propelled by air. This text devotes 230 stanzas to the building of these machines, and their uses in peace and war. Quoting from the text:

"Strong and durable must the body be made, like a great flying bird, of light material. Inside it one must place the *Mercury-engine* with its iron heating apparatus beneath. By means of the *power latent in the mercury* which sets the driving *whirlwind* in motion, a man sitting inside may travel a great distance in the sky in a most marvelous manner.

"Similarly by using the prescribed processes one can build a vimana as large as the temple of the God-in-motion. Four strong *mercury* containers must be built into the interior structure. When these have been heated by controlled fire from iron containers, the vimana develops thunder-power through the mercury. And at once it becomes a pearl in the sky.

Moreover, if this iron engine with properly welded joints be filled with mercury, and the fire be conducted to the upper part it develops power with the roar of a lion."

Sanderson then goes on to make the basic observation that a circular dish of mercury revolves in a contrary manner to a naked flame circulated below it, and that it gathers speed until it exceeds the speed of revolution of said flame. Sanderson's observation of revolving mercury is one of the first references to what we now call *Mercury Vortex Engines.*

THE CADUCEUS

Mercury, the Messenger of the Gods, carried with him his magic wand or caduceus, the winged staff with which he could perform many wondrous feats. In one form or another, the ancient symbol has appeared throughout the world, though its actual origin remains a mystery. The caduceus staff of the God *Mercury* (Hermes to the Greeks) was a rod entwined by two serpents and topped with a winged sphere. Clendenon[16] likens the entwined serpents to an identical energy as that of the kundalini energy of India.

Today the caduceus is used by the medical profession as their symbol, a practice that apparently stems from the Middle Ages. Probably, the use of the caduceus as a medical symbol stems from the symbolism of the wings for speedy medical attention and the entwined snakes as chemical or medical symbols.

The mythical god Mercury was a messenger of the Gods, he flew through the air rapidly bearing important tidings and official news from kings, gods, or sovereign powers. It was said that if the gods wanted to communicate, carry on commerce, to move things swiftly from one place to another over a long distance safely, they made use of Mercury to accomplish their goals.

Researcher Clendenon [16] believes that the caduceus is an ancient symbol of "electromagnetic flight and cosmic energy." The entwined snakes are the vortex coils of the propellant, the rod the mercury boiler/starter/antenna and the wings symbolical of flight.

Clendenon's basic turbo-pump engine has four main sections: compressor, combustion (or heat chambers), turbo-pump and exhaust. Burning gases are exhausted through the turbo-pump wheel to generate power to turn the electric generator:

1. Propellant tanks will be filled with liquid air obtained directly from the atmosphere by on-board reduction equipment.

2. Liquid air may be injected into expansion chambers and heated by the metal working-fluid mercury confined in a boiler coupled to a heat exchanger.

3. the super heated magneto-hydrodynamic plasma (or air) will expand through propellant cooled nozzles.

4. the ship may recharge its propellant tanks with liquid air and condensate water collected directly from the upper

atmosphere by the on-board reducing plant.

Clendenon's interpretation of the *Samarangana Sutradhara* is then as follows: "*Inside the circular air frame, place the mercury-engine with its electric/ultrasonic mercury boiler at the bottom center.*" — Inside the circular air frame, place the mercury-engine with its electric/ultrasonic mercury boiler at the bottom center.

"By means of the power latent in the mercury which sets the driving whirlwind in motion a man sitting inside may travel a great distance in the sky in a most marvelous manner." — The unchained heat unchained heat energy from the hot mercury vapor sets the air pump/turbine in motion.

"Four strong mercury containers must be built into the interior structure. When these have been heated by controlled fire from iron containers, the vimana develops thunder-power through the mercury. And at once it becomes like a pearl in the sky." — One mercury boiler and three mercury flux valve sensor units must be installed in the propulsion system within the center of the circular air frame. When these mercury containers have been heated by electrically-controlled fire (hot mercury vapor) from the containers, the aircraft develops ultrasonic power through the mercury. And at once, the ionized recirculating air flow flow becomes like a pearl in the sky because of magneto-hydrodynamic plasma.[16]

The ball of light that surrounds the scout ship is the magneto-hydrodynamic plasma, a hot, continuously recirculating air flow through the the ship's gas turbine and is ionized (electrically conducting). According to Clendenon, at times a shimmering mirage-like effect caused by heat, accompanied by pulsations of the ball of light makes the craft appear to be alive and breathing. This has, at times, suggests Clendenon, made witnesses to certain UFOs think that they were seeing a living thing. For some of the above reasons, the ship may seem to suddenly disappear from view, though it is actually still there and not de-materialized. The ionized bubble of air surrounding the UFO may be controlled by a computerized rheostat so the the ionization of the air may shift through every color of the spectrum obscuring the aircraft from view. Clendenon's view of a great deal of discoid craft seen since 1947 is that many are *vimanas*, either of ancient manufacture, or modern manufacture. He believes that the famous "scout ship" observed by George Adamski (and later by other witnesses) is neither a hoax or an interplanetary space craft. His mercury vortex engines are not capable of interplanetary flight, he says, but, like this version of a vimana, are for terrestrial flight only.

ELECTROMAGNETIC LIFT AND REPULSION

Clendenon's *vimana*, modeled after Adamski's scout ship, consists of a circular air frame that is partly a powerful electromagnet though which is passed a rapidly pulsating direct current.

The Electromagnetic field coil which consists of the closed circuit heat exchanger/condenser coil circuit containing the liquid metal mercury and/or its hot vapor, is placed with its core axis vertical to the craft.

A ring conductor (directional gyro-armature) is placed around the field coil (heat exchanger) windings so that the core of the vertical heat exchanger coils protrudes through the center of the ring conductor (directional gyro-armature).

When the electromagnet (heat exchanger coils) is energized, the ring conductor (or armature) is instantly shot into the air, taking the craft as a complete unit along with it.

If the current is controlled by a computerized resistance (rheostat), the ring conductor armature and craft can be made to hover or float in the Earth's atmosphere.

The electromagnet (heat exchanger) hums and the armature ring (or torus) becomes quite hot. In fact, if the electrical current is high enough, the ring will glow dull red or rust orange with heat.

The phenomenon (outward sign of a working law of

257

nature) is brought about by an induced current effect identical with an ordinary transformer.

As the repulsion between the electromagnet (heat exchanger) and the ring conductor (armature) is mutual, one can imagine the craft being effected and responding to the repulsion phenomenon as a complete unit.

Lift or repulsion is generated because of close proximity of the field magnet (heat exchanger) to the ring conductor (armature). Clendenon says that lift would always be vertically opposed to the gravitational pull of the planet Earth, but repulsion can be employed to cause fore and aft propulsion. For more information on Clendenon's technical details on his proposed craft, see his book, *Mercury, UFO Messenger of the Gods*.[16]

VORTEX PROPULSION

Once a vortex field has been created, the propulsion of the craft is seemingly quite natural.

A number of authors, including John Walker in his article on vortex technology in *Anti-Gravity & the Unified Field*[91] point out that a vortex IS a gravity focal point. That the very motion of rotating or spinning indicates an exchange is taking place between the center and the outside of the motion.

Walker discusses the "Searl Ether Converter" and then tells how he would build a vortex craft: "John Searl was living in England in 1949 and employed at the time as an electrical fitter and cultivated much interest in electricity even though he had no formal education on the subject other than required by his job. Undaunted by conventional ideas he carried out his own investigations into electrical motors and generators. During work on this he noticed that a small EMF was produced by spinning metal parts whereby he proceeded to augment the effect by using slip rings in various ways. He noticed that when the annulus were spinning freely his hair bristled in the field created. He decided to build a generator based on the principle.

"By 1952, the first generator (converter of ether) had been constructed and tested by Searl and a friend. It was about three feet in diameter and was set in motion by a small engine. The device produced the expected electrical power, but at an unexpectedly high potential on the order of 100,000 volts. While still speeding up the generator broke loose from the engine and rose to a height of about 50 feet. Here the rotor stayed for a while, still speeding up, with the air in the immediate vicinity of the rotor turning a pink like halo around it. Finally the whole works accelerated at a fantastic rate and is thought to have gone off into space. Since that day, Searl and others have made a number of small flying craft, some of which have also been lost. A form of control was developed and later craft 12 to 30 feet in diameter have been built.

"Some interesting side light to the effects produced by the craft are:

"1. Levity

"2. Very high electrostatic fields.

"3. The fields generated interact with radio receivers in the area.

"4. Once the machine passes a threshold of potential, the energy output exceeds the energy input.

"5. Above threshold potential, the generator (read: converter) becomes inertia free. It has no apparent mass.

"6. The effects of the field around the craft that ionize the local air, also produce a near vacuum around it. However, the effects especially around the equatorial plane of the craft, have a tendency to push outside matter away from it. A type of force field as it were.

"7. The preferred direction of travel at ultra-high speeds is away from the planet, the plane of the generator-rotor being at 90 degrees to the gravity field. When in horizontal flight the craft takes up an angle to the gravity field suggestive of the balance between two similar vector fields. In other words, the craft tilts or dips in the horizontal direction it is going.

"8. Matter snatch during acceleration. This occurs when the craft is on the ground, and the drive is suddenly turned on. The rising craft takes part of the ground with it. If it were flying low over water, the water would peak up toward the bottom of the craft. The device cannot possibly be pushing itself away from the Earth if it is picking up matter from underneath.

"9. If the craft hovers low to the ground too long, the ground becomes warm and the grass burnt. Also when flying in humid conditions precipitation or slight small cloud formations occur on the top side or around the craft.

"The last effect, precipitation, was also noted by Nikola Tesla in his laboratory, for his energy producing coils were spiral configurations which created gravity focal points where water molecules became attracted above and around the top of the coil.

"It should be pointed out with Searl's craft, that only a small amount of space fabric (ether) is converted for energy. However, small changes in the ether lead to large physical effects because of the wave energy's high potential.

"What I've listed above have been noted at one time or another as being effects from UFO activity as well. The Searl Ether Converter is real and is being worked on somewhere in the world. I can explain ALL of these effects simply by overlapping them with Gravity Vortex Mechanics."[91]

Walker goes on to say, "If I were to build a ring or rotor based motion system, the most natural type of vessel to contain it in would be round like a common motor. If I were to design my rotor like a flat plate, naturally my containment vessel would be saucer or convex lens shaped. The fact that it is lens shaped also assists the whole craft to act as a focussing instrument. If you've ever seen a magnifying lens used to make a fire, the smoke allows you to see light streams pass through the lens to create a cone. Where the cone is smallest at its apex, that's the energy concentration point.

"Essentially the form of a saucer follows exactly its

function to create a rotating potential — gravity vortex. It works with nature. The reason a disc craft would have more of a structure to it on the top side indicates room for pilot quarters and focal control coils, or in the case of remote craft, just the coils.

"If you just build a flat rotor that produced a rotating field, space would curve in toward the center and then it would curve back out again. However, if you added a couple of more coils above the rotor, the top one being smallest, now you are shaping the field. A good example for a model would be a 3 foot rotor, a 2 foot coil above that, and your top coil is say - 9 inches in diameter. Now space curves in and is confined to smaller and smaller concentric rings. By the time it is leaving the topside it is almost pointed. It is focused. Focusing coils are not a new concept I just thought of. If you know even the basics of television you would know that focus coils are utilized to pinpoint and direct the tube electron beam against the screen. The principles speak for themselves."[91]

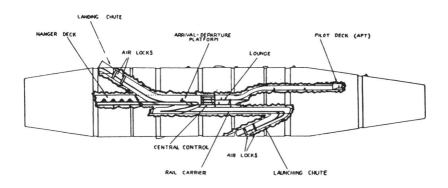

A technical drawing of the interior of the spaceship that George Adamski claimed to have traveled in.

261

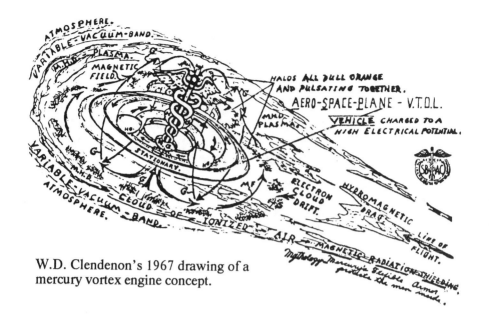

W.D. Clendenon's 1967 drawing of a
mercury vortex engine concept.

A medieval Rosicrucian alchemical diagram in which mercury plays
an important part. The symbols and concentric circles seem to
correspond to various elements as well as the electromagnetic fields
of an atom. According to the legend, "Whoever deciphers the
alchemical riddle will be able to journey through lands otherwise
inaccessible."

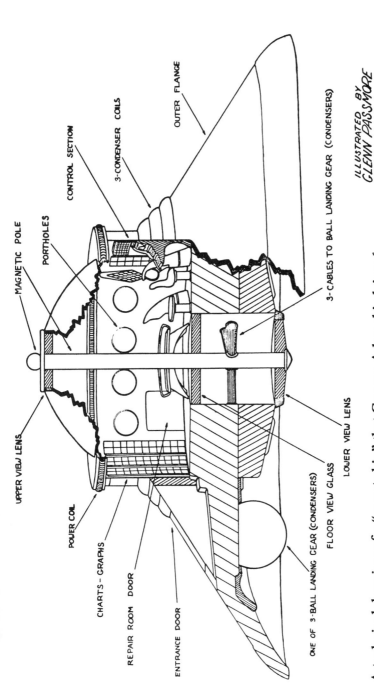

MAGNETIC POLE

PORTHOLES

CONTROL SECTION

3-CONDENSER COILS

OUTER FLANGE

UPPER VIEW LENS

POWER COIL

CHARTS - GRAPHS

REPAIR ROOM DOOR

ENTRANCE DOOR

ONE OF 3-BALL LANDING GEAR (CONDENSERS)

FLOOR VIEW GLASS

LOWER VIEW LENS

3-CABLES TO BALL LANDING GEAR (CONDENSERS)

ILLUSTRATED BY
GLENN PASSMORE

A technical drawing of a "scout ship" that George Adamski claimed to have ridden in during the early 1950's. Clendenon argues that this craft was powered by Mercury Vortex motors utilizing the condensers, coils and electromagnetic fields set up within the craft.

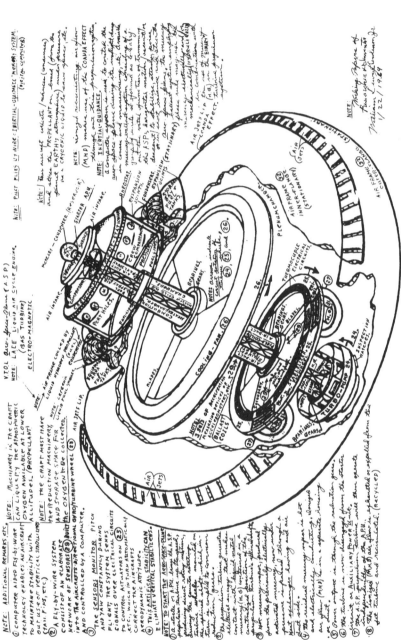

W.D. Clendenon's illustration of his concept of a Mercury Vortex Discoid craft. This is his basic concept of the propulsion of at least one type of Vimana. Many current UFOs may well use a variant on this design. Clendenon believes that George Adamski's craft was also a Mercury Vortex Vimana.

At 3:00 in the afternoon on March 8, 1964, Harry Hauxler of West Germany took this photo of discoid craft through the window of a train near Oberwesel. Note the whirling dark vortex beneath the rising craft. This craft may well be a Vimana with a mercury vortex propulsion system. Photo courtesy of UFO Photo Archives, Tuscon, Arizona.

At about 4:30 in the afternoon on July 19, 1952, Customs Inspector Domingo Troncoso took this photo at Puerto Maldonado, Peru. The object was estimated to be over 100 feet long with a thick vapor, smoke or whitish substance coming out of the back. At a time when cylindrical airships were no longer being manufactured (officially) this craft seems very similar to many vimanas and vailxi as described in texts. Photo courtesy of UFO Photo Archives, Tuscon, Arizona.

DIRECTIONAL GYRO

Flew along the path defined by a space stabilized
directional gyro, it would be flying straight in space. This
could not be the same as flying North, since flying North is
a curved line in space. This effect is sometimes called
apparent drift due to meridian convergence. It is also
called North steaming error--and the amount of error depends
upon speed and latitude.

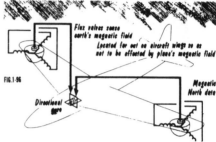

FIG.1-96

Flux valves sense earth's magnetic field
Located far out on aircraft wings so as not to be affected by plane's magnetic field

Directional gyro

Magnetic North data

NOTE: "Two ping pong balls on bottom side of airplane
wing." B. Clendenon

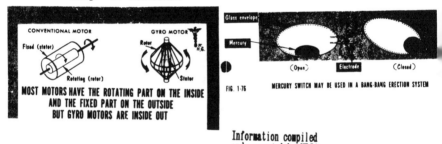

CONVENTIONAL MOTOR

Fixed (stator)

Rotating (rotor)

GYRO MOTOR

Rotor

Stator

MOST MOTORS HAVE THE ROTATING PART ON THE INSIDE
AND THE FIXED PART ON THE OUTSIDE
BUT GYRO MOTORS ARE INSIDE OUT

FIG. 1-76

Glass envelope

Mercury

(Open) Electrode (Closed)

MERCURY SWITCH MAY BE USED IN A BANG-BANG ERECTION SYSTEM

Information compiled
and arranged by WDCjr
(including notations)

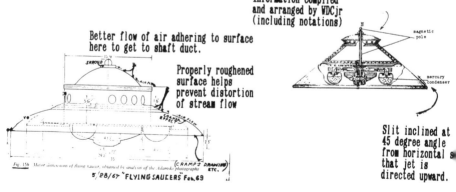

Better flow of air adhering to surface
here to get to shaft duct.

Properly roughened
surface helps
prevent distortion
of stream flow

magnetic pole

mercury condenser

Fig. 156 *Major dimensions of flying Saucer, obtained by analysis of the Adamski photographs*

(CRAMPS DRAWING ETC.)

5/28/67 "FLYING SAUCERS Feb.69

Slit inclined at
45 degree angle
from horizontal s
that jet is
directed upward.

Clendenon claims that directional gyros are already in use in many craft

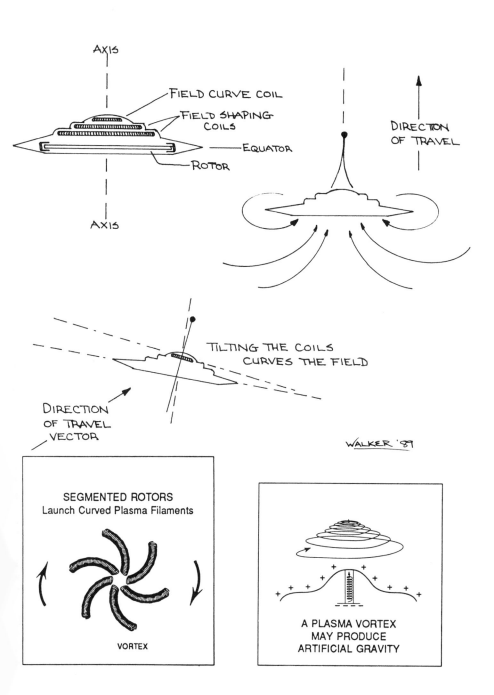

AXIS

FIELD CURVE COIL

FIELD SHAPING COILS

EQUATOR

ROTOR

AXIS

DIRECTION OF TRAVEL

TILTING THE COILS CURVES THE FIELD

DIRECTION OF TRAVEL VECTOR

WALKER '89

SEGMENTED ROTORS
Launch Curved Plasma Filaments

VORTEX

A PLASMA VORTEX
MAY PRODUCE
ARTIFICIAL GRAVITY

DISC DYNAMICS - Shaping and directing the vortex for travel by levity.

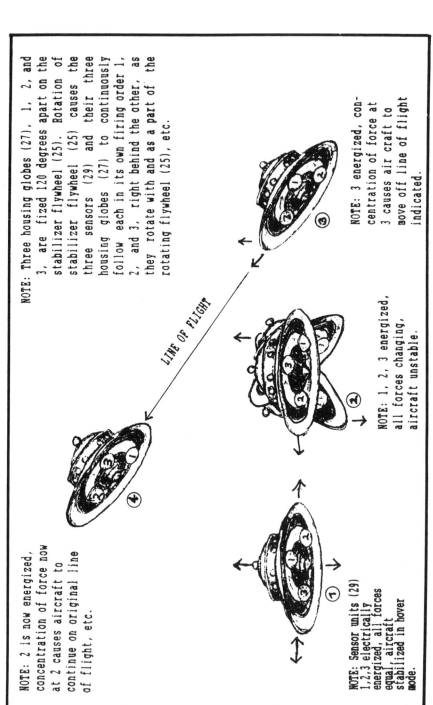

NOTE: Three housing globes (27), 1, 2, and 3, are fixed 120 degrees apart on the stabilizer flywheel (25). Rotation of stabilizer flywheel (25) causes the three sensors (29) and their three housing globes (27) to continuously follow each in its own firing order 1, 2, and 3, right behind the other, as they rotate with and as a part of the rotating flywheel (25), etc.

NOTE: 3 energized, concentration of force at 3 causes air craft to move off line of flight indicated.

NOTE: 2 is now energized, concentration of force now at 2 causes aircraft to continue on original line of flight, etc.

LINE OF FLIGHT

NOTE: 1, 2, 3 energized, all forces changing, aircraft unstable.

NOTE: Sensor units (29) 1,2,3 electrically energized, all forces equal, aircraft stabilized in hover mode.

Clendenon's illustration of how a discoid Vimana would use the electrified mercury vortex housing globes (directional gyros) for travel.

7

ATLANTIS
& THE
ATLANTEAN VAILX

You were an engineer and manufacturer
during many of your incarnations in the *Poseid
Empire.* The device for taking motive power
directly from the atmosphere was perfected about
twenty thousand years ago, and you were among
the many who understood its workings. Perhaps
you may be instrumental in its rediscovery.

—*The mysterious Dr. White to a young man
in the 1963 book, The Ultimate Frontier*[46]

§§§

The subject of Atlantis and the aircraft allegedly used by
this famous, though controversial, lost civilization is a far
more difficult topic to discuss than that of Vimana's used in
ancient India. While authentic texts still exist from ancient
India with which we can base our study of ancient Indian
aircraft, the same cannot be said for Atlantis.

It is the advantage of ancient India over other ancient

269

civilizations that many of the ancient books have been kept safe and retranslated from the distant days of the Rama Empire, while most other nations of the time have had most of their ancient records destroyed, such as in China, Egypt, Central America, Peru and other areas. Many of these ancient nations are now either desert wastelands, swallowed by thick jungle or literally at the bottom of some ocean or sea. Yet, India, despite devastation by wars and invasion, managed to maintain a large part of its ancient history.

It is not the purpose of this book to argue for or against the existence of a former continent in the Atlantic Ocean called Atlantis. Rather, for the sake of the discussion at hand, that of ancient aircraft used approximately six to sixteen thousand years ago, we will assume that such a nation existed and that they had a high form of technology similar to that of ancient India.

The knowledge of this technology comes largely from metaphysical texts such as Edgar Cayce, the Theosophical Society, the Lemurian Fellowship and other similar groups. For this book we will focus largely on two sources, that of Edgar Cayce and the books *A Dweller On Two Planets* and *An Earth Dweller Returns.*

Known as the "sleeping clairvoyant," Edgar Cayce was born on March 18, 1877 on a farm near Hopkinskinville, Kentucky. Even as a child he displayed powers of perception which seem to extend beyond the normal range of perception. In 1898 at the age of twenty-one he became a salesman for a wholesale stationery company and developed a gradual paralysis of the throat muscles which threatened the loss of his voice. When doctors were unable to find a cause for the strange paralysis, he began to see a hypnotist. During a trance, the first of many for Cayce, he recommended medication and manipulative therapy which successfully restored his voice and cured his throat trouble.

He began doing readings for people, mostly of a medical nature, for people and on October 9, 1910, *The New York*

Times carried two pages of headlines and pictures on the Cayce phenomenon. By the time Edgar Cayce died on January 3, 1945, in Virginia Beach, Virginia, he left well over fourteen thousand documented stenographic records of the telepathic-clairvoyant statements he had given for more than eight thousand different people over a period of forty-three years. These typewritten documents are referred to as "readings". Important to our discussion in this book is that many of these "readings" concern Atlantis, persons former lives in Atlantis, and the airships and motive power used in Atlantis.[65]

In reading 2437-1; Jan. 23, 1941 told his subject: "in Atlantean land during those periods of greater expansion as to ways, means and manners of applying greater conveniences for the people of the land—things of transportation, the aeroplane as called today, but then as ships of the air, for they sailed not only in the air but in other elements also."

A number of persons who came to Cayce for individual life readings were, according to Cayce's reading, once navigators or engineers on these aircraft: "in Atlantean land when there were the developments of those things as made for motivative forces as carried the peoples into the various portions of the land and to other lands. Entity a navigator of note then." (2124-3, Oct. 2, 1931)

"in Atlantean land when peoples understood the the law of universal forces entity able to carry messages through space to the other lands, guided crafts of that period." (2494-1; Feb. 76, 1930)

Cayce called the motive power used in these vessels the "nightside of life.": "in Atlantean land or Poseidia—entity ruled in pomp and power and in understanding of the mysteries of the application of that often termed the nightside of life, or in applying the universal forces as understood in that period." (2897-1; Dec. 15, 1929)

"in Atlantean period of those peoples that gained much in understanding of mechanical laws and application of nightside of life for destruction." (2896-1; May 2, 1930)

Cayce speaks of the use of crystals or "firestones" for energy and related applications. He also speaks of the misuse of power and warnings of destruction to come: "in Atlantean land during the periods of exodus due to foretelling or foreordination of activities which were bringing about destructive forces. Among those who were not only in Yucatan but in the Pyrenees and Egyptian land, for the manners of transportation and communications through airships of that period were such as Ezekiel described at a much later date." (4353-4; Nov. 26, 1939. See Ezekiel 1:15-25, 10:9-17 RSV.)

"...in Atlantis when there were activities that brought about the second upheaval in the land. Entity was what would be in the present the electrical engineer—applied those forces or influences for airplanes, ships, and what you would toady call radio for constructive or destructive purposes." (1574-1; April 19, 1938)

"...in Atlantean land before the second destruction when there was the dividing of islands, when the temptations were begun in activities of Sons of Belial and children of the Law of One. Entity among those that interpreted the messages received through the crystals and the fires that were to be the eternal fires of nature. New developments in air and water travel are no surprise to this entity as these were beginning development at that period for escape." (3004-1; May 15, 1943)

"...in Atlantean land at time of development of electrical forces that dealt with transportation of craft from place to place, photographing at a distance, overcoming gravity itself, preparation of the crystal, the terrible mighty crystal; much of this brought destruction." (519-1; Feb. 20, 1934)

"...in city of Peos in Atlantis—among people who gained understanding of application of nightside of life or negative influences in the earth's spheres, of those who gave much understanding to the manner of sound, voice

272

and picture and such to peoples of that period." (2856-1; June 7, 1930)

"...in Poseidia the entity dwelt among those that had charge of the storage of the motivative forces from the great crystals that so condensed the lights, the forms of the activities, as to guide the ships in the sea and in the air and in conveniences of the body as television and recording voice." (813-1; Feb. 5, 1935)

The use of crystals as an important part of the technology is mentioned in a very long reading from Dec. 29, 1933: "About the firestone—the entity's activities then made such applications as dealt both with the constructive as well as destructive forces in that period. It would be well that there be given something of a description of this so that it may be understood better by the entity in the present.

"In the center of a building which would today be said to be lined with nonconductive stone—something akin to asbestos, with . . . other nonconductors such as are now being manufactured in England under a name is well known to many of those who deal in such things.

"The building above the stone was oval; or a dome wherein there could be . . . a portion for rolling back, so that the activity of the stars—the concentration of energies that emanate from bodies that are on fire themselves, along with elements that are found and not found in the earth's atmosphere.

"The concentration through the prisms or glass (as would be called in the present) was in such manner that it acted upon the instruments which were connected with the various modes of travel through induction methods which made much the [same] character of control as would in the present day be termed remote control through radio vibrations or directions; though the kind of force impelled from the stone acted upon the motivation forces in the crafts themselves.

"The building was constructed so that when the dome was rolled back there might be little or no hindrance in the

273

direct application of power to various crafts that were to be impelled through space—whether within the radius of vision or whether directed under water or under other elements, or through other elements.

"The preparation of this stone was solely in the hands of the initiates at the time; and the entity was among those directed the influences of radiation which arose, in the form of rays that were invisible to the eye but acted upon the stones themselves as set in the motivating forces — whether the aircraft were lifted by the gases of the period; or whether for guiding the more-of-pleasure vehicles that might pass along close to the earth, or crafts on the water or under the water.

"These, then, were impelled by the concentration of rays from the stone which was centered in the middle of the power station, or powerhouse (as would be the term in the present).

"In the active forces of these, the entity brought destructive forces by setting up—in various portions of the land—the kind that was to act in producing powers for the various forms of the people's activities in the same cities, the towns, and the countries surrounding same. These, not intentionally, were tuned too high; and brought the second period of destructive forces to the people of the land—and broke up the land into those isles which later became the scene of further destructive forces in the land.

"Through the same form of fire the bodies of individuals were regenerated; by burning—through application of rays from the stone—the influences that brought destructive forces to an animal organism. Hence the body often rejuvenated itself; and it remained in that land until the eventual destruction; joining with the peoples who made for the breaking up of the land—or joining with Belial, at the final destruction of the land. In this, the entity lost. At first it was not the intention nor desire for destructive forces. Later it was for ascension of power itself.

"As for a description of the manner of construction of

the stone: we find it was a large cylindrical glass (as would be termed today); cut with facets in such manner that the capstone on top of it made for centralizing the power or force that concentrated between the end of the cylinder and the capstone itself. As indicated, the records as to ways of constructing same are in three places in the earth, as it stands today: in the sunken portion of Atlantis, or Poseidia, where a portion of the temples may yet be discovered under the slime of ages of sea water—near what is known as Bimini, off the coast of Florida. And (secondly) in the temple records that were in Egypt, where the entity acted later in cooperation with others towards preserving the records that came from the land where these had been kept. Also (thirdly) in records that were carried to what is now Yucatan, in America, where these stones (which they know so little about) are now—during the last few months—being uncovered." (440-5; Dec. 20, 1933)

§§§

Even more specific material on the airships of Atlantis, or Poseid, as the country was allegedly known to it occupants, can be found in two unusual books, A *Dweller On Two Planets*[71] and *An Earth Dweller Returns.* [72]

A Dweller On Two Planets was first dictated in 1884 by "Phylos the Thibetan" to a young Californian named Frederick Spencer Oliver who wrote the dictations down in manuscript form in 1886. The book was not published until 1899, when it was finally released as a book. In 1940, the sequel, *An Earth Dweller Returns* was published by The Lemurian Fellowship of Ramona, California. Also accredited to "Phylos the Thibetan" this book was allegedly dictated to Beth Nimrai. Both books are the long and complicated history of a number of persons and the karma created by each of them during their many lives, especially the karmic relationships and events of the "amanuensis" Frederick Spencer Oliver and his different lives as

Rexdahl, Aisa and Mainin with the many lives of "Phylos" as Ouardl, Zo Lahm, Zailm and Walter Pierson.

Both books are a complicated, and often difficult to follow collection of past lives and the cycles of karma and rebirth between no less then eight people, men and women, which also includes Beth Nimrai, the amanuensis of the later book *An Earth Dweller Returns.*

An Earth Dweller Returns is largely an attempt to correct and clarify much of the material in *A Dweller On Two Planets* and both books contain a great deal of detailed information on the life, times, culture and technology of ancient Atlantis, including the airships which were called Vailxi in plural and Vailx in singular.

A Dweller On Two Planets has remained a popular occult book for a nearly a century largely because it contains detailed descriptions of devices and technology which were unquestionably well in advance of the time frame in which it was written. As the book cover of one of the editions of the book states "One of the greatest wonders of our times is the uncanny way in which *A Dweller On Two Planets* predicted inventions which modern technology fulfilled after the writing of the book."[71]

Among the inventions and devices mentioned in both books are Air Conditioners, to overcome deadly and noxious vapors; Airless Cylinder Lamps, tubes of crystal illuminated by the "night side forces"; Electric Rifles, guns employing electricity as a propulsive force (rail-guns are similar, and very new invention); Mono-Rail Transportation; Water Generators, an instrument for condensing water from the atmosphere; and the Vailx, an aerial ship governed by forces of levitation and repulsion.

Much of the wording and terms are identical to the Edgar Cayce readings, such as "night side forces" and the term "Poseid" for Atlantis. While verification of any of the information in both books is impossible, the material is fascinating and of definite interest to any student of the Vimanas of ancient India. In chapter two of *A Dweller On*

276

Two Planets the hero, Zailm (an earlier incarnation of Phylos and Walter Pierson) visits Caiphul, the capital of Atlantis, and views many wonderful electronic devices and the monorail system.

In chapter four the electromagnetic airships of Atlantis are introduced along with radio and television (don't forget, this book was written in 1886). It is explained that the airships, similar to zeppelins, but more like a cigar-shaped airship, are electro-magnetic-gravitational and are capable of entering the water as a submarine or traveling through the air. Later, in chapter sixteen, Zailm takes a journey via Vailx to "Suern" which is apparently ancient India or thereabouts.

In chapter eighteen Zailm visit "Umaurean" (present day American) colonies of Poseid. In a fascinating portion of the book, the Vailx stops for the night to visit a building on the summit of the Tetons. According to the text, "On the tallest of these had stood, perhaps for five centuries, a building made of heavy slabs of granite. It had originally been erected for the double purpose of worship of Incal (the Sun, or God), and astronomical calculations, but was used in my day as a monastery. There was no path up the peak, and the sole means of access was by vailx."

Frederick Spencer Oliver then alleges in a break in the story that such massive, granite slab-walls were discovered in 1886 by a Professor Hayden, allegedly the first person to climb Grand Teton. Whether such massive granite slabs, certainly in poor condition and probably thought to be naturally, do indeed exist on or near the summit of Grand Teton, I have no way of knowing.

Afterwards they visit the ancient copper mines of the Lake Superior region (which do indeed exist and are archaeological fact, nor satisfactorily explained) and then return to Poseid, making part of the journey underwater.

Back in Atlantis (Poseid) Zailm makes the mistake of getting involved with two women at the same time and karmic repercussions are severe when, about to marry one of the women, the other exposes him and tragedy follows when both women are killed. One commits suicide and the other stands in the Maxin Light, a kind-of super energy beam in the center of the great temple, analogous to the similar Edgar Cayce reading (440-5; Dec. 20, 1933). This Maxin Light is also similar to the giant energy towers designed by the great inventor Nikola Tesla to be built in the 1930s, but never produced.

In chapter eighteen, Zailm speeds away in his private Vailx and wanders for a time searching for gold in South America, using an electronic mineral detector, a water generator and an electric rifle. While searching for gold he is trapped in a small cavern by the evil priest Mainin (who is an early incarnation of Frederick Spencer Oliver, the amaneusis of the book) and dies.

Later in the book, a few incarnations later, Zailm (Phylos) is taken astral traveling to Venus, hence the title of the book *A Dweller On Two Planets* This part of the book is somewhat reminiscent of the Hari Krishna publication *Easy Journey To Other Planets* by Swami Prabhupada.[77]

The second book, *An Earth Dweller's Return*,[72] much of the text is used in explaining elements of *A Dweller On Two Planets* that was left unexplained, particularly the karmic relationship between Phylos himself and Frederick Spencer Oliver. However a great deal of this book goes into the science of Atlantis including the cause of gravitational attraction; heat, magnetism and motion, transmutation of matter, the Maxin Light, another energy tower known as the Maxt, airless cylinder light, levitation and much more.

Part Five of the book is entitled *Description Of A Journey By Vailx* According to the text, "the Atlantean vailx was an air vessel motivated by currents derived from the Night Side of Nature.

"Altitude was dependent wholly upon pleasure. For this reason wide views were possible with a great variety of scenery. The rooms of the vailx were warmed by *Navaz* (Night Side of Nature) forces and furnished with the

278

proper density of air by the same means. So rapidly did the aspect of things change beneath, that the spectator, looking backwards, gazed upon a dissolving view.

"The currents, derived from the Night Sides of Nature, permitted the attainment of the same rate of speed as the diurnal rotation of the earth. For example, suppose we were at an altitude of ten miles and that the time was the instant of the sun's meridian. At that meridian moment, we could remain indefinitely bows on, while the earth revolved beneath at approximately seventeen miles per minute. Or the reverse direction keys could be set, and our vailx would rush away from its position at the same almost frightful speed—frightful to one unused to it, but not so to the returning Atlanteans who, in the Aquarian Age to come, will travel the highways of the land, sea and air without a thought of fear."[72]

On the trip in the Vailx is beset by a storm: "The repulse keys were set., and presently we were so high in the air that all about our now closed ship were cirrus clouds—clouds of hail held aloft by the uprising of the winds which were severe enough to have been dangerous had our vessel been propelled by wings, fans, or gas reservoirs.

"But as we derived our forces of propulsion and repulsion from Nature's Night Side, or in Poseid phraseology, from *Navaz*, our long white aerial spindles feared no storm however severe. . . .The evening had not far advanced when it was suggested that the storm would most likely be wilder near the earth, and so the repulse keys were set to a fixed degree, making nearer approach to the ground impossible as an accidental occurrence."

The chapter continues to speak of the journey, mentioning the destination, Suernis (India) and the air dispensers with wheels and pistons that pressurize the cabin. In Section 418 of the text it states, "The vailx used was about the middle traffic size. these vessels were made in four standard lengths; number one, about twenty-five feet; number two, eighty feet; number three about one hundred

279

fifty-five feet; while the largest was approximately three hundred feet in length.

"These long spindles were round, hollow needles of aluminum, comprising an outer and an inner shell between which were placed many thousands of double 'T' braces, an arrangement productive of intense rigidity and strength. Other partitions made other braces of additional resistant force. From amidships the vessels tapered toward either end to sharp points. Most vailxi were provided with an arrangement which allowed an open promenade deck at one end. The vailx which Zailm used was about fifteen feet and seven inches in diameter.

"Crystal windows of enormous resistant strength were arranged in rows like port holes along the sides, with a few on top and several others set in the floor, thus affording a view in all directions."[72]

What is fascinating in reading descriptions of so-called Atlantean Vailxi in these books, as well as there brief descriptions in the Edgar Cayce readings, is their similarity to the descriptions of Vimanas in ancient Indian texts and their similarity with a number of UFO craft seen in present times.

As the back cover paragraph on *A Dweller On Two Planets* points out, this book, and its description of a long, cylindrical, cigar-shaped aircraft, is a haunting premonition of not only many UFOs seen today, but of a type of craft that may yet be produced by a manufacturer in the near future!

At least several types of Vimana aircraft is described by the ancient texts as circular in characteristics, which can either mean it is discoid, as in the mercury vortex type of propulsion, or it is cylindrical, as in the Vailx type of craft allegedly of Atlantis. That some of the UFO sightings of similar type craft of the past forty years might somehow be Atlantean or Indian type Vailx or Vimana is a fantastic notion that apparently has never been considered by either the scientific community nor by current UFO investigators.

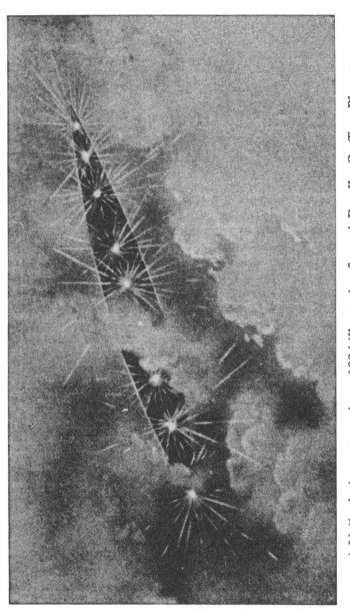

A Vailx during a storm in an 1884 illustration from *A Dweller On Two Planets.*
Note the lights along the side of the craft.

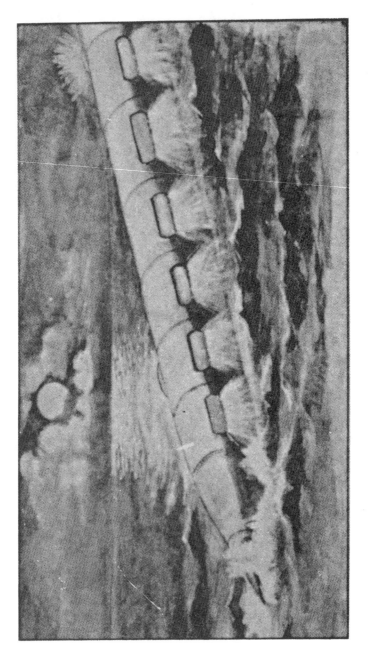

A Vailx enters the water in an 1884 illustration from *A Dweller On Two Planets*. Note the lights along the side of the craft.

bove: An Atlantean Vailx leaves the shore upon a journey. Notice its similarity to certain
edleshaped UFOs. Below: An electro-odic transit carriage scene from Atlantis illstrating
me of the technology. Both drawings from the 1940 book *An Earth Dweller's Return.*

Atlantean Inventions

AIR CONDITIONER — *Deadly and noxious vapors overcome by purification.*

AIRLESS CYLINDER LAMPS — *Tubes of crystal illuminated by the Night Side Forces.*

BOOK MACHINE — *A psychic apparatus to reproduce the voice of characters in literature.*

CALORIVEYANT INSTRUMENT — *Heat producing apparatus powered by the Night Side of Nature.*

CRIME CURING APPARATUS — *A machine designed to transmute desires of convicted criminals.*

ELECTRIC RIFLES — *Guns employing electricity as propulsive force.*

GRAND ORGAN — *Color and tone instrument soon to be rediscovered.*

IRIDESCENT LIGHTS — *High tension odic-electric lamps diffusing a multi-colored radiance.*

MAXIN LIGHT — *An Unfed Light sustained by super physical power.*

MONO-RAIL TRANSPORTATION — *Locomotion in use for high speed transit.*

NAIM — *Radio and Television*

NOISELESS MACHINERY — *Machines cushioned by synthetic shock absorbers.*

TRANSMUTATION OF METALS — *Apparatus powered by electrical action.*

VAILX — *An aerial ship governed by forces of levitation and repulsion.*

WATER GENERATOR — *An instrument for condensing water from the atmosphere.*

VOCAL NEWS RECORD — *A machine for printing the spoken word.*

From the Lemurian Fellowship, 1940.

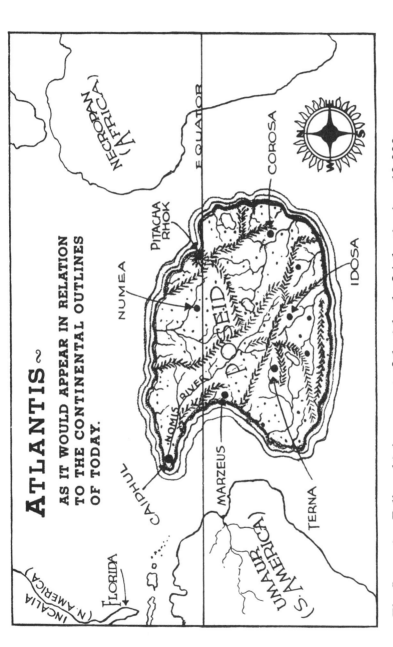

ATLANTIS ~

AS IT WOULD APPEAR IN RELATION TO THE CONTINENTAL OUTLINES OF TODAY.

INCALIA (N. AMERICA)

FLORIDA

CAIPHUL

NOMIS RIVER

NUMEA

POSEID

PITACA RHOK

NECROPAN (AFRICA)

EQUATOR

COROSA

IDOSA

MARZEUS

UMAURICA (S. AMERICA)

TERNA

N
E
W
S

The Lemurian Fellowship's concept of the island of Atlantis circa 10,000 B.C. It includes several major cities that supposedly existed at that time.

The giant Maxt Light that radiated power into the atmosphere as a kind of radio station sending out electricity to the world. From the Lemurian Fellowship, 1940.

This drawing of Nikola Tesla's Warcliff Tower being built in Long Island, New York, appeared in the June, 1919 issue of Electrical Experimenter. Like the alleged Maxt or Maxin Light of Atlantis, it was to broadcast power to the world. An anti-gravity airship, drawing power from the tower, hovers nearby. Note the powerful searchlight on the front of the ship.

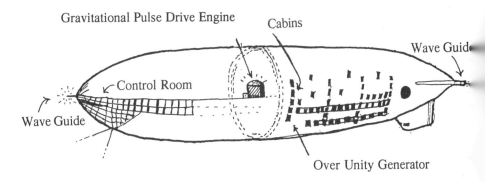

Gravitational Pulse Drive Engine   Cabins

Wave Guide

Control Room

Wave Guide

Over Unity Generator

Two concepts of a cylindrical vimana craft powered by electo-gravitic motors and devices.

8

VIMANAS TODAY

§§§

In the late years of the last century, a number of unusual airship sightings were made which may well have been of Vimana craft. In 1873 at Bonham, Texas, workers in a cotton field suddenly saw a shiny, silver object that came streaking down from the sky at them. Terrified, they ran away, while the "great silvery serpent" as some people described it, swung around and dived at them again. A team of horses ran away the driver was thrown beneath the wheels of the wagon and killed. A few hours later that same day in Fort Riley, Kansas, a similar "airship" swooped down out of the skies at a cavalry parade and terrorized the horses to such an extent that the cavalry drill ended in a tumult.

The great "Airship Flap of 1897" actually started in November, 1896 in San Francisco, California when hundreds of residents saw a large, elongated, dark object that used brilliant searchlights and moved against the wind, traveling northwest across Oakland. A few hours later reports came from other northern California cities: Santa Rosa, Chico, Sacramento and Red Bluff—all describing what appears to be the same airship, a cigar shaped craft. It is quite possible that this craft was heading for Mount Shasta in northern California.

The airship moved very slowly and majestically, flying low at times, and at night, shining its powerful searchlight on the ground. It is worth noting here, as Jacques Vallee did in his book *Dimensions*,[25] that the airship could do exactly as it cared to, because unlike today, it ran no risk of being pursued. There were no jet squadrons to be scrambled after the aerial intruder, nor anti-aircraft guns or surface to air missiles to shoot down this trespassing craft in the sky.

However, the airship, clearly not a typical balloon or gas-filled airship of the time, did at times move erratically, sometimes it would depart "as a shot out of a gun," change course abruptly, change altitude at great speed, circle and land and, as previously mentioned, use powerful searchlights to sweep the countryside.[25]

These mysterious airships were seen across the United States, from California to Nebraska, Texas, Colorado, Kansas, Iowa, Missouri, Wisconsin and Minnesota, including many heavily populated urban areas such as Omaha and Milwaukee. On April 10, 1897, thousands of people in Chicago reported seeing a cigar shaped airship.

It is generally agreed that the many accounts of the airship could not be attributed to known airships or technology of the time. The first powered flight was Giffard's steam airship built in 1852, while the Tissandier brothers built the first electric airship in 1883. Renard and Kreb's electric airship, the *La France*, was first flown at Chalais-Meudon in 1884. The Schwartz aluminum rigid airship was first flown at Tempelhofer Field, Germany, in 1897 and the first "successful" airship, the *Lebaudy* was test flown in Paris in 1903.[83]

A great deal has been made of the airship flap of 1897 in UFO circles, typically seeking to prove that the airships were extraterrestrial vehicles. Yet, as Jacques Vallee points out in *Dimensions*,25 the evidence does not point toward extraterrestrial occupants because those airship operators who engaged in conversation with witness "were indistinguishable from the average American population of the time."

Many of the occupants did indeed converse with locals and occasionally they offered earth bound spectators rides—though no one ever seemed to take up the offers. In a curious incident at Hot Springs, Arkansas (a sight of natural crystals, essential for Vimanas, according to Indian texts) on the night of May 6, 1897, Constable Sumpter and Deputy Sheriff McLemore witnessed an airship land on a rainy night. Drawing their Winchesters they demanded an occupant to identify himself and the airship. A man with a long dark beard came forth with a lantern in his hand (possibly electric?) and "on being informed who we were proceeded to tell us that he and the others—a young man and a woman—were traveling through the country in an airship. We could plainly distinguish the outlines of the vessel, which was cigar-shaped and about sixty feet long, and looking just like the the cuts that have appeared in the papers recently. It was dark and raining and the young man was filling a big sack with water about thirty yards away, and the woman was particular to keep back in the dark. She was holding an umbrella over her head. The man with the whiskers invited us to take a ride, saying that he could take us where it was not raining. We told him we believed we preferred to get wet.

"Asking the man why the brilliant light was turned on and off so much, he replied that the light was so powerful that it consumed a great deal of his motive power... Being in a hurry we left and upon our return, about forty minutes later, nothing was to be seen. We did not hear or see the airship when it departed."[25]

In another fascinating and revealing report, this one from the *Houston Post* of April 22, 1897, a Mr. John M. Barclay living near Houston witnessed an airship on the ground on the night of April 21 at about 11:00 P.M. "It was a peculiar shaped body, with an oblong shape, with wings and side attachments of various sizes and shapes. There were bright lights, which appeared much brighter than electric lights. When he first saw it, it seemed perfectly stationary about five yards from the ground. It circled a few times and gradually descended to the ground in a pasture adjacent to his house. He took his Winchester and went down to investigate. As soon as the ship, or whatever it might be, alighted, the lights went out.

The night was bright enough for a man to be distinguished several yards away, and when within about thirty yards of the ship he was met by an ordinary mortal, who requested him to lay his gun aside as no harm was intended. Whereupon the following conversation ensued. Mr. Barclay inquired: "Who are you and what do you want?" "Never mind about my name, call it Smith. I want some lubricating oil and a couple of cold chisels if you can get them, and some bluestone. I suppose the saw mill hard by has the two former articles and the telegraph operator has the bluestone. Here is a ten-dollar bill: take it and get us these articles and keep the change for your trouble."

"Mr. Barclay said, "What have you got down there? Let me go and see it." He who wanted to be called Smith said: "No, we cannot permit you to approach any nearer, but do as we request you and your kindness will be appreciated, and we will call you some future day and reciprocate your kindness by taking you on a trip."

"Mr. Barclay went and procured the oil and cold chisels, but could not get the bluestone. They had no change and Mr. Barclay tendered him the the ten-dollar bill, but same was refused. The man shook hands with him and thanked him cordially and asked that he not follow him to the vessel. As he left Mr. Barclay called him and asked him where he was from and where he was going. He replied, "From anywhere, but we will be in Greece day after tomorrow." He got on board, when there was again the whirling noise, and the thing was gone, as Mr. Barclay expresses it, like a shot out of a gun. Mr. Barclay is perfectly reliable."[25,84]

While such incidents are baffling to most people, in the context of a Vimana, they do not seem so extraordinary. Jacques Vallee thinks the statement from the stranger that he is "From anywhere, but we will be in Greece day after tomorrow," is absurd. Yet what is absurd about a vague answer as to one's origins and that he plans to be in Greece in two days? In 1897, by the airship technology of the time this was impossible, and what extraterrestrial, asks Vallee, would state that they would be in Greece in two days? For a human Vimana pilot on his way to Greece, the answer seems quite sensible, and that would probably be the amount of time for such a trip.

The airship wave of 1896/1897 will never be fully solved. Of the 100 or so reported sightings across the country, some were obvious hoaxes and fabrications based on the many newspaper articles appearing at the time. Yet, with those genuine sightings, considerable doubt remains as to the nature of these craft. Says Wallace Chariton at the end of his book *The Great Texas Airship Mystery*: "Many 1897 witnesses said they heard a peculiar whirring or whizzing sound that could not be identified. There were several reports that the flying machine hovered in one spot for some time then quickly disappeared traveling at a high rate of speed. There was always at least one light that was frequently described as being the brightest light the witnesses had ever seen and was often said to be considerably more powerful than any incandescent light, which was the only kind they had in 1897. Some witnesses said they saw a bright, fluorescent glow about the ship and many others claimed there were multicolored lights along the sides. If you do any research into reported modern UFO sightings you will find that similar statements occur frequently."

§§§

Closer to our own time period are other disturbingly familiar encounters with ordinary humans in unusual craft. At approximately 11:00 A.M. on April 18, 1961, sixty-year-old chicken farmer Joe Simonton of Eagle River, Wisconsin had a highly unusual encounter. He was attracted outside by a peculiar noise similar to "knobby tires on a wet pavement." Stepping into his yard, he faced a silvery saucer-shaped object, "brighter than chrome," which appeared to be hovering close to the ground without actually touching it. The object was about twelve feet high and thirty feet in diameter.

A hatch opened about five feet from the ground and Simonton saw three men inside the machine. One was dressed in a black two-piece suit. The occupants were about five feet tall. Smooth-shaven, they appeared to "resemble Italians." They had dark hair and skin and wore outfits with turtleneck tops and knit helmets.

One of the men held up a jug apparently made of the same material as the saucer. His motioning to Joe Simonton seemed to indicate that he needed water. Simonton took the jug, went inside the house, and filled it. As he returned, he saw that one of the men inside the saucer was "frying food on a flameless grill of some sort." The interior of the ship was black, "the color of wrought iron." Simonton saw several instrument panels and heard a slow humming sound, similar to the hum of a generator. When he made a motion indicating he was interested in the food, one of the men, who was also dressed in black but with a narrow red trim along the trousers, handed him three cookies, about three inches in diameter and perforated with small holes.

The whole affair lasted about five minutes. Finally, the man closest to the witness attached a kind of belt to a hook in his clothing and closed the hatch in such a way that Simonton could scarcely detect its outline. Then the object rose about twenty feet from the ground before taking off straight south, causing a blast of air that bent some nearby pine trees.

Along the edge of the saucer, the witness recalls, were exhaust pipes six or seven inches in diameter. The hatch was about six feet high and thirty inches wide, and, although the object has always been described as a saucer, its actual shape was that of two inverted bowls.

Simonton later reported to two Sheriff's deputies that he ate one of the cakes, and thought it "tasted like cardboard." The United States Air Force, which examined the remaining two cakes put it more scientifically: "The cake was composed of hydrogenated fat, starch, buckwheat hulls, soya bean hulls, wheat bran. Bacteria and radiation reading were normal for this material. Chemical, infrared and other destructive type tests were run on this material. The Food and Drug Laboratory of the U.S. Department of Health, Education and Welfare concluded that the material was an ordinary pancake of terrestrial origin."[25]

To well-known UFO investigator Jacques Vallee, this case is credible, yet absurd! What sort of extraterrestrials look like ordinary humans, wear coveralls (Oshkosh-by-gosh!) and hand out perfectly ordinary buckwheat pancakes to chicken farmers in Wisconsin? Interdimensional ones, he concludes.

It is interesting to put this unusual UFO case into the context of Vimanas, which have a terrestrial, although admittedly unusual, origin. One wonders what sort of kitchen facilities might be inside a Vimana, and what do its occupants eat while on a journey. We can dispel (I think) the idea of a stewardess warming up some tasteless, pre-prepared meal. Ancient Indians and Tibetans might have gotten by with a handful of nuts and dried fruits while cruising the Asian skies, yet a simple electric griddle with which to fry pancakes and flat breads makes a great deal of sense. It is curious that the occupants did not speak to Simonton, perhaps this is because they were aware that Simonton did not speak ancient Sanskrit or Dravidian, and they did not speak English!

Many of the UFO cases reported in Vallee's book *Dimensions*25 are puzzling to Vallee because they appear to be contacts with ordinary humans, rather than extraterrestrials.

On December 3, 1967, a patrolman named Herb Schirmer, of Ashland, Nebraska, had an unusual experience. After writing in his logbook that he "saw a flying saucer at the junction of highways 6 and 63. Believe it or not," he realized that twenty minutes were missing in his life. Later, he was put under hypnosis.

Schirmer reported he had seen an object with a row of flickering lights takeoff from the highway. The patrolman decided to follow it and drove up a dirt road toward the intense light. He tried to call the police in Wahoo, Nebraska, but his radio would not work. His car died (typical of being around a strong electromagnetic field) and he starred at the object which was metallic and football shaped and surrounded by a silvery glow. It was making a "whooshing" sound, and the lights were flickering rapidly. Legs appeared under the craft, and it landed. Schirmer wanted to drive home, but he was "prevented by something in his mind."

The occupants of the craft came toward the car. He was unable to draw his revolver. A greenish gas was shot toward the car and an occupant pulled a small object from a holster, flashed a bright light at him, and he passed out.

The next thing Schirmer remembered, under hypnosis, was rolling down the car window and talking to the occupant of the craft, who pressed something against the side of his neck and asked him: "Are you the watchman over this place?" He then pointed to a powerplant that was visible and asked him, "Is this the only source of power you have?"

295

Schrimer was taken aboard the craft. He saw control panels and computer-like machines. The occupants appeared to be normal human beings and were wearing coveralls with an emblem of a *winged-serpent*. They told him their craft operated by reverse electromagnetism and they drew their power from *large water reservoirs*.

"To a certain extent they want to puzzle people," Schrimer reported under hypnosis. In an apparent attempt at disinformation, they told him they were from another galaxy, that he would not remember being inside the ship, and concluded: "You will not speak wisely about this night. We will return to see you two more times."

And at one point, one of the men took Schirmer to the large window of the ship, pointed to the deserted landscape around them and said gravely, "Watchman, someday you will see the Universe!"[25]

In a similar incident near Temple, Oklahoma on March 23, 1966, an instructor in aircraft electronics at Sheppard Air Force Base was driving to work at 5:00 A.M. on Route 65 and approached the intersection with Highway 70. In a telephone interview he told UFO researcher Jacques Vallee, "One mile before the intersection I saw a very bright light a mile or so to my right, and I supposed it was a truck having trouble on the highway. I went on to turn west on Highway 70. I went a quarter of a mile or so, and changed my mind and thought that it was a house that was being moved down the highway in the early morning hours.

"...It was parked on the highway and I got within a hundred yards of it and stopped, got out of the car, and started trotting towards the object, leaving the car lights on and my engine running. I got about fifteen steps or so, and I happened to think I had a Kodak on the front seat, and I would like to get a picture. I hesitated just a second, and while I did, why this man that was dressed in military fatigues, which I thought was a master sergeant... this insignia was on his right arm, and he had a kind of cap with the bill turned up, weighed approximately 180 pounds and about 5'9" ...."

"He looked perfectly ordinary?" asked Jacques Vallee.

"Oh, yes, he was just a plain old G.I. mechanic... or a crew chief or whatever he might happen to be on that crew. He had a flashlight in his hand, and he was almost kneeling on his right knee, with his left hand touching the bottom of the fuselage."

The object looked like an aluminum airliner with no wings or tail and with no seams along the fuselage. It lifted up vertically for about fifty feet and headed southeast almost straight backward, off by about ten degrees, at a speed estimated to be about 720 mph, judging by the barns it illuminated along its path across the valley. It was the size of a cargo plane, but had no visible means of propulsion. The witness was grilled by a roomful of officers at the Air Force base. A truck driver down the road had observed the same object.

Concludes Vallee on this sighting, "Whoever he was, the man in the baseball cap was no interplanetary explorer. This is only one of many sightings in which the pilots are described as ordinary humans. Whatever they are, the occupants of such craft are not genuine extraterrestrials."[25]

What is fascinating about these and many other encounters, is that aside from the "fact" that each involves an aircraft of a completely different design than we are accustomed to seeing in this century, each of these events appears to be a highly mundane encounter with perfectly normal human beings of this planet who are neither threatening or even apparently observing the witnesses, but merely going about their own business (whatever that may be) or repairing some malfunction on their craft.

In the case of Ashland, Nebraska sighting, the occupants may have been looking for a source of power or something to refuel their ship. Upon seeing the electrical generating station they were prompted to ask (perhaps in surprise at its primitiveness) "Is this the only source of power you have?" Later when Schrimer is informed that "one day he will see the universe," this may merely mean that space travel is within the easy reach of all mankind.

Each one of these reports describes human-occupied craft that corresponds to descriptions of ancient Vimanas from Indian texts as well as the descriptions of Vailxi from Atlantis. One solution is that some of this craft has been lingering, secretly, for the last several millennium, while another suggestion is that we have some sort of time travel phenomenon.

297

§§§

That some lingering Vimanas were still around several thousand years after the destruction of Rama and Atlantis is evidenced by certain "UFO" accounts in ancient history. According to several researchers such as Frank Edwards, when Alexander the Great invaded India in 326 B.C., two shining silvery shields spitting fire around the rims dived repeatedly on the Greek columns descending the mountain-passes into the Punjab, stampeding horses and elephants. The shields then returned to the skies and vanished. Alexander's men refused to go further than the river they had been attempting to cross, and Alexander's conquest of India was abandoned. Alexander personally led his army back through the desert, reaching Susa in Persia in 324 B.C., dying one year later at the age of 33. Were these left-over Vimanas still in use 2300 years ago, and many thousands of years after the decline of the Rama Empire?[19, 21]

Curiously, several ancient texts on *Vimanas* state that *Vimanas* are especially suited to the purpose of frightening armies of war elephants! The Sanskrit scholar V. Raghavavan, the author of *Yantras or Mechanical Contrivances in Ancient India*,96 comments on one text: "A heavier (*alaghu*) Daru-vimana is then described (97-98); it contains, not one as in the previous case, but four pitchers of mercury over iron ovens. The boiling mercury ovens produce a terrific noise which is put to use in battle to scare away elephants; by strengthening the mercury chambers, the roar could be increased so that by it elephants are thrown completely out of control. This specific military use of aircraft against elephants tempts one to suggest that the *Hasti-yantra* advocated by Kautilya against elephants was something like the heavier *Daru-vimana* described by Bhoja."[96]

§§§

The incredible search for Vimanas today leads us to highly remote areas of the world and on an intellectual journey bound to stretch the

298

very fabric of reality for many people. We are led on an occult trip through Tibet, China, the remote Himalayas, Hindu Kush and Karakoram mountains. We must examine areas of the Gobi, remote arctic areas of Siberia, Alaska and the Yukon. The trail leads to remote mountain and jungle areas of South America, and even to such well known areas as Mount Shasta and the Bermuda Triangle. Ancient legend exists that the Vimanas of ancient India and Atlantis have not completely disappeared. Some are kept today in remote caves and "hollowed-out" mountains, similar to Cheyenne Mountain outside of Colorado Springs where the NORAD defense command is currently located.

While some ancient Vimanas may still be sitting idle beneath the Potala Palace in Tibet, and even more astonishing thought is that some of these Vimanas are still in use today! One can only wonder, what kind of group is operating these craft and who are their pilots? Are they reincarnated pilots who continue to keep coming back so they can pilot the ancient craft. Are the pilots kept in suspended animation to be awakened whenever a trip is to be made? Do we have an ancient Brotherhood of Masters who routinely fly their craft from Vimana hangers in Tibet to visit their friends at other Vimana bases in Mount Shasta or the Andes? Perhaps the moon or the "Hollow Earth" has whole cities of ancient Masters where they and certain extraterrestrial races meet and talk about the old days.

Interestingly, Vallee quotes from the twenty century old Indian book of astronomy called the Surya Siddhanta which says that, "Below the moon and above the clouds revolve the Siddhas (perfected men) and the Vidyaharas (possessors of knowledge)." Vallee goes on to quote the late Australian writer Andrew Tomas who says that Indian tradition holds that the Siddhas could become "very heavy at will or as light as a feather, travel through space and disappear from sight."[25]

Vallee also quotes from the Archbishop of Lyons, Agobard, who was born in Spain in 779 and came to France when three years old, became archbishop at thirty-seven and died in 840, "one of the most celebrated and learned prelates of the ninth century."

Says Agobard of a peculiar incident: "We have seen and heard many men plunged in such great stupidity, sunk in such depths of folly, as to believe that there is a certain region, which they call Magonia, whence ships sail the clouds, in order to carry back to that region those fruits of the earth which are destroyed by hail or tempests; the sailors paying rewards to the storm wizards, and themselves receiving corn and other produce. Out of the number of those whose blind folly was deep enough to allow them to believe these things possible, I saw several exhibitions in a certain concourse of people, four persons in bonds—three men and a woman who they said had fallen from these same ships; after keeping them in captivity they brought them before the assembled multitude, as we have said, in our presence to be stoned. But truth prevailed."[25]

That ancient *Siddhas* have roamed the skies in ancient airships throughout history right up to modern times is an amazing theory!

That the "land," or secret base of their origin was called *Magonia* by Medieval Europeans is curious. Perhaps this is a corruption of the word Mongolia. Is it possible that some Vimanas are coming from a secret, inaccessible region on Central Asia? Buddhist and other Asian legend says that such a secret area exists, and it is sometimes called Shambhala, Agartha, Valley of the Immortals or the land of Hsi Wang Mu.

Information on Shambhala and Agartha is widely varied and contradictory. In some texts, Agartha and Shambhala are said to be underground cities, or kingdoms, somewhere in Central Asia where occults live and study. Shambhala is said to be north of Lhasa, possibly in the Gobi Desert, perhaps in Mongolia. Shambhala and Agartha are sometimes said to be at odds. In some traditions Agartha is the right-hand path, the "white occult" group, while Shambhala is the left-hand path, or "black occult" group. Also, it is conversely said that Agartha is occupied by dark forces and Shambhala is the abode of the "Masters of the World" and a place of goodness.[38, 33, 29]

Sometimes Shambhala is associated with The Great White Brotherhood, and the "Valley of the Immortals." Much information indicates that some sort of "black occult" group is operating out of Central Asia, and they usually call themselves the Shambhala. The term "Shambhala," like the term, "Great White Brotherhood," are quite ambiguous, and can be used by anyone. The term Shambhala may have originally been used by a group of adepts in Central Asia, and then the name corrupted and used by other groups for their own purposes.

Shambhala is sometimes associated with Shangri-la, a fictional valley of wise initiates in Tibet described in the book *Lost Horizon*. According to ancient legends, familiar to the occult societies at the turn of the century, and related in the book *Le Roi du Monde* by Rene Guenon, there was a cataclysm in the Gobi desert, so the "Sons of Intelligences of Beyond" took up their abode in the vast underground encampment under the Himalayas. There inside these caves, they split up into two groups; one, the Agarthi, supposedly following the "right-hand way" of meditation and goodness, and the other, the Shambalists, following the "left-hand way" of evil and violence.

Shambhala, according to Guenon, was a city of black occults located underground whose forces commanded the elements and the masses of humanity through telepathic hypnosis, mediumship and other occult means, hastening the arrival of the human race to the "turning point in time," which might be construed to mean "Armageddon."[20]

A story is told of a Polish nobleman who was studying in Tibet entering a smoking cavern and penetrating it into Shambhala. Upon his return to the monastery where he was staying, he began to disclose the location of the cave community, but the lamas immediately cut out his tongue to prevent him from telling the secret of Shambhala.[38]

Tradition places Shambhala to the north of Lhasa, possibly in the Gobi Desert. Apparently, the Buddhists of Lhasa and the Bon had an uneasy truce. The Dalai Lama used to go every year to Mongolia, and at one point their caravan stopped as the animals all began trembling for no apparent reason. The reason, the Dalai Lama explained, was that they were passing through the forbidden territory of Shambhala.[38]

The Hungarian philologist, Csoma de Koros, who spent four years in a Buddhist monastery in Tibet from 1827 to 1830, gave the location

301

of Shambhala as 45 to 50 degrees latitude, beyond the river Syr Daria, which would place Shambhala in southern Mongolia. The Panchen Lama, head of the Tashi Lhunpo monastic citadel near Shigatse and no great friend of the Dalai Lama's, was said to be able to issue passports to Shambhala, though he would never disclose its location. According to tradition, both Shambhala and Agartha were connected to all the major monasteries of Tibet by a system of underground tunnels, and the monastery of Shigastse is either near, or at the actual entrance to Agartha.[38]

§§§

It is quite possible that the occult cities of Shambhala and Agartha are really crude, dirty hovels in some remote area, probably underground in extensive caves, quite possibly beneath Kanchenjunga or the Shigatse Monastery for the Agarthi, and in other caves to the north for the Shambalists. The occultists who lived there, so legend goes, had the ability to create, in the minds of their visitors, visions of a magnificent city by use of a kind of telepathic hypnosis. They might even create hypnotic visions of aircraft, UFOs, alien encounters and the like, if their legendary mental powers are any indication of reality.

Shambhala, in many traditions, is said to be a wonderful, lush valley in the high mountains with a tall, ornate solid jade tower from which a brilliant light shines. In Agartha and Shambhala, fantastic inventions and artifacts could theoretically be seen; and visitors came away absolutely stunned by the splendor and beauty of these places, through it was, apparently, a mental illusion.[38]

In contrast, a real secret headquarters, called the "Valley of the Immortals" may be located in the Kun Lun Mountains of north western Tibet. While the cave communities may be illusions, an actual "secret city" may in fact exist somewhere. Here really are ancient artifacts of a time gone by watched over by "Masters." Yet, it is unlikely that any person not chosen specifically by those who are the caretakers of this repository, would be allowed inside. Nor would those who had entered (such as possibly Nicholas Roerich) ever reveal the location or what they had seen there.

Other such secret retreats are said to exist in other remote areas, much like Superman's *Fortress of Solitude*, complete with crystal library and special machines. One such place that also has a strong reputation for mysterious people as well as strange craft is Mount Shasta, located in northern California. It has been said to be (or have been) the location of a group of "Masters" and within their secret fortress deep within Mount Shasta are said to be a few aircraft, spacecraft or airships. Might we call them *Vimanas*? It is an amusing to note the similarities between the Sanskrit work *shastra* and the native Indian word for the mountain, *Shasta*.

As incredible as it may seem, it is quite possible that some ancient aircraft from the Rama Empire has survived to this day and is kept in the secret headquarters of a fraternity of adepts who are watching over mankind. Are their ancient airships still cruising the skies, perhaps on a mission or visit to others of their fraternity?

In a letter to *Strange Magazine* (issue No. 6, 1990, page 2), Charles A. Dunphy, Sr. of Gardner, Massachusetts told of a wartime experience that he and a friend had during World War II. "It was in the year 1943, in Gordonvale, Australia. I do not remember the month. I was a soldier in the 503rd Parachute Inf. Regiment. My friend Nickolai Valvanis and I were lying in our cots. The rest of the Co. D had gone out on some night maneuvers. We had been left behind. I can't remember the reason why. It was dark. Some people came into the tent and went over to where Valvanis was.

"I heard a commotion and then they were leaving. I got up and followed along. We went out to where there was an open area, there was this strange ship with stairs going up to it. It was a flying saucer. They had not named them as yet. We all went into the ship.

"It was not large, but circular. There were about five men and an officer, Valvanis and I. The officer was in a light blue uniform and on his hat was a white star. The men were in green uniforms, a fatigue type of uniform.

"They were Asiatic or Oriental. There were no words spoken. The Officer was sitting across from me. He turned his head towards his right shoulder and I saw his lips sort of move, but no sound.

"After that, there was sensation, and I knew that we were moving. There was not any sound. After a short while, and I can't say how long, we were landed somewhere, we all got out, and Valvanis and I ran like Hell.

"It was a place called the Markham Valley, about 15 miles behind Lae, New Guinea. The reason I know this is because later that year my regiment parachuted in that area, our first time in combat. I recognized the area when we jumped there.

"I must be very honest with you, I do not know how Valvanis and I ever got back to Gordonvale, Australia.

Valvanis always said that I saved his life. His hands were bound and I cut him loose."

Charles Dunphy, Sr. then concludes his bizarre letter with these final three sentences: "These people were not from Outer Space. They looked Japanese. But they did have a white star on their hats."

It does not appear that the visitors meant any harm and it seems strange that the two should be taken to an area where they were later to parachute into during combat. If there is anything more than fantasy to this story (unverified, to say the least) then we might conjecture that the occupants were not Japanese, that they were possibly Tibetan, and that perhaps modern day pilots of Vimanas wear hats with a little white star!

§§§

The Rama Empire reaches to us and is in the news to this very day. As of the spring of 1991, the nation of India was in severe political and religious turmoil directly related the *Ramayana*, Rama and his capital city, Ayodhya. Since Ayodhya was the glittering capital of a golden age of India gone-by, a modern Hindu revival has threatened split India in two and plunge the country into civil war.

TIME magazine ran a special story on Ayodhya and Rama in its November 12, 1990 issue: "Militant Hindus marching on the town last week were bent on reclaiming what they believe to be Rama's birthplace, a site now occupied by a dilapidated mosque. If Moslems note that their shrine has stood there for centuries, Hindu revivalists cite as proof nothing less than divine lightning and the appearance of a mysterious black icon.

"Supposedly, it was on the night of Dec. 22, 1949, that a thunderbolt struck Ayodhya and an eerie light emanated from the rear of the Babri mosque's central prayer hall. A bystander, so the story goes, witnessed the brief appearance of a child at the light's source, a spot where later investigation discovered a black stone *murti*, or divine likeness. In Hinduism, Rama was not just a celebrated warrior and king; he was an incarnation of *Vishnu the Preserver*, one of the trinity of supreme gods. As such, his victorious labors in pursuit of Sita—aided by the ingenious Hanuman, magical king of the monkeys—ushered in a golden age of righteousness known as the Ram Rajya.

"As the Ramayana describes Ayodhya, it was a palatial metropolis of broad avenues, brilliant gardens and mighty walls. Historically, however, the site of present-day Ayodhya became a mini-Jerusalem, a holy place for many faiths where the Buddha's legendary Toothbrush Tree grew and where a Jain saint was born. In the 16th century, Islam arrived. The commingled armies of Babur, a Central Asian warlord, swept down from Afghanistan to found the Mughal dynasty in northern India. And in 1528, Mir Baqi, on of Babur's commanders, established in Ayodhya the Babri mosque, named for his emperor.

"It stands today as one of the religious world's strangest hybrids: a triple-domed Islamic edifice with statuary portraying Rama inside, an outer courtyard reserved for Hindu devotions and, beyond that, a high-fenced, barbed-wire security perimeter monitored by closed-circuit TV".

Continued the *TIME* report, "The mosque was declared off-limits in 1949 following the reputed appearance of the child Rama. In the wake of gruesome Hindu-Muslim massacres accompanying the partition of British India in 1947, a local magistrate feared that the incident would inflame animosities. Many Hindus continue to accept the vision as a miracle, but others, with backing from the police report, say that Hindu militants sneaked inside the mosque, placed the *murti* in its strategic niche and then spread a supernatural tale.

"Wonders aside, defenders of the site as Rama's birthplace point to what they call hard evidence: column sections in the mosque that predate its construction and feature ornaments in a much older Indian style. As believers see it, these formed part of an ancient Rama shrine, one superseding, perhaps, the original temple of legend that was built of black stone fetched from Lanka by Rama's simian lieutenant.

"Moslems opposing the campaign to remove the mosque dismiss such claims and have won support from some prominent historians and social activists. Last year a report by 25 distinguished Indian historians found what Romila Thapar, a scholar on ancient India, called "really no evidence" suggesting that the site is one of great antiquity linked to Rama. She added, "There is also no record of the destruction of a temple." In the panel's view, the mosque's Hindu or Jain structural elements could have been collected from ruins elsewhere."

The *TIME* article concludes: "The dispute is under review by the state high court. Whatever the facts, however, to militant Hindus the birthplace theory is an article of faith. Since a court granted them access to the site in 1986, they have intensified their movement to build a new temple after relocating the mosque or, failing that, destroying it. In the words of Murli Manohar Joshi, one of the movement's top ideologues, Rama "is not a Hindu god but a national hero, and every Indian irrespective of his religion must accept that."

"Scholars believe that the Ramayana records some of the earliest conquests of southern India by the proto-Hindu Aryans sometime before 500 B.C. By contrast, the Babri mosque symbolizes Islam's later triumph. If Hindu revivalists have their way, they would turn the tables decisively by upsetting modern India's secular political order. Of the temple dispute, political commentator M.N. Buch concludes, "It is immaterial who wins, because India will lose in any case."

As militant Hindu groups marched on Ayodhya to demolish the mosque and build a new shrine to Rama, the Indian army blocked roads into Ayodhya, battles with the police occurred in which at least

80 persons were killed and Lal Kishen Advani, the political head of the Bharatiya Janata Party (BJP) was arrested in November, 1990.

Advani actually toured India raising support for the new temple to Rama in a "flying chariot" from the Ramayana; that is, a *Vimana!* It was not a real Vimana, of course, but a wooden model with swans as the sort of Vimana that Rama and Sita had returned to Ayodhya from Lanka in.

While the glory, history and incredible technology of the ancient Rama empire of India is missed by most journalists and western educated "Indiologists," most Hindus in India are firm believers in the reality of Rama, his exploits and Ayodhya as the former capital city.

The *Ramayana,* as *TIME* says, is not the depiction of the Aryan invasion of India (Bharat), as the Ramayana was probably written many thousands of years earlier in Dravidian, and clearly states the time of the events of the Ramayana as still earlier. More correctly, it is the *Rg Veda* (*Rig Veda*) that is a chronicle of the Aryan invasion of India.

While India breaks into a religious war trying to regain a glorious past, the legacy of the ancient Rama empire and its fantastic technology lives on. Yet, it seems that mankind has not learned even the most basic lesson of the ancient Indian chronicles: that war does not solve mankind's problems, and we must learn to cooperate with our neighbors and live in peace!

Top: Stone lintel at the Egyptian temple of Abydos in southern Egypt. It has several curious and unexplained hieroglyphs, including one that looks like a helicopter and one that looks like a modern jet (left).

Got 'Cakes' from Saucer Men
Is Claim of Joe Simonton

Report Stirs State, Then Much of U.S.

By A STAFF WRITER

The alleged landing and contact between three men in a "flying saucer" and Joe Simonton, 54 year old Eagle River plumber, has rocketed to nationwide, and then nationwide attention since it broke to the public shortly after noon Saturday.

Many residents of this community are surprised and almost bewildered by the tremendous interest in the report which was wired from the News-Review office Saturday morning to the Milwaukee Journal.

Simonton claims he received several small pancake-shaped pieces of food from the visitors from outer space. He turned over one of the cakes—about three inches in diameter and perforated with many small holes, to Judge Frank Carter, who said he sent them to a Washington, D. C. organization investigating "unidentified flying objects."

The national press services became interested in the story picked it up and received confirmation from Washington that the "cakes" had been received there—but a lab report however on an analysis of the cake would be unavailable until Friday, April 18, or as late as Monday of next week.

MEANWHILE the story simmers, and the question repeats—what is behind the incredible report from Joe Simonton?

The claimed landing of the "flying saucer" was said to have occurred about 11 a.m., Tuesday April 18—but Simonton said he was reluctant to spread the word, realizing some would ridicule his experience was preposterous.

He said he was attracted to his yard when he heard a noise outside, and the noise—he...

United Press International, and leading television stations and metropolitan newspapers. One of the cakes has been sent by Judge Frank W. Carter to Donald E. Keyhoe, director of the National Investigating Committee on Aerial Phenomena, Washington, D. C. Keyhoe...

In 1961, Joe Simonton of Wisconsin was given buckwheat pancakes from two strange men in a flying saucer, he claimed.

A vimana depicted in a temple relief at Ellora Caves, India.

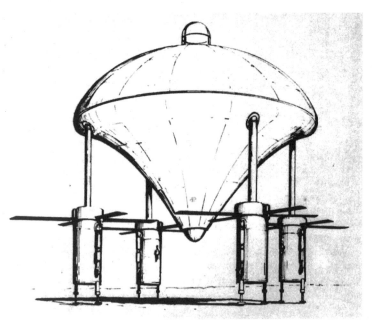

Ezekiel's Biblical vision as interpreted by NASA engineer Joseph F. Blumrich. Was it a helicopter-like vimana?

Schwartz aluminium rigid airship at Tempelhofer Field, 1897

The first successful airship: the Lebaudy lands on the Champs de Mars, Paris, 1903

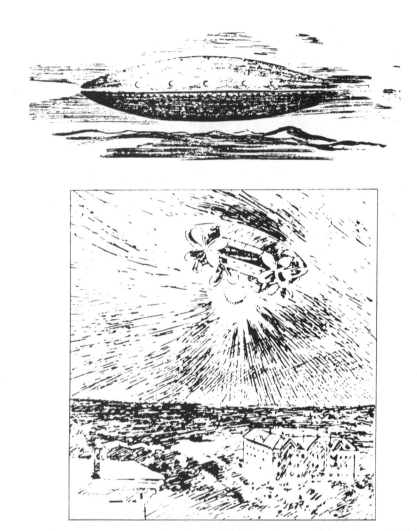

Two drawings from the 1896 airship flap in California, Texas and throughout the U.S. Notic
the powerful searchlights on the aircraft and their cylindrical shape, with window or ligh
along the sides, much as Vailx and Vimanas have been described.

C. A. SMITH.
AIR SHIP.

No. 565,805.

Patented Aug. 11, 1896.

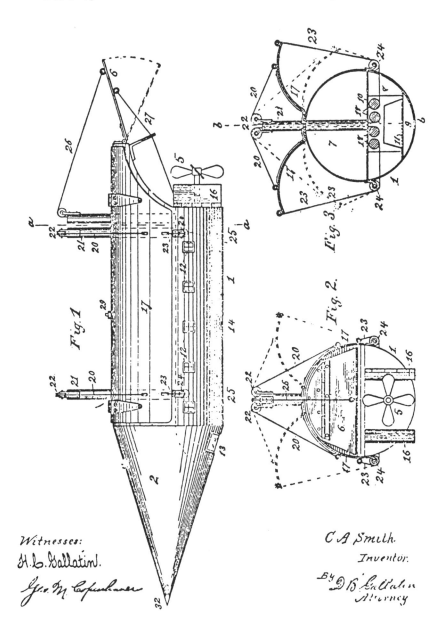

Witnesses:

H. G. Gallatin.

Geo. M. Carpenter

C. A. Smith.
Inventor.

By D. B. Gallatin
Attorney

C.A. Smith's 1896 patent for an airship powered by a propeller.

A 1910 cover illustration from the *Chicago Ledger*. Note the discoid craft, looking like flying shields or saucers in a story about early adventurers on a quest to Halley's Comet which was passing close to earth at the time. Even in 1910 the concept of discoid craft was already being popularized!

During World War I, the fear of German airship attacks led to illustrations such as these. The airship flap of 1896 and earlier Vailx reports were nearly identical in nature. Note the powerful searchlights always depicted in conjunction with such cylindrical craft. Was some of it some sort of premonition or have tubular craft existed for thousands of years?

A German zeppelin spotlights the seaside town of Yarmouth, England, during World War I, in a composite photograph (1915). UPI

he German airship scare: current fears reflected in the popular press. [*The Queen,* 1913]

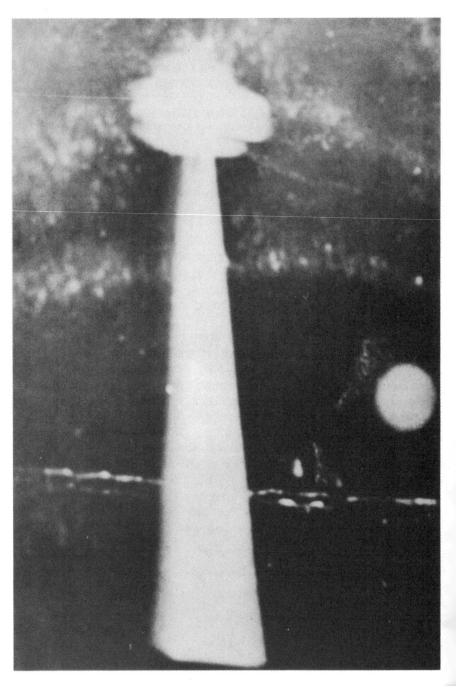

On a late January night in 1966, this photograph of a UFO with a powerf
searchlight and an apparent vortex underneath it was taken at the Wanaq
Resevoir in New Jersey. Sightings went on for weeks at a time.

On June 3, 1967 at 7:15 in the evening, Joseph L. Ferriere took the above photo, printed in two densities, at Cumberland, Rhode Island. Notice the long cylindrical shape, its similarity to Adamski's craft and how it matches the desription of even earlier craft.

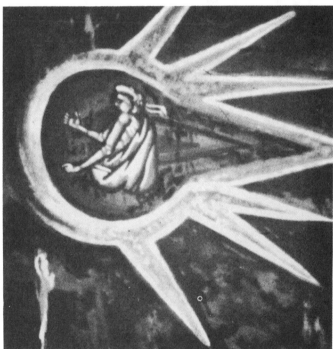

Medieval mural of a "saint" or Angel flying through the air in what appears to be a spherical machine. Might we call this a "vimana"? From the Desani Monastery in Jugoslavia.

In his travel diary of 1926 Nicholas Roerich, a well-known artist and explorer, told of a strange sighting in northern China:

On August 5th–something remarkable! We were in our camp in the Kukunor district not far from the Humboldt Chain. In the morning about half-past nine some of our caravaneers noticed a remarkably big black eagle flying above us. Seven of us began to watch this unusual bird. At this same moment another of our caravaneers remarked, "There is something far above the bird." And he shouted in his astonishment. We all saw, in a direction from north to south, something big and shiny reflecting the sun, like a huge oval moving at great speed. Crossing our camp this thing changed in its direction from south to southwest. And we saw how it disappeared in the intense blue sky. We even had time to take our field glasses and saw quite distinctly an oval form with shiny surface, one side of which was brilliant from the sun. [Nicholas Roerich, *Altai-Himalaya: A Travel Diary*, pp.361–62]

Nicholas Roerich was a Russian landscape painter and archeologist who traveled widely in India and Asia from 1923 until 1928. New York City's Roerich Museum houses several hundred of his paintings.

1942, Tientsien, Hopeh Province, North China. A Chinese street photographer captured this photograph of a cone-shaped structured craft of considerable size flying down the street of the city. A witness in the picture points to the object as the picture is taken.

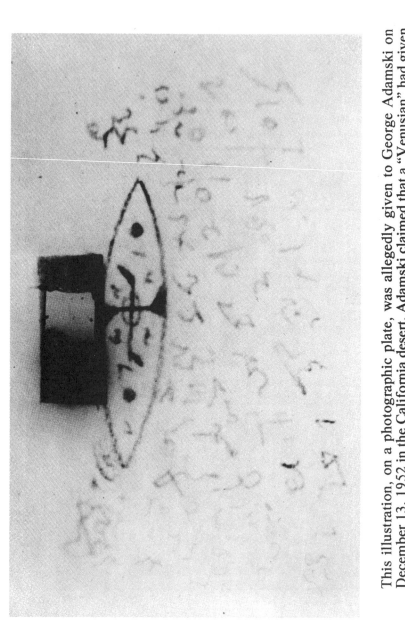

This illustration, on a photographic plate, was allegedly given to George Adamski on December 13, 1952 in the California desert. Adamski claimed that a "Venusian" had given it to him and that it contained "writing from another planet." It is possible that it shows the concept of a Mercury Vortex engine, written in an ancient language that is now extinct. Note the Swastika (running to the right, rather than the left as Nazi and Bon Swastikas run) of the vortex movement and the possible Central Asian origin of the text.

Appendix A: Aerial Warfare In Ancient India

by Ramachandra Dikshitar
From *War In Ancient India*
First published 1944
by the University of Madras
Chapter VII, pages 277-286

No question can be more interesting in the present circumstances of the world than India's contribution to the science of aeronautics. There are numerous illustrations in our vast Purāṇic and epic literature to show how well and wonderfully the ancient Indians conquered the air. To glibly characterize everything found in this literature as imaginary and summarily dismiss it as unreal has been the practice of both Western and Eastern scholars until very recently. The very idea indeed was ridiculed and people went so far as to assert that it was physically impossible for man to use flying machines. But to-day what with balloons, aeroplanes and other flying machines[1] a great change has come over our ideas on the subject.

The use and value of air forces is not hard to assess. Their chief use lay until recently in the rapidity and skill with which the men flying did the scouting and reported to headquarters. They located the position of the enemy, which enabled them to direct the attack. We know from modern history that the French were the first to use balloons for this purpose. The discovery of aeroplanes has revolutionised the realm of strategy and

[1] See in this connexion Golikere: *Through Wonderlands of the Universe* (1933), esp. ch. vi ff.

321

tactics. The present World War has demonstrated that before the air arm everything else pales into insignificance.

Turning to Vedic literature, in one of the *Brāhmaṇas* occurs the concept of a ship that sails heavenwards. The ship is the Agnihotra of which the Āhavanīya and Gārhapatya fires represent the two sides bound. heavenward, and the steersman is the Agnihotrin who offers milk to the three Agnis.[2] Again in the still earlier *Ṛg Veda Saṁhitā* we read that the Aśvins conveyed the rescued Bhujya safely by means of winged ships.[3] The latter may refer to the aerial navigation in the earliest times.

In the recently published *Samarāṅgaṇa Sūtradhāra* of Bhoja, a whole chapter of about 230 stanzas[4] is devoted to the principles of construction underlying the various flying machines and other engines used for military and other purposes. The various advantages of using machines, especially flying ones, are given elaborately. Special mention is made of their attacking visible as well as invisible objects, of their use at one's will and pleasure, of their uninterrupted movements, of their strength and durability, in short of their capability to do in the air all that is done on earth. After enumerating and explaining a number of other advantages, the author concludes that even impossible things could be effected through them. Three movements are usually ascribed to these machines,—ascending, cruising thousands of miles in different directions in the atmos-

---

2 *Satapatha Brāhmaṇa*, II, 3, 3, 15.

3 *Ṛg Veda*, I. 117. 14 and 15. Here ' wings ' may be ' sails '.

4 Ch. 31. (Gaekwad Oriental Series).

phere and lastly descending. It is said that in an aerial
car one can mount up to the Sūryamaṇḍala, 'solar
region' and the Nakṣatra maṇḍala (stellar region) and
also travel throughout the regions of air above the sea
and the earth. These cars are said to move so fast as
to make a noise that could be heard faintly from the
ground.[5] Still some writers have expressed a doubt and
asked 'Was that true?' But the evidence in its favour
is overwhelming.

The make of machines for offence and defence to be
used on the ground and in the air is described. Some
of these are water machines, musical instruments, door-
keeper machines, streets, houses and pillars by means of
'yantra' or machine, and other varieties. These require
separate study. Considering briefly some of the flying
machines alone that find distinct mention in this work,
we find that they were of different shapes like those of
elephants, horses, monkeys, different kinds of birds, and
chariots. Such vehicles were made usually of wood. We
quote in this connexion the following stanzas so as to
give an idea of the materials and size, especially as we
are in the days of rigid airships navigating the air for
a very long time and at a long distance as well.

यन्त्राणामाकृतिस्तेन निगंतुं नैव शक्यते ।
यथावद्बीजसंयोगः सौश्लिष्टयं श्लक्ष्णतापि च ।
अलक्षता निर्वहणं लघुत्वं शब्दहीनता ।
शब्दे साध्ये तदाधिक्यमशैथिल्यमगाढता ॥
वहनीषु समस्तासु सौश्लिष्टयं चास्खलद्गति ।
यथाभीष्टार्थकारित्वं लयतालानुगामिता ॥

5 *Samar.* Ch. 31, 45-79.

जायन्ते यन्त्रानिर्माणाद् विविधानोप्सितानि च ।
दुष्करं यद्यदन्यश्च तच्चद् यन्त्रात् प्रसिध्यति ॥ 31. 45-79.

An aerial car[6] is made of light wood looking like
a great bird with a durable and well-formed body
having mercury inside and fire at the bottom. It has
two resplendent wings, and is propelled by air. It flies
in the atmospheric regions for a great distance and
carries several persons along with it. ˙The inside
construction resembles heaven created by Brahmā himself. Iron, copper, lead and other metals are also used
for these machines. All these show how far art was
developed in ancient India in this direction· Such
elaborate descriptions ought to meet the criticism that
the vimānas and similar aerial vehicles mentioned in
ancient Indian literature should be relegated to the
region of myth.

The ancient writers could certainly make a distinction between the mythical which they designated daiva
and the actual aerial wars designated mānuṣa. Some

6 लघुदारुमयं महाविहङ्ग दृढसुश्लिष्टतनुं विधाय तस्य ।
उदरे रसयन्त्रमादधोत ज्वलनाधारमधोऽस्यचाग्निपूर्णम् ।
तत्रारूढः पुरुषस्तस्य पक्षद्वन्द्वोच्चालप्रोज्झितेनानिलेन ।
सुप्तस्वान्तः पारदस्यास्य शक्त्या चित्रं कुर्वन्नम्बरे याति दूरम् ॥
इत्थमेव सुरमन्दिरतुल्यं सञ्चलस्य लघुदारुविमानम् ।
आदधीत विधिना चतुरोऽन्तस्तस्य पारदभृतान् दृढकुम्भान् ॥
अयःकपालहितमन्दवह्निमत्तत्कुम्भभुवा गुणेन ।
व्योम्नों श्रगित्याभरणत्वमेति सन्तप्तगजेंद्रसराजशक्त्या ॥
वृत्तसन्धितमथायसयन्त्रं तद् विधाय रसपूरितमन्तः ।
उच्चदेशविनिधापिततसं सिंहनादमुरजं विदधाति ॥ *Ibid.*, 95-99.

wars mentioned in ancient literature belong to the daiva form, as distinguished from the mānuṣa. An example of the daiva form is the encounter between Sumbha and the goddess Durgā. Śumbha was worsted and he fell headlong to the ground. Soon he recovered and flew up again and fought desperately until at last he fell dead on the ground.[7] Again, in the famous battle between the celestials and the Asuras elaborately described in the *Harivaṁśa,* Māya flung stones, rocks and trees from above, though the main fight took place in the field below.[8] The adoption of such tactics is also mentioned in the war between Arjuna and the Asura Nivātakavaca,[9] and in that between Karṇa and the Rākṣasa[10] in both of which, arrows, javelins, stones and other missiles were freely showered down from the aerial regions.

King Śatrujit was presented by a Brahman Gālava with a horse named Kuvalaya which had the power of conveying him to any place on the earth.[11] If this had any basis in fact it must have been a flying horse. There are numerous references both in the *Viṣṇupurāṇa* and the *Mahābhārata* where Kṛṣṇa is said to have navigated the air on the Garuḍa.[12] Either the accounts are imaginary or they are a reference to an eagle-shaped machine flying in the air. Subrahmaṇya used a peacock as his vehicle and Brahmā a swan. Further, the Asura, Māya by name, is said to have owned an animated golden car with four

7 *Mākaṇḍeya Purāṇa,* ch. 90.
8 *Harivaṁśa.* ch. 56.
9 *Vana.* ch. 172. Cp. *Rāma,* V. 47.5, 33: VI. 50.51.
10 *Droṇa.* ch. 176, 50.
11 *Mārkaṇḍeya Purāṇa,* ch. 20.
12 *Viṣṇu Purāṇa,* IV, ch. 30, 64-66; *Harivaṁśa,* ch. 44.

strong wheels and having a circumference of 12,000 cubits, which possessed the wonderful power of flying at will to any place. It was equipped with various weapons and bore huge standards. And in the battle between the Devas and the Asuras in which Māya took a leading part, several warriors are represented as riding birds.[13]

In the *Rāmāyaṇa* when Rāvaṇa was flying with Sītā in his aerial car to Lankā, Jaṭāyu, a giant bird, charged him and his car and this led to a duel between the bird and the Rākṣasa king. Golikere draws attention to a number of instances where fierce duels have been fought between man and bird of prey resulting in the damage of the aeroplane and its inmates, in some cases leading to a forced landing.[14] Again, the Rākṣasa Droṇamukha offers his services to Rāvaṇa in his encounter with the vānara hosts to fight them either on the sea or in the sky or in subterranean regions.[15] After the great victory of Rāma over Lankā, Vibhīṣaṇa presented him with the Puṣpaka vimāna which was furnished with windows, apartments, and excellent seats. It was capable of accommodating all the vānaras besides Rāma, Sītā and Lakṣmaṇa.[16] Rāma flew to his capital Ayodhyā pointing to Sītā from above the places of encampment, the town of Kiṣkindhā and others on the way. Again Vālmīki beautifully compares the city of Ayodhyā to an aerial car.[17]

13 *Harivaṁśa,* ch. 43.
14 *Through the Wonderlands of the Universe,* pp. 124-126.
15 *Yuddha.* ch. 8.
16 *Ibid.,* ch. 123.
17 *Bāla.,* ch. 5.

This is an allusion to the use of flying machines as transport apart from their use in actual warfare. Again in the *Vikramaurvaśīya*, we are told that king Purūravas rode in an aerial car to rescue Urvaśī in pursuit of the Dānava who was carrying her away. Similarly in the *Uttararāmacarita* in the fight between Lava and Candraketu (Act VI) a number of aerial cars are mentioned[18] as bearing celestial spectators. There is a statement in the *Harṣacarita*[19] of Yavanas being acquainted with aerial machines. The Tamil work *Jīvakacintāmani* refers to Jīvaka flying through the air.[20]

But it has to be inferred that being very costly, their use was more or less the exclusive privilege of kings and aristocrats. Another reason why they did not become common is found in the following lines from the *Samarānganasūtradhāra*:

यन्त्राणां घटना नोक्ता
गुप्त्यर्थं नाज्ञतावशात्
तत्र हेतुरयं ज्ञेयो व्यक्ता नैते फलप्रदाः
कथितान्यत्र बीजानि यन्त्राणां घटना न यत् *Ibid.*

This supplies a certain clue to the right understanding of the decline of this art. The make and construction of these contrivances were usually kept secret lest others should get a knowledge of them and use them for wrong ends.

---

18 *Uttarārāmacarita*, Act. VI.

19 Daṇḍopanatayavana nirmitena Nabhastalayāvinā yantra-yānena : VI ucchvāsa.

20 XIII. 2614 (5).

But to the common people and even to the military officials, the use of carrier-pigeons was of the utmost importance. There is enough to show that their use was well known to ancient peoples. Pliny relates that Brutus sent these pigeons, at the siege of Modena in 43 B.C., to his friends for help. Again, we find that they were used in 1167 A.D. as a means of communication between Syria and Bagdad. The letters were usually fastened to the wings. Despite the improved methods of communication by post and telegraph, even to-day they have their value. For when wars break out, there is every possibility that postal and telegraphic communication will be cut off or otherwise interrupted to the great detriment of the belligerent parties. But no one can prevent these birds from carrying information to the desired destination. Therefore even to-day in some countries in Europe the shooting and hunting of these birds is treated as an offence and severely punished.[21] Coming to our own country, Kauṭalya also makes a side reference to pigeon houses that served as military stations, an indication of the use of the birds in early days. This is perhaps why we find them among the several presents given to kings.[22]

To conclude, the flying vimāṇa of Rāma or Rāvaṇa was set down as but a dream of the mythographer till aeroplanes and zeppelins of the present century saw the light of day. The mohanāstra or the " arrow of unconsciousness " of old was until very recently a creature of legend till we heard the other day of bombs discharging poisonous gases. We owe much to the energetic scientists and researchers who plod persistently and carry their torches deep down into the caves and excavations of old and dig out valid testimonials pointing to the misty antiquity of the wonderful creations of humanity.[23]

21 Hildebrandt, *Airships Past and Present.*
22 *Cambridge History of India,* Vol. I, p. 399.
23 *Introduction to Indian Architecture,* Vol. III.

APPENDIX B:
BIBLIOGRAPHY
&
FOOTNOTES

1. **Flying Saucers Have Landed**, Desmond Leslie and George Adamski, 1953, The British Book Centre, New York.
2. **Sensitive Chaos**, Theodore Schwenk, 1965, Rudolph Steiner Press, London.
3. **Vimana In Ancient India**, Dileep Kumar Kanjilal, 1985, Sanskrit Pustak Bhandar, Calcutta.
4. **Atlantis, The Antidiluvian World**, Ignatius Donnelly, 1882, Harper & Row, NYC.
5. **War In Ancient India**, Ramachandra Dikshitar, 1944, Motilal Banarsidass, Delhi.
6. **The Bhagavad Gita**, translated by Juan Mascaro, 1962, Penguin Books, NYC.
7. **The Book of the Damned**, Charles Fort, 1919, Ace Books, NYC.
8. **Children of Mu**, James Churchward, 1931, Ives Washburn Inc, NYC.
9. **Doomsday 1999 A.D.**, Charles Berlitz, 1981, Doubleday & Co., Garden City, NJ.
10. **Fate Magazine**, Sept. 1983, Highland Park, IL.
11. **Forgotten Worlds**, Robert Charroux, 1971, Popular Library, NYC.
12. **The Four Books**, Confucius, various translations and editions.
13. **Gods of Air and Darkness**, Richard Mooney, 1975, Stein & Day, NYC.
14. **The Gods Unknown**, Robert Charroux, 1969, Berkley Books, NYC.
15. **Van Nostrand's Scientific Encyclopedia**, Douglas Considine, Ed., 1983, Van Nostrand Reinhold Co. New York.
16. **Mercury, UFO Messenger of the Gods**, William Clendenon, 1990, Adventure Survival Productions, Biloxi, Mississippi.
17. **Invisible Residents**, Ivan T. Sanderson, 1970, World Publishing, Cleveland, Ohio.
18. **Inside the Spaceships**, George Adamski, 1955, Adelard-Schuman, New York City.
19. **Stranger Than Science**, Frank Edwards, 1959, Lyle Stuart, NYC.

20. **Legacy of the Gods**, Robert Charroux, 1965, Robert Laffont Inc., NYC.
21. **Gods and Spacemen in the Ancient East**, W. Raymond Drake, 1968, Sphere Books, London.
22. **Gods, Demons, and Others**, R.K. Narayan, 1964, Bantam Classic Editions, Bantam Books, NY.
23. **Levitation** , Steve Richards, 1980, The Aquarian Press, Wellingborough, Northamptonshire, England.
24. **The Lost Continent of Mu**, James Churchward, 1931, Ives Washburn Inc., NYC.
25. **Dimensions**, Jacques Vallee, 1988, Ballantine Books, NY.
26. **The Mahabharata**, translated by Protap Chandra Roy, 1889, Calcutta.
27. **Masters of the World**, Robert Charroux, 1967, Berkeley Books, NYC.
28. **Mysteries of Time & Space**, Brad Steiger, 1974, Prentice Hall, NYC.
29. **The Morning of the Magicians**, Louis Pauwels & Jacques Bergier, 1960, Stein & Day, NYC.
30. **The Edicts of Asoka**, N.A. Kikam & Richard McKeon, 1959, University of Chicago Press.
31. **Not Of This World**, Peter Kolosimo, 1971, University Books, Seacaucus, NJ.
32. **Lost Cities of China, Central Asia & India**, David Hatcher Childress, 1987, AUP, Stelle, Illinois.
33. **One Hundred Thousand Years of Man's Unknown History**, Robert Charroux, 1965, Robert Laffont Inc., NYC.
34. **The Queen of Sheba aznd Her Only Son Menyelek** (Kebra Nagast), translated by Sir E.A. Wallis Budge, 1932, Dover, London.
35. **The Ramayana**, R.C. Prasad, 1988, Motilal Banarsidass, Delhi.
36. **Legends of the World**, R. Cavendish, 1982, Orbis Publishing, London.
37. **Secrets of the Past**, Reader's Digest, 1980, Berkeley Books, NYC.
38. **Shambala**, Andrew Tomas, 1977, Sphere Books, London.
39. **The Atlas of Archaeology**, 1982, St. Martin's Press, NYC
40. **Tao Te Ching**, Lao Tzu, various translations and editions.
41. **The Land & People of Ceylon**, Donald Wilber, 1963, Lippincott Co. Philadelphia.
42. **Great Temple of the East**, Sacherell Sitwell, 1962, Obolensky Inc. NYC.
43. **Timeless Earth**, Peter Kolosimo, 1973, Bantam Books, NYC.

44. The Maldive Mystery, Thor Heyerdahl, 1986, Adler-Adler, Bethesda, MD.
45. 2000 AC Distruzione Atomica (Atomic Destruction 2000 BC), David Davenport, 1979, Milan, Italy.
46. The Ultimate Frontier, Eklal Kueshana, 1963, The Stelle Group, Stelle, Illinois.
47. Vanished Civilizations, Max Parrish, 1963, Thames & Hudson, London
48. Vymaanika-Shaastra Aeronautics, Maharishi Bharadwaaja, translated and published 1973 by G.R. Josyer, Mysore, India.
49. The World Almanac Second Book of the Strange, 1981, NYC.
50. Lost World's, Alastair Service, 1981, Arco Publishing, Ny.
51. The World's Last Mysteries, Reader's Digest, 1976, Pleasantville, NY.
52. The World Alamanac First Book of the Strange, 1977, Signet, NYC.
53. We Are Not the First, Andrew Tomas, 1971, Souvineer Press, London.
54. Mysteries of Ancient South America, Harold Wilkins, 1946, Citadel, NYC.
55. Lost Cities & Ancient Mysteries of South America, David Hatcher Childress, 1986, AUP, Stelle, Illinois.
56. Christ In Kashmir, Aziz Kashmiri, 1973, Roshni Publications, Srinigar, India.
57. Lost Continents, L. Sprague de Camp, 1954, Ballantine Books, NYC.
58. Science Digest, August 1981, Hearst Corp., NYC.
59. Discovery of Lost Worlds, J. Thorndike Jr.,ed., 1979, American Heritage, NYC.
60. The Lemurian Fellowship Lessons, 1936, Lemurian Fellowship, Ramona, CA.
61. The Ancient Hydraulic Civilization of Sri Lanka in Relation to its Natural Resources, A.D. Fernando, 1982, Journal of the Sri Lanka Branch of the Royal Asiatic Society (Colombo), Vol. XXVII.
62. Magic and Mystery in Tibet, Alexandra David-Neel, 1929, Dover, NYC.
63. Himalayas: Abode of Light, Nicholas Roerich, 1930, Roerich Museum, NYC.
64. Into the Unknown, 1981, Readers Digest Ass., Pleasantville, NY.
65. Edgar Cayce On Atlantis, Hugh Lynn Cayce, 1968, A.R.E., Virginia Beach, VA.

66. **Analects**, Confucius (Kung-Fu-Tzu), various translations.
67. **Chuang Tzu**, Chuang Tzu , various translations & publishers.
68. **The Dictionary of Imaginary Places**, A. Manguel & G. Guadalupi, 1980, Macmillian, NYC.
69. **Shambala**, Nicholas Roerich, 1930, Roerich Museum, NYC.
70. **A Tagore Reader**, Edited by Amiya Chakravarty, 1961, Macmillan Company, NY.
71. **A Dweller On Two Planets**, Phylos the Thibetan, 1884, Borden Publishing, Alhambra, California.
72. **An Earth Dweller's Return**, Phylos the Thibetan, 1940, Lemurian Fellowship, Ramona, CA & Borden Publishing, Alhambra, CA.
73. **The Encyclopedia of the Strange**, Daniel Cohen, 1985, Avon Books, NYC.
74. **The Dark Gods**, A. Roberts, G. Gilbertson, 1980, Panther, London.
75. **Secret of the Ages**, Brinsley Le Poer Trench, 1974, Pinnacle, NYC.
76. **Lost Cities**, Leonard Cottrell, 1957, Robert Hale & Co., London.
77. **Easy Journey to Other Planets**, Swami Prabhupada, 1970, Bhaktivedanta Book Trust (ISKCON), Los Angeles.
78. **The Silk Road**, Irene Franck & David Brownstone, 1986, Facts On File Pub., NYC.
79. **From Earthquake, Fire & Flood**, R. Hewitt, 1958, Scientific Book Club, London.
80. **Life and Teaching of the Masters of the Far East**, Vol. 1 - 5, Baird T. Spalding, 1924, DeVorss & Co. Santa Monica, CA.
81. **Pathways To the Gods**, Erich von Daniken, 1982, Berkley Pub., NYC.
82. **A Search In Secret India**, Paul Brunton, 1935, Dutton & Co., NYC.
83. **The Aeronauts**, L.T. C. Rolt, 1966, Walker & Co. New York.
84. **The Great Texas Airship Mystery**, Wallace O. Chariton, 1991, Wordware Publishing, Plano, Texas.
85. **The Mysticism and Magic of India**, Ormond McGill, 1977, Barnes & Co., Cranbury, NJ.
86. **The Fringe of the Unknown**, L. Sprague de Camp, 1986, Prometheus, Buffalo, NY.
87. **Spaceships in Prehistory**, Peter Kolosimo, 1975, University Books, Seacaucus, NJ.
88. **2000 Years of Space Travel**, Russell Freedman, 1963, Collins, London, UK.
89. **Anti-Gravity & the World Grid**, D.H. Childress, ed. 1987, Adventures Unlimited Press, Stelle, Illinois.

90. **Altai-Himalaya: A Travel Diary**, Nicholas Roerich, 1929, Roerich Museum, New York.
91. **Anti-Gravity & the Unified Field**, D.H. Childress, ed. 1990, AUP, Stelle, Illinois.
92. **UFOs Over Modern China**, P. Dong, W. Stevens, 1983, UFO Photo Archives, Tuscon, AZ.
93. **Heart of Asia**, Nicholas Roerich, 1930, Roerich Museum, NYC.
94. **On Eastern Crossroads**, J. Saint-Hilair (H. Roerich), 1930, Roerich Museum, NYC.
95. **The Genius of China: 3,000 Years of Science, Discovery and Invention**, Robert Temple, 1987, Simon & Schuster, NYC.
96. **Yantras or Mechanical Contrivances in Ancient India**, V. Raghavan, 1956, Indian Institute of Culture, Bangalore, India.

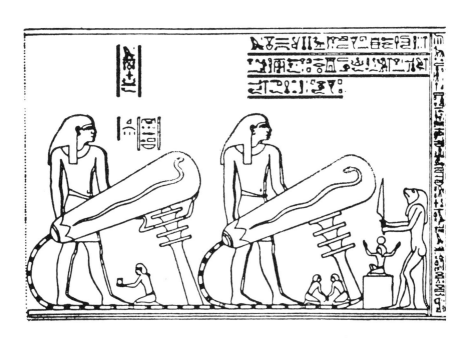

The following item appeared on the internet in 1998 concerning the U.S. government's secret aircraft called the TR-3B which was claimed to be powered by a mercury vortex drive as described in the Vimanika Shastra:

The TR-3B Triangular Anti-Gravity Craft, by Ed Fouche

A very important speech was given by Ed Fouche to the 1998 Summer Sessions at the International UFO Congress, describing the 200 foot across (600 foot operational model?) triangular UFO "anti-gravity" craft being built and tested in area S-4 inside Area 51 in Nevada. Supposedly uses a heated mercury vortex to offset gravity "mass."

A PLASMA VORTEX
MAY PRODUCE
ARTIFICIAL GRAVITY

ROSWELL AND THE REICH
The Nazi Connection
By Joseph P. Farrell
Farrell has meticulously reviewed the best-known Roswell research from UFO-ET advocates and skeptics alike, as well as some little-known source material, and comes to a radically different scenario of what happened in Roswell, New Mexico in July 1947, and why the US military has continued to cover it up to this day. Farrell presents a fascinating case sure to disturb both ET believers and disbelievers, namely, that what crashed may have been representative of an independent postwar Nazi power—an extraterritorial Reich monitoring its old enemy, America, and the continuing development of the very technologies confiscated from Germany at the end of the War.
540 pages. 6x9 Paperback. Illustrated. $19.95. Code: RWR

SECRETS OF THE UNIFIED FIELD
The Philadelphia Experiment, the Nazi Bell, and the Discarded Theory
by Joseph P. Farrell
Farrell examines the now discarded Unified Field Theory. American and German wartime scientists and engineers determined that, while the theory was incomplete, it could nevertheless be engineered. Chapters include: The Meanings of "Torsion"; Wringing an Aluminum Can; The Mistake in Unified Field Theories and Their Discarding by Contemporary Physics; Three Routes to the Doomsday Weapon: Quantum Potential, Torsion, and Vortices; Tesla's Meeting with FDR; Arnold Sommerfeld and Electromagnetic Radar Stealth; Electromagnetic Phase Conjugations, Phase Conjugate Mirrors, and Templates; The Unified Field Theory, the Torsion Tensor, and Igor Witkowski's Idea of the Plasma Focus; tons more.
340 pages. 6x9 Paperback. Illustrated. $18.95. Code: SOUF

NAZI INTERNATIONAL
The Nazi's Postwar Plan to Control Finance, Conflict, Physics and Space
by Joseph P. Farrell
Beginning with prewar corporate partnerships in the USA, including some with the Bush family, he moves on to the surrender of Nazi Germany, and evacuation plans of the Germans. He then covers the vast, and still-little-known recreation of Nazi Germany in South America with help of Juan Peron, I.G. Farben and Martin Bormann. Farrell then covers Nazi Germany's penetration of the Muslim world including Wilhelm Voss and Otto Skorzeny in Gamel Abdul Nasser's Egypt before moving on to the development and control of new energy technologies including the Bariloche Fusion Project, Dr. Philo Farnsworth's Plasmator, and the work of Dr. Nikolai Kozyrev. Finally, Farrell discusses the Nazi desire to control space, and examines their connection with NASA, the esoteric meaning of NASA Mission Patches.
412 pages. 6x9 Paperback. Illustrated. $19.95. Code: NZIN

ARKTOS
The Polar Myth in Science, Symbolism & Nazi Survival
by Joscelyn Godwin
Explored are the many tales of an ancient race said to have lived in the Arctic regions, such as Thule and Hyperborea. Progressing onward, he looks at modern polar legends: including the survival of Hitler, German bases in Antarctica, UFOs, the hollow earth, and the hidden kingdoms of Agartha and Shambala. Chapters include: Prologue in Hyperborea; The Golden Age; The Northern Lights; The Arctic Homeland; The Aryan Myth; The Thule Society; The Black Order; The Hidden Lands; Agartha and the Polaires; Shambhala; The Hole at the Pole; Antarctica; more.
220 Pages. 6x9 Paperback. Illustrated. Bib. Index. $16.95. Code: ARK

REICH OF THE BLACK SUN
Nazi Secret Weapons & the Cold War Allied Legend
by Joseph P. Farrell

Why were the Allies worried about an atom bomb attack by the Germans in 1944? Why did the Soviets threaten to use poison gas against the Germans? Why did Hitler in 1945 insist that holding Prague could win the war for the Third Reich? Why did US General George Patton's Third Army race for the Skoda works at Pilsen in Czechoslovakia instead of Berlin? Why did the US Army not test the uranium atom bomb it dropped on Hiroshima? Why did the Luftwaffe fly a non-stop round trip mission to within twenty miles of New York City in 1944? *Reich of the Black Sun* takes the reader on a scientific-historical journey in order to answer these questions. Arguing that Nazi Germany actually won the race for the atom bomb in late 1944,

352 PAGES. 6X9 PAPERBACK. ILLUSTRATED. BIBLIOGRAPHY. $16.95. CODE: ROBS

THE GIZA DEATH STAR
The Paleophysics of the Great Pyramid & the Military Complex at Giza
by Joseph P. Farrell

Was the Giza complex part of a military installation over 10,000 years ago? Chapters include: An Archaeology of Mass Destruction, Thoth and Theories; The Machine Hypothesis; Pythagoras, Plato, Planck, and the Pyramid; The Weapon Hypothesis; Encoded Harmonics of the Planck Units in the Great Pyramid; High Freqquency Direct Current "Impulse" Technology; The Grand Gallery and its Crystals: Gravito-acoustic Resonators; The Other Two Large Pyramids; the "Causeways," and the "Temples"; A Phase Conjugate Howitzer; Evidence of the Use of Weapons of Mass Destruction in Ancient Times; more.

290 PAGES. 6X9 PAPERBACK. ILLUSTRATED. $16.95. CODE: GDS

THE GIZA DEATH STAR DEPLOYED
The Physics & Engineering of the Great Pyramid
by Joseph P. Farrell

Farrell expands on his thesis that the Great Pyramid was a maser, designed as a weapon and eventually deployed—with disastrous results to the solar system. Includes: Exploding Planets: A Brief History of the Exoteric and Esoteric Investigations of the Great Pyramid; No Machines, Please!; The Stargate Conspiracy; The Scalar Weapons; Message or Machine?; A Tesla Analysis of the Putative Physics and Engineering of the Giza Death Star; Cohering the Zero Point, Vacuum Energy, Flux: Feedback Loops and Tetrahedral Physics; and more.

290 PAGES. 6X9 PAPERBACK. ILLUSTRATED. $16.95. CODE: GDSD

THE GIZA DEATH STAR DESTROYED
The Ancient War For Future Science
by Joseph P. Farrell

Farrell moves on to events of the final days of the Giza Death Star and its awesome power. These final events, eventually leading up to the destruction of this giant machine, are dissected one by one, leading us to the eventual abandonment of the Giza Military Complex—an event that hurled civilization back into the Stone Age. Chapters include: The Mars-Earth Connection; The Lost "Root Races" and the Moral Reasons for the Flood; The Destruction of Krypton: The Electrodynamic Solar System, Exploding Planets and Ancient Wars; Turning the Stream of the Flood: the Origin of Secret Societies and Esoteric Traditions; The Quest to Recover Ancient Mega-Technology; Non-Equilibrium Paleophysics; Monatomic Paleophysics; Frequencies, Vortices and Mass Particles; "Acoustic" Intensity of Fields; The Pyramid of Crystals; tons more.

292 pages. 6x9 paperback. Illustrated. $16.95. Code: GDES

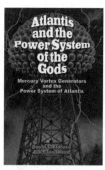

ATLANTIS & THE POWER SYSTEM OF THE GODS
by David Hatcher Childress and Bill Clendenon
Childress' fascinating analysis of Nikola Tesla's broadcast system in light of Edgar Cayce's "Terrible Crystal" and the obelisks of ancient Egypt and Ethiopia. Includes: Atlantis and its crystal power towers that broadcast energy; how these incredible power stations may still exist today; inventor Nikola Tesla's nearly identical system of power transmission; Mercury Proton Gyros and mercury vortex propulsion; more. Richly illustrated, and packed with evidence that Atlantis not only existed—it had a world-wide energy system more sophisticated than ours today.
246 PAGES. 6x9 PAPERBACK. ILLUSTRATED. $15.95. CODE: APSG

THE ANTI-GRAVITY HANDBOOK
edited by David Hatcher Childress

The new expanded compilation of material on Anti-Gravity, Free Energy, Flying Saucer Propulsion, UFOs, Suppressed Technology, NASA Cover-ups and more. Highly illustrated with patents, technical illustrations and photos. This revised and expanded edition has more material, including photos of Area 51, Nevada, the government's secret testing facility. This classic on weird science is back in a new format!
230 PAGES. 7x10 PAPERBACK. ILLUSTRATED. $16.95. CODE: AGH

ANTI-GRAVITY & THE WORLD GRID
Is the earth surrounded by an intricate electromagnetic grid network offering free energy? This compilation of material on ley lines and world power points contains chapters on the geography, mathematics, and light harmonics of the earth grid. Learn the purpose of ley lines and ancient megalithic structures located on the grid. Discover how the grid made the Philadelphia Experiment possible. Explore the Coral Castle and many other mysteries, including acoustic levitation, Tesla Shields and scalar wave weaponry. Browse through the section on anti-gravity patents, and research resources.

274 PAGES. 7x10 PAPERBACK. ILLUSTRATED. $14.95. CODE: AGW

ANTI-GRAVITY & THE UNIFIED FIELD
edited by David Hatcher Childress
Is Einstein's Unified Field Theory the answer to all of our energy problems? Explored in this compilation of material is how gravity, electricity and magnetism manifest from a unified field around us. Why artificial gravity is possible; secrets of UFO propulsion; free energy; Nikola Tesla and anti-gravity airships of the 20s and 30s; flying saucers as superconducting whirls of plasma; anti-mass generators; vortex propulsion; suppressed technology; government cover-ups; gravitational pulse drive; spacecraft & more.
240 PAGES. 7x10 PAPERBACK. ILLUSTRATED. $14.95. CODE: AGU

THE TIME TRAVEL HANDBOOK
A Manual of Practical Teleportation & Time Travel
edited by David Hatcher Childress
The Time Travel Handbook takes the reader beyond the government experiments and deep into the uncharted territory of early time travellers such as Nikola Tesla and Guglielmo Marconi and their alleged time travel experiments, as well as the Wilson Brothers of EMI and their connection to the Philadelphia Experiment—the U.S. Navy's forays into invisibility, time travel, and teleportation. Childress looks into the claims of time travelling individuals, and investigates the unusual claim that the pyramids on Mars were built in the future and sent back in time. A highly visual, large format book, with patents, photos and schematics. Be the first on your block to build your own time travel device!
316 PAGES. 7x10 PAPERBACK. ILLUSTRATED. $16.95. CODE: TTH

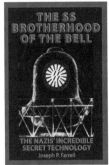

THE SS BROTHERHOOD OF THE BELL
The Nazis' Incredible Secret Technology
by Joseph P. Farrell
In 1945, a mysterious Nazi secret weapons project code-named "The Bell" left its underground bunker in lower Silesia, along with all its project documentation, and a four-star SS general named Hans Kammler. Taken aboard a massive six engine Junkers 390 ultra-long range aircraft, "The Bell," Kammler, and all project records disappeared completely, along with the gigantic aircraft. It is thought to have flown to America or Argentina. What was "The Bell"? What new physics might the Nazis have discovered with it? How far did the Nazis go after the war to protect the advanced energy technology that it represented?

456 pages. 6x9 Paperback. Illustrated.References. $16.95.

Code: SSBB

SECRETS OF THE HOLY LANCE
The Spear of Destiny in History & Legend
by Jerry E. Smith
Secrets of the Holy Lance traces the Spear from its possession by Constantine, Rome's first Christian Caesar, to Charlemagne's claim that with it he ruled the Holy Roman Empire by Divine Right, and on through two thousand years of kings and emperors, until it came within Hitler's grasp—and beyond! Did it rest for a while in Antarctic ice? Is it now hidden in Europe, awaiting the next person to claim its awesome power? Neither debunking nor worshiping, *Secrets of the Holy Lance* seeks to pierce the veil of myth and mystery around the Spear. Mere belief that it was infused with magic by virtue of its shedding the Savior's blood has made men kings. But what if it's more? What are "the powers it serves"?

312 PAGES. 6X9 PAPERBACK. ILLUSTRATED. BIBLIOGRAPHY. $16.95.
CODE: SOHL

MAPS OF THE ANCIENT SEA KINGS
Evidence of Advanced Civilization in the Ice Age
by Charles H. Hapgood
Charles Hapgood has found the evidence in the Piri Reis Map that shows Antarctica, the Hadji Ahmed map, the Oronteus Finaeus and other amazing maps. Hapgood concluded that these maps were made from more ancient maps from the various ancient archives around the world, now lost. Not only were these unknown people more advanced in mapmaking than any people prior to the 18th century, it appears they mapped all the continents. The Americas were mapped thousands of years before Columbus. Antarctica was mapped when its coasts were free of ice.

316 PAGES. 7X10 PAPERBACK. ILLUSTRATED. BIBLIOGRAPHY & INDEX. $19.95. CODE: MASK

PATH OF THE POLE
Cataclysmic Pole Shift Geology
by Charles H. Hapgood
Maps of the Ancient Sea Kings author Hapgood's classic book *Path of the Pole* is back in print! Hapgood researched Antarctica, ancient maps and the geological record to conclude that the Earth's crust has slipped on the inner core many times in the past, changing the position of the pole. *Path of the Pole* discusses the various "pole shifts" in Earth's past, giving evidence for each one, and moves on to possible future pole shifts.

356 PAGES. 6X9 PAPERBACK. ILLUSTRATED. $16.95. CODE: POP

THE COSMIC WAR
Interplanetary Warfare, Modern Physics, and Ancient Texts
By Joseph P. Farrell

There is ample evidence across our solar system of catastrophic events. The asteroid belt may be the remains of an exploded planet! The known planets are scarred from incredible impacts, and teeter in their orbits due to causes heretofore inadequately explained. Included: The history of the Exploded Planet hypothesis, and what mechanism can actually explode a planet. The role of plasma cosmology, plasma physics and scalar physics. The ancient texts telling of such destructions: from Sumeria (Tiamat's destruction by Marduk), Egypt (Edfu and the Mars connections), Greece (Saturn's role in the War of the Titans) and the ancient Americas.

436 Pages. 6x9 Paperback. Illustrated. Bibliography. $18.95. Code: COSW

TECHNOLOGY OF THE GODS
The Incredible Sciences of the Ancients
by David Hatcher Childress

Childress looks at the technology that was allegedly used in Atlantis and the theory that the Great Pyramid of Egypt was originally a gigantic power station. He examines tales of ancient flight and the technology that it involved; how the ancients used electricity; megalithic building techniques; the use of crystal lenses and the fire from the gods; evidence of various high tech weapons in the past, including atomic weapons; ancient metallurgy and heavy machinery; the role of modern inventors such as Nikola Tesla in bringing ancient technology back into modern use; impossible artifacts; and more.

356 PAGES. 6x9 PAPERBACK. ILLUSTRATED. BIBLIOGRAPHY. $16.95. CODE: TGOD

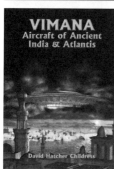

VIMANA AIRCRAFT OF ANCIENT INDIA & ATLANTIS
by David Hatcher Childress, introduction by Ivan T. Sanderson

In this incredible volume on ancient India, authentic Indian texts such as the *Ramayana* and the *Mahabharata* are used to prove that ancient aircraft were in use more than four thousand years ago. Included in this book is the entire Fourth Century BC manuscript *Vimaanika Shastra* by the ancient author Maharishi Bharadwaaja. Also included are chapters on Atlantean technology, the incredible Rama Empire of India and the devastating wars that destroyed it.

334 PAGES. 6x9 PAPERBACK. ILLUSTRATED. $15.95. CODE: VAA

LOST CONTINENTS & THE HOLLOW EARTH
I Remember Lemuria and the Shaver Mystery
by David Hatcher Childress & Richard Shaver

Shaver's rare 1948 book *I Remember Lemuria* is reprinted in its entirety, and the book is packed with illustrations from Ray Palmer's *Amazing Stories* magazine of the 1940s. Palmer and Shaver told of tunnels running through the earth—tunnels inhabited by the Deros and Teros, humanoids from an ancient spacefaring race that had inhabited the earth, eventually going underground, hundreds of thousands of years ago. Childress discusses the famous hollow earth books and delves deep into whatever reality may be behind the stories of tunnels in the earth. Operation High Jump to Antarctica in 1947 and Admiral Byrd's bizarre statements, tunnel systems in South America and Tibet, the underground world of Agartha, the belief of UFOs coming from the South Pole, more.

344 PAGES. 6x9 PAPERBACK. ILLUSTRATED. $16.95. CODE: LCHE

ANCIENT ALIENS ON THE MOON
By Mike Bara
What did NASA find in their explorations of the solar system that they may have kept from the general public? How ancient really are these ruins on the Moon? Using official NASA and Russian photos of the Moon, Bara looks at vast cityscapes and domes in the Sinus Medii region as well as glass domes in the Crisium region. Bara also takes a detailed look at the mission of Apollo 17 and the case that this was a salvage mission, primarily concerned with investigating an opening into a massive hexagonal ruin near the landing site. Chapters include: The History of Lunar Anomalies; The Early 20th Century; Sinus Medii; To the Moon Alice!; Mare Crisium; Yes, Virginia, We Really Went to the Moon; Apollo 17; more. Tons of photos of the Moon examined for possible structures and other anomalies.
248 Pages. 6x9 Paperback. Illustrated. $19.95. Code: AAOM

ANCIENT TECHNOLOGY IN PERU & BOLIVIA
By David Hatcher Childress
Childress speculates on the existence of a sunken city in Lake Titicaca and reveals new evidence that the Sumerians may have arrived in South America 4,000 years ago. He demonstrates that the use of "keystone cuts" with metal clamps poured into them to secure megalithic construction was an advanced technology used all over the world, from the Andes to Egypt, Greece and Southeast Asia. He maintains that only power tools could have made the intricate articulation and drill holes found in extremely hard granite and basalt blocks in Bolivia and Peru, and that the megalith builders had to have had advanced methods for moving and stacking gigantic blocks of stone, some weighing over 100 tons.
340 Pages. 6x9 Paperback. Illustrated.. $19.95 Code: ATP

THE ILLUSTRATED DOOM SURVIVAL GUIDE
Don't Panic!
By Matt "DoomGuy" Victor
With over 500 very detailed and easy-to-understand illustrations, this book literally shows you how to do things like build a fire with whatever is at hand, perform field surgeries, identify and test foodstuffs, and form twine, snares and fishhooks. In any doomsday scenario, being able to provide things of real value—such as clothing, tools, medical supplies, labor, food and water—will be of the utmost importance. This book gives you the particulars to help you survive in any environment with little to no equipment, and make it through the first critical junctures after a disaster. Beyond any disaster you will have the knowledge to rebuild shelter, farm from seed to seed, raise animals, treat medical problems, predict the weather and protect your loved ones.
356 Pages. 6x9 Paperback. Illustrated. $20.00. Code: IDSG

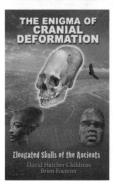

THE ENIGMA OF CRANIAL DEFORMATION
Elongated Skulls of the Ancients
By David Hatcher Childress and Brien Foerster
In a book filled with over a hundred astonishing photos and a color photo section, Childress and Foerster take us to Peru, Bolivia, Egypt, Malta, China, Mexico and other places in search of strange elongated skulls and other cranial deformation. The puzzle of why diverse ancient people—even on remote Pacific Islands—would use head-binding to create elongated heads is mystifying. Where did they even get this idea? Did some people naturally look this way—with long narrow heads? Were they some alien race? Were they an elite race that roamed the entire planet? Why do anthropologists rarely talk about cranial deformation and know so little about it?
250 Pages. 6x9 Paperback. Illustrated. $19.95. Code: ECD

LBJ AND THE CONSPIRACY TO KILL KENNEDY
By Joseph P. Farrell
Farrell says that a coalescence of interests in the military industrial complex, the CIA, and Lyndon Baines Johnson's powerful and corrupt political machine in Texas led to the events culminating in the assassination of JFK. Farrell analyzes the data as only he can, and comes to some astonishing conclusions. Chapters include: Oswald, the FBI, and the CIA: Hoover's Concern of a Second Oswald; Oswald and the Anti-Castro Cubans; The Mafia; Hoover, Johnson, and the Mob; The FBI, the Secret Service, Hoover, and Johnson; The CIA and "Murder Incorporated"; Ruby's Bizarre Behavior; The French Connection and Permindex; Big Oil; The Dead Witnesses: Jack Zangretti, Maurice Gatlin, Guy Bannister, Jr., Mary Pinchot Meyer, Rose Cheramie, Dorothy Killgallen, Congressman Hale Boggs; LBJ and the Planning of the Texas Trip; LBJ: A Study in Character, Connections, and Cabals; LBJ and the Aftermath: Accessory After the Fact; The Requirements of Coups D'État; more.
342 Pages. 6x9 Paperback. $19.95 Code: LCKK

THE FREE-ENERGY DEVICE HANDBOOK
A Compilation of Patents and Reports
by David Hatcher Childress
A large-format compilation of various patents, papers, descriptions and diagrams concerning free-energy devices and systems. *The Free-Energy Device Handbook* is a visual tool for experimenters and researchers into magnetic motors and other "over-unity" devices. With chapters on the Adams Motor, the Hans Coler Generator, cold fusion, superconductors, "N" machines, space-energy generators, Nikola Tesla, T. Townsend Brown, and the latest in free-energy devices. Packed with photos, technical diagrams, patents and fascinating information, this book belongs on every science shelf.
292 PAGES. 8X10 PAPERBACK. ILLUSTRATED. $16.95. CODE: FEH

LEY LINE & EARTH ENERGIES
An Extraordinary Journey into the Earth's Natural Energy System
by David Cowan & Chris Arnold
The mysterious standing stones, burial grounds and stone circles that lace Europe, the British Isles and other areas have intrigued scientists, writers, artists and travellers through the centuries. How do ley lines work? How did our ancestors use Earth energy to map their sacred sites and burial grounds? How do ghosts and poltergeists interact with Earth energy? How can Earth spirals and black spots affect our health? This exploration shows how natural forces affect our behavior, how they can be used to enhance our health and well being.
368 PAGES. 6x9 PAPERBACK. ILLUSTRATED. $18.95. CODE: LLEE

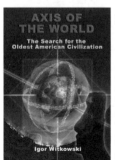

AXIS OF THE WORLD
The Search for the Oldest American Civilization
by Igor Witkowski
Witkowski's research reveals remnants of a high civilization that was able to exert its influence on almost the entire planet, and did so with full consciousness. Sites around South America show that this was not just one of the places influenced by this culture, but a place where they built their crowning achievements. Easter Island, in the southeastern Pacific, constitutes one of them. The Rongo-Rongo language that developed there points westward to the Indus Valley. Taken together, the facts presented by Witkowski provide a fresh, new proof that an antediluvian, great civilization flourished several millennia ago.
220 pages. 6x9 Paperback. Illustrated. $18.95. Code: AXOW

GRAVITATIONAL MANIPULATION OF DOMED CRAFT
UFO Propulsion Dynamics
by Paul E. Potter

Potter's precise and lavish illustrations allow the reader to enter directly into the realm of the advanced technological engineer and to understand, quite straightforwardly, the aliens' methods of energy manipulation: their methods of electrical power generation; how they purposely designed their craft to employ the kinds of energy dynamics that are exclusive to space (discoverable in our astrophysics) in order that their craft may generate both attractive and repulsive gravitational forces; their control over the mass-density matrix surrounding their craft enabling them to alter their physical dimensions and even manufacture their own frame of reference in respect to time. Includes a 16-page color insert.

624 pages. 7x10 Paperback. Illustrated. References. $24.00. Code: GMDC

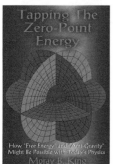

TAPPING THE ZERO POINT ENERGY
Free Energy & Anti-Gravity in Today's Physics
by Moray B. King

King explains how free energy and anti-gravity are possible. The theories of the zero point energy maintain there are tremendous fluctuations of electrical field energy imbedded within the fabric of space. This book tells how, in the 1930s, inventor T. Henry Moray could produce a fifty kilowatt "free energy" machine; how an electrified plasma vortex creates anti-gravity; how the Pons/Fleischmann "cold fusion" experiment could produce tremendous heat without fusion; and how certain experiments might produce a gravitational anomaly.

180 PAGES. 5x8 PAPERBACK. ILLUSTRATED. $12.95. CODE: TAP

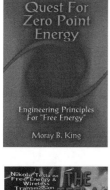

QUEST FOR ZERO-POINT ENERGY
Engineering Principles for "Free Energy"
by Moray B. King

King expands, with diagrams, on how free energy and anti-gravity are possible. The theories of zero point energy maintain there are tremendous fluctuations of electrical field energy embedded within the fabric of space. King explains the following topics: TFundamentals of a Zero-Point Energy Technology; Vacuum Energy Vortices; The Super Tube; Charge Clusters: The Basis of Zero-Point Energy Inventions; Vortex Filaments, Torsion Fields and the Zero-Point Energy; Transforming the Planet with a Zero-Point Energy Experiment; Dual Vortex Forms: The Key to a Large Zero-Point Energy Coherence. Packed with diagrams, patents and photos.

224 PAGES. 6x9 PAPERBACK. ILLUSTRATED. $14.95. CODE: QZPE

THE TESLA PAPERS
Nikola Tesla on Free Energy &
Wireless Transmission of Power
by Nikola Tesla, edited by David Hatcher Childress

David Hatcher Childress takes us into the incredible world of Nikola Tesla and his amazing inventions. Tesla's fantastic vision of the future, including wireless power, anti-gravity, free energy and highly advanced solar power. Also included are some of the papers, patents and material collected on Tesla at the Colorado Springs Tesla Symposiums, including papers on: •The Secret History of Wireless Transmission •Tesla and the Magnifying Transmitter •Design and Construction of a Half-Wave Tesla Coil •Electrostatics: A Key to Free Energy •Progress in Zero-Point Energy Research •Electromagnetic Energy from Antennas to Atoms •Tesla's Particle Beam Technology •Fundamental Excitatory Modes of the Earth-Ionosphere Cavity

325 PAGES. 8x10 PAPERBACK. ILLUSTRATED. $16.95. CODE: TTP

ORDER FORM

**10% Discount
When You Order
3 or More Items!**

One Adventure Place
P.O. Box 74
Kempton, Illinois 60946
United States of America
Tel.: 815-253-6390 • Fax: 815-253-6300
Email: auphq@frontiernet.net
http://www.adventuresunlimitedpress.com

ORDERING INSTRUCTIONS

✓ Remit by USD$ Check, Money Order or Credit Card

✓ Visa, Master Card, Discover & AmEx Accepted

✓ Paypal Payments Can Be Made To:

    info@wexclub.com

✓ Prices May Change Without Notice

✓ 10% Discount for 3 or More Items

SHIPPING CHARGES

United States

✓ Postal Book Rate { $4.50 First Item
                 50¢ Each Additional Item

✓ POSTAL BOOK RATE Cannot Be Tracked!
    Not responsible for non-delivery.

✓ Priority Mail { $6.00 First Item
            $2.00 Each Additional Item

✓ UPS { $7.00 First Item
        $1.50 Each Additional Item

    NOTE: UPS Delivery Available to Mainland USA Only

Canada

✓ Postal Air Mail { $15.00 First Item
               $2.50 Each Additional Item

✓ Personal Checks or Bank Drafts MUST BE
    US$ and Drawn on a US Bank

✓ Canadian Postal Money Orders OK

✓ Payment MUST BE US$

All Other Countries

✓ Sorry, No Surface Delivery!

✓ Postal Air Mail { $19.00 First Item
               $6.00 Each Additional Item

✓ Checks and Money Orders MUST BE US$
    and Drawn on a US Bank or branch.

✓ Paypal Payments Can Be Made in US$ To:
    info@wexclub.com

SPECIAL NOTES

✓ RETAILERS: Standard Discounts Available

✓ BACKORDERS: We Backorder all Out-of-
    Stock Items Unless Otherwise Requested

✓ PRO FORMA INVOICES: Available on Request

✓ DVD Return Policy: Replace defective DVDs only

ORDER ONLINE AT: www.adventuresunlimitedpress.com

**10% Discount When You Order
3 or More Items!**

Please check: ✓

☐ This is my first order		☐ I have ordered before		

Name

Address

City

State/Province   Postal Code

Country

Phone: Day   Evening

Fax   Email

Item Code	Item Description	Qty	Total

Please check: ✓

	Subtotal ▶
	Less Discount-10% for 3 or more items ▶
☐ Postal-Surface	Balance ▶
☐ Postal-Air Mail (Priority in USA)	Illinois Residents 6.25% Sales Tax ▶
	Previous Credit ▶
☐ UPS	Shipping ▶
(Mainland USA only)	Total (check/MO in USD$ only) ▶

☐ Visa/MasterCard/Discover/American Express

Card Number:

Expiration Date: Security Code:

✓ SEND A CATALOG TO A FRIEND: